THE HERITAGE GUIDE
TO THE
CONSTITUTION

Cataloging-in-Publication Data on file with the Library of Congress

ISBN 1-59698-001-X

Published in the United States by
Regnery Publishing, Inc.
An Eagle Publishing Company
One Massachusetts Avenue, NW
Washington, DC 20001

The Heritage Foundation
214 Massachusetts Ave., NE
Washington, DC 20002
202-546-4400 • heritage.org

Visit us at www.regnery.com

Printed on acid-free paper

Manufactured in the United States of America

10

Books are available in quantity for promotional or premium use. Write to Director of Special Sales, Regnery Publishing, Inc., One Massachusetts Avenue, NW, Washington, DC 20001, for information on discounts and terms, or call (202) 216-0600.

Editorial and Production Staff
Charissa Kersten, Assistant Executive Editor
Therese Pennefather, Production Editor
Alex Adrianson, Interior Design and Composition

THE HERITAGE GUIDE
TO THE
CONSTITUTION

Edwin Meese III
Chairman of the Editorial Advisory Board

David F. Forte
Senior Editor

Matthew Spalding
Executive Editor

Editorial Advisory Board

Contents

CONTRIBUTORS

Albert W. Alschuler
Julius Kreeger Professor of Law and Criminology
The University of Chicago Law School

Dennis W. Arrow
Professor of Law
Oklahoma City University School of Law

John Baker
Dale E. Bennet Professor of Law
Louisiana State University,
Paul M. Hebert Law Center

Rachel E. Barkow
Assistant Professor of Law
New York University School of Law

Herman Belz
Professor of History
University of Maryland

Thomas Berg
Professor of Law
University of St. Thomas School of Law

David Bernstein
Professor of Law
George Mason University School of Law

Joseph Bessette
Alice Tweed Tuohy Professor of Government
and Ethics
Claremont McKenna College

G. Robert Blakey
William and Dorothy O'Neill Professor of Law
Notre Dame Law School

Gerard V. Bradley
Professor of Law
Notre Dame Law School

James L. Buckley
Senior Judge
United States Court of Appeals,
District of Columbia Circuit

Lee Casey
Partner
Baker & Hostetler, LLP

Michael A. Carrier
Associate Professor of Law
Rutgers University School of Law, Camden

Eric Chiappinelli
Professor of Law
Seattle University School of Law

Roger Clegg
Vice President and General Counsel
Center for Equal Opportunity

Charles Cooper
Attorney, Founding Partner
Cooper & Kirk, PLLC

Douglas Cox
Partner
Gibson, Dunn & Crutcher, LLP

Robert Delahunty
Associate Professor of Law
University of St. Thomas School of Law

Brannon P. Denning
Associate Professor of Law
Cumberland School of Law, Samford University

John G. Douglass
Professor of Law
University of Richmond School of Law

Donald Dripps
Professor of Law
University of San Diego School of Law

John C. Eastman
Professor of Law
Chapman University School of Law

Einer Elhauge
Professor of Law
Harvard Law School

James W. Ely, Jr.
Milton R. Underwood Professor of Law
Vanderbilt University Law School

David Engdahl
Professor of Law
Seattle University School of Law

Trent England
Legal Policy Analyst
The Heritage Foundation

Richard A. Epstein
James Parker Hall Distinguished Service
Professor of Law
The University of Chicago Law School

Edward Erler
Professor of Political Science
California State University, San Bernardino

John Feerick
Dean and Professor of Law
Fordham University School of Law

David F. Forte
Charles R. Emrick Jr. - Calfee, Halter &
Grisworld Endowed Professor of Law
Cleveland-Marshall College of Law
Cleveland State University

Matthew Franck
Professor of Political Science
Radford University

Charles Fried
Beneficial Professor of Law
Harvard Law School

Richard W. Garnett
Associate Professor of Law
Notre Dame Law School

Todd Gaziano
Director, Center for Legal and Judicial Studies
The Heritage Foundation

Michael J. Gerhardt
Hanson Professor of Law
The College of William and Mary,
Marshall-Wythe School of Law

Douglas Ginsburg
Chief Judge
United States Court of Appeals,
District of Columbia Circuit

Andrew S. Gold
Assistant Professor of Law
DePaul University College of Law

Jack L. Goldsmith III
Professor of Law
Harvard Law School

Eric Grant
Attorney at Law
Sweeney and Grant, LLP

Michael S. Greve
John G. Searle Scholar
American Enterprise Institute

Arthur Hellman
Professor of Law
University of Pittsburgh School of Law

James C. Ho
Majority Chief Counsel
United States Senate Judiciary Subcommittee
on the Constitution

Erik M. Jensen
David L. Brennan Professor of Law
Case Western Reserve University Law School

Tiffany Jones
Assistant Professor of Political Science
University of Dallas

Patrick Kelley
Professor of Law
Southern Illinois University School of Law

Gary Kepplinger
Deputy General Counsel
Government Accountability Office

Vasan Kesavan
Attorney
Highbridge/Zwirn Partners

Charles Kesler
Professor of Government
Claremont McKenna College

Douglas W. Kmiec
Professor of Constitutional Law
Pepperdine University School of Law

Adam Kurland
Professor of Law
Howard University School of Law

Tadahisa Kuroda
Professor of History
Skidmore College

Joan L. Larsen
Visiting and Adjunct Faculty
University of Michigan Law School

Gary Lawson
Professor of Law
Boston University School of Law

Andrew Leipold
Professor, Galowich-Huizenga Faculty Scholar
University of Illinois College of Law

Robert Levy
Senior Fellow in Constitutional Studies
Cato Institute

Nelson Lund
Patrick Henry Professor of Constitutional Law
and the Second Amendment
George Mason University School of Law

Earl Maltz
Distinguished Professor of Law
Rutgers University School of Law, Camden

Calvin Massey
Professor of Law
University of California Hastings College of
the Law

Thomas McAffee
Professor of Law
University of Nevada, Las Vegas,
William S. Boyd School of Law

Forrest McDonald
Distinguished University Professor
University of Alabama

John McGinnis
Class of 1940 Research Professor of Law
Northwestern University School of Law

Thomas Merrill
Charles Keller Beckman Professor of Law
Columbia Law School

Paul Moreno
William and Berniece Grewcock Chair in the
Constitution of the United States
Hillsdale College

Andrew P. Morriss
Galen J. Roush Professor of Business Law and
Regulation
Case Western Reserve University Law School

Thomas Nachbar
Associate Professor of Law
University of Virginia School of Law

John Copeland Nagle
Professor of Law
Notre Dame Law School

Robert G. Natelson
Professor of Law
University of Montana School of Law

Erin O'Hara
Professor of Law
Vanderbilt University Law School

Mackubin Owens
Professor of National Security Affairs
United States Naval War College

Bruce Peabody
Assistant Professor of American Politics and
the Judicial Process
Fairleigh Dickinson University

Anthony Peacock
Associate Professor
Utah State University

Terence Pell
President
Center for Individual Rights

Richard Peltz
Associate Professor of Law
University of Arkansas at Little Rock,
William H. Bowen School of Law

Ronald Pestritto
Associate Professor of Politics
University of Dallas

James Pfiffner
Professor of Public Policy
George Mason University

Sai Prakash
Professor of Law
University of San Diego School of Law

Stephen B. Presser
Raoul Berger Professor of Legal History
Northwestern University School of Law

Claire Priest
Assistant Professor of Law
Northwestern University School of Law

Robert J. Pushaw, Jr.
James Wilson Endowed Professor
Pepperdine University School of Law

Michael D. Ramsey
Professor of Law
University of San Diego School of Law

Michael B. Rappaport
Professor of Law
University of San Diego School of Law

Paul Rosenzweig
Senior Legal Research Fellow
The Heritage Foundation

Ralph Rossum
Salvatori Professor of Political Philosophy &
the American Constitution
Claremont McKenna College

Ronald Rotunda
George Mason University Foundation Professor
of Law
George Mason University School of Law

Stephen Safranek
Professor of Law
Ave Maria School of Law

Stephen Saltzburg
Wallace and Beverley Woodbury University
Professor of Law
The George Washington University Law School

Peter W. Schramm
Professor of Political Science
Ashland University

J. Gregory Sidak
Resident Scholar
American Enterprise Institute

Jeffrey Sikkenga
Associate Professor of Political Science
Ashland University

Bradley Smith
Professor of Law
Capital University Law School

Loren Smith
Senior Judge
United States Court of Federal Claims

David Smolin
Professor of Law
Cumberland School of Law, Samford University

Matthew Spalding
Director, B. Kenneth Simon Center for
American Studies
The Heritage Foundation

Andrew Spiropoulos
Professor of Law
Oklahoma City University School of Law

William J. Stuntz
Professor of Law
Harvard Law School

Paul Taylor
Chief Counsel
House Subcommittee on the Constitution

George Thomas
Professor of Law and Judge Alexander P. Waugh
Senior Distinguished Scholar
Rutgers School of Law, Newark

Daniel Troy
Partner in the Life Sciences Practice and
Appellate Litigation Group
Sidley, Austin, Brown & Wood LLP

Jonathan Turley
J.B. and Maurice Shapiro Professor of Public
Interest Law
The George Washington University Law School

Michael Uhlmann
Professor of Political Science
Claremont Graduate University

Paul Verkuil
Professor of Law
Yeshiva University,
Benjamin N. Cardozo School of Law

Adrian Vermeule
Bernard Meltzer Professor of Law
The University of Chicago Law School

Eugene Volokh
Professor of Law
University of California, Los Angeles
School of Law

David Wagner
Associate Professor of Law
Regent University School of Law

Bradley C. S. Watson
Philip M. McKenna Chair in American and
Western Political Thought
Saint Vincent College

John Yoo
Professor of Law
University of California-Berkley,
Boalt Hall School of Law

Ernest A. Young
Judge Benjamin Harrison Powell Professor in
Law
The University of Texas at Austin School of Law

Todd Zywicki
Professor of Law
George Mason University School of Law

PREFACE

The Heritage Guide to the Constitution is intended to provide a brief and accurate explanation of each clause of the Constitution as envisioned by the Framers and as applied in contemporary law. Its particular aim is to provide lawmakers with a means to defend their role and to fulfill their responsibilities in our constitutional order. Yet while the *Guide* will provide a reliable reference for lawmakers and policy-makers, and be especially useful for the trained jurist, it is written to be explanatory and educational, accessible and helpful for informed citizens and students of the Constitution generally.

To create such a unique line-by-line analysis of our supreme law, we set about finding an expert to write on each clause identified in the Constitution, from the Preamble to the Twenty-seventh Amendment. Each contributor was asked to write a brief essay on a particular clause, with two objectives. First, provide a description of the original understanding of the clause, as far as it can be determined. If within the standard of original understanding there are credible and differing interpretations, they were to be noted and explained. (The concept of "originalism" is discussed in the introductory essay, "The Originalist Perspective.") Second, the article was to provide an explanation of the current state of the law regarding the clause and, where appropriate, to give brief explanations of the historical development of current doctrine.

At the end of each essay, the authors have added cross-references to other clauses in the Constitution, suggestions for further research, and a listing of significant cases concerning that clause. (A complete index of cases referenced throughout the *Guide* is provided in Appendix A.)

In addition to the text of the Constitution itself, and as reflected by extensive references throughout the *Guide*, we have taken three widely recognized sources to be especially authoritative in this project. First, *The Records of the Federal Convention of 1787*, the definitive collection of the records and debates of the Constitutional Convention, written by participants of the Convention, including in particular the extensive notes taken by James Madison. Second, *The*

Federalist Papers, the great series of essays written by Alexander Hamilton, John Jay, and James Madison in 1787 and 1788 to defend the Constitution during the debates over the document's ratification. And third, Joseph Story's *Commentaries on the Constitution of the United States*, a classic and substantive work on the meaning of the U.S. Constitution, written in 1833 by one of its best scholars and one of the greatest justices of the Supreme Court.

*****

In the long process of creating this book, innumerable individuals deserve acknowledgment for their ideas, comments, and substantive contributions. The project began in conversations with then Heritage Vice President Adam Meyerson, and continued under the steady guidance of Edwin Meese III, the Ronald Reagan Distinguished Fellow in Public Policy at The Heritage Foundation. Mr. Meese acted as the Chairman of this project's Editorial Advisory Board, which included four distinguished scholars who read and commented on the essay's as they were being produced and edited: Jim Bond of Seattle University School of Law, Gary Lawson of Boston University School of Law, John O. McGinnis of Northwestern University School of Law, and Ronald Rotunda of George Mason University School of Law.

Charissa Kersten was invaluable as Assistant Executive Editor for the project, tracking essays through the process, checking case citations, and generally keeping a very complicated project organized. Lien O'Neill fulfilled this role in the initial phase of the project, and Carolyn Garris assisted in its final stages. We are especially thankful to Todd Gaziano, Paul Rosenzweig, and Trent England of the Center for Legal and Judicial Studies at The Heritage Foundation who, in addition to contributing to the work, provided recommendations, counsel, and support throughout.

The publishing group at The Heritage Foundation, under the direction of Jonathan Larsen, was crucial to developing and producing the final work, beginning in its early iterations with Daryl Malloy, and then with our indefatigable Production Editor Therese Pennefather, along with the help of Senior Desktop Publishing Specialist Alex Adrianson, and Graphic Designer Carolyn Belefski.

Heritage's Vice President for Communications and Marketing, Rebecca Hagelin, also played a vital role in the publication of the *Guide*. Her marketing insights and leadership were invaluable to this project.

Throughout, we have used *The Chicago Manual of Style* and *The Bluebook: A Uniform System of Citations* as style guides. For the text of the Constitution, we used the National Archives' transcription of the document in its original form. Each essay herein represents the views of its author or authors and does not represent the views of any government entity.

A succession of talented student researchers has supported the project while interning at The Heritage Foundation: David Barnes of Yale University, Mary Elizabeth Davis of Messiah College, David Derksen of Carleton College, Rachel Hanson of Trinity University, Jana Hardy of Claremont McKenna College, Tim Holbert of Miami University of Ohio, Audrey Jones of Patrick Henry College, Joseph Lindsley of Notre Dame University, Rebeccah Ramey of Ashland University, Stephen Roberts of Calvin College, Lydia Sullivan of Loyola University (Chicago), and Claire Wendt of Pepperdine University.

Several researchers also supported the project, working with Dr. Forte at Cleveland-Marshall College of Law: Catherine Bozell, Max Dehn, Otto Elkins, John Friedmann, Siegmund Fuchs, Sara Govrik, Krista Kaleps, Sara Menefee, Terrell Menefee, Susan Owens, Joseph Patituce, Stephen Tylman, and Steven Vargo.

On several occasions a number of scholars, some of whom are also contributors, were consulted as advisors or as outside readers on particular essays: Herman Belz (The University of Maryland), Roger Clegg (Center for Equal Opportunity), Stephen J. Darmody (Shook, Hardy & Bacon, L.L.P.), Steven J. Eagle (George Mason University School of Law), John Eastman (Chapman University School of Law), Joel Finer (Cleveland-Marshall College of Law), Rick Garnett (Notre Dame School of Law), Deborah Geier (Cleveland-Marshall College of Law), Arthur Hellman (University of Pittsburgh School of Law), Nelson Lund (George Mason School of Law), Phillip Muñoz (Tufts University), Kevin O'Neill (Cleveland-Marshall College of Law), Stephen Safranek (Ave Maria School of Law), Steven Steinglass (Cleveland-Marshall College of Law), Adam Thurschwald (Cleveland-Marshall College of Law), and Seth Tillman (Clerk, United States Court of Appeals, Third Circuit).

The Heritage Guide to the Constitution was made possible by two self-made entrepreneurs and generous philanthropists. Born in Italy, Henry Salvatori founded the Western Geophysical Company, one of the most successful oil-exploration and contracting enterprises in the world. B. Kenneth Simon was a marine during the Second World War before founding and building a thriving business called All-Pak to distribute, design, and contract the manufacture of packaging materials. Later in life, both dedicated their time and considerable fortunes to strengthening the underpinnings of American liberty and constitutionalism. That dedication continues because of endowments they created at The Heritage Foundation.

David F. Forte
Matthew Spalding

The Meaning of the Constitution

Edwin Meese III

*T*he Constitution of the United States has endured for over two centuries. It remains the object of reverence for nearly all Americans and an object of admiration by peoples around the world. William Gladstone was right in 1878 when he described the U.S. Constitution as "the most wonderful work ever struck off at a given time by the brain and purpose of man."

Part of the reason for the Constitution's enduring strength is that it is the complement of the Declaration of Independence. The Declaration provided the philosophical basis for a government that exercises legitimate power by "the consent of the governed," and it defined the conditions of a free people, whose rights and liberty are derived from their Creator. The Constitution delineated the structure of government and the rules for its operation, consistent with the creed of human liberty proclaimed in the Declaration.

Justice Joseph Story, in his *Familiar Exposition of the Constitution* (1840), described our Founding document in these terms:

> We shall treat [our Constitution], not as a mere compact, or league, or confederacy, existing at the mere will of any one or more of the States, during their good pleasure; but, (as it purports on its face to be) as a Constitution of Government, framed and adopted by the people of the United States, and obligatory upon all the States, until it is altered, amended, or abolished by the people, in the manner pointed out in the instrument itself.

By the diffusion of power—horizontally among the three separate branches of the federal government, and vertically in the allocation of power between the central government and the states—the Constitution's Framers devised a structure of government strong enough to ensure the nation's future strength and prosperity but without sufficient power to threaten the liberty of the people.

1

The Constitution and the government it establishes "has a just claim to [our] confidence and respect," George Washington wrote in his Farewell Address (1796), because it is "the off-spring of our choice, uninfluenced and unawed, adopted upon full investigation and mature deliberation, completely free in its principles, in the distribution of its powers uniting security with energy, and containing, within itself, a provision for its own amendment."

The Constitution was born in crisis, when the very existence of the new United States was in jeopardy. The Framers understood the gravity of their task. As Alexander Hamilton noted in the general introduction to *The Federalist*,

> [A]fter an unequivocal experience of the inefficacy of the subsisting federal government, [the people] are called upon to deliberate on a new Constitution for the United States of America. The subject speaks its own importance; comprehending in its consequences nothing less than the existence of the Union, the safety and welfare of the parts of which it is composed, the fate of an empire in many respects the most interesting in the world.

Several important themes permeated the completed draft of the Constitution. The first, reflecting the mandate of the Declaration of Independence, was the recognition that the ultimate authority of a legitimate government depends on the consent of a free people. Thomas Jefferson had set forth the basic principle in his famous formulation:

> We hold these truths to be self-evident, that all men are created equal, that they are endowed by their Creator with certain unalienable Rights, that among these are Life, Liberty, and the pursuit of Happiness. That to secure these rights, Governments are instituted among Men deriving their just powers from the consent of the governed.

That "all men are created equal" means that they are equally endowed with unalienable rights. Nature does not single out who is to govern and who is to be governed; there is no divine right of kings. Nor are rights a matter of legal privilege or the benevolence of some ruling class. Fundamental rights exist by nature, prior to government and conventional laws. It is because these individual rights are left unsecured that governments are instituted among men.

Consent is the means by which equality is made politically operable and whereby arbitrary power is thwarted. The natural standard for judging if a government is legitimate is whether that government rests on the consent of the governed. Any political powers not derived from the consent of the governed are, by the laws of nature, illegitimate and hence unjust.

The "consent of the governed" stands in contrast to "the will of the majority," a view more current in European democracies. The "consent of the governed" describes a situation where the people are self-governing in their communities, religions, and social institutions, and into which the government may intrude only with the people's consent. There exists between the people and limited government a vast social space in which men and women, in their individual and corporate capacities, may exercise their self-governing liberty. In Europe, the "will of the majority" signals an idea that all decisions are ultimately political and are routed through the government. Thus, limited government is not just a desirable objective; it is the essential bedrock of the American polity.

A second fundamental element of the Constitution is the concept of checks and balances. As James Madison famously wrote in *The Federalist* No. 51,

> In framing a government which is to be administered by men over men, the great difficulty lies in this: You must first enable the government to controul the governed; and in the next place oblige it to controul itself. A dependence on the people is, no doubt, the primary controul on the government; but experience has taught mankind necessity of auxiliary precautions.

These "auxiliary precautions" constitute the improved science of politics offered by the Framers and form the basis of their "Republican remedy for the diseases most incident to Republican Government" (*The Federalist* No. 10).

The "diseases most incident to Republican Government" were basically two: democratic tyranny and democratic ineptitude. The first was the problem of majority faction, the abuse of minority or individual rights by an "interested and overbearing" majority. The second was the problem of making a democratic form of government efficient and effective. The goal was limited but energetic government. The constitutional object was, as the late constitutional scholar Herbert Storing said, "a design of government with the powers to act and a structure to make it act wisely and responsibly."

The particulars of the Framers' political science were catalogued by Madison's celebrated collaborator in *The Federalist*, Alexander Hamilton. Those particulars included such devices as representation, bicameralism, independent courts of law, and the "regular distribution of powers into distinct departments," as Hamilton put it in *The Federalist* No. 9; these were "means, and powerful means, by which the excellencies of republican government may be retained and its imperfections lessened or avoided."

Central to their institutional scheme was the principle of separation of powers. As Madison bluntly put it in *The Federalist* No. 47, the "preservation of liberty requires that the three great departments of power should be separate and distinct," for, as he also wrote, "The accumulation of all powers, legislative, executive, and judiciary, in the same hands, whether of one, a few, or many, and whether hereditary, self-appointed or elective, may justly be pronounced the very definition of tyranny."

Madison described in *The Federalist* No. 51 how structure and human nature could be marshaled to protect liberty:

> [T]he great security against a gradual concentration of the several powers in the same department, consists in giving to those who administer each department, the necessary constitutional means, and personal motives to resist encroachments of the others.

Thus, the separation of powers frustrates designs for power and at the same time creates an incentive to collaborate and cooperate, lessening conflict and concretizing a practical community of interest among political leaders.

Equally important to the constitutional design was the concept of federalism. At the Constitutional Convention there was great concern that an overreaction to the inadequacies of the Articles of Confederation might produce a tendency toward a single centralized and all-powerful national government. The resolution to such fears was, as Madison described it in *The Federalist*, a government that was neither wholly federal nor wholly national but a composite of the two. A half-century later, Alexis de Tocqueville would celebrate democracy in America as precisely the result of the political vitality spawned by this "incomplete" national government.

The institutional design was to divide sovereignty between two different levels of political entities, the nation and the states. This would prevent an unhealthy concentration of power in a single government. It would provide, as Madison said in *The Federalist* No. 51, a "double security . . . to the rights of the people." Federalism, along with separation of powers, the Framers thought, would be the basic principled matrix of American constitutional liberty. "The different governments," Madison concluded, "will controul each other; at the same time that each will be controulled by itself."

But institutional restraints on power were not all that federalism was about. There was also a deeper understanding—in fact, a far richer understanding—of why federalism mattered. When the delegates at Philadelphia convened in May 1787 to revise the ineffective Articles of Confederation, it was a foregone conclusion that the basic debate would concern the proper role of the states. Those who favored a diminution of state power, the Nationalists, saw unfettered state sovereignty under the Articles as the problem; not only did it allow the states to undermine congressional efforts to govern, it also rendered individual rights insecure in the hands of "interested and overbearing majorities." Indeed, Madison, defending the Nationalists' constitutional handiwork, went so far as to suggest in *The Federalist* No. 51 that only by way of a "judicious modification" of the federal principle was the new Constitution able to remedy the defects of popular, republican government.

The view of those who doubted the political efficacy of the new Constitution was that good popular government depended quite as much on a political community that would promote civic or public virtue as on a set of institutional devices designed to check the selfish impulses of the majority. As Herbert Storing has shown, this concern for community and civic virtue tempered and tamed somewhat the Nationalists' tendency toward simply a large nation. Their reservations, as Storing put it, echo still through our political history.[1]

It is this understanding, that federalism can contribute to a sense of political community and hence to a kind of public spirit, that is too often ignored in our public discussions about federalism. But in a sense, it is this understanding that makes the American experiment in popular government truly the novel undertaking the Framers thought it to be.

At bottom, in the space left by a limited central government, the people could rule themselves by their own moral and social values, and call on local political institutions to assist them. Where the people, through the Constitution, did consent for the central government to have a role, that role would similarly be guided by the people's sense of what was valuable and good as

---

[1] Herbert J. Storing, "The Constitution and the Bill of Rights," in Joseph M. Bessette, ed., *Toward a More Perfect Union: Writings of Herbert J. Storing* (Washington, D.C.: The AEI Press, 1995).

articulated through the political institutions of the central government. Thus, at its deepest level popular government means a structure of government that rests not only on the consent of the governed, but also on a structure of government wherein the views of the people and their civic associations can be expressed and translated into public law and public policy, subject, of course, to the limits established by the Constitution. Through deliberation, debate, and compromise, a public consensus is formed about what constitutes the public good. It is this consensus on fundamental principles that knits individuals into a community of citizens. And it is the liberty to determine the morality of a community that is an important part of our liberty protected by the Constitution.

In *The Heritage Guide to the Constitution*, we seek to present the Founders' understanding of the Constitution and its various provisions, and examine the judicial interpretations and political circumstances that make up the historical development of constitutional law.

The Constitution is our most fundamental law. It is, in its own words, "the supreme Law of the Land." Its translation into the legal rules under which we live occurs through the actions of all government entities, federal and state. The entity we know as "constitutional law" is the creation not only of the decisions of the Supreme Court, but also of the various Congresses and of the President.

Yet it is the court system, particularly the decisions of the Supreme Court, that most observers identify as providing the basic corpus of "constitutional law." This body of law, this judicial handiwork, is, in a fundamental way, unique in our scheme, for the Court is charged routinely, day in and day out, with the awesome task of addressing some of the most basic and most enduring political questions that face our nation. The answers the Court gives are very important to the stability of the law so necessary for good government. But as constitutional historian Charles Warren once noted, what is most important to remember is that "however the Court may interpret the provisions of the Constitution, it is still the Constitution which is the law, not the decisions of the Court."[2]

By this, of course, Warren did not mean that a constitutional decision by the Supreme Court lacks the character of binding law. He meant that the Constitution remains the Constitution and that observers of the Court may fairly consider whether a particular Supreme Court decision was right or wrong. There remains in the country a vibrant and healthy debate among the members of the Supreme Court, as articulated in its opinions, and between the Court and academics, politicians, columnists and commentators, and the people generally, on whether the Court has correctly understood and applied the fundamental law of the Constitution. We have seen throughout our history that when the Supreme Court greatly misconstrues the Constitution, generations of mischief may follow. The result is that, of its own accord or through the mechanism of the appointment process, the Supreme Court may come to revisit some of its doctrines and try, once again, to adjust its pronouncements to the commands of the Constitution.

This recognition of the distinction between constitutional law and the Constitution itself produces the conclusion that constitutional decisions, including those of the Supreme Court,

---

[2] Charles Warren, *The Supreme Court in United States History* (Boston: Little, Brown, and Company, 1922–1924), 3 vols., 470–471.

need not be seen as the last words in constitutional construction. A correlative point is that constitutional interpretation is not the business of courts alone but is also, and properly, the business of all branches of government. Each of the three coordinate branches of government created and empowered by the Constitution—the executive and legislative no less than the judicial—has a duty to interpret the Constitution in the performance of its official functions. In fact, every official takes a solemn oath precisely to that effect. Chief Justice John Marshall, in *Marbury v. Madison* (1803), noted that the Constitution is a limitation on judicial power as well as on that of the executive and legislative branches. He reiterated that view in *McCullough v. Maryland* (1819) when he cautioned judges never to forget it is a constitution they are expounding.

The Constitution—the original document of 1787 plus its amendments—is and must be understood to be the standard against which all laws, policies, and interpretations should be measured. It is our fundamental law because it represents the settled and deliberate will of the people, against which the actions of government officials must be squared. In the end, the continued success and viability of our democratic Republic depends on our fidelity to, and the faithful exposition and interpretation of, this Constitution, our great charter of liberty.

THE FORMATION OF THE CONSTITUTION

MATTHEW SPALDING

*T*he creation of the United States Constitution—John Adams described the Constitutional Convention as "the greatest single effort of national deliberation that the world has ever seen"—was a seminal event in the history of human liberty. The story of that creation in the summer of 1787 is itself a significant aspect in determining the meaning of the document.

In June 1776, amid growing sentiment for American independence and after hostilities with the British army had commenced at Lexington, Massachusetts, Richard Henry Lee of Virginia introduced a resolution in the Second Continental Congress for the colonies to collectively dissolve political connections with Great Britain, pursue foreign alliances, and draft a plan of confederation. These actions resulted in the Declaration of Independence of 1776, the Franco-American Alliance of 1778, and the Articles of Confederation, which were proposed in 1777 and ratified in 1781.

From its conception, the inherent weaknesses of the Articles of Confederation made it awkward at best and unworkable at worst. Each state governed itself through elected representatives, and the state representatives in turn elected a weak national government. There was no independent executive, and the Congress lacked authority to impose taxes to cover national expenses. Because all thirteen colonies had to ratify amendments, one state's refusal prevented structural reform; nine of thirteen states had to approve important legislation, which meant five states could thwart any major proposal. And although the Congress could negotiate treaties with foreign powers, all treaties had to be ratified by the states.

The defects of the Articles became more and more apparent during the "critical period" of 1781–1787. By the end of the war in 1783, it was clear that the new system was, as George Washington observed, "a shadow without the substance." Weakness in international affairs and in the face of continuing European threats in North America, the inability to enforce the peace treaty or collect enough taxes to pay foreign creditors, and helplessness in quelling domestic disorder, such as Shays's Rebellion—all intensified the drive for a stronger national government.

If that were not enough, the Americans faced an even larger problem. Absolutely committed to the idea of popular rule, they knew that previous attempts to establish such a government had almost always led to majority tyranny—that of the overbearing many disregarding the rights of the few. In *The Federalist* No. 10, James Madison famously described this as the problem of faction, the latent causes of which are "sown in the nature of man." Previous solutions usually rendered government weak, and thus susceptible to all the problems with which the Founders were most concerned. This was the case in the individual states, which, dominated by their popular legislatures, routinely violated rights of property and contract and limited the independence of the judiciary.

In 1785, representatives from Maryland and Virginia, meeting at George Washington's Mount Vernon to discuss interstate trade, requested a meeting of the states to discuss trade and commerce generally. Although only five states met at Annapolis in 1786, James Madison and Alexander Hamilton used the failed conference to issue a clarion call for a general convention of all the states "to render the constitution of government adequate to the exigencies of the Union." After several states, including Virginia and Pennsylvania, chose delegates for the meeting, the Congress acquiesced with a narrower declaration that the "sole and express purpose" of the upcoming Convention would be to revise the Articles of Confederation.

The next year, from May 25 to September 17, 1787, state delegates met in what is now called Independence Hall, in Philadelphia, Pennsylvania—as it says in the Constitution's Preamble—to "form a more perfect Union." It was an impressive group. Not only were there leaders in the fight for independence, such as Roger Sherman and John Dickinson, and leading thinkers just coming into prominence, such as Madison, Hamilton, and Gouverneur Morris, but also already-legendary figures, such as Washington and Benjamin Franklin. Every state was represented, except for one: Rhode Island, fearful that a strong national government would injure its lucrative trade, opposed revising the Articles of Confederation and sent no delegates. Patrick Henry and Samuel Adams, both of whom opposed the creation of a strong central government, did not attend. Notably absent were John Jay, who was then U.S. secretary of foreign affairs, and John Adams and Thomas Jefferson, who were out of the country on government missions. Nonetheless, Jefferson described the gathering as "an assembly of demigods."

The Constitutional Convention

As its first order of business, the delegates unanimously chose Washington as president of the Convention. Having initially hesitated in attending the Convention, once decided, Washington pushed the delegates to adopt "no temporizing expedient" but instead to "probe the defects of the Constitution to the bottom, and provide radical cures." While they waited in Philadelphia for a quorum, Washington presided over daily meetings of the Virginia delegation (composed of Washington, George Mason, George Wythe, John Blair, Edmund Randolph, James McClurg, and James Madison) to consider strategy and the reform proposals that would become the plan presented at the outset of the Convention. Although he contributed to formal debate only once at the end of the Convention, Washington was actively involved throughout the three-and-a-half-month proceedings.

There were three basic rules of the Convention: voting was to be by state, with each state, regardless of size or population, having one vote; proper decorum was to be maintained at all times; and the proceedings were to be strictly secret. To encourage free and open discussion and debate, the Convention shifted back and forth between full sessions and meetings of the Committee of the Whole, a parliamentary procedure that allowed informal debate and flexibility in deciding and reconsidering individual issues. Although the Convention hired a secretary, the best records of the debate—and thus the most immediate source of the intended meaning of the clauses—are the detailed notes of Madison, which, in keeping with the pledge of secrecy, were not published until 1840.

As soon as the Convention agreed on its rules, Edmund Randolph of the Virginia delegation presented a set of fifteen resolutions, known as the Virginia Plan, which set aside the Articles of Confederation and created in its stead a supreme national government with separate legislative, executive, and judicial branches. This was largely the work of James Madison, who came to the Convention extensively prepared and well-versed in the ancient and modern history of republican government. (See his memorandum on the "Vices of the Political System of the United States.") The delegates generally agreed on the powers that should be lodged in a national legislature, but disagreed on how the states and popular opinion should be reflected in it. Under the Virginia Plan, population would determine representation in each of the two houses of Congress.

To protect their equal standing, delegates from less-populous states rallied around William Paterson's alternative New Jersey Plan to amend the Articles of Confederation, which would preserve each state's equal vote in a one-house Congress with slightly augmented powers. When the delegates rejected the New Jersey Plan, Roger Sherman proffered what is often called "the Great Compromise" (or the Connecticut Compromise, after Sherman's home state) that the House of Representatives would be apportioned based on population and each state would have an equal vote in the Senate. A special Committee of Eleven (one delegate from each state) elaborated upon the proposal, and then the Convention adopted it. As a precaution against having to assume the financial burdens of the smaller states, the larger states exacted an agreement that revenue bills could originate only in the House, where the more populous states would have greater representation.

In late July, a Committee of Detail (composed of John Rutledge of South Carolina, Edmund Randolph of Virginia, Nathaniel Gorham of Massachusetts, Oliver Ellsworth of Connecticut, and James Wilson of Pennsylvania) reworked the resolutions of the expanded Virginia Plan into a draft Constitution; the text now included a list of eighteen powers of Congress, a "necessary and proper" clause, and a number of prohibitions on the states. Over most of August and into early September, the Convention carefully worked over this draft and then gave it to a Committee of Style (William Johnson of Connecticut, Alexander Hamilton of New York, Gouverneur Morris of Pennsylvania, James Madison of Virginia, and Rufus King of Massachusetts) to polish the language. The notable literary quality of the Constitution, most prominently the language of the Preamble, is due to Morris's influence. The delegates continued revising the final draft until September 17 (now celebrated as Constitution Day), when delegates signed the Constitution and sent it to the Congress of the Confederation, and the Convention officially adjourned.

Some of the original fifty-five delegates had returned home over the course of the summer and were not present at the Convention's conclusion. Of the forty-one that were, only three delegates—Edmund Randolph and George Mason of Virginia and Elbridge Gerry of Massachusetts—opposed the Constitution and chose not to sign. Randolph (who had introduced the Virginia Plan) thought in the end that the Constitution was not sufficiently republican, and was wary of creating a single executive. Mason and Gerry (who later supported the Constitution and served in the First Congress) were concerned about the lack of a declaration of rights. Despite these objections, George Washington thought that it was "little short of a miracle" that the delegates had agreed on a new Constitution. Thomas Jefferson, who was also concerned about the lack of a bill of rights, nevertheless wrote that the Constitution "is unquestionably the wisest ever yet presented to men."

On September 28, Congress sent the Constitution to the states to be ratified by popular conventions. *See* Article VII (Ratification). Delaware was the first state to ratify the Constitution, on December 7, 1787; the last of the thirteen original colonies to ratify was Rhode Island, on May 29, 1790, two-and-a-half years later. It was during the ratification debate in the state of New York that Hamilton, Madison, and John Jay wrote a series of newspaper essays under the pen name of Publius, later collected in book form as *The Federalist*, to refute the arguments of the Anti-Federalist opponents of the proposed Constitution. With the ratification by the ninth state—New Hampshire, on June 21, 1788—Congress passed a resolution to make the new Constitution operative, and set dates for choosing presidential electors and the opening session of the new Congress.

There had been some discussion among the delegates of the need for a bill of rights, a proposal that was rejected by the Convention. The lack of a bill of rights like that found in most state constitutions, however, became a rallying cry for the Anti-Federalists, and the advocates of the Constitution (led by James Madison) agreed to add one in the first session of Congress. Ratified on December 15, 1791, the first ten amendments—called the Bill of Rights—include sweeping restrictions on the federal government and its ability to limit certain fundamental rights and procedural matters. The Ninth and Tenth Amendments briefly encapsulate the twofold theory of the Constitution: the purpose of the Constitution is to protect *rights*, which stem not from the government but from the people themselves; and the powers of the national government are limited to only those delegated to it by the Constitution on behalf of the people.

Auxiliary Precautions

In addition to the provisions of the document, three important unstated mechanisms are at work in the Constitution: the extended Republic, the separation of powers, and federalism. The Founders believed that citizen virtue was crucial for the success of republican government but they knew that passion and interest were permanent parts of human nature and could not be controlled by parchment barriers alone. "A dependence on the people is, no doubt, the primary control on the government," Madison explained in *The Federalist* No. 51, "but experience has taught mankind the necessity of auxiliary precautions." Rather than hoping for the best, the Founders designed a system that would harness these opposite and rival interests to supply "the defect of better motives."

The effect of representation—of individual citizens being represented in the government rather than ruling through direct participatory democracy—is to refine and moderate public opinion through a deliberative process. Extending the Republic, literally increasing the size of the nation, would take in a greater number and variety of opinions, making it harder for a majority to form on narrow interests contrary to the common good. The majority that did develop would be more settled and, by necessity, would encompass (and represent) a wider diversity of opinion. This idea that bigger is better reversed the prevailing assumption that republican government could work only in small states.

The Founders also knew, again as Madison explained in *The Federalist* No. 48, that "the accumulation of all powers, legislative, executive, and judiciary, in the same hands, whether of one, a few, or many, and whether hereditary, self-appointed, or elective, may justly be pronounced the very definition of tyranny." In order to distribute power and prevent its accumulation, they created three separate branches of government, each performing its own functions and duties and sharing a few powers—as when the President shares the legislative power through the veto—so that they would have an incentive to check each other. Jefferson called the "republican form and principles of our Constitution" and "the salutary distribution of powers" in the Constitution the "two sheet anchors of our Union." "If driven from either," he predicted, "we shall be in danger of foundering."

And although national powers were clearly enhanced by the Constitution, the federal government was to exercise only delegated powers, the remainder being reserved to the states or the people. Despite the need for additional national authority, the Framers remained distrustful of government in general and of a centralized federal government in particular. "The powers delegated by the proposed Constitution to the federal government are few and defined," Madison wrote in *The Federalist* No. 45. "Those which are to remain in the State governments are numerous and indefinite." To give the states more leverage against the national government, equal state representation in the Senate was blended into the national legislature (and guaranteed in Article V). "This balance between the National and State governments ought to be dwelt on with peculiar attention, as it is of the utmost importance," Hamilton argued at the New York state ratifying convention. "It forms a double security to the people. If one encroaches on their rights they will find a powerful protection in the other. Indeed, they will both be prevented from overpassing their constitutional limits by a certain rivalship, which will ever subsist between them."

A Momentous Work

When the Constitutional Convention assembled on the morning of September 17, 1787, the completed document was read aloud to the delegates for one last time. Thereupon Benjamin Franklin, the eighty-one-year-old patriarch of the group, rose to speak. He declared his support for the new Constitution—"with all its faults, if they are such"—because he thought a new government was necessary for the young nation. Franklin continued:

> I doubt too whether any other convention we can obtain may be able to make a better Constitution. For when you assemble a number of men to have the advantage of their

joint wisdom, you inevitably assemble with those men, all their prejudices, their passions, their errors of opinion, their local interests, and their selfish views. From such an Assembly can a perfect production be expected? It therefore astonishes me, Sir, to find this system approaching so near to perfection as it does; and I think it will astonish our enemies. . . . Thus I consent, Sir, to this Constitution because I expect no better, and because I am not sure, that it is not the best.

As the delegates came forward, one at a time, to sign their names to the final document, Madison recorded Franklin's final comment, just before the Constitutional Convention was dissolved. Referring to the sun painted on the back of Washington's chair, Franklin said that he had

often in the course of the Session, and the vicissitudes of my hopes and fears as to its issue, looked at that behind the President without being able to tell whether it was rising or setting. But now at length I have the happiness to know that it is a rising and not a setting Sun.

"The business being thus closed," George Washington recorded in his private diary, the delegates proceeded to City Tavern, where they

dined together and took a cordial leave of each other; after which I returned to my lodgings, did some business with and received the papers from the Secretary of the Convention, and retired to meditate on the momentous work which had been executed. . . .

THE ORIGINALIST PERSPECTIVE

DAVID F. FORTE

*W*ritten constitutionalism implies that those who make, interpret, and enforce the law ought to be guided by the meaning of the United States Constitution—the supreme law of the land—as it was originally written. This view came to be seriously eroded over the course of the last century with the rise of the theory of the Constitution as a "living document" with no fixed meaning, subject to changing interpretations according to the spirit of the times.

In 1985, Attorney General Edwin Meese III delivered a series of speeches challenging the then-dominant view of constitutional jurisprudence and calling for judges to embrace a "jurisprudence of original intention." There ensued a vigorous debate in the academy, as well as in the popular press, and in Congress itself over the prospect of an "originalist" interpretation of the Constitution. Some critics found the idea too vague to be pinned down; others believed that it was impossible to find the original intent that lay behind the text of the Constitution. Some rejected originalism in principle, as undemocratic (though it is clear that the Constitution was built upon republican rather than democratic principles), unfairly binding the present to the choices of the past.

As is often the case, the debate was not completely black and white. Some nonoriginalists do not think that the Framers intended anything but the text of the Constitution to be authoritative, and they hold that straying beyond the text to the intentions of various Framers is not an appropriate method of interpretation. In that, one strain of originalism agrees. On the other hand, many prominent nonoriginalists think that it is not the text of the Constitution per se that ought to be controlling but rather the principles behind the text that can be brought to bear on contemporary issues in an evolving manner.

Originalism, in its various and sometimes conflicting versions, is today the dominant theory of constitutional interpretation. On the one hand, as complex as an originalist jurisprudence may be, the attempt to build a coherent nonoriginalist justification of Supreme Court decisions (excepting the desideratum of following *stare decisis*, even if the legal principle had been wrongly begun) seems to have failed. At the same time, those espousing originalism have profited from the criticism of nonoriginalists, and the originalist enterprise has become more nuanced and self-critical as research into the Founding period continues to flourish. Indeed, it is fair to say that this generation of scholars knows more about what went into the Constitution than any other since the time of the Founding. To paraphrase Thomas Jefferson, in a significant sense "we are all originalists" now.

This is true of both "liberal" and "conservative" judges. For example, in *United States Term Limits, Inc. v. Thornton* (1995), Justices John Paul Stevens and Clarence Thomas engaged in a debate over whether the Framers intended the Qualifications Clauses (Article I, Section 2, Clause 2 and Article I, Section 3, Clause 3) to be the upper limit of what could be required of a person running for Congress. In *Wallace v. Jaffree* (1985), Justice William H. Rehnquist expounded on the original understanding of the Establishment Clause (Amendment I), which Justice David Souter sought to rebut in *Lee v. Weisman* (1992). Even among avowed originalists, fruitful debate takes place. In *McIntyre v. Ohio Elections Commission* (1995), Justices Thomas and Antonin Scalia disputed whether the anonymous pamphleteering of the Founding generation was evidence that the free speech guarantee of the First Amendment was meant to protect such a practice.

Originalism is championed for a number of fundamental reasons. First, it comports with the nature of a constitution, which binds and limits any one generation from ruling according to the passion of the times. The Framers of the Constitution of 1787 knew what they were about, forming a frame of government for "ourselves and our Posterity." They did not understand "We the people" to be merely an assemblage of individuals at any one point in time but a "people" as an association, indeed a number of overlapping associations, over the course of many generations, including our own. In the end, the Constitution of 1787 is as much a constitution for us as it was for the Founding generation.

Second, originalism supports legitimate popular government that is accountable. The Framers believed that a form of government accountable to the people, leaving them fundamentally in charge of their own destinies, best protected human liberty. If liberty is a fundamental aspect of human nature, then the Constitution of 1787 should be defended as a successful champion of human freedom. Originalism sits in frank gratitude for the political, economic, and spiritual prosperity midwifed by the Constitution and the trust the Constitution places in the people to correct their own errors.

Third, originalism accords with the constitutional purpose of limiting government. It understands the several parts of the federal government to be creatures of the Constitution, and to have no legitimate existence outside of the Constitution. The authority of these various entities extends no further than what was devolved upon them by the Constitution. "[I]n all free States the Constitution is fixd," Samuel Adams wrote, "& as the supreme Legislative derives its Power & Authority from the Constitution, it cannot overleap the Bounds of it without destroying its own foundation."

Fourth, it follows that originalism limits the judiciary. It prevents the Supreme Court from asserting its will over the careful mix of institutional arrangements that are charged with making policy, each accountable in various ways to the people. Chief Justice John Marshall, overtly deferring to the intention of the Framers, insisted that "that the framers of the constitution contemplated that instrument, as a rule for the government of courts, as well as of the legislature." In words that judges and academics might well contemplate today, Marshall said,

> Why otherwise does it direct the judges to take an oath to support it? This oath certainly applies, in an especial manner, to their conduct in their official character. How immoral to impose it on them, if they were to be used as the instruments, and the knowing instruments, for violating what they swear to support! (*Marbury v. Madison*)

Fifth, supported by recent research, originalism comports with the understanding of what our Constitution was to be by the people who formed and ratified that document. It affirms that the Constitution is a coherent and interrelated document, with subtle balances incorporated throughout. Reflecting the Founders' understanding of the self-motivated impulses of human nature, the Constitution erected devices that work to frustrate those impulses while leaving open channels for effective and mutually supporting collaboration. It is, in short, a remarkable historical achievement, and unbalancing part of it could dismantle the sophisticated devices it erected to protect the people's liberty.

Sixth, originalism, properly pursued, is not result-oriented, whereas much nonoriginalist writing is patently so. If evidence demonstrates that the Framers understood the commerce power, for example, to be broader than we might wish, then the originalist ethically must accept the conclusion. If evidence shows that the commerce power was to be more limited than it is permitted to be today, then the originalist can legitimately criticize governmental institutions for neglecting their constitutional duty. In either case, the originalist is called to be humble in the face of facts. The concept of the Constitution of 1787 as a good first draft in need of constant revision and updating—encapsulated in vague phrases such as the "living Constitution"—merely turns the Constitution into an unwritten charter to be developed by the contemporary values of sitting judges.

Discerning the Founders' original understanding is not a simple task. There are the problems of the availability of evidence; the reliability of the data; the relative weight of authority to be given to different events, personalities, and organizations of the era; the relevance of subsequent history; and the conceptual apparatus needed to interpret the data. Originalists differ among themselves on all these points and sometimes come to widely divergent conclusions. Nevertheless, the values underlying originalism do mean that the quest, as best as we can accomplish it, is a moral imperative.

How does one go about ascertaining the original meaning of the Constitution? All originalists begin with the text of the Constitution, the words of a particular clause. In the search for the meaning of the text and its legal effect, originalist researchers variously look to the following:

- The evident meaning of the words.
- The meaning according to the lexicon of the times.
- The meaning in context with other sections of the Constitution.
- The meaning according to the words by the Framer suggesting the language.

- The elucidation of the meaning by debate within the Constitutional Convention.
- The historical provenance of the words, particularly their legal history.
- The words in the context of the contemporaneous social, economic, and political events.
- The words in the context of the revolutionary struggle.
- The words in the context of the political philosophy shared by the Founding generation, or by the particular interlocutors at the Convention.
- Historical, religious, and philosophical authority put forward by the Framers.
- The commentary in the ratification debates.
- The commentary by contemporaneous interpreters, such as Publius in *The Federalist*.
- The subsequent historical practice by the Founding generation to exemplify the understood meaning (e.g., the actions of President Washington, the First Congress, and Chief Justice Marshall).
- Early judicial interpretations.
- Evidence of long-standing traditions that demonstrate the people's understanding of the words.

As passed down by William Blackstone and later summarized by Joseph Story, similar interpretive principles guided the Framing generation itself. It is the legal effect of the words in the text that matters, and its meaning is to be determined by well-known and refined rules of interpretation supplemented, where helpful, by the understanding of those who drafted the text and the legal culture within which they operated. As Chief Justice Marshall put it,

> To say that the intention of the instrument must prevail; that this intention must be collected from its words; that its words are to be understood in that sense in which they are generally used by those for whom the instrument was intended; that its provisions are neither to be restricted into insignificance, nor extended to objects not comprehended in them, nor contemplated by its framers; — is to repeat what has been already said more at large, and is all that can be necessary. (*Ogden v. Saunders,* Marshall, C. J., dissenting, 1827)

Marshall's dialectical manner of parsing a text, seeking its place in the coherent context of the document, buttressed by the understanding of those who drafted it and the generally applicable legal principles of the time are exemplified by his classic opinions in *Marbury v. Madison* (1803), *McCulloch v. Maryland* (1819), *Gibbons v. Ogden* (1824), and *Barron v. Baltimore* (1833). Both Marshall's ideological allies and enemies, such as Alexander Hamilton and Thomas Jefferson, utilized the same method of understanding.

Originalism does not remove controversy, or disagreement, but it does cabin it within a principled constitutional tradition that makes real the Rule of Law. Without that, we are destined, as Aristotle warned long ago, to fall into the "rule of men."

With its format of brief didactic essays, the work that follows does not seek to be a thorough defense of originalism against its critics, nor does it choose which strains of originalism or which authorities are to be accorded greater legitimacy than others. But it does respect the originalist endeavor. Each contributor was asked to include a description of the original understanding of the meaning of the clause, as far as it can be determined, and to note and explain any credible and differing originalist interpretations.

It is within this tradition that this volume is respectfully offered to the consideration of the reader.

The Constitution of the United States

THE CONSTITUTION
OF THE UNITED STATES

WE THE PEOPLE of the United States, in Order to form a more perfect Union, establish Justice, insure domestic Tranquility, provide for the common defense, promote the general Welfare, and secure the Blessings of Liberty to ourselves and our Posterity, do ordain and establish this Constitution for the United States of America.

Preamble

ARTICLE. I.

Section. 1.

All legislative Powers herein granted shall be vested in a Congress of the United States, which shall consist of a Senate and House of Representatives.

Legislative Powers

Section. 2.

The House of Representatives shall be composed of Members chosen every second Year by the People of the several States, and the Electors in each State shall have the Qualifications requisite for Electors of the most numerous Branch of the State Legislature.

House of Representatives

No Person shall be a Representative who shall not have attained to the Age of twenty five Years, and been seven Years a Citizen of the United States, and who shall not, when elected, be an Inhabitant of that State in which he shall be chosen.

Requirements of Office

[Representatives and direct Taxes shall be apportioned among the several States which may be included within this Union, according to their respective Numbers, which shall be determined by adding to the whole Number of free Persons, including those bound to Service for a

Changed by Section 2 of the Fourteenth Amendment

Term of Years, and excluding Indians not taxed, three fifths of all other Persons.] The actual Enumeration shall be made within three Years after the first Meeting of the Congress of the United States, and within every subsequent Term of ten Years, in such Manner as they shall by Law direct. The Number of Representatives shall not exceed one for every thirty Thousand, but each State shall have at Least one Representative; and until such enumeration shall be made, the State of New Hampshire shall be entitled to chuse three, Massachusetts eight, Rhode-Island and Providence Plantations one, Connecticut five, New-York six, New Jersey four, Pennsylvania eight, Delaware one, Maryland six, Virginia ten, North Carolina five, South Carolina five, and Georgia three.

When vacancies happen in the Representation from any State, the Executive Authority thereof shall issue Writs of Election to fill such Vacancies.

Speaker

Impeachment

The House of Representatives shall chuse their Speaker and other Officers; and shall have the sole Power of Impeachment.

Section. 3.

Senate

Changed by the Seventeenth Amendment

The Senate of the United States shall be composed of two Senators from each State, [chosen by the Legislature thereof] for six Years; and each Senator shall have one Vote.

Immediately after they shall be assembled in Consequence of the first Election, they shall be divided as equally as may be into three Classes. The Seats of the Senators of the first Class shall be vacated at the Expiration of the second Year, of the second Class at the Expiration of the fourth Year, and of the third Class at the Expiration of the sixth Year, so that one third may be chosen every second Year; [and if Vacancies happen by Resignation, or otherwise, during the Recess of the Legislature of any State, the Executive thereof may make temporary Appointments until the next Meeting of the Legislature, which shall then fill such Vacancies.]

Changed by the Seventeenth Amendment

Requirements of Office

No Person shall be a Senator who shall not have attained to the Age of thirty Years, and been nine Years a Citizen of the United States, and who shall not, when elected, be an Inhabitant of that State for which he shall be chosen.

Role of Vice President

The Vice President of the United States shall be President of the Senate, but shall have no Vote, unless they be equally divided.

The Senate shall chuse their other Officers, and also a President pro tempore, in the Absence of the Vice President, or when he shall exercise the Office of President of the United States.

Impeachment

The Senate shall have the sole Power to try all Impeachments. When sitting for that Purpose, they shall be on Oath or Affirmation. When the President of the United States is tried, the Chief Justice shall preside: And no Person shall be convicted without the Concurrence of two thirds of the Members present.

Judgment in Cases of Impeachment shall not extend further than to removal from Office, and disqualification to hold and enjoy any Office of honor, Trust or Profit under the United States: but the Party convicted shall nevertheless be liable and subject to Indictment, Trial, Judgment and Punishment, according to Law.

Section. 4.

The Times, Places and Manner of holding Elections for Senators and Representatives, shall be prescribed in each State by the Legislature thereof; but the Congress may at any time by Law make or alter such Regulations, except as to the Places of chusing Senators.

Elections

The Congress shall assemble at least once in every Year, and such Meeting shall [be on the first Monday in December,] unless they shall by Law appoint a different Day.

Changed by Section 2 of the Twentieth Amendment

Section. 5.

Each House shall be the Judge of the Elections, Returns and Qualifications of its own Members, and a Majority of each shall constitute a Quorum to do Business; but a smaller Number may adjourn from day to day, and may be authorized to compel the Attendance of absent Members, in such Manner, and under such Penalties as each House may provide.

Each House may determine the Rules of its Proceedings, punish its Members for disorderly Behaviour, and, with the Concurrence of two thirds, expel a Member.

Rules of Proceedings

Each House shall keep a Journal of its Proceedings, and from time to time publish the same, excepting such Parts as may in their Judgment require Secrecy; and the Yeas and Nays of the Members of either House on any question shall, at the Desire of one fifth of those Present, be entered on the Journal.

Neither House, during the Session of Congress, shall, without the Consent of the other, adjourn for more than three days, nor to any other Place than that in which the two Houses shall be sitting.

Adjournment

Section. 6.

The Senators and Representatives shall receive a Compensation for their Services, to be ascertained by Law, and paid out of the Treasury of the United States. They shall in all Cases, except Treason, Felony and Breach of the Peace, be privileged from Arrest during their Attendance at the Session of their respective Houses, and in going to and returning from the same; and for any Speech or Debate in either House, they shall not be questioned in any other Place.

Privilege from Arrest

No Senator or Representative shall, during the Time for which he was elected, be appointed to any civil Office under the Authority of the United States, which shall have been created, or the Emoluments whereof shall have been encreased during such time; and no Person holding any Office under the United States, shall be a Member of either House during his Continuance in Office.

Section. 7.

All Bills for raising Revenue shall originate in the House of Representatives; but the Senate may propose or concur with Amendments

Revenue Bills

as on other Bills.

Presentment Clause   Every Bill which shall have passed the House of Representatives and the Senate, shall, before it become a Law, be presented to the President of the United States: If he approve he shall sign it, but if not he **Veto** shall return it, with his Objections to that House in which it shall have originated, who shall enter the Objections at large on their Journal, and proceed to reconsider it. If after such Reconsideration two thirds of that House shall agree to pass the Bill, it shall be sent, together with the Objections, to the other House, by which it shall likewise be reconsidered, and if approved by two thirds of that House, it shall become a Law. But in all such Cases the Votes of both Houses shall be determined by yeas and Nays, and the Names of the Persons voting for and against the Bill shall be entered on the Journal of each House respec- **Pocket Veto** tively. If any Bill shall not be returned by the President within ten Days (Sundays excepted) after it shall have been presented to him, the Same shall be a Law, in like Manner as if he had signed it, unless the Congress by their Adjournment prevent its Return, in which Case it shall not be a Law.

Every Order, Resolution, or Vote to which the Concurrence of the Senate and House of Representatives may be necessary (except on a question of Adjournment) shall be presented to the President of the United States; and before the Same shall take Effect, shall be approved by him, or being disapproved by him, shall be repassed by two thirds of the Senate and House of Representatives, according to the Rules and Limitations prescribed in the Case of a Bill.

Section. 8.

Enumerated Powers of Congress   The Congress shall have Power To lay and collect Taxes, Duties, Imposts and Excises, to pay the Debts and provide for the common **Spending** Defence and general Welfare of the United States; but all Duties, Imposts and Excises shall be uniform throughout the United States;

To borrow Money on the credit of the United States;

Commerce   To regulate Commerce with foreign Nations, and among the several States, and with the Indian Tribes;

Naturalization   To establish an uniform Rule of Naturalization, and uniform Laws on the subject of Bankruptcies throughout the United States;

To coin Money, regulate the Value thereof, and of foreign Coin, and fix the Standard of Weights and Measures;

To provide for the Punishment of counterfeiting the Securities and current Coin of the United States;

To establish Post Offices and post Roads;

To promote the Progress of Science and useful Arts, by securing for limited Times to Authors and Inventors the exclusive Right to their respective Writings and Discoveries;

Inferior Courts   To constitute Tribunals inferior to the supreme Court;

To define and punish Piracies and Felonies committed on the high Seas, and Offences against the Law of Nations;

War Power   To declare War, grant Letters of Marque and Reprisal, and make Rules concerning Captures on Land and Water;

To raise and support Armies, but no Appropriation of Money to that Use shall be for a longer Term than two Years;

To provide and maintain a Navy;

To make Rules for the Government and Regulation of the land and naval Forces;

To provide for calling forth the Militia to execute the Laws of the Union, suppress Insurrections and repel Invasions;

To provide for organizing, arming, and disciplining, the Militia, and for governing such Part of them as may be employed in the Service of the United States, reserving to the States respectively, the Appointment of the Officers, and the Authority of training the Militia according to the discipline prescribed by Congress;

To exercise exclusive Legislation in all Cases whatsoever, over such District (not exceeding ten Miles square) as may, by Cession of particular States, and the Acceptance of Congress, become the Seat of the Government of the United States, and to exercise like Authority over all Places purchased by the Consent of the Legislature of the State in which the Same shall be, for the Erection of Forts, Magazines, Arsenals, dock-Yards, and other needful Buildings; — And **District of Columbia**

To make all Laws which shall be necessary and proper for carrying into Execution the foregoing Powers, and all other Powers vested by this Constitution in the Government of the United States, or in any Department or Officer thereof. **Necessary and Proper Clause**

Section. 9.

The Migration or Importation of such Persons as any of the States now existing shall think proper to admit, shall not be prohibited by the Congress prior to the Year one thousand eight hundred and eight, but a Tax or duty may be imposed on such Importation, not exceeding ten dollars for each Person.

The Privilege of the Writ of Habeas Corpus shall not be suspended, unless when in Cases of Rebellion or Invasion the public Safety may require it. **Habeas Corpus**

No Bill of Attainder or ex post facto Law shall be passed. **Ex Post Facto Laws**

No Capitation, or other direct, Tax shall be laid, [unless in Proportion to the Census or enumeration herein before directed to be taken.] **Changed by the Sixteenth Amendment**

No Tax or Duty shall be laid on Articles exported from any State.

No Preference shall be given by any Regulation of Commerce or Revenue to the Ports of one State over those of another; nor shall Vessels bound to, or from, one State, be obliged to enter, clear, or pay Duties in another.

No Money shall be drawn from the Treasury, but in Consequence of Appropriations made by Law; and a regular Statement and Account of the Receipts and Expenditures of all public Money shall be published from time to time. **Appropriations**

No Title of Nobility shall be granted by the United States: And no Person holding any Office of Profit or Trust under them, shall, without the Consent of the Congress, accept of any present, Emolument, **No Titles of Nobility**

Office, or Title, of any kind whatever, from any King, Prince, or foreign State.

Section. 10.

Restrictions on States

No State shall enter into any Treaty, Alliance, or Confederation; grant Letters of Marque and Reprisal; coin Money; emit Bills of Credit; make any Thing but gold and silver Coin a Tender in Payment of Debts; pass any Bill of Attainder, ex post facto Law, or Law impairing the Obligation of Contracts, or grant any Title of Nobility.

No State shall, without the Consent of the Congress, lay any Imposts or Duties on Imports or Exports, except what may be absolutely necessary for executing it's inspection Laws: and the net Produce of all Duties and Imposts, laid by any State on Imports or Exports, shall be for the Use of the Treasury of the United States; and all such Laws shall be subject to the Revision and Controul of the Congress.

No State shall, without the Consent of Congress, lay any Duty of Tonnage, keep Troops, or Ships of War in time of Peace, enter into any Agreement or Compact with another State, or with a foreign Power, or engage in War, unless actually invaded, or in such imminent Danger as will not admit of delay.

ARTICLE. II.

Section. 1.

Executive Power

The executive Power shall be vested in a President of the United States of America. He shall hold his Office during the Term of four Years, and, together with the Vice President, chosen for the same Term, be elected, as follows:

The Electoral College

Each State shall appoint, in such Manner as the Legislature thereof may direct, a Number of Electors, equal to the whole Number of Senators and Representatives to which the State may be entitled in the Congress: but no Senator or Representative, or Person holding an Office of Trust or Profit under the United States, shall be appointed an Elector.

[The Electors shall meet in their respective States, and vote by Ballot for two Persons, of whom one at least shall not be an Inhabitant of the same State with themselves. And they shall make a List of all the Persons voted for, and of the Number of Votes for each; which List they shall sign and certify, and transmit sealed to the Seat of the Government of the United States, directed to the President of the Senate. The President of the Senate shall, in the Presence of the Senate and House of Representatives, open all the Certificates, and the Votes shall

Changed by the Twelfth Amendment

then be counted. The Person having the greatest Number of Votes shall be the President, if such Number be a Majority of the whole Number of Electors appointed; and if there be more than one who have such Majority, and have an equal Number of Votes, then the House of Representatives shall immediately chuse by Ballot one of them for President; and if no Person have a Majority, then from the five highest on the List the said House shall in like Manner chuse the President. But in chusing the President, the Votes shall be taken by States, the Representation from each State having one Vote; A quorum for this purpose shall consist of a Member or Members from two thirds of the States, and a Majority of all the States shall be necessary to a Choice. In every Case, after the Choice of the President, the Person having the greatest Number of Votes of the Electors shall be the Vice President. But if there should remain two or more who have equal Votes, the Senate shall chuse from them by Ballot the Vice President.]

The Congress may determine the Time of chusing the Electors, and the Day on which they shall give their Votes; which Day shall be the same throughout the United States.

No Person except a natural born Citizen, or a Citizen of the United States, at the time of the Adoption of this Constitution, shall be eligible to the Office of President; neither shall any Person be eligible to that Office who shall not have attained to the Age of thirty five Years, and been fourteen Years a Resident within the United States.

Requirements of Office

[In Case of the Removal of the President from Office, or of his Death, Resignation, or Inability to discharge the Powers and Duties of the said Office, the Same shall devolve on the Vice President, and the Congress may by Law provide for the Case of Removal, Death, Resignation or Inability, both of the President and Vice President, declaring what Officer shall then act as President, and such Officer shall act accordingly, until the Disability be removed, or a President shall be elected.]

Changed by the Twenty-fifth Amendment

The President shall, at stated Times, receive for his Services, a Compensation, which shall neither be increased nor diminished during the Period for which he shall have been elected, and he shall not receive within that Period any other Emolument from the United States, or any of them.

Before he enter on the Execution of his Office, he shall take the following Oath or Affirmation: — "I do solemnly swear (or affirm) that I will faithfully execute the Office of President of the United States, and will to the best of my Ability, preserve, protect and defend the Constitution of the United States."

Oath of Office

Section. 2.

The President shall be Commander in Chief of the Army and Navy of the United States, and of the Militia of the several States, when called into the actual Service of the United States; he may require the Opinion, in writing, of the principal Officer in each of the executive Departments, upon any Subject relating to the Duties of their respective Offices, and he shall have Power to grant Reprieves and Pardons for Offences against the United States, except in Cases of Impeachment.

Commander in Chief

Reprieves and Pardons

He shall have Power, by and with the Advice and Consent of the Senate, to make Treaties, provided two thirds of the Senators present concur; and he shall nominate, and by and with the Advice and Consent of the Senate, shall appoint Ambassadors, other public Ministers

Treaty Power

Nominations and Appointments

and Consuls, Judges of the supreme Court, and all other Officers of the United States, whose Appointments are not herein otherwise provided for, and which shall be established by Law: but the Congress may by Law vest the Appointment of such inferior Officers, as they think proper, in the President alone, in the Courts of Law, or in the Heads of Departments.

Recess Appointments   The President shall have Power to fill up all Vacancies that may happen during the Recess of the Senate, by granting Commissions which shall expire at the End of their next Session.

Section. 3.

State of the Union   He shall from time to time give to the Congress Information of the State of the Union, and recommend to their Consideration such Measures as he shall judge necessary and expedient; he may, on extraordinary Occasions, convene both Houses, or either of them, and in Case of Disagreement between them, with Respect to the Time of Adjournment, he may adjourn them to such Time as he shall think proper; he shall receive Ambassadors and other public **Take Care Clause**   Ministers; he shall take Care that the Laws be faithfully executed, and shall Commission all the Officers of the United States.

Section. 4.

Impeachment   The President, Vice President and all civil Officers of the United States, shall be removed from Office on Impeachment for, and Conviction of, Treason, Bribery, or other high Crimes and Misdemeanors.

ARTICLE III.

Section. 1.

Judicial Power   The judicial Power of the United States shall be vested in one supreme Court, and in such inferior Courts as the Congress may from time to time ordain and establish. The Judges, both of the supreme and inferi-**Tenure**   or Courts, shall hold their Offices during good Behaviour, and shall, at stated Times, receive for their Services a Compensation, which shall not be diminished during their Continuance in Office.

Section. 2.

Jurisdiction, Cases, and   The judicial Power shall extend to all Cases, in Law and Equity, arising **Controversies**   under this Constitution, the Laws of the United States, and Treaties made, or which shall be made, under their Authority; — to all Cases affecting Ambassadors, other public Ministers and Consuls; — to all Cases of admiralty and maritime Jurisdiction; — to Controversies to which the United States shall be a Party; — to Controversies between **Changed by the Eleventh**   two or more States; — [between a State and Citizens of another State; **Amendment**   —] between Citizens of different States; — between Citizens of the same State claiming Lands under Grants of different States, [and **Changed by the Eleventh**   between a State, or the Citizens thereof, and foreign States, Citizens or **Amendment**   Subjects.]

In all Cases affecting Ambassadors, other public Ministers and Consuls, and those in which a State shall be Party, the supreme Court shall have original Jurisdiction. In all the other Cases before mentioned, the supreme Court shall have appellate Jurisdiction, both as to Law and Fact, with such Exceptions, and under such Regulations as the Congress shall make.

Original Jurisdiction

Appellate Jurisdiction

The Trial of all Crimes, except in Cases of Impeachment, shall be by Jury; and such Trial shall be held in the State where the said Crimes shall have been committed; but when not committed within any State, the Trial shall be at such Place or Places as the Congress may by Law have directed.

Trial by Jury

Section. 3.

Treason against the United States, shall consist only in levying War against them, or in adhering to their Enemies, giving them Aid and Comfort. No Person shall be convicted of Treason unless on the Testimony of two Witnesses to the same overt Act, or on Confession in open Court.

Treason

The Congress shall have Power to declare the Punishment of Treason, but no Attainder of Treason shall work Corruption of Blood, or Forfeiture except during the Life of the Person attainted.

ARTICLE. IV.

Section. 1.

Full Faith and Credit shall be given in each State to the public Acts, Records, and judicial Proceedings of every other State. And the Congress may by general Laws prescribe the Manner in which such Acts, Records and Proceedings shall be proved, and the Effect thereof.

Relations Among the States

Section. 2.

The Citizens of each State shall be entitled to all Privileges and Immunities of Citizens in the several States.

Privileges and Immunities

A Person charged in any State with Treason, Felony, or other Crime, who shall flee from Justice, and be found in another State, shall on Demand of the executive Authority of the State from which he fled, be delivered up, to be removed to the State having Jurisdiction of the Crime.

Extradition

[No Person held to Service or Labour in one State, under the Laws thereof, escaping into another, shall, in Consequence of any Law or Regulation therein, be discharged from such Service or Labour, but shall be delivered up on Claim of the Party to whom such Service or Labour may be due.]

Changed by the Thirteenth Amendment

Section. 3.

New States may be admitted by the Congress into this Union; but no new State shall be formed or erected within the Jurisdiction of any

Admission of New States

other State; nor any State be formed by the Junction of two or more States, or Parts of States, without the Consent of the Legislatures of the States concerned as well as of the Congress.

Territories

The Congress shall have Power to dispose of and make all needful Rules and Regulations respecting the Territory or other Property belonging to the United States; and nothing in this Constitution shall be so construed as to Prejudice any Claims of the United States, or of any particular State.

Section. 4.

Republican Form of Government

The United States shall guarantee to every State in this Union a Republican Form of Government, and shall protect each of them against Invasion; and on Application of the Legislature, or of the Executive (when the Legislature cannot be convened), against domestic Violence.

ARTICLE. V.

Procedures for Amending the Constitution

The Congress, whenever two thirds of both Houses shall deem it necessary, shall propose Amendments to this Constitution, or, on the Application of the Legislatures of two thirds of the several States, shall call a Convention for proposing Amendments, which, in either Case, shall be valid to all Intents and Purposes, as Part of this Constitution, when ratified by the Legislatures of three fourths of the several States, or by Conventions in three fourths thereof, as the one or the other Mode of Ratification may be proposed by the Congress; Provided that no Amendment which may be made prior to the Year One thousand eight hundred and eight shall in any Manner affect the first and fourth Clauses in the Ninth Section of the first Article; and that no State, without its Consent, shall be deprived of its equal Suffrage in the Senate.

ARTICLE. VI.

All Debts contracted and Engagements entered into, before the Adoption of this Constitution, shall be as valid against the United States under this Constitution, as under the Confederation.

Supreme Law of the Land

This Constitution, and the Laws of the United States which shall be made in Pursuance thereof; and all Treaties made, or which shall be made, under the Authority of the United States, shall be the supreme Law of the Land; and the Judges in every State shall be bound thereby, any Thing in the Constitution or Laws of any State to the Contrary notwithstanding.

Oath to Support Constitution

The Senators and Representatives before mentioned, and the Members of the several State Legislatures, and all executive and judicial Officers, both of the United States and of the several States, shall be bound by Oath or Affirmation, to support this Constitution; but no religious Test shall ever be required as a Qualification to any Office or public Trust under the United States.

No Religious Test

ARTICLE. VII.

The Ratification of the Conventions of nine States, shall be sufficient for the Establishment of this Constitution between the States so ratifying the Same.

Ratification

   Done in Convention by the Unanimous Consent of the States present the Seventeenth Day of September in the Year of our Lord one thousand seven hundred and Eighty seven and of the Independence of the United States of America the Twelfth In witness whereof We have hereunto subscribed our Names,

Attest William Jackson, Secretary

Go. Washington – Presidt
and deputy from Virginia

Delaware
   Geo: Read
   Gunning Bedford jun
   John Dickinson
   Richard Bassett
   Jaco: Broom

Maryland
   James McHenry
   Dan of St Thos. Jenifer
   Danl. Carroll

Virginia
   John Blair
   James Madison Jr.

North Carolina
   Wm. Blount
   Richd. Dobbs Spaight
   Hu Williamson

South Carolina
   J. Rutledge
   Charles Cotesworth Pinckney
   Charles Pinckney
   Pierce Butler

Georgia
   William Few
   Abr Baldwin

New Hampshire
   John Langdon
   Nicholas Gilman

Massachusetts
   Nathaniel Gorham
   Rufus King

Connecticut
   Wm. Saml. Johnson
   Roger Sherman

New York
   Alexander Hamilton

New Jersey
   Wil: Livingston
   David Brearley
   Wm. Paterson
   Jona: Dayton

Pennsylvania
   B Franklin
   Thomas Mifflin
   Robt. Morris
   Geo. Clymer
   Thos. FitzSimons
   Jared Ingersoll
   James Wilson
   Gouv Morris

AMENDMENTS TO THE CONSTITUTION
OF THE UNITED STATES OF AMERICA

AMENDMENT I

The First Ten Amendments—
the Bill of Rights—Were
Ratified Effective December
15, 1791

Religion, Speech, Press,
Assembly, and Petition

Congress shall make no law respecting an establishment of religion, or prohibiting the free exercise thereof; or abridging the freedom of speech, or of the press; or the right of the people peaceably to assemble, and to petition the Government for a redress of grievances.

AMENDMENT II

Right to Bear Arms

A well regulated Militia, being necessary to the security of a free State, the right of the people to keep and bear Arms, shall not be infringed.

AMENDMENT III

Quartering of Troops

No Soldier shall, in time of peace be quartered in any house, without the consent of the Owner, nor in time of war, but in a manner to be prescribed by law.

AMENDMENT IV

Searches and Seizures

The right of the people to be secure in their persons, houses, papers, and effects, against unreasonable searches and seizures, shall not be violated, and no Warrants shall issue, but upon probable cause, supported by Oath or affirmation, and particularly describing the place to be searched, and the persons or things to be seized.

AMENDMENT V

Grand Juries, Double Jeopardy,
Self Incrimination, Due Process

Taking of Property

No person shall be held to answer for a capital, or otherwise infamous crime, unless on a presentment or indictment of a Grand Jury, except in cases arising in the land or naval forces, or in the Militia, when in actual service in time of War or public danger; nor shall any person be subject for the same offence to be twice put in jeopardy of life or limb; nor shall be compelled in any criminal case to be a witness against himself, nor be deprived of life, liberty, or property, without due process of law; nor shall private property be taken for public use, without just compensation.

AMENDMENT VI

In all criminal prosecutions, the accused shall enjoy the right to a speedy and public trial, by an impartial jury of the State and district wherein the crime shall have been committed, which district shall have been previously ascertained by law, and to be informed of the nature and cause of the accusation; to be confronted with the witnesses against him; to have compulsory process for obtaining witnesses in his favor, and to have the Assistance of Counsel for his defence.

Criminal Court Procedures

AMENDMENT VII

In Suits at common law, where the value in controversy shall exceed twenty dollars, the right of trial by jury shall be preserved, and no fact tried by a jury, shall be otherwise re-examined in any Court of the United States, than according to the rules of the common law.

Trial by Jury in Civil Cases

AMENDMENT VIII

Excessive bail shall not be required, nor excessive fines imposed, nor cruel and unusual punishments inflicted.

Bail, Cruel and Unusual Punishments

AMENDMENT IX

The enumeration in the Constitution, of certain rights, shall not be construed to deny or disparage others retained by the people.

Other Rights of the People

AMENDMENT X

The powers not delegated to the United States by the Constitution, nor prohibited by it to the States, are reserved to the States respectively, or to the people.

Powers Reserved to the States, or the People

AMENDMENT XI

(Ratified February 7, 1795)

The Judicial power of the United States shall not be construed to extend to any suit in law or equity, commenced or prosecuted against one of the United States by Citizens of another State, or by Citizens or Subjects of any Foreign State.

Suits Against States

(Ratified June 15, 1804)

Election of the President

AMENDMENT XII

The Electors shall meet in their respective states and vote by ballot for President and Vice-President, one of whom, at least, shall not be an inhabitant of the same state with themselves; they shall name in their ballots the person voted for as President, and in distinct ballots the person voted for as Vice-President, and they shall make distinct lists of all persons voted for as President, and of all persons voted for as Vice-President, and of the number of votes for each, which lists they shall sign and certify, and transmit sealed to the seat of the government of the United States, directed to the President of the Senate; — the President of the Senate shall, in the presence of the Senate and House of Representatives, open all the certificates and the votes shall then be counted; — The person having the greatest number of votes for President, shall be the President, if such number be a majority of the whole number of Electors appointed; and if no person have such majority, then from the persons having the highest numbers not exceeding three on the list of those voted for as President, the House of Representatives shall choose immediately, by ballot, the President. But in choosing the President, the votes shall be taken by states, the representation from each state having one vote; a quorum for this purpose shall consist of a member or members from two-thirds of the states, and a majority of all the states shall be necessary to a choice. [And if the House of Representatives shall not choose a President whenever the right of choice shall devolve upon them, before the fourth day of March next following, then the Vice-President shall act as President, as in case of the death or other constitutional disability of the President. —] The person having the greatest number of votes as Vice-President, shall be the Vice-President, if such number be a majority of the whole number of Electors appointed, and if no person have a majority, then from the two highest numbers on the list, the Senate shall choose the Vice-President; a quorum for the purpose shall consist of two-thirds of the whole number of Senators, and a majority of the whole number shall be necessary to a choice. But no person constitutionally ineligible to the office of President shall be eligible to that of Vice-President of the United States.

Superseded by Section 3 of the Twentieth Amendment

(Ratified December 6, 1865)

AMENDMENT XIII

Prohibition of Slavery

Section 1.
Neither slavery nor involuntary servitude, except as a punishment for crime whereof the party shall have been duly convicted, shall exist within the United States, or any place subject to their jurisdiction.

Section 2.
Congress shall have power to enforce this article by appropriate legislation.

AMENDMENT XIV

(Ratified July 9, 1868)

Section 1.

All persons born or naturalized in the United States, and subject to the jurisdiction thereof, are citizens of the United States and of the State wherein they reside. No State shall make or enforce any law which shall abridge the privileges or immunities of citizens of the United States; nor shall any State deprive any person of life, liberty, or property, without due process of law; nor deny to any person within its jurisdiction the equal protection of the laws.

Citizenship

Privileges and Immunities

Due Process

Equal Protection

Section 2.

Representatives shall be apportioned among the several States according to their respective numbers, counting the whole number of persons in each State, excluding Indians not taxed. But when the right to vote at any election for the choice of electors for President and Vice-President of the United States, Representatives in Congress, the Executive and Judicial officers of a State, or the members of the Legislature thereof, is denied to any of the male inhabitants of such State, [being twenty-one years of age,] and citizens of the United States, or in any way abridged, except for participation in rebellion, or other crime, the basis of representation therein shall be reduced in the proportion which the number of such male citizens shall bear to the whole number of male citizens twenty-one years of age in such State.

Apportionment

Superseded by Section 1 of the Twenty-sixth Amendment

Section 3.

No person shall be a Senator or Representative in Congress, or elector of President and Vice-President, or hold any office, civil or military, under the United States, or under any State, who, having previously taken an oath, as a member of Congress, or as an officer of the United States, or as a member of any State legislature, or as an executive or judicial officer of any State, to support the Constitution of the United States, shall have engaged in insurrection or rebellion against the same, or given aid or comfort to the enemies thereof. But Congress may by a vote of two-thirds of each House, remove such disability.

Disqualification for Rebellion

Section 4.

The validity of the public debt of the United States, authorized by law, including debts incurred for payment of pensions and bounties for services in suppressing insurrection or rebellion, shall not be questioned. But neither the United States nor any State shall assume or pay any debt or obligation incurred in aid of insurrection or rebellion against the United States, or any claim for the loss or emancipation of any slave; but all such debts, obligations and claims shall be held illegal and void.

Debts Incurred During Rebellion

Section 5.

The Congress shall have the power to enforce, by appropriate legislation, the provisions of this article.

(Ratified February 3, 1870)

AMENDMENT XV

Section 1.
The right of citizens of the United States to vote shall not be denied
Suffrage—Race   or abridged by the United States or by any State on account of race,
color, or previous condition of servitude —

Section 2.
The Congress shall have the power to enforce this article by appropriate legislation.

(Ratified February 3, 1913)

AMENDMENT XVI

Federal Income Tax   The Congress shall have power to lay and collect taxes on incomes,
from whatever source derived, without apportionment among the
several States, and without regard to any census or enumeration.

(Ratified April 8, 1913)

AMENDMENT XVII

Popular Election of Senators   The Senate of the United States shall be composed of two Senators
from each State, elected by the people thereof, for six years; and
each Senator shall have one vote. The electors in each State shall
have the qualifications requisite for electors of the most numerous
branch of the State legislatures.

When vacancies happen in the representation of any State in
the Senate, the executive authority of such State shall issue writs of
election to fill such vacancies: *Provided,* That the legislature of any
State may empower the executive thereof to make temporary
appointments until the people fill the vacancies by election as the
legislature may direct.

This amendment shall not be so construed as to affect the election or term of any Senator chosen before it becomes valid as part
of the Constitution.

(Ratified January 16, 1919)
Repealed by the Twenty-first
Amendment

AMENDMENT XVIII

Prohibition   **Section 1.**
After one year from the ratification of this article the manufacture,
sale, or transportation of intoxicating liquors within, the importation thereof into, or the exportation thereof from the United States
and all territory subject to the jurisdiction thereof for beverage
purposes is hereby prohibited.

Section 2.
The Congress and the several States shall have concurrent power
to enforce this article by appropriate legislation.

Section 3.

This article shall be inoperative unless it shall have been ratified as an amendment to the Constitution by the legislatures of the several States, as provided in the Constitution, within seven years from the date of the submission hereof to the States by the Congress.

AMENDMENT XIX

(Ratified August 18, 1920)

The right of citizens of the United States to vote shall not be denied or abridged by the United States or by any State on account of sex.

Suffrage—Sex

Congress shall have power to enforce this article by appropriate legislation.

AMENDMENT XX

(Ratified January 23, 1933)

Section 1.

The terms of the President and the Vice President shall end at noon on the 20th day of January, and the terms of Senators and Representatives at noon on the 3d day of January, of the years in which such terms would have ended if this article had not been ratified; and the terms of their successors shall then begin.

Lame-duck Amendment

Section 2.

The Congress shall assemble at least once in every year, and such meeting shall begin at noon on the 3d day of January, unless they shall by law appoint a different day.

Section 3.

If, at the time fixed for the beginning of the term of the President, the President elect shall have died, the Vice President elect shall become President. If a President shall not have been chosen before the time fixed for the beginning of his term, or if the President elect shall have failed to qualify, then the Vice President elect shall act as President until a President shall have qualified; and the Congress may by law provide for the case wherein neither a President elect nor a Vice President shall have qualified, declaring who shall then act as President, or the manner in which one who is to act shall be selected, and such person shall act accordingly until a President or Vice President shall have qualified.

Presidential Succession

Section 4.

The Congress may by law provide for the case of the death of any of the persons from whom the House of Representatives may choose a President whenever the right of choice shall have devolved upon them, and for the case of the death of any of the persons from whom the Senate may choose a Vice President whenever the right of choice shall have devolved upon them.

Section 5.

Sections 1 and 2 shall take effect on the 15th day of October following the ratification of this article.

Section 6.

This article shall be inoperative unless it shall have been ratified as an amendment to the Constitution by the legislatures of three-fourths of the several States within seven years from the date of its submission.

(Ratified December 5, 1933)

AMENDMENT XXI

Section 1.

Repeal of Prohibition

The eighteenth article of amendment to the Constitution of the United States is hereby repealed.

Section 2.

The transportation or importation into any State, Territory, or Possession of the United States for delivery or use therein of intoxicating liquors, in violation of the laws thereof, is hereby prohibited.

Section 3.

This article shall be inoperative unless it shall have been ratified as an amendment to the Constitution by conventions in the several States, as provided in the Constitution, within seven years from the date of the submission hereof to the States by the Congress.

(Ratified February 27, 1951)

AMENDMENT XXII

Section 1.

Limit on Presidential Terms

No person shall be elected to the office of the President more than twice, and no person who has held the office of President, or acted as President, for more than two years of a term to which some other person was elected President shall be elected to the office of President more than once. But this Article shall not apply to any person holding the office of President when this Article was proposed by Congress, and shall not prevent any person who may be holding the office of President, or acting as President, during the term within which this Article becomes operative from holding the office of President or acting as President during the remainder of such term.

Section 2.

This article shall be inoperative unless it shall have been ratified as an amendment to the Constitution by the legislatures of three-fourths of the several States within seven years from the date of its submission to the States by the Congress.

AMENDMENT XXIII

Section 1.

The District constituting the seat of Government of the United States shall appoint in such manner as Congress may direct:

Presidential Electors for the District of Columbia

A number of electors of President and Vice President equal to the whole number of Senators and Representatives in Congress to which the District would be entitled if it were a State, but in no event more than the least populous State; they shall be in addition to those appointed by the States, but they shall be considered, for the purposes of the election of President and Vice President, to be electors appointed by a State; and they shall meet in the District and perform such duties as provided by the twelfth article of amendment.

Section 2.

The Congress shall have power to enforce this article by appropriate legislation.

AMENDMENT XXIV

Section 1.

The right of citizens of the United States to vote in any primary or other election for President or Vice President, for electors for President or Vice President, or for Senator or Representative in Congress, shall not be denied or abridged by the United States or any State by reason of failure to pay poll tax or other tax.

Prohibition of the Poll Tax

Section 2.

The Congress shall have power to enforce this article by appropriate legislation.

AMENDMENT XXV

Section 1.

In case of the removal of the President from office or of his death or resignation, the Vice President shall become President.

Presidential Succession

Section 2.

Whenever there is a vacancy in the office of the Vice President, the President shall nominate a Vice President who shall take office upon confirmation by a majority vote of both Houses of Congress.

Vice Presidency

Section 3.

Whenever the President transmits to the President pro tempore of the Senate and the Speaker of the House of Representatives his written declaration that he is unable to discharge the powers and

Incapacity to Perform Duties of Office

duties of his office, and until he transmits to them a written declaration to the contrary, such powers and duties shall be discharged by the Vice President as Acting President.

Section 4.
Whenever the Vice President and a majority of either the principal officers of the executive departments or of such other body as Congress may by law provide, transmit to the President pro tempore of the Senate and the Speaker of the House of Representatives their written declaration that the President is unable to discharge the powers and duties of his office, the Vice President shall immediately assume the powers and duties of the office as Acting President.

Thereafter, when the President transmits to the President pro tempore of the Senate and the Speaker of the House of Representatives his written declaration that no inability exists, he shall resume the powers and duties of his office unless the Vice President and a majority of either the principal officers of the executive department or of such other body as Congress may by law provide, transmit within four days to the President pro tempore of the Senate and the Speaker of the House of Representatives their written declaration that the President is unable to discharge the powers and duties of his office. Thereupon Congress shall decide the issue, assembling within forty-eight hours for that purpose if not in session. If the Congress, within twenty-one days after receipt of the latter written declaration, or, if Congress is not in session, within twenty-one days after Congress is required to assemble, determines by two-thirds vote of both Houses that the President is unable to discharge the powers and duties of his office, the Vice President shall continue to discharge the same as Acting President; otherwise, the President shall resume the powers and duties of his office.

(Ratified July 1, 1971)

AMENDMENT XXVI

Section 1.

Suffrage—Age

The right of citizens of the United States, who are eighteen years of age or older, to vote shall not be denied or abridged by the United States or by any State on account of age.

Section 2.
The Congress shall have power to enforce this article by appropriate legislation.

(Ratified May 7, 1992)

Proposed September 25, 1789 as part of the original Bill of Rights

Congressional Compensation

AMENDMENT XXVII

No law, varying the compensation for the services of the Senators and Representatives, shall take effect, until an election of representatives shall have intervened.

The Heritage Guide to
the Constitution

PREAMBLE

We the People of the United States, in Order to form a more perfect Union, establish Justice, insure domestic Tranquility, provide for the common defense, promote the general Welfare, and secure the Blessings of Liberty to ourselves and our Posterity, do ordain and establish this Constitution for the United States of America.

∼

*T*he Preamble was placed in the Constitution more or less as an afterthought. It was not proposed or discussed on the floor of the Constitutional Convention. Rather, Gouverneur Morris, a delegate from Pennsylvania who as a member of the Committee of Style actually drafted the near-final text of the Constitution, composed it at the last moment. It was Morris who gave the considered purposes of the Constitution coherent shape, and the Preamble was the capstone of his expository gift. The Preamble did not, in itself, have any substantive legal meaning. The understanding at the time was that preambles are merely declaratory and are not to be read as granting or limiting

power—a view sustained by the Supreme Court in *Jacobson v. Massachusetts* (1905).

Nevertheless, the Preamble has considerable potency by virtue of its specification of the purposes for which the Constitution exists. It distills the underlying values that moved the Framers during their long debates in Philadelphia. As Justice Joseph Story put it in his celebrated *Commentaries on the Constitution of the United States,* "its true office is to expound the nature and extent and application of the powers actually conferred by the Constitution." Alexander Hamilton, in *The Federalist* No. 84, went so far as to assert that the words "secure the Blessings of Liberty to ourselves and our Posterity" were "a better recognition of popular rights, than volumes of those aphorisms, which make the principal figure in several of our state bills of rights."

An appreciation of the Preamble begins with a comparison of it to its counterpart in the compact the Constitution replaced, the Articles of Confederation. There, the states joined in "a firm league of friendship, for their common defence, the security of their liberties, and their mutual and general welfare" and bound themselves to assist one another "against all force offered to, or attacks made upon them, or any of them, on account of religion, sovereignty, trade, or any other pretence whatever." The agreement was among states, not people, and the military protection and the liberties to be secured were of the states as such.

The very opening words of the Constitution mark a radical departure: "We the People of the United States." That language was at striking variance with the norm, for in earlier documents, including the 1778 treaty of alliance with France, the Articles of Confederation, and the 1783 Treaty of Paris recognizing American independence, the word "People" was not used, and the phrase "the United States" was followed immediately by a listing of the states ("viz., New Hampshire, Massachusetts Bay, Rhode Island and Providence Plantations," and so on down to Georgia).

The new phraseology was necessary, given the circumstances. The Constitutional Convention had provided that whenever the popularly elected ratifying conventions of nine states approved the Constitution, it would go into effect for those nine, irrespective of whether any of the remaining states ratified. In as much as no one could know which states would and which would not ratify, the Convention could not list all thirteen. Moreover, names could scarcely be added to the Preamble retroactively as they were admitted. Even so, the phrase set off howls of protest from a number of opponents of ratification, notably Patrick Henry. Henry charged that the failure to follow the usual form indicated an intention to create a "consolidated" national government instead of the system that James Madison described in *The Federalist* No. 39 as being "neither a national nor a federal constitution; but a composition of both." Henry's assertion was made in the Virginia ratifying convention and was promptly and devastatingly rebutted by Governor Edmund Randolph: "The government is for the people; and the misfortune was, that the people had no agency in the government before.... If the government is to be binding on the people, are not the people the proper persons to examine its merits or defects?"

The Preamble's first-mentioned purpose of the Constitution, "to form a more perfect Union," was likewise subjected to misreading by Anti-Federalists. "More perfect" may strike modern readers as a solecism or as an ambigu-

ous depiction, for "perfect" is now regarded as an absolute term. At the time of the Framing, however, it had no such connotation. For example, Sir William Blackstone, in his widely read *Commentaries on the Laws of England*, could assert that the constitution of England was perfect but steadily improving. Thus a more perfect union was simply a better and stronger one than had preexisted the Constitution. Yet a New York Anti-Federalist who wrote under the pseudonym Brutus professed to believe that to carry out the mandate it would be "necessary to abolish all inferior governments, and to give the general one compleat legislative, executive and judicial powers to every purpose." Madison disposed of that patent exaggeration in *The Federalist* No. 41 by demonstrating that "the powers proposed to be lodged in the new federal government, are as little formidable to those reserved to the individual states as they are indispensably necessary to accomplish the purposes of the union."

> [A]ll those alarms which have been sounded, or a mediated and consequential annihilation of the state governments, must, on the most favourable interpretation, be ascribed to the chimerical fears of the authors of them.

In the second stated objective, to "establish Justice," the key word is "establish," clearly implying that justice, unlike union, was previously nonexistent. On the face of it, that implication seems hyperbolic, for the American states and local governments had functioning court systems with independent judges, and trial by jury was the norm. But Gouverneur Morris chose the word carefully and meant what he wrote; he and many other Framers thought that the states had run amok and had trampled individual liberties in a variety of ways. The solution was twofold: the establishment of an independent Supreme Court and the provision for a federal judiciary superior to those of the states; and outright prohibition of egregious state practices.

The third avowed purpose, to "insure domestic Tranquility," was in a general sense prompted by the long-standing habit of Americans to take up arms against unpopular government measures and was more immediately a response to Shays's Rebellion in Massachusetts (1786–1787) and lesser uprisings in New Hampshire and Delaware. The most important constitutional provisions directed toward that end give Congress ultimate control over the militias (*see* Article I, Section 8) and guarantee each state a republican form of government and protection against domestic violence (*see* Article IV, Section 4). One should bear in mind that two rebellions broke out during the first decade under the Constitution, the Whiskey Rebellion (1794) and Fries's Rebellion (1799), both of which were speedily crushed without the shedding of blood.

The fourth purpose, to "provide for the common defense," is obvious—after all, it was the reason the United States came into being. But the matter cannot be dismissed lightly. For the better part of a century Americans had been possessed by a fear of "standing armies," insisting that armed forces adequate to defend the nation would also be adequate to enslave it. Besides, ordinary Americans could believe that, since the War for Independence had been won over the best fighting force in Europe under the aegis of the Confederation, further provision was unnecessary as well as dangerous. Anti-Federalists clearly thought along those lines. By and large, those who agreed had seen little of the fighting during the war, whereas veterans of actual combat and people who had served in Congress or the administration during the darkest hours of the war knew differently. They expected that other wars would occur and were determined to be prepared to fight them. The Framers did, however, take fears of standing armies into account, hence their commitment to civilian control of things military.

The fifth purpose, to "promote the general Welfare," had a generally understood meaning at the time of the Constitution. The concept will be developed fully in the discussion of the Spending Clause of Article I, Section 8, but a few comments are germane here. The salient point is that its implications are negative, not positive—a limitation on power, not a grant of power. By definition "general" means applicable to the whole rather than to particular parts or special interests. A single example will illustrate the point. In the late 1790s Alexander Hamilton, an outspoken advocate of loose construction of the Constitution as well as of using the Necessary and Proper Clause to justify a wide range of "implied powers," became convinced that a federally financed system of what would soon be called internal improvements—building roads, dredging rivers, digging canals—was in the national interest. But, since each project would be of immediate advantage only to the area where it was located, none could properly be regarded as being in the general welfare. Accordingly, Hamilton believed a constitutional amendment would be necessary if internal improvements were to be undertaken. James Madison, in his second term as President, would veto a congressional bill on precisely that ground.

The sixth purpose of the Constitution is to "secure the Blessings of Liberty to ourselves and our Posterity." In broad terms the securing of liberty is a function of the whole Constitution, for the Constitution makes possible the establishment of a government of laws, and liberty without law is meaningless. Special provisions, however, in Article I, Sections 9 and 10, and Article III were designed to prevent specific dangers to liberty about which history had warned the Framers. Those in Section 9 were drawn from the example of English history: the prohibitions against suspending the writ of habeas corpus, against bills of attainder and ex post facto laws, and against granting titles of nobility. In addition, Article III, Section 2, guaranteed trial by jury in criminal cases, and Section 3 defined treason extremely narrowly and prohibited corruption of the blood. These protections of liberty are of individual liberty, not of the states' liberty as under the Articles of Confederation.

The restrictions in Article I, Section 10, apply to the state governments and were born of more recent history. The states are forbidden, among other things, to issue paper money, to make anything but gold and silver legal tender, or to pass bills of attainder, ex post facto laws, or laws impairing the obligation of contracts. All these mischievous kinds of laws had in fact been enacted by the states since the Declaration of Independence.

That brings us back to another point about the "general Welfare" and enables us to arrive at a broader understanding of the Preamble than is possible through a provision-by-provision analysis. Some historians have argued that the philosophy or ideology of the Constitution was at variance with that of the Declaration; indeed, several have described the adoption of the Constitution as a counter-Revolution. But consider this. The Declaration refers to God-given rights to life, liberty, and the pursuit of happiness. The Preamble introduces a document whose stated purpose is to secure the rights of life and liberty. And what of happiness? Once again the word "Welfare" is crucial: in the eighteenth century the definition of welfare included well-being, but it also and equally encompassed happiness.

The Preamble as a whole, then, declares that the Constitution is designed to secure precisely the rights proclaimed in the Declaration. The Constitution was therefore not the negation of the Revolution; it was the Revolution's fulfillment.

Forrest McDonald

See Also

Significant Case

Jacobson v. Massachusetts, 197 U.S. 11 (1905)

ARTICLE I

Legislative Vesting Clause

All legislative Powers herein granted shall be vested in a Congress of the United States, which shall consist of a Senate and House of Representatives.

(ARTICLE I, SECTION 1)

*A*rticles I, II, and III of the Constitution respectively vest the legislative, executive, and judicial powers each in a separate department of the federal government. This separation of powers, which draws upon ideas advanced by John Locke, Baron de Montesquieu, and Sir William Blackstone, reflects the Framers' intention that undue power not be combined in any one department lest, being unchecked, it become tyrannical. The separation, by which each department may exercise only its own constitutional powers, is fundamental to the idea of a limited government accountable to the people. The principle is particularly noteworthy in regard to the Congress. The Constitution declares that the Congress may exercise only those legislative powers "herein granted." That the power assigned to each branch must remain with that branch, and may be expressed only by that branch, is central to the theory.

This basic principle is enforced by the Constitution's scheme of enumerated powers. The President and the federal courts are vested with the executive and judicial powers, respectively. Neither power includes a general power of lawmaking. Nor can the Congress confer such a lawmaking power by statute, for the simple reason that the Congress has no enumerated power to create lawmakers. (The exceptions are in the Enclave Clause and the Property Clause, where the Congress has essentially plenary powers, and in foreign affairs, where, in light of the President's inherent executive powers, delegation is of little concern. *United States v. Curtiss-Wright Export Corp.* (1936).)

The executive necessarily has a range of discretion in the manner of effectuating a law. But some decisions are legislative by nature; otherwise, the distinction among legislative, executive, and judicial powers that is fundamental to the Constitution's structure would be meaningless. Accordingly, the question arises whether and when laws that confer discretion upon the executive call for the executive to exercise legislative power.

The Supreme Court has wrestled with that difficult question from early in the history of the Republic to the present day. In the 1825 case of *Wayman v. Southard*, the Court acknowledged that "[t]he line has not been exactly drawn which separates those important subjects, which must be entirely regulated by the legislature itself, from those of less interest, in which a general provision may be made, and power given to [others] to fill up the details." In another early case the Court held that a conditional exercise of the legislative power—by enactment of a statute with a provision that takes effect only upon the President's making a certain factual finding—does not unlawfully delegate that power. *Cargo of the Brig Aurora v. United States* (1813).

In 1928, the Court upheld a statute delegating to the President the power to adjust tariffs to any rate, within a wide range, he found necessary to "equalize the . . . differences in costs of production in the United States and the principal competing country." *J.W. Hampton, Jr. & Co. v. United States*. In that case, the Court for the first time set out what remains the governing standard: a "legislative action is not a forbidden delegation of legislative power" if the "Congress shall lay down by legislative act an intelligible principle to which the person or body [to whom power is delegated] is directed to conform."

Twice in 1935 the Court held that a statute delegating sweeping regulatory power to the President violated this standard. In *Panama Refining Co. v. Ryan* (1935), the Court held unconstitutional a section of the National Industrial Recovery Act that permitted the President broadly to ban interstate transportation of quantities of oil in excess of state law production limitations: "[T]he Congress has declared no policy, has established no standard, has laid down no rule. There is no requirement, no definition of circumstances and conditions in which the transportation is to be allowed or prohibited." Four months later in *A.L.A. Schechter Poultry Corp. v. United States* (1935), the Court unanimously struck down a section of the same act that gave the President virtually unbridled power to regulate the economy by approving so-called codes of fair competition for industry. Justice Benjamin N. Cardozo, the lone dissenter in the prior case, described the code system at issue in *Schechter Poultry* as "delegation running riot" because the statutory provision delegated to the President "anything that Congress may do within the limits of the commerce clause for the betterment of business."

Schechter Poultry marks the last time the Court held a statute unconstitutional under Article I, Section 1. In 1980, however, then-Justice William H. Rehnquist expressed his doubts about the lengths to which the Congress had gone in delegating its authority to the Occupational Safety and Health Administration in the Department of Labor. The Court in *Industrial Union Department, AFL-CIO v. American Petroleum Institute* (1980), known as *The Benzene Case*, vacated an OSHA regulation limiting the amount of benzene to which an employer may expose its employees, on the ground that the regulation was not authorized by the statute. Justice Rehnquist, in a concurring opinion, expressed the view that the statute—which authorized the Secretary of Labor to "set the standard which most adequately assures, to the extent feasible" that no employee would suffer material harm from exposure—was itself standardless and therefore an unconstitutional delegation of legislative power.

The Court has since moved toward an entirely hands-off approach to delegation. In 1989 it upheld the Congress's delegation to the United States Sentencing Commission of authority to issue "guidelines" prescribing the range of sentences for every federal crime. *Mistretta v. United States* (1989). Justice Antonin Scalia, the lone dissenter, considered the statute an impermissible delegation because the standards given to the Commission were not "related to the exercise of executive or judicial powers; they [were], plainly and simply, standards for further legislation." He criticized the Court's emphasis upon whether the statute contained an intelligible principle, arguing that a court cannot practically police the uncertain boundary between proper and improper delegations. In its most recent delegation decision, *Whitman v. American Trucking Ass'ns, Inc.* (2001), the Court as a matter of form continued to apply the requirement of an intelligible principle, but it seems in substance to have joined Justice Scalia in abandoning any serious effort to police the boundary between proper and improper delegations. The Court found in *Whitman v. American Trucking Ass'ns, Inc.* an intelligible principle in Congress's directive to the Environmental Protection Agency to promulgate air quality standards "requisite to protect the public health" with "an adequate margin of safety." Because no standard could eliminate all significant adverse effects to health, the statute effectively delegated to an unelected and unaccountable agency the decision how far our society should go and how many billions of dollars should be spent to reduce the adverse health effects of industrial pollution, a decision that seems quintessentially legislative, but undoubtedly one for which legislators would prefer to avoid responsibility. In that case, Justice Clarence Thomas suggested that "there are cases in which the principle is intelligible and yet the significance of the delegated decision is simply too great for the decision to be called anything other than 'legislative.'"

The Supreme Court, by failing to prevent delegations of legislative authority, forgoes a significant opportunity to maintain the structure of government prescribed by the Constitution. As a result, legislators may and do delegate difficult and divisive legislative issues to agencies in the executive and judicial branches far removed from political accountability.

Douglas Ginsburg

See Also

Article I, Section 8, Clause 17 (Enclave Clause)
Article I, Section 8, Clause 18 (Necessary and Proper Clause)
Article II
Article III
Article IV, Section 3, Clause 2 (Property Clause)

Suggestions for Further Research

Douglas H. Ginsburg, *Delegation Running Riot*, 1 Reg. 83 (1995)
Gary Lawson, *Delegation and Original Meaning*, 88 Va. L. Rev. 327 (2002)
David Schoenbrod, Power Without Responsibility (1993)

Significant Cases

Cargo of the Brig Aurora v. United States, 11 U.S. (7 Cranch) 382 (1813)
Wayman v. Southard, 23 U.S. (10 Wheat.) 1 (1825)
United States v. Klein, 80 U.S. (13 Wall.) 128 (1871)
J.W. Hampton, Jr. & Co. v. United States, 276 U.S. 394 (1928)
A.L.A. Schechter Poultry Corp. v. United States, 295 U.S. 495 (1935)
Panama Refining Co. v. Ryan, 293 U.S. 388 (1935)
United States v. Curtiss-Wright Export Corp., 299 U.S. 304 (1936)
Industrial Union Department, AFL-CIO v. American Petroleum Institute, 448 U.S. 607 (1980)
Mistretta v. United States, 488 U.S. 361 (1989)
Whitman v. American Trucking Ass'ns, Inc., 531 U.S. 457 (2001)

House of Representatives

The House of Representatives shall be composed of Members chosen every second Year by the People of the several States....

(Article I, Section 2, Clause 1)

~

*T*hree issues—length of terms, equal versus proportional representation of states, and method of selection—dominated the Constitutional

Convention's debate over the makeup of the House of Representatives. They each were resolved in the language of Article I, Section 2.

The two-year term of office for the House was a straightforward compromise between those who preferred annual elections and those who favored a longer, three-year term. The original Virginia Plan envisaged that both branches of the federal legislature would be directly or indirectly accountable to "the People." In the end, however, the Convention determined that the states would be represented in the Senate and the people in the House of Representatives. During the debate over equal or proportional state representation in the House, several delegates, notably James Wilson, James Madison, and George Mason, argued for population as the just basis of apportionment. That later became conflated with the related but distinct question on the manner of selection.

What the Framers intended in providing for election "by the People" can be better understood in terms of the alternatives that they rejected. The Committee of the Whole vigorously debated and discarded a counter resolution that the House be selected by "the State Legislatures, and not the People." Elbridge Gerry suggested that Members be selected by state legislatures from among candidates "nominated by the people." Another compromise, proposed by Charles Cotesworth Pinckney, provided for the House to be selected "in such manner as the legislature of each state shall direct." Against these proposals, Madison and Wilson argued that selection by the people was necessary to link citizens directly to the national government and to prevent the states from overpowering the central authority. Article I, Section 2, secured direct popular election of the House.

The scope of the phrase "by the People," however, was neither debated nor defined at the Convention. It appears to have meant the direct popular election with a relatively broad right of suffrage as determined by the states' own practices. Madison described electoral accountability to the people as "the republican principle." *The Federalist* No. 10. Responding to charges that the House would not represent "the mass of the people," Madison argued in *The Federal-ist* No. 57 that "the electors are to be the great body of people of the United States. They are to be the same who exercise the right in every State of electing the corresponding branch of the legislature of the State." Leading Anti-Federalists, such as Melancton Smith and the anonymous Brutus, used the term in a similar fashion, affirming the broadly accepted meaning. Thomas Jefferson defined "the People" as no particular class but, rather, "the mass of individuals composing the society."

Comments at both the Convention and at state ratifying conventions indicate substantial support for the general proposition that Representatives should be apportioned in a manner roughly equal to population. Nevertheless, it seems evident that the delegates did not intend to place any particular principle, such as "one person, one vote," into the Constitution. "One person, one vote" was not the norm in the states at the time of the Convention. Although most states established districts roughly according to population, none came close to the "one person, one vote" standard. Geography, history, and local political boundaries cut against equally populated districts. Similarly, in the Northwest Ordinance of 1787, Congress provided for up to one Representative per 500 persons, but based on townships and counties. Furthermore, besides the celebrated compromise providing each state with equal representation in the Senate, the Constitution specifically grants each state, no matter how small its population, one Representative in the House.

The Constitution, however, does not require Representatives to be elected by districts. In the beginning, many states had their Representatives elected at large. If a state chose its Representatives at large, then they were more likely to speak with one voice, thus increasing the influence of the state in the House of Representatives. Congress then responded by requiring states to elect its Representatives by district. For a brief time, some states required their Representatives to reside in the district from which they were elected, but that requirement no longer exists.

There was a limit, however, to what the states could do in fashioning congressional districts.

The Framers did, in fact, disapprove of "rotten boroughs" in Great Britain, districts with no more than a few inhabitants that nevertheless held seats in Parliament equal, in some cases, to large cities. But they decided to address inequities in representation by leaving it to Congress's discretion to "alter" the "Times, Places, and Manner" of choosing Members. (*See* Article I, Section 4.) Madison argued that this clause was a necessary safeguard against state-created inequalities in federal representation.

For most of the nation's history, Section 4 was indeed held to be the sole remedy to malapportionment. However, in the early twentieth century, rural state legislators in many states simply stopped redistricting in order to avoid transferring power to more populous urban areas. In 1962, the Supreme Court held in *Baker v. Carr* that such questions were justiciable in the courts. In *Wesberry v. Sanders*, decided in 1964, the Court held that Article I, Section 2, mandated that congressional districts be equal in population "as nearly as is practicable." In doing so, the Court relied heavily on statements made at the Convention in favor of representation according to population. These comments, however, were made during debate over the proportional representation of the states in Congress, not the manner in which Representatives would be selected according to the first paragraph of Article I, Section 2. Nevertheless, later that year, in *Reynolds v. Sims*, the Court extended the doctrine of "one person, one vote" to state legislatures, based on the Equal Protection Clause of the Fourteenth Amendment. In *Lucas v. 44th General Assembly of Colorado*, decided the same day as *Reynolds*, the Court applied the equal population rule to a state districting plan the state's voters had specifically approved, including a majority of voters in those parts of the state underrepresented by the plan.

The Court has since held to the principle of precise mathematical equality when congressional districting is at issue. Most notably, *Karcher v. Daggett* (1983) struck down a New Jersey plan in which the average district population variation was 726 people, or 0.1384 percent, a difference well within the believed margin of error in the census count. State redistricting plans, scrutinized under the Fourteenth Amendment rather than Article I, have been granted more leeway. The Court has upheld state legislative districts with population variances up to ten percent with no state justification at all, *Gaffney v. Cummings* (1973), and variations to nearly twenty percent are permissible where the state demonstrates a rational basis for its plan, such as drawing districts to follow municipal lines. *Mahan v. Howell* (1973). Consideration of group or economic interests is not, however, an accepted justification. *Swann v. Adams* (1967).

The Court has also applied the "one person, one vote" rule to local governments. *Avery v. Midland County* (1968). In a few limited circumstances, however, where the entity in question does not exercise "a traditional element of governmental sovereignty," as in the case of a water storage district, the Court has not required the "one person, one vote" rule. *Ball v. James* (1981).

In recent years, the reapportionment decisions have drawn renewed scholarly attention. Critics claim that they have inhibited the formation of regional government consortiums to deal with metropolitan-wide problems; removed traditional constraints on gerrymandering, such as adherence to political jurisdictions or geographic regions; and imposed a particular theory of representation on the states and Congress that is not grounded in the Constitution. Critics also note that equal population does not correspond to an equal number of voters, due to differing numbers of children, immigrants, and other nonvoters in a district. Thus votes are still not weighted equally. Nonetheless, the standard of "one person, one vote" remains Supreme Court doctrine, and there is little evidence that the Court is prepared to reassess its jurisprudence in the area.

Bradley Smith

See Also

Amendment XIV, Section 2 (Apportionment of Representatives)

Suggestions for Further Research

GORDON E. BAKER, THE REAPPORTIONMENT REVOLUTION: REPRESENTATION, POLITICAL POWER AND THE SUPREME COURT (1966)

ROBERT G. DIXON, JR., DEMOCRATIC REPRESENTATION: REAPPORTIONMENT IN LAW & POLITICS (1968)

Michael W. McConnell, *Voting Rights, Equality, and Racial Gerrymandering: The Redistricting Cases: Original Mistakes and Current Consequences*, 24 HARV. J.L. & PUB. POL'Y 103 (2000)

James L. McDowell, *"One Person, One Vote" and the Decline of Community*, 23 LEGAL STUD. F. 131 (1999)

NELSON W. POLSBY, ED., REAPPORTIONMENT IN THE 1970s (1971)

Scott A. Reader, *One Person, One Vote Revisited: Choosing a Population Basis to Form Political Districts*, 17 HARV. J.L. & PUB. POL'Y 521 (1994)

Significant Cases

Baker v. Carr, 369 U.S. 186 (1962)

Lucas v. 44th General Assembly of Colorado, 377 U.S. 713 (1964)

Reynolds v. Sims, 377 U.S. 533 (1964)

Wesberry v. Sanders, 376 U.S. 1 (1964)

Swann v. Adams, 385 U.S. 440 (1967)

Avery v. Midland County, 390 U.S. 474 (1968)

Gaffney v. Cummings, 412 U.S. 735 (1973)

Mahan v. Howell, 410 U.S. 315 (1973)

Ball v. James, 451 U.S. 355 (1981)

Karcher v. Daggett, 462 U.S. 725 (1983)

Elector Qualifications

... the Electors in each State shall have the Qualifications requisite for Electors of the most numerous Branch of the State Legislature.

(ARTICLE I, SECTION 2, CLAUSE 1)

~

*A*t the Constitutional Convention, the Framers debated whether the electors of the House of Representative should be limited to freeholders, or whether they should incorporate state voting laws by requiring that whoever the state decided is eligible to vote for "the most numerous Branch of the State Legislature" is also eligible to vote for the House of Representatives. The majority of the delegates preferred to defer to the states and approved the Elector Qualifications Clause. As James Wilson summarized in records of the Convention, "It was difficult to form any uniform rule of qualifications for all the States." Unnecessary innovations, he thought, should also be avoided: "It would be very hard & disagreeable for the same persons, at the same time, to vote for representatives in the State Legislature and to be excluded from a vote for those in the Natl. Legislature."

Thus, the Constitution gives authority for determining elector qualifications to the states. The Seventeenth Amendment adopted the same qualifications language to apply to the popular election of United States Senators. This authority is superseded only insofar as the Constitution itself forbids the denial of equal protection and the exclusion of voters on specific grounds, such as race (Fifteenth Amendment), sex (Nineteenth Amendment), failure to pay a poll tax or other tax (Twenty-fourth Amendment), and, for those eighteen years old or older, age (Twenty-sixth Amendment).

Article I, Section 4, allows Congress to "make or alter such [state] Regulations" regarding "the Times, Places and Manner of holding Elections for Senators and Representatives," but, as a textual matter, Congress's power is about "holding Elections"—not about who votes, which is the express focus of Section 2. Both Alexander Hamilton and James Madison believed the two clauses to be independent in this way. Hamilton, in *The Federalist* No. 60, said of Article I, Section 4, that the national government's "authority would be expressly restricted to the regulation of the *times*, the *places*, and the *manner* of elections. The qualifications of the persons who may choose or may be chosen ... are defined and fixed in the Constitution; and are unalterable by the [national] legislature." (Emphasis in original.) In *The Federalist* No. 52, Madison wrote of Article I, Section 2: "To have left it [the definition of the right of suffrage] open for the occasional regulation of Congress, would have been improper. . . ." Hamilton and Madison believed that generally the state constitutions, and certainly not Congress, would determine who could vote.

The Supreme Court has applied the Equal Protection Clause of the Fourteenth Amendment to invalidate certain state regulations that excluded classes of voters from the franchise. In *Kramer v. Union Free School District No. 15* (1969), the Court declared that it was unconstitutional to limit school district elections to property holders or to those who had children enrolled in the district schools.

The Court has also upheld congressional regulation of federal elections over contrary state laws. In *Oregon v. Mitchell* (1970), a decision of limited precedential value, five Justices in a highly fractured series of opinions voted to uphold federal legislation—passed prior to the adoption of the Twenty-sixth Amendment, which was ratified a little over six months after the Court's decision—that required the states to allow eighteen-year-olds to vote in federal elections. While it is true that in this case a majority of the Justices did vote to uphold a statute that dictated who could vote in federal elections, only one of the five Justices who did so—Justice Hugo L. Black—relied on Article I, Section 4 (power of Congress to regulate the times, manner, and places of elections). The other four relied on interpretations of Congress's enforcement authority under the Fourteenth and Fifteenth Amendments. In *City of Boerne v. Flores* (1997), the Court ruled that Congress may not assert authority under Section 5 of the Fourteenth Amendment "to enforce" the amendment by prohibiting state actions not closely related to violations of the amendment. The Court has not yet directly applied this principle to congressional statutes regulating suffrage.

Accordingly, it would seem that reliance on Article I, Section 4, to trump Article I, Section 2, lacks textual support, and only Justice Harry A. Blackmun endorsed it in 1970. "Rather, the general rule is that Congress may pass laws superseding the states' determination of elector qualifications only when confronted with a deliberate denial of either a specific constitutional guarantee of the right to vote or of equal protection under the Fourteenth Amendment."

In *Tashjian v. Republican Party of Connecticut* (1986), the Supreme Court, by a 5–4 majority, used the First Amendment to restrict the application of the Elector Qualifications Clause in primary elections. In that case, a Connecticut law that required a closed primary conflicted with a Connecticut Republican Party rule that permitted *independent* voters to vote in Republican primaries for federal and statewide offices. The Court said that the Connecticut law violated freedom of association.

The majority also held that the implementation of party rules—that had established qualifications for voting in congressional elections differing from the voting qualifications in elections for the more numerous house of the state legislature—did not violate the Elector Qualifications Clause (or the Seventeenth Amendment). Primaries are subject to these clauses, the Court said, but the purpose of those clauses is satisfied "if all those qualified to participate in the selection of members of the more numerous branch of the state legislature are also qualified to participate in the election of Senators and Members of the House of Representatives." There is no need for "perfect symmetry." Justice John Paul Stevens, joined by Justice Antonin Scalia, dissented: "The Court nevertheless separates the federal qualifications from their state counterparts, inexplicably treating the mandatory 'shall have' language of the clauses as though it means only that the federal voters 'may but need not have' the qualifications of state voters."

Roger Clegg

See Also

Significant Cases

United States v. Classic, 313 U.S. 299 (1941)

Carrington v. Rash, 380 U.S. 89 (1965)

Kramer v. Union Free School District No. 15, 395 U.S. 621 (1969)

Oregon v. Mitchell, 400 U.S. 112 (1970)

Tashjian v. Republican Party of Connecticut, 479 U.S. 208 (1986)

City of Boerne v. Flores, 521 U.S. 507 (1997)

Qualifications for Representatives

No Person shall be a Representative who shall not have attained to the Age of twenty five Years, and been seven Years a Citizen of the United States, and who shall not, when elected, be an Inhabitant of that State in which he shall be chosen.

(ARTICLE I, SECTION 2, CLAUSE 2)

~

When Edmund Randolph of Virginia presented the Virginia Plan at the beginning of the Constitutional Convention, he suggested, among other things, that Representatives should meet certain qualifications. It was some time, however, before the delegates turned to the issue. When they had completed their consideration, the Framers had opted for only a few restrictions.

The Framers considered and rejected property, wealth, and indebtedness qualifications. On republican grounds, the Framers cut loose from the British practice of multiple qualifications and limitations. They settled on only three. First, there must be a minimum age of twenty-five years so that the office-holder would possess some modicum of life's experience to season his judgment. Second, a Representative must be a citizen for seven years, a compromise among widely different views, but seemingly long enough to prevent foreign nations from infiltrating the halls of Congress with persons holding alien allegiances. Third, the Member of the House must be an inhabitant of the state in

which he is chosen, a change from "resident," which word might, according to James Madison, "exclude persons absent occasionally for a considerable time on public or private business." Although a Representative must be an inhabitant of the state in which he is chosen, according to the Constitution, he need not be an inhabitant of the district from which he is elected. When the Constitution was before the state ratifying conventions, delegates paid little attention to the issue of qualifications, and although disputes occasionally arose over the seating of a Member of the House, the clause attracted no judicial attention for nearly two centuries.

Judicial involvement in the clause did not occur until the latter part of the twentieth century. The question of whether the House of Representatives could, through Article I, Section 5, Clause 1, add to or define for itself what constituted "qualifications" reached the Supreme Court in *Powell v. McCormack* (1969). Finding that an elected Representative, Adam Clayton Powell, Jr., had engaged in serious misconduct, the House refused to seat him, even though Powell had met the formal qualifications of Article I, Section 2, Clause 2. In its decision, the Supreme Court held that Congress had no constitutional authority to alter the qualifications for Representatives as stated in the Constitution. So far as Congress was concerned, the constitutional qualifications were fixed. The Congress could not validly exclude Powell.

The *Powell* decision left open the question whether the states could add to the qualifications stated in the Constitution. Were the qualifications in the Constitution a floor on which the states could erect other requirements, or were they the sum of all qualifications, brooking no alteration from any source?

This issue came to a head in the 1990s when a popular movement to limit the terms of Members of Congress swept the country. In *United States Term Limits v. Thornton* (1995), the Court struck down those attempts. The Court ruled that the qualifications in the Constitution were in fact exclusive and could not be added to or altered.

In his opinion for the majority, Justice John Paul Stevens reaffirmed the historical argument in *Powell* that Congress did not have the power to alter the qualifications. He then extended that rationale to reach the issue *Powell* had not decided: whether any given state could impose additional qualifications. The Court held that the historical record demonstrated that the qualifications were exclusive in relation to the states as well. Stevens argued that Framers and early commentators, such as John Dickinson, James Madison, and Justice Joseph Story, thought that the states could not add additional qualifications, that the federal government was a creature of the people and not of the states, and that, consequently, the Members of the House of Representatives were accountable to the people and not to the states. He added that after ratification of the Constitution, the states retained the power to add certain qualifications for voters, such as property, but had no power to add qualifications for Representatives beyond what the Constitution prescribed. Quoting earlier cases and Alexander Hamilton, Stevens's central argument was "that the people should choose whom they please to govern them."

Justice Clarence Thomas, speaking for the four-person dissent, developed a contrary history and argued that the federal government was created by the people, not as a whole, but of the several states. Whatever powers not given to the federal government were thus retained by the states. Consequently, the states retained the power to add qualifications to Representatives elected within their respective jurisdictions. As Thomas noted, the text of the clause limits the power of Congress, not that of the states. In addition, neither in the Constitutional Convention nor in the state ratifying conventions was there a statement that the states could not add qualifications. The Court's majority, on the other hand, stated that creating qualifications for federal Representatives did not derive from the states and there was, consequently, no such power that was retained by the states.

David F. Forte and Stephen Safranek

See Also
Article I, Section 2, Clause 3 (Allocation of Representatives)

Article I, Section 5, Clause 1 (Qualifications and Quorum)

Suggestions for Further Research
Roderick Hills, *A Defense of State Constitutional Limits on Federal Congressional Terms*, 52 U. PITT. L. REV. 97 (1991)

David Hays Lowenstein, *Congressional Term Limits and the Constitution*, in THE POLITICS AND LAW OF TERM LIMITS 125–140 (Edward H. Crane & Roger Pilon eds., 1994)

Ronald D. Rotunda, *Rethinking Term Limits for Federal Legislators in Light of the Structure of the Constitution*, 73 OR. L. REV. 561 (1994)

Ronald D. Rotunda & Stephen Safranek, *An Essay on Term Limits and a Call for a Constitutional Convention*, 80 MARQ. L. REV. 227 (1996)

STEPHEN SAFRANEK, THE CONSTITUTIONAL CASE FOR TERM LIMITS (1993)

Significant Cases
Powell v. McCormack, 395 U.S. 486 (1969)

United States Term Limits v. Thornton, 514 U.S. 779 (1995)

Three-fifths Clause

Representatives and direct Taxes shall be apportioned among the several States which may be included within this Union, according to their respective Numbers, which shall be determined by adding to the whole Number of free Persons, including those bound to Service for a Term of Years, and excluding Indians not taxed, three fifths of all other Persons.

(**ARTICLE I, SECTION 2, CLAUSE 3**)

~

*T*he three-fifths rule for counting slaves is often misunderstood. When the Constitutional Convention debated the issue of how to count population for the purposes of representation, the *Southern* delegates to the Convention would have been pleased if nonvoting slaves had been counted as full persons. That way, the Southern states would have had a greater representation in the House of Representatives. In contrast, some Northern delegates resisted counting slaves at all. Why, asked Elbridge Gerry, "shd. the blacks, who were property in the South, be in the rule of representation more than the cattle & horses of the North?" Among other things, counting slaves provided an incentive to import still more slaves.

Nor was the three-fifths rule new at the Convention. It was derived from a mechanism adopted in 1783 to apportion requisitions (the national government's only revenue source under the Articles of Confederation) among the states. That rule was intended to provide rough equality between the North and the South, and when the idea first appeared at the Convention, no one suggested that another fraction would be more appropriate. Indeed, the rule was included in a June 11 motion, made by James Wilson of Pennsylvania and seconded by Charles Pinckney of South Carolina, suggesting that a compromise had already occurred behind the scenes.

By itself, however, the three-fifths compromise for representation was not enough. Facing deadlock at the Convention, Gouverneur Morris (representing Pennsylvania) moved on July 12 to add a "proviso that taxation shall be in proportion to Representation" (later limited to *direct* taxation), the purpose of which, wrote James Madison, was to "lessen the eagerness on one side, & the opposition on the other, to the share of Representation claimed by the [Southern] States on account of the Negroes." Morris subsequently said he meant his motion only "as a bridge to assist us over a certain gulph," but tying apportionment to both taxation and representation turned out to be crucial. Slaves were to be counted as less than whites for representation, which was not in the interests of the South. Slaves were, however, also to be counted as less than whites for measuring a state's apportioned direct-tax liability, and that was a benefit to the South. A fuller account of how the Framers dealt with the issue of slavery can be ascertained by considering the other clauses of the Constitution that deal with slavery. (*See* Article I, Section 9, Clause 1; Article IV, Section 2, Clause 3; and Article V.)

Furthermore, the compromise protected the integrity of the census, as Madison explained in *The Federalist* No. 54: "The States should feel as little bias as possible to swell or to reduce the amount of their numbers.... By extending the rule to both [taxation and representation], the States will have opposite interests which will control and balance each other and produce the requisite impartiality."

The three-fifths rule does not directly affect litigation today, but it affects how scholars interpret the apportionment requirement for direct taxes. It has been argued, for example, that the direct-tax clauses should be ignored because they are tainted by slavery, or because, with slavery ended, there is no longer reason to honor any part of the compromise. In light of the entire history that led to the Revolution and the Constitution, however, it would go too far to assume that in a world without slavery, the Founders would have been indifferent to the dangers of national taxation.

Furthermore, understood in context, the apportionment rule was not proslavery. Even though slaves were property under the laws of the Southern states, the Constitution itself acknowledged that they were persons. In addition, by tying both representation and direct taxation to apportionment, the Framers removed any sectional benefit, and thus any proslavery taint, from the special counting rule.

Erik M. Jensen

See Also

Article I, Section 8, Clause 1 (Spending Clause and Uniformity Clause)

Article I, Section 9, Clause 4 (Direct Taxes)

Article II, Section 2, Clause 3 (Recess Appointments Clause)

Article V (Prohibition on Amendment: Slave Trade)

Suggestions for Further Research

Bruce Ackerman, *Taxation and the Constitution*, 99 COLUM. L. REV. 1 (1999)

ROGER H. BROWN, REDEEMING THE REPUBLIC: FEDERALISTS, TAXATION, AND THE ORIGINS OF THE CONSTITUTION 195–197 (1993)

Erik M. Jensen, *The Apportionment of "Direct Taxes": Are Consumption Taxes Constitutional?*, 97 Colum. L. Rev. 2334 (1997)

Enumeration Clause

The actual Enumeration shall be made within three Years after the first Meeting of the Congress of the United States, and within every subsequent Term of ten Years, in such Manner as they shall by Law direct.

(ARTICLE I, SECTION 2, CLAUSE 3)

~

*T*his section, as amended by Section 2 of the Fourteenth Amendment, requires, for the purpose of apportioning the House of Representatives, that a census be taken of the whole number of persons in the nation. Congress has followed the Constitution's command, even extending the census into territories and appending long lists of additional inquiries, although it is questionable as to what power Congress possesses to ask non-apportionment-related questions.

The central question regarding the original meaning of this section is whether the Constitution requires that this census consist only of an actual counting of individuals or whether the national government may rely on estimates of the national population to apportion the House. There was no direct discussion at the Constitutional Convention regarding whether there should be an actual count. The Committee of Detail's draft of the section stated that the number of inhabitants "shall ... be taken in such manner as ... [Congress] shall direct." That phrasing was modified to "as they shall by Law direct," and the Committee of Style subsequently added the phrase "actual Enumeration."

Those who contend that this section allows the use of estimates of the population argue that this phrase "actual Enumeration" likely means the most accurate possible calculation. When this phrase, so defined, is read together with the words "in such Manner as they shall by Law direct," they conclude that the Framers intended to grant Congress complete discretion to choose whatever method of census taking they thought would result in the most accurate calculation of population, including the use of estimating methods. Alternatively, the word "actual" refers to the first census to be conducted three years after the meeting of the first Congress, as opposed to the less formal enumeration the Framers relied upon in apportioning the first and second Congresses.

Those who maintain that the phrase "actual Enumeration" means actual counting of individuals as opposed to the use of estimating methods argue, as Justice Antonin Scalia did in *Department of Commerce v. United States House of Representatives* (1999), that the words mean "counting 'singly,' 'separately,' 'number by number,' 'distinctly.'" The distinction between actual counting and estimating was well known and thoroughly discussed in both debates in eighteenth-century English politics and in controversies between the American colonies and England. Indeed, the participants in these debates used the precise terms at issue; those who criticized the use of estimates in calculating population figures demanded instead that an enumeration—an actual count—be taken.

In *The Federalist* No. 36, Alexander Hamilton, in attempting to reassure his audience that the population figures upon which taxation would be based would not be subject to political manipulation, stated that "an actual census or enumeration of the people must furnish the rule, a circumstance which effectively shuts the door to partiality or oppression." Similarly, Thomas Jefferson, in a 1791 letter discussing the first census, indicated that the census "is founded on actual returns" as opposed to being " conjectured." George Washington, in a letter to Gouverneur Morris in the same year, contrasted an estimate with an enumeration, commenting that an "estimate" he had given "of the number of inhabitants which would probably be found in the United States on enumeration, was too large." Finally, the Census Act of 1790, establishing the first census, required an actual counting;

census takers were required to swear an oath to "truly cause to be made, a just and perfect enumeration and description of all persons resident within [their] districts."

The Supreme Court, after avoiding the constitutional question in previous cases challenging the use of advanced statistical methods, decided the question of whether an actual counting is required in *Utah v. Evans* (2002), a case involving the use of a methodology that infers that households not actually counted in the census have the same population characteristics as their geographic neighbors that were counted. Justice Stephen Breyer, writing for the majority, concluded that the Framers "did not write detailed census methodology into the Constitution," and therefore methods, such as the one used in this case, that are based on inference and not actual counting are constitutionally valid. Justice Clarence Thomas, writing in dissent, lamented the Court's decision. He concluded: "Well familiar with methods of estimation, the Framers chose to make an 'actual Enumeration' part of the constitutional structure. Today, the Court undermines their decision, leaving the basis of our representative government vulnerable to political manipulation."

Andrew Spiropoulos

See Also

Article I, Section 9, Clause 4 (Direct Taxes)

Amendment XIV, Section 2 (Apportionment of Representatives)

Suggestions for Further Research

Margo Anderson & Stephen E. Feinberg, *Census 2000: Politics and Statistics*, 32 U. Tol. L. Rev. 19 (2002)

Thomas R. Lee, *The Original Understanding of the Census Clause: Statistical Estimates and the Constitutional Requirement of an "Actual Enumeration,"* 77 Wash. L. Rev. 1 (2002)

Significant Cases

Wisconsin v. City of New York, 517 U.S. 1 (1996)

Department of Commerce v. United States House of Representatives, 525 U.S. 316 (1999)

Utah v. Evans, 536 U.S. 452 (2002)

Allocation of Representatives

The Number of Representatives shall not exceed one for every thirty Thousand, but each State shall have at Least one Representative; and until such enumeration shall be made, the State of New Hampshire shall be entitled to chuse three, Massachusetts eight, Rhode-Island and Providence Plantations one, Connecticut five, New-York six, New Jersey four, Pennsylvania eight, Delaware one, Maryland six, Virginia ten, North Carolina five, South Carolina five, and Georgia three.

(ARTICLE I, SECTION 2, CLAUSE 3)

~

*I*n Philadelphia, the Framers spent untold hours discussing the basis of representation for the new government and then fell to haggling over the number of Representatives to be elected from each state for the House of Representatives. A majority of delegations set the initial size of the House at a modest sixty-five Members, defeating James Madison's wish to have it doubled. They wished to leave Congress the flexibility to set numbers in the future, making sure that Congress would not allow for more than one Representative for every 30,000 persons, a last minute modification of the original floor of 40,000 persons.

At the ratifying conventions, the Anti-Federalists were extremely exercised over the clause. George Mason, for example, inveighed against the small number of Representatives during the debates at the Virginia ratifying convention. James Madison accurately summarized their objections in *The Federalist* No. 55:

[F]irst, that so small a number of representatives will be an unsafe depositary of the public interests; secondly, that they will not possess a proper knowledge of the local circumstances of their numerous constituents; thirdly, that they will be taken from that class of citizens which will sympathize least with the feelings of the mass of the people, and be most likely to aim at a permanent elevation of the few on the depression of the many; fourthly, that defective as the number will be in the first instance, it will be more disproportionate, by the increase of the people, and the obstacles which will prevent a correspondent increase of the representatives.

Madison spent much time rebutting these objections. "Nothing can be more fallacious than to found our political calculations on arithmetical principles," he declared. He assured his audience that Congress would increase the number of Representatives as the population grew; that the Senate would not stand in the way; that there was more danger in a cabal of the few forming in a large assembly than in a small one; that there were sufficient checks against corruption within the Constitution; and that Representatives needed knowledge only over subjects they could legislate upon, namely, commerce, taxation, and the militia.

Behind the debate between the Federalists and the Anti-Federalists lay different understandings of the future course of American republicanism. The Anti-Federalists did not believe that the country could grow and still remain republican, a proposition rebutted in Madison's classic argument in *The Federalist* No. 10. At the Constitutional Convention, Madison resisted any built-in increase to the numbers of Representatives, arguing that population growth would "render the number of Representatives excessive." Nathaniel Gorham of Massachusetts responded, "It is not to be supposed that the Gov't will last so long as to produce this effect. Can it be supposed that this vast Country including the Western territory will 150 years hence remain one nation?"

In response to Anti-Federalist objections, Congress sent twelve amendments to the states for ratification, the first of which changed the method of calculating the number of Representatives. Instead of there being *no more than* one Representative for 30,000 people, the amendment would have required *at least* one Representative for 30,000, or later, 40,000 and 50,000 as the population grew. But the amendment failed to achieve ratification, the only one of the original twelve never to have been approved by the states. The Federalist vision of the Union prevailed.

True to Madison's prediction, Congress dutifully increased the number of Representatives as the population grew. By 1833, Justice Joseph Story would write in his *Commentaries on the Constitution of the United States* that the dire predictions of the Anti-Federalists "have all vanished into air, into thin air." After the Civil War, Southern representation increased with the ending of slavery and the three-fifths rule. Congress, however, failed to enforce Section 2 of the Fourteenth Amendment, written to compel the Southern states to enfranchise blacks or lose representation. Finally, in 1929, after being unable to make a reapportionment after the census of 1920, Congress decided to cap the number of Representatives at 435.

Since 1790, Congress has applied five different methods of apportioning Representatives among the states. The present "Hill Method," with its complex formula determining when a state may gain or lose a seat, has been in use since 1940. It has been twice challenged before the Supreme Court. In *Franklin v. Massachusetts* (1992), the Court upheld the inclusion of federal military and civil personnel and their dependents in the apportioned populations. In *United States Department of Commerce v. Montana* (1992), the Court unanimously approved the "Hill Method" in the face of a challenge by Montana, which lost one seat in favor of Washington after the 1990 census.

David F. Forte

See Also

Article I, Section 2, Clause 1 (House of Representatives)

Amendment XIV, Section 2 (Apportionment of Representatives)

Suggestions for Further Research

David P. Currie, *The Constitution in Congress: The Second Congress 1791–1793*, 90 Nw. U. L. Rev. 606 (1996)

David B. Goldin, *Number Wars: A Decade of Census Litigation*, 32 U. Tol. L. Rev. 1 (2000)

Significant Cases
Franklin v. Massachusetts, 505 U.S. 788 (1992)
United States Department of Commerce v. Montana, 503 U.S. 442 (1992)

Executive Writs of Election

When vacancies happen in the Representation from any State, the Executive Authority thereof shall issue Writs of Election to fill such Vacancies.

(ARTICLE I, SECTION 2, CLAUSE 4)

~

*A*lthough the phrasing of the Executive Writs of Election Clause varied until the Committee of Style established its final wording, there was no dispute among the Framers as to the necessity of having vacant House seats filled by special election. Justice Joseph Story wrote of the clause that "[i]t is obvious, that such a power ought to reside in some public functionary" and that the Constitution vests such power with "the State Executive, which is best fitted to exercise it with promptitude and discretion." In fact, the clause combined the principles of those who did not want to see "the people" unrepresented in any part of the government with those who desired to continue to support state authority over the electoral process.

The Seventh Circuit Court of Appeals has ruled that the clause imposes a mandatory duty on governors to issue writs of election to fill vacancies in the United States House of Representatives. *Jackson v. Ogilvie* (1970). More specifically, the court held that in performing that duty, the governor has the discretion to choose one day of the week over another on which to issue writs of election, but he does not have the discretion to decide against issuing the writs of election altogether. Similarly, in *United States Term Limits, Inc. v. Thornton* (1995), Justice Clarence Thomas for the four-person dissent indicated that the clause prescribed an affirmative duty on the state executive to issue a writ whenever a vacancy occurred. Nonetheless, in *ACLU v. Taft* (2002), the district court held that the governor enjoyed substantial discretion as to the timing of special elections and, further, that if the unexpired term were exceedingly short, the governor possessed discretion to forgo calling the election at all.

Paul Taylor

See Also
Article I, Section 4, Clause 1 (Election Regulations)
Amendment XVII (Vacancies in the Senate)

Suggestion for Further Research
Paul Taylor, *Alternatives to a Constitutional Amendment: How Congress May Provide for the Quick, Temporary Filling of House Member Seats in Emergencies by Statute*, 10 J.L. & POL'Y 373 (2002)

Significant Cases
Jackson v. Ogilvie, 426 F.2d 1333 (7th Cir. 1970)
United States Term Limits v. Thornton, 514 U.S. 779 (1995) (Thomas, J., dissenting)
ACLU of Ohio v. Taft, 217 F. Supp. 2d 842 (S.D. Ohio 2002)

Speaker of the House

The House of Representatives shall chuse their Speaker and other Officers....

(ARTICLE I, SECTION 2, CLAUSE 5)

~

A "Speaker of the House" has been an organic part of the Anglo-American legislative process for centuries. The British House of Commons elects its Speaker, but the Crown, at least formally, must approve of the selection. Prior to independence, colonial assemblies also had speakers, but the royally appointed governors maintained control over the elective process.

Under Article IX of the Articles of Confederation (1781), the Congress of the United States had the power "to appoint one of their number to preside, provided that no person be allowed to serve in the office of president more than one year in any term of three years." At the Constitutional Convention, however, the Framers undoubtedly drew on the model of the Massachusetts Constitution of 1780, which provided that "the House of Representatives... shall choose their own Speaker, appoint their own officers, and settle the rules and order of proceeding in their own House." The language in the Massachusetts Constitution emphasizing "their own" was to declare the legislature free from the kind of gubernatorial control under which state legislatures had labored during the colonial period. The more succinct language of Article I, Section 2, Clause 5, of the Constitution carried the same meaning and clearly established the House's power to choose its leadership free from the executive and Senate power conferred in the Recess Appointments Clause of Article II, Section 2, Clause 3.

The House of Representatives elects its Speaker as the first order of business at the start of each two-year term or when a Speaker dies or resigns during the legislative term. The practice is customary, for it occurs before the House formally adopts its rules of procedure for the legislative term. Until 1839, the House elected the Speaker by ballot, but since that time the election has been by roll call. The party caucuses, however, predetermine the result by meeting and selecting the candidates to be voted upon. The successful candidate must obtain a majority of the votes cast. Only when party discipline breaks down, or a third party has sufficient strength, is there the possibility for multiple ballots. In 1923, for example, when the Progressive Party held a number of seats, the House took nine ballots before electing Frederick Gillett, a Republican.

Unlike British practice and unlike the President Pro Tempore of the Senate, the Speaker of the House is the primary legislative leader of the body. As the leader of the majority party, the Speaker declares and defends the legislative agenda of the majority party. However, the Speaker traditionally refrains from debating or voting in most circumstances and does not sit

on any standing committees in the House. The Constitution does not state the duties of the Speaker, and the role of the Speaker has largely been shaped by traditions and customs that evolved over time. During much of the nineteenth century, the Speaker possessed enormous power, including the power to appoint members and chairmen of all committees and to control the timing and content of bills brought before the House. But in a Republican revolt against Speaker Joseph Cannon in 1910, the Speaker's power was reduced, and chairmen came to be appointed primarily by reason of seniority. Thereafter, power within the House was concentrated within the chairmen of the committees until the mid-1970s, when the House restored many of the Speaker's powers.

The House also elects other officers such as the Clerk, Sergeant-at-Arms, Chief Administrative Officer, and Chaplain, whereas the Speaker appoints the Historian of the House, the General Counsel, and the Inspector General.

David F. Forte

See Also

Article I, Section 3, Clause 5 (President Pro Tempore)
Article II, Section 2, Clause 3 (Recess Appointments Clause)

Suggestion for Further Research

Alfred T. Zubrov, Speakers of the House 1789–2002 (2002)

Impeachment

The House of Representatives... shall have the sole Power of Impeachment.
(**Article I, Section 2, Clause 5**)

⁓

*I*n the debates in the Constitutional Convention, the delegates were attempting to craft a mechanism that would allow for the disciplining of a President who abused his constitutional responsibilities without creating a weapon by which the President would be prevented from carrying them out. At bottom, it was a question of how to refine and make effective the separation of powers.

Article II, Section 4, says that the President, Vice President, and "all civil Officers of the United States"—which includes judges—can be impeached. Members of Congress can be expelled by their own respective body. (*See* Article I, Section 5, Clause 2.)

Early on, some delegates expressed the apprehension that those serving in the federal government would be disinclined to monitor each other. Accordingly, John Dickinson proposed "that the Executive be made removeable by the National Legislature on the request of a majority of the Legislatures of individual States." James Madison opposed the idea because it would subject the executive to the "intrigues" of the states. After defeating Dickinson's proposal, the members of the Convention also turned aside George Mason's and Gouverneur Morris's initial fears that the impeachment power might render the executive the servant of the legislature. Instead, the Framers opted for the procedure that had been followed by the English and by the constitutions of most of the states. The appropriate place of bringing charges of impeachment, which power is analogous to the bringing of criminal charges by a grand jury, is in the lower house of the legislature. Just as the grand and petit juries are popular institutions, so it made sense to have the branch closest to the people charged with this indictment-like power.

The Constitution does not specify how impeachment proceedings are to be initiated. Early in our history, a Member would rise on the floor of Congress and propose an impeachment, which would then be assigned to a committee. In recent years, Members of the House Judiciary Committee have initiated the proceeding and then made recommendations for the whole House's consideration. If the House votes an impeachment resolution, the Chairman of the Judiciary Committee recommends a slate of "managers," whom the House subsequently approves by resolution, and who then become prosecutors in the trial in the Senate.

For a time there was legislation enabling the Attorney General to appoint a "special prosecutor" with the power to recommend impeachments to Congress, but dissatisfaction with the power of such an unchecked independent counsel led to the expiration of the authorizing statute. Even the most famous "independent counsel," Judge Kenneth Starr, who recommended the impeachment of President William Jefferson Clinton to Congress, had consistently argued against the practice of appointing such independent counsels.

There have not been many instances of impeachment over the years—a few dozen in all, mostly of corrupt federal judges. The most notable impeachments—Justice Samuel Chase, Presidents Andrew Johnson and William Jefferson Clinton—have ended in acquittals by the Senate. There were proceedings and hearings at the House Judiciary Committee and a bill of impeachment reported to the House against President Richard M. Nixon. Nixon resigned before the full House could vote on the impeachment charges against him.

The near-unanimous view of constitutional commentators is that the House of Representatives' "sole power" of impeachment is a political question and therefore not reviewable by the judiciary. The House is constitutionally obligated to base a bill of impeachment on the standards set out in Article II. (*See* Article II, Section 4.) However, the fact that the Constitution's text grants the House the "sole power," and the fact that such a review is not clearly within the Article III power of the federal judiciary indicate that this responsibility is the House's alone. The Supreme Court has found that the Senate's "sole power" to try impeachments is not justiciable. *Nixon v. United States* (1993).

That leaves the question of whether the clause imposes an affirmative duty on the House to monitor the conduct of those subject to impeachment, and, when evidence of impeachable offenses is manifest, to initiate proceedings. It has been the general American practice regarding criminal law to grant considerable discretion to prosecutors, so that by analogy one could argue that the House has complete discretion to decide whether to initiate impeachment proceedings. On the other hand, Alexander Hamilton, in *The Federalist* No. 77, argued that the nation would find "republican" safety from a presidential abuse of power by the mode of his election and by his "being at all times liable to impeachment." There is no doubt that the Framers saw impeachment as a part of the system of checks and balances to maintain the separation of powers and the republican form of government. The implication is that when the President (or other impeachable official) has committed an impeachable offense, the Members of the House, bound by the oaths they take to uphold the Constitution, are under a particular obligation to deal with the miscreant's offenses, irrespective of whether their bill of impeachment may or may not lead to a conviction in the Senate.

Stephen B. Presser

See Also

Article I, Section 3, Clause 6 (Trial of Impeachment)

Article I, Section 3, Clause 7 (Punishment for Impeachment)

Article I, Section 5, Clause 2 (Rules and Expulsion Clause)

Article II, Section 4 (Standards for Impeachment)

Article III

Suggestions for Further Research

MICHAEL J. GERHARDT, THE FEDERAL IMPEACHMENT PROCESS: A CONSTITUTIONAL AND HISTORICAL ANALYSIS (2d ed. 2000)

Michael J. Gerhardt, *Rediscovering Nonjusticiability: Judicial Review of Impeachments after Nixon*, 44 DUKE L.J. 231 (1994)

Stephen B. Presser, *Would George Washington Have Wanted Bill Clinton Impeached?*, 67 GEO. WASH. L. REV. 666 (1999)

Ronald D. Rotunda, *An Essay on the Constitutional Parameters of Federal Impeachment*, 76 KY. L. REV. 707 (1988)

Jonathan Turley, *Congress as Grand Jury: The Role of the House of Representatives in the Impeachment*

of an American President, 67 GEO. WASH. L. REV. 735 (1999)

Significant Case

Nixon v. United States, 506 U.S. 224 (1993)

Senate

The Senate of the United States shall be composed of two Senators from each State, chosen by the Legislature thereof for six Years; and each Senator shall have one Vote.

(ARTICLE I, SECTION 3, CLAUSE 1)

~

*T*he formulation of the Senate was the result of the famous Connecticut Compromise at the Constitutional Convention, which provided for proportional representation of the states in the House and equal representation of the states in the Senate. Each state was to have two Senators, who would be elected by its state legislature, serve for staggered six-year terms, and vote per capita. By these devices, the Framers intended to protect the interests of the states as states.

Equal representation of all states in the Senate ensured that the ability of the smaller states to protect their interests would not be seriously impaired. Combined with the bicameral system created by the Constitution, it required that all legislation would have to be ratified by two independent power sources: Representatives of the people in the House and Representatives of the states (regardless of their respective size) in the Senate.

The mode of election impelled Senators to preserve the original federal design and to protect the interests not only of their own states, but, concomitantly, of the states as political and legal entities within the federal system. As Alexander Hamilton declared during the New York ratifying convention in 1788, "When you take a view of all the circumstances which have been recited, you will certainly see that the senators will constantly look up to the state governments with an eye of dependence and affection. If they are ambitious to continue in office, they will make every prudent arrangement for this purpose, and, whatever may be their private sentiments or politics, they will be convinced that the surest means of obtaining reelection will be a uniform attachment to the interests of their several states."

On first blush, per capita voting seems, as Luther Martin argued in the Constitutional Convention, to depart "from the idea of the *States* being represented in the second branch." However, the Framers knew from their experiences with block voting under the Articles of Confederation that states had often gone unrepresented because of an evenly divided delegation. They also appreciated that per capita voting could often represent a state's interests better than block voting, even if occasionally that state's Senators split their vote. Because their six-year terms of office were to be staggered, and because they were elected by state legislatures which, as James Madison observed in *The Federalist* No. 63, were continuously "regenerate[d]" by "the periodic change of members," a state's two Senators would end up representing somewhat different political moods and sentiments. Elected by shifting majorities in the state legislature, the two Senators, voting per capita, would be able to reflect more accurately the shifting political sentiments of the people in their home states than if they were required to vote as a block.

The Seventeenth Amendment profoundly altered Article I, Section 3, by providing for direct election of the Senate. Four interrelated factors explain its ratification: (1) legislative deadlocks over the election of Senators brought about when one party controlled the state assembly or house and another the state senate; (2) scandals brought on by charges of bribery and corruption in the election of Senators; (3) the growing strength of the Populist movement, with its deep-seated suspicion of wealth and influence and its penchant for describing the Senate as "an unrepresentative, unresponsive 'millionaires club,' high on parti-

sanship but low in integrity"; and (4) the rise of Progressivism and its conviction that the solution to the problems of democracy was more democracy—in this case, popular election of Senators.

Ralph Rossum

See Also

Article I, Section 3

Amendment XVII (Popular Election of Senators)

Suggestions for Further Research

Jay S. Bybee, *Ulysses at the Mast: Democracy, Federalism, and the Sirens' Song of the Seventeenth Amendment*, 91 Nw. U. L. Rev. 500 (1997)

George H. Haynes, The Election of Senators (1906)

George H. Haynes, The Senate of the United States: Its History and Practice (2 vols. 1938)

Ralph A. Rossum, Federalism, the Supreme Court, and the Seventeenth Amendment: The Irony of Constitutional Democracy (2001)

Senatorial Classes and Vacancies Clause

Immediately after they shall be assembled in Consequence of the first Election, they shall be divided as equally as may be into three Classes. The Seats of the Senators of the first Class shall be vacated at the Expiration of the second Year, of the second Class at the Expiration of the fourth Year, and of the third Class at the Expiration of the sixth Year, so that one third may be chosen every second Year; and if Vacancies happen by Resignation, or otherwise, during the Recess of the Legislature of any State, the Executive thereof may make temporary Appointments until the

next Meeting of the Legislature, which shall then fill such Vacancies.
(ARTICLE I, SECTION 3, CLAUSE 2)

∽

*W*ell before the delegates to the Constitutional Convention had reached "the Great Compromise" that accorded the states equal votes in the Senate, they had already decided much about the upper house. They determined that the state legislatures would choose the Members of the Senate from their respective states; that it would have fewer Members than the lower house; and that the Members of the Senate would serve longer terms. By these mechanisms, the delegates integrated the states into the national legislative process, "protected" and "preserved" the states, provided for a forum to represent "the great mercantile interest," and made the Senate's membership more "permanent," in order to modify the more "transient impressions" that would influence the House. They perceived the Senate to be a more deliberative body. The House of Representatives, the Framers thought, would initiate most legislation, whereas the Senate was to be a corrective and a refinement of what emanated from the House.

Various delegates suggested terms ranging from three to nine years. James Madison argued for a longer term "to give the Govt. that stability which was every where called for." Most delegates seemed to support a term of seven years, but after Alexander Hamilton proposed a complex system of rotation, Hugh Williamson of North Carolina suggested a term of six years "as more convenient for Rotation then 7 years." After some hesitation, the delegates agreed to six-year staggered terms.

The first Senate was able to reach a quorum on April 6, 1789, and immediately counted the electoral ballots that elected George Washington President. On May 13, they divided themselves into three geographically balanced classes, with no two Senators from the same state in the same class. Then, the Senate resolved that "three papers of an equal size, numbered 1, 2, and 3, be, by the Secretary, rolled up and put into a box," and drawn by three Senators representing the previously assigned classes. The class

drawing "1" would vacate at the end of two years, "2" at the end of four, and "3" at the end of six. New states' Senators would be allocated among the classes. Thus began the institution of staggered terms by which the Senate continues to be elected, now through the terms of the Seventeenth Amendment.

At the Convention, only James Wilson had objected to granting governors the power to make appointments to the Senate if there were a sudden vacancy and the legislature was not in session. He thought the device contrary to the principle of the separation of powers. Edmund Randolph, however, declared that the provision was "necessary in order to prevent inconvenient chasms in the Senate," and the Convention agreed.

David F. Forte

See Also

Article I, Section 3, Clause 1 (Senate)
Article I, Section 3, Clause 3 (Qualifications for Senators)
Amendment XVII (Popular Election of Senators)

Suggestion for Further Research

DANIEL WIRLS & STEPHEN WIRLS, THE INVENTION OF THE UNITED STATES SENATE (2004)

Qualifications for Senators

No person shall be a Senator who shall not have attained to the Age of thirty Years, and been nine Years a Citizen of the United States, and who shall not, when elected, be an Inhabitant of that State for which he shall be chosen.
(ARTICLE I, SECTION 3, CLAUSE 3)

∽

*T*he Framers understood that the frequent elections for Members of the House meant that Congress as a whole would be subject to the dangers of faction, unless a "responsible" Senate were added to the legislature. Publius in *The Federalist* No. 63 agreed, and argued that the role of the Senate ensures that "the cool and deliberate sense of the community" prevails in Congress over the potential tyranny of momentary passions. The more advanced age of Senators and their longer period of citizenship make them better suited for the "senatorial trust, which, requiring greater extent of information and stability of character, requires at the same time that the senator should have reached a period of life most likely to supply these advantages." *The Federalist* No. 62. Before the Constitutional Convention settled on a nine-year compromise, Gouverneur Morris had pressed for a fourteen-year period of citizenship. It would take at least that long, Morris argued, for foreigners to learn the American Constitution and its system of laws. James Madison, Benjamin Franklin, and James Wilson opposed a period of such length, arguing that it would make the Constitution too "illiberal."

The age, residency, and citizenship requirements for the Senate have not, themselves, been the subject of judicial dispute. The clause makes it clear that one must be a resident of the state at the time of election, but the Senate has adopted the practice of receiving into its membership Senators who attain the minimum age or length of citizenship subsequent to their election but prior to assuming office.

In the aftermath of the Civil War, both Houses of Congress did occasionally deny individuals their seats if they could not swear that they had never been disloyal to the union. The question of Congress's power to consider qualifications in addition to those stated in Article I remained open until 1969, when Chief Justice Earl Warren wrote in *Powell v. McCormack* that "in judging the qualifications of its members Congress is limited to the standing qualifications prescribed in the Constitution."

The question whether states could add to the Constitution's list of requirements was the focus of *United States Term Limits v. Thornton* (1995). Previously, both the House and the Senate had seated Members who were not in compliance with an additional state requirement. For example, in 1856 the Senate seated Lyman Trumbull from Illinois, even though, as a sitting state judge,

Trumbull was forbidden by the Illinois Constitution from serving in any other state or federal office. A 1970 circuit opinion by Justice Hugo L. Black in *Davis v. Adams* upheld a lower court's determination that the state of Florida could not require a candidate for Congress to resign his state office prior to assuming his federal candidacy. In writing for the Court in *Thornton*, Justice John Paul Stevens concluded that "the Framers intended the Constitution to be the exclusive source of qualifications for members of Congress, and that the Framers thereby 'divested' States of any power to add qualifications."

Ronald Pestritto

See Also

Article I, Section 2, Clause 2 (Qualifications for Representatives)

Article I, Section 5, Clause 1 (Qualifications and Quorum)

Suggestion for Further Research

John C. Eastman, *Open to Merit of Every Description? An Historical Assessment of the Constitution's Qualifications Clauses*, 73 Denv. U. L. Rev. 89 (1995)

Significant Cases

Powell v. McCormack, 395 U.S. 486 (1969)

Davis v. Adams, 400 U.S. 1203 (1970)

United States Term Limits v. Thornton, 514 U.S. 779 (1995)

Vice President as Presiding Officer

> The Vice President of the United States shall be President of the Senate, but shall have no Vote, unless they be equally divided.
>
> (**Article I, Section 3, Clause 4**)

~

*E*xcepting the duty to receive the tally of electoral votes for President, the only regular responsibility assigned to the office of the Vice President by the Constitutional Convention was to preside over the Senate and to cast tie-breaking votes. Because this seemed to give the Vice President some legislative responsibility, George Mason argued during the Convention that this was a violation of the separation of powers, that "it mixed too much" the executive and legislative powers. But Roger Sherman responded: "If the Vice President were not to be President of the Senate, he would be without employment."

Yet it was agreed that allowing the Vice President to preside over the Senate, and to vote in case of a tie, solved two important problems. First, it allowed that body—at all times—to come to a definitive resolution, because the President of the Senate would break tie votes. Second, it preserved the equality of the states in the Senate. Should a Senator be chosen to preside over the body, and should that Senator cast the tie-breaking vote, a state would, in effect, increase its representation. Joseph Story, *Commentaries on the Constitution of the United States.*

Alternatively, if the Senator as presiding President would be allowed to vote only in case of a tie, a state would end up losing half its representation during normal votes. *The Federalist* No. 68. There have been over two hundred occasions when the Vice President has had to cast a tie-breaking vote, but most occurred early in the history of the Republic. In fact, the first Vice President, John Adams, cast the highest number of such votes.

Early in the Republic the Vice President took seriously his constitutional duty of presiding over the Senate, and John Adams and Thomas Jefferson did much to shape the presider's role. Rarely, however, does the Vice President sit in modern times. The President Pro Tempore of the Senate is the formal substitute, but normally a junior member of the Senate is assigned to sit in the chair. Instead, under the broad discretion the Constitution leaves to each branch to develop its own structure, the political influence of Vice Presidents in the executive branch has increased as modern Presidents have delegated many functions to their Vice Presidents.

Peter W. Schramm

See Also

Article II, Section 1, Clause 3 (Electoral College)
Article II, Section 1, Clause 6 (Presidential Succession)
Amendment XII (Electoral College)
Amendment XXII (Presidential Term Limit)
Amendment XXV (Presidential Succession)

Suggestions for Further Research

Mark O. Hatfield, Vice Presidents of the United States, 1789–1993 (1997)
Paul C. Light, Vice-Presidential Power: Advice and Influence in the White House (1984)
L. Edward Purcell, The Vice Presidents: A Biographical Dictionary (1998)

President Pro Tempore

The Senate shall chuse their other Officers, and also a President pro tempore, in the Absence of the Vice President, or when he shall exercise the Office of President of the United States.

(Article I, Section 3, Clause 5)

$\sim$

*T*o maintain the appropriate ordering of the legislative process in the Senate, the Constitution provided for the appointment of a temporary presiding officer when the Vice President was absent from the body. As with Article I, Section 1, Clause 2, vesting the appointment of the Speaker and other officers in the House of Representatives, this clause avoids any inference that the Appointments Clause (Article II, Section 2, Clause 2), might apply to legislative officers. It is, in other words, another carefully drafted provision to protect the separation of powers.

At first, the Senate elected a President Pro Tempore each time the Vice President absented himself from the chair, the office ending upon the return of the Vice President. In 1792, John Adams began the custom of vacating the presidential chair shortly before the end of each day's session, permitting the Senate to elect a President Pro Tempore who would be in place in case the Vice

President died or assumed the functions of the President of the United States. The Senate codified that practice by resolution in 1876.

In 1890, the Senate adopted the procedure that continues today of electing a President Pro Tempore who holds the office until replaced. By custom, the Senate elects the Member of the majority party who is senior in terms of length of service. By statute, the office is third in succession to the presidency after the Vice President and the Speaker of the House of Representatives.

The President Pro Tempore is not a legislative leader. He supervises the Senate and makes procedural rulings while in the chair. He appoints substitutes from the Members to sit in the chair when he steps down. Often the daily roster of substitutes includes younger Senators in order to acquaint them with the procedures of the Senate.

"Other Officers" of the Senate include the majority and minority leaders who have the primary responsibility of directing the flow of legislation, party secretaries, the Sergeant at Arms and Doorkeeper, Chaplain, Secretary of the Senate, Chief Clerk, and Executive Clerk.

David F. Forte

See Also

Suggestion for Further Research

Richard C. Sachs, The President Pro Tempore of the Senate: History and Authority of the Office (2001)

Trial of Impeachment

The Senate shall have the sole Power to try all Impeachments. When sitting for that Purpose, they shall be on Oath or Affirmation. When the President of the United States is tried, the Chief Justice shall preside: And no Person shall be convicted without the Concurrence of two thirds of the Members present.

(**Article I, Section 3, Clause 6**)

～

The essential powers and procedures for Senate impeachment trials are set forth in this clause. The Framers vested the Senate with the "sole Power to try Impeachments" for several reasons. First, they believed Senators would be better educated, more virtuous, and more high-minded than Members of the House of Representatives and thus uniquely able to decide responsibly the most difficult of political questions. Second, the Framers vested the Senate rather than the judiciary with the authority to try impeachments because they favored, as Alexander Hamilton explained in *The Federalist* No. 65, a "numerous court for the trial of impeachments." He believed such a body would be well suited to handle the procedural demands of an impeachment trial, in which it, unlike judges, should "never be tied down by such strict rules, either in the delineation of the offense by the prosecutor, or in the construction of it by judges, as in the common cases serve to limit the discretion of courts in favor of personal security." Hamilton explained further that "[t]he awful discretion which a court of impeachments must necessarily have to doom to honor or infamy the most confidential and the most distinguished characters of the community forbids the commitment of the trust to a small number of persons."

There are three special requirements for impeachment trials. The requirement that Senators be on Oath or Affirmation in impeachment trials was plainly designed to impress upon them the extreme seriousness of the occasion. The requirement for the Chief Justice to preside over presidential impeachment trials underscores the solemnity of the occasion and aims to avoid the possible conflict of interest of a Vice President's presiding over the proceeding for the removal of the one official standing between him and the presidency. Moreover, the supermajority requirement was designed to facilitate serious deliberation and to make removal possible only through a consensus that cuts across factional divisions. This requirement's impact is apparent in the fact that the Senate has convicted only seven of sixteen people impeached by the House. It was instrumental in Andrew Johnson's trial, as the majority fell one vote short of removing him from office. In President William Jefferson Clinton's trial, there was never a question of his removal so long as all forty-five Democrats in the Senate uniformly opposed his ouster.

In addition to the requirements in the Constitution's text, three significant questions have arisen about Senate authority to try impeachments. The first is the minimum the Senate must do once the House impeaches someone. This question arose after the House's first impeachment in 1797. One day after the House impeached Senator William Blount, the Senate expelled him by a vote of 25–1. Blount claimed the Senate lacked authority to try him because Senators were not impeachable and, in any event, he no longer occupied an office from which he could be removed. The Senate voted to dismiss the impeachment resolution against the expelled Blount for lack of jurisdiction. Subsequently, many Senators have construed this vote as supporting their authority to dismiss an impeachment without a full-scale trial.

The second question is the extent of the Chief Justice's authority as presiding officer to render unilateral rulings. In the first presidential impeachment trial in 1868, Chief Justice Salmon Chase claimed the authority to decide certain procedural questions on his own, but the Senate challenged several of his rulings and overruled him at least twice. In President Clinton's impeachment trial in 1999, Chief Justice William H. Rehnquist ruled on some procedural questions, but the Senate never challenged, much less overruled, any of these rulings.

A third question revolves around which procedures the Senate must employ in impeachment trials. Because the Constitution both provides the Senate with the "sole power to try impeachments" and empowers "Each House . . . to determine the Rules of its Proceed-

ings," the Senate has formulated its own special impeachment trial procedures (first written down by Thomas Jefferson when he was Vice President). In President Johnson's impeachment trial, the Senate formulated an additional set of rules that have largely remained intact ever since and were followed by the Senate in President Clinton's impeachment trial.

In 1936, the Senate amended these rules to include Rule XI, which allows the appointment of a small number of Senators to operate as a trial committee to gather evidence and take testimony. The Senate has used trial committees on only three occasions in the 1980s to assist with fact-finding regarding impeachment articles approved by the House against three federal district judges. Before the Senate and in federal court, all three judges challenged the legitimacy of trial committees. They argued the Senate's "power to try impeachments" imposed on the full Senate the obligation to conduct a full trial. The Senate countered that it had complete authority over how to fashion proceedings and that Senators' political accountability was the only check on this authority. Ultimately, the Supreme Court accepted the Senate's arguments in *Nixon v. United States* (1993) on the principal ground that the Senate's power to try impeachments included the nonreviewable final discretion to determine how to conduct its trials. The Court did not address the propriety of judicial review of the Senate's possible deviation from any explicit safeguard required by the Constitution for impeachment trials.

The Senate settled some other procedural questions raised in the 1980s, including the applicability of the Fifth Amendment Due Process Clause to and the requisite rules of evidence and burden of proof for impeachment trials. The Senate ruled that adopting a uniform rule on these questions was impractical because it lacked the means for enforcing any such rule against Senators. It decided that each question was a matter for the Senators to decide for themselves.

The Constitution fastens the responsibility of trying impeachments upon the Senate. Yet some Senators have doubted whether they have the requisite competence to try impeachments. Rule XI was adopted as a response to poor attendance and preparation by Senators in impeachment trials in the early twentieth century. Yet even in the 1980s, some Senators claimed that they had not bothered to prepare before voting, and such proceedings diverted their energies away from legislative business of greater concern to their constituents. Others argued the proceedings restored their confidence in the Senate's institutional competence to conduct them. In any event, the Framers of the Constitution vested that task in the Senate and nowhere else.

The last question is the continuing debate over how effective impeachment is as a remedy for executive or judicial misconduct. After the acquittal of President Clinton, some commentators have wondered whether impeachment is a meaningful option for dealing with a popular President's misconduct. Some believe that Clinton's acquittal strengthened the presidency because it makes it less likely future Presidents will face serious impeachment attempts for private misconduct. Others think Clinton's acquittal reflects an appropriate compromise that was consistent with the structure: he had been impeached by the House and therefore disgraced for his misconduct but not removed from office. Validation of these competing views must await future impeachment trials.

Michael J. Gerhardt

See Also

Article I, Section 2, Clause 5 (Impeachment)

Article I, Section 3, Clause 7 (Punishment for Impeachment)

Article I, Section 5, Clause 2 (Rules and Expulsion Clause)

Article II, Section 4 (Standards for Impeachment)

Article III, Section 1 (Good Behavior Clause)

Suggestions for Further Research

Raoul Berger, Impeachment: The Constitutional Problems (1974)

Charles L. Black, Impeachment: A Handbook (1998)

Rebecca Brown, *When Political Questions Affect Individual Rights: The Other* Nixon v. United States, 1993 Sup. Ct. Rev. 125

Michael J. Gerhardt, The Federal Impeachment Process: A Constitutional and Historical Analysis (2d ed. 2000)

Peter Charles Hoffer & N.E.H. Hull, Impeachment in America, 1635–1801 (1984)

Buckner F. Melton, Jr., The First Impeachment: The Constitution's Framers and the Case of Senator William Blount (1998)

Richard Posner, An Affair of State: The Investigation, Impeachment and Trial of President Clinton (1999)

William H. Rehnquist, Grand Inquests: The Historic Impeachments of Justice Samuel Chase and President Andrew Johnson (1992)

Ronald D. Rotunda, *An Essay on the Constitutional Parameters of Federal Impeachment*, 76 Ky. L. Rev. 707 (1988)

Significant Cases

Powell v. McCormack, 395 U.S. 486 (1969)

Hastings v. United States, 802 F. Supp. 490 (D.D.C. 1992), *revised and remanded* Order No. 92-5327 (D.C. Cir. March 2, 1993); 837 F. Supp. 3 (D.D.C. 1993)

Nixon v. United States, 506 U.S. 224 (1993)

Punishment for Impeachment

Judgment in Cases of Impeachment shall not extend further than to removal from Office, and disqualification to hold and enjoy any Office of honor, Trust or Profit under the United States: but the Party convicted shall nevertheless be liable and subject to Indictment, Trial, Judgment and Punishment, according to Law.

(Article I, Section 3, Clause 7)

$\sim$

*T*he Punishment for Impeachment Clause sets forth the scope and nature of the punishments that the Senate may impose in impeachment trials. In fashioning this clause, the delegates to the Constitutional Convention deliberately distinguished impeachment in this country from the British system by limiting the punishments in the federal Constitution to those typically found in state constitutions, that is, removal and disqualification, in contrast to the House of Lords' practice of imposing any punishment, including death, in an impeachment proceeding.

Since ratification, four troublesome questions have arisen under this clause. The first was whether the Senate may impose the sanctions of removal and disqualification separately and, if so, how. The Senate claims that it may impose these sanctions by separate votes: (1) removal, involving the ouster of an official from the office he occupies at the time of his impeachment trial, and (2) disqualification barring the person from ever serving again in the federal government. In 1862 and 1913, the Senate took separate votes to remove and disqualify judges West Humphreys and Robert Archbald, respectively. For each judge, a supermajority first voted to convict followed by a simple majority vote to disqualify. The Senate defended this practice on the ground that the clause mentioning disqualification does not specify the requisite vote for its imposition, although Article II, Section 4, mentions removal as following conviction. The Senate in 1862 and 1913 considered that the supermajority requirement was designed as a safeguard against removal that, once satisfied, did not extend to the separate imposition of disqualification.

The second question involves the proper sequence of impeachment and criminal proceedings. It is clear from practice and judicial interpretation that officials other than the President may be convicted and even imprisoned before impeachment. The question is whether a sitting President, though not singled out in the text of the Constitution, is immune from trial and conviction in the ordinary courts before impeachment and removal from office. The provision that a convicted official is "liable and subject to Indictment, Trial, Judgement and Punishment, according to Law" gives rise to two constructions. Alexander Hamilton in *The Federalist* No. 69 construed the clause as requiring that a President would first be impeached and removed from office and "would afterwards be liable to prosecution and punishment in the course of law." The

argument, made by many of President William Jefferson Clinton's defenders during his impeachment and trial, is that prosecuting Presidents poses a unique risk not applicable to prosecuting the leaders of other branches because the executive branch is the only federal branch overseen by a single individual and thus prosecuting its leader—the President—uniquely risks paralyzing the entire branch he oversees.

The counter-arguments seem at least as strong. First, the clause could be read not as requiring that impeachment precede prosecution, but as reflecting an expectation that impeachments generally might but are not required to precede prosecutions. In other words, the Constitution merely provides that these proceedings are mutually exclusive. Second, the President is not above the law, and a President is subject to the same legal requirements and burdens as any citizen, as implied by two unanimous Supreme Court decisions: *United States v. Nixon* (1974) (the President is not immune to subpoenas for evidence in a federal criminal trial) and *Clinton v. Jones* (1997) (the President is not immune from civil litigation based on his personal, unofficial conduct). Third, several judges have been prosecuted (and even imprisoned) before being impeached. Indeed, several courts rejected their efforts to bar their prosecutions before being impeached. On the other hand, an impeachable offense (such as abuse of office) may not be a crime. If an impeachable offense had to be first enacted into a criminal code, then the House of Representatives would not have the "sole" power to impeach because a criminal law would first have to be passed and therefore approved by the other branches of government.

The third question involves the interpretation of the provision that "Judgment in Cases of Impeachment shall not extend further than to removal from Office, and disqualification to hold and enjoy any Office of honor, Trust or Profit under the United States." Throughout President Clinton's impeachment proceedings, Members of Congress considered whether this language permitted the Congress to impose a sanction against him short of impeachment and removal, such as a resolution passed by the House or Senate denouncing him for his misconduct. The congressional and academic debates at the time remain the most extensive yet on the legitimacy of censure.

There are strong arguments against censure. First, the Constitution does not explicitly authorize censure. Second, the vesting of the impeachment power in Congress arguably implies the exclusion of other means by which to punish officials who have committed impeachable offenses. Third, the use of censure would undermine the Framers' objective to narrow the range of permissible sanctions in an impeachment trial. Fourth, allowing censure could upset the delicate system of checks and balances by making it easier for Congress to harass or embarrass a President. Fifth, censure conceivably constitutes a bill of attainder (a legislative imposition of a punishment that only a court should have been authorized to impose after a trial).

There are also arguments supporting censure. First, the relevant text seems to imply that "lesser" punishments than removal or disqualification are permissible. Second, other clauses of the Constitution (including the Speech and Debate Clause, the First Amendment's freedom of speech guarantee, and the vesting of power in the House and the Senate to keep journals of their respective proceedings) empower Members of Congress to enter critical comments about public figures into the congressional record. While a "censure" consisting of mere words may or may not be thought a meaningful punishment, such expression could be easily accomplished outside of the impeachment process as a matter of collective speech of Senators and Representatives. Third, historical practices support censure. The House and Senate have passed over a dozen such resolutions, including resolutions condemning Presidents James K. Polk and Andrew Jackson. Hence, the debates over censure, like those over the other questions about the appropriate sanctions the Senate may impose for presidential misconduct, are likely to persist until historical practice resolves the matter.

Michael J. Gerhardt

See Also

Article I, Section 2, Clause 5 (Impeachment)
Article I, Section 3, Clause 6 (Trial of Impeachment)

Article II, Section 4 (Standards for Impeachment)
Article III, Section 1

Suggestions for Further Research

Raoul Berger, Impeachment: The Constitutional Problems (1974)

Arthur Bestor, *Impeachment*, 49 Wash. L. Rev. 255 (1973) (reviewing R. Berger, Impeachment: The Constitutional Problems (1973))

Charles L. Black, Impeachment: A Handbook (1998) (with an introduction by Akhil Reed Amar)

Michael J. Gerhardt, The Federal Impeachment Process: A Constitutional and Historical Analysis (2000)

Richard Posner, An Affair of State: The Investigation, Impeachment and Trial of President Clinton (1999)

Ronald D. Rotunda, *An Essay on the Constitutional Parameters of Federal Impeachment*, 76 Ky. L.J. 707 (1988)

Emily Field Van Tassel, Impeachable Offenses: A Documentary History 1787 to the Present (1999)

Significant Cases

United States v. Isaacs, 493 F.2d 1124 (1974)
United States v. Nixon, 418 U.S. 683 (1974)
Nixon v. Fitzgerald, 457 U.S. 731 (1982)
Clinton v. Jones, 520 U.S. 681 (1997)

Election Regulations

The Times, Places and Manner of holding Elections for Senators and Representatives, shall be prescribed in each State by the Legislature thereof; but the Congress may at any time by Law make or alter such Regulations, except as to the Places of chusing Senators.

(Article I, Section 4, Clause 1)

～

$\mathcal{T}$he purpose of this provision of the Constitution was twofold. First, it made clear the division of responsibility with respect to the conduct of the election of federal Senators and

Representatives. That responsibility lay primarily with the states and secondarily with Congress. Second, the clause lodged the power to regulate elections in the respective legislative branches of the states and the federal government, not with the executive or judicial.

Opponents to the Constitution hotly contested the clause during the ratification debates. The concern of the Anti-Federalists was that the default prerogatives to Congress would result in Members of Congress manipulating election laws so that they could stay in office indefinitely. Alternatively, Congress might alter the times and places of elections so as to make it extremely difficult to vote, undermining the franchise. On the other hand, defenders of the clause argued that if Congress did not retain residual power to control federal elections, state officials might effectively destroy Congress by failing to make rules for the election of its Members. As Alexander Hamilton remarked in *The Federalist* No. 59, "every government ought to contain within itself the means of its own preservation." Hamilton argued that the provision was a reasonable compromise that gave Congress default powers that would be exercised "whenever extraordinary circumstances might render that interposition necessary to its safety." In addition, the fact that Congress as a whole, and not any single house of Congress, was authorized to make or alter regulations under the clause meant that a national consensus between the people's or "democratic" branch of the federal government and the Senate, representing the states, would have to take place before any changes could occur.

Since ratification of the Constitution, there have been many legal developments that have altered the provisions of Article I, Section 4, the most significant of which came after the Civil War. The Fifteenth Amendment (1870) prohibited voter discrimination on the basis of race. The Enforcement Act of 1870 had some beneficial effect in curbing the abuse of the electoral process, particularly in the South, but with its evisceration in *United States v. Reese* (1875) and *United States v. Cruikshank* (1876), Southern states were able effectively to disenfranchise black citizens.

The Voting Rights Act of 1965 resurrected tough legal prohibitions on racial discrimination in voting and transformed Southern politics and American politics in the process. The most important and controversial of the act's original provisions, Sections 4 and 5, required states predominantly in the South (covered by Section 4) to seek "preclearance" (under Section 5) from the federal Department of Justice or U.S. District Court for the District of Columbia for any new voting practices or procedures postdating November 1, 1964. The constitutionality of these provisions was upheld in *South Carolina v. Katzenbach* (1966). The 1970 Voting Rights Act proposed to reduce the voting age in national, state, and local elections to eighteen. In *Oregon v. Mitchell* (1970), the Court upheld this provision as it applied to national elections but disallowed it as it applied to state and local elections. The Twenty-sixth Amendment effectively overruled this latter holding. The scope of the Voting Rights Act's coverage has increased over the decades and continues to impose significant constraints on states covered by the act, particularly when it comes to redistricting.

In addition to statutory constraints, Congress and the people have altered the electoral process through the amending process. The Seventeenth Amendment altered the manner of conducting the elections of Senators by requiring their popular election. The Nineteenth Amendment prohibited voter discrimination on the basis of sex. The Twenty-fourth Amendment prohibited poll taxes in federal elections, and the Twenty-sixth Amendment gave eighteen-year-olds the right to vote.

Despite Alexander Hamilton's assurance that Congress would regulate elections only in "extraordinary circumstances," congressional intervention has been significant. In 1842, Congress required the election of Members of the House of Representatives by district. Repealed in 1929, the single-Member district rule was restored by Congress in 1967. Also, until 1929 Congress required that each district's territory be compact and contiguous with substantially the same number of inhabitants. *Wood v. Broom* (1932).

In recent decades, the Supreme Court has stepped into the electoral process. In *Wesberry v. Sanders* (1964), the Supreme Court determined that, despite congressional practice, Article I, Section 2, Clause 1, mandated that the "one person, one vote" formula be applied to each congressional district. Critics of the Court's decision have noted that it ignored the language of Article I, Section 4, Clause 1, which appeared to leave questions of reapportionment and redistricting to the legislative, not judicial, branch of government. Under the Fourteenth Amendment's Equal Protection Clause, the Court has also indicated that gerrymandered districts can be an indication of an unconstitutional, racially motivated redistricting plan. *Shaw v. Reno* (1993). However, the Court has not yet required, as a constitutional matter, that districts be compact and contiguous. *Shaw v. Reno* and *Miller v. Johnson* (1995) also highlighted the potential conflict between the demands of the Voting Rights Act for the creation of "safe minority seats" and the constitutional prohibition on redistricting in which race is the predominant factor motivating the redistricting.

Beginning with the Tillman Act in 1907, Congress has imposed a growing number of restrictions on elections and campaign financing. The most significant piece of legislation has been the 1971 Federal Election Campaign Act, amended in 1974. It was this legislation that was at issue in the Supreme Court's seminal decision, *Buckley v. Valeo* (1976), which, in the face of a First Amendment challenge, set the ground rules for campaign finance legislation, generally disallowing restrictions on expenditures by candidates, but permitting restrictions on contributions by individuals and corporations.

Anthony Peacock

See Also

Article I, Section 5, Clause 1 (Qualifications and Quorum)

Article II, Section 1, Clause 2 (Presidential Electors)

Amendment XV (Suffrage—Race)

Amendment XIX (Suffrage—Sex)

Amendment XXIV (Poll Taxes)

Amendment XXVI (Suffrage—Age)

Suggestions for Further Research

WARD E.Y. ELLIOTT, THE RISE OF GUARDIAN DEMOCRACY: THE SUPREME COURT'S ROLE IN VOTING RIGHTS DISPUTES, 1845–1969 (1974)

DANIEL HAYS LOWENSTEIN & RICHARD L. HASEN, ELECTION LAW: CASES & MATERIALS (2d ed. 2001)

ANTHONY A. PEACOCK, ED., AFFIRMATIVE ACTION AND REPRESENTATION: SHAW V. RENO AND THE FUTURE OF VOTING RIGHTS (1997)

Significant Cases

United States v. Reese, 92 U.S. 214 (1875)

United States v. Cruikshank, 92 U.S. 542 (1876)

Wood v. Broom, 287 U.S. 1 (1932)

Smith v. Allwright, 321 U.S. 649 (1944)

Wesberry v. Sanders, 376 U.S. 1 (1964)

South Carolina v. Katzenbach, 383 U.S. 301 (1966)

Oregon v. Mitchell, 400 U.S. 112 (1970)

Beer v. United States, 425 U.S. 130 (1976)

Buckley v. Valeo, 424 U.S. 1 (1976)

Karcher v. Daggett, 462 U.S. 725 (1983)

Thornburg v. Gingles, 478 U.S. 30 (1986)

Shaw v. Reno, 509 U.S. 630 (1993)

Miller v. Johnson, 515 U.S. 900 (1995)

Georgia v. Ashcroft, 539 U.S. 461 (2003)

McConnell v. FEC, 540 U.S. 93 (2003)

Meetings of Congress Clause

The Congress shall assemble at least once in every Year, and such Meeting shall be on the first Monday in December, unless they shall by Law appoint a different Day.

(**ARTICLE I, SECTION 4, CLAUSE 2**)

~

*E*ver mindful of federalism and the separation of powers, the delegates to the Constitutional Convention believed that the scheduling of congressional sessions was a significant issue. There was no thought given to the British model, in which the executive called Parliament to meet.

The Framers did allow the President to convene Congress in a special session for "extraordinary Occasions" (Article II, Section 3), but they fixed the date of Congress's regular sessions to keep it free from executive control.

James Madison submitted that the "Legislature shall meet on the first Monday in December in every year" and the delegates added a provision to allow for a different date "appointed by law" (thus permitting the possibility of executive veto). At first, the delegates argued over the date on the basis of convenience or for extrinsic concerns. Gouverneur Morris moved to substitute May for December because the United States would likely legislate in response to Europe's measures, which were generally planned during the winter and would likely arrive in the United States by spring. Madison changed his mind and stated that he also preferred May because the season would be more agreeable to traveling to and from the capital. In contrast, James Wilson and Oliver Ellsworth argued that requiring the legislature to assemble in December would be more convenient for private business, because most of the Members would be involved with agriculture during the spring and summer.

Edmund Randolph, however, turned the debate to concerns for the structural integrity of the polity. He noted that the state elections would better coincide with the December date, and the vote to require assembly in the month of May did not pass. The issue was not closed, however. Madison was in favor of annual meetings, but of leaving the date to "be fixed or varied by law." Gouverneur Morris and Rufus King believed yearly meetings were not necessary, for there would not be enough legislative business for Congress to deal with annually.

Nathaniel Gorham of Massachusetts focused the delegates' attention once again on the structural needs of the new government. He argued that the time should be fixed to prevent disputes from arising within the legislature, and to allow the states to adjust their elections to correspond with the fixed date. A fixed date also corresponded to the tradition in the states of having annual meetings. Finally, Gorham concluded that the legislative branch should be required to meet at least once a year to act as a check upon the executive department.

Ultimately, Article I, Section 4, Clause 2, bound legislative discretion and placed the requirement for annual legislative sessions "beyond the power of faction, and of party, of power, and of corruption," according to Justice Joseph Story in *Commentaries on the Constitution of the United States*. In practice, prior to the passage of the Twentieth Amendment in 1933, each numbered Congress existed from March 4 of the odd-numbered year to March 3 of the next odd-numbered year, but the regular sessions began on the first Monday in December and generally lasted well into spring.

David F. Forte

See Also

Qualifications and Quorum

Each House shall be the Judge of the Elections, Returns and Qualifications of its own Members, and a Majority of each shall constitute a Quorum to do Business; but a smaller Number may adjourn from day to day, and may be authorized to compel the Attendance of absent Members, in such Manner, and under such Penalties as each House may provide.

(Article I, Section 5, Clause 1)

～

*T*he tradition of permitting a legislative body to judge its own elections, returns, and qualifications was fairly uniform throughout England and America. At the time of the Constitutional Convention, eight states had similar clauses in their state constitutions and the Framers approved the provision without debate. According to Justice

Joseph Story in his *Commentaries on the Constitution of the United States*, it was a necessary attribute of the separation of powers. If that power, Justice Story wrote, were "lodged in any other, than the legislative body itself, its independence, its purity, and even its existence and action may be destroyed, or put into imminent danger." Further, Story declared, the power allowed each House to "sustain the free choice of its constituents." The only objections to the clause in the state ratifying conventions were by those who wanted the power to judge elections to reside with the state legislatures, as it had under the Articles of Confederation.

The power to judge elections extends to investigations of fraud. It includes the power to subpoena witnesses and to impose punishment for perjury. In *Morgan v. United States* (1986), then-Circuit Judge Antonin Scalia declared that the House's determination as to which of two candidates had been elected was nonjusticiable under this clause, a position supported in dicta by previous Supreme Court cases. However, when the House of Representatives sought to expand the definition of "qualifications" beyond those expressly listed in Article I, Section 2, Clause 2, that it was judging under this clause, then the Court not only found the issue justiciable, but struck down the action by the House. *Powell v. McCormack* (1969).

The second section of the clause, dealing with the numbers necessary to constitute a quorum, caused more concern. All agreed that the two-thirds requirement under the Articles of Confederation had been a major hindrance. Nathaniel Gorham, however, objected to even a simple majority, as it might cause a "great delay" in the legislature's business. Most of the debate revolved around the fear of factions. John Mercer of Maryland thought that "[s]o great a number will put it in the power of a few by seceding at a critical moment." George Mason answered that by having a quorum set at less than a majority would "allow a small number of members of the two houses to make laws." The attempt to fix a specific number of votes for a quorum failed and the majority provision remained in the text. The provision allowing day-to-day adjournment by a smaller number permits the business of each house to lie over without the need of continually calling for a quorum.

For some decades after the Constitution, the House of Representatives did not pass legislation unless a full quorum of the House approved the bill. Those present but not voting could prevent a quorum. In 1890, the House changed its rules to determine that a quorum is satisfied if a majority of members are present, even if they withhold their votes on a particular bill. The Supreme Court upheld that procedure in *United States v. Ballin* (1892), and it continues to the present.

The third and final part of the clause, authorizing each house "to compel the attendance of absent members," introduced by John Randolph and James Madison, also passed without debate. It was an additional guard against the power of a minority to abuse the quorum process. Justice Joseph Story declared that the provision did away with any apprehension that a minority could "subvert the fundamental principle of a republican government" by intentionally preventing the formation of a quorum. Under current practice, fifteen Members of the House of Representatives or a majority of the Senate may order the Sergeant at Arms of each respective chamber to compel the attendance of absent Members.

David F. Forte

See Also

Article I, Section 2, Clause 2 (Qualifications for Representatives)

Article I, Section 5, Clause 2 (Rules and Expulsion Clause)

Suggestion for Further Research

Congressional Quarterly's Guide to the Congress (4th ed. 1991)

Significant Cases

United States v. Ballin, 144 U.S. 1 (1892)

Reed v. County Commissioners, 277 U.S. 376 (1928)

Barry v. United States *ex rel.* Cunningham, 279 U.S. 597 (1929)

Powell v. McCormack, 395 U.S. 486 (1969)

Roudebush v. Hartke, 405 U.S. 15 (1972)

Morgan v. United States, 801 F.2d 445 (U.S. App. D.C. 1986)

Rules and Expulsion Clause

Each House may determine the Rules of its Proceedings, punish its Members for disorderly Behaviour, and, with the Concurrence of two thirds, expel a Member.

(ARTICLE I, SECTION 5, CLAUSE 2)

~

By confirming each House's power to set its own procedures, the Framers strengthened the independence of each branch of Congress against the other as well as against the executive and the judiciary. Although the original proposal to give each House of Congress the power to expel lacked a supermajority requirement, James Madison, pointing out the danger that a majority faction could abuse its power by expelling Members of the minority, successfully moved to insert the two-thirds rule. Unlike the exclusion power of Article I, Section 5, Clause 1, there are no judicially enforceable constitutional standards limiting the use of the expulsion power other than the supermajority requirement. *In re Chapman* (1897). Moreover, the courts generally regard disputes arising from the procedural rules of Congress as non-justiciable, unless Congress "ignores constitutional restraints or violates fundamental rights." *United States v. Ballin* (1892). *Powell v. McCormack* (1969), for example, assumed that the case would be nonjusticiable if two-thirds of the House had "expelled" Congressman Adam Clayton Powell instead of "excluding" him.

The Rules and Expulsion Clause stands as the analog to the impeachment clauses. It is the only constitutional mechanism by which a sitting Member of Congress can be removed from office. Alexander Hamilton assumed that Members of the legislature could be impeached, and

some comments in the ratifying conventions presumed the same, but historical practice has been to the contrary. In 1797, the Senate expelled William Blount, but it later refused to convict him on a bill of impeachment because it concluded that there was a lack of jurisdiction. Subsequent interpretation of the Senate's action, supported in particular by Justice Joseph Story, has found the Senate's action dispositive: Members of each branch of Congress may be expelled by their own respective body, but they cannot be impeached. Story's position is supported at least in part by the text of the Constitution. The existence of the specific removal provisions for Members of Congress negates any inference that impeachment exists as an alternative removal mechanism.

Since 1789, the Senate has had nine expulsion proceedings out of which fifteen Senators were expelled, most of them early in the Civil War on grounds of supporting the rebellion. The House has also proceeded against twenty-nine of its Members but has expelled only five, two for corruption and three for supporting the rebellion.

More frequent have been instances when each House has punished its respective Members by a simple majority. Punishments have included censure (or the somewhat lesser "denouncement"), reprimand, loss of seniority, removal from committee or subcommittee chairmanship, and fine. In addition, when a Member of Congress is convicted of a crime, he is expected to refrain from voting unless and until his conviction is overturned or he is re-elected.

David F. Forte

See Also

Article I, Section 5, Clause 1 (Qualifications and Quorum)

Suggestions for Further Research

ANNE M. BUTLER & WENDY WOLFF, UNITED STATES SENATE ELECTION, EXPULSION AND CENSURE CASES, 1793–1990 (1995)

Laura Krugman Ray, *Discipline through Delegation: Solving the Problem of Congressional Housecleaning*, 55 U. PITT. L. REV. 389 (1994)

John C. Roberts, *Are Congressional Committees Constitutional?: Radical Textualism, Separation of Powers, and the Enactment Process*, 52 CASE W. RES. L. REV. 489 (2001)

Significant Cases

United States v. Ballin, 144 U.S. 1 (1892)
In re Chapman, 166 U.S. 661 (1897)
Powell v. McCormack, 395 U.S. 486 (1969)

House Journal

Each House shall keep a Journal of its Proceedings, and from time to time publish the same, excepting such Parts as may in their Judgment require Secrecy; and the Yeas and Nays of the Members of either House on any question shall, at the Desire of one fifth of those Present, be entered on the Journal.

(ARTICLE I, SECTION 5, CLAUSE 3)

∽

*T*he requirement to publish a journal of each House's proceedings occasioned little debate either in the Constitutional Convention or at the ratifying conventions. As Justice Joseph Story commented in his *Commentaries on the Constitution of the United States*, "The object of the whole clause is to ensure publicity to the proceedings of the legislature, and a correspondent responsibility of the members to their respective constituents."

The provision for secrecy, however, raised more problems. At the Convention, Oliver Ellsworth unsuccessfully moved to have the secrecy option deleted, while at the Virginia ratifying convention, Patrick Henry railed, "The liberties of a people never were, nor ever will be, secure, when the transactions of their rulers may be concealed from them." Others feared that, even aside from the secrecy provision, the permission to publish a journal "from time to time" would allow either branch of the Congress to conceal its doings. James Madison assured his fellow Virginians that the discretion was only to allow flexibility for the purposes of accuracy and convenience.

For all the concern about secrecy, the official journals of each House, even when published, turn out not to have some of the most valuable information for constituents, namely, debates on the floor of Congress and testimony before congressional committees. For example, the journals contain a list of the bills and resolutions that are introduced, but they do not normally include the text. Rather, the secrecy provision applies to whether a House will have its daily proceedings accessible to the public.

Both history and judicial opinion have determined that each House possesses complete discretion over what proceedings shall be secret. *Field v. Clark* (1892). For the first twenty years of the country, secret sessions were frequent. Beginning with the War of 1812, however, both Houses have kept most of their proceedings open to the public. The Senate is most likely to hold secret sessions, but over the last seventy-five years, it has done so only during debates over impeachment, classified information, and national defense. The Senate kept its committee sessions closed, however, until the 1970s.

Although not mandated to do so by the Constitution, Congress initiated the *Congressional Record* in 1873. It records the debates on the floor of each House nearly verbatim, and can include undelivered remarks and documents. A federal judge has held that the rules allowing a Member of Congress to edit his remarks before publication are unreviewable by the courts. *Gregg v. Barrett* (1985).

Prior to the *Congressional Record*, mostly paraphrased remarks were carried in the *Annals of Congress* (1789–1824), the *Abridgement of the Debates of Congress* (1789–1850), the *Register of the Debates in Congress* (1824–1837), and the *Congressional Globe* (1833–1873). In the very early years, newspaper reporters had free access to the floor to record the statements of the Members. In recent years, radio and television have increased the public's access to Congress's proceedings.

David F. Forte

See Also

Article I, Section 6, Clause 1 (Speech and Debate Clause)

Suggestion for Further Research

N. David Bleisch, *The Congressional Record and the First Amendment: Accuracy Is the Best Policy*, 12 B.C. ENVTL. AFF. L. REV. (1985)

Significant Cases

Field v. Clark, 143 U.S. 649 (1892)

Gregg v. Barrett, 248 U.S. App. D.C. 347 (1985)

Adjournment

Neither House, during the Session of Congress, shall, without the Consent of the other, adjourn for more than three days, nor to any other Place than that in which the two Houses shall be sitting.

(ARTICLE I, SECTION 5, CLAUSE 4)

~

$\mathcal{D}$ividing the legislative department into two equal branches was one of the most important checks on the legislative power that the Framers devised. At the same time, the Framers believed that it was vital to the affairs of the nation that one House not be permitted to keep Congress as a whole from meeting and performing its functions. Under this clause, neither House can use its power to adjourn to another time or to another place in order to check the actions of the other branch of the legislature. If the two Houses cannot agree on a time of adjournment, then pursuant to Article II, Section 3, Clause 1, the President can "adjourn them to such Time as he shall think proper." At the Virginia ratifying convention, James Monroe and George Mason worried that the clause might give the Senate the power to prevent House Members from returning home, but James Madison opined that the President's power to resolve the dispute would prevent the Senate from keeping the House hostage to its will. Since the time of

the First Congress, the two branches have always reached agreement, and the President has never had to intervene.

At the Constitutional Convention, Rufus King raised a different concern. He worried that the two Houses of Congress could actually move the seat of government merely by agreeing upon the place to which they would adjourn. The Convention decided that Congress could by law establish the seat of government (*see* Article I, Section 8, Clause 17), but the Framers left Congress the option of making temporary moves in the face of exigencies. Thus, during the times of yellow-fever outbreaks in the 1790s, the three departments moved from Philadelphia to Trenton. Of course, during the War of 1812, the government fled from Washington.

Congress has followed the text of the Adjournment Clause. Either House may adjourn or recess for up to three days on its own motion. Longer adjournments or recesses, or adjournments *sine die*, ending a session, require the concurrent resolution of both Houses. An adjournment of whatever length ends the "legislative day," requiring much legislative business to be recommenced when the chamber reconvenes. In the Senate, introduced bills must lie over one legislative day before they can be considered. Recesses do not interrupt the legislative process.

David F. Forte

See Also

Article I, Section 4, Clause 2 (Meetings of Congress Clause)

Article I, Section 8, Clause 17 (Enclave Clause)

Article II, Section 3 (Convening of Congress)

Compensation Clause

The Senators and Representatives shall receive a Compensation for their Services, to be ascertained by

Law, and paid out of the Treasury
of the United States.
(ARTICLE I, SECTION 6, CLAUSE 1)

∽

*T*he Framers of the Constitution included the
Compensation Clause (also known as the Ascertainment Clause) in an attempt to structure the
incentives facing Senators or Representatives in
desirable ways. Two questions were critical:
Would federal legislators be paid at all? If so,
would they be paid by their respective states, or
by the federal government?

First, as to whether federal legislators would
be paid, the Constitutional Convention feared
that unpaid legislators would turn to corruption to supplement their incomes. As Justice
Joseph Story put it in his *Commentaries on the
Constitution of the United States*, "they might be
compelled by their necessities, or tempted by
their wants, to yield up their independence, and
perhaps their integrity, to the allurements of the
corrupt, or the opulent." Thus, supporters of the
federal legislative salary argued that providing
no salary would not attract candidates motivated only by a sense of duty, but would instead
permit only wealthy candidates, creating a de
facto legislative plutocracy.

The second question involved the source of
the payment. Under the Articles of Confederation, the states, rather than Congress, had paid
the salaries of delegates to Congress. Most of the
delegates to the Convention, by contrast, hoped
that requiring federal legislators to be paid
according to federal law, and out of federal
funds rather than state funds, would make them
less beholden to state governments. As Edmund
Randolph put it, "[I]f the States were to pay the
members of the National Legislature, a dependence would be created that would vitiate the
whole system."

Modern controversies over the Compensation Clause have focused on different questions.
Who should be able to change the level of legislative compensation, and how may the changes be
made? The leading case is the 1988 decision of
the Court of Appeals for the District of Columbia Circuit in *Humphrey v. Baker*. Under the
mechanism for legislative compensation then in

place, established by the Federal Salary Act of
1967, a "Quadrennial Commission" would make
recommendations for salary increases to the
President, who in turn had statutory authority to
recommend increases to the Congress. The presidential recommendations become effective as
law unless Congress enacted a joint resolution of
disapproval within thirty days. After this procedure brought about a legislative pay raise effective in 1987, Senator Gordon Humphrey and five
Members of the House sued the Secretary of the
Treasury, claiming that the Salary Act violated
both the Compensation Clause and the nondelegation doctrine. Relying heavily on precedent,
the Court of Appeals rejected both claims. It read
the Salary Act as fully complying with the clause;
because the procedure that produced the pay
increase (namely the delegation to the President
followed by the disapproval option) was itself
"ascertained" by statute, the clause was satisfied.
Humphrey's capacious reading of the clause suggests that Congress has broad flexibility in
designing schemes of legislative compensation,
subject to the restrictions of the Twenty-seventh
Amendment, which now prevents a sitting Congress from giving itself a pay raise to take effect
during its term.

Adrian Vermeule

See Also

Article II, Section 1, Clause 7 (Compensation)
Article III, Section 1 (Judicial Compensation Clause)
Amendment XXVII (Congressional Compensation)

Suggestions for Further Research

Articles of Confederation, Article V
L. Anthony Sutin, *Check, Please: Constitutional
Dimensions of Halting the Pay of Public Officials*,
26 J. LEGIS. 221 (2000)
Adrian Vermeule, *The Constitutional Law of Official
Compensation*, 102 COLUM. L. REV. 501 (2002)

Significant Cases

Pressler v. Simon, 428 F. Supp. 302 (D.D.C. 1976)
(three judge court), *aff'd sub nom.* Pressler v. Blu-
menthal, 434 U.S. 1028 (1978)
Humphrey v. Baker, 848 F.2d 211 (D.C. Cir. 1988)

Privilege from Arrest

The Senators and Representatives...shall in all Cases, except Treason, Felony, and Breach of the Peace, be privileged from Arrest during their Attendance at the Session of their respective Houses, and in going to and returning from the same....

(ARTICLE I, SECTION 6, CLAUSE 1)

~

*T*he Privilege from Arrest Clause provides a Member of Congress a privilege from civil arrest only, but not from other civil processes. Even the privilege from civil arrest would be valid only while Congress is in session.

Civil arrest is the physical detainment of a person, by lawful authority, to answer a civil demand against him. At the time the Constitution was adopted, civil arrests were common. *Long v. Ansell* (1934). The Framers likely feared this tool could be misused to interfere with the legislative process. Civil arrest is rarely, if ever, practiced, so this clause is virtually obsolete and has little application today.

The Supreme Court interpreted the language "in all Cases, except Treason, Felony, and Breach of the Peace" to encompass all crimes. *Williamson v. United States* (1908). Tracing the origins of the clause to parliamentary privilege, the Court found this identical language was used to qualify Parliament's privilege from arrest so that the members of Parliament were not immune from criminal prosecution. The Court concluded that the Framers' use of the identical phrase, without any explanation, indicated that Congress's privilege was to have the same limitation regarding criminal actions as did the parliamentary privilege from which the language was borrowed. The clause, therefore, does not provide Congress with any immunity from criminal prosecution.

The Supreme Court, applying the Framers' intent, later declared that the clause also did not provide any privilege from civil process. *Long v. Ansell*. Hence, civil litigants can compel Members of Congress to appear in a court of proper jurisdiction to defend against civil actions. Fur-

thermore, the Court has so narrowly interpreted the clause that Members of Congress may even be compelled by subpoena to testify in criminal and civil actions while Congress is in session.

David F. Forte

Suggestion for Further Research
Louis S. Raveson, *Unmasking the Motives of Government Decisionmakers: A Subpoena for Your Thoughts?*, 63 N.C. L. REV. 879 (June 1985)

Significant Cases
Williamson v. United States, 207 U.S. 425 (1908)
Long v. Ansell, 293 U.S. 76 (1934)

Speech and Debate Clause

...for any Speech or Debate in either House, [Senators and Representatives] shall not be questioned in any other Place.

(ARTICLE I, SECTION 6, CLAUSE 1)

~

*T*he right of legislators to speak their minds with impunity while engaged in legislative work was acknowledged by the British Bill of Rights of 1689, written into the Articles of Confederation, and, after the Revolution, guaranteed by state constitutions as well as by the Speech and Debate Clause. James Wilson, who was one of the principal architects of the Constitution, explained the purpose of the clause as follows:

In order to enable and encourage a representative of the publick to discharge his publick trust with firmness and success, it is indispensably necessary, that he should enjoy the fullest liberty of speech, and that he should be protected from the resentment of every one, however powerful, to whom the exercise of that liberty may occasion offence. Lecture on Law (1791).

In his *Commentaries on the Constitution of the United States*, Justice Joseph Story wrote that in England the privilege was "strictly confined to things done in the course of parliamentary proceedings, and [did] not cover things done beyond the place and limits of duty." To illustrate this limitation, he noted that although a libelous speech delivered in the House of Commons was privileged, if a Member republished that speech elsewhere, the libeled party was free to bring him to court. He then added that "the same principles seem applicable to the privilege of debate and speech in congress."

Although the only early case to deal with the privilege dealt with a virtually identical provision of a state constitution, rather than with the clause itself, the Massachusetts Supreme Court agreed that the privilege was limited to actions taken by a legislator "in the exercise of the functions of [his] office." *Coffin v. Coffin* (1808). This view of the scope of the privilege is certainly consistent with that of another delegate to the Constitutional Convention, Charles Pinckney, who later observed in remarks in the U.S. Senate that the Framers "knew that in free countries very few privileges were necessary for the undisturbed exercise of legislative duties....They therefore not only intended, but did confine their privileges within the narrow limits mentioned in the Constitution."

Over the past fifty years, the Supreme Court has reaffirmed that the purpose of the clause is to protect the independence of Congress when exercising the legislative responsibilities assigned to it by the Constitution, *Eastland v. United States Servicemen's Fund* (1975); and that it will interpret the clause broadly to that effect. *United States v. Johnson* (1966). The Court has also consistently limited its application to activities that are "clearly a part of the legislative process." *United States v. Brewster* (1972).

An activity is deemed to be within the legislative sphere if it is "an integral part of the deliberative and communicative processes by which Members participate in committee and House proceedings with respect to the consideration and passage or rejection of proposed legislation or with respect to other matters which the Constitution places within the jurisdiction of either House." *Gravel v. United States* (1972). Thus, the Court has held that the clause protects such acts as voting, the conduct of committee hearings, the issuance and distribution of committee reports, the subpoenaing of information required in the course of congressional investigations, and even the reading of stolen classified materials into a subcommittee's public record. *Doe v. McMillan* (1973). Conversely, speech and debate immunity will not protect Members engaged (even in their official capacities) in such nonlegislative activities as negotiations with federal agencies, the issuance of press releases and newsletters, and the delivery of speeches in their home districts. *Gravel v. United States*; *Hutchinson v. Proxmire* (1979).

If a Member's actions meet the "legislative process" test, his immunity is absolute; and that is so even if he has acted contrary to law. Accordingly, although the government may prosecute a Member for a criminal act, such as accepting a bribe, it may not pursue the case if proof of the crime "depend[s] on his legislative acts or his motive for performing them." *United States v. Brewster*. Thus, the government may not prove that the Member voted a particular way on the House floor in exchange for a bribe; the government, however, may prove (by other means) that the Member *promised* to vote a particular way in exchange for the bribe. The former requires proof of what happened on the House floor whereas the latter does not. Members must be shielded not only from the consequences of litigation, but also from its burdens, because engagement in litigation of any kind "creates a distraction and forces Members to divert their time, energy, and attention from their legislative tasks." *Eastland v. United States Servicemen's Fund* (1975). Consequently, a Member may immediately appeal a trial court's denial of a Member's motion to dismiss a case based on a claim of speech and debate so that the Member may be spared the burden of a trial if his motion proves to be valid. *Helstoski v. Meanor* (1979).

Although the clause speaks only of "Senators and Representatives," in order to effect its purpose, the Court in *Gravel* declared that it applies "not only to a Member but also to his aides insofar as the conduct of the latter would be a protected legislative act if performed by the Member himself." An aide who carries out congressional instructions that are found to be unlawful, however, is responsible for his acts even though the legislators who issued the instructions continue to be protected. *Powell v. McCormack* (1969); *Doe v. McMillan.*

In *Eastland*, the Supreme Court acknowledged that the clause may shield Members from civil or criminal liability "even though their conduct, if performed in other than legislative contexts, would in itself be unconstitutional or otherwise contrary to criminal or civil statutes." The risk of such abuse, however, "was the conscious choice of the Framers' buttressed and justified by history." Errant Members nevertheless remain subject to disciplinary action by their respective Houses for "disorderly behavior"—and, of course, by their constituents on Election Day.

James L. Buckley

See Also

Article I, Section 1 (Legislative Vesting Clause)

Article I, Section 5, Clause 2 (Rules and Expulsion Clause)

Suggestion for Further Research

2 Philip P. Kurland & Ralph Lerner, The Founders' Constitution 318–345 (1987)

Significant Cases

Coffin v. Coffin, 4 Mass. 1 (1808)

United States v. Johnson, 383 U.S. 169 (1966)

Powell v. McCormack, 395 U.S. 486 (1969)

Gravel v. United States, 408 U.S. 606 (1972)

United States v. Brewster, 408 U.S. 501 (1972)

Doe v. McMillan, 412 U.S. 306 (1973)

Eastland v. United States Servicemen's Fund, 421 U.S. 491 (1975)

United States v. Powell, 423 U.S. 87 (1975)

Helstoski v. Meanor, 442 U.S. 500 (1979)

Hutchinson v. Proxmire, 443 U.S. 111 (1979)

United States v. Helstoski, 442 U.S. 477 (1979)

Sinecure Clause

No Senator or Representative shall, during the Time for which he was elected, be appointed to any civil Office under the Authority of the United States, which shall have been created, or the Emoluments whereof shall have have been encreased during such time....

(Article I, Section 6, Clause 2)

∽

*D*etermined to avoid corruption and self-dealing in the legislative process, the Framers kept all appointive powers out of the hands of Congress. (*See* Article II, Section 2, Clause 2.) But corruption could come not only from self-dealing but also from the blandishments of the executive. Consequently, in order to prevent a repetition of the British Crown's practice of "buying" support by creating offices and sinecures to give to members of Parliament, Robert Yates proposed to the Constitutional Convention a ban on Members of Congress from "any office established by a particular State, or under the authority of the U. States ... during the term of service, and under the national Government for the space of one year after its expiration."

All the delegates in Philadelphia agreed that no Member of Congress should serve in an appointive position while he was sitting, but Nathaniel Gorham, James Wilson, and Alexander Hamilton wanted no bar at all, once a person was no longer in Congress. Hamilton argued that since passion drives all men, the executive should be able to satisfy the desires of the better qualified men by inducing them to serve in appointive offices.

James Madison proposed a solution that sought to reconcile the divergent concerns of the Framers: "that no office ought to be open to a member, which may be created or augmented while he is in the legislature." For some time, the delegates debated whether this idea was too restrictive or not restrictive enough. Madison responded that "the unnecessary creation of offices, and increase of salaries, were the evils most experienced, & that if the door was shut agst. them, it might properly be left open for the appointt. of members to other offices as an encouragmt. to the Legislative service." Eventually, the delegates accepted Madison's view, but they deleted the prohibition from holding state office (the state might need the Member's services) and the one-year bar after leaving office (it was not long enough to be of any significant effect). They also limited the bar to "civil" offices so that the military could have the service of all when the country was in danger.

As adopted, the relatively limited bar of this clause reinforces the separation of powers and the federal structure of the union. Of the separation of powers, Madison famously wrote in *The Federalist* No. 51: "Ambition must be made to counteract ambition. The interest of the man must be connected with the constitutional rights of the place." The clause puts an obstacle to the President's ability to shift a Congress Member's ambition from the legislative to the executive. Of the federal structure of the union, Madison had warned of "the unnecessary creation of offices"—obviously beyond what was appropriate for the central government—that could occur if the clause were not adopted.

The clause establishes a number of formal requirements: (1) It applies to those Members who have actually taken their seats, not to those who were elected but not yet sworn in. (2) "Appointed" means at the moment of nomination for civil office, not at the time of approval. *Marbury v. Madison* (1803). (3) The bar cannot be evaded by resignation from Congress. In a written opinion of Attorney General Benjamin Brewster in 1882, the clause applies for the term "for which he was elected," not the time during which the member actually holds office. (4) "Civil office" is one in which the appointee exercises an authoritative role. It does not apply to temporary, honorific, advisory, or occasional postings. *United States v. Hartwell* (1868). (5)

"Emoluments" means more than salary, *McLean v. United States* (1912), but it is unclear how much more. In 1937, the Senate approved the appointment of Hugo L. Black to the Supreme Court even though Congress had passed legislation significantly augmenting the pensions of Supreme Court justices during the Senate term in which Black served. Later, under Presidents Lyndon B. Johnson and James Earl Carter, the Department of Justice opined that it did not matter when Congress passed legislation increasing the salary for an office, so long as the former Member of Congress was nominated before the salary increase went into effect. The courts have dismissed suits contesting the appointments of Justice Hugo L. Black and Judge Abner Mikva on lack of standing grounds. *Ex parte Levitt* (1937); *McClure v. Carter* (1981).

In his *Commentaries on the Constitution of the United States*, Justice Joseph Story, even in his panegyric, was hesitant about the clause: "It has been deemed by one commentator as admirable provision against venality, though not perhaps sufficiently guarded to prevent evasion." For well over a century, Presidents and their attorneys general had rigorously followed the formal requirements of the clause. In 1973, however, Congress and the executive devised an effective stratagem to avoid the limitations of the clause. Termed the "Saxbe fix," it copied an idea invented during the Taft administration. President Richard M. Nixon appointed Senator William Saxbe to be Attorney General even though Saxbe had been a Senator when Congress raised the Attorney General's salary from $35,000 to $60,000. Under an opinion from acting Attorney General Robert H. Bork, the Congress "fixed" the violation of the clause by returning the Attorney General's salary to the $35,000 level.

Presidents Gerald R. Ford, Carter (appointing Senator Edmund Muskie as Secretary of State), and William Jefferson Clinton (appointing Senator Lloyd Bentsen as Secretary of the Treasury) went further and utilized "temporary Saxbe fixes," persuading Congress to reduce the salary of a position to which a Member had been appointed but only until the date when the Member's term would have ended. Only under Attorney General Edwin Meese III did the Department of Justice eschew this end run around the formal requirements of the Sinecure Clause. In 1987, the Office of Legal Counsel issued an opinion that Senator Orrin Hatch would be ineligible for nomination to the Supreme Court because Congress had raised the salaries for Associate Justices during Hatch's term. President Ronald Reagan chose to nominate Judge Robert H. Bork, whom the Senate did not approve.

Justice Joseph Story had also written, "It has sometimes been a matter of regret, that the disqualification had not been made co-extensive with the supposed mischief; and thus to have for ever excluded members from the possession of offices created, or rendered more lucrative, by themselves." Yet he still adds ambivalently: "Perhaps there is quite as much wisdom in leaving the provision, where it now is." The upshot is that fidelity to the Constitution by any of the branches of the government is as much a function of internal commitment as it is of external constraint.

David F. Forte

See Also

Article II, Section 2, Clause 2 (Appointments Clause)

Suggestions for Further Research

3 Op. Off. Legal Counsel 286 (1979)

17 Op. Att'y Gen. 365 (1882)

33 Op. Att'y Gen. 88 (1922)

42 Op. Att'y Gen. 381 (1969)

John F. O'Connor, *The Emoluments Clause: An Anti Federalist Intruder in a Federalist Constitution*, 24 HOFSTRA L. REV. 89 (1995)

Michael S. Paulsen, *Is Lloyd Bentsen Unconstitutional?*, 46 STAN. L. REV. 907 (1994)

Significant Cases

Marbury v. Madison, 5 U.S. (1 Cranch) 137 (1803)

United States v. Hartwell, 73 U.S. (6 Wall.) 385 (1868)

McLean v. United States, 226 U.S. 374 (1912)

Ex parte Levitt, 302 U.S. 633 (1937)

McClure v. Carter, 513 F. Supp. 265 (D.C. Idaho 1981), *aff'd*, 454 U.S. 1025 (1981)

Incompatibility Clause

...no Person holding any Office under the United States, shall be a Member of either House during his Continuance in Office.

(ARTICLE I, SECTION 6, CLAUSE 2)

∾

*T*he Constitution establishes several limitations on a person's ability to serve in Congress. For example, Article I, Sections 2 and 3, limit the class of persons eligible to serve in Congress by imposing age, citizenship, and residency requirements. The Incompatibility Clause of Article I, Section 6, imposes a further limitation: it forbids federal executive and judicial officers from simultaneously serving in Congress.

The Framers of the Constitution understood the Incompatibility Clause primarily as an anticorruption device. Painfully familiar with the system of "royal influence," whereby the English kings had "purchased" the loyalty of Members of Parliament with appointment to lucrative offices, the Framers sought to limit the corrupting effect of patronage and plural office holding in the new Republic. Drawing on examples provided by the bans on plural office holding contained in contemporaneous state constitutions, and in the Articles of Confederation, the Framers crafted a ban on dual office holding, which Alexander Hamilton described in *The Federalist* No. 76 as "an important guard against the danger of executive influence upon the legislative body."

It is easy, in modern times, to underestimate the importance of the Incompatibility Clause. There has been virtually no litigation involving its meaning. In *Schlesinger v. Reservists Committee to Stop the War* (1974), the Supreme Court held that citizens who had filed a civil action to challenge the reserve membership of some Members of Congress were asserting only a "generalized grievance about the conduct of government," and thus lacked standing to sue. That is not to say that the Incompatibility Clause would be judicially unenforceable if it were violated, for example, if a sitting Member of Congress who was also an Officer of the United

States took official action that adversely affected an individualized private interest. But such cases rarely, if ever, arise, perhaps because the rule the clause announces is relatively straightforward.

The Incompatibility Clause nonetheless serves a vital function in the American system of separated powers. By preventing joint legislative and executive office holding, the clause forecloses any possibility of parliamentary government in America, and thus preserves a hallmark of American constitutional government: the independence of the executive and the Congress.

Beyond this vital structural function, what is perhaps most interesting about the clause is what it does not, by its terms, prohibit. Neither the clause itself nor any other constitutional provision expressly prohibits joint service in the federal executive and judiciary, or joint service in federal and state office. The latter issue is largely handled as a matter of state constitutional law, which generally forbids most forms of dual federal–state office holding. As for the question of simultaneous service in federal executive and judicial offices, the constitutionality of the practice is suggested not only by the lack of a textual prohibition, but by a few prominent examples of such service in the early days of the Republic, such the simultaneous service of Chief Justices John Marshall, John Jay, and Oliver Ellsworth in judicial and executive posts. Nonetheless, examples of joint service in the executive and the judiciary have been a rarity in American history, and a strong tradition has developed disfavoring the practice. Moreover, some might argue that generalized notions of the separation of powers, such as those expressed by the Supreme Court in *Mistretta v. United States* (1989), render the practice constitutionally suspect.

Joan L. Larsen

See Also

Suggestions for Further Research
Steven G. Calabresi & Joan L. Larsen, *One Person, One Office: Separation of Powers or Separation of Personnel?*, 79 CORNELL L. REV. 1045 (1994)

Daniel H. Pollitt, *Senator/Attorney-General Saxbe and the "Ineligibility Clause" of the Constitution: An Encroachment upon the Separation of Powers*, 53 N.C. L. REV. 111 (1974)

Russell Wheeler, *Extrajudicial Activities of the Early Supreme Court*, 1973 SUP. CT. REV. 123

Significant Cases
Schlesinger v. Reservists Committee to Stop the War, 418 U.S. 208 (1974)

Mistretta v. United States, 488 U.S. 361 (1989)

Origination Clause

All Bills for raising Revenue shall originate in the House of Representatives; but the Senate may propose or concur with Amendments as on other Bills.

(ARTICLE I, SECTION 7, CLAUSE 1)

~

Consistent with the English requirement that money bills must commence in the House of Commons, the Framers expected that the Origination Clause would ensure that "power over the purse" would lie with the legislative body closer to the people. Under the Articles of Confederation, the national government could not tax individuals, and the clause was one of several provisions meant to cabin the national revenue power created under the Constitution. The clause was also part of a critical compromise between large and small states, helping to temper the large states' unhappiness with equal representation in the

Senate by leaving the power to initiate tax bills with the House of Representatives, where the large states had greater influence.

The final version of the clause was much weaker than the form proposed by Elbridge Gerry of Massachusetts, which would have required all "money bills" (including appropriations) to originate in the House and would have given the Senate no power to amend. Gerry feared that the Senate would become an aristocratic body because of its small size, its selection by legislatures rather than by election, and its six-year term of office. "It was a maxim," he said, "that the people ought to hold the purse-strings."

The strongest proponents of national power opposed the clause in any form. As James Wilson of Pennsylvania explained at the Convention, "If both branches were to say yes or no, it was of little consequence which should say yes or no first." What survived the contentious debates was closer to Wilson's vision than to Gerry's. The clause was restricted to bills for raising revenue, and the Senate was given the amendment power (which, Gerry thought, gutted the provision of any real effect).

Even in weakened form, however, the Origination Clause was not meaningless. James Madison, no supporter of the clause at the Convention, gave it a generous interpretation in *The Federalist* No. 58: "The House of Representatives cannot only refuse, but they alone can propose the supplies requisite for the support of the government. . . . This power over the purse may, in fact, be regarded as the most complete and effectual weapon with which any constitution can arm the immediate representatives of the people, for obtaining a redress of every grievance, and for carrying into effect, every just and salutary measure."

As it turned out, the Origination Clause has had little effect. For one thing, many revenue bills have their intellectual genesis in the Treasury Department, not in Congress. Furthermore, Elbridge Gerry's fears were well founded: the Senate's power to amend is generally understood in practice to be so broad that the Senate can replace the entire text of a bill that technically originates in the House.

The understanding that the clause is a nullity reflects practice, however, not doctrine. In its most recent Origination Clause case, *United States v. Munoz-Flores* (1990), a divided Supreme Court rejected the argument that origination issues are nonjusticiable political questions. The Court held that a plaintiff with standing may pursue a claim that a revenue statute improperly originated in the Senate. In *Munoz-Flores*, however, the Court did not reach the larger issues, concluding that a bill to impose a user's fee, where raising revenue was a secondary concern, was not a "bill for raising revenue." The larger issues await another case where a taxpayer subject to an unquestioned revenue statute can raise serious questions about the statute's origin.

Erik M. Jensen

See Also

Article I, Section 7
Article I, Section 8, Clause 1 (Spending Clause)

Significant Cases

Millard v. Roberts, 202 U.S. 429 (1906)
Rainey v. United States, 232 U.S. 310 (1914)
United States v. Munoz-Flores, 495 U.S. 385 (1990)

Presentment Clause

Every Bill which shall have passed the House of Representatives and the Senate, shall, before it become a Law, be presented to the President of the United States: If he approve he shall sign it, but if not he shall return it, with his Objections to that House in which it shall have originated, who shall enter the Objections at large on their Journal, and proceed to reconsider it. If after such Reconsideration two thirds of that House shall agree to pass the Bill, it shall be sent, togeth-

er with the Objections, to the other House, by which it shall likewise be reconsidered, and if approved by two thirds of that House, it shall become a Law. But in all such Cases the Votes of both Houses shall be determined by yeas and Nays, and the Names of the Persons voting for and against the Bill shall be entered on the Journal of each House respectively. If any Bill shall not be returned by the President within ten Days (Sundays excepted) after it shall have been presented to him, the Same shall be a Law, in like Manner as if he had signed it, unless the Congress by their Adjournment prevent its Return, in which Case it shall not be a Law.

(ARTICLE I, SECTION 7, CLAUSE 2)

≈

The Presentment Clause is commonly viewed as a provision that protects the President's veto power, an association reinforced by the clause's name. Yet, the Presentment Clause has a broader function: The clause prescribes the exclusive method for passing federal statutes, indicating that all bills must pass both Houses of Congress and be subject to the President's veto. Thus, with some justification, one might call the provision the Lawmaking Clause.

The Presentment or Lawmaking Clause was often debated during the Founding, but the discussions generally focused on issues not relevant to current interpretive controversies. In the Constitutional Convention, the principal focus was on how difficult it should be for Congress to override the President's veto and on whether the President should possess the veto alone or should share it with the judiciary in a council of revision. During the ratification debates, the Federalists sought to justify the veto and bicameralism as devices for restraining the legislature from invading executive power and for limiting the enactment of hasty and unwise legislation.

The Presentment Clause ultimately drafted by the Convention was one of the most formal

provisions in the Constitution. The Framers apparently feared that factions would attempt to depart from the constitutional method for passing laws and therefore they spelled out that method in one of the document's longest provisions. The clause describes the specifics of the lawmaking process, including that the President's veto can be overridden by two-thirds of both Houses, that the President has ten days to decide whether to veto a bill, and that congressional adjournments should not deprive the President of his ability to veto measures. The Framers even mentioned that Sundays should not be counted in the ten-day period, and James Madison had the phrase "after it shall have been presented to him" inserted into the clause to "prevent a question whether the day on which the bill be presented, ought to be counted or not as one of the ten days." Moreover, to preclude Congress from bypassing the President by calling a bill by another name, Madison also persuaded the Convention to take the extraordinary step of adding a second Presentment Clause that required submission to the President of "Every Order, Resolution, or Vote to which the Concurrence of the Senate and House of Representatives may be necessary." (*See* Article I, Section 7, Clause 3.) Clearly, the Framers believed that lawmaking was so important that they could not take any chances that the Congress might try to circumvent the President's role in the legislative process.

There are two ways that the Presentment Clause might be violated. First, Congress might pass statutes that authorize the legislative Houses or the President to take legislative-type actions without conforming to bicameralism and presentment. Second, Congress or the President might take legislative-type actions on their own initiative without statutory authority. The Framers' efforts have largely proved successful in preventing this second type of Presentment Clause violation. Thus, Congress has rarely if ever attempted to pass laws without either the approval of both Houses or presentment to the President. In addition, the President's assertions of the constitutional authority to take legislative-type actions in the domestic sphere have been relatively rare and, when they do occur, have often been restrained by the courts. *Youngstown Sheet & Tube Co. v. Sawyer* (1952); *but see In re Debs* (1895).

The Constitution has been less successful, however, in preventing Congress from authorizing departures from bicameralism and presentment through the enactment of legislation, such as through statutory delegations of administrative discretion to the executive. These statutes raise complex questions and therefore may sometimes be constitutional. Still, as a general matter, it seems unlikely that the Framers would have allowed Congress to bypass the bicameralism and presentment requirements simply by passing legislation.

One important statutory departure from the traditional lawmaking process was the legislative veto, in which Congress usually granted each house the authority to nullify administrative actions taken by the executive. One might view the legislative veto from several different perspectives, but in each case the veto is unconstitutional. If the legislative veto is conceptualized as executive power, then it is unconstitutional because the legislators who wield it are not executive officials. If the veto is viewed as involving the power to pass legislation, then it clearly violates the Presentment Clause, because the veto does not conform to the requirements of bicameralism or presentment. Finally, the veto might be viewed as an exercise of the power of an individual House, but such powers are either mentioned in the Constitution, such as the power of each House to pass legislative rules, or can be reasonably inferred because they are traditionally possessed by legislative Houses, as with the power of investigation. The legislative veto, however, falls under neither category. The Supreme Court has largely conformed to the Constitution's original meaning and held legislative vetoes to be unconstitutional. *I.N.S. v. Chadha* (1983); *Metropolitan Washington Airports Authority v. Citizens for the Abatement of Aircraft Noise* (1991).

The most common departure from bicameralism and presentment has involved the statutory delegation to the executive of administrative discretion. Although such delegations certainly do not conform to the Presentment Clause, there is a plausible originalist argument that these delegations are constitutional either under the Necessary and Proper Clause or because they confer executive power rather than legislative power. Nonetheless, many originalists reject these arguments and conclude that broad delegations are constitutionally problematic because they give to the executive either legislative or nonexecutive power. The Supreme Court, however, currently holds that these delegations are constitutional, based in part on the nonoriginalist argument that the modern administrative state requires them. *Mistretta v. United States* (1989).

Recently, the Supreme Court has reviewed a different departure from the traditional lawmaking process—the conferral of cancellation authority on the executive—and held it to be unconstitutional as a violation of the Presentment Clause. *Clinton v. City of New York* (1998). In 1995, Congress enacted the Line Item Veto Act, which despite its name, did not provide the President with veto authority, but instead authorized him to cancel certain spending provisions. This cancellation authority was similar to an ordinary delegation of administrative authority in that it conferred discretion on the executive, subject to a statutory standard, to take certain actions. Cancellation authority, however, differs from an ordinary delegation since it is generally narrower. Whereas an ordinary delegation allows the executive to promulgate a rule of his choosing, cancellation authority permits him only to accept or reject a statutory rule. For example, in the appropriation law area, ordinary delegations under traditional appropriation laws permit the President to spend any sum *between* the amount appropriated and zero, whereas cancellation authority only permits him the choice to spend the appropriated amount or to cancel the appropriation and spend nothing.

Reviewing the cancellation authority provided by the Line Item Veto Act, the Supreme Court found it unconstitutional. In the Court's view, cancellation authority was similar to the power to repeal a law, because the authority could eliminate an appropriation. The exercise of cancellation authority therefore needed to conform to the Presentment Clause. Of course, if cancellation authority is similar to repealing an appropriation, then the executive's authority under a traditional appropriation to decide how much to spend is similar to enacting an appropriation, because the executive can "legislate" the amount that should be spent. Under the Court's reasoning, then, ordinary delegations may also logically violate the Presentment Clause, but the Court continues regularly to permit such delegations. The Court has yet to resolve this double standard whereby cancellation authority is unconstitutional even though such authority is generally narrower than ordinary delegations.

Several other matters raise questions under the Presentment Clause. First, some have argued that the clause defines *bill* as a provision relating to a single subject; consequently, if Congress were to combine two separate subjects in a measure, that would really be two bills and the President could therefore exercise a kind of item veto by vetoing one of the bills, while approving the other. Historical and structural evidence reveals, however, that the original meaning of bill was a measure that included whatever provisions Congress placed within it. Second, the Line Item Veto Act provided that the President would receive cancellation authority only as to bills that he signed but that he would lack such authority if he vetoed the bill, a provision that arguably places an unconstitutional burden on the President's veto power. Finally, it has been argued that the Presentment Clause requires that Congress pass bills under a majority voting rule, but the clause's language, which simply refers to every bill "which shall have passed" the legislative houses, combined with its structure and history, indicates that each house can employ supermajority rules to govern the passage of bills.

Michael B. Rappaport

See Also

Article I, Section 1 (Legislative Vesting Clause)
Article I, Section 7, Clause 3 (Presentment of Resolutions)

Article I, Section 8, Clause 18 (Necessary and Proper Clause)
Article II, Section 1, Clause 1 (Executive Vesting Clause)

Suggestions for Further Research

Gary Lawson, *Delegation and Original Meaning*, 88 Va. L. Rev. 327 (2002)

John O. McGinnis & Michael B. Rappaport, *The Rights of Legislators and the Wrongs of Interpretation: A Further Defense of the Constitutionality of Legislative Supermajority Rules*, 47 Duke L.J. 327 (1997)

Saikrishna B. Prakash, *Deviant Executive Lawmaking*, 67 Geo. Wash. L. Rev. 1 (1998)

Michael B. Rappaport, *The President's Veto and the Constitution*, 87 Nw. U. L. Rev. 735 (1993)

Michael B. Rappaport, *The Selective Nondelegation Doctrine and the Line Item Veto: A New Approach to the Nondelegation Doctrine and Its Implications for* Clinton v. City of New York, 76 Tul. L. Rev. 265 (2001)

Michael B. Rappaport, *Veto Burdens and the Line Item Veto Act*, 91 Nw. U. L. Rev. 771 (1997)

J. Gregory Sidak & Thomas A. Smith, *Four Faces of the Item Veto: A Reply to Tribe and Kurland*, 84 Nw. U. L. Rev. 437 (1990)

Significant Cases

In re Debs, 158 U.S. 564 (1895)

Youngstown Sheet & Tube Co. v. Sawyer, 343 U.S. 579 (1952)

I.N.S. v. Chadha, 462 U.S. 919 (1983)

Mistretta v. United States, 488 U.S. 361 (1989)

Metropolitan Washington Airports Authority v. Citizens for the Abatement of Aircraft Noise, 501 U.S. 252 (1991)

Clinton v. City of New York, 524 U.S. 417 (1998)

Pocket Veto

If any Bill shall not be returned by the President within ten Days (Sundays excepted) after it shall have been presented to him, the Same shall be a Law, in like Manner

as if he had signed it, unless the Congress by their Adjournment prevent its Return, in which Case it shall not be a Law.

(ARTICLE I, SECTION 7, CLAUSE 2)

∾

*I*n order to ensure the vitality of the separation of powers, the Framers gave the Executive, as James Madison wrote in *The Federalist* No. 47, a "partial agency" in the legislative process. Under Article II, Section 3, Clause 1, the President can propose measures to Congress, and under Article I, Section 7, Clause 2, the President can approve or veto bills that the Congress must present to him. If he does veto the bill, he must return it to Congress, which may then override his veto by a two-thirds vote. What happens, however, if the President refuses to approve or to return the bill to Congress? What happens if Congress adjourns, preventing a return of the bill?

In order to solve these two problems, the Framers crafted this part of the Pocket Veto Clause. If the President refuses to approve or return the bill within ten days (not including Sunday), the bill automatically becomes law. If, in the interim, Congress has adjourned, the bill dies and the legislation must be reintroduced and passed again when Congress reconvenes. Later termed by Andrew Jackson the "Pocket Veto," the clause has been the subject of much controversy between the President and the Congress.

There is an ambiguity as to which kinds of adjournments the clause covers: (1) *sine die* adjournments when a Congress comes to an end, and a newly elected Congress must convene; (2) intersession adjournments between the two sessions of the same Congress; and (3) intrasession adjournments when Congress takes a break within a session. There is virtually unanimous agreement that the President may pocket veto a bill when Congress adjourns *sine die*. Although some Members of Congress have disputed the validity of intersession and intrasession pocket vetoes, the Congress as a whole has acquiesced in these kinds of presidential pocket vetoes during such adjournments.

As a model for the veto power, the Framers used the constitution of the state of New York of 1777 but omitted the section that would have prohibited intersession pocket vetoes:

> that if any bill shall not be returned ... within ten days after it shall have been presented, the same shall be a law, unless the legislature shall, by their adjournment, render a return of the said bill within ten days impracticable; *in which case the bill shall be returned on the first day of the meeting of the legislature after the expiration of the said ten days* [emphasis added].

Other parts of the Constitution refer to adjournments of differing lengths, but the Framers did not particularize which adjournments would or would not be subject to the pocket veto. Textually, therefore, it seems that the clause permits the President to exercise a pocket veto any time the Congress as a whole adjourns.

On the other hand, advocates for the view that the clause applies only to *sine die* adjournments hold that the purpose of the Pocket Veto Clause was to permit the President and the Congress to continue to engage in the legislative process if at all practicable. Just as the President is not permitted to veto a law simply by not signing it, so should he not be permitted to veto a law simply because Congress has recessed for a few days. The advocates for greater congressional authority assert that an intrasession adjournment (and perhaps even an intersession adjournment) does not "prevent a return" as the clause states it. It merely postpones the return until Congress reconvenes. Further, many holding this view have also asserted that so long as Congress appoints an agent to receive the return while it is adjourned, the President may not pocket veto the legislation.

President James Madison exercised the first pocket veto during an intersession; Andrew Jackson, the first pocket veto after a final adjournment (prompting an objection from Henry Clay); and President Andrew Johnson, the first intrasession vetoes (rejecting five bills). In response to Johnson's action, the Senate passed a bill regulating the presidential return of bills, excluding intrasession recesses from the definition of adjournment. The bill never made it through the House. That action typifies the history of the dispute. From time to time, Members of Congress seek legislation limiting the President's use of the pocket veto, but none of these efforts has ever ripened into law.

Meanwhile, the use of the pocket veto accelerated. By 1929, 479 bills had been thus vetoed, about one-fourth during intersession adjournments but only eight during intrasession breaks. In that year, the Supreme Court decided *The Pocket Veto Case*. During a five-month intersession adjournment, President Calvin Coolidge had pocket vetoed a bill that would have given entitlements to a group of Indian tribes. The tribes sought to claim their rights, asserting that the President's veto was invalid and that therefore the bill had become law. The Court upheld the President's action. It found no constitutional distinction among the various types of adjournment. The President, the Court declared, could not return a bill to a Congress that was not actually sitting. It was Congress's choice whether to adjourn before the ten-day period could run. In *Wright v. United States* (1938), however, the Court held that a three-day recess by a single House did not meet the clause's definition of adjournment.

Beginning with Franklin D. Roosevelt's tenure, presidential power increased and so did the use of the pocket veto. From 1930 until 1972, seventy-six bills fell to vetoes during intrasession breaks and 143 others during intersession adjournments. Presidents accompanied many vetoes with messages explaining the reason for the rejection. Congress continued to acquiesce in the practice.

The congressional counterattack began during President Richard M. Nixon's administration. In *Kennedy v. Sampson* (1974), a federal court declared invalid an intrasession pocket veto. Two years later another dispute, *Kennedy v. Jones* (1976), produced an agreement between Congress and the President limiting the use of the pocket veto to only *sine die* adjournments. In each case, the federal courts tried to distinguish *The Pocket Veto Case* by claiming that modern Congresses were no longer in recess or

adjournment for such a lengthy time as to "prevent a return."

President Ronald Reagan, however, renounced that agreement and made pocket vetoes during intersession adjournments, the latter resulting in the D.C. Circuit's prohibition of intersession vetoes when Congress has appointed an agent to receive a return. *Barnes v. Kline* (1985). The Supreme Court, however, vacated the decision as moot. Following the action by the Supreme Court, the Department of Justice declared its opinion that the President's pocket-veto power extends to any adjournment of longer than three days. President George H.W. Bush continued to exercise the power, as did President William Jefferson Clinton, and repeated attempts in Congress to pass legislation stating its view of the power have failed to pass. Recently, Congress has treated pocket vetoes as regular vetoes and has scheduled override votes, but none have succeeded. When Presidents now exercise the pocket veto, they do so with a "protective return": a message declaring the objections to the bill so that if, perchance, a court holds the pocket veto invalid, the bill will be treated as vetoed in the regular manner, rather than becoming law by default.

David F. Forte

See Also

Article I, Section 5, Clause 1 (Qualifications and Quorum)

Article I, Section 5, Clause 4 (Adjournment)

Article I, Section 7, Clause 2 (Pocket Veto)

Article II, Section 3 (Recommendations Clause)

Article II, Section 3 (Convening of Congress)

Suggestion for Further Research

Butler C. Derrick, Jr., *Stitching the Hole in the President's Pocket: A Legislative Solution to the Pocket-Veto Controversy*, 31 Harv. J. Legis. 371 (1994)

Significant Cases

The Pocket Veto Case, 279 U.S. 655 (1929)

Wright v. United States, 302 U.S. 583 (1938)

Kennedy v. Sampson, 511 F.2d 430 (D.C. Cir. 1974)

Kennedy v. Jones, 412 F. Supp. 353 (D.D.C. 1976)

Barnes v. Kline, 759 F.2d 21 (D.C. Cir. 1985)

Presentment of Resolutions

Every Order, Resolution, or Vote to which the Concurrence of the Senate and House of Representatives may be necessary (except on a question of Adjournment) shall be presented to the President of the United States; and before the Same shall take Effect, shall be approved by him, or being disapproved by him, shall be repassed by two thirds of the Senate and House of Representatives, according to the Rules and Limitations prescribed in the Case of a Bill.

(ARTICLE I, SECTION 7, CLAUSE 3)

~

*D*uring the Constitutional Convention, James Madison noted that Congress could evade the possibility of a presidential veto by simply denominating a "bill" as a "resolution." Although his motion to insert the words *or resolve* after the word *bill* in the Presentment of Resolutions Clause was defeated, the following day Edmund Randolph proposed a freestanding clause with more exacting language, and the Convention approved it. Justice Joseph Story, writing prior to the posthumous publication of Madison's Convention record, in his *Commentaries on the Constitution of the United States*, appears to have taken a view similar to Madison's: "[C]ongress, by adopting the form of an order or resolution, instead of a bill, might have effectually defeated the president's qualified negative in all the most important portions of legislation." Nearly all commentators have agreed with that interpretation.

Nonetheless, not all resolutions of Congress require presidential approval because not all are intended to be law. Generally, *joint resolutions* do require presentment to the President as they are designed to have the force of law. They differ from bills only in that they usually deal with a single subject, such as a declaration of war. Congressionally proposed amendments to the Constitution are also styled as joint resolutions, but they are not presented to the President. Under the form of the amending process in Article V that has been followed in all cases, Congress proposes and three-quarters of the legislatures of the several states approve. Thus, no presidential involvement is necessary for a joint resolution proposing an amendment to the Constitution. *Hollingsworth v. Virginia* (1798).

Concurrent resolutions, passed by both Houses, apply only to subjects affecting the procedures of both houses, such as fixing the time for adjournment, or to express "the sense of the Congress" on an issue of public policy, or to set revenue and spending goals. Simply put, concurrent resolutions are not "law" and are not presented to the President. Similarly, *simple resolutions* (sometimes just known as *resolutions*) do not have the force of law and apply only to the operations of a particular branch of Congress dealing with its internal procedures, imposing censure on a Member, setting spending limits for particular committees, or expressing the viewpoint of one House on a public issue. A bill of impeachment passed by the House of Representatives could technically be seen as in the form of a simple resolution (as might also be Senate approval of treaties and presidential appointments), although it may not officially be designated as such. The Senate's resolution to convict is similar. In *I.N.S. v. Chadha* (1983) the Supreme Court invalidated the use of a resolution by one House (or by extension, a joint resolution by both Houses) to "veto" an executive action as violative of the Presentment of Resolutions Clause.

David F. Forte

See Also

Article I, Section 7, Clause 2 (Presentment Clause)
Article V

Suggestion for Further Research

CONGRESSIONAL QUARTERLY'S GUIDE TO CONGRESS (4th ed. 1991)

Gary Lawson, Comment, *Burning Down the House (and Senate): A Presentment Requirement for*

Legislative Subpoenas Under the Orders, Resolutions, and Votes Clause, 83 Tex. L. Rev. 1373 (2005)

Seth Barrett Tillman, *A Textualist Defense of Article I, Section 7, Clause 3: Why* Hollingsworth v. Virginia *Was Rightly Decided, and Why* I.N.S. v. Chadha *Was Wrongly Resolved,* 83 Tex. L. Rev. 1373 (2005)

Significant Cases

Hollingsworth v. Virginia, 3. U.S. (3 Dall.) 378 (1798)

I.N.S. v. Chadha, 462 U.S. 919 (1983)

Spending Clause

The Congress shall have Power To lay and collect Taxes, Duties, Imposts and Excises, to pay the Debts and provide for the common Defence and general Welfare of the United States....

(Article I, Section 8, Clause 1)

∾

*A*lthough the Spending Clause is the source of congressional authority to levy taxes, it permits the levying of taxes for two purposes only: to pay the debts of the United States, and to provide for the common defense and general welfare of the United States. Taken together, these purposes have traditionally been held to imply and constitute the "Spending Power."

To many today, those two purposes are so broad as to amount to no limitation at all. The contemporary view is that Congress's power to provide for the "general Welfare" is a power to spend for virtually anything that Congress itself views as helpful. To be sure, some of the Founders, most notably Alexander Hamilton, supported an expansive spending power during the Constitutional Convention; but such proposals, including an explicit attempt to authorize spending by the federal government for internal improvements, were rejected by the Convention. Hamilton continued to press his case by arguing during George Washington's administration for an expansive interpretation of the clause (which Washington adopt-

ed). In his "Report on Manufactures" (1791), Hamilton contended that the only limits on the tax-and-spend power were the requirements that duties be uniform, that direct taxes be apportioned by population, and that no tax should be laid on articles exported from any state. The power to raise money was otherwise "plenary, and indefinite," he argued, "and the objects to which it may be appropriated are no less comprehensive."

Hamilton's broad reading met with opposition from many of the other Founders. James Madison repeatedly argued that the power to tax and spend did not confer upon Congress the right to do whatever it thought to be in the best interest of the nation, but only to further the ends specifically enumerated elsewhere in the Constitution, a position supported by Thomas Jefferson.

There was also a third, more intermediate, interpretation, recognized later even by Alexander Hamilton. According to this view, the "common Defence and general Welfare" language is not, as Madison contended, a shorthand way of limiting the power to tax and spend in furtherance of the powers elsewhere enumerated in Article I, Section 8; but it does contain its own limitation, namely, that spending under the clause be for the "general" (that is, national) welfare and not for purely local or regional benefit. President James Monroe later adopted this position—albeit with more teeth than Hamilton had been willing to give it—in his 1822 message vetoing a bill to preserve and repair the Cumberland Road. Monroe contended that Congress's power to spend was restricted "to purposes of common defence, and of general, national, not local, or state, benefit."

There are relatively few examples from the early Congresses of debate over the scope of the spending power, but the few that do exist are enlightening. The First Congress refused to make a loan to a glass manufacturer after several Members expressed the view that such an appropriation would be unconstitutional, and the Fourth Congress did not believe it had the power to provide relief to the citizens of Savannah, Georgia, after a devastating fire destroyed the entire city. The debates do not reflect whether Congress thought such appropriations unconstitutional because they did not further other enumerated powers (Madison's position) or because they were of local rather than national benefit (Monroe's position), but they reflect a rejection of the broad interpretation of the spending power originally proffered by Hamilton.

On the other hand, some appropriations for apparently local projects were approved, but it can be argued that those projects were of general benefit or specifically tied to other enumerated powers, and hence within the authority conferred by Article I, Section 8. At the same time it was denying a request to fund the dredging of the Savannah River, for example, Congress approved an appropriation for a lighthouse at the entrance of the Chesapeake Bay. Both measures were important for navigation, but the lighthouse was of benefit to the coastal trade of the entire nation (and hence to *interstate* commerce), while the dredging operation was primarily of local, *intrastate* benefit to the people of Georgia and hence fell on the "local" rather than the "general" side of the public welfare line.

Congress approved various appropriations to fund a road across the Cumberland Gap, but it rejected as unconstitutional a larger appropriation for internal improvements of which the Cumberland Gap road project was a part. Congress accepted the view that it had no power under the Constitution to open roads and canals in any state; its power to fund the Cumberland Road was the result of the compact with Ohio "for which the nation receive[d] an equivalent," namely, Ohio's promise not to tax for five years any lands sold by the federal government in Ohio. Moreover, as George Washington had repeatedly urged while President, the opening of a road across the Cumberland Gap was strategically necessary to keep the western territories allied with the coastal states (rather than with the foreign powers that controlled the Mississippi river region at the time), something critically important to the security of the entire nation and not just the people of Ohio. The Cumberland Gap road was an example of a local project that directly benefited the nation. Appropriations for other local projects such as public education and local roads and canals, the "general" benefit of which was less direct, were viewed as

unconstitutional, and a proposal in Jefferson's 1806 State of the Union Address to amend the Constitution to permit funding for such internal improvements was never adopted.

In sum, although Alexander Hamilton and other leaders of the Federalist Party argued for an expansive reading of the spending power, their reading was, on the whole, rejected both by Congress and, after the election of 1800, by the executive. Indeed, the differing views on the scope of federal power was a principal ground on which the 1800 presidential-election contest between Jefferson and incumbent Federalist President John Adams was waged. As Jefferson would note in an 1817 letter to Albert Gallatin, the different interpretations of the Spending Clause put forward by Hamilton, on the one hand, and Madison and Jefferson, on the other, were "almost the only landmark which now divides the federalists from the republicans." Jefferson won that election, and, save for a brief interlude during the one-term presidency of John Quincy Adams, the more restrictive interpretation of spending power was adopted by every President until the Civil War.

President Madison vetoed as unconstitutional an internal improvements bill that was passed by Congress at the very end of his presidency. President James Monroe also rejected the expansive Hamiltonian view of the Spending Clause (albeit on slightly different grounds than Madison had), vetoing various attempts at internal improvement bills during most of his two terms. But in the last year of his presidency, James Monroe, finding the line between "general" welfare and local welfare a hard one to define, signed a few bills to fund surveys for some local internal improvement projects. He thus opened a gate through which flowed a flood of spending on local projects during the administration of President John Quincy Adams. But Adams's resurrection of the Hamiltonian position became the focus of the next presidential election, contributing to Adams's defeat at the hands of Andrew Jackson, who promptly put to rest "this dangerous doctrine" by vetoing a $200 million appropriation for the purchase of stock in the Maysville and Lexington Turnpike Company and for the direct construction of other "ordinary" roads and canals by the government itself. So strong was his veto message that for four years Congress did not even try to pass another such bill, and when in 1834 it passed an act to improve the navigation of the Wabash River, Jackson again responded forcefully, rejecting as a "fallacy" the contention that the Spending Clause conferred upon Congress the power to do whatever seemed "to conduce to the public good."

In 1847 and 1857, Presidents James K. Polk and James Buchanan, respectively, vetoed subsequent congressional efforts to fund internal improvements. Polk vetoed a bill strikingly similar to much of the pork-barrel legislation to which we have grown accustomed in modern times. It provided $6,000 for projects in the Wisconsin territory—constitutionally permissible because of Congress's broader powers over federal territories—but it also included $500,000 for a myriad of projects in the existing states. Polk contended that to interpret the Spending Clause to permit such appropriations would allow "combinations of individual and local interests [that would be] strong enough to control legislation, absorb the revenues of the country, and plunge the government into a hopeless indebtedness."

Similarly, in his message vetoing the college land grant bill, President Buchanan took it as a given that the funds raised by Congress from taxation were "confined to the execution of the enumerated powers delegated to Congress." The idea that the resources of the federal government—either taxes or the public lands—could be diverted to carry into effect any measure of state domestic policy that Congress saw fit to support "would be to confer upon Congress a vast and irresponsible authority, utterly at war with the well-known jealousy of Federal power which prevailed at the formation of the Constitution."

Thus, while there were clearly voices urging for an expansive spending power before the Civil War, the interpretation held by Jefferson, Madison, and Monroe is the one that prevailed for most of the first seventy years after adoption of the Constitution.

Modern-day jurisprudence on the Spending Clause begins with the 1936 New Deal-era case of *United States v. Butler*. In that case, both parties relied upon the Hamiltonian position, despite the history recounted above. Both the majority and dissenting opinions of the Court facially accepted the correctness of Hamilton's position even though the majority ruled that the particular tax and regulatory program at issue in the case was unconstitutional because its purpose was to regulate and control agricultural production, "a matter beyond the powers delegated to the federal government"—a holding much more in line with Madison's interpretation of the spending power than Hamilton's.

Moreover, the Hamiltonian position purportedly adopted by the Court was not the expansive view that Congress could do whatever it deemed to be in the public interest, but the much more limited view that the limits on spending were contained in the Spending Clause itself and not in the remainder of Article I, Section 8. "While, therefore, the power to tax is not unlimited," Justice Owen J. Roberts wrote, "its confines are set in the clause which confers it, and not in those of Section 8 which bestow and define the legislative powers of the Congress." In other words, the only limitation on Congress's power to tax and spend was that the spending be for the "general Welfare"—the position actually advocated by James Monroe. What really makes *Butler* a departure from the early interpretation of the clause, then, was that it gave virtually unlimited discretion to Congress to determine what was in the "general welfare"—a holding that, practically speaking, is much more in line with the expansive Hamiltonian position than the positions advocated either by Monroe or by Madison and Jefferson.

Since *Butler*, the courts have essentially treated whatever limitation the clause might impose as essentially a nonjusticiable political question. In the 1987 case of *South Dakota v. Dole*, for example, the Supreme Court noted that "the level of deference to the congressional decision is such that the Court has more recently questioned whether 'general welfare' is a judicially enforceable restriction at all." Instead, the courts have focused not on the constitutionality of spending programs themselves, but on whether various conditions imposed on the receipt of federal funds—conditions designed to achieve ends concededly not within Congress's enumerated powers—were constitutionally permissible. In *South Dakota v. Dole*, the Court adopted a four-prong test against which it assesses the constitutionality of spending conditions: (1) the spending power must be in pursuit of the "general Welfare," a requirement that the Court left to Congress's judgment to satisfy because, in its view, "the concept of welfare or the opposite is shaped by Congress"; (2) whether the conditions imposed were unambiguous; (3) whether they were related to the particular national projects or programs being funded (thus far, the Court has not invalidated a spending restriction on the grounds that it is too unrelated to the programs being funded); and (4) whether there are other constitutional provisions that provide an independent bar to the conditional grant of federal funds. For example, Congress could not impose as a condition that a state receiving federal funds for its welfare programs require welfare recipients to waive their Fourth Amendment rights.

Of these four requirements, the "relatedness" and the independent constitutional bar prongs are the only ones that at present have any prospect of actually imposing a real limit on spending. Yet in the facts of *South Dakota v. Dole* itself, the Court concluded that conditioning receipt of federal highway funds on a state's adoption of a twenty-one-year-old drinking age was sufficiently related to the funding program. Eighteen-year-old residents of states with a twenty-one-year-old drinking age would drive to border states where the drinking age was eighteen and procure their liquor, the argument went. When driving back, the drivers had an increased risk of drunk driving on the highways paved by federal funds, and that was a sufficient connection for the Court.

Both Justices William J. Brennan, Jr., and Sandra Day O'Connor dissented. Justice O'Connor noted in her *South Dakota v. Dole* dissent: "If the spending power is to be limited only by Congress' notion of the general welfare, the reality . . . is that the Spending Clause gives 'power to the Congress . . . to become a parliament of the whole people, subject to no restrictions save such as are self-

imposed.' This . . . was not the Framers' plan and it is not the meaning of the Spending Clause."

While the Court has recently restored some limits to other powers delegated to Congress (such as the Commerce Clause), it has not yet done so with the Spending Power. This does not prevent Congress from adopting on its own a view of its power to spend that is more in accord with those of the Founders.

John C. Eastman

See Also

Article I, Section 8, Clause 1 (Uniformity Clause)

Article I, Section 8, Clause 3 (Commerce Among the States)

Article I, Section 8, Clause 17 (Enclave Clause)

Article I, Section 8, Clause 18 (Necessary and Proper Clause)

Article I, Section 9, Clause 4 (Direct Taxes)

Article I, Section 9, Clause 5 (Export Taxation Clause)

Article IV, Section 3, Clause 2 (Property Clause)

Suggestions for Further Research

Lynn A. Baker, *Conditional Federal Spending After Lopez*, 95 Colum. L. Rev. 1911 (1995)

Erwin Chemerinsky, *Protecting the Spending Power*, 4 Chapman L. Rev. 89 (2001)

John C. Eastman, *Restoring the "General" to the General Welfare Clause*, 4 Chapman L. Rev. 63 (2001)

David E. Engdahl, *The Spending Power*, 44 Duke L.J. 1 (1994)

Celestine Richards McConville, *Federal Funding Conditions: Bursting Through the Dole Loopholes*, 4 Chapman L. Rev. 163 (2001)

Robert G. Natelson, *The General Welfare Clause and the Public Trust: An Essay in Original Understanding*, 52 U. Kan. L. Rev. 1 (2003)

Jeffrey T. Renz, *What Spending Clause? (Or the President's Paramour): An Examination of the Views of Hamilton, Madison and Story on Article I, Section 8, Clause 1 of the United States Constitution*, 33 J. Marshall L. Rev. 81 (1999)

Significant Cases

United States v. Butler, 297 U.S. 1 (1936)

South Dakota v. Dole, 483 U.S. 203 (1987)

Uniformity Clause

...all Duties, Imposts and Excises
shall be uniform throughout the
United States....
(ARTICLE I, SECTION 8, CLAUSE 1)

～

*A*mong the unsatisfactory aspects of the Confederation government were its inability to regulate interstate and foreign commerce and its weak powers of taxation. The Constitution cured these defects, but thereby created a new danger: the greatly strengthened national government might abuse its powers by oppressing politically weaker groups and strangling the economic activity that the Framers hoped to promote.

At the Constitutional Convention, the Uniformity Clause was initially joined with what is now the Port Preference Clause (Article I, Section 9, Clause 6), which forbids Congress to give preferences "by any Regulation of Commerce or Revenue" to the ports of one state over those of another. Along with other provisions restricting congressional power over taxes and commercial regulations, these two were designed to forestall economically oppressive discrimination. The Port Preference Clause limits both the commerce and taxing powers, whereas the Uniformity Clause applies to the taxing power alone. Their common origin, however, is a sign of their common purpose: each was meant to prevent geographic discrimination that would give one state or region a competitive advantage or disadvantage in its commercial relations with the others.

Because the goods and activities that can be taxed are distributed unequally through the country, virtually all duties, imposts, and excises have nonuniform effects. A tax on oil production, for example, will affect certain regions more severely than others. Because the Constitution expressly empowers Congress to levy these taxes, it must also permit some of the nonuniform effects that inevitably accompany them. The principal challenge in interpreting the Uniformity Clause is to distinguish between the kind of nonuniformity that is forbidden by the Constitution and the inevitable nonuniform effects that accompany legitimate duties, imposts, and excises.

In its earliest exposition, the Supreme Court declared that a tax is uniform if it "operates with the same force and effect in every place where the subject of it is found." *Edye v. Robertson* (1884). This rule correctly recognized that the Uniformity Clause was meant to forbid geographically nonuniform taxes without outlawing all geographically nonuniform effects. But the formula is inadequate, because it does not describe the limits on Congress's discretion to define the "subjects" of taxation. Suppose, for example, that Congress chose to define the subject of an excise tax as "oil produced in Alaska." The rule would be formally satisfied, but the most flagrant geographic discrimination would be possible.

In *United States v. Ptasynski* (1983), a unanimous Court concluded (1) that any tax in which the subject is defined in nongeographic terms satisfies the Uniformity Clause, and (2) that where the subject is defined in geographic terms, the tax will be scrutinized for "actual geographic discrimination."

The first part of this test creates a very large safe harbor for discriminatory taxes, which can almost always be framed without using overtly geographic terminology (for example, "oil whose production might affect caribou populations"). Nor is it clear that the second part of the test puts any real limit on Congress's power to impose discriminatory and oppressive taxes, for the Court nowhere defined "actual geographic discrimination." In fact, the Court went out of its way to emphasize that review of statutes using geographic terminology would be highly deferential. With no promise of effective judicial enforcement, the Uniformity Clause has, at least for the present, apparently been rendered nugatory, save for Congress's own sense of its obligations under the Constitution.

Nelson Lund

See Also

Article I, Section 8, Clause 1 (Spending Clause)

Article I, Section 8, Clause 3 (Commerce with Foreign
　Nations)

Article I, Section 8, Clause 3 (Commerce Among the
    States)
Article I, Section 9, Clause 5 (Export Taxation Clause)
Article I, Section 9, Clause 6 (Port Preference Clause)

Suggestions for Further Research

RICHARD A. EPSTEIN, TAKINGS: PRIVATE PROPERTY AND
    THE POWER OF EMINENT DOMAIN 289–293 (1985)
Nelson Lund, Comment, *The Uniformity Clause*, 51
    U. CHI. L. REV. 1193 (1984)

Significant Cases

Edye v. Robertson, 112 U.S. 580 (1884)
Knowlton v. Moore, 178 U.S. 41 (1900)
United States v. Ptasynski, 462 U.S. 74 (1983)

Borrowing Clause

**The Congress shall have Power
To ... borrow Money on the credit
of the United States ....**
(ARTICLE I, SECTION 8, CLAUSE 2)

~

*T*he power to borrow money is essential to the
existence and survival of a national government. In the Founding era, political leaders
expected that in peacetime the Congress would
craft the federal government's budget so that
revenues equaled or surpassed expenditures.
Indeed, the Treasury Department strictly complied with a policy of earmarking all revenues
for particular government programs. Nonetheless, the nation could not successfully defend
itself militarily without the power to borrow
quickly and extensively when the need arose.
The Framers therefore drafted the Borrowing
Clause without an express limitation.

The Borrowing Clause, however, has a practical corollary. The terms upon which a nation
could borrow money depended upon its credit
standing. George Washington's Farewell Address
captures the general sentiment of the times:

> As a very important source of strength
> and security, cherish public credit. One

method of preserving it is to use it as sparingly as possible: avoiding occasions of
expense by cultivating peace, but remem-
bering also that timely disbursements to
prepare for danger frequently prevent
much greater disbursements to repel it;
avoiding likewise the accumulation of
debt, not only by shunning occasions of
expense, but by vigorous exertions in time
of peace to discharge the debts which
unavoidable wars may have occasioned,
not ungenerously throwing upon posterity the burden which we ourselves ought
to bear.

Although Federalists and Republicans agreed
on the need to maintain the public credit, they
diverged considerably on how the borrowing
power should be implemented. Indeed, the core
differences in the visions of the Federalists and
Republicans in the Founding era relate to contrasting views of this power. Alexander Hamilton sought to assure a strong central government
by interpreting the Borrowing Clause as authorizing Congress to charter the First Bank of the
United States (established in 1791), which maintained federal control over the federal reserves
and issued debt instruments that circulated like
money. Hamilton viewed large federal issues of
debt instruments as an essential stimulant to
commerce, providing a source of capital to a cap-
ital-poor society, and equally important for revenue collection purposes. The Constitution,
however, did not expressly authorize Congress to
charter corporations, and the constitutionality
of the bank was widely debated.

Thomas Jefferson dismantled much of Hamilton's program. To the Jeffersonian Republicans,
a balanced budget reflected a popular desire to
limit the size and power of the federal government and to protect states' rights. Jefferson
repealed Hamilton's internal taxes (which provided security for the federal debt) and appointed Albert Gallatin as Secretary of the Treasury
with a mandate to pay down the federal debt.
With a few exceptions, subsequent administrations also prioritized balancing the federal
budget, and Andrew Jackson successfully paid
down the federal debt in 1834.

Wartime exigencies and economic crises led the country toward the modern interpretation of the Borrowing Clause. A financial emergency that threatened national security during the War of 1812 led to the bipartisan acceptance of the need for federal government control of its reserves through the Bank of the United States, which was held constitutional in Justice John Marshall's expansively written *McCulloch v. Maryland* (1819). With respect to a federal currency, the Report of the Committee of Detail (debated at the Constitutional Convention) gave Congress the power to "borrow money, and emit bills on the credit of the United States." The delegates voted to strike the power to "emit bills," which strongly suggests that Congress was not authorized to borrow by means of a paper money, although it is clear that interest-bearing debt instruments were permissible. The Union's financial crisis during the Civil War, however, led to the attempt by the federal government to issue and make legal tender a paper-money currency, which was held constitutional in the *Legal Tender Cases* (1871). Financial problems during the Great Depression led Congress to define what constitutes legal tender. In 1933, a congressional joint resolution prohibited the enforcement of gold clauses in both contracts between the government and individuals and in private contracts, thereby making Federal Reserve notes the exclusive legal tender. The Supreme Court held the resolution constitutional in *The Gold Clause Cases* (1935).

Legal disputes dealing with the Borrowing Clause today involve two issues. The most litigated issue involves the principle of intergovernmental-taxation immunity. The Supreme Court has held that the Supremacy Clause (Article VI, Clause 2) prohibits state and municipal governments from directly or indirectly taxing the interest income on federal government debt and thereby interfering with the federal government's power under the Borrowing Clause. *See State ex rel. Missouri Insurance Co. v. Gehner* (1930).

The clause also implicitly requires Congress to maintain the public credit. The Supreme Court has invoked the clause in treating the government like a private party in its contractual dealings and in vesting Congress with the power to contract against subsequent repudiation or impairment of its obligations by future Congresses even in the exercise of independent substantive powers authorized under the Constitution. In *Perry v. United States* (1935), the Court cautioned that the power to borrow money is

> a power vital to the government, upon which in an extremity its very life may depend. The binding quality of the promise of the United States is of the essence of the credit which is so pledged. Having this power to authorize the issue of definite obligations for the payment of money borrowed, the Congress has not been vested with authority to alter or destroy those obligations.

In *United States v. Winstar Corp.* (1996), the Court held, among other things, that contractual obligations of the government would be enforced unless doing so blocked the exercise of one of the government's essential sovereign powers.

Because the Constitution imposes no express limits on the borrowing power, the political branches must decide the issue. As in the Founding era, the question of the extent to which the government should run deficits and maintain a large federal debt are at the essence of contrasting views about the proper scope of the federal government.

Claire Priest

See Also

Article I, Section 8, Clause 5 (Coinage Clause)
Article I, Section 10, Clause 1
Article VI, Clause 2 (Supremacy Clause)
Amendment XIV, Section 4 (Debts Incurred During Rebellion)

Suggestions for Further Research

Albert S. Bolles, The Financial History of the United States, 1774–1885 (Vols. 1–3, reprinted 1969)

Kenneth W. Dam, *The Legal Tender Cases*, 1981 Sup. Ct. Rev. 367

James Macdonald, A Free Nation Deep in Debt: The Financial Roots of Democracy (2003)

James D. Savage, Balanced Budgets and American Politics (1988)

Significant Cases

Scope of the Borrowing Clause:
McCulloch v. Maryland, 17 U.S. (4 Wheat.) 316 (1819)

Maintaining the Public Credit:
Perry v. United States, 294 U.S. 330 (1935)
United States v. Winstar Corp., 518 U.S. 839 (1996)

Authority to Determine Legal Tender:
Bronson v. Rodes, 74 U.S. (7 Wall.) 229 (1868)
Veazie Bank v. Fenno, 75 U.S. (8 Wall.) 533 (1869)
Legal Tender Cases, 79 U.S. (12 Wall.) 457 (1871), *overruling in part* Hepburn v. Griswold, 75 U.S. (8 Wall.) 603 (1870)
Julliard v. Greenman, 110 U.S. 421 (1884)

The Gold Clause Cases:
Norman v. Baltimore and Ohio Railroad, 294 U.S. 240 (1935)
Nortz v. United States, 294 U.S. 317 (1935)
Perry v. United States, 294 U.S. 330 (1935)

Intergovernmental Taxation Immunity:
State of Missouri *ex rel.* Missouri Insurance Co. v. Gehner, 281 U.S. 313 (1930)
New Jersey Realty Title Insurance Co. v. Division of Tax Appeals, 338 U.S. 665 (1950)

Commerce with Foreign Nations

The Congress shall have Power To . . . regulate Commerce with foreign Nations. . . .

(**Article I, Section 8, Clause 3**)

$\approx$

*E*ven before the Constitutional Convention, James Madison had long argued that exclusive power over foreign commerce should be vested in the national government. Under the Articles of Confederation, the states had the power to raise tariffs against goods from others states and from foreign nations, creating "rival, conflicting and angry regulations." Thus Great Britain had been able to use its power over duties and tariffs to monopolize trade in its favor without the United States government having the ability to respond.

At Philadelphia, there was unanimity that one of the general powers of the new government should be to regulate foreign commerce. Even Anti-Federalist Luther Martin, who later left the Convention to oppose the Constitution, had no doubts about it. In fact, in *The Federalist* No. 42, one of Madison's arguments for lodging the power to regulate commerce among the states with Congress was that "without this supplemental provision, the great and essential power of regulating foreign commerce, would have been incompleat, and ineffectual."

Some delegates, particularly from the South, wanted any regulation of foreign commerce to be effective only through a supermajority vote in Congress, but Madison successfully countered that a supermajority would cripple the government if it were necessary to retaliate against discriminatory tariffs from a foreign country.

Although Madison undoubtedly believed that the power to regulate foreign commerce was exclusive to the federal government, the proposition is not obvious from the text. Elsewhere, the Constitution denies the states certain powers over foreign commerce (no treaties or other agreements and no tariffs except under very limited circumstances). The text of the Commerce Clause does not differentiate between Congress's power "to regulate" foreign commerce from its power over interstate commerce, and some Justices on the Supreme Court have opined that Congress's power to regulate interstate commerce is coextensive with its power over foreign commerce. Nonetheless, a number of other opinions have held that Congress's power over foreign commerce is qualitatively greater than its power to regulate commerce among the states, because it is part of the federal government's complete sovereign power over foreign relations, in which the states have no standing. *Brolan v. United States* (1915).

In *Board of Trustees of University of Illinois v. United States* (1933), the Court stated: "In international relations and with respect to foreign intercourse and trade the people of the United States act through a single government with unified and adequate national power." And in *Japan Line, Ltd. v. County of Los Angeles* (1979), the Court declared that "[f]oreign commerce is preeminently a matter of national concern." As early as 1827, in *Brown v. Maryland*, Chief Justice John Marshall held that both the Import-Export Clause and the Commerce with Foreign Nations Clause precluded a state from burdening an imported good with a tax or license so long as the good remained in the ownership of the importer and "in the original form or package," though the Court permitted states to prohibit dangerous or noxious foreign goods. *Compagnie Francaise de Navigation a Vapeur v. Louisiana Board of Health* (1902).

Today, the Court allows the states less power to tax foreign commerce than they have to tax interstate commerce. In *Complete Auto Transit, Inc. v. Brady* (1977), the Supreme Court declared that a state tax affecting interstate commerce would be valid only if it were (1) nondiscriminatory, (2) applied to an interstate activity that had a "substantial nexus" with the state, (3) apportioned fairly, and (4) connected to services that the state provided. Later, in *Japan Line*, the Court added two further considerations to taxation of a foreign instrumentality: (1) the danger of multiple taxation and (2) the danger that the tax may damage the need for federal uniformity. Even though the Court has been somewhat more generous in recent years in permitting state taxation that involves foreign commerce, the rules continue to suggest a greater federal constitutional interest in foreign commerce than in commerce among the states, where the background principles of federalism still have some presence.

David F. Forte

See Also

Article I, Section 8, Clause 3 (Commerce Among the States; Commerce with the Indian Tribes)

Article I, Section 10, Clause 1 (State Treaties)

Article I, Section 10, Clause 2 (Import-Export Clause)

Suggestions for Further Research

Albert S. Abel, *The Commerce Clause in the Constitutional Convention and in Contemporary Comment*, 25 Minn. L. Rev. 432 (1941)

Saikrishna Prakash, *Our Three Commerce Clauses and the Presumption of Intrasentence Uniformity*, 55 Ark. L. Rev. 1149 (2003)

Significant Cases

Brown v. Maryland, 25 U.S. (12 Wheat.) 419 (1827)

Compagnie Francaise de Navigation a Vapeur v. Louisiana Board of Health, 186 U.S. 380 (1902)

Buttfield v. Stranahan, 192 U.S. 470 (1904)

Brolan v. United States, 236 U.S. 216 (1915)

Board of Trustees of University of Illinois v. United States, 289 U.S. 48 (1933)

Michelin Tire Corp. v. Wages, 423 U.S. 276 (1976)

Complete Auto Transit, Inc. v. Brady, 430 U.S. 274 (1977)

Japan Line, Ltd. v. County of Los Angeles, 441 U.S. 434 (1979)

Container Corp. of America v. Franchise Tax Board, 463 U.S. 159 (1983)

Itel Containers International Corp. v. Huddleston, 507 U.S. 60 (1993)

Commerce among the States

The Congress shall have Power To . . . regulate Commerce . . . among the several States . . . .

(Article I, Section 8, Clause 3)

∼

*T*he Commerce Among the States Clause operates both as a power delegated to Congress and as a constraint upon state legislation. No clause in the 1787 Constitution has been more disputed, and it has generated more cases than any other.

To this day, the debate over the extent of the commerce power centers on the definitions of "to regulate," "Commerce," and "among the several States."

The narrowest definition of "to regulate" is to "make regular," that is, to facilitate the free flow of goods, but not, except in cases of danger, to prohibit the flow of any good. The Supreme Court has never accepted this narrow definition. From the beginning, Chief Justice John Marshall in *Gibbons v. Ogden* (1824) saw the power to regulate as coextensive with the other delegated powers of Congress. He declared: "This power, like all others vested in Congress, is complete in itself, may be exercised to its utmost extent, and acknowledges no limitations, other than are prescribed in the constitution." The manner in which Congress decides to regulate commerce, Marshall said, is completely at the discretion of Congress, subject only to the political check of the voters. This power, as it later turned out, includes the power to prohibit the transportation of articles, as well as to control their exchange and transportation. *Champion v. Ames* (1903).

In generally ascending order of breadth, various writers and Justices have defined "commerce" as

1. The trafficking and trading of economic commodities
2. The trafficking and trading of economic commodities and the modes of their transportation
3. The trafficking and trading of any kind of commodity and the mode of its transportation
4. The movement of any thing or any person and its mode of transportation
5. Economic activity that substantially or causally impacts on the trafficking, trading, or transportation of commodities
6. Any human activity or other phenomenon that has any ultimate impact on activities in more states than one.

In *Gibbons*, Marshall held that commerce is "something more" than traffic. The term, he said, "describes the commercial intercourse between nations, and parts of nations, in all its branches." His description of the term did not settle matters, for the issue of what constitutes commerce was to exercise the Court from his time until the present.

Some commentators have defined "among the several States" as the trading and movement of goods between two or more states. But Chief Justice Marshall (again in *Gibbons*) thought *among* had a wider purview than would the word *between*: "Comprehensive as the word 'among' is, it may very properly be restricted to that commerce which concerns more States than one." Although this was a broader concept, Marshall nonetheless saw that there is some commerce that Congress cannot reach: "The enumeration presupposes something not enumerated; and that something, if we regard the language or the subject of the sentence, must be the exclusively internal commerce of a State." Purely local activities, therefore, remain outside of the reach of Congress under the Commerce Among the States Clause.

After *Gibbons v. Ogden*, there was little occasion for the Supreme Court to investigate the breadth of federal commerce power until the late nineteenth century and the advent of national economic legislation. (However, the Court considered many cases involving the so-called dormant commerce power: the power of the states to enact legislation that affects interstate commerce when Congress is silent, i.e., has not enacted any legislation.) From 1895 on, the Court experimented with differing notions of the commerce power until 1938, when it signaled that it was abdicating any serious role in monitoring Congress's exercise of this delegated power.

In *United States v. E.C. Knight Co.* (1895), the Supreme Court declared that the Sherman Antitrust Act could not constitutionally be interpreted to apply to monopolies in manufacturing, for the commerce power did not reach manufacturing. "Manufacturing is transformation—the fashioning of raw materials into a change of form for use . . . . The buying and selling and the transportation incidental thereto constitute commerce." Any effect manufacturing has on commerce was merely "indirect" and could not be reached under the commerce power. This *qualitative* distinction between manufacturing and commerce held for forty years, but the Court was not ungenerous in otherwise upholding federal regulatory legislation.

If companies engaged in price-fixing and marketing schemes, the Court held them to be "in commerce" and subject to Congress's power to regulate commerce. *Addyston Pipe & Steel Co. v. United States* (1899). In an expansionary gloss to the qualitative distinction, the Court also held that goods in the "stream of commerce," such as cattle at the Chicago stockyards and slaughterhouses on the way from farm to nationwide distribution, also fell under the commerce power. *Swift & Co. v. United States* (1905); *Stafford v. Wallace* (1922).

In *Champion v. Ames*, the Court also eschewed any scrutiny on whether the purpose of congressional regulation of interstate commerce was economic. So long as the good traveled across state lines, the Court held, Congress could regulate or prohibit it, even if Congress's purpose was moral. The dissenters pointed out unsuccessfully that legislation to regulate morals had been traditionally left to the states under their police power. Soon thereafter, on this basis the Court upheld the Pure Food and Drug Act, *Hipolite Egg Co. v. United States* (1911); legislation restricting interstate prostitution, *Hoke v. United States* (1913); and even personal immorality connected with interstate commerce, *Caminetti v. United States* (1917).

Thus, the Court only applied a qualitative test to legislation, the purpose and effect of which was to regulate manufacturing, as in the laws regulating child labor, *Hammer v. Dagenhart* (1918), and railroad retirement plans, *Railroad Retirement Board v. Alton Railroad Co.* (1935), if Congress sought to regulate goods after their interstate transportation had come to rest, *A.L.A. Schechter Poultry Corp. v. United States* (1935), or before transportation had begun, *Carter v. Carter Coal Co.* (1936). As limited as the Court's use of the qualitative test was, an alternative test had begun to develop that would have approved even more congressional legislation. Traditionally ascribed to the *Shreveport Rate Case* (1914), which permitted federal regulation of intrastate railroad rates to harmonize with interstate railroad rates, this *quantitative* test asserted that Congress could regulate a local activity, even manufacturing, if that local activity had a "substantial" effect on interstate

commerce. Over the next two decades, a minority of Justices continued to argue in favor of a quantitative test. The dispute between those espousing a qualitative version of the power and those supporting a quantitative interpretation increased during the 1930s as more extensive federal regulatory legislation came before the Supreme Court.

In 1935, Justice Benjamin N. Cardozo, concurring in the unanimous opinion in *Schechter*, suggested a test that would allow the government to regulate local activities if they had a proximate or foreseeable effect on interstate commerce: "The law is not indifferent to considerations of degree. Activities local in their immediacy do not become interstate and national because of distant repercussions." The following year, in striking down the Bituminous Coal Conservation Act, the Court accepted Cardozo's proximate cause test. (Cardozo dissented from the decision on procedural grounds.) Writing for the majority, Justice George Sutherland declared: "The word 'direct' implies that the activity or condition invoked or blamed shall operate proximately—not mediately, remotely, or collaterally—to produce the effect. It connotes the absence of an efficient intervening agency or condition."

A year later, in *NLRB v. Jones & Laughlin Steel Corp.* (1937), Chief Justice Charles Evans Hughes, in upholding the National Labor Relations Act's regulation of factory working conditions, filled his opinion with overlapping justifications, but the proximate cause language was prominent. The commerce power could not reach activities that were "indirect and remote." Federal power could reach those activities that have a "close and intimate effect" on interstate commerce. An industry organized on a national level had such an effect, he declared. Soon, however, Justice Cardozo died, and other Justices retired. By 1941, in *United States v. Darby*, it was clear that the new majority had embraced a very expansive quantitative test and, as events were to show, these Justices were able to find that any local activity, taken either separately or in the aggregate, *Wickard v. Filburn* (1942), always had a sufficiently substantial effect on interstate commerce to justify congressional legislation. By these means, the Court turned the commerce power into the equivalent of a general regulatory power and undid the Framers' original structure of limited and delegated powers, as also observed by Justice Clarence Thomas in his dissent in *Gonzales v. Raich* (2005).

The commerce power was also invoked to expand federal criminal legislation, as well as for major social reforms such as the Civil Rights Act of 1964. But in *United States v. Lopez* (1995) and *United States v. Morrison* (2000), the Supreme Court limited Congress's power under the Commerce Among the States Clause for the first time since in the 1930s. In *Lopez*, Chief Justice William H. Rehnquist wound his way among the Court's precedents to strike down a federal law that had criminalized the possession of a gun near a school. He declared that the commerce power extends to (1) "the use of the channels of interstate commerce"; (2) the regulation of "instrumentalities of interstate commerce, or person or things in interstate commerce"; and (3) a local commercial activity having a "substantial relation" to interstate commerce. Possessing a gun is not a commercial activity, even though gun violence affects commerce. More importantly, he argued that the effects prong of the commerce power applies when the activity is a commercial activity. He insisted that the rule of *substantial* effects must be observed.

Justice Stephen G. Breyer, for the dissent, agreed that there are limits to the commerce power—it does not grant a general federal police power. But he could not find those limits. He argued that there is a sufficient connection between guns near schools, the impact on the educational process, and the eventual connection to the nation's economy to justify the regulation, but he could not, under his formula, put forward any activity that could not thus be reached by Congress under the Commerce Among the States Clause. Concurring with the majority, Justice Clarence Thomas suggested that, upon the proper occasion, the Court should reexamine some of its more expansionary precedents dealing with the "affects" test. Subsequent to the decision, Congress amended the law, requiring that the particular gun found in possession near to a school must be shown to have traveled in interstate commerce.

In *Morrison*, the Court struck down a suit for damages for rape, even though the suit would have been permitted under the Violence Against Women Act. Here, Chief Justice Rehnquist explained *Lopez* by emphasizing that noneconomic activities (violence against women, or violence against men, or violence in general) could not be aggregated to establish a substantial connection to interstate commerce.

In recent decades, scholars have investigated anew the Framers' view of the commerce power. Randy Barnett argues that, to the Framers, commerce meant the trade or exchange of goods, including the means of transporting them. Richard Epstein finds that the commerce power includes "interstate transportation, navigation and sales, and the activities closely incident to them. All else should be left to the states." Raoul Berger opines that "the Founders conceived of 'commerce' as 'trade,' the interchange of goods by one state with another." Grant Nelson and Robert Pushaw assert a somewhat broader view. They interpret the founding documents as providing Congress the authority to regulate or prohibit "any market-based activity that affects more than one state," which includes the manufacturing, farming, environmental, safety, financial, and labor effects of commercial activity.

In the worldview of the Framers, informed by their struggle with England and their experience with the Articles of Confederation, the direction of economic policy centered on two powers: the regulation of commerce and the regulation of the money supply. (Taxation, on the other hand, was primarily for raising revenue.) The Constitution removed from the states the power of coining money and the power over interstate commerce and lodged both with the Congress, with the proviso that Congress could not discriminate against any state or region in the exercise of those powers. The Framers believed that both those powers were sufficient for the Congress to shepherd national economic policy. The Framers felt no need to give the Congress the direct power to regulate local activities not otherwise included in its delegated powers. As Justice Marshall put it in *Gibbons v. Ogden* (1824):

> The genius and character of the whole government seem to be, that its action is to be applied to all the external concerns of the nation, and to those internal concerns which affect the states generally; but not to those which are completely within a particular state, which do not affect other states, and with which it is not necessary to interfere, for the purpose of executing some of the general powers of the government. The completely internal commerce of a state, then, may be considered as reserved for the state itself.

Lurking behind the debate over the commerce power and occasionally hinted at in some of the Court's opinions is the Necessary and Proper Clause (Article I, Section 8, Clause 18). In the preceding quote, Chief Justice Marshall noted that there may be some "internal concerns" with which it may be "necessary to interfere, for the purpose of executing some of the general powers of the government." Thus, even if the commerce power in and of itself cannot reach particular local activities, Congress may still be able to regulate them if to do so has an appropriate connection to commerce. As Marshall said five years before *Gibbons* in *McCulloch v. Maryland* (1819):

> Let the end be legitimate [for example, the protection of interstate commerce], let it be within the scope of the constitution, and all means which are appropriate, which are plainly adapted to that end, which are not prohibited, but consist with the letter and spirit of the constitution, are constitutional.

As Marshall stated it, the required connection between the regulation of the local activity and the protection of Congress's policy on interstate commerce produces a connection similar to the proximate cause test devised by Justice Cardozo and developed by Justice Sutherland. But the modern Court has ignored it.

One should also recall Marshall's limitation, again from *McCulloch v. Maryland*, on the uses of the Necessary and Proper Clause:

> Should Congress, in the execution of its powers, adopt measures which are prohibited by the constitution; or should Congress, under the pretext of executing its powers, pass laws for the accomplishment of objects not entrusted to the government; it would become the painful duty of this tribunal, should a case requiring such a decision come before it, to say that such an act was not the law of the land.

It would follow that Congress could regulate a local activity only if its purpose comports with its delegated power to regulate commerce and the regulation is plainly adapted to its interstate commerce purpose. So concluded Justice Antonin Scalia in his concurrence in *Gonzales v. Raich* (2005), upholding federal regulation of locally grown and consumed marijuana, otherwise legal under state law.

Although Justice Scalia has contested the proposition, *Tyler Pipe Industries v. Department of Revenue* (1987), the traditional view is that the Constitution grants Congress plenary power over interstate commerce. The Commerce Among the States Clause, therefore, operates as an extrinsic restraint on the legislative powers of the states. If Congress has legislated upon a subject within its commerce power, then, due to the Supremacy Clause, any state law to the contrary falls. Congress may even consent to state regulation that directly regulates interstate commerce. But to what extent may a state legislate upon a subject that impacts interstate commerce in the absence of congressional action? Does it matter if the state law *discriminates* against interstate commerce, either in purpose or effect?

It was inevitable that the states, even in the honest exercise of their police powers, would trench on interstate commerce. How far the states can even incidentally intrude upon interstate commerce has been the subject of literally hundreds of Supreme Court cases, often with inconsistent holdings. A detailed treatment of that complicated history is beyond the scope of this essay, but in 1970 in *Pike v. Bruce Church, Inc.*, the Court consolidated its dormant Commerce Clause jurisprudence into the following test: "Where the [state] statute regulates evenhandedly to effectuate a legitimate local public interest, and its effects on interstate commerce are only incidental, it will be upheld unless the burden imposed on such commerce is clearly excessive in relation to the putative local benefits."

A few decades ago, some scholars opined that the *Pike* test was a codification of an ad hoc balancing test. More recent scholarship, however, has indicated that the Supreme Court rarely, if ever, decides a dormant Commerce Clause case on balancing grounds since it would be attempting to compare incommensurables. Rather, the *Pike* test describes a series of separate standards by which a state statute can be determined to be within its constitutional powers.

Those determinative principles are as follows:

1. The statute must have a "legitimate" and "public" purpose. It must be within the state's police power, and not designed either to regulate interstate commerce as such, or to discriminate against out-of-state economic interests in favor of private in-state interests.
2. The effect on interstate commerce must be "incidental," rather than the primary purpose of the statute.
3. The interest must be "local." It must regulate elements that are peculiar to the state, such as its harbors, and not impose a pattern of "multiple inconsistent burdens" with other states' conflicting laws on an interstate enterprise.
4. The statute must "regulate evenhandedly." The state must be regulating an activity as part of its police powers. If it is only a "market participant" similar to a private entity, the dormant Commerce Clause is not a bar to its economic decisions even if they impact or discriminate against interstate commerce, though the Privileges and Immunities Clause of Article IV may

be a constraint. Moreover, if a state is, in fact, regulating even in the pursuit of a legitimate interest, the state may not discriminate against out-of-staters, absent compelling reasons.

5. The statute must "effectuate" its local public interest. If there is little evidence of such a result, the court may infer that the interstate impact was intentional and hence unconstitutional, after all.

If a state statute survives all these criteria, it will be upheld unless the burden imposed on interstate commerce is "clearly excessive" in relation to the asserted local benefits. This last clause is indeed a balancing test (weighted in favor of the state), but the Court rarely, if ever, reaches it, preferring to decide the issue on one of the antecedent principles.

Justica Scalia does not believe the Court should be monitoring the states' impact on interstate commerce, outside of discrimination against interstate commerce or creating multiple inconsistent burdens. *CTS Corp. v. Dynamics Corp. of America* (1987) (Scalia, J., dissenting.) He believes that the Constitution gives the power to the Congress to cure (or approve of) any excessive state action by legislation. Justice Thomas would rather use the Import-Export Clause to strike down state discriminations against interstate commerce. *Camps Newfound/Owatonna, Inc. v. Town of Harrison* (1997) (Thomas, J., dissenting).

David F. Forte

See Also

Suggestions for Further Research

Albert Abel, *The Commerce Clause in the Constitutional Convention and in Contemporary Comment*, 25 Minn. L. Rev. 432 (1941)

Randy E. Barnett, *New Evidence of the Original Meaning of the Commerce Clause*, 55 Ark. L. Rev. 847 (2003)

Randy E. Barnett, *The Original Meaning of the Commerce Clause*, 68 U. Chi. L. Rev. 101 (2001)

Raoul Berger, *Judicial Manipulation of the Commerce Clause*, 74 Tex. L. Rev. 695 (1996)

Barry Cushman, Rethinking the New Deal Court: The Structure of a Constitutional Revolution (1998)

Brannon P. Denning, *Why the Privileges and Immunities Clause of Article IV Cannot Replace the Dormant Commerce Clause Doctrine*, 88 Minn. L. Rev. 384 (2003)

Richard A. Epstein, *The Proper Scope of the Commerce Power*, 73 Va. L. Rev. 1387 (1987)

Robert J. Pushaw & Grant S. Nelson, *A Critique of the Narrow Interpretation of the Commerce Clause*, 96 Nw. U. L. Rev. 695 (2002)

Martin H. Redish & Shane V. Nugent, *The Dormant Commerce Clause and the Constitutional Balance of Federalism*, 1987 Duke L.J. 569 (1987)

Donald Regan, *The Supreme Court and State Protectionism: Making Sense of the Dormant Commerce Clause*, 84 Mich. L. Rev. 1091 (1986)

Significant Cases

McCulloch v. Maryland, 17 U.S. (4 Wheat.) 316 (1819)

Gibbons v. Ogden, 22 U.S. (9 Wheat.) 1 (1824)

Cooley v. Board of Wardens, 53 U.S. (12 How.) 299 (1851)

United States v. E.C. Knight Co., 156 U.S. 1 (1895)

Addyston Pipe & Steel Co. v. United States, 175 U.S. 211 (1899)

Champion v. Ames, 188 U.S. 321 (1903)

Swift & Co. v. United States, 196 U.S. 375 (1905)

Hipolite Egg Co. v. United States, 220 U.S. 45 (1911)

Hoke v. United States, 227 U.S. 308 (1913)

Shreveport Rate Case, 234 U.S. 342 (1914)

Caminetti v. United States, 242 U.S. 470 (1917)

Hammer v. Dagenhart, 247 U.S. 251 (1918)

Stafford v. Wallace, 258 U.S. 495 (1922)

A.L.A. Schechter Poultry Corp. v. United States, 295 U.S. 495 (1935)

Railroad Retirement Board v. Alton Railroad Co., 295 U.S. 330 (1935)

Carter v. Carter Coal Co., 298 U.S. 238 (1936)

NLRB v. Jones & Laughlin Steel Corp., 301 U.S. 1 (1937)

United States v. Darby, 312 U.S. 100 (1941)

Wickard v. Filburn, 317 U.S. 111 (1942)

H.P. Hood & Sons v. Du Mond, 336 U.S. 525 (1949)

Dean Milk v. Madison, 340 U.S. 349 (1951)

Heart of Atlanta Motel v. United States, 379 U.S. 241 (1964)

Katzenbach v. McClung, 379 U.S. 294 (1964)

Pike v. Bruce Church, Inc., 397 U.S. 137 (1970)

Hughes v. Alexandria Scrap Corp., 426 U.S. 794 (1976)

Hunt v. Washington State Apple Advertising Commission, 432 U.S. 333 (1977)

Philadelphia v. New Jersey, 437 U.S. 617 (1978)

Reeves, Inc. v. Stake, 447 U.S. 429 (1980)

Kassel v. Consolidated Freightways Corp. of Delaware, 450 U.S. 662 (1981)

Minnesota v. Clover Leaf Creamery Co., 449 U.S. 456 (1981)

South-Central Timber Development, Inc. v. Wunnicke, 467 U.S. 82 (1984)

CTS Corp. v. Dynamics Corp. of America, 481 U.S. 69 (1987)

Tyler Pipe Industries v. Department of Revenue, 483 U.S. 232 (1987)

United States v. Lopez, 514 U.S. 549 (1995)

Camps Newfound/Owatonna, Inc. v. Town of Harrison, 520 U.S. 564 (1997)

United States v. Morrison, 529 U.S. 598 (2000)

Gonzales v. Raich, 125 S. Ct. 2195 (2005)

Commerce with the Indian Tribes

> The Congress shall have Power To . . . regulate Commerce . . . with the Indian Tribes. . . .
>
> (Article I, Section 8, Clause 3)

～

*T*he Commerce Clause grants Congress plenary power to regulate commerce between the United States and three other forms of sovereign entities: the states, foreign nations, and the Indian tribes.

At the Constitutional Convention, there were several different drafts describing how the

Indians should be incorporated into the Constitution. Finding a single formula was not easy, because Indians resided within the United States as well as within the states. A troubling precedent was the ambiguous relationship between Congress, the states, and the Indians in the Articles of Confederation. Thus, the Framers gave the power of regulating commerce solely to Congress, without reference to the states. For Justice Joseph Story, the power to regulate trade and commerce with the Indian tribes passed naturally from the Crown to the federal government after the Revolution, and this clause confirmed that proposition. In *Worcester v. Georgia* (1832), Chief Justice John Marshall confirmed the supremacy of federal authority over the states in regard to the Indians.

One can derive the plenary authority of Congress over the Indians from the Commerce Clause, the Treaty Clause (Article II, Section 2, Clause 2), the Property Clause (Article IV, Section 3, Clause 2), and from the nature of the sovereign power of federal government in relation to the Indians. For the first century following the ratification of the Constitution, Congress regulated Indian affairs through the Trade and Intercourse Acts and through treaties. Tribes had juridical existence, not as foreign states, but as "domestic dependent nations," *Cherokee Nation v. Georgia* (1831), and were entitled to rights in property and self-rule, subject to the will of Congress. *Johnson v. McIntosh* (1823). The Court declared Indians as "wards" in a trust relationship with the United States government. *Cherokee Nation v. Georgia*; *United States v. Kagama* (1886).

Federal policy toward the Indians has developed through a number of phases, punctuated by treaties (until 1871), legislation, and conflict, but it has consistently rejected state incursions into federal authority. Expansion of lands for settlement and Indian removal from east of the Mississippi dominated congressional attention until 1850. Thereafter, the government attempted to move the western tribes to reservations, followed, beginning in 1887, with a policy of assimilation. In 1924, Congress granted citizenship to all Indians born in the United States who had not been made citizens under a prior treaty. In the Indian "New Deal" beginning in 1934, the government ended the assimilation policy and sought to reorganize and maintain tribal structure. In the 1950s, however, policy veered again, this time toward ending tribal status and integrating the Indians into the political structure as individuals. In 1953, Congress began allowing some states to extend their jurisdiction to Indian areas within their borders, but beginning in 1968, policy once again reversed when the Indian Civil Rights Act extended constitutional guarantees to Indians in relation to their own tribal governments. At the same time, Congress sought to expand the areas of Indian local self-rule. Under the Indian Gaming Regulatory Act (1988), Indian tribes throughout the country have been able to establish gambling institutions on their lands under compacts entered into with the states.

The Supreme Court has been highly deferential to congressional control of relations with the Indian tribes, and the Court closely monitors under the Supremacy Clause any state legislation affecting the Indians. Furthermore, the Court has increasingly required the executive to abide by specific undertakings found in the laws and treaties dealing with the Indians, particularly in upholding Indian monetary claims. However, the Court has never enforced a trust arrangement between the Indians and the government as a ubiquitous legal rule.

David F. Forte

See Also

Article I, Section 8, Clause 3 (Commerce with Foreign Nations and Commerce Among the States)
Article II, Section 2, Clause 2 (Treaty Clause)
Article IV, Section 3, Clause 2 (Property Clause)
Article VI, Clause 2 (Supremacy Clause)

Suggestions for Further Research

Gerard N. Magliocca, *The Cherokee Removal and the Fourteenth Amendment*, 53 Duke L.J. 875 (2003)

Nell Jessup Newton, *Federal Power Over Indians: Its Sources, Scope, and Limitations*, 132 U. Pa. L. Rev. 195 (1984)

Saikrishna B. Prakash, *Against Tribal Fungibility*, 89 Cornell L. Rev. 1069 (2004)

Mark Savage, *Native Americans and the Constitution: The Original Understanding*, 16 AMERICAN INDIAN L. REV 57(1991)

Significant Cases

Johnson v. McIntosh, 21 U.S. (8 Wheat.) 543 (1823)

Cherokee Nation v. Georgia, 30 U.S. (5 Pet.) 1 (1831)

Worcester v. Georgia, 31 U.S. (6 Pet.) 515 (1832)

Ex parte Crow Dog, 109 U.S. 556 (1883)

United States v. Kagama, 118 U.S. 375 (1886)

Talton v. Mayes, 163 U.S. 376 (1896)

Lone Wolf v. Hitchcock, 187 U.S. 553 (1903)

United States v. Creek Nation, 295 U.S. 103 (1935)

Seminole Nation v. United States, 316 U.S. 286 (1942)

Williams v. Lee, 358 U.S. 217 (1959)

McClanahan v. State Tax Commission of Arizona, 411 U.S. 164 (1973)

Morton v. Mancari, 417 U.S. 535 (1974)

Oliphant v. Suquamish Indian Tribe, 435 U.S. 191 (1978)

Santa Clara Pueblo v. Martinez, 436 U.S. 49 (1978)

United States v. Wheeler, 435 U.S. 313 (1978)

United States v. Mitchell, 445 U.S. 535 (1980)

Montana v. United States, 450 U.S. 544 (1981)

United States v. Mitchell, 463 U.S. 206 (1983)

California v. Cabazon Band of Mission Indians, 480 U.S. 202 (1987)

Brendale v. Confederated Tribes and Bands of Yakima, 492 U.S. 408 (1989)

Nevada v. Hicks, 533 U.S. 353 (2001)

Naturalization

The Congress shall have Power To . . . establish an uniform Rule of Naturalization . . . .

(ARTICLE I, SECTION 8, CLAUSE 4)

~

*F*ew powers are more fundamental to sovereignty than the control over immigration and the vesting of citizenship in aliens (naturalization). According to the Declaration of Independence, "obstructing the Laws for the Naturalization of Foreigners" was one of the grievances that led the American colonists to break with Britain.

Under the Articles of Confederation, each state retained authority over the naturalization of aliens. This resulted in widely varying state practices, which James Madison in *The Federalist* No. 42 called a "fault" and "defect" of the Confederation. At the Constitutional Convention, there was virtually no opposition to moving the naturalization power from the states to the new national government, and in the ratification debates only a handful of Anti-Federalists even raised the issue. James Madison seemed to speak the sentiment of most when at the Convention he expressed his wish "to invite foreigners of merit & republican principles among us. America was indebted to emigration for her settlement & prosperity."

Congress passed the first "uniform Rule of Naturalization" under the new Constitution in March 1790. It allowed "any alien, being a free white person" and "of good character" who had resided in the United States for two years to become a "citizen of the United States" by taking an oath in court "to support the constitution of the United States." Although Alexander Hamilton had argued in *The Federalist* No. 32 that the power to establish "an uniform rule of naturalization . . . must necessarily be exclusive; because if each State had power to prescribe a distinct rule, there could not be a uniform rule," some states continued to naturalize foreigners even after Congress had acted. In 1795, Congress claimed exclusive authority over naturalization by establishing new conditions—"and not otherwise"—for aliens "to become a citizen of the United States, or any of them." In *Chirac v. Lessee of Chirac* (1817), the Supreme Court affirmed that "the power of naturalization is exclusively in congress," notwithstanding any state laws to the contrary.

Individual naturalizations following Congress's "uniform Rule" were not the only avenues to citizenship for those who were not American citizens by birth. The incorporation of the Louisiana Territory and Florida into the Union in the first decades of the nineteenth century raised the issue of whether the national government through treaty or law could vest citizenship collectively. A federal circuit court in 1813 and then the Supreme Court in *American Insurance*

Co. v. 356 Bales of Cotton (1828) upheld collective naturalization. Moreover, in 1848 the Treaty of Guadalupe Hidalgo, which ended the Mexican-American War, offered the Mexican inhabitants of the territories ceded to the United States the option of maintaining their Mexican citizenship or, if they made no such request, becoming American citizens.

From the beginning, American naturalization law and practice assumed that a free citizen of one country had the right to transfer his allegiance to another if the latter allowed: hence, the provision of the 1795 law that required the new citizen to "absolutely and entirely renounce" any previous allegiance. However, this essential element of social-contract theory—that political communities are the free association of individuals to promote their mutual security and happiness—violated settled European norms. Sir William Blackstone had written in *Commentaries on the Laws of England* that the "natural allegiance" owed by all those born within the sovereign's domain could not be "forfeited, cancelled, or altered" by any act of the subject himself, including moving to another country and "swearing allegiance to another."

This conflict of views on the legitimacy of voluntary expatriation led to considerable conflict between the new nation and both Britain and France, especially when the latter two nations captured on the high seas and impressed into their naval service former nationals who had moved to the United States. This was one of the American grievances that led to the War of 1812. As late as the 1860s, the British government refused to recognize the American naturalization of former Irish subjects. In response, Congress passed the Expatriation Act of 1868, which declared that "the right of expatriation is a natural and inherent right of all people, indispensable to the enjoyment of the rights of life, liberty, and the pursuit of happiness."

Key criteria for citizenship of the Naturalization Act of 1795 remain part of American law. These include (1) five years of (lawful) residence within the United States; (2) a "good moral character, attached to the principles of the Constitution of the United States, and well disposed to the good order and happiness of the United States"; (3) the taking of a formal oath to support the Constitution and to renounce any foreign allegiance; and (4) the renunciation of any hereditary titles.

Current law, which is much more detailed than the first naturalization statutes, also requires competency in the English language and excludes those who advocate world communism or the violent overthrow of the government of the United States. Also, current law prohibits discrimination in naturalization on the basis of race, sex, or marital status. The elements of the oath have been expanded to include a solemn commitment "to support and defend the Constitution and the laws of the United States against all enemies, foreign and domestic; ... to bear true faith and allegiance to the same; and ... to bear arms on behalf of the United States when required by law, or ... to perform noncombatant service in the Armed Forces of the United States when required by law" (with exceptions for conscientious objectors).

Federal law and regulations establish procedures, administered by the Department of State, by which Americans can voluntarily renounce their citizenship. In addition, federal law lists a variety of acts that shall result in the loss of citizenship if "voluntarily perform[ed] ... with the intention of relinquishing United States nationality." These include obtaining naturalization in a foreign state; declaring allegiance to a foreign state; serving in the armed forces of a foreign state as an officer or when the foreign state is engaged in hostilities against the United States; and, in some cases, serving in governmental office in a foreign state.

Prior to several important Supreme Court decisions in the last half of the twentieth century, federal law had also required loss of citizenship for, among other acts, voting in a foreign election; deserting during wartime; leaving the country during wartime to evade military service; and, for those who acquired dual nationality at birth, voluntarily seeking or claiming the benefits of foreign nationality and residing in the foreign state for three years continuously after the age of twenty-two.

Although the Supreme Court in *MacKenzie v. Hare* (1915) upheld Congress's power to expatriate, in 1958 the Court began to cut back on Congress's power in a number of closely decided cases. Although it upheld expatriation for voting in a foreign election, *Perez v. Brownell* (1958), it overturned expatriations for desertion from the military during wartime, *Trop v. Dulles* (1958), and for service by a dual national in the Japanese army during World War II, *Nishikawa v. Dulles* (1958). In 1963, in *Kennedy v. Mendoza-Martinez*, the Court ruled that a citizen could not be expatriated for fleeing the country during wartime to evade military service. The following year, it extended the limits on expatriation to naturalized citizens who returned to their native countries and resided there for at least three years. *Schneider v. Rusk* (1964). Then in *Afroyim v. Rusk* (1967), it overturned *Perez v. Brownell* by ruling that a naturalized American citizen who relocated to Israel and voted in an election for the Israeli Knesset could not lose his citizenship as a result.

In *Rogers v. Bellei* (1971), however, the Court did uphold a statute requiring that if a person acquires United States citizenship by virtue of having been born abroad to an American citizen, he shall lose his citizenship unless he resides in the United States continuously for five years between the ages of fourteen and twenty-eight. But this statute applied only to a person who was neither born in the United States nor naturalized in the United States. In any event, in 1978, Congress removed from federal law the residency requirements upheld in *Rogers v. Bellei*.

Finally, in *Vance v. Terrazas* (1980), the Court clarified its decision in *Afroyim* by holding that it was not enough to show that an individual voluntarily committed an act that Congress determined was inconsistent with American citizenship. It was necessary also to show independently that the individual "intended to relinquish his citizenship." Given the broad language of the more recent cases, it seems that no involuntary expatriations are lawful. The one exception, which applies only to naturalized Americans, is the denaturalization (and deportation) of those who became citizens through fraud or illegality. It has been applied most notably in recent decades to former Nazis who engaged in war crimes during World War II and later lied about

their wartime activities either when they entered the United States as "displaced persons" or when they applied for citizenship.

Until recent decades, American public policy consistently prohibited dual citizenship. Since 1795, Congress has required that all candidates for naturalization formally renounce allegiance to their native land and any other foreign power. That requirement remains a part of national law and is an integral element of the citizenship oath. The rationale for these policies is that citizenship requires undivided loyalty to one country.

Yet today there are millions of American citizens who are also citizens of other countries. Many are naturalized American citizens whose native countries do not recognize the renunciation of loyalty that their native citizens make in the American citizenship oath. Others are the offspring of one American parent and one foreign parent, deriving citizenship from both sides, or foreign-born children adopted by American parents. Because the courts now prohibit the government from expatriating those who maintain an active citizenship in a foreign nation (some American citizens have even held political office in other countries), dual citizenship has become a fact of American life, despite statutory law.

Joseph Bessette

See Also

Article IV, Section 2, Clause 1 (Privileges and Immunities Clause)

Amendment XIV, Section 1 (Citizenship)

Suggestions for Further Research

Leonard Dinnerstein & David M. Reimers, Ethnic Americans: A History of Immigration (4th ed. 1999)

James H. Kettner, The Development of American Citizenship, 1608–1870 (1978)

Arthur Mann, The One and the Many: Reflections on the American Identity (1979)

Significant Cases

Chirac v. Lessee of Chirac, 15 U.S. (2 Wheat.) 259 (1817)

American Insurance Co. v. 356 Bales of Cotton, 26
    U.S. (1 Pet.) 511 (1828)
Boyd v. State of Nebraska, 143 U.S. 135 (1892)
MacKenzie v. Hare, 239 U.S. 299 (1915)
Nishikawa v. Dulles, 356 U.S. 129 (1958)
Perez v. Brownell, 356 U.S. 44 (1958)
Trop v. Dulles, 356 U.S. 86 (1958)
Kennedy v. Mendoza-Martinez, 372 U.S. 144 (1963)
Schneider v. Rusk, 377 U.S. 163 (1964)
Afroyim v. Rusk, 387 U.S. 253 (1967)
Rogers v. Bellei, 401 U.S. 815 (1971)
Vance v. Terrazas, 444 U.S. 252 (1980)

Bankruptcy Clause

The Congress shall have Power To...establish...uniform Laws on the subject of Bankruptcies throughout the United States....
(ARTICLE I, SECTION 8, CLAUSE 4)

∽

*T*he Bankruptcy Clause of the Constitution was one of Congress's several delegated powers in Article I, Section 8, that were designed to encourage the development of a commercial republic and to temper the excesses of pro-debtor state legislation that proliferated under the Articles of Confederation. Both state legislation and state courts tended to use debtor-creditor laws to redistribute money from out-of-state and urban creditors to rural agricultural interests. Under the Articles of Confederation, the states alone governed debtor-creditor relations, and that led to diverse and contradictory state laws. It was unclear, for instance, whether a state law that purported to discharge a debtor of a debt prohibited the creditor from trying to collect the debt in another state. Pro-debtor state laws also interfered with the reliability of contracts, and creditors confronted still further obstructions in trying to use state courts to collect their judgments, especially when debtors absconded to other states to avoid collection.

A coherent and consistent bankruptcy regime for merchants was also required for the United States to flourish as a commercial republic. The Framers were so convinced of the need for a national power over bankruptcy that there was hardly any debate over the issue at the Constitutional Convention. The Bankruptcy Clause helped to further the goals of uniformity and predictability within the federalist system. As James Madison observed in *The Federalist* No. 42, "The power of establishing uniform laws of bankruptcy is so intimately connected with the regulation of commerce, and will prevent so many frauds where the parties or their property may lie or be removed into different States that the expediency of it [i.e., Congress's power to regulate bankruptcy] seems not likely to be drawn into question." As Madison suggests, there was little debate over and little opposition to the Bankruptcy Clause at the Constitutional Convention. Although state law continued to govern most routine debtor-creditor relations, Congress had the authority to override state laws dealing with insolvency.

Following ratification of the Constitution, the mercantile northeastern states spearheaded the movement for a national bankruptcy law. The first bankruptcy law was passed under the Federalists in 1800, but it lasted only until 1803. Other bankruptcy laws existed from 1841 to 1843 and from 1867 to 1878. The first permanent bankruptcy law was enacted in 1898 and remained in effect, with amendments, until being replaced with a comprehensive new law in 1978, the essential structure of which continues today.

Subsequent to the ratification of the Constitution, it remained unclear where the line between the state and federal power should be drawn. English law relied upon a traditional distinction between "bankruptcies" on one hand and "insolvency" on the other. Under English law, only merchants and traders could be declared "bankrupt," which enabled them to have their debts discharged upon the satisfaction of certain requirements. By contrast, non-merchants had to seek refuge under "insolvency" laws, which did little more than to release a debtor from debtor's prison but did not discharge the debtor from his indebtedness. Thus, many understood the Constitution's grant of power to Congress to regulate "bankruptcies" as creating federal power to regulate only with respect to merchants and traders and not with respect to those individuals traditionally subject to "insolvency" laws, which remained under state control. Others argued that this traditional distinction had disappeared by the mid-eighteenth century, such that by the time of the Constitution, the terms became interchangeable so as to give Congress the power to regulate all insolvent debtors. In 1819, the Supreme Court held in *Sturges v. Crowninshield* that the use of the term *bankruptcy* in the Constitution did not limit Congress's jurisdiction, thereby permitting Congress to regulate both of these realms. In *Ogden v. Saunders* (1827), the Court further restricted the states' concurrent power, prohibiting discharge of debts owed to citizens of another state, but permitting discharge of debts owed to a citizen of the same state so long as the law operated prospectively so as not to impair contract obligations.

Still, the original understanding of the Bankruptcy Clause placed several clear constraints on Congress's authority to regulate on the subject of debtor-creditor relations. First, Congress's power under the Bankruptcy Clause is limited to the adjustment of the debts of *insolvent* debtors and their creditors and does not extend to the general regulation of debtor-creditor law. Previous bankruptcy laws required that the debtor be insolvent as a condition for bankruptcy, but the current Bankruptcy Code contains no such limitation. Second, Congress's bankruptcy power was limited to the adjustment of relations between a debtor and its creditors and does not extend to the protection or benefit of third parties, except to the extent that such protection is ancillary to the adjustment of the debts of an insolvent debtor. This original limitation is also ineffective today.

The Bankruptcy Code thus represents a tenuous accommodation between federal and state law. Most of the nonbankruptcy law that governs debtor-creditor relations remains state law, and federal bankruptcy law honors these state-law substantive entitlements, unless federal law and policy expressly preempts them. Moreover, the Bankruptcy Code expressly incorporates some elements of state law into the Code itself, such as in the treatment of a debtor's property exemptions. This interaction between state and federal law guarantees that creditors and debtors will be treated differently depending on the state that determines their rights.

At the same time, any bankruptcy legislation enacted by Congress must also be "uniform...throughout the United States." In *Hanover National Bank v. Moyses* (1902), the Supreme Court held that this "personal" nonuniformity in treatment among individuals was permissible, so long as "geographical" uniformity was preserved. Thus, debtors and creditors in *different states* may receive different treatment, so long as the debtors and creditors within the *same state* are treated the same. The "uniformity" requirement does, however, forbid "private" bankruptcy laws that affect only particular debtors.

Todd Zywicki

See Also

Article I, Section 8, Clause 3 (Commerce Among the States)

Article I, Section 10, Clause 1 (Obligation of Contract)

Article III

Article IV, Section 1 (Full Faith and Credit Clause)

Amendment V (Takings Clause)

Amendment VII (Right to Jury in Civil Cases)

Amendment XI (Suits Against a State)

Suggestions for Further Research

Peter J. Coleman, Debtors and Creditors in America: Insolvency, Imprisonment for Debt, and Bankruptcy, 1607–1900 (1999)

Frank R. Kennedy, *Bankruptcy and the Constitution*, in Blessings of Liberty: The Constitution and the Practice of Law, 131–174 (1988)

Judith Schenck Koffler, *The Bankruptcy Clause and Exemption Laws: A Reexamination of the Doctrine of Geographic Uniformity*, 58 N.Y.U. L. Rev. 22 (1983)

Kurt H. Nadelmann, *On the Origin of the Bankruptcy Clause*, 1 Am. J. Legal Hist. 215 (1957)

Thomas E. Plank, *The Constitutional Limits of Bankruptcy*, 63 Tenn. L. Rev. 487 (1996)

DAVID A. SKEEL, JR., DEBT'S DOMINION: A HISTORY OF BANKRUPTCY LAW IN AMERICA (2001)

Charles Jordan Tabb, *The History of the Bankruptcy Laws in the United States*, 3 AM. BANKR. INST. L. REV. 5 (1995)

CHARLES WARREN, BANKRUPTCY IN UNITED STATES HISTORY (1935)

Significant Cases

Sturges v. Crowninshield, 17 U.S. (4 Wheat.) 122 (1819)

Ogden v. Saunders, 25 U.S. (12 Wheat.) 213 (1827)

Hanover National Bank v. Moyses, 186 U.S. 181 (1902)

Louisville Joint Stock Land Bank v. Radford, 295 U.S. 555 (1935)

Northern Pipeline Construction Co. v. Marathon Pipe Line Co., 458 U.S. 50 (1982)

Coinage Clause

The Congress shall have Power To ... coin Money, regulate the Value thereof, and of foreign Coin ....

(ARTICLE I, SECTION 8, CLAUSE 5)

~

*C*ongress's power to coin money is exclusive: under Article I, Section 10, the states are not permitted to "coin Money; emit Bills of Credit; [or] make any Thing but gold and silver Coin a Tender in Payment of Debts...." Whereas the prohibitions on the states are clear and detailed, Congress's grant of power under the Coinage Clause is open-ended.

Nonetheless, certain elements are clear. First, Congress is granted the authority to "coin money," which authorizes Congress to coin money from precious metals such as gold and silver. Under the Articles of Confederation, the power to coin money was a concurrent power of Congress and the states. To create a more standardized monetary system and reduce the costs of running mints, the Constitution granted this power to Congress exclusively. The elimination of the states' power to coin money and the exclusive grant to Congress provoked controversy because the power to coin money was tradition-

ally understood as a symbol of political sovereignty. Second, Congress is empowered to regulate the value of the coins struck domestically and to set the value of foreign coins. Under the Articles, Congress held the former power but not the latter. The Constitution gave both powers to Congress to encourage domestic and foreign commerce by preventing the states from attaching disparate valuations to circulating coins.

Beyond these simple issues, however, the scope of the federal government's powers under the Coinage Clause is unclear. In particular, although the Coinage Clause empowers Congress to *coin* money from precious metals, it is not clear whether the federal government could also issue *paper* money. Linguistic and conceptual usage during the Founding era distinguished between several different concepts: the power to "coin" specie money (i.e., money backed by gold or silver), the power to borrow money through the issuance of interest-bearing "notes," and the issuance of "Bills of Credit." Unlike coined money, whose value was inherent in the metal that composed the coin, and unlike "notes" that accrued interest, a bill of credit was non–interest-bearing paper money issued on the good credit of the United States with no tangible backing in precious metal.

Under the Articles of Confederation, both the federal and state governments were guilty of rampant inflationary issuance of bills of credit to finance the Revolutionary War. In response to the revolutionary history, Article I, Section 10, of the Constitution expressly prohibits the states from issuing bills of credit. With respect to Congress's power, however, the issue is not as clear. At the Constitutional Convention, it was proposed to give the federal government the power to "emit bills on the credit of the United States," but the language was defeated as being too prone to abuse. As a result, the Constitution's monetary clauses expressly grant Congress the power to coin money and to borrow money by issuing "notes" (i.e., interest-bearing government bonds), but not to issue bills of credit. Given the Framers' general hostility to paper money (James Madison, for instance, bemoaned its "pestilent effects" under the Articles), it is likely that the Framers' intended to prohibit the federal government from issuing bills of credit, just as they expressly barred the states from doing so. Moreover, the Constitution itself created a government of enumerated powers; thus, absent an express grant, Congress lacked the power to act. In fact, both those who spoke for and those who spoke against the proposed language to grant this power to the federal government understood that striking the language amounted to a prohibition on Congress's power to issue paper money.

The monetary system that prevailed throughout most of the eighteenth and nineteenth centuries up until the Civil War comprised a hodgepodge of different types of money. Circulating money consisted of specie, coins minted by the government; privately minted coins; certain foreign coins; and paper banknotes issued by state-chartered private banks and backed by those institutions. Congress regulated the weight of gold and silver required to be contained in coins, but these ratios were often manipulated for political purposes. There were also several private mints, which stamped coins whose value reflected their intrinsic weight in specie. The dominant form of circulating money for most of this period was currency issued by state-chartered private banks and redeemable in gold or silver from the banks. Privately stamped "token" money, often made of copper, also circulated as an instrument for low-value exchange.

In general, the federal government did not issue fiat money (paper money not backed by specie) prior to the Civil War. Issuances were usually short-lived and were intended to be temporary solutions for government finance needs during a war or to shore up the bank system during a crisis. They were receivable for payment of government obligations and taxes, but none of these issuances were declared legal tender for private debts, although they did circulate for private transactions to some degree. Issuances usually were interest-bearing and of relatively large denominations that discouraged the circulation of the notes as money. The federal government issued large denomination interest-bearing notes at the outset of the War of 1812, but subsequent issuances declined in denomination and did not pay interest. Interest-bearing notes also were issued in response

to the Panic of 1837. Notwithstanding the Framers' opposition to paper money and principles of constitutional interpretation that suggest that Congress is barred from issuing paper money, in *Veazie Bank v. Fenno* (1869), the Supreme Court held that the federal government's issuance of bills of credit to fund government operations was a valid exercise of the Necessary and Proper Clause.

To fund the Civil War, Congress also passed the Legal Tender Act of 1862. Unlike earlier issuances that were used to pay government obligations (as well as the paper money issued by the Confederate government), Civil War "greenbacks" (for which redemption in gold was "postponed") were for the first time declared legal tender for all debts, public or private. Even if the federal government had the authority to issue bills for payment of government obligations, it was a distinct question whether the federal government could also force private individuals to accept them for private contracts, an issue specifically withheld in *Veazie Bank*.

The Framers believed that in prohibiting the authority of the federal government from issuing bills of credit, they also were prohibiting their recognition as legal tender by definition. Moreover, they also separately and expressly barred the states from recognizing anything as legal tender other than gold or silver, which was generally understood as further evidence of the Framer's hostility to legal tender laws. Even those at the Constitutional Convention who supported Congress's power to issue bills of credit opposed granting the power to declare them legal tender.

In a series of nineteenth-century cases dubbed *The Legal Tender Cases*, the Supreme Court addressed the federal government's power to order its bills of credit to be accepted as legal tender for all debts, public and private. In *Hepburn v. Griswold* (1870), the Court held it a violation of the Obligation of Contract Clause to retroactively alter contract terms by permitting payment in "greenbacks" of an obligation incurred in gold dollars. Greenbacks were not immediately redeemable in gold. Following a dramatic change in membership, however, just one year later in the *Knox v. Lee* (1871), the Court expressly overruled *Hepburn* and upheld the Legal Tender Act as applied to both prospective and retrospective debts. Pointing to the crisis occasioned by the Civil War, *Knox* upheld the power to declare paper money to be legal tender. In *Julliard v. Greenman* (1884), the Supreme Court extended *Knox*, upholding the validity of legal tender laws during peacetime. The Court held that the federal government's monetary power was inherent in its sovereignty; thus it need not be enumerated in the Constitution. Justice Stephen Field's blunt dissent declared, "If there be anything in the history of the Constitution which can be established with moral certainty, it is that the framers of that instrument intended to prohibit the issue of legal tender notes both by the general government and by the States; and thus prevent interference with the contracts of private parties." The recognition of Congress's expansive discretion on monetary issues in *The Legal-Tender Cases* was later used to support the federal government's invalidation of gold clauses in private contracts in the 1930s.

Todd Zywicki

See Also

Article I, Section 8, Clause 2 (Borrowing Clause)
Article I, Section 8, Clause 18 (Necessary and Proper Clause)
Article I, Section 10, Clause 1 (State Coinage)
Article I, Section 10, Clause 1 (Obligation of Contract)

Suggestions for Further Research

Kenneth W. Dam, *The Legal Tender Cases*, 12 Sup. Ct. Rev. 367 (1982)

Bernard H. Siegan, The Supreme Court's Constitution: An Inquiry into Judicial Review and Its Impact on Society (1987)

James B. Thayer, *Legal Tender*, 1 Harv. L. Rev. 73 (1887–1888)

Richard Timberlake, Gold, Greenbacks, and the Constitution (1991)

Thomas Wilson, The Power "to Coin" Money: The Exercise of Monetary Powers by the Congress (1992)

Significant Cases

Craig v. Missouri, 29 U.S. (4 Pet.) 410 (1830)
Bronson v. Rodes, 74 U.S. (7 Wall.) 229 (1868)
Veazie Bank v. Fenno, 75 U.S. (8 Wall.) 533 (1869)
Hepburn v. Griswold, 75 U.S. (8 Wall.) 603 (1870), *overruled in part by* Legal Tender Cases (Knox v. Lee) 79 U.S. (12 Wall.) 457 (1871); *sub nom.* The Legal-Tender Cases (Julliard v. Greenman), 110 U.S. 421 (1884)

Weights and Measures

The Congress shall have Power To . . . fix the Standard of Weights and Measures . . . .
(Article I, Section 8, Clause 5)

∼

*T*he Articles of Confederation was the immediate source that gave the central government "the sole and exclusive right and power of . . . fixing the Standard of Weights and Measures throughout the United States." Article IX, Section 4. More remotely, the power to establish national standards of weights and measures resided in the English Crown or Parliament from the late eleventh century, although it appears that official standards were frequently ignored throughout England. The phrase itself dates from the late fourteenth century.

By the time of the Constitutional Convention, it appears that the Weights and Measures Clause was not an attempt to remedy a situation in which various standards obtained in various parts of the country. There already existed a customary uniformity. Rather, the purpose in granting this power was to facilitate domestic and international commerce by permitting the federal government to adopt and enforce national measurement standards based upon the prevailing consensus. The clause excited no controversy among the Framers or in the ratifying conventions.

During their respective tenures as Secretary of State, Thomas Jefferson and John Quincy Adams, as well as a House Committee, produced extensive studies calling for congressional adoption of uniform standards. The reports by the House and Adams rejected adopting the metric system of France and proposed no federal enforcement mechanism, leaving the application of the standards to the executives of the several states. Nonetheless, Congress did not adopt any systems of weights or measures, although the Treasury Department established standards for the pound, yard, gallon, and bushel for customs purposes.

In the face of congressional inaction, many states defined standard measures for trade purposes. No Supreme Court case has explicitly held that the states are free to establish such standards in the absence of congressional action, although Justice Oliver Wendall Holmes intimated as much in *Massachusetts State Grange v. Benton* (1926).

Congress has acquiesced in (though never authorized) the use of the traditional English system of weights and measures in nonbusiness activities. In 1866, Congress authorized, but did not mandate, the use of the metric system and, since 1975, the metric system has been the "preferred system" for trade and commerce. The National Institute of Standards and Technology of the Department of Commerce periodically publishes standards for English and metric weights and measures.

Eric Chiappinelli

See Also

Article I, Section 8, Clause 1 (Uniformity Clause)

Article I, Section 8, Clause 3 (Commerce with Foreign Nations)

Article I, Section 8, Clause 3 (Commerce Among the States)

Article I, Section 8, Clause 8 (Patent and Copyright Clause)

Article I, Section 8, Clause 18 (Necessary and Proper Clause)

Amendment X (Reserved Powers of the States)

Suggestions for Further Research

David P. Currie, *Weights & Measures*, 2 Green Bag 2d 261 (1999)

Lewis V. Judson, Weights and Measures Standards of the United States (1976)

Significant Cases

The Miantinoni, 17 F. Cas. 254 (C.C.W.D. Pa. 1855) (No. 9521)

Massachusetts State Grange v. Benton, 272 U.S. 525 (1926)

Counterfeiting

The Congress shall have Power To . . . provide for the Punishment of counterfeiting the Securities and current Coin of the United States . . . .
(**Article I, Section 8, Clause 6**)

∾

*A*t the Constitutional Convention, Gouverneur Morris voiced concern that "[b]ills of exchange . . . might be forged in one State and carried into another." Another delegate feared that the counterfeiting of "foreign paper" might embarrass foreign relations. Consequently, when Oliver Ellsworth moved to allow Congress the power to punish "counterfeiting the securities and current coin of the U. States," it was unanimously approved. Yet in light of the Necessary and Proper Clause, it is not clear why there was a need for this power to be defined in the Constitution at all. Justice Joseph Story later declared in his *Commentaries on the Constitution of the United States* that "this power [to provide for the punishment of counterfeiting] would naturally flow, as an incident, from the antecedent powers to borrow money and regulate the coinage; and, indeed, without it those powers would be without any adequate sanction."

Nonetheless, there are three reasons why a separate delegated power to punish counterfeiting is appropriate. First, the Framers took pains to undo the British law on treason, which included counterfeiting and was often punished by parliamentary bills of attainder. Thus, the Constitution defines the crime of treason in terms that leave Congress no power to expand it. The Constitution also prohibits bills of attainder. But the Framers did want authority over the remaining formerly treasonous crime of counterfeiting to be left in the hands of the national legislature. Otherwise, having denied Congress the power to define treason, it might be inferred that the Constitution also denied Congress the power to legislate against counterfeiting.

Second, the Framers lodged all the incidents of the foreign-affairs power in the national government. Counterfeiting of foreign securities was a serious breach of international comity. The clause empowers Congress to deal with an important element of the nation's international obligations.

Third, the clause betokens federal supremacy in the field of monetary policy. In *The Federalist* No. 42, James Madison includes the power over counterfeiting as among those powers "which provide for the harmony and proper intercourse among states." The implication is that, like commerce, the power over counterfeiting is exclusive and plenary. Justice Joseph Story was explicit: "this power would seem to be exclusive of that of the States, since it grows out of the Constitution, as an appropriate means to carry into effect other delegated powers, not antecedently existing in the States."

In the hands of the judiciary, however, the power became limited and eventually superfluous. In *Fox v. Ohio* (1847), the Supreme Court upheld an Ohio law that punished the "passing" or "uttering" of counterfeited money. The Court reasoned that the actual act of counterfeiting was an offense directed at the federal government, whereas uttering counterfeited money was a "private harm" within a state's police power. As the Supreme Court of South Carolina explained in *State v. Tutt* (1831): "The offence against the Government of the United States consists in discrediting its currency. That against the State in defrauding its citizens. The offence against the State is certainly of the more palpable and dangerous character." The result is that although the federal government has exclusive power to punish the actual act of counterfeiting, states have the concurrent power to punish the passing of counterfeited currency. The federal and state governments possess concurrent power to punish the possession of devices for making counterfeited money. *Baender v. Barnett* (1921).

In cases upholding the right of Congress to punish counterfeiting coinage, *United States v.*

Marigold (1850), and counterfeiting foreign currency, *United States v. Arjona* (1887), the Court justified Congress's power under the Coinage Clause, the Necessary and Proper Clause, the Commerce Clause, and the Counterfeiting Clause. In practical terms, there seems little if any activity that can be reached under the Counterfeiting Clause that could not also be reached by other congressional powers. The Court, however, does apply the First Amendment to legislation passed under the Counterfeiting Clause. In *Regan v. Time, Inc.* (1984), the Court struck down a portion of the statute permitting limited reproduction of United States currency "for philatelic, numismatic, educational, historical, or newsworthy purposes" as being content-based.

Congress passed the first anti-counterfeiting statute in 1790. The current federal prohibition on counterfeiting is found in 18 U.S.C. §§ 470–513 (2004), which generally provides for an unspecified fine or imprisonment of not more than twenty years, or both, for its violation.

David F. Forte

See Also

Article I, Section 8, Clause 3 (Commerce Among the States)
Article I, Section 8, Clause 5 (Coinage Clause)
Article I, Section 8, Clause 18 (Necessary and Proper Clause)
Article I, Section 10, Clause 1 (State Coinage)

Suggestion for Further Research

Nathan K. Cummings, *The Counterfeit Buck Stops Here: National Security Issues in the Redesign of U.S. Currency*, 8 S. Cal. Interdisc. L.J. 539 (1999)

Significant Cases

State v. Tutt, 18 S.C.L. (2 Bail.) 44 (1831)
Fox v. Ohio, 46 U.S. (5 How.) 410 (1847)
United States v. Marigold, 50 U.S. (9 How.) 560 (1850)
United States v. Arjona, 120 U.S. 479 (1887)
Sexton v. California, 189 U.S. 319 (1903)
Baender v. Barnett, 255 U.S. 224 (1921)
Regan v. Time, Inc., 468 U.S. 641 (1984)

Post Office

The Congress shall have Power
To...establish Post Offices and
post Roads....
(ARTICLE I, SECTION 8, CLAUSE 7)

≈

Under the Articles of Confederation, Congress possessed the power to establish and regulate post offices. The Framers easily transferred the power into the Constitution and gave Congress the additional authority to establish postal roads. At the Constitutional Convention, Benjamin Franklin suggested that Congress should also have the "power to provide for cutting canals where deemed necessary," and James Madison sought to enlarge the power "to grant charters of incorporation where the interest of the U.S. might require & the legislative provisions of individual States may be incompetent." However, the Founders turned aside these extensions on the ground that such powers were already assumed in the power to regulate trade.

Following the adoption of the Constitution, the Act of September 22, 1789 (1 Stat. 70), established (at first temporarily) a post office and created the Office of the Postmaster General. By that time, seventy-five post offices and over 2000 miles of post roads already existed. What was originally thought to be a rather simple and benign power soon turned controversial; legislatures disagreed over whether this power merely enabled Congress to direct where post offices should be located and on what roads mail should be carried, or whether it authorized Congress to construct and maintain roads and post offices within the states. Thomas Jefferson and James Monroe doubted whether the clause granted Congress the power to construct roads, whereas many in Congress asserted that it did have such power. In fact, most congressional enactments merely designated post roads, but in 1833, Justice Joseph Story declared in his *Commentaries on the Constitution of the United States* that the words "to establish" encompass a power to create roads as well as to designate them. Story maintained, however, that once built, a post road is subject to the laws of the state. In 1845, in the case of *Searight v. Stokes*, Chief Justice Roger B. Taney held that mail carriages are immune to state road taxes on the Cumberland Road, but, over the dissent of Justice Peter V. Daniel, he specifically avoided the question of the power of Congress to construct post roads.

Story's view has stronger textual support than does Jefferson's. The power "to establish an uniform Rule of Naturalization, and uniform Laws on the subject of Bankruptcies" (Article I, Section 8, Clause 4), and the power of Congress to "establish" inferior federal courts (Article III, Section 1) clearly contemplate the creation of such laws and courts, respectively. Congress would seem to have a similar creative power in establishing post roads.

The Supreme Court has consistently interpreted the Post Office Clause broadly. In *Ex parte Jackson* (1877), the Supreme Court held that congressional power over the mail is indeed far-reaching, including the right to determine what can and cannot be mailed:

> The validity of legislation describing what should be carried, and its weight and form, and the charges to which it should be subjected, has never been questioned.... The power possessed by Congress embraces the regulation of the entire Postal System of the country. The right to designate what shall be carried necessarily involves the right to determine what shall be excluded.

In *In re Rapier* (1892), the Court held that Congress has exclusive jurisdiction over the mail, which includes the right to prohibit the circulation of materials that are immoral and injurious, such as lottery tickets. The Court in *Brennan v. United States Postal Service* (1978) reaffirmed the government's monopoly over the postal system; and in *United States Postal Service v. Council of Greenburgh Civic Ass'ns* (1981), the Court upheld a federal law prohibiting the placing of unstamped mail in home mailboxes.

During World War I, the government's power to ban incendiary and disloyal material figured largely in prosecutions under the Espionage Act of 1917. *See Masses Publishing Co. v. Patten* (1917). Later cases dealt with laws prohibiting the mailing of obscene material. *Roth v. United States* (1957); *United States v. Reidel* (1971). Meanwhile, lower courts added that regulations governing what materials could be mailed are subject to First Amendment scrutiny. *See United States v. Handler* (1974). The Supreme Court has affirmed that, like all other delegated powers, the post-office power is subject to extrinsic restraints such as the First Amendment. For example, in *Postal Service v. Council of Greenburgh Civic Ass'ns*, the Supreme Court acknowledged the broad sweep of the Post Office Clause, all the while holding that its broad power cannot be exercised in a way that abridges the rights protected under the First Amendment.

Another area of recent contention relevant to the Post Office Clause is the franking privilege, which exempts all federal governmental officials from paying postage when conducting official business. The frank itself is a reproduction of the Member's signature, which is affixed to the mailed item in lieu of a stamp. Members of the House of Commons and Members of the Continental Congress enjoyed the privilege. The First Congress retained the privilege in 1789. The act of 1895, 28 Stat. 601, 622 § 85, restricted the use of the privilege only for correspondence on "official business," to be interpreted by the Post Office Department, which would issue advisory opinions on whether a contemplated mailing could be franked. By 1971, the Post Office Department relinquished any responsibility to give advisory opinions. This led to a number of lawsuits by disgruntled candidates who ran against incumbent Members who used their franking privileges in mass mailings to constituents. Abuses became more flagrant, and the Franking Act of 1973, Pub. L. No. 93–191, 39 U.S.C. § 3210, was enacted to limit "official business" to "cover all matters which directly or indirectly pertain to the legislative process...." The Act also laid out a noninclusive list of what constitutes official business, and established two special commissions, the House Commission on Congressional Mailing Standards and the Select Committee

on Standards and Conduct of the Senate, to provide advisory opinions as to whether certain business is official or not.

David F. Forte

See Also

Article I, Section 8, Clause 4 (Naturalization)

Article III, Section 1 (Inferior Courts)

Significant Cases

Searight v. Stokes, 44 U.S. (3 How.) 151 (1845)

Ex parte Jackson, 96 U.S. 727 (1877)

In re Rapier, 143 U.S. 110 (1892)

Masses Publishing Co. v. Patten, 244 F. 535 (S.D.N.Y. 1917), *rev'd* 246 F. 24 (2d Cir. 1917)

Roth v. United States, 354 U.S. 476 (1957)

United States v. Reidel, 402 U.S. 351 (1971)

United States v. Handler, 383 F. Supp. 1267 (D. Md. 1974)

Brennan v. United States Postal Service, 439 U.S. 1345 (1978)

United States Postal Service v. Council of Greenburgh Civic Ass'ns, 453 U.S. 114 (1981)

Patent and Copyright Clause

The Congress shall have Power To... promote the Progress of Science and useful Arts, by securing for limited Times to Authors and Inventors the exclusive Right to their respective Writings and Discoveries....

(ARTICLE I, SECTION 8, CLAUSE 8)

≈

There is little direct evidence about the Patent and Copyright Clause's original meaning. The clause neither represented a legal tradition of great historical and practical significance to the Framers, unlike the availability of habeas corpus (*see* Article I, Section 9, Clause 2), nor was it one of the great structural innovations of the Constitution that attracted so much attention because of its gravity and novelty.

Rather, the clause appears to have been largely an afterthought.

What little direct evidence we have about the circumstances of the clause's adoption has been of little help in resolving the disputes that have arisen, many of them quite recently, over its meaning. The clause was the subject of little debate during the Constitutional Convention, nor was it a major topic of discussion during the ratification debates. James Madison, in his wrap-up of "miscellaneous powers" in *The Federalist* No. 43, devoted only a single paragraph to the clause, justifying it both on the need to provide a national, uniform standard of intellectual property regulation as well as on the merits of the protection itself. "The copy right of authors," Madison wrote, "has been solemnly adjudged in Great Britain to be a right at Common Law. The right to useful inventions seems with equal reason to belong to the inventors." On this point Madison was mistaken; the House of Lords had decided in 1774 that copyright was not a common-law right, and invention patents had always been granted as a matter of crown or parliamentary discretion. In the very same breath as he extolled a natural-rights view of intellectual property, however, Madison also struck upon an incentives-based approach, justifying intellectual property regulation by its contribution to the public, as well as private, benefit. Madison concluded, "The public good coincides in both cases with the claims of individuals." He did not address the question of what to do in cases in which the public's good is not served by extending intellectual property rights.

In the end, no one appears to have objected seriously to the clause. George Mason and Thomas Jefferson (privately to Madison), along with a few other Anti-Federalists, raised concerns over the granting of state-sanctioned monopolies, which the Framers certainly disfavored as a general matter. But no one took the clause to authorize federal trade monopolies, and such objections were rebuffed by Federalists (in Jefferson's case by Madison himself) by reference to the value of granting copyright and patents and the need for national uniformity, which no one appears to have questioned.

The clause's text has been of limited help in resolving modern disputes over its meaning.

Although some commentators have developed complex textual arguments about the clause, courts have been wary of applying the many limits potentially to be mined from its wording. In fact, with one early exception, the Court has deferred to Congress's view of its own powers under the clause. For example, in *Eldred v. Ashcroft* (2003), the Court upheld not only Congress's extension of the duration of copyrights to almost five times what it was in the 1790 copyright act, it also ruled that the requirement that copyrights be for "limited Times" did not prevent Congress from extending the copyright term for a work already under protection. The Court's rationale was largely based on historical practice. The exception was the *In re Trade-Mark Cases* (1879), in which the Supreme Court held that the clause did not provide authority for federal trademark legislation. Even that limit was eventually circumvented by Congress's use of the commerce power as authority for trademark legislation.

The Court has, nevertheless, shed light on some of the clause's terms. In *Burrow-Giles Lithographic Co. v. Sarony* (1884), the Court held that protection for photographs was within the clause even though the clause limits copyright to "Writings" and "Authors," partly because the first Congress granted copyright protection to other graphical works (such as maps and charts) and partly because the Court decided that "author" was more accurately defined as "originator" rather than "writer." The Court later extended this logic to allow protection for sculptures as well.

Other statements of the Court have suggested intrinsic limits to the clause. Thus, in *Graham v. John Deere Co.* (1966), the Court declared that Congress may not grant patents "without regard to the innovation, advancement or social benefit gained thereby" or "whose effects are to remove information from the public domain or to restrict free access to materials already available." More generally, it concluded that the patent system as adopted must "promote the Progress of . . . useful Arts." In *Feist Publications, Inc. v. Rural Telephone Service Co.* (1991), the Court stated that because the clause permits copyright protection only for creative works, facts cannot be copyrighted. But neither *Graham* nor *Feist* involved challenges to Congress's power; neither case required the Court to apply the limits it had found in the clause. The Court has frequently repeated its statement in *Graham* that "[t]he clause is both a grant of a power and a limitation," but at the same time it has explained that "it is generally for Congress, not the courts, to decide how best to pursue the Copyright Clause's objectives." *Eldred v. Ashcroft.*

It would seem that the courts would not approve of a facially perpetual grant, although many would argue that the current copyright term is already functionally equivalent to perpetual. More problematical are situations in which Congress either has granted or may grant exclusive rights to items that have up until now been considered to be outside the clause's traditional reach, such as database protection, protection for inventions not reaching the standard for patentability, or renewed protection for some works that have fallen into the public domain.

It is possible that, given the strongly deferential approach in *Eldred*, the Court will permit some of these new grants under the clause when it finally has to confront them, particularly if Congress supports them with thoughtful inquiry and findings. Nevertheless, proponents of such measures might rely on constitutional powers unencumbered by the Patent and Copyright Clause's many limitations. Two have sprung to the forefront: the power to regulate interstate commerce and, because some of these new grants are intended to bring the United States into compliance with international intellectual property conventions, the treaty power. Courts have so far approached the problem with caution, finding authority in other parts of the Constitution for Congress to grant exclusive rights but in part because they found that, while the Patent and Copyright Clause did not authorize the grants, they were nonetheless consistent with it. The issue is still being litigated and is far from settled.

Just as proponents of broader exclusive rights have looked to other parts of the Constitution, so too have their opponents. In *Harper & Row Publishers, Inc. v. Nation Enterprises* (1985), the Court acknowledged the possibility that copyright legislation might result in so heavy a burden on speech as to run afoul of the First Amendment. So far, however, the Court has held that copyright in its current form presents, on its face, no First Amendment problem. With the ever-increasing importance of information to the economy, it is safe to say that constitutional challenges to intellectual property laws will become more frequent.

Thomas Nachbar

See Also

Article I, Section 8, Clause 3 (Commerce Among the States)

Article I, Section 9, Clause 2 (Habeas Corpus)

Article II, Section 2, Clause 2 (Treaty Clause)

Amendment I (Freedom of Speech and of the Press)

Suggestions for Further Research

Bruce W. Bugbee, Genesis of American Patent and Copyright Law (1967)

Jane C. Ginsburg, *No "Sweat"? Copyright and Other Protection of Works of Information after* Feist v. Rural Telephone, 92 Colum. L. Rev. 338 (1992)

Paul J. Heald & Suzanna Sherry, *Implied Limits on the Legislative Power: The Intellectual Property Clause as an Absolute Constraint on Congress*, 2000 U. Ill. L. Rev. 1119 (2000)

Thomas B. Nachbar, *Intellectual Property and Constitutional Norms*, 104 Colum. L. Rev. 272 (2004)

Tyler T. Ochoa & Mark Rose, *The Anti-Monopoly Origins of the Patent and Copyright Clause*, 84 J. Pat. & Trademark Off. Soc'y 909 (2002)

Edward C. Walterscheid, The Nature of the Intellectual Property Clause: A Study in Historical Perspective (2002)

Significant Cases

In re Trade-Mark Cases, 100 U.S. 82 (1879)

Burrow-Giles Lithographic Co. v. Sarony, 111 U.S. 53 (1884)

Graham v. John Deere Co., 383 U.S. 1 (1966)

Harper & Row Publishers, Inc. v. Nation Enterprises, 471 U.S. 539 (1985)

Feist Publications, Inc. v. Rural Telephone Service Co., 499 U.S. 340 (1991)

United States v. Moghadam, 175 F.3d 1269 (11th Cir. 1999)

Eldred v. Ashcroft, 537 U.S. 186 (2003)

Inferior Courts

The Congress shall have Power To
...constitute Tribunals inferior to
the supreme Court....
(ARTICLE I, SECTION 8, CLAUSE 9)

∾

*W*hile the Constitutional Convention agreed
that the new central government should include
a permanent judiciary, there was disagreement
over its size. The original proposal (the Virginia
Plan) called for "one or more supreme tribunals" as well as "inferior tribunals." (In English and American usage at that time, "supreme"
and "inferior" were normally used to indicate
different breadths of geographic or subject matter competence, rather than appellate hierarchy;
Virginia, for example, had four "supreme"
courts, with a complex of relations among
them.) Many of the delegates, however, believed
it would be sufficient to have a single national
court, empowered to review certain state court
judgments. By successive amendments, those
delegates succeeded first in reducing the number of "supreme" courts to one and then in eliminating the reference to "inferior" courts.

The latter vote was very close, however; James
Madison moved as a compromise "that the
National Legislature be empowered to institute
inferior tribunals." Madison repeated his earlier
argument that "unless inferior tribunals were
dispersed throughout the Republic with *final*
jurisdiction in *many* cases" [the words are
emphasized in Madison's own notes], there
would be docket overload and oppressive
expense. The delegates' approval of this compromise resulted in three separate but related constitutional provisions: the Inferior Courts Clause
in Article I, granting Congress power (and discretion) to constitute "inferior" tribunals; the
phrase in Article III, alluding to "such inferior
Courts as the Congress may from time to time
ordain and establish"; and the Appellate Jurisdiction Clause in Article III, Section 2, Clause 2,
which provides that judgments may be excluded
by Congress from Supreme Court review.

Some commentaries and judicial opinions
have maintained that the Inferior Courts Clause

implies congressional discretion to determine
how much of the subject-matter jurisdiction
authorized by Article III should actually be vested in federal courts. The Framers, however,
rejected every attempt to give such discretion to
Congress. Instead they insisted upon specifying
in the Constitution itself the subject-matter
extent of "the judicial Power of the United
States" and directed in mandatory language that
it "shall be vested" in the national judiciary (to
consist of the one "supreme" and whatever "inferior" courts Congress might establish). Indeed,
the Framers specifically voted down a succession
of proposals that would have empowered Congress to exclude subject matters from the inferi-
or courts; with regard to the "supreme" court,
though, they included the Appellate Jurisdiction
Clause, so that if Congress did create "inferior"
courts, these could be given "*final* jurisdiction in
many cases," as Madison had urged.

It does not follow that every inferior court
must have the full range of competence prescribed by Article III. Barely a week before final-
izing the scope of subject-matter jurisdiction,
the delegates had approved the Necessary and
Proper Clause (Article I, Section 8, Clause 18),
which the Committee of Detail had devised, in
part, for the very purpose of empowering Congress to organize the judicial branch. It must
have been obvious that, if inferior tribunals
were created at all, this Necessary and Proper
Clause would enable Congress to *distribute* the
jurisdiction prescribed by Article III without
diminishing the collective competence of the
federal judiciary as a whole. It logically follows
that Congress may constitute specialized tribunals for admiralty, bankruptcy, or diversity
cases, for example, so long as it makes one or
another federal tribunal available for each subject matter on the Article III list.

Congress's power to organize the judicial
branch goes beyond constituting inferior courts
and distributing the Article III subject-matter
jurisdiction. Congress also may designate some
courts for trials, others for appeals, and (if it
chooses) some for both; it may facilitate,
restrict, or preclude appellate review, and prescribe its procedural course; and it may legislate
rules of evidence and practice.

As to the latter, ever since the Justices affirmed the argument of Attorney General Edmund Randolph regarding process and service in *Chisholm v. Georgia* (1793), it has been understood that, where Congress is silent, federal courts can establish procedures of their own, but that legislation regarding procedure prevails by virtue of the Supremacy Clause. Congressional discretion over procedural matters is not unlimited, however. If its power were really derived from the Tribunals Clause (which contains no intrinsic limit), Congress could even dictate procedures impeding the judiciary or impairing the independence at which the judicial tenure and salary guarantees of the Constitution are aimed. Because this power actually comes from the Necessary and Proper Clause, however, laws regarding the judiciary must satisfy the requirement that they be "necessary and proper for carrying into Execution the . . . Powers vested by this Constitution in [the judicial] department . . . ." This intrinsic limit leaves ample discretion to Congress as to whether and how to assist, but if judges find a procedure enacted by Congress incompatible with the independent performance of their own constitutional duties, it would seem that they are bound by their oaths to disregard it.

While the judges of inferior federal courts have the same tenure and compensation guarantees as Supreme Court Justices, it may not necessarily follow that they must be nominated or appointed in the same political manner. Lower federal court judges might be considered "inferior Officers," whose appointment Congress is empowered by the Appointments Clause to vest "in the President alone, in the Courts of Law, or in the Heads of Departments." In any event, Congress has not yet attempted to dispense with either presidential appointment or Senate confirmation for life-tenured inferior court judges.

The Judiciary Act of 1789, drafted in the first Congress by a Senate committee—half of whose members had participated at the Constitutional Convention—established a federal court system very different from that which is familiar today. Reflection on that system helps one understand how much discretion the Constitution gives Congress regarding judicial system design. Single-judge district courts heard admiralty matters, tried civil "forfeiture" proceedings (a category which, at the time, embraced federal question claims), and exercised concurrent jurisdiction over minor federal crimes. Three-judge circuit courts were the principal federal tribunals; they tried diversity cases and most federal crimes, heard cases removed from state courts, and could review most of the single-judge district courts' decisions. Supreme Court Justices spent most of their time presiding at the several circuit courts. They gathered only briefly twice each year to try matters within the Supreme Court's scant original jurisdiction and to hear a few appellate cases. However, Supreme Court review was not available for any criminal case (unless by habeas corpus) or for civil cases that had begun in a district court. Except for federal question cases from state courts, no other case could reach the Supreme Court unless the amount in controversy exceeded a sum that very few Americans at that time could hope to earn in a year.

Supreme Court review of inferior federal courts was rare. Statistics confirm that most federal court litigation began and ended in the circuit courts. The establishment thus conformed to Madison's model of "inferior tribunals . . . dispersed throughout the Republic with *final* jurisdiction in *many* cases . . . ." So decentralized a judiciary, while certainly able to give the laws concrete applications, could hardly be a political organ. It was consistent with Alexander Hamilton's prediction in *The Federalist* No. 78 that the judiciary could "take no active resolution whatever" and "may truly be said to have neither Force nor Will, but merely judgment."

This basic framework of 1789, with slight modifications, was still in place when Alexis de Tocqueville visited America in 1831. Tocqueville described the practice of judicial review in this distinctly nonhierarchical judicial system as "one of the most powerful barriers ever erected against the tyranny of political assemblies." He observed that when any judge, from constitutional conviction, "refuses to apply a law in a case, it loses at once part of its moral force," prompting other litigants to contest it, too. Then, should other judges reach the same conclusion, the force of that law would be further diminished; but, Tocqueville observed, "it is only gradually, under repeated judicial blows, that it finally succumbs." Thus the accumulation of independent judgments, rather than any central, authoritative pronouncement, safeguarded the Constitution. At the same time, the consequences of an ill-considered ruling would probably be confined to the particular parties and case.

Not everyone was pleased with the decentralized judiciary. James Wilson, a participant at the Convention who became one of the original Associate Justices, criticized the federal judiciary as "a very uncommon establishment," and urged in his law lectures that instead it "should resemble a pyramid.... [O]ne supreme tribunal should superintend and govern all others." By 1801, this argument had persuaded the Federalist Congress to remodel the judicial branch; but the Federalist overhaul was repealed by Thomas Jefferson's Republicans the next year. Jefferson's own Congress, however, soon enacted some piecemeal revisions that gradually, but significantly, began to pyramid the judicial branch: Justices' circuit-riding duties were reduced, enabling them to focus on appellate work; restrictions on appellate review were relaxed; and a process was enacted for certifying to the Supreme Court any question of law over which the two or more judges presiding at a Circuit Court proceeding disagreed. Thus did the wish for uniform resolution of legal questions begin to eclipse the original conception of conscientious, oath-bound, and independent adjudication of each litigant's case.

Nonstatutory developments—like the increasing availability of Supreme Court opinions once official publication started in 1817, and the widespread respect gained by Chief Justice John Marshall—helped make the centralization of judicial authority seem safe and desirable. Soon another development occurred, however, which nobody could have foreseen.

A decade before the American Revolution, English legal scholar Sir William Blackstone had written that a judge is "not delegated to pronounce a new law, but to maintain and expound the old one." A few years earlier, Baron de Montesquieu had seen English judges as "no more than the mouth that pronounces the words of the law, mere passive beings, incapable of moderating either its force or its rigour." That is why, in discussing the separation of powers, Montesquieu put aside the judiciary as "next to nothing" and focused on the three *political* elements—executive, commons, and lords. During the early decades of the nineteenth century, however, the possibility that judges might actually revise the law by their decisions began to be recognized; and some frankly embraced the potential. Before long, new appointees brought this new instrumentalism to the Supreme Court.

Gradually, instrumentalist jurisprudence operating in an increasingly hierarchical system made the federal judiciary a different institution from what the Framers had conceived. This combination enabled judges to make effective throughout the nation their honorably held, but not always predominantly shared, opinions on controversial questions of public policy linked to some constitutional phrase or ideal.

Harmonization of legal opinion may be a beneficial effect of a hierarchical judiciary in certain areas, but its persistence in whole or in part is at Congress's option. A pyramided judicial branch is not constitutionally ordained, although not prohibited either. Centralized judicial decision of controversial public issues, under the rubric of constitutional generalities, frequently stirs vigorous dissent. At times, Members of Congress have urged that categories of jurisdiction be stripped from the judicial branch as a whole. The Framers refused to allow that, of course; when a divestment law was actually enacted in 1867, inferior courts ignored it and proceeded with the forbidden cases anyway. *See Beckwith v. Bean* (1878). In contrast, laws that de-pyramid by making exceptions to Supreme Court appellate jurisdiction are valid because of the Appellate Jurisdiction Clause, so long as the excepted cases have access to the inferior federal courts structured by Congress for carrying into execution the federal judicial power.

David Engdahl

See Also

Article I, Section 8, Clause 18 (Necessary and Proper Clause)

Article III, Section 1 (Inferior Courts)

Article III, Section 2, Clause 2 (Appellate Jurisdiction Clause)

Suggestions for Further Research

Significant Cases

Define and Punish Clause

The Congress shall have Power To ...define and punish Piracies and Felonies committed on the high Seas, and Offences against the Law of Nations....

(Article I, Section 8, Clause 10)

~

The power to "define and punish Piracies and Felonies committed on the high Seas" attracted little discussion at the Founding and has not proven controversial. Although the Constitution authorizes Congress to "define" piracy, the Framers and later commentators, such as James Madison, James Kent, and Justice Joseph Story, opined that piracy was so well defined in international law that a general statute punishing the crime would be valid. Although there has been a federal piracy statute since 1790, the parent of the present piracy statute was enacted in 1819. The current statute provides: "Whoever, on the high seas, commits the crime of piracy as defined by the law of nations, and is afterwards brought into or found in the United States, shall be imprisoned for life." 18 U.S.C. § 1651. In a decision involving the 1819 statute, the Supreme Court, in an opinion by Justice Story, held that Congress's definition of piracy by reference to the law of nations was sufficiently precise. *United States v. Smith* (1820). Story reasoned that the crime of piracy had a definite meaning in international law and that "Congress may as well define by using a term of a known and determinate meaning as by an express enumeration of all the particulars included in that term."

The Framers were more concerned with Congress's power to "define and punish... Offenses against the Law of Nations." The define-and-punish power grew out of the Founders' concern that the states might not adequately punish infractions of the law of nations (such as attacks on ambassadors) and, in failing to do so, might thereby implicate the international responsibility of the entire United States. This concern led the Continental Congress to pass a resolution in 1781 recommending that the states "provide expeditious, exemplary and adequate punishment... for the infractions of the immunities of ambassadors and other public ministers authorized and received as such by the United States in Congress assembled." At the Constitutional Convention in 1787, Edmund Randolph stated that one of the defects of the Articles of Confederation was that Congress "could not cause infractions of treaties or of the law of nations, to be punished [and]: that particular states might by their conduct provoke war without controul...."

When the Define and Punish Clause was being drafted, James Wilson expressed concern about the implications of Congress's power to "define" the law of nations: "To pretend to *define* the law of nations which depended on the authority of all the Civilized Nations of the World, would have the look of arrogance, that would make us look ridiculous." Gouverneur Morris responded: "The word *define* is proper when applied to *offenses* in this case; the law of (nations) being often too vague and deficient to be a rule." (In contrast to piracy, Justice Story wrote in *United States v. Smith*, "Offences, too, against the law of nations, cannot, with any accuracy, be said to be completely ascertained and defined in any public code recognized by the common consent of nations."

The Supreme Court in *United States v. Arjona* (1887) read the Define and Punish Clause broadly not only to permit Congress to punish actual violations of the law of nations but also to punish offenses that would trigger the international responsibility of the United States if left unpunished. Similarly, in *Ex parte Quirin* (1942), the Court upheld Congress's "authority to define and punish offenses against the law of nations by sanctioning, within constitutional limitations, the jurisdiction of military commissions to try persons for offenses which, according to the rules and precepts of the law of nations, and more particularly the law of war, are cognizable by such tribunals."

There are two potential limits on the Define and Punish Clause. The first limit is based on the protections within the Bill of Rights. For example, in *Boos v. Barry* (1988), the Supreme Court held that a statute enacted pursuant to the Define and Punish Clause that prohibited the display of certain flags or banners within 500 feet of an embassy violated the First Amendment. A second possible limit is the clause's reference to "punish," which might textually signify that Congress only has criminal enforcement authority, but not the authority to regulate civil suits. Nonetheless, Congress has invoked the Define and Punish Clause as a basis for enacting important civil legislation relating to foreign affairs, including the Foreign Sovereign Immunities Act, 28 U.S.C. § 1601 et seq., and the Torture Victim Protection Act, 28 U.S.C. § 1350 note.

Jack L. Goldsmith III

Suggestions for Further Research
1 RECORDS OF THE FEDERAL CONVENTION OF 1787, at 19, 25 (Max Farrand ed., 1911)

2 RECORDS OF THE FEDERAL CONVENTION OF 1787, at 614–615 (Max Farrand ed., 1911)

21 JOURNALS OF THE CONTINENTAL CONGRESS 1136 (1781)

29 JOURNALS OF THE CONTINENTAL CONGRESS 654–666 (1785)

Charles D. Siegal, *Deference and Its Dangers: Congress' Power to "Define…Offenses Against the Law of Nations*, 21 VAND. J. TRANSNAT'L L. 865, 874–879 (1988)

Beth Stephens, *Federalism and Foreign Affairs: Congress's Power to "Define and Punish…Offenses Against the Law of Nations*," 42 WM. & MARY L. REV. 447 (2000)

Significant Cases
United States v. Smith, 18 U.S. (5 Wheat.) 153 (1820)

United States v. Arjona, 120 U.S. 479 (1887)

Ex parte Quirin, 317 U.S. 1 (1942)

Reid v. Covert, 354 U.S. 1 (1957)

Boos v. Barry, 485 U.S. 312 (1988)

Declare War

The Congress shall have Power To …declare War….
(ARTICLE I, SECTION 8, CLAUSE 11)

~

*I*t is well accepted that the conduct of war is an "executive Power," vested by Article II in the President, who also serves as Commander in Chief of the Armed Forces. Both at the time of the Framing of the Constitution and afterward, there has been agreement that the President has the power to repel invasions. Intimately familiar with the treatises on international law, the Framers were undoubtedly aware of the general rule that, as Hugo Grotius had put it, "By the law of nature, no declaration is required when one is repelling an invasion." *The Law of War and Peace* (1646). The debate, instead, has centered on the location of the power to initiate war.

Advocates of congressional power contend that the President cannot initiate hostilities because the Constitution expressly vests the power to "declare War" in Congress. In support of that view, they note that, according to his notes from the Constitutional Convention, James Madison successfully advocated that Congress be given the power, not to "make" war but to "declare" war, to "leav[e] to the Executive the power to repel sudden attacks." In 1862, the Supreme Court opined that the President "has no power to initiate or declare a war," but if there were an invasion, "the President is not only authorized but bound to resist force by force...without waiting for any special legislative authority." *Prize Cases* (1863).

On the other hand, the Constitution distinguishes between "declaring" war and "engaging in" (*see* Article I, Section 10, Clause 3) or "levying" war (*see* Article III, Section 3, Clause 1). Moreover, there is no express requirement of legislative consent in other sections of the Constitution or in earlier documents before the President may commence hostilities.

Accordingly, much of the debate over the power to initiate hostilities focuses on understanding the meaning of the words, "declare War." Supporters of presidential authority contend that the Founders were well aware of the long British practice of undeclared wars. They assert that the Constitution likewise does not require formal war declarations for the President to authorize hostilities as a matter of domestic constitutional power.

Under this view, Congress's power to declare war was established for an altogether different purpose. Declarations of war alter legal relationships between subjects of warring nations and trigger certain rights, privileges, and protections under the laws of war. According to Grotius, declarations gave notice of the legal grounds for the war and the opportunity for enemy nations to make amends and thereby avoid the scourge of war. It served notice on the enemy's allies that they would be regarded as cobelligerents and their shipping subject to capture. Under a declaration of war, one's own navy and privateers could not be treated as pirates by the enemy,

but on the other hand one's own citizens were subject to prosecution if they dealt with the enemy.

Furthermore, under previous practice, declarations of war triggered other legal actions, such as the internment or expulsion of enemy aliens, the breaking of diplomatic relations, and the confiscation of the enemy's property. In short, the power to declare war was designed as a power to affect legal rights and duties in times of hostilities. It is not a check on executive power to engage in such hostilities in the first place.

Congressional power supporters respond that the Declaration of War Clause must be given a broader interpretation, particularly in light of contemporaneous statements by prominent Founding era figures. They contend that the clause was intended to include the power not only to issue formal declarations, but also to confer authority to decide upon any engagement of hostilities, whether declared or otherwise. Therefore, they argue, the Declaration of War Clause must be construed to deprive the President of power to initiate hostilities absent congressional consent.

There have been only five congressionally declared wars in the history of the United States. Of those, only the first, the War of 1812, constituted an affirmative declaration of war. The remaining four, the Mexican-American War of 1846, the Spanish-American War of 1898, World War I, and World War II, merely declared the prior existence of a state of war. Notably, those declarations were accompanied by express authorizations of use of force, suggesting a distinction between declarations of war and authorizations of force.

Numerous other hostilities have been specifically authorized by Congress through instruments other than formal declarations. For example, offensive actions taken by the United States during its first real "war"— against Tripoli in 1802—were statutorily authorized but not accompanied by a formal declaration. Congress also expressly authorized the use of force in the Quasi War with France in 1798, against Iraq in 1991 and 2002, and against the perpetrators of the September 11,

2001, attacks, all without issuing a formal declaration of war.

Early in American history, in an era of limited peacetime budgets for military resources, Presidents tended to defer to Congress. In modern times, the debate over the allocation of war powers between Congress and the President is dramatically affected by the institution of a large United States peacetime military force following World War II. Starting with the Korean War, modern Presidents have been more aggressive in asserting unilateral authority to engage in war without declaration or other congressional authorization. In 1973, Congress attempted to affirm its control over war through passage, over President Richard M. Nixon's veto, of the War Powers Resolution. Presidents have generally refused to recognize the constitutional operation of the War Powers Resolution, although Presidents have often taken actions "consistent" with the War Powers Resolution to avoid unnecessary conflict with Congress.

The Supreme Court has never intervened to stop a war that a President has started without congressional authorization. Some federal courts of appeals have held that at least some level of congressional authorization is constitutionally required before the President may conduct military hostilities. *See, e.g., Orlando v. Laird* (1971). Other courts have found the issue nonjusticiable. *See, e.g., Mitchell v. Laird* (1973).

Whatever the domestic constitutional implications for presidential power to initiate hostilities, the Declaration of War Clause gives to Congress certain powers under international and domestic statutory law. Nonetheless, with the growth of international law, the significance of formal declarations has declined. For example, the Geneva Conventions of 1949, which guarantee various enumerated rights to lawful combatants, prisoners of war, and civilians, explicitly apply to all armed conflicts between contracting nations and not just to declared wars. Congress's power to declare war continues to have important statutory ramifications, nonetheless. A particularly dramatic example is the Alien Enemy Act (1 Stat. 577 (1798), codified in 50 U.S.C. § 21 (2003)), which authorizes the President to detain and deport citizens of enemy nations, but only following either a declaration of war or an attack upon the United States.

John Yoo and James C. Ho

See Also

Article I, Section 10, Clause 3 (Compact Clause)
Article II, Section 2, Clause 1 (Commander in Chief)
Article III, Section 3, Clause 1 (Treason)

Suggestions for Further Research

Ellen C. Collier, ed., Congressional Research Service, Instances of Use of United States Forces Abroad, 1798-1993 (1993)

Louis Fisher, Congressional Abdication on War & Spending (2000)

Louis Henkin, Foreign Affairs and the U.S. Constitution (2d ed. 1996)

Harold Hongju Koh, The National Security Constitution: Sharing Power After the Iran-Contra Affair (1990)

Montgomery Kosma, *Our First Real War*, 2 Green Bag 2d 169 (1999)

C. Kevin Marshall, *Putting Privateers in Their Place: The Applicability of the Marque and Reprisal Clause to Undeclared Wars*, 64 U. Chi. L. Rev. 953 (1997)

Michael D. Ramsey, *Textualism and War Powers*, 69 U. Chi. L. Rev. 1543 (2002)

Robert F. Turner, *War and the Forgotten Executive Power Clause of the Constitution: A Review Essay of John Hart Ely's War and Responsibility*, 34 Va. J. Int'l L. 903 (1994)

John C. Yoo, *Clio at War: The Misuse of History in the War Powers Debate*, 70 U. Colo. L. Rev. 1169 (1999)

John C. Yoo, *The Continuation of Politics by Other Means: The Original Understanding of War Powers*, 84 Cal. L. Rev. 167 (1996)

John C. Yoo, *War and Constitutional Texts*, 69 U. Chi. L. Rev. 1639 (2002)

Significant Cases

Prize Cases, 67 U.S. (2 Black) 635 (1863)
Orlando v. Laird, 443 F.2d 1039 (2d Cir. 1971)
Mitchell v. Laird, 488 F.2d 611 (D.C. Cir. 1973)

Marque and Reprisal

The Congress shall have Power To
...grant Letters of Marque and
Reprisal....
(ARTICLE I, SECTION 8, CLAUSE 11)

∼

*T*he Marque and Reprisal Clause plays an important supporting role in the debate over the original allocation of war powers between the President and Congress. At the time of the Founding, the sovereign authorized holders of letters of marque and reprisal to engage in hostile actions against enemies of the state. The common understanding of "Reprisal" is a seizure of property (or sometimes persons) of a foreign state for redressing an injury committed by that state. Because the word marque is the French equivalent of reprisal, many scholars believe that the constitutional term "Marque and Reprisal" is best understood as a single phrase.

The only serious debate over the meaning of the Marque and Reprisal Clause is whether it extends only to authorizing private parties (known as "privateers") to engage in reprisals for private, commercial gain, or whether it also gives Congress the power to authorize reprisals by the armed forces of the United States for public purposes.

That debate mirrors the larger war powers debate over the Declare War Clause. Congressionalists construe the Declare War Clause and the Marque and Reprisal Clause jointly to cover all forms of hostilities and thereby to deny the President any power whatsoever to initiate hostilities. They contend that the Declare War Clause requires Congress to authorize wars, whereas the Marque and Reprisal Clause requires Congress to authorize lower level hostilities, whether by public forces or by privateers.

Citing revolutionary practice, presidentialists maintain that the Marque and Reprisal Clause was originally understood to give Congress the power to vest sovereign authority to use force against enemy nations and their subjects with private parties only. Exercising that power, Congress could authorize so-called privateers to engage in military hostilities, with neither government funding nor oversight (other than after-the-fact judicial determinations of prizes by the prize courts). Thus, according to presidentialists, the Marque and Reprisal Clause is best read in conjunction with Congress's power over the purse. They argue that the clause is consistent with their overall structural theory of the Constitution, under which Congress has exhaustive authority over all funding of military hostilities, whether through public appropriations or private letters of reprisal, but no power to control directly the President's ability to initiate hostilities with whatever resources Congress has previously made available to him. Under this framework, locating the Marque and Reprisal Clause in Article I prevents the President from engaging in hostilities free from congressional control over resources, whether in the form of public appropriations or the issuance of letters of marque and reprisal. The clause thus helps fill a hole that would otherwise exist in Congress's control over the provision of military resources.

Outside of the law reviews and scholarly debates over the allocation of war powers between Congress and the President, the Marque and Reprisal Clause has played little if any role in modern law. The United States has not issued letters of marque and reprisal since the War of 1812, and has not seriously considered doing so since Andrew Jackson's presidency. In addition, the 1856 Declaration of Paris prohibits privateering as a matter of international law. Although the United States has not ratified the Declaration, it has upheld the ban in practice.

During the Iran-Contra controversy of Ronald Reagan's administration, Members of Congress objected to the President's private financing of hostilities, absent prior congressional consent. Congress did not expressly invoke the Marque and Reprisal Clause, however, in objecting to executive branch action.

John Yoo and James C. Ho

See Also

Article I, Section 10, Clause 3 (Compact Clause)
Article II, Section 2, Clause 1 (Commander in Chief)

Article III, Section 3, Clause 1 (Treason)

Article III, Section 3, Clause 2 (Punishment of Treason)

Suggestions for Further Research

Ellen C. Collier, ed., Congressional Research Service, Instances of Use of United States Forces Abroad, 1798–1993 (1993)

Louis Fisher, Congressional Abdication on War & Spending (2000)

Louis Henkin, Foreign Affairs and the U.S. Constitution (2d ed. 1996)

Harold Hongju Koh, The National Security Constitution: Sharing Power After the Iran-Contra Affair (1990)

Montgomery Kosma, *Our First Real War*, 2 Green Bag 2d 169 (1999)

C. Kevin Marshall, *Putting Privateers in Their Place: The Applicability of the Marque and Reprisal Clause to Undeclared Wars*, 64 U. Chi. L. Rev. 953 (1997)

Michael D. Ramsey, *Textualism and War Powers*, 69 U. Chi. L. Rev. 1543 (2002)

Robert F. Turner, *War and the Forgotten Executive Power Clause of the Constitution: A Review Essay of John Hart Ely's War and Responsibility*, 34 Va. J. Int'l L. 903 (1994)

John C. Yoo, *Clio at War: The Misuse of History in the War Powers Debate*, 70 U. Colo. L. Rev. 1169 (1999)

John C. Yoo, *The Continuation of Politics by Other Means: The Original Understanding of War Powers*, 84 Cal. L. Rev. 167 (1996)

John C. Yoo, *War and Constitutional Texts*, 69 U. Chi. L. Rev. 1639 (2002)

Captures Clause

The Congress shall have Power To ...make Rules concerning Captures on Land and Water....

(Article I, Section 8, Clause 11)

~

*U*nder the Captures Clause, Congress has the power to make rules for the confiscation, disposition, and distribution of captured enemy property. Although nothing in the text of the clause precludes its application to captures of enemy persons, it has never been so applied by either courts or Congress.

The roots of the clause can be traced to Article IX of the Articles of Confederation, which vested in Congress the power "of establishing rules for deciding in all cases, what captures on land or water shall be legal, and in what manner prizes taken by land or naval forces in the service of the united states shall be divided or appropriated." Read as a unit, this clause suggests that Congress alone has the power to establish rules governing the circumstances under which wartime "captures" will be adjudged lawful "prizes," to which the captors are entitled at least partial title. This construction is supported by the fact that, during the Revolution, captors could not claim lawful title to captured property until after a prize court had granted it.

Under this interpretation, the term *captures*, as understood by the Framers of the Constitution, includes only enemy property. The term could not include captured enemy soldiers, as persons can neither be "divided" nor "appropriated." This approach is bolstered by the fact that the term *capture* was understood under international law, as listed in Bouvier's Law Dictionary (1914), as "the taking of property by one belligerent from another or from an offending neutral."

Presidentialists may read the Captures Clause in conjunction with the Marque and Reprisal Clause to conclude that the Captures Clause authorizes Congress to regulate captures by private parties only and not by the armed forces of the United States. Revolutionary practice suggests such a view, as letters of marque and reprisal were frequently issued by the Continental Congress exclusively to privateers "to make Captures of British Vessels and Cargoes," pursuant to rules established by Congress.

Although the executive's power to conduct war necessarily includes the power to seize persons and property on the battlefield, the Supreme Court has construed the Captures Clause to deny the executive constitutional power to seize enemy property off the battlefield. In *Brown v. United States* (1814), the Court concluded that, by virtue of the Captures Clause, the executive lacks inherent constitutional authority to confiscate property owned by subjects of enemy nations, and must seek congressional authorization in order to do so. Congress has long conferred such power upon the executive by enacting laws such as the Trading with the Enemy Act.

John Yoo and James C. Ho

See Also

Article I, Section 10, Clause 3 (Compact Clause)
Article II, Section 2, Clause 1 (Commander in Chief)
Article III, Section 3, Clause 1 (Treason)
Article III, Section 3, Clause 2 (Punishment of Treason)

Suggestions for Further Research

Ellen C. Collier, ed., Congressional Research Service, Instances of Use of United States Forces Abroad, 1798–1993 (1993)

Louis Fisher, Congressional Abdication on War & Spending (2000)

Louis Henkin, Foreign Affairs and the U.S. Constitution (2d ed. 1996)

Harold Hongju Koh, The National Security Constitution: Sharing Power After the Iran-Contra Affair (1990)

Montgomery Kosma, *Our First Real War*, 2 Green Bag 2d 169 (1999)

C. Kevin Marshall, *Putting Privateers in Their Place: The Applicability of the Marque and Reprisal Clause to Undeclared Wars*, 64 U. Chi. L. Rev. 953 (1997)

Michael D. Ramsey, *Textualism and War Powers*, 69 U. Chi. L. Rev. 1543 (2002)

Robert F. Turner, *War and the Forgotten Executive Power Clause of the Constitution: A Review Essay of John Hart Ely's War and Responsibility*, 34 Va. J. Int'l L. 903 (1994)

John C. Yoo, *Clio at War: The Misuse of History in the War Powers Debate*, 70 U. Colo. L. Rev. 1169 (1999)

John C. Yoo, *The Continuation of Politics by Other Means: The Original Understanding of War Powers*, 84 Cal. L. Rev. 167 (1996)

John C. Yoo, *War and Constitutional Texts*, 69 U. Chi. L. Rev. 1639 (2002)

Significant Cases

Brown v. United States, 12 U.S. (8 Cranch) 110 (1814)

Prize Cases, 67 U.S. (2 Black) 635 (1863)

Army Clause

The Congress shall have Power To ...raise and support Armies, but no Appropriation of Money to that Use shall be for a longer Term than two Years....
(Article I, Section 8, Clause 12)

∼

*F*or most Americans after the Revolution, a standing army was one of the most dangerous threats to liberty. In thinking about the potential dangers of a standing army, the Founding generation had before them the precedents of Rome and England. In the first case, Julius Caesar marched his provincial army into Rome, overthrowing the power of the Senate, destroying the republic, and laying the foundation of empire. In the second, Cromwell used the army to abolish Parliament and to rule as dictator. In addition, in the period leading up to the Revolution, the British Crown had forced the American colonists to quarter and otherwise support its troops, which the colonists saw as nothing more than an army of occupation. Under British practice, the king was not only the commander in chief; it was he who raised the armed forces. The Framers were determined not to lodge the power of raising an army with the executive.

Many of the men who met in Philadelphia to draft the Constitution, however, had the experience of serving with the Continental Line, the army that ultimately bested the British for our independence. Founders like George Washington, James Madison, and Alexander Hamilton were also acutely aware of the dangers external enemies posed to the new republic. The British and Spanish were not only on the frontiers of the new nation. In many cases they were within the frontiers, allying with the Indians and attempting to induce frontier settlements to split off from the country. The recent Shays's Rebellion in Massachusetts had also impelled the Framers to consider the possibility of local rebellion.

The "raise and support Armies" clause was the Framers' solution to the dilemma. The Constitutional Convention accepted the need for a standing army but sought to maintain control by the appropriations power of Congress, which the Founders viewed as the branch of government closest to the people.

The compromise, however, did not satisfy the Anti-Federalists. They largely shared the perspective of James Burgh, who, in his *Political Disquisitions* (1774), called a "standing army in times of peace, one of the most hurtful, and most dangerous of abuses." The Anti-Federalist paper *A Democratic Federalist* called a standing army "that great support of tyrants." And *Brutus*, the most influential series of essays opposing ratification, argued that standing armies "are dangerous to the liberties of a people . . . not only because the rulers may employ them for the purposes of supporting themselves in any usurpation of powers, which they may see proper to exercise, but there is a great hazard, that any army will subvert the forms of government, under whose authority, they are raised, and establish one, according to the pleasure of their leader." During the Virginia ratifying convention, George Mason exclaimed, "What havoc, desolation, and destruction, have been perpetrated by standing armies!" The Anti-Federalists would have preferred that the defense of the nation remain entirely with the state militias.

The Federalists disagreed. For them, the power of a government to raise an army was a dictate of prudence. Thus, during the Pennsylvania ratifying convention, James Wilson argued that "the power of raising and keeping up an army, in time of peace, is essential to every government. No government can secure its citizens against dangers, internal and external, without possessing it, and sometimes carrying it into execution." In *The Federalist* No. 23, Hamilton argued, "These powers [of the federal government to provide for the common defense] ought to exist without limitation: because it is impossible to foresee or define the extent or variety of national exigencies, or the correspondent extent & variety of the means which may be necessary to satisfy them."

Nonetheless, both Federalists and Anti-Federalists alike expressed concerns about a standing army, as opposed to a navy or the militia. Accordingly, this is the only clause related to military affairs that includes a time limit on appropriations. The appropriations power of Congress is a very powerful tool, and one that the Framers saw as particularly necessary in the case of a standing army. Indeed, some individuals argued that army appropriations should be made on a yearly basis. During the Constitutional Convention, Elbridge Gerry raised precisely this point. Roger Sherman replied that the appropriations were *permitted*, not required, for two years. The problem, he said, was that in a time of emergency, Congress might not be in session when an annual army appropriation was needed.

Since the time of the Constitution, legal developments based on the clause have been legislatively driven, and barely the subject of judicial interpretation. With the establishment of a Department of Defense in 1947, Army appropriations have been subsumed by a single department-wide appropriation that includes the Army, the Navy, and the Air Force (established in 1947), as well as other agencies of the department. Despite periodic congressional efforts to move to a two-year appropriations cycle, the annual appropriations for the military are the rule, although not for the reasons that animated Elbridge Gerry during the Constitutional Convention. In addition, the Armed Services Committees of Congress have taken on the responsibility of authorizing almost all aspects of the defense budget as well as appropriating the funds for the services.

The character of the United States Army has changed significantly since the constitutional period in two fundamental ways. The first was its way of mobilizing. The second was its orientation and purpose.

With respect to wartime mobilization, Hamilton and later John C. Calhoun envisioned the United States Army as an "expansible" force. A small peacetime establishment would serve as the foundation for a greatly expanded force in times of emergency. The emergency ended, the citizen-soldiers would demobilize and return to their civilian occupations. With modifications, this was essentially the model for mobilization from the Mexican War through World War II. During the Cold War, the United States for the first time in its history maintained a large military establishment during peacetime. Even so, the fact that soldiers were drafted meant that citizen-soldiers continued to be the foundation of the Army. But with the end of the draft in 1973, the citizen-soldier was superseded by the long-term professional.

The draft, of course, has been a controversial issue. Although compulsory military service can be traced to the colonial and revolutionary period in America, it usually involved the states obligating service in the militia. The United States did not have a national draft until the Civil War, and did not resort to a peacetime draft until 1940. Opponents of a draft have used a number of constitutional arguments in support of their position. The Supreme Court has ruled, however, that a draft is constitutional. This includes a draft during peacetime and the power to dispatch draftees overseas. Nor does a draft intrude on the state's right to maintain a militia. *Selective Draft Law Cases* (1918). An example of the Court's reasoning is found in *Holmes v. United States* (1968): "the power of Congress to raise armies and to take effective measures to preserve their efficiencies, is not limited by the Thirteenth Amendment or the absence of a military emergency." Nonetheless, the Court has, for some time now, been broadening exemptions to the draft, such as those with conscientious objections to war.

The purpose of the United States Army has not always been primarily to win the nation's wars, but to act as a constabulary. Soldiers were often used during the antebellum period to enforce the fugitive slave laws and suppress domestic violence. The Fugitive Slave Act of 1850 permitted federal marshals to call on the *posse comitatus* to aid in returning a slave to his owner, and Attorney General Caleb Cushing issued an opinion that included the Army in the *posse comitatus*.

In response, Congress enacted the Posse Comitatus Act (1878), which prohibited the use of the military to aid civil authorities in enforcing the law or suppressing civil disturbances unless expressly ordered to do so by the President. The Army welcomed the legislation. The use of soldiers as a posse removed them from their own chain of command and placed them in the uncomfortable position of taking orders

from local authorities who had an interest in the disputes that provoked the unrest in the first place. As a result, many officers came to believe that the involvement of the Army in domestic policing was corrupting the institution.

In 1904, Secretary of War Elihu Root reoriented the Army away from constabulary duties to a mission focused on defeating the conventional forces of other states. This view has shaped United States military culture since at least World War II and continues to this day. Whether the exigencies of a modern war against terrorism once again changes the military's mission towards domestic order is yet to be seen.

Mackubin Owens

See Also

Article I, Section 8, Clause 11 (Declare War)
Article I, Section 8, Clause 13 (Navy Clause)
Article I, Section 8, Clause 14 (Military Regulations)
Article I, Section 8, Clause 16 (Organizing the Militia)
Article II, Section 2, Clause 1 (Commander in Chief)

Suggestions for Further Research

Kenneth Hagan & William J. Roberts, eds., Against All Enemies: Interpretations of American Military History from Colonial Times to the Present (1986)

Richard H. Kohn, Eagle and Sword: The Federalists and the Creation of the Military Establishment in America, 1783–1802 (1975)

Richard Kohn, ed., The United States Military Under the Constitution of the United States, 1789–1989 (1991)

Allan Millet & Peter Maslowski, For the Common Defense: A Military History of the United States of America (2d ed. 1994)

Emory Upton, Military Policy of the United States (1968)

Karl-Friedrich Walling, Republican Empire: Alexander Hamilton on War and Free Government (1999)

Significant Cases

Selective Draft Law Cases, 245 U.S. 366 (1918)
Witmer v. United States, 348 U.S. 375 (1955)

United States v. Seeger, 380 U.S. 163 (1966)

Hart v. United States, 391 U.S. 956 (1968)

Holmes v. United States, 391 U.S. 936 (1968)

United States v. O'Brien, 391 U.S. 367 (1968)

Navy Clause

The Congress shall have Power To
...provide and maintain a Navy....
(ARTICLE I, SECTION 8, CLAUSE 13)

∼

*B*ecause the Founding generation considered navies to be less dangerous to republican liberty than standing armies, the Navy Clause did not elicit the same level of debate as did the Army Clause (*see* Article I, Section 8, Clause 12). Their experience taught them that armies, not navies, were the preferred tools of tyrants. Readers of Thucydides could view a navy as particularly compatible with democratic institutions. They were also aware of how much the economic prosperity and even the survival of the country depended upon sea-going trade. Consequently, the Framers of the Constitution imposed no time limit on naval appropriations as they did in the case of the army.

Both Federalists and Anti-Federalists believed that maritime trade was necessary if the United States was to maintain its independence of action, but they disagreed over how to protect this trade. After the Revolution, the United States possessed one of the principal merchant fleets in the world, but it was largely defenseless. In June 1785 Congress voted to sell the one remaining ship of the Continental Navy, a frigate, leaving the fledgling nation with only a fleet of small Treasury Department revenue cutters for defense.

Federalists such as Alexander Hamilton argued for a federal navy, which "if it could not vie with those of the great maritime powers, would at least be of respectable weight if thrown into the scale of either of two contending parties." Hamilton argued that without a navy, "a nation, despicable by its weakness, for-

feits even the privilege of being neutral." *The Federalist* No. 11.

Anti-Federalists argued that instead of defending American commerce and guaranteeing American neutrality, creating a navy would provoke the European powers and invite war. They were also concerned about the expense of maintaining a navy and the distribution of that expense. During the Virginia ratifying convention, William Grayson argued that, despite the fact that a navy would not appreciably reduce the vulnerability of southern ports, the South would bear the main burden of naval appropriations.

The wisdom of granting Congress the power to provide and maintain a navy became evident during the two decades after the framing and ratification of the Constitution. As Europe once again erupted in war, American merchantmen increasingly found themselves at the mercy of British and French warships and the corsairs of the Barbary States. Only the rapid creation of a navy permitted the United States to hold its own in the Quasi War with France (1798–1800) and the War of 1812 with the British.

The Navy Clause has changed little, if at all, in practice. Neither have the arguments for and against naval power. Indeed, many of the major debates over foreign policy that have taken place since the middle of the nineteenth century were adumbrated by those between Federalists and Anti-Federalists during the framing of the Constitution.

Similarly, despite vast technological changes, the character of the Navy as a service, in contrast to the Army, has also changed very little. While the "citizen soldier" envisioned by the Founders has virtually disappeared from the Army of today, today's sailor, both officer and enlisted, has much in common with his predecessor who manned the Navy of the Constitution, technical expertise of course excepted. Although service reforms beginning in the latter decades of the nineteenth century created a powerful Navy, the foundation of this Navy was laid by the likes of Hamilton, Benjamin Stoddert, the first Secretary of the Navy, and other Federalists who recognized the shortcomings of a navy limited to coastal defense alone.

The main changes affecting the Navy, if not the Navy Clause, have to do with defense organization, primarily the National Security Act of 1947 (and subsequent modifications). These include downgrading the Department of the Navy from a Cabinet department and the creation of the Air Force as a separate branch of the armed forces.

Mackubin Owens

See Also

Suggestions for Further Research

George Baer, One Hundred Years of Sea Power (1994)

Demetrios Caraley, The Politics of Military Unification: A Study of Conflict and the Policy Process (1966)

Alice Cole et al., eds., The Department of Defense: Documents on Establishment and Organization, 1944–1978 (1978).

Marshall Smelser, The Congress Founds a Navy, 1787–1798 (1973)

Craig Symonds, Navalists and Antinavalists: The Naval Policy Debate in the United States, 1785–1826 (1980)

Robert W. Tucker & David C. Hendrickson, Empire of Liberty: The Statecraft of Thomas Jefferson (1990)

Military Regulations

The Congress shall have Power To ...make Rules for the Government and Regulation of the land and naval Forces....

(Article I, Section 8, Clause 14)

$\sim$

*I*n his *Commentaries on the Constitution of the United States*, Justice Joseph Story remarked that Congress's power to govern and regulate the land and naval forces is "a natural incident to the preceding powers to make war, to raise armies, and to provide and maintain a navy." Yet the Framers had overlooked this "natural incident" until after the Committee of Detail submitted its draft. Only then was a motion made from the floor to copy the language from the Articles of Confederation into the new Constitution, making explicit the grant of plenary power to Congress. It passed without controversy. By placing the power in Congress, the Framers helped to define the respective roles of the legislature, the executive, and the judiciary over the Armed Forces and thus lessened the chances for serious conflict. Story explains: "The whole power is far more safe in the hands of congress, than of the executive; since otherwise the most summary and severe punishments might be inflicted at the mere will of the executive." The central purpose of the clause is the establishment of a system of military law and justice outside of the ordinary jurisdiction of the civil courts. Tradition and experience taught the Framers that the necessities of military discipline require a system of jurisprudence separate from civilian society.

The American experience with military law predates the Constitution. In 1775, the Continental Congress adopted codes of military law for the Army and the Navy—largely based on corresponding British codes. John Adams, then a Massachusetts representative to the Continental Congress and chairman of its Naval Committee, wrote both *Rules for the Regulation of the Navy of the United Colonies* (1775) and the *American Articles of War* (1775). Following the adoption of the Constitution, the First Congress decided that both of these codes would continue in force. The *American Articles of War*, although revised several times, remained the basic code for the United States Army until 1917. Revisions included changes to punishments; rules governing the appointment of courts-martial; and, during the Civil War, the expansion of military jurisdiction over crimes and persons leading to major contests in the courts of law.

A common criticism of the *Articles* was that they were too harsh. This criticism remained even after the *Articles* were significantly modified in 1917 to deal with a mass army of citizen-soldiers. Critics charged that punishments were disproportionate to the crimes and that military authorities had too much discretion. For instance, following a race riot in Houston in 1917, the military hastily executed thirteen black enlisted soldiers. The same complaint arose during World War II, leading to the Elston Act of 1948, which modified the *Articles*. Such criticisms and the creation of a unified Department of Defense finally led Congress to enact the Uniform Code of Military Justice (UCMJ) in 1950. The Navy code followed a similar path.

The UCMJ is a compilation of federal statutes that establish uniform policies, procedures, and penalties within the military justice system. Congress's objective in creating the UCMJ was to eliminate disparities between the codes of the Army and Navy and to reduce, insofar as it was possible, "command influence," considered by critics to be the bane of a fair military justice system.

Throughout the history of the United States, the civil courts have been highly deferential to decisions of the military justice system. That is particularly true in the enforcement of military orders. The more difficult question is determining whether the military or civilian courts have jurisdiction over military personnel charged with "ordinary" or "civilian" crimes such as murder, or robbery, or rape. Most civilian court reviews of courts-martial center on whether the military had proper jurisdiction over the cause.

Although commanders in the field have always possessed authority to punish infractions of military discipline, it was not until 1863 that Congress permitted the trial during wartime of soldiers who were charged with committing civil crimes such as murder. Until that time, soldiers had been turned over to state courts for trial. Subsequently, Congress expanded court-martial jurisdiction over civil offenses. After the Korean War, however, the Supreme Court and the federal appeals courts have limited the reach of the military's jurisdiction to those acts that are "service connected."

There is no dispute that a civilian offense committed by a soldier on a military base, or in the theatre of war, or overseas is service con-nected and falls under military jurisdiction. Civilian dependents charged with crimes during peacetime, however, may not be tried by court-martial, *Reid v. Covert* (1957), *Grisham v. Hagan* (1960), at least while the civil courts are still in operation. *Ex parte Milligan* (1866). To avoid such civilians being charged by host nations abroad, in 2000, Congress passed the Military Extraterritorial Jurisdiction Act. That law imposes federal jurisdiction for crimes allegedly committed by civilians accompanying U.S. Armed Forces abroad, and also for military personnel charged with civil crimes but over whom the military has no further control.

Outside of these categories, federal courts consider a number of factors to determine if the act of the accused member of the military was service connected. *O'Callahan v. Parker* (1969). Among others, the factors considered include (1) whether the victim of the crime was a member of the military, (2) whether the accused was properly off base when the crime occurred, (3) whether military property was involved, and (4) whether the act by the accused was within his military duties. When reviewing the jurisdiction of a military court, the federal courts utilized these and similar factors on a case-by-case basis. However, in *Solorio v. United States* (1987), the Supreme Court reversed *O'Callahan* and found that the military status of the defendant was sufficient by itself to establish the jurisdiction over the person irrespective of whether the offense was service connected. Subsequent to *Solorio*, military courts obtained more jurisdiction over cases that had been previously tried by the civilian courts. Judicial deference toward military exigencies goes beyond respect for the different rules, procedures, and liabilities in the UCMJ. Deference also includes allowances for military orders and regulations that would hardly be constitutional in a civilian context.

The military courts and tribunals authorized by Congress are established pursuant to Congress's powers under Article I. They do not have the same protections and independence as Article III courts. Military courts fall into two jurisdictional categories: (1) martial and military courts of inquiry, which deal with military personnel; and (2) military commissions (or tribunals) and provost courts, which deal with civilians who have fallen under military jurisdiction. Depending on the degree of punishment attached to the offense, the military courts of first instance are the summary court-martial, the special court-martial, and the general court-martial, each of which may be convened by a successively more senior military authority. Following the decision of the court-martial, the convening authority reviews the decision and may revise it but only in favor of the defendant. The record is then further reviewed by a Judge Advocate general and, in cases of a serious sentence, is reviewed yet again by the Court of Military Review for the appropriate service. The UCMJ established a Court of Military Appeals (renamed in 1994 as the U.S. Court of Appeals for the Armed Forces), which, for the first time in United States history, created a civilian court with appellate jurisdiction over military justice. The U.S. Court of Appeals for the Armed Forces may review decisions of the Court of Military Review. Finally, upon a writ of certiorari, the Supreme Court can hear petitions from decisions by the U.S. Court of Appeals for the Armed Forces.

Collateral appeal to the federal courts is also available, normally through a writ of habeas corpus. They cannot review the factual basis of the decision, and their collateral review is limited to issues of jurisdiction, whether the proceeding denied fundamental constitutional rights, *Burns v. Wilson* (1953) (*see* the Fifth Amendment), and whether the military court gave full and fair consideration to the constitutional issue raised. Moreover, collateral review on a petition for habeas corpus is only available if the petitioner is in actual military custody, and he has exhausted all available military-justice remedies.

As events after 9/11 indicate, a controversial aspect of military justice is the establishment of military tribunals. Military tribunals established in occupied territory are governed by international law. In *Dow v. Johnson* (1880), the Court ruled that the law governing an army invading an enemy's country is not the civil law of the invaded country or of the conquering country "but military law—the law of war."

The Court has upheld the authority of the President to try enemy aliens (and United States

citizens working with them) by military tribunal in *Ex parte Quirin* (1942). The Court held that enemy aliens (in this case saboteurs, who had entered the United States in secret for the purpose of committing hostile acts) are not entitled to prisoner-of-war status, but are unlawful combatants who can be tried by military tribunal. The Court, in *Rasul v. Bush* (2004), relying on *Burns* and other cases, held that the federal habeas statute confers federal district court jurisdiction to hear challenges of alien detainees held at Guantanamo Bay. However, the Court explicitly did not decide the substance of those rights and limited the habeas extra-territorial reach to Guantanamo Bay, which it said had a unique relationship to the United States. At the same time, in *Rumsfeld v. Padilla* (2004), the Court, on jurisdictional grounds, avoided ruling on the extent of the President's power to keep a U.S. citizen in military custody as an enemy combatant; but in *Hamdi v. Rumsfeld* (2004) the Court decided, without a majority opinion, that the government must give a U.S. citizen held in the United States some type of hearing at which he may contest the facts on which the government decided to treat him as an enemy combatant.

David F. Forte and Mackubin Owens

See Also

Article I, Section 8, Clause 11 (Declare War)
Article I, Section 8, Clause 12 (Army Clause)
Article I, Section 8, Clause 15 (Militia Clause)
Article I, Section 8, Clause 16 (Organizing the Militia)
Article II, Section 2, Clause 1 (Commander in Chief)
Amendment V (Grand Jury Requirement)
Amendment VI (Jury Trial)

Suggestions for Further Research

Jonathan Lurie, Arming Military Justice: The Origins of the United States Court of Appeals for the Armed Forces, 1775–1950 (1992)

Jonathan Lurie, Pursuing Military Justice: The History of the United States Court of Appeals for the Armed Forces, 1951–1980 (1998)

Jonathan Lurie, *The Role of the Federal Judiciary in the Governance of the American Military: The*

United States Supreme Court and Civil Rights and Supervision over the Armed Forces, in RICHARD KOHN, ED., THE UNITED STATES MILITARY UNDER THE CONSTITUTION OF THE UNITED STATES, 1789–1989 (1991)

Glenn R. Schmitt, *Closing the Gap in Criminal Jurisdiction over Civilians Accompanying the Armed Forces Abroad—A First Person Account of the Creation of the Military Extraterritorial Jurisdiction Act of 2000*, 51 CATH. U. L. REV. 55 (2001)

WILLIAM WINTHROP, MILITARY LAW AND PRECEDENTS (1979)

Significant Cases

Dynes v. Hoover, 61 U.S. (20 How.) 65 (1857)
Ex parte Vallandigham, 68 U.S. (1 Wall.) 243 (1864)
Ex parte Milligan, 71 U.S. (4 Wall.) 2 (1866)
Dow v. Johnson, 100 U.S. 158 (1880)
Ex parte Quirin, 317 U.S. 1 (1942)
Duncan v. Kahanamoku, 327 U.S. 304 (1946)
In re Yamashita, 327 U.S. I (1946)
United States v. Clay, 1 C.M.R. 74 (1951)
Burns v. Wilson, 346 U.S. 137 (1953)
Toth v. Quarles, 350 U.S. 11 (1955)
Reid v. Covert, 354 U.S. 1 (1957)
Grisham v. Hagan, 361 U.S. 278 (1960)
United States *ex rel.* Kinsella v. Singleton, 361 U.S. 234 (1960)
United States *ex rel.* McElroy v. Guagliardo, 361 U.S. 281 (1960)
United States v. Jacoby, 29 C.M.R. 244 (1960)
United States v. Tempia, 37 C.M.R. 249 (1967)
O'Callahan v. Parker, 395 U.S. 258 (1969)
Parker v. Levy, 417 U.S. 733 (1974)
Middendorf v. Henry, 425 U.S. 25 (1976)
Rostker v. Goldberg, 453 U.S. 57 (1981)
Solorio v. United States, 483 U.S. 435 (1987)
Hamdi v. Rumsfeld, 124 S. Ct. 2633 (2004)
Rasul v. Bush, 124 S. Ct. 2686 (2004)
Rumsfeld v. Padilla, 124 S. Ct. 2711 (2004)

Militia Clause

The Congress shall have Power To ...provide for calling forth the Militia to execute the Laws of the Union, suppress Insurrections and repel Invasions....

(ARTICLE I, SECTION 8, CLAUSE 15)

~

*F*or the Founders, the militia arose from the *posse comitatus*, constituting the people as a whole and embodying the Anglo-American idea that the citizenry is the best enforcer of the law. "A militia when properly formed," wrote Richard Henry Lee in his *Letters From the Federal Farmer*, "are in fact the people themselves...and include all men capable of bearing arms." From its origins in Britain, the *posse comitatus* (meaning to be able to be an attendant) was generally understood to constitute the constabulary of the "shire." When order was threatened, the "shire-reeve," or sheriff, would raise the "hue and cry," and all citizens who heard it were bound to render assistance in apprehending a criminal or maintaining order. The Framers transferred the power of calling out the militia from local authorities to the Congress.

The Anti-Federalists were not pleased. They wanted the militia to remain under state control as a check on the national government. Many feared that an institution intended for local defense could be dispatched far from home. As Luther Martin objected:

> As it now stands, the Congress will have the power, if they please, to march the *whole* militia of Maryland to the *remotest* part of the union, and keep them in service as long as they think proper, without being in any respect *dependent* upon the *government of Maryland for this unlimited exercise of power over its citizens.* "Genuine Information," 1788.

In the "Calling Forth" Act of 1792, Congress exercised its powers under the Militia Clause and delegated to the President the authority to call out the militia and issue it orders when invasion appeared imminent or to suppress insurrections. While the act gave the President a relatively free hand in case of invasion, it constrained his authority in the case of insurrections by requiring that a federal judge certify that the civil authority and the *posse comitatus* were powerless to meet the exigency. The President had also to order the insurgents to disband before he could mobilize the militia. This was the procedure that President George Washington followed during the Whiskey Rebellion of 1794.

In 1795, Congress refined the language authorizing the President to federalize the militia:

> [W]henever the United States shall be invaded, or be in imminent danger of invasion from any foreign nation or Indian tribe, it shall be lawful for the president to call forth such number of the militia of the state, or states most convenient to the place of danger, or scene of action, as he may judge necessary to repel such invasion, and to issue his orders for that purpose to such officer or officers of the militia, as he shall think proper.

But even such clear language was insufficient to prevent a challenge to presidential authority during the War of 1812. At the outset of the conflict, President James Madison ordered the governors of Connecticut and Massachusetts to provide militia detachments for the defense of the maritime frontiers of the United States. These governors, however, were Federalists who opposed the war. They claimed that they, not the President, had the authority to determine whether an emergency existed. Governor Caleb Strong of Massachusetts requested an opinion of his state's Supreme Judicial Court, which concluded that this right was "vested in the commanders-in-chief of the militia of the several states." Op. of Justices 8 Mass. 548 (1812)

The issue was finally resolved by the Supreme Court in 1827 in *Martin v. Mott*. Although the case explicitly concerned the validity of a court-martial of a militiaman, the decision rendered by Justice Joseph Story validated the claim that the President had the exclusive right to judge whether there was an exigency sufficient for calling forth the militia.

State governors, however, retain concurrent authority to call out their respective militias to handle civil and military emergencies. *Houston v. Moore* (1820).

Mackubin Owens

See Also

Article I, Section 8, Clause 11 (Declare War)
Article I, Section 8, Clause 12 (Army Clause)
Article I, Section 8, Clause 14 (Military Regulations)
Article I, Section 8, Clause 16 (Organizing the Militia)
Article II, Section 2, Clause 1 (Commander in Chief)
Amendment II (To Keep and Bear Arms)

Suggestions for Further Research

Lawrence Delbert Cress, Citizens in Arms: The Army and militia in American Society to the War of 1812 (1982)

J. Norman Heath, *Exposing the Second Amendment: Federal Preemption of State Militia Legislation*, 79 U. Detroit Mercy L. Rev. 39 (2001)

Richard H. Kohn, *The Constitution and National Security: The Founders' Intent*, in Richard H. Kohn, ed., The United States Military Under the Constitution of the United States, 1789–1989 (1991)

Richard H. Kohn, ed., Military Laws of the United States from the Civil War Through the War Powers Act of 1973 (1979)

Allan Millett & Peter Maslowski, For the Common Defense: A Military History of the United States of America (2d ed. 1994)

Op. of Justices 8 Mass. 548 (1812)

Significant Cases

Meade v. Deputy Marshal, 16 F. Cas 1291 (C.C.D. Va. 1815) (No. 9372)
Houston v. Moore, 3 S. & R. (Pa.) 169 (1817), *aff'd*, Houston v. Moore, 18 U.S. (5 Wheat.) 1 (1820)
Martin v. Mott, 25 U.S. (12 Wheat.) 19 (1827)
Texas v. White, 74 U.S. (7 Wall.) 700 (1869)
Tarble's Case, 80 U.S. (13 Wall.) 397 (1872)
Dunne v. People, 94 Ill. 120 (1879)
Cox v. Wood, 247 U.S. 3 (1918)
Selective Draft Law Cases, 245 U.S. 366 (1918)
Perpich v. Department of Defense, 496 U.S. 334 (1990)

Organizing the Militia

The Congress shall have Power To ...provide for organizing, arming, and disciplining, the Militia, and for governing such Part of them as may be employed in the Service of the United States, reserving to the States respectively, the Appointment of the Officers, and the Authority of training the Militia according to the discipline prescribed by Congress....

(ARTICLE I, SECTION 8, CLAUSE 16)

The militia, long a staple of republican thought, loomed large in the deliberations of the Framers, many of whom were troubled by the prospect of a standing army in times of peace. For the Founders, a militia, composed of a "people numerous and armed," was the ultimate guardian of liberty. It was a means to enable citizens not only to protect themselves against their fellows but also, particularly for the Anti-Federalists, to protect themselves from an oppressive government. "The militia is our ultimate safety," said Patrick Henry during the Virginia ratifying convention. "We can have no security without it. The great object is that every man be armed.... Every one who is able may have a gun." Both the Pennsylvania and Vermont constitutions asserted that "the people have a right to bear arms for the defense of themselves and the state...."

The Anti-Federalists feared that Congress would permit the militia to atrophy, leaving the states defenseless against the central government. In the Virginia ratifying convention, George Mason, while advocating a stronger central control over the militia, nevertheless argued that there was a danger that Congress could render the militia useless "by disarming them. Under various pretences, Congress may neglect to provide for arming and disciplining the militia; and the state governments cannot do it, for Congress has an exclusive right to arm them &c." The desire to prevent enfeebling state militias, which provided a check to a standing army, prompted the ratifying conventions to call for an amendment guaranteeing the right of citizens to bear arms. The First Congress responded, but the Second Amendment did not remove national control over armed forces or the state militias.

Federal preemption of state-militia legislation commenced very early in the history of the Republic. In *Houston v. Moore* (1820), the Supreme Court stated that the federal government's power over the militia "may be exercised to any extent that may be deemed necessary by Congress."

Despite the generally poor performance of the militia during the Revolution, Federalists recognized that without a militia, there would be no United States military establishment. They believed, however, that they could minimize the weaknesses of the militia by creating a select militia corps in each state and establishing federal control over officership and training. The ultimate Federalist goal was to turn the militia into a national reserve of uniform, interchangeable units. In 1792, Congress passed the Uniform Militia Act, which remained the basic militia law of the United States until the twentieth century. This act established an "obligated" militia, based on universal military service. All able-bodied white men between the ages of eighteen and forty-five were required to enroll. But the act fell far short of Federalist goals. It did not create select state corps and, most importantly, did not impose penalties on the states or individuals for noncompliance. For the most part, the states ignored the provisions of the act. The abysmal performance of the militia during the War of 1812 ensured the demise of the obligated reserve as established by the Founding generation.

The obligated militia was succeeded by the "uniformed" militia, local volunteer units generally equipped and supported by their own members. In addition, the states continued to provide volunteer citizen-soldiers when the regular U.S. Army had to be expanded, as was the case during the Mexican War and the Civil War. After the Civil War, the uniformed militia reemerged as the National Guard, but, unhappy with their largely domestic constabulary role, guardsmen lobbied for the mission of a national reserve. In the Militia Act of 1903 (the Dick Act), amended and expanded in 1908, Congress divided the eligible male population into an "organized militia" (the National Guard of the several states) and a "reserve," or "unorganized," militia.

In response to an opinion by the Attorney General that the Militia Clause and the Dick Act precluded the employment of guardsmen outside of United States borders, Congress included in the National Security Act of 1916 (amended in 1920 and 1933) provisions that explicitly "federalized" the National Guard. This act, as amended, has continued to govern federal-state military relations. By giving the United States Army extensive control of National Guard officers and units, and by making state forces available for duty overseas, the National Security Act of 1916 essentially stripped the states of all of their militia powers. It effectively repealed the power of the states to appoint officers by limiting such appointments to those who "shall have successfully passed such tests as to . . . physical, moral and professional fitness as the President shall prescribe." The law stated that the army of the United States now included both the regular army and "the National Guard while in the service of the United States." In *Cox v. Wood* (1918), the Supreme Court validated the action of Congress, holding that the plenary power to raise armies was "not qualified or restricted by the provisions of the Militia Clause."

The World War I draft completely preempted state sovereignty regarding the militia by drafting individual guardsmen directly into the United States Army. In *The Selective Draft Law Cases* (1918), the Court held that the states held sway over the militia only "to the extent that such actual control was not taken away by the exercise by Congress of its power to raise armies."

The transition of the National Guard into a national reserve reached its completion during the Cold War. Despite the existence of a large regular army, Guard units were included in most war plans. But with federal funding, which covered about ninety-five percent of the costs, came federal control. While governors continued to call up the Guard to quell domestic dis-turbances and to aid in disaster relief, they discovered that their control was trumped by federal demands. For instance, in protest against United States actions in Central America during the 1980s, several governors attempted to prevent units from their states from deploying to Honduras and El Salvador for training. In response, Congress passed a law "prohibiting a governor from withholding consent to a unit of the National Guard's being ordered to active duty outside the United States on the ground that the governor objects to the location, purpose, type, or schedule of that duty." In such cases as *Perpich v. Department of Defense* (1990), the Court supported Congress's position.

With the end of the Cold War, the National Guard's role as a national reserve was called into question. As a result of the terrorist attacks of September 11, 2001, some observers believed that the Guard could return to a domestic constabulary role. On the other hand, extensive military commitments abroad have required the Guard to remain an active element in the United States armed forces.

Mackubin Owens

See Also

Article I, Section 8, Clause 11 (Declare War)
Article I, Section 8, Clause 12 (Army Clause)
Article I, Section 8, Clause 14 (Military Regulations)
Article I, Section 8, Clause 15 (Militia Clause)

Suggestions for Further Research

Lawrence Delbert Cress, Citizens in Arms: The Army and Militia in American Society to the War of 1812 (1982)

J. Norman Heath, *Exposing the Second Amendment: Federal Preemption of State Militia Legislation*, 79 U. Detroit Mercy L. Rev. 39 (2001)

Richard H. Kohn, *The Constitution and National Security: The Founders' Intent*, in Richard H. Kohn, ed., The United States Military Under the Constitution of the United States, 1789–1989 (1991)

Richard H. Kohn, ed., Military Laws of the United States from the Civil War through the War Powers Act of 1973 (1979)

A L L A N M I L L E T T & P E T E R M A S L O W S K I , F O R T H E
C O M M O N D E F E N S E : A M I L I T A R Y H I S T O R Y O F T H E
U N I T E D S T A T E S O F A M E R I C A (2d ed. 1994)

Significant Cases

Meade v. Deputy Marshal, 16 F. Cas. 1291 (C.C.D. Va. 1815)

Houston v. Moore, 3 S. & R. (Pa.) 169 (1817), *aff'd*, Houston v. Moore, 18 U.S. (5 Wheat.) 1 (1820)

Tarble's Case, 80 U.S. (13 Wall.) 397 (1872)

Dunne v. People, 94 Ill. 120 (1879)

Cox v. Wood, 247 U.S. 3 (1918)

The Selective Draft Law Cases, 245 U.S. 366 (1918)

Perpich v. Department of Defense, 496 U.S. 334 (1990)

Enclave Clause

The Congress shall have Power To ... exercise exclusive Legislation in all Cases whatsoever, over such District (not exceeding ten Miles square) as may, by Cession of particular States, and the Acceptance of Congress, become the Seat of the Government of the United States....

(ARTICLE I, SECTION 8, CLAUSE 17)

~

*I*n *The Federalist* No. 43, James Madison explained the need for a "federal district," subject to Congress's exclusive jurisdiction and separate from the territory, and authority, of any single state:

The indispensable necessity of compleat authority at the seat of Government carries its own evidence with it. It is a power exercised by every Legislature of the Union, I might say of the world, by virtue of its general supremacy. Without it, not only the public authority might be insulted and its proceedings be interrupted, with impunity; but a dependence of the members of the general Government, on the State comprehending the seat of the Government for protection in the exer-

cise of their duty, might bring on the national councils an imputation of awe or influence, equally dishonorable to the Government, and dissatisfactory to the other members of the confederacy.

Madison's concerns about insults to the "public authority" were not speculative. In June 1783, several hundred unpaid and angry Continental soldiers had marched on Philadelphia, menacing Congress in Independence Hall itself. Pennsylvania refused all requests for assistance and, after two days, Congress adjourned. Its Members fled into New Jersey.

The incident made a lasting impression. The Framers referenced it over and again in defending their provision for a "federal town," which Anti-Federalists persisted in visualizing as a sink of corruption and a potential nursery for tyrants. In fact, however, the need for a territory in which the general government exercised full sovereignty, not beholden to any state, was probably inherent in the federal system itself.

At the time, the location of the new capital was more contentious than its necessity. Both New York and Pennsylvania were desperate for the plum—with Benjamin Franklin urging Pennsylvania's legislature to grant the land moments after the proposed Constitution was first read to that body. In the event, a "Southern" site was selected, near the fall line of the Potomac River. In exchange, the Southern states agreed that the new federal government would assume the states' Revolutionary War debts, which were more burdensome to the Northern states. That arrangement was sealed in a meeting between Alexander Hamilton and Thomas Jefferson in which the South gained the capital, but the federal government obtained economic prowess. Maryland and Virginia ceded "ten miles square" on their respective sides of the river, and the government finally moved to its permanent seat in 1800.

In 1846, the Virginia portion of the original territory of Columbia, encompassing Old Town Alexandria and Arlington County, was "retroceded" by Congress to the Commonwealth. The constitutionality of this act has never been determined. In 1875, the Supreme

Court dismissed, for lack of standing, a case brought by a Virginia taxpayer who argued that he was properly subject to the District's then less-onerous tax burden. The Court noted that the plaintiff sought to "vicariously raise a question" that neither Virginia nor the federal government had "desire[d] to make." *Phillips v. Payne* (1875).

The week before John Adams left the presidency in 1801, Congress established a government for the District, dividing it into two counties, Washington and Alexandria. The law provided that the laws then existing in the two counties, deriving from Virginia and Maryland, respectively, would remain in force until modified by Congress. A realization that the original bill would have left the District without a judiciary prompted Congress to provide for justices of the peace to be appointed by the President. Over the last two centuries, Congress has experimented with varying methods of home rule, as well as with direct rule. Today, the most controversial aspect of Congress's authority over the District is the fact that Washington, D.C., residents cannot elect Members to Congress. The Twenty-third Amendment gave the District the right to participate in presidential elections but not in congressional elections. Instead, the residents elect a nonvoting "delegate" to the House of Representatives.

Because of the District's unique character as the federal city, neither the Framers nor Congress accorded the inhabitants the right to elect Members of the House of Representatives or the Senate. In exchange, however, the District's residents received the multifarious benefits of the national capital. As Justice Joseph Story noted in *Commentaries on the Constitution of the United States*, "there can be little doubt, that the inhabitants composing [the District] would receive with thankfulness such a blessing, since their own importance would be thereby increased, their interests be subserved, and their rights be under the immediate protection of the representatives of the whole Union." In effect, the Framers believed that the residents were "virtually" represented in the federal interest for a strong, prosperous capital.

There have been a number of efforts to change this original design, including a proposed constitutional amendment (passed by Congress in 1977) that would have granted the District of Columbia congressional voting representation "as if it were a state." This amendment, however, was not ratified in the seven-year period established by Congress. Other proposals have included a retrocession of most, or all, of the District to Maryland—a plan that Attorney General Robert F. Kennedy in 1964 deemed impractical and unconstitutional—and the admission of Washington, D.C., to the Union as the fifty-first state.

In 2000, the courts rejected a series of arguments suggesting that the District's inhabitants were, on various constitutional and policy grounds, entitled to voting representation in Congress without an amendment. *See Adams v. Clinton* (2000). More recently, the courts have rejected application of the Second Amendment to the District of Columbia, reasoning that the right to keep and bear arms was for the benefit of *state* militias, and efforts to invalidate a congressionally imposed limit on the District's ability to tax nonresident commuters. *See Seegars v. Ashcroft* (2004); *Banner v. United States* (2004). In the latter case, the court noted that, "simply put . . . the District and its residents are the subject of Congress' unique powers, exercised to address the unique circumstances of our nation's capital."

Statehood is now the clear preference of District of Columbia voting-rights advocates, but the proposal has never excited much support in Congress and would, in any case, also require a constitutional amendment since an independent territory, subject to the ultimate authority of Congress, was a critical part of the Framers' original design for an indestructible federal union of indestructible states.

Lee Casey

See Also

Amendment XXIII (Electors for the District of Columbia)

Suggestions for Further Research

Bob Arnebeck, Through A Fiery Trial: Building Washington 1790–1800 (1991)

WILHELMUS B. BRYAN, A HISTORY OF THE NATIONAL
　　CAPITAL (1914)

Peter Raven-Hansen, *The Constitutionality of D.C.
　　Statehood*, 60 GEO. WASH. L. REV. 160 (1991)

U.S. Department of Justice, Office of Legal Policy,
　　*Report to the Attorney General: The Question of
　　Statehood for the District of Columbia* (1987)

Significant Cases

Phillips v. Payne, 92 U.S. 130, 133 (1875)

Albaugh v. Tawes, 233 F. Supp. 576 (D.C. Md. 1964),
　　aff'd, 379 U.S. 27 (1964) (per curiam)

Evans v. Cornman, 398 U.S. 419 (1970)

Adams v. Clinton, 90 F. Supp. 2d 35 (D.D.C. 2000),
　　aff'd, 531 U.S. 941 (2000)

Adams v. Clinton, 90 F. Supp. 2d 27 (D.D.C. 2000),
　　cert. denied, 154 L. Ed. 2d 15 (2002)

Banner v. United States, 303 F. Supp. 2d 1 (D.D.C. 2004)

Seegars v. Ashcroft, 297 F. Supp. 2d 201 (D.D.C. 2004)

Military Installations

**The Congress shall have Power To
...exercise like Authority over all
Places purchased by the Consent of
the Legislature of the State in
which the Same shall be, for the
Erection of Forts, Magazines, Arsenals, dock-Yards, and other needful
Buildings ....**
(ARTICLE I, SECTION 8, CLAUSE 17)

～

*I*n addition to the permanent seat of government, established by 1800 in the District of
Columbia, the Constitution gave Congress exclusive legislative authority over certain federal
installations. Like the federal district, the purpose
of this grant was to accommodate and guarantee
the independence of both federal and state sovereignties. As Justice Joseph Story noted in his *Commentaries on the Constitution of the United States*:

The public money expended on such
places, and the public property deposited
in them, and the nature of the military

duties, which may be required there, all
demand, that they should be exempted
from state authority. In truth, it would be
wholly improper, that places, on which the
security of the entire Union may depend,
should be subjected to the control of any
member of it. The power, indeed, is wholly
unexceptionable; since it can only be exercised at the will of the state; and it is therefore placed beyond all reasonable scruple.

Federal "enclave" jurisdiction, obtained under
this provision, must be distinguished from
instances where the federal government has
obtained only a "proprietarial" interest in a particular building or parcel of land through purchase—although federal authority over such
areas may be nearly as broad under the Territories Clause (Article IV, Section 3, Clause 2).
Enclave jurisdiction also may exist as a result of a
federal reservation of legislative authority over an
area at the time a state is admitted to the Union,
or based upon a particular cession by the state of
that authority. Federal enclave jurisdiction may
apply to individual buildings, or parts of buildings (such as the U.S. Customs House, and the
northern portion of the U.S. mint, located in
Denver, Colorado), or to vast territories (such as
the 200-square-mile Camp Pendleton in California). Federal enclaves include such varying installations as the National Institutes of Health in
Bethesda, Maryland, and Cape Canaveral, Florida, as well as certain national parks, national
cemeteries, lighthouses, and locks and dams.

The case law dealing with federal enclaves is
complex. Such areas are subject to the "special
maritime and territorial jurisdiction of the United States," 18 U.S.C. § 2243, and criminal offenses
committed within an enclave are subject to federal prosecution, although the substantive offense
may well be grounded in the surrounding state's
law pursuant to the Assimilative Crimes Act, 18
U.S.C. § 13(a). The ceding state retains no authority in a federal enclave unless it specifically
reserved such rights at the time it consented to
the purchase, or made the cession. In fact, most
states have reserved at least the right to serve state
civil and criminal process in federal enclaves, and
they may also retain certain regulatory authority.

Paul v. United States (1963). At the same time, although a state's rights vis-á-vis a federal enclave depend upon the terms of the original cession, the Supreme Court has ruled that federal enclave residents are entitled to vote as residents of the surrounding state. *Evans v. Cornman* (1970).

Lee Casey

See Also

Article IV, Section 3, Clause 2 (Property Clause)

Suggestions for Further Research

David E. Engdahl, *State and Federal Power over Federal Property*, 18 Ariz. L. Rev. 283 (1976)

Jurisdiction over Federal Areas Within the States: Report of the Interdepartmental Committee for the Study of Jurisdiction over Federal Areas Within the States (April 1956)

Significant Cases

Fort Leavenworth Railroad Co. v. Lowe, 114 U.S. 525 (1885)

James v. Dravo Contracting Co., 302 U.S. 134 (1937)

James Stewart & Co. v. Sadrakula, 309 U.S. 94 (1940)

Paul v. United States, 371 U.S. 245, 268 (1963)

Evans v. Cornman, 398 U.S. 419 (1970)

Lewis v. United States, 523 U.S. 155 (1998)

Necessary and Proper Clause

> The Congress shall have Power To ...make all Laws which shall be necessary and proper for carrying into Execution the foregoing Powers, and all other Powers vested by this Constitution in the Government of the United States, or in any Department or Officer thereof.
>
> (Article I, Section 8, Clause 18)

≈

*A*t the Constitutional Convention, the Committee of Detail took the Convention's resolutions on national legislative authority and particular-

ized them into a series of enumerated powers. This originated the principle of enumerated powers, under which federal law can govern only as to matters within the terms of some power-granting clause of the Constitution. By including the Necessary and Proper Clause, the Framers set the criterion for laws that, even if they are not within the terms of other grants, serve to make other federal powers effective.

In *McCulloch v. Maryland* (1819), Chief Justice John Marshall noted that other grants of power by themselves "according to the dictates of reason" would "imply" a "means of execution." He went on, however, to declare that the Constitution "has not left the right of Congress to employ the necessary means for the execution of the powers conferred on the Government to general reasoning." For the Chief Justice, the Necessary and Proper Clause makes express a power that otherwise would only have been implied and thus might have been subject to cavil. By implanting the clause among the powers of Congress, the Framers confirmed that Congress may act to make the constitutional plan effective. In his parsing of the words of the clause, he concluded that the Necessary and Proper Clause authorizes laws enacted as means "really calculated to effect any of the objects intrusted to the government." Arguments for laws that lack this crucial means-to-end characteristic find no support in Marshall's opinion or in the Necessary and Proper Clause.

The Framers crafted the Necessary and Proper Clause to serve two great purposes. The first was to facilitate organization of the government, such as empowering Congress to organize the judicial branch (*see* Article I, Section 8, Clause 9). The second was to help effectuate the other enumerated powers of Congress. As to the first, the Constitution could not prescribe all points of government organization, so Detail Committee member Edmund Randolph proposed empowering Congress to "organize the government." James Wilson proposed the "necessary and proper" clause as a substitute, authorizing laws "for carrying into Execution" the other federal powers. The committee, and then the Convention, approved. The organizational function of this clause was recognized from the outset. Among Congress's first acts were establishing executive departments and staffs, determining the number of Justices of the Supreme Court, and allocating the judicial power among federal courts. The Supreme Court acknowledged this clause as the source of Congress's power to legislate about judicial process and procedure. Without this clause (or some equivalent), statutes organizing the other branches not only would have violated the principle of enumerated powers, but also would have offended the principle of separation of powers.

As to the second and more significant purpose, the clause also supports laws for carrying into execution "the foregoing Powers," that is, those specified for the legislature itself in Article I, Section 8. It thus enhances the other powers given to Congress. During the ratification debates, opponents dubbed it the "sweeping clause" and the "general clause," arguing that it subverted the principle of enumerated powers by sweeping general legislative competence to Congress. The critic Brutus, for example, said it "leaves the national legislature at liberty, to do every thing, which in their judgment is best." In *The Federalist* No. 33, Alexander Hamilton replied that the clause is tautological but harmless, meaning nothing more than that Congress may exercise its legislative powers by making laws. Hamilton soon abandoned that simplistic view, however.

At Pennsylvania's ratification convention, James Wilson, the author of the clause, explained that the words "necessary and proper" are "limited, and defined by the following, 'for carrying into execution the foregoing powers.' It is saying no more than that the powers we have already particularly given, shall be effectually carried into execution." It authorizes what is "necessary to render effectual the particular powers that are granted." Congress thus can make laws about something otherwise outside the enumerated powers, insofar as those laws are "necessary and proper" to effectuate federal policy for something within an enumerated power. Although not independently valid under another enumerated power, such laws are supported by this clause to the extent that they constitute a means by which federal policy can be executed under an enumerated power.

On this principle, Hamilton, as Treasury Secretary, urged Congress in 1790 to establish a private banking corporation to facilitate tax collection and support of the army, to promote commerce among the states, and to answer the government's own borrowing needs. The Supreme Court confirmed the indispensable means-to-end nature of the necessary and proper power in *McCulloch v. Maryland* (1819). Writing for the Court, Chief Justice John Marshall upheld the Second Bank of the United States, utilizing the very rationale that Secretary Hamilton, and Wilson before him, had employed. Marshall rejected Thomas Jefferson's view that the clause limits Congress to "those means without which the grant of power would be nugatory." That would have precluded Congress from deliberating alternatives, and the Court read the clause instead as vesting "discretion, with respect to the means by which the powers it confers are to be carried into execution." *McCulloch* countenanced "any means calculated to produce the end," giving Congress "the capacity to avail itself of experience, to exercise its reason, and to accommodate its legislation to circumstances." According to *McCulloch*, unless otherwise inconsistent "with the letter and spirit of the constitution," any law that is "appropriate," "plainly adapted to that end," and "really calculated to effect any of the objects entrusted to the federal government" is valid under the Necessary and Proper Clause. For the judiciary "to inquire into the degree of its necessity," Marshall said, "would be . . . to tread on legislative ground."

So long as a law promotes an end within the scope of some enumerated power, extraneous objectives do not render it unconstitutional. Indeed, one means might be preferred over others precisely because it advances another objective as well. For example, besides helping Congress effectuate various enumerated powers, a bank could make private loans to augment business capital or to satisfy consumer wants; while these extraneous ends could provide no independent constitutional justification, Hamilton urged them as principal reasons why Congress should incorporate a bank. Record-keeping and reporting requirements regarding drug transactions, if apt as means to enforce federal taxes on those transactions, are no less valid because crafted for police ends that are not within any enumerated power. Extraneous objectives are constitutionally immaterial; but to invoke the Necessary and Proper Clause, a sufficient link to some enumerated-power end is constitutionally indispensable.

The Necessary and Proper Clause allows Congress to decide whether, when, and how to legislate "for carrying into Execution" the powers of another branch; but it respects and even reinforces the principle of separation of powers. Unlike Randolph's authorization to "organize the government"—which the Committee of Detail had replaced with Wilson's more exacting phrase—"laws...for carrying into Execution" the powers (and thus discretion) reposed in another branch can only mean laws to help effectuate the discretion of that other branch. It gives Congress no power to instruct or impede another branch in the performance of that branch's constitutional role. Of course, when the clause is invoked to effectuate ends within Congress's own powers, it compounds Congress's discretion: not only the selection of means, but also the selection of policy ends, rests in Congress's own discretion.

McCulloch remains the classic elucidation of this clause, but it has been elaborated in many other cases, such as in the proceedings concerning the Legal Tender Act of 1862. Congress, in an effort to stabilize commerce and support military efforts during the Civil War, determined that new paper currency must be accepted at face value as legal tender. The Supreme Court, in the *Legal Tender Cases* (1871), affirmed Congress's discretion to choose among means thought conducive to enumerated-power ends. The Court upheld Congress's choice, even though better means might have been chosen, and though the legal tender clause proved to be of little help: "The degree of the necessity for any Congressional enactment, or the relative degree of its appropriateness, if it has any appropriateness, is for consideration in Congress, not here," said the Court.

The basic operation of the Necessary and Proper Clause is the same in every context. For example, federal tax lien and collection laws; record-keeping, reporting, and filing requirements; and civil and criminal penalties for non-payment are not themselves exertions of Congress's power to tax, but are laws "necessary and proper for carrying into Execution" the federal

taxing power. That is why "provisions extraneous to any tax need" are not rendered valid simply by inclusion in a tax statute. *United States v. Kahriger* (1953); *see also Linder v. United States* (1925). Similarly, with regard to federal condemnation of property, "the really important question to be determined" is whether "it is necessary or appropriate to use the land in the execution of any of the powers granted to it by the constitution." *United States v. Gettysburg Electric Railway Co.* (1896). "Public use" alone is not sufficient, but if the proposed use is the kind of public use embraced by one of the enumerated federal powers, "the provision comes within the rule laid down by Chief Justice Marshall, in *McCulloch v. Maryland*...."

This clause's enhancement of Congress's power over commerce among the states had been judicially recognized decades before Congress began to exercise that power extensively. *See Gilman v. Philadelphia* (1866). Its means-to-end logic underlay the Supreme Court's approval of antitrust prosecutions for local monopolies when the government could prove a purpose to restrain interstate trade, *Addyston Pipe & Steel v. United States* (1899), but not when the government omitted to prove such a purpose, *United States v. E.C. Knight Co.* (1895). The same rationale sustained an amendment to the Safety Appliance Act, which prescribed safety equipment for railcars used only within a state, because the amendment increased safety for interstate cars and cargos on the same rails. *Southern Railway v. United States* (1911). Likewise, the Interstate Commerce Commission could authorize carriers to disregard state limits on rates for trips within a state, as a means to eliminate price discrimination against interstate commerce. *Shreveport Rate Case* (1914). Upholding the wage and hour provisions of the Fair Labor Standards Act on this ground in *United States v. Darby* (1941), the Court cited not only those older cases but also *NLRB v. Jones & Laughlin Steel Corp.* (1937) as illustrating the rationale of the Necessary and Proper Clause.

Often the Supreme Court has not articulated this Necessary and Proper Clause basis of its so-called affecting commerce doctrine. This has led to one of the most confused areas of all constitutional law. Justice Sandra Day O'Connor, however, did emphasize it: first in her dissent in *Garcia v. San Antonio Metropolitan Transit Authority* (1985), and then for the majority in *New York v. United States* (1989). The rule against federal "commandeering" of state officials, applied both in that New York case and in *Printz v. United States* (1997), was attributed to the word "proper" in the Necessary and Proper Clause, as interpreted in *McCulloch* to mean consistency with "the spirit of the constitution."

It should be emphasized, however that the Necessary and Proper Clause authorizes Congress to enact laws that are "appropriate" and plainly adapted for carrying into execution Congress's enumerated powers; it does not authorize Congress to enact any law that Congress thinks is "reasonable."

Thus, although a measure can be sustained under this clause, even if Congress's means-to-end judgment proves wrong, as Justice Robert H. Jackson said in *United States v. Five Gambling Devices* (1953), it must appear that the means-to-end relation "has been considered by Congress and has been explicitly and deliberately resolved."

The Necessary and Proper Clause does not confer general authority over a matter simply because its regulation in some respects might serve an enumerated-power end; it only supports the particular regulations that have such an effect. For example, what mattered in *NLRB v. Jones & Laughlin Steel Corp* (1937) was not that steel manufacturing impacts interstate commerce, but rather that applying the particular NLRA provisions prohibiting those factories' unfair labor practices would promote Congress's policy of uninterrupted interstate commerce in steel. Similarly, in *Heart of Atlanta Motel v. United States* (1964), Title II of the 1964 Civil Rights Act was held applicable, not because hotels affect interstate commerce, but because prohibiting racial discrimination by hotels promotes Congress's interstate commerce policy of unimpeded travel.

The Necessary and Proper Clause served as the model for the "enforcement" clauses of the Thirteenth, Fourteenth, and Fifteenth Amendments, and the latter have always been construed as analogous to the former. *See Civil Rights Cases* (1883); *Katzenbach v. Morgan* (1966) ("the *McCulloch v. Maryland* standard is the measure for what constitutes 'appropriate legislation' under Section 5 of the Fourteenth Amendment"). Recent cases have held that to invoke Enforcement Clause support, a law must be "congruent" and "proportional" to the amendment violation it aims to redress. *City of Boerne v. Flores* (1997); *Board of Trustees of the University of Alabama v. Garrett* (2001). These can be seen as elaborations of the *McCulloch* principle—to invoke the Necessary and Proper Clause, a law must be "plainly adapted" to an enumerated end—a principle that for almost a century has been exhibited in "affecting commerce" cases as the requirement of "substantial effect." This substantial effect test was raised to new prominence in *United States v. Lopez* (1995). If the analogy between this clause and the various enforcement clauses is to hold, perhaps the same principles of congruence and proportionality must also be applied in so-called affecting commerce cases and in other contexts of the Necessary and Proper Clause.

David Engdahl

See Also

Suggestions for Further Research

Randy E. Barnett, *Necessary and Proper*, 44 UCLA L. Rev. 745 (1997)

David E. Engdahl, *The Necessary and Proper Clause as an Intrinsic Restraint on Federal Lawmaking Power*, 22 Harv. J.L. & Pub. Pol'y 107 (1998)

David E. Engdahl, *Sense and Nonsense About State Immunity*, 2 Const. Comment. 93 (1985)

Stephen A. Gardbaum, *Rethinking Constitutional Federalism*, 74 Tex. L. Rev. 795 (1996)

Gary Lawson & Patricia B. Granger, *The Proper Scope of Federal Power: A Jurisdictional Interpretation of the Sweeping Clause*, 43 Duke L.J. 267 (1993)

Significant Cases

McCulloch v. Maryland, 17 U.S. (4 Wheat.) 316 (1819)

Gilman v. Philadelphia, 70 U.S. (3 Wall.) 713 (1866)

Legal Tender Cases, 79 U.S. (12 Wall.) 457 (1871)

Civil Rights Cases, 109 U.S. 3 (1883)

United States v. E.C. Knight Co., 156 U.S. 1 (1895)

United States v. Gettysburg Electric Railway Co., 160 U.S. 668 (1896)

Addyston Pipe & Steel v. United States, 175 U.S. 211 (1899)

Southern Railway v. United States, 222 U.S. 20 (1911)

Shreveport Rate Case, 234 U.S. 342 (1914)

Linder v. United States, 268 U.S. 5 (1925)

NLRB v. Jones & Laughlin Steel Corp., 301 U.S. 1 (1937)

United States v. Darby, 312 U.S. 100 (1941)

United States v. Five Gambling Devices, 346 U.S. 441 (1953)

United States v. Kahriger, 345 U.S. 22 (1953)

Heart of Atlanta Motel v. United States, 379 U.S. 241 (1964)

Katzenbach v. Morgan, 384 U.S. 641 (1966)

Garcia v. San Antonio Metropolitan Transit Authority, 469 U.S. 528 (1985)

New York v. United States, 488 U.S. 1041 (1989)

United States v. Lopez, 514 U.S. 549 (1995)

City of Boerne v. Flores, 521 U.S. 507 (1997)

Printz v. United States, 521 U.S. 898 (1997)

Board of Trustees of the University of Alabama v. Garrett, 531 U.S. 356 (2001)

Slave Trade

The Migration or Importation of such Persons as any of the States now existing shall think proper to admit, shall not be prohibited by the Congress prior to the Year one thousand eight hundred and eight, but a Tax or duty may be imposed on such Importation, not exceeding ten dollars for each Person.

(ARTICLE I, SECTION 9, CLAUSE 1)

∼

*A*lthough the first debate over slavery at the Constitutional Convention concerned representation (*see* Article I, Section 2, Clause 3), the second debate arose when Southern delegates objected that an unrestricted congressional power to regulate commerce could be used against Southern commercial interests to restrict or outlaw the slave trade. That the resulting provision was an important compromise is underscored by the fact that the clause stands as the first independent restraint on congressional powers, prior even to the restriction on the power to suspend the writ of habeas corpus.

Taking Southern concerns into consideration, the draft proposed by the Committee of Detail (chaired by John Rutledge of South Carolina) dealt with trade issues as well as those relating to slavery. The draft permanently forbade Congress to tax exports, to outlaw or tax the slave trade, or to pass navigation laws without two-thirds majorities in both houses of Congress. Several delegates strongly objected to the proposal, including Gouverneur Morris, who delivered one of the Convention's most spirited denunciations of slavery, calling it a "nefarious institution" and "the curse of heaven."

When the issue came up for a vote, the Southern delegates themselves were sharply divided. George Mason of Virginia condemned the "infernal traffic," and Luther Martin of Maryland saw the restriction of Congress's power over the slave trade as "inconsistent with the principles of the Revolution and dishonorable to the American character." But delegates from Georgia and South Carolina announced that they would not support the Constitution without the restriction, with Charles Pinckney arguing that failing to include the clause would trigger "an exclusion of South Carolina from the Union."

Unresolved, the issue was referred to the Committee of Eleven (chaired by William Livingston of New Jersey), which took the opposite position and recognized a congressional power over the slave trade, but recommended that it be restricted for twelve years, and allowed a tax on slave importation. Although that was a significant change from the Committee of Detail's original proposal, Southern delegates accepted the new arrangement with the extension of the time period to twenty years, from 1800 to 1808.

Agitation against the slave trade was the leading cause espoused by the antislavery movement at the time of the Constitutional Convention, so it is not surprising that this clause was the most immediately controversial of the so-called slave clauses of the proposed Constitution (*see* Article I, Section 2, Clause 3; Article IV, Section 2, Clause 3; and Article V). Although some denounced the Slave Trade Clause as a major concession to slavery interests, most begrudged it to be a necessary and prudent compromise. James Madison, for example, argued at the Convention that the twenty-year exemption was "dishonorable," but in *The Federalist* No. 42, he declared that it was "a great point gained in favor of humanity, that a period of twenty years may terminate for ever within these States" what he called an "unnatural traffic" that was "the barbarism of modern policy."

Some claimed that the Commerce Clause gave Congress the power to regulate both the interstate and the foreign slave trade once the twenty-year period had lapsed. James Wilson of Pennsylvania argued, "yet the lapse of a few years, and Congress will have power to exterminate slavery from within our borders." Though the question was not clearly resolved at the time, Madison denied this interpretation during the First Congress. Not even Abraham Lincoln claimed that congressional power to regulate commerce could be used to restrict interstate commerce in slaves.

In *Dred Scott v. Sandford* (1857), Chief Justice Roger B. Taney pointed to this clause, along with the so-called Fugitive Slave Clause (Article IV, Section 2, Clause 3), as evidence that slaves were not citizens but were to be considered property according to the Constitution. Observers are virtually unanimous that those clauses did not address the question of citizenship at all. Although protection of the slave trade was a major concession demanded by proslavery delegates, the final clause was not a permanent element of the constitutional structure, but a temporary restriction of a delegated federal power. Moreover the restriction applied only to states existing at the time, not to new states or territories, and it did not prevent

states from restricting or outlawing the slave trade for themselves. As the dissent in *Dred Scott* points out, there were freed blacks who were citizens in a number of Northern states and who had voted to ratify the new constitution.

It is significant that the words *slave* and *slavery* are not used in the Constitution of 1787, and that the Framers used the word *person* rather than *property*. This would assure, as Madison explained in *The Federalist* No. 54, that a slave would be regarded "as a moral person, not as a mere article of property." It was in the context of the slave trade debate at the Constitutional Convention that Madison argued that it was "wrong to admit in the Constitution the idea that there could be property in men."

Although Southern delegates hoped opposition would weaken with time, the practical effect of the clause was to create a growing expectation of federal legislation against the practice. Congress passed, and President Thomas Jefferson signed into law, a federal prohibition of the slave trade, effective January 1, 1808, the first day that Article I, Section 9, Clause 1, allowed such a law to go into effect.

Matthew Spalding

See Also

Suggestions for Further Research

Walter Berns, *The Constitution and the Migration of Slaves*, 78 YALE L.J. 198 (1968)

DON E. FEHRENBACHER, THE SLAVEHOLDING REPUBLIC: AN ACCOUNT OF THE UNITED STATES GOVERNMENT'S RELATIONS TO SLAVERY (2001)

DONALD L. ROBINSON, SLAVERY IN THE STRUCTURE OF AMERICAN POLITICS, 1765–1820 (1971)

Ronald D. Rotunda & John E. Nowak, *Joseph Story: A Man for All Seasons, in* 1990 YEARBOOK OF THE SUPREME COURT HISTORICAL SOCIETY (1990)

Herbert J. Storing, *Slavery and the Moral Foundations of the American Republic, in* ROBERT H. HORWITZ, THE MORAL FOUNDATIONS OF THE AMERICAN REPUBLIC (1986)

Significant Cases

The Amistad, 40 U.S. (15 Pet.) 518 (1841)
Prigg v. Pennsylvania, 41 U.S. (16 Pet.) 539 (1842)
Jones v. Van Zandt, 46 U.S. (5 How.) 215 (1847)
Moore v. Illinois, 55 U.S. (14 How.) 13 (1852)
Dred Scott v. Sandford, 60 U.S. (19 How.) 393 (1857)
Ableman v. Booth, 62 U.S. (21 How.) 506 (1859)
Osborn v. Nicholson, 80 U.S. (13 Wall.) 654 (1871)

Habeas Corpus

The Privilege of the Writ of Habeas Corpus shall not be suspended, unless when in Cases of Rebellion or Invasion the public Safety may require it.

(ARTICLE I, SECTION 9, CLAUSE 2)

∼

*T*he writ of habeas corpus, or the "Great Writ," is an order by a common-law court to require a person holding a prisoner to demonstrate the legal and jurisdictional basis for continuing to hold the prisoner. If there is no legal basis for detention or incarceration, the court orders the release of the prisoner. In English practice, the writ addressed detentions before trial, not defects that might have occurred during trial, but American practice has greatly expanded its sweep and availability. The scope and meaning of the Habeas Corpus Clause has been controversial since its ratification—this often-heated public debate remains one of the longest running in American history.

The Great Writ was one of the many imports from England, where Sir William Blackstone described it in his *Commentaries on the Laws of England* as "the glory of the English law." The right of citizens to demand review of their incarceration was an essential protection against government abuse, which,

Blackstone noted, "does not always arise from the ill-nature, but sometimes from the mere inattention, of government." The colonial governments agreed, and, despite the Crown's position that habeas was not available in the colonies, writs of habeas corpus (literally, you shall have the body) were issued before the Revolution.

In *The Federalist* No. 84, Alexander Hamilton stressed the importance of the writ of habeas corpus to protect against "the favorite and most formidable instruments of tyranny." By 1787, several state constitutions already guaranteed habeas corpus, and there was fairly uniform agreement that it would be one of the basic guarantees in the American Republic.

At the Constitutional Convention and the later state ratification conventions, one of the most divisive issues was the failure to ban absolutely any suspension of the writ. Luther Martin argued that the power would be "an engine of oppression" that could be used by the federal government to declare any state opposition to federal law, "however arbitrary and unconstitutional," an act of rebellion. Nonetheless, a general consensus emerged: there could be circumstances where the writ had to be suspended in the most extreme conditions of war or invasion. It is clear from this record that some delegates understood the Habeas Corpus Clause to mean that the Congress could not suspend the authority of *state* courts (as well as federal courts) in the exercise of the writ except in cases of rebellion or invasion. Some delegates also believed that the state courts could exercise habeas authority to review the custody of federal prisoners. Consistent with this understanding, various state courts did exercise habeas jurisdiction over federal prisoners well into the nineteenth century. State court habeas power over federal prisoners soon lapsed. Chief Justice John Marshall concluded in *Ex parte Bollman* (1807) that the Judiciary Act of 1789 granted only federal courts the power to issue writs for federal prisoners, and ruled that the Habeas Corpus Clause dealt only with prisoners in federal authority. The Supreme Court has built the modern view of habeas around this interpretation. This included decisions that effectively prevented any state court from exercising habeas authority over a federal prisoner. In 1859, for example, the Taney Court unanimously rejected a state court's claim of habeas authority over federal prisoners in *Ableman v. Booth*. In 1953, the Supreme Court reaffirmed the authority of the federal courts over state courts in *Brown v. Allen*. The Court held that the Supremacy Clause of the Constitution dictated that federal courts would hear federal claims raised in state courts, even though state courts could not grant release of federal prisoners.

One of the most obvious ambiguities in the Habeas Corpus Clause is the absence of an affirmative grant of the right to suspend habeas corpus. Written in the negative, the clause only described the conditions under which it could be suspended. While controversial during the ratification debate, it has been generally accepted that a right to suspend the writ is implied in the language. The next ambiguity arises from the fact that the clause does not affirmatively state who can suspend the writ. Originally, Charles Pinckney proposed the clause with the words "shall not be suspended *by the Legislature*." This reference to Congress was dropped in the later debate, allowing some to argue that either Congress or the President could suspend habeas corpus. However, it is notable that the Committee of Style moved the clause from Article III (dealing with the judicial branch) to Article I (dealing with the legislative branch), suggesting that suspension was viewed as a legislative power. Later, President Abraham Lincoln's unilateral suspension of the writ was met with such political and judicial opposition until he obtained congressional authorization. *See Ex parte Merryman* (1861).

Another debate focused on the authority of the courts to issue the writ, a power not expressly given in the Constitution. In *Bollman*, Chief Justice Marshall indicated that it was up to Congress to authorize the writ, though he suggested Congress was under an obligation to do so. He observed that "[a]cting under the immediate influence of [the Habeas Corpus Clause], [Congress] must have felt, with peculiar force, the obligation of providing efficient means by which this great constitutional privilege should receive life and activity; for if the means be not in existence, the privilege itself would be lost, although no law for its suspension should be enacted."

Since that time, Congress has suspended the writ only three times: South Carolina in 1871 (to deal with the Ku Klux Klan); the Philippines in 1905 (in connection with the local revolt); and Hawaii during World War II. Conversely, beginning in 1789, Congress passed a number of statutes providing habeas relief for a growing category of prisoners. Along the way Congress also statutorily granted federal courts the power to issue writs for the release of state prisoners. Though the first Judiciary Act of 1789 only authorized issuance of the writ for federal prisoners, the writ was made available in federal court to state prisoners through the Habeas Corpus Act of 1867. *Ex parte McCardle* (1869). Those statutes filled a real need in the federal criminal-justice system, for there was no direct appeal from criminal cases in the federal system until 1875. Thus, in the early years of the Republic, habeas relief was the only means by which the federal courts could review the conviction of a prisoner who had his constitutional rights denied in his criminal trial. In fact, a prisoner could raise a constitutional challenge both at the trial and later through a habeas petition. Recent changes in statutory and case law have served to limit the number of challenges a petitioner can make.

From the time of the Civil War, the Supreme Court continuously expanded the availability of habeas relief. Under the common-law tradition, habeas relief obtained only when the court (or the sheriff or warden) could not show jurisdiction over the prisoner. Federal courts, however, expanded habeas relief to include a broader definition of "custody" than mere arrest, including most defects found at trial. In *Brown v. Allen*, the Supreme Court dispensed with earlier limitations and accorded habeas relief to any person held in violation of the Constitution.

Federal habeas power reached its high-water mark in 1963. In three cases dealing with habeas petitions, the Supreme Court directed lower federal courts to hold evidentiary hearings, allowed for successive claims on the same facts, and held that a prisoner is entitled to lodge a habeas petition, even if he failed state law requirements to raise his substantive objectives in a timely manner during trial. *Sanders v. United States* (1963); *Townsend v. Sain* (1963); *Fay v. Noia* (1963).

Subsequently, however, both Congress and the Supreme Court have narrowed the availability of criminal appeals and habeas relief and reversed some of the previous holdings. In cases such as *Stone v. Powell* (1976), the Supreme Court deferred to state courts in the adjudication of certain claims so long as the claims were properly considered in the state system. The next year, in *Wainwright v. Sykes* (1977), Justice William H. Rehnquist emphasized that habeas corpus was a form of equitable relief that courts have the power to expand or contract as is needed. These and later cases have resulted in a shift back to the state courts as the primary guarantors of constitutional protections and due process. The Antiterrorism and Effective Death Penalty Act of 1996, among other things, placed curbs on the filing of successive and frivolous petitions, and required federal courts to presume that state court factual determinations are correct. Although there remains significantly less authority for state courts than envisioned in the eighteenth century, this judicial and legislative shift represents a significant enhancement of the state court authority over state prisoners.

With new national security measures following the attacks of September 11, 2001, the legal protections of "the Great Writ" persist. Congress must declare any suspension of the writ by statute, which it has not done. Accordingly, the writ is available to civilian and military prisoners claiming jurisdictional barriers to their continued detention or incarceration. Indeed, "the Great Writ" is already at the forefront of the long American debate over the balancing of national security interests and individual liberties.

Jonathan Turley

See Also
Article VI, Clause 2 (Supremacy Clause)

Suggestions for Further Research
Paul Bator, *Finality in Criminal Law and Habeas Corpus for State Prisoners*, 76 HARV. L. REV. 441 (1963)

A Native of Virginia, *Observations upon the Proposed Plan of Federal Government, reprinted in* 9 DOCUMENTARY HISTORY OF THE RATIFICATION OF THE CONSTITUTION 655 (John P. Kaminiski & Gaspare J. Saldino eds., 1984)

Significant Cases
Ex parte Bollman, 8 U.S. (4 Cranch) 75 (1807)

Ableman v. Booth, 62 U.S. (21 How.) 506 (1859)

Ex parte Merryman, 17 F. Cas. 144 (C.C. Md. 1861) (No. 9487)

Ex parte McCardle, 74 U.S. (7 Wall.) 506 (1869)

Brown v. Allen, 344 U.S. 443 (1953)

Fay v. Noia, 372 U.S. 391 (1963)

Sanders v. United States, 373 U.S. 1 (1963)

Townsend v. Sain, 372 U.S. 293 (1963)

Stone v. Powell, 428 U.S. 465 (1976)

Wainwright v. Sykes, 433 U.S. 72 (1977)

I.N.S. v. Enrico St. Cyr, 533 U.S. 289 (2001)

Bill of Attainder

No Bill of Attainder...shall be passed.

(**ARTICLE I, SECTION 9, CLAUSE 3**)

∾

*T*he Constitution prohibits both the federal government (in this clause) and the states (in Article I, Section 10, Clause 1) from passing either bills of attainder or ex post facto laws. The Framers considered freedom from bills of attainder and ex post facto laws so important that these are the only two individual liberties that the original Constitution protects from both federal *and* state intrusion. As James Madison said in *The Federalist* No. 44, "Bills of attainder, ex post facto laws, and laws impairing the obligation of contracts, are contrary to the first principles of the social compact, and to every principle of sound legislation."

In common law, bills of attainder were legislative acts that, without trial, condemned specifically designated persons or groups to death. Bills of attainder also required the "corruption of blood"; that is, they denied to the condemned's heirs the right to inherit his estate. Bills of pains and penalties, in contrast, singled out designated persons or groups for punishment less than death, such as banishment or disenfranchisement. Many states had enacted both kinds of statutes after the Revolution.

The Framers forbade bills of attainder as part of their strategy of undoing the English law of treason, and to contend with what they regarded as the most serious historical instances of legislative tyranny by state or national legislatures. Professor Raoul Berger argues that the bill of attainder clauses (*see also* Article I, Section 10, Clause 1) protect only against legislative actions that affect the *life* of the individual, not his property, which was the province of bills of pains and penalties. Beginning with Chief Justice John Marshall, however, the Supreme Court has insisted that "a Bill of Attainder may affect the life of an individual, or may confiscate his property, or may do both." *Fletcher v. Peck* (1810).

Marshall and his successors saw the Bill of Attainder Clause as an element of the separation of powers. As the decisions of the Court in *Marbury v. Madison* (1803) and *United States v. Klein* (1871) made clear, only a court can hold a trial, evaluate the evidence, and determine the merits of the claim or accusation. The Constitution forbade the Congress from "exercis[ing] the power and office of judge." *Cummings v. Missouri* (1867). In *United States v. Brown* (1965), the Court specifically rejected a "narrow historical approach" to the clauses and characterized the Framers' purpose as to prohibit "legislative punishment, of any form or severity, of specifically designated persons or groups."

Even with an expansive definition, the Bill of Attainder Clause provides only limited protection against retroactive civil legislation. The modern Court rarely invokes the clause's protection; it has not invalidated legislation on bill-of-attainder grounds since 1965. Moreover, the only laws that the Court has invalidated as bills of attainder have been bars on the employment of specific individuals or groups of individuals.

The Court devised a three-part test to determine when a piece of legislation violates the Bill of Attainder Clause: such legislation specifies the affected persons (even if not done in terms within the statute), includes punishment, and lacks a judicial trial. Because of the Court's relatively narrow definition of punishment, however, it rarely, if ever, invalidates legislation on this basis. For example, the Court has held that the denial of noncontractual government benefits such as financial aid was not punishment, *Selective Service System v. Minnesota Public Interest Research Group* (1984), nor did an act requisitioning the recordings and material of President Richard M. Nixon and several of his aides constitute punishment. *Nixon v. Administrator of General Services* (1977). Exclusion from employment, however, is a form of punishment. *United States v. Brown* (1965).

Daniel Troy

See Also

Article I, Section 9, Clause 3 (Ex Post Facto)
Article I, Section 10, Clause 1 (State Bill of Attainder)
Article I, Section 10, Clause 1 (State Ex Post Facto)

Suggestions for Further Research

Raoul Berger, *Bills of Attainder: A Study of Amendment by the Court*, 63 CORNELL L. REV. 355 (1978)
DANIEL E. TROY, RETROACTIVE LEGISLATION (1998)

Significant Cases

Marbury v. Madison, 5 U.S. (1 Cranch) 137 (1803)
Fletcher v. Peck, 10 U.S. (6 Cranch) 87 (1810)
Cummings v. Missouri, 71 U.S. (4 Wall.) 277 (1867)
United States v. Klein, 80 U.S. (13 Wall.) 128 (1871)
United States v. Lovett, 328 U.S. 303 (1946)
United States v. Brown, 381 U.S. 437 (1965)
Nixon v. Administrator of General Services, 433 U.S. 425 (1977)
Selective Service System v. Minnesota Public Interest Research Group, 468 U.S. 841 (1984)

Ex Post Facto

No…ex post facto Law shall be passed.

(ARTICLE I, SECTION 9, CLAUSE 3)

∼

*A*s generally understood, a law that is ex post facto—literally, after the fact—is one that criminally punishes conduct that was lawful when it was done. It is an aspect of the fundamental maxim, *nulla poena sine lege:* there can be no punishment without law—in this case, without pre-existing law. Despite the fact that the prohibition against such laws had worked its way into English law (as celebrated by Sir William Blackstone), Parliament had, nonetheless, claimed the right to enact ex post facto laws in the form of bills of attainder against unpopular groups and persons. In addition, prior to the Constitutional Convention, some states themselves had passed ex post facto laws. (The prohibition of ex post facto state laws is found in Article I, Section 10, Clause 1.)

Nevertheless, opposition to ex post facto laws was a bedrock principle among the Framers. In *The Federalist* No. 78, Alexander Hamilton noted that "the subjecting of men to punishment for things which, when they were done, were breaches of no law" is among "the favorite and most formidable instruments of tyranny." Thomas Jefferson noted in an 1813 letter to Isaac McPherson "the sentiment that ex post facto laws are against natural right."

In Philadelphia, the Framers debated the issue vigorously. Some thought an explicit ban on ex post facto laws an absolute necessity. Others, such as Oliver Ellsworth of Connecticut, echoed the natural law tradition and "contended that there was no lawyer, no civilian who would not say that ex post facto laws were void of themselves. It cannot then be necessary to prohibit them." James Wilson declared that the prohibition against ex post facto laws in the state constitutions had been ineffective and would be likewise "useless" in the national constitution. Hugh Williamson then pointed to North Carolina's prohibition of ex post facto laws. He acknowledged that the prohibition had been violated, but argued that "it has done good

there & may do good here, because the Judges can take hold of it." The delegates then approved the clause, seven states to three.

Later, James Dickinson reported that, on examining Blackstone's *Commentaries on the Laws of England*, he found that "the terms 'ex post facto' related to criminal cases only; that they would not consequently restrain the states from retrospective laws in civil cases and that some further provision for this purpose would be requisite." After the Committee of Style had reported the ex post facto law clauses in their current form, George Mason of Virginia moved to strike the prohibition against ex post facto laws because the clause might apply to civil laws "and no Legislature ever did or can altogether avoid them in Civil cases." Elbridge Gerry seconded the motion because he wanted a clearer statement that prohibition did in fact apply to "Civil cases." Mason's motion was unanimously rejected.

The Court addressed the issue of the scope of the clause in one of its earliest constitutional decisions. *Calder v. Bull*, decided in 1798, involved a determination by the Connecticut legislature that a judicial decree should be set aside and a new trial held regarding a contested will. Without dissent, the Court held that the Connecticut legislature's action was not an ex post facto law forbidden under Article I, Section 10. Justice Samuel Chase defined ex post facto laws as:

1st. Every law that makes an action done before the passing of the law, and which was innocent when done, criminal; and punishes such action. 2d. Every law that aggravates a crime, or makes it greater than it was, when committed. 3d. Every law that changes the punishment, and inflicts a greater punishment, than the law annexed to the crime, when committed. 4th. Every law that alters the legal rules of evidence, and receives less, or different testimony, than the law required at the time of the commission of the offence, in order to convict the offender. All these, and similar laws, are manifestly unjust and oppressive.

Chase also made the point that, had the ex post facto law clauses barred all retroactive civil laws, the prohibition on the impairment of contracts by states (Article I, Section 10, Clause 1) and on uncompensated takings by the federal government (the Fifth Amendment's Takings Clause) would have been unnecessary.

Although some believe that the question of the scope of the Ex Post Facto Clause had not been squarely presented in *Calder v. Bull*, the Supreme Court adopted and upheld Justice Chase's position in *Carpenter v. Pennsylvania* (1855). Since that time, a few commentators and two Justices, William Johnson in *Satterlee v. Matthewson* (1829) and Clarence Thomas in *Eastern Enterprises v. Apfel* (1998), have voiced doubt over the accepted rule that the Ex Post Facto Clause applies only to criminal legislation. In *Apfel*, citing Justice Joseph Story, Thomas contended that the Ex Post Facto Clause, even more clearly than the Takings Clause, reflects the principle that retrospective laws are "generally unjust." He continued:

Since *Calder v. Bull*, . . . this Court has considered the Ex Post Facto Clause to apply only in the criminal context. I have never been convinced of the soundness of this limitation, which in *Calder* was principally justified because a contrary interpretation would render the Takings Clause unnecessary . . . . In an appropriate case, therefore, I would be willing to reconsider *Calder* and its progeny to determine whether a retroactive civil law that passes muster under our current Takings Clause jurisprudence is nonetheless unconstitutional under the Ex Post Facto Clause.

The weight of precedent and scholarly opinion, however, supports Justice Chase's view.

While the Supreme Court has hewn to the position that the Ex Post Facto Clause prohibits criminal penalties only, it has also applied the clause in civil cases where criminal penalties are disguised as civil disabilities. As the Court has said, "it is the effect, not the form, of the law that determines whether it is ex post facto." *Weaver v. Graham* (1980).

When undertaking this inquiry, courts assess whether the ostensibly civil fine or penalty is penal in nature. As Justice Felix Frankfurter articulated the inquiry:

The mark of an ex post facto law is the imposition of what can fairly be designated punishment for past acts. The question in each case where unpleasant consequences are brought to bear upon an individual for prior conduct, is whether the legislative aim was to punish that individual for past activity, or whether the restriction of the individual comes about as a relevant incident to a regulation of a present situation, such as the proper qualifications for a profession. *De Veau v. Braisted* (1960).

The issue of what constitutes "punishment" involves other clauses of the Constitution as well. For example, recent interpretations of the Double Jeopardy Clause of the Fifth Amendment may have implications for the Ex Post Facto Clause. In *United States v. Halper* (1989), the Supreme Court said that if "civil proceedings . . . advance punitive as well as remedial goals," they do not constitute punishment that is prohibited under the Double Jeopardy Clause. In *United States v. Ursery* (1996), the Court found that confiscating the home of an individual convicted for growing marijuana was a "civil remedial sanction" rather than a civil penalty. On the other hand, the Court has found that an imposed forfeiture constitutes a punitive sanction under the Eighth Amendment's excessive fines clause. *United States v. Bajakajian* (1998).

Most recently, in *Smith v. Doe* (2003), the Court (by a 6–3 decision) rejected the claim that Alaska's sex offender registration and notification law constituted retroactive punishment forbidden by the Ex Post Facto Clause (of the analogue Article I, Section 10, Clause 1). The Court focused on the legislature's "intention" and applied the following analytical framework:

If the intention of the legislature was to impose punishment, that ends the inquiry. If, however, the intention was to enact a regulatory scheme that is civil and non-punitive, we must further examine whether the statutory scheme is so punitive either in purpose or effect as to negate [the State's] intention to deem it civil. Because we ordinarily defer to the legislature's stated intent, only the clearest proof will suffice to override legislative intent and transform what has been denominated a civil remedy into a criminal penalty.

A possible problem with the Court's current interpretation of the Ex Post Facto Clause is the fact that many criminal laws could be rephrased as civil. As currently understood, the Ex Post Facto Clause thus guards against only the most severe use of the legislature's power to make laws retroactive. They do so effectively where personal liberty is at issue. But the clause is of little use to those who are aggrieved by most forms of retroactive civil legislation, which frequently affect property rights of one form or another.

The clause applies only to criminal statutes, not judicial decisions having a retroactive effect. Retroactive judicial decisions, however, can be challenged under the Due Process Clause. *See Rogers v. Tennessee* (2001). Retroactive procedural statutes that work to deny a defense, bar the practice of law, increase punishment, or increase the likelihood of conviction may violate the Ex Post Facto Clause. *See Cummings v. Missouri* (1867); *Ex parte Garland* (1867); *Carmell v. Texas* (2000). In *Stogner v. California* (2003), the Court struck down a California law that revived prosecutions for sexual abuse of children after the statute of limitations had expired.

A statutory increase in punishment is also an impermissible ex post facto law. *Collins v. Youngblood* (1990). The clause prohibits, for example, applying new sentencing guidelines to a defendant who committed the crime prior to their promulgation, *Miller v. Florida* (1987); or canceling early-release credits after they have been awarded, *Lynce v. Mathis* (1997); but not a retroactive decrease in the availability of parole hearings, *California Department of Corrections v. Morales* (1995); nor a change in the place of trial, *Cook v. United States* (1891); nor deportation, *Mahler v. Eby* (1924). The Court found no increase in punishment in a change of method

of execution from hanging to electrocution, *Malloy v. South Carolina* (1915); or in imposing civil commitment on a sexual predator after sentence, *Kansas v. Hendricks* (1997).

Daniel Troy

See Also

Suggestions for Further Research

Wayne A. Logan, *"Democratic Despotism" and Constitutional Constraint: An Empirical Analysis of Ex Post Facto Claims in State Courts*, 12 Wm. & Mary Bill Rts. J. 439 (2004)

Wayne A. Logan, *The Ex Post Facto Clause and the Jurisprudence of Punishment*, 35 Am. Crim. L. Rev. 1262 (1998)

Robert G. Natelson, *Statutory Retroactivity: The Founders' View*, 39 Idaho L. Rev. 489 (2003)

R. Brian Tanner, *Legislative Miracle: Revival Prosecution and the Ex Post Facto Clauses*, 50 Emory L.J. 307 (2001)

Daniel E. Troy, Retroactive Legislation (1998)

Daniel E. Troy, *When Does Retroactivity Cross the Line? Winstar, Eastern Enterprises and Beyond: Toward a Definition and Critique of Retroactivity*, 51 Ala. L. Rev. 1329 (2000)

Significant Cases

Calder v. Bull, 3 U.S. (3 Dall.) 386 (1798)
Satterlee v. Mathewson, 27 U.S. (2 Pet.) 380 (1829)
Carpenter v. Pennsylvania, 58 U.S. (17 How.) 456 (1855)
Cummings v. Missouri, 71 U.S. (4 Wall.) 277 (1867)
Ex parte Garland, 71 U.S. (4 Wall.) 333 (1867)
Cook v. United States, 138 U.S. 157 (1891)
Johannessen v. United States, 225 U.S. 227 (1912)
Frank v. Magnum, 237 U.S. 309 (1915)
Malloy v. South Carolina, 237 U.S. 180 (1915)
Mahler v. Eby, 264 U.S. 32 (1924)
Lindsey v. State of Washington, 301 U.S. 397 (1937)
Harisiades v. Shaughnessy, 342 U.S. 580 (1952)
De Veau v. Braisted, 363 U.S. 144, 160 (1960)

Dobbert v. Florida, 432 U.S. 282 (1977)

Weaver v. Graham, 450 U.S. 24 (1981)

Miller v. Florida, 482 U.S. 423 (1987)

United States v. Halper, 490 U.S. 435 (1989)

Collins v. Youngblood, 497 U.S. 37 (1990)

California Department of Corrections v. Morales, 514 U.S. 499 (1995)

United States v. Ursery, 518 U.S. 267 (1996)

Kansas v. Hendricks, 521 U.S. 346 (1997)

Lynce v. Mathis, 519 U.S. 433 (1997)

Eastern Enterprises v. Apfel, 524 U.S. 498 (1998)

United States v. Bajakajian, 524 U.S. 321 (1998)

Carmell v. Texas, 529 U.S. 513 (2000)

Rogers v. Tennessee, 532 U.S. 451 (2001)

Smith v. Doe, 538 U.S. 84 (2003)

Stogner v. California, 539 U.S. 607 (2003)

Direct Taxes

No Capitation, or other direct, Tax shall be laid, unless in Proportion to the Census or enumeration herein before directed to be taken.

(Article I, Section 9, Clause 4)

～

*T*he Constitution was intended to give the national government greater power to raise revenue—the Articles of Confederation had been a fiscal disaster—but many Framers remained fearful of taxation. Indirect taxes (generally understood as falling on articles of consumption) did not lend themselves to congressional abuse (for reasons that will be described presently), but the Framers believed that "direct taxes" needed to be cabined. The cumbersome apportionment rule, requiring that a direct tax be apportioned among the states on the basis of population (so that, for example, a state with twice the population of another state would have to pay twice the tax, even if the more populous state's share of the national tax base were smaller), made the more dangerous taxes politically difficult for Congress to impose.

The effectiveness of apportionment as a limitation on congressional power obviously depends on the levies to which it applies, and students of the Founding disagree on this point. At one extreme, some scholars, citing Rufus King's unanswered question at the Constitutional Convention ("Mr King asked what was the precise meaning of *direct* taxation? No one answd."), have argued that "direct taxes" had no agreed-upon meaning, or, much the same thing, that the Framers did not think through what they were doing. They created an apportionment scheme so unworkable that a cramped definition of "direct taxes" became necessary to prevent the collapse of the system.

Those views overstate the extent of the confusion in 1787. No interpretation of "direct taxes" can be consistent with all statements made at the time, but the Founding debates are full of references to two forms of taxation for which apportionment was clearly intended: capitation taxes (specifically denominated as direct in the Constitution) and taxes on land (generally including slaves as well). Although intended to be difficult, apportionment was not impossible. Between 1798 and 1861, Congress enacted several real-estate taxes, all with complex schemes for apportionment.

The serious question is whether "direct taxes" includes anything beyond capitation and land taxes. The conventional wisdom is that it does not, based on dicta in *Hylton v. United States* (1796), which held that a tax on carriages was an excise rather than a direct tax. Justice William Paterson, for example, thought the provision was designed to allay Southern fears of a federal tax on their lands and slaves—nothing more. Because the Federalist justices were themselves among the Framers, these dicta are often accepted as evidence of original understanding. Not all significant Framers thought the concept of "direct taxes" was so limited—James Madison voted against the carriage tax in Congress because he thought it needed to be apportioned—but, based on the *Hylton* dicta, the Supreme Court in the nineteenth century upheld unapportioned federal taxes on insurance company receipts, *Pacific Insurance Co. v. Soule* (1869); on notes of state-chartered banks, *Veazie Bank v. Fenno* (1869); on inheritances of real estate, *Scholey v. Rew*

(1875); and on the Civil War income tax, *Springer v. United States* (1881).

What looked to be a revolutionary change occurred in 1895, when, in *Pollock v. Farmers' Loan & Trust Co.* (1895), a divided Court accepted a broader conception of "direct taxes" and concluded that an unapportioned 1894 income tax—which largely reached income from property—was invalid. In rejecting the notion that nothing but a capitation or land tax could be direct, the Court stressed that a limitation on congressional power ought not to be interpreted in a way that destroys the limitation. Although the Court after *Pollock* continued to approve a large number of unapportioned federal taxes, calling them "excises," *Pollock* unquestionably hampered the government's ability to raise revenue. In 1913, the Sixteenth Amendment was ratified, exempting "taxes on incomes" from apportionment.

Recent judicial authority provides little further guidance on the meaning of "direct taxes." The Sixteenth Amendment made worrying about new sources of revenue less pressing for the federal government. Nonetheless, it seems that any direct tax other than an income tax should still be subject to the apportionment rule. At a minimum, that would include capitation and land taxes. In its most recent statement on the subject, in 1934, the Supreme Court emphasized, in dictum, that a tax on the value of real estate would be direct. *Helvering v. Independent Life Insurance Co.* (1934).

And, after *Pollock*, "direct taxes" could include much more. In fact, a broad interpretation of "direct taxes" can reconcile the clear original understanding that capitation and land taxes were direct with the equally clear intention that apportionment should have bite. The Constitution divided governmental levies into two mutually exclusive categories: indirect taxes subject to the uniformity requirement, and direct taxes subject to apportionment. Indirect taxes, which the Framers assumed would fund the national government in ordinary circumstances, were "Duties, Imposts, and Excises"— generally taxes on articles of consumption. These taxes were considered safe because, regardless of who collected them, the burden

was thought to be shifted to consumers. If Congress became greedy and raised rates too high, fewer taxed goods would be purchased and revenue would decrease. It was thus in the "nature of the thing," wrote Alexander Hamilton in *The Federalist* No. 21, that further constitutional protection against congressional overreaching was unnecessary.

Direct taxes, which were expected to be used only in emergencies, did not have the built-in protections characteristic of indirect taxes. Direct taxes were imposed directly on individuals, who, it was assumed, could not shift their liability to others. If a tax was not indirect, the Framers thought it should be apportioned. Capitation and land taxes were direct under this understanding, but so might other taxes be, whether known in 1787 or not. If nothing else, a broader understanding of "direct taxes" should require that the constitutional character of any proposed tax be studied before it is enacted in an unapportioned form.

Erik M. Jensen

See Also

Article I, Section 2, Clause 3 (Allocation of Representatives)
Article I, Section 8, Clause 1 (Spending Clause)
Article I, Section 8, Clause 1 (Uniformity Clause)
Amendment XVI (Income Tax)

Suggestions for Further Research

Bruce Ackerman, *Taxation and the Constitution*, 99 Colum. L. Rev. 1 (1999)

Erik M. Jensen, *The Apportionment of "Direct Taxes": Are Consumption Taxes Constitutional?*, 97 Colum. L. Rev. 2334 (1997)

Calvin H. Johnson, *Apportionment of Direct Taxes: The Foul-Up in the Core of the Constitution*, 7 Wm. & Mary Bill Rts. J. 1 (1998)

Significant Cases

Hylton v. United States, 3 U.S. (3 Dall.) 171 (1796)
Pacific Insurance Co. v. Soule, 74 U.S. (7 Wall.) 433 (1869)
Veazie Bank v. Fenno, 75 U.S. (8 Wall.) 533 (1869)
Scholey v. Rew, 90 U.S. (23 Wall.) 331 (1875)

Springer v. United States, 102 U.S. 586 (1881)

Pollock v. Farmers' Loan & Trust Co., 157 U.S. 429, 158 U.S. 601 (1895)

Helvering v. Independent Life Insurance Co., 292 U.S. 371 (1934)

Export Taxation Clause

No Tax or Duty shall be laid on Articles exported from any State.

(Article I, Section 9, Clause 5)

∾

The Export Taxation Clause was one of the many accommodations that the Framers made to cement unity among the various sections of the union. Many of the Southern delegates at the Constitutional Convention regarded the clause as a prerequisite to gaining their approval of the Constitution. As the primary exporter of goods in the late eighteenth century, the South would have borne a disproportionate burden from export taxes. In addition to their disproportionate burden argument, George Mason voiced the South's fear that a tax on exports would create a mechanism through which the more numerous Northern states could overwhelm the Southern states' economies. They also worried that export taxes could be used indirectly to attack slavery. They were joined by Northerners such as Oliver Ellsworth, who declared that export taxes would stifle industry.

In response, some of the most distinguished delegates at the Convention, including James Madison, Alexander Hamilton, George Washington, Gouverneur Morris, and James Wilson, favored export taxes. They argued variously that export taxes were a necessary source of revenue, that they were a necessary means for the federal government to regulate trade, that they could become a necessary source of income for the central government, and that the South's disproportionate need for naval protection justified its disproportionate share of export taxes. Attempts to limit the absolute prohibition on export taxes failed. James Madison's attempt to

require a supermajority for passage of an export tax was barely defeated by a 6–5 vote. The absolute prohibition on export taxation then passed by a 7–4 vote. It provoked little discussion during the ratifying conventions.

Cases interpreting the Export Taxation Clause have made clear that the clause "strictly prohibits any tax or duty, discriminatory or not, that falls on exports during the course of exportation," and that the protection extends to "services and activities closely related to the export process." *United States v. IBM Corp.* (1996). Unlike its analysis of Commerce Clause cases, the Court has kept distinct what is intended for export and what remains available for local trade. Although a product may ultimately be intended for export, the Export Taxation Clause does not prohibit federal taxation of goods and services before they enter the course of exportation, or even of services and activities only tangentially related to the export process. Thus, the Court has invalidated taxes on bills of lading, ship charters, and marine insurance; but it has upheld federal assessments on preexport goods and services, such as an excise tax on manufactured tobacco, a tax on the manufacturing of cheese intended for export, and a corporate income tax on exporters.

Although the Export Taxation Clause was integral to the evaluation of numerous levies between 1876 and 1923, the clause did not make its way back onto the Court's docket until 1996. After over seven decades of obscurity, the Court utilized the Export Taxation Clause twice between 1996 and 1998 to strike down federal tax statutes. In *United States v. IBM Corp.*, the Court relied on the Export Taxation Clause to strike down a nondiscriminatory federal excise tax on insurance premiums paid for the purpose of insuring goods against loss during exportation. The Court also expressly rejected the government's arguments that the dormant Commerce Clause and Import-Export Clause jurisprudence altered or governed the interpretation of the Export Taxation Clause. In *United States v. United States Shoe Corp.* (1998), a unanimous Court relied on the Export Taxation Clause to strike down, to the extent it applied to exports, the Harbor Maintenance Tax. The tax was an excise imposed on any "port use." The Court rejected the government's contention that the charge was a valid user fee rather than a tax.

Although the original purpose of the Export Taxation Clause was to prevent sectional favoritism by Congress, the Court has chosen to enforce the flat ban that the Framers placed into the Constitution's text, rather than seeking to measure an export tax's discriminatory effect. Under the Commerce Clause, Congress retains the power to regulate exports, even to the extent of creating embargoes. It may not, however, utilize export taxes as a means of regulation.

David F. Forte

See Also

Article I, Section 8, Clause 3 (Commerce with Foreign Nations)

Article I, Section 8, Clause 3 (Commerce Among the States)

Article I, Section 10, Clause 2 (Import-Export Clause)

Suggestion for Further Research

Erik M. Jensen, *The Export Clause*, 6 FLA. TAX. REV. 1 (2003)

Significant Cases

Turpin v. Burgess, 117 U.S. 504 (1886)

Fairbank v. United States, 181 U.S. 283 (1901)

Cornell v. Coyne, 192 U.S. 418 (1904)

Thames & Mersey Marine Insurance Co. v. United States, 237 U.S. 19 (1915)

United States v. Hvoslef, 237 U.S. 1 (1915)

W.E. Peck & Co. v. Lowe, 247 U.S. 165 (1918)

United States v. IBM Corp., 517 U.S. 843 (1996)

United States v. United States Shoe Corp., 523 U.S. 360 (1998)

Port Preference Clause

No Preference shall be given by any Regulation of Commerce or Revenue to the Ports of one State over those of another; nor shall Vessels bound to, or from, one State, be obliged to enter, clear, or pay Duties in another.

(ARTICLE I, SECTION 9, CLAUSE 6)

~

*L*ike the Uniformity Clause, with which it was initially joined at the Constitutional Convention, and the Export Taxation Clause, the Port Preference Clause was meant to interfere with the natural tendency of legislatures to become instruments through which powerful commercial interests injure their politically weaker rivals.

The impetus for the Port Preference Clause came from the Maryland delegation, whose members were especially worried that vessels bound to or from the port of Baltimore might be required to stop in Virginia. Some other delegates objected that Congress should not have its hands tied, lest it be unable to deal adequately with problems such as smuggling on long rivers like the Delaware. The issue was referred to a committee, which included a delegate from each state, and which recommended language nearly identical to the final version now in the Constitution. This was not sufficient for Maryland's Luther Martin, who became a leading Anti-Federalist. He objected that Congress might easily violate the spirit of the provision, perhaps by limiting Maryland to one inappropriate port of entry on the Potomac: this would effectively require Baltimore shipping to stop in Virginia.

The language of the Port Preference Clause sweeps beyond the specific concerns that motivated its proponents at the Convention. The Supreme Court, however, has construed the Port Preference Clause very narrowly, holding that Congress may grant enormous "incidental" preferences to the ports of certain states through devices such as making improvements (like dredging) or creating obstructions (like bridges) in one place rather than another. *Pennsylvania v. Wheeling & Belmont Bridge Co.* (1856) ("*Wheeling Bridge II*"); *South Carolina v. Georgia* (1876). The Supreme Court has indicated that the clause would be violated by naked discrimination between all the ports of one state and those of another. *Wheeling Bridge II.* But even this prohibition is essentially toothless: it has been read to allow Congress to impose a tax that affected all the ports of some states and no ports in some others. *Augusta Towing Co., Inc. v. United States* (1984).

A dissent in the seminal Supreme Court case complained that the majority's interpretation rendered the clause a dead letter. *Wheeling Bridge II* (McLean, J., dissenting). More recently, Justice Clarence Thomas suggested in a concurrence that a natural reading of the constitutional language "prohibits Congress from using its commerce power to channel commerce through certain favored ports." *United States v. Lopez* (1995) (Thomas, J., concurring). As the case law stands, however, Congress is on its honor to comply with the spirit of the clause by refraining from politically motivated favoritism that distorts the natural economic competition among American ports.

Nelson Lund

See Also

Article I, Section 8, Clause 1 (Uniformity Clause)

Article I, Section 8, Clause 3 (Commerce Among the States)

Article I, Section 9, Clause 5 (Export Taxation Clause)

Suggestion for Further Research

3 THE FOUNDERS' CONSTITUTION 370–373 (Philip B. Kurland & Ralph Lerner eds., 1987)

Significant Cases

Pennsylvania v. Wheeling & Belmont Bridge Co., 59 U.S. (18 How.) 421 (1856)

South Carolina v. Georgia, 93 U.S. 4 (1876)

Augusta Towing Co., Inc. v. United States, 5 Cl. Ct. 160 (1984)

United States v. Lopez, 514 U.S. 549 (1995) (Thomas, J., concurring)

Appropriations Clause

No Money shall be drawn from the Treasury, but in Consequence of Appropriations made by Law; and

a regular Statement and Account of the Receipts and Expenditures of all public Money shall be published from time to time.

(ARTICLE I, SECTION 9, CLAUSE 7)

~

*T*he Appropriations Clause is the cornerstone of Congress's "power of the purse." It assigns to Congress the role of final arbiter of the use of public funds. The source of Congress's power to spend derives from Article I, Section 8, Clause 1. The Appropriations Clause provides Congress with a mechanism to control or to limit spending by the federal government. The Framers chose the particular language of limitation, not authorization, for the first part of the clause and placed it in Section 9 of Article I, along with other restrictions on governmental actions to limit, most notably, executive action.

The Virginia Plan offered at the opening of the Constitutional Convention did not contain an appropriations clause, although the plan did refer, albeit indirectly, to Congress's authority under the Articles of Confederation to appropriate public funds. The Appropriations Clause first appeared at the Convention as part of a proposed division of authority between the House and the Senate. A part of that proposal declared that all bills raising or appropriating money— "money bills"—were to originate in the House, and were not subject to alteration or amendment in the Senate. Further, no money could be drawn from the "public Treasury, but in pursuance of appropriations to be originated in the House of Representatives." The Convention rejected both the provision vesting exclusive control of money bills in the House of Representatives (resolved in Article I, Section 7, Clause 2) and the associated appropriations clause. Late in the Convention, the Committee of Eleven, appointed to consider unresolved parts of the Constitution, offered a compromise to permit the Senate to amend or concur in amendments of money bills, provided that "no Money shall be drawn from the Treasury, but in Consequence of Appropriations made by Law." The Convention incorporated the proposal, resulting, with only minor changes made by the Committee of

Style and Arrangement, in the final language of the first part of the Appropriations Clause.

In *The Federalist* No. 58, James Madison described the centrality of the power of the purse's role in the growth of representative government and its particular importance in the Constitution's governmental structure:

> The House of Representatives cannot only refuse, but they alone can propose the supplies requisite for the support of the government. They, in a word, hold the purse—that powerful instrument by which we behold, in the history of the British Constitution, an infant and humble representation of the people gradually enlarging the sphere of its activity and importance, and finally reducing, as far as it seems to have wished, all the overgrown prerogatives of the other branches of government. This power over the purse may, in fact, be regarded as the most complete and effectual weapon with which any constitution can arm the immediate representatives of the people, for obtaining a redress of every grievance, and for carrying into effect every just and salutary measure.

Under the Articles of Confederation, under which Congress possessed the power to appropriate, there was no independent executive authority. With the creation of an executive under the Constitution, the Founders decided, in the words of Justice Joseph Story in *Commentaries on the Constitution of the United States*, "to preserve in full vigor the constitutional barrier between each department...that each should possess equally...the means of self-protection." An important means of self-protection for the legislative department was its ability to restrict the executive's access to public resources "but in Consequence of Appropriations made by Law." Justice Story continues:

> And the [legislature] has, and must have, a controlling influence over the executive power, since it holds at its own command all the resources by which a chief magistrate could make himself formidable. It

possesses the power over the purse of the nation and the property of the people. It can grant or withhold supplies; it can levy or withdraw taxes; it can unnerve the power of the sword by striking down the arm that wields it.

The second part of the clause, the "Statement and Account" provision, resulted from an amendment offered by George Mason of Virginia in the final days of the Convention. Mason proposed that "an Account of the public expenditures should be annually published." Questions concerning the wisdom and practicality of this proposal led to the adoption of an amendment, offered by James Madison, to substitute the less-demanding "from time to time" for "annually." This "would enjoin the duty of frequent publication," Madison argued, "but leave enough to the discretion of the legislature." The requirement for a "Statement and Account," said Justice Story, makes Congress's responsibility as guardian of the public treasure "complete and perfect" by requiring an account of receipts and expenditures "that the people may know what money is expended, for what purposes, and by what authority." Today, the "discretion of the legislature" is a "plenary power to exact any reporting and accounting [the Congress] considers appropriate in the public interest." *Richardson v. United States* (1974).

The courts have consistently recognized the primacy given to Congress by the Appropriations Clause in allocating the resources of the Treasury. As the Supreme Court declared in *Cincinnati Soap Co. v. United States* (1937), the Appropriations Clause "was intended as a restriction upon the disbursing authority of the Executive department." It means simply that "no money can be paid out of the Treasury unless it has been appropriated by an act of Congress." In *United States v. MacCollom* (1976), the Court articulated an "established rule" that "the expenditure of public funds is proper only when authorized by Congress, not that public funds may be expended unless prohibited by Congress."

The power reserved to Congress by the Appropriations Clause is "a most complete and effectual weapon" because "any exercise of the power granted by the Constitution to one of the other Branches of Government is limited by a valid reservation of congressional control over funds in the Treasury." *Office of Personnel Management v. Richmond* (1990). *See also Knote v. United States* (1877). For example, because public funds may only be paid out of the Treasury "according to the letter of the difficult judgments reached by Congress," private litigants may not use equitable principles of estoppel to require the payment of benefits for which there is no appropriation. *Office of Pers. Mgmt. v. Richmond.* Similarly, a court may no more order the obligation or a payment of funds for which there is no appropriation, *Reeside v. Walker* (1850), than it may make or order an appropriation. *Rochester Pure Water District v. United States Environmental Protection Agency* (1992); *National Ass'n of Regional Councils v. Costle* (1977).

Congress has broad authority to give meaning to the Appropriations Clause. As a technical matter, Congress regularly enacts statutes, specifically styled as appropriations acts, of varying types, durations, and effect. To satisfy the Appropriations Clause, however, Congress need do no more than enact a law expressly directing a payment out of a designated fund or source in the Treasury. As the Court of Claims explained, an appropriation is "per se nothing more than the legislative authorization prescribed by the Constitution for money to be paid out at the Treasury." *Campagna v. United States* (1891).

Congress also may, and does, adjust, suspend, or repeal various provisions of law through appropriations acts. *United States v. Dickerson* (1940); *Robertson v. Seattle Audubon Society* (1992); *United States v. Bean* (2002). The Supreme Court has insisted, however, that Congress must clearly articulate its purposes when it uses the appropriations process to adjust, suspend, or repeal other provisions of law. *United States v. Will* (1980). Nevertheless, Congress has "wide discretion . . . in prescribing details of expenditures," *Cincinnati Soap Co. v. United States* (1937), and indeed has a long and consistent practice of setting conditions on the expenditure of appropriations. One particularly noteworthy example was the Boland Amendments of the 1980s, which limited the use of appropriated funds by any agency

or entity of the United States involved in intelligence activities to support the Nicaraguan insurgency against the Sandinista regime.

There are limits to the length to which Congress may go in its exercise of the appropriations power. Congress's power, in this respect, like all of its other powers, is subject to the Bill of Rights and other constraints in the Constitution. Congress may not, for example, in the guise of appropriating, subject named individuals to bills of attainders explicitly prohibited by the Constitution. *United States v. Lovett* (1946). It may not preclude or direct an act in derogation of an individual's First Amendment rights. *Legal Service Corp. v. Velasquez* (2001). Similarly, just as a presidential pardon may not effect payment of a claim out of the Treasury barred by act of Congress, *Hart v. United States* (1886), or permit the recovery of the proceeds of confiscated property deposited in the Treasury, *Knote v. United States*, the Congress cannot, through a rider in an appropriations act, impair the express and enumerated power of the President to grant pardons. *United States v. Klein* (1871).

Gary Kepplinger

See Also

Suggestions for Further Research
J. Gregory Sidak, *The President's Power of the Purse*, 1989 Duke L.J. 1162 (1989)
Kate Stith, *Congress's Power of the Purse*, 97 Yale L.J. 1343 (1988)
Charles Tiefer, Congressional Practice and Procedure (1989)
U.S. Gen. Accounting Office, Principles of Federal Appropriations Law, Office of General Counsel (2d ed. 1991)

Significant Cases
Reeside v. Walker, 52 U.S. (11 How.) 272 (1850)
United States v. Klein, 80 U.S. (13 Wall.) 128 (1871)

Knote v. United States, 95 U.S. 149 (1877)

Hart v. United States, 118 U.S. 62, 67 (1886)

Campagna v. United States, 26 Ct. Cl. 316, 317 (1891)

Cincinnati Soap Co. v. United States, 301 U.S. 308 (1937)

United States v. Dickerson, 310 U.S. 554 (1940)

United States v. Lovett, 328 U.S. 303 (1946)

Richardson v. United States, 415 U.S. 971 (1974)

United States v. MacCollom, 426 U.S. 317 (1976)

National Ass'n of Regional Councils v. Costle, 564 F.2d 583 (D.C. Cir. 1977)

United States v. Will, 449 U.S. 200 (1980)

Office of Personnel Management v. Richmond, 496 U.S. 414 (1990)

Robertson v. Seattle Audubon Society, 503 U.S. 429 (1992)

Rochester Pure Water District v. United States Environmental Protection Agency, 960 F.2d 180 (D.C. Cir. 1992)

Legal Service Corp. v. Velazquez, 531 U.S. 533 (2001)

United States v. Bean, 537 U.S. 71 (2002)

Emoluments Clause

No Title of Nobility shall be granted by the United States: And no Person holding any Office of Profit or Trust under them, shall, without the Consent of the Congress, accept of any present, Emolument, Office, or Title, of any kind whatever, from any King, Prince, or foreign State.

(**Article I, Section 9, Clause 8**)

$\sim$

*A*rticle VI of the Articles of Confederation was the source of the Constitution's prohibition on federal titles of nobility and the so-called Emoluments Clause. The clause sought to shield the republican character of the United States against corrupting foreign influences.

The prohibition on federal titles of nobility—reinforced by the corresponding prohibition on state titles of nobility in Article I, Section 10, and more generally by the republican Guarantee Clause in Article IV, Section 4—was designed to

underpin the republican character of the American government. In the ample sense James Madison gave the term in *The Federalist* No. 39, a republic was "a government which derives all its powers directly or indirectly from the great body of the people, and is administered by persons holding their offices during good behavior."

Republicanism so understood was the ground of the constitutional edifice. The prohibition on titles of nobility buttressed the structure by precluding the possibility of an aristocracy, whether hereditary or personal, whose members would inevitably assert a right to occupy the leading positions in the state.

Further, the prohibition on titles complemented the prohibition in Article III, Section 3, on the "Corruption of Blood" worked by "Attainder[s] of Treason" (i.e., the prohibition on creating a disability in the posterity of an attained person upon claiming an inheritance as his heir, or as heir to his ancestor). Together these prohibitions ruled out the creation of certain caste-specific legal privileges or disabilities arising solely from the accident of birth.

In addition to upholding republicanism in a political sense, the prohibition on titles also pointed to a durable American social ideal. This is the ideal of equality; it is what David Ramsey, the eighteenth-century historian of the American Revolution, called the "life and soul" of republicanism. The particular conception of equality denied a place in American life for hereditary distinctions of caste—slavery being the most glaring exception. At the same time, however, it also allowed free play for the "diversity in the faculties of men," the protection of which, as Madison insisted in *The Federalist* No. 10, was "the first object of government." The republican system established by the Founders, in other words, envisaged a society in which distinctions flowed from the unequal uses that its members made of equal opportunities: a society led by a natural aristocracy based on talent, virtue, and accomplishment, not by an hereditary aristocracy based on birth. "Capacity, Spirit and Zeal in the Cause," as John Adams said, would "supply the Place of Fortune, Family, and every other Consideration, which used to have Weight with Mankind." Or as the Jeffersonian St. George Tucker put it in 1803:

"A Franklin, or a Washington, need not the pageantry of honours, the glare of titles, nor the pre-eminence of station to distinguish them.... Equality of rights...precludes not that distinction which superiority of virtue introduces among the citizens of a republic."

Similarly, the Framers intended the Emoluments Clause to protect the republican character of American political institutions. "One of the weak sides of republics, among their numerous advantages, is that they afford too easy an inlet to foreign corruption." *The Federalist* No. 22 (Alexander Hamilton). The delegates at the Constitutional Convention specifically designed the clause as an antidote to potentially corrupting foreign practices of a kind that the Framers had observed during the period of the Confederation. Louis XVI had the custom of presenting expensive gifts to departing ministers who had signed treaties with France, including American diplomats. In 1780, the King gave Arthur Lee a portrait of the King set in diamonds above a gold snuff box; and in 1785, he gave Benjamin Franklin a similar miniature portrait, also set in diamonds. Likewise, the King of Spain presented John Jay (during negotiations with Spain) with the gift of a horse. All these gifts were reported to Congress, which in each case accorded permission to the recipients to accept them. Wary, however, of the possibility that such gestures might unduly influence American officials in their dealings with foreign states, the Framers institutionalized the practice of requiring the consent of Congress before one could accept "any present, Emolument, Office, or Title, of any kind whatever, from...[a] foreign State."

Like several other provisions of the Constitution, the Emoluments Clause also embodies the memory of the epochal constitutional struggles in seventeenth-century Britain between the forces of Parliament and the Stuart dynasty. St. George Tucker's explanation of the clause noted that "in the reign of Charles the [S]econd of England, that prince, and almost all his officers of state were either actual pensioners of the court of France, or supposed to be under its influence, directly, or indirectly, from that cause. The reign of that monarch has been, accordingly, proverbially disgraceful to his memory." As these remarks imply, the clause was directed not merely at American diplomats serving abroad, but more generally at officials throughout the federal government.

The Emoluments Clause has apparently never been litigated, but it has been interpreted and enforced through a long series of opinions of the Attorneys General and by less-frequent opinions of the Comptrollers General. Congress has also exercised its power of "Consent" under the clause by enacting the Foreign Gifts and Decorations Act, which authorizes federal employees to accept foreign governmental benefits of various kinds in specific circumstances.

Robert Delahunty

See Also

Suggestions for Further Research

Applicability of Emoluments Clause to Employment of Government Employees by Foreign Public Universities, 18 Op. Off. Legal Counsel 13 (1994)

Applicability of the Emoluments Clause to Non-Government Members of ACUS, 17 Op. Off. Legal Counsel 114 (1993)

Gifts from Foreign Prince, 24 Op. Att'y Gen. 116 (1902)

President Reagan's Ability to Receive Retirement Benefits from the State of California, 5 Op. Off. Legal Counsel 187 (1981)

State Treaties

No State shall enter into any Treaty, Alliance, or Confederation; grant Letters of Marque and Reprisal....
(ARTICLE I, SECTION 10, CLAUSE 1)

~

*I*n addition to granting the government powers to regulate trade and raise revenue that it either lacked or could not enforce under the Articles of Confederation, the Framers intended the Constitution to centralize much, if not all, power over foreign affairs. Many of the federal government's enumerated powers relate to foreign affairs and have corresponding restrictions on states in Article I, Section 10. Article VI of the Articles of Confederation had permitted the states to conclude treaties with foreign governments with the consent of Congress. States could also grant letters of marque and reprisal after Congress had declared war. While some of Article I, Section 10's proscriptions, like the ability to levy tonnage duties or enter into "compacts or agreements," may be permitted by Congress, others, like the prohibitions described here, are absolute.

Treaties, as well as alliances and confederations, are formal, binding agreements between nations that are the subjects of international law. "Compacts and agreements" are usually made by governmental officials, such as the executive, or by subsidiary governmental units, such as states or municipalities. In the late eighteenth century, governments issued letters of marque and reprisal to authorize private ships to attack certain foreign shipping and gain booty for their efforts. Issuing them was regarded as an act of war.

In *The Federalist* No. 44, James Madison noted that these proscriptions (like the prohibition on treaties) either "need[ed] no explanation" or (like the restrictions on letters of marque and reprisal) were "fully justified by the advantage of uniformity in all points which relate to national powers; and of immediate responsibility to the nation in all those for whose conduct the nation itself is to be responsible." Justice Joseph Story concurred, writing in his *Commentaries on the Constitution of the United States* that the state marque and reprisal restriction "is appropriately confined to the national government" because "the protection of the whole Union is confided to the national arm, and the national power," and no state "should possess military means to overawe the Union, or to endanger the general safety." As noted foreign-affairs scholar Louis Henkin remarked, "these restrictions are as clear as words can make them and have raised no issues...."

The courts have had little occasion to deal with the clause, though in *Holmes v. Jennison* (1840), Justice Roger B. Taney, writing for himself and three other Justices, commented that the clause "positively and unconditionally" forbade states from entering into treaties, and that "even the consent of Congress could not authorize" them to do so. He also distinguished formal "treaties," which were expressly forbidden to states, from "agreements" and "compacts" that Congress could authorize.

Brannon P. Denning

See Also
Article I, Section 8, Clause 11 (Marque and Reprisal)
Article I, Section 10, Clause 3 (Compact Clause)
Article II, Section 2, Clause 2 (Treaty Clause)

Suggestion for Further Research
Louis Henkin, Foreign Affairs and the U.S. Constitution (2d ed. 1996)

Significant Case
Holmes v. Jennison, 39 U.S. (14 Pet.) 540 (1840)

State Coinage

No State shall...coin Money; emit Bills of Credit; make any Thing but gold and silver Coin a Tender in Payment of Debts....
(Article I, Section 10, Clause 1)

~

*T*he prohibition on the states to create any form of money signaled the shift of the power to make economic policy from the states to the federal government. In the late eighteenth century, money and trade were the prime mechanisms for regulating the economy, and the Constitution gave both exclusively to the new central government.

"Bills of Credit" was the generic name for various forms of paper money not backed by gold or silver (known as "specie"). Up until near the end of the Revolution, the states had managed, as they had when they were colonies, the issuance of paper money as a means of stimulating and cooling the economy, not unlike the practice of the modern Federal Reserve. After issuing a currency to increase investment, the colony or state would later call in, or "sink," the currency by levying taxes payable in that particular issue. The colony would then issue a new currency (sometimes overlapping with the collection of the previous one) to begin (or maintain) the cycle again. Inevitably, currencies became depreciated, and the complexities of determining who owed how much in which currency to whom confounded transactions and the courts. *See Deering v. Parker* (1760).

During the latter half of the eighteenth century, Parliament laid increasing monetary regulations on the colonies until 1764, when, as part of its program of centralizing control in London, it put a complete ban on making bills of credit legal tender. During the Revolution, the states began issuing paper currencies again, having a somewhat better record in financing the war than Congress had. After 1783, however, specie dried up in a popular rush to purchase imported goods, and the states' currency issues exacerbated the serious depression of 1784. In early 1787, Massachusetts, which had resisted currency issues, was faced with Shays's Rebellion, whose partisans demanded new currency. In Philadelphia, the Framers were determined to put an end to the practice that they believed had contributed to so much economic and political dislocation. Rhode Island, a major issuer of paper money, refused to send delegates to the Constitutional Convention precisely because it feared monetary reform.

At the Convention, the delegates found a proposal to allow the states to issue bills of credit with the approval of Congress not stringent enough, and James Wilson and Roger Sherman successfully moved to insert the current language. In the ratifying conventions, the Anti-Federalists quickly saw what was afoot. The states could no longer debase the currency with new issues of paper tender. Luther Martin asserted that the states would no longer be able

"to prevent the wealthy creditor and the monied man from totally destroying the poor though even industrious debtor." After ratification, the full force of the constitutional changes soon came to fruition; Alexander Hamilton pushed through a program by which the federal government absorbed all previous federal and state debt, established a national bank, and levied new tariffs and internal taxes.

The need for circulating currency, however, did not abate. Soon, private and state chartered banks were issuing bank notes redeemable in specie. States still could not enter the monetary field directly. In *Craig v. Missouri* (1830), the Supreme Court struck down state loan offices that had issued loan-office certificates, but in *Briscoe v. Bank of Kentucky* (1837), the Court upheld the constitutionality of bank notes issued from a state-chartered bank because they were not formally issued by the state. By the time of the Civil War, there were more than 1,600 state-chartered banks in the country. With never enough specie to back the notes, their value fluctuated widely. In order to control these problems and support the adoption of a federal currency, the Congress levied a ten percent tax on state bank notes. After the Supreme Court upheld the tax in *Veazie Bank v. Fenno* (1869), state bank notes began their journey to extinction. State banks then turned to more modern financial devices, such as deposit accounts and checks, to stay in business.

David F. Forte

See Also

Article I, Section 8, Clause 1 (Spending Clause)

Article I, Section 8, Clause 2 (Borrowing Clause)

Article I, Section 8, Clause 3 (Commerce Among the States)

Article I, Section 8, Clause 5 (Coinage Clause)

Article I, Section 8, Clause 6 (Counterfeiting)

Suggestions for Further Research

Gerald T. Dunne, Monetary Decisions of the Supreme Court (1960)

William W. Folwell, *The Evolution of Paper Money in the United States*, 8 Minn. L. Rev. 561 (1924)

Robert S. Getman, *The Right to Use Gold Clauses*, 42 Brook. L. Rev. 487 (1976)

Ali Khan, *The Evolution of Money: A Story of Constitutional Nullification*, 67 U. Cin. L. Rev. 393 (1999)

Significant Cases

Deering v. Parker, 4 Dall. App. xxiii (P.C. 1760)

Craig v. Missouri, 29 U.S. (4 Pet.) 410 (1830)

Byrne v. Missouri, 33 U.S. (8 Pet.) 40 (1834)

Briscoe v. Bank of Kentucky, 36 U.S. (11 Pet.) 257 (1837)

Griffin v. Thompson, 43 U.S. (2 How.) 244 (1844)

Gwin v. Breedlove, 43 U.S. (2 How.) 29 (1844)

Darrington v. Bank of Alabama, 54 U.S. (13 How.) 12 (1851)

Veazie Bank v. Fenno, 75 U.S. (8 Wall.) 533 (1869)

The Legal-Tender Cases, 110 U.S. 421 (1884)

Poindexter v. Greenhow, 114 U.S. 269 (1885)

Chaffin v. Taylor, 116 U.S. 567 (1886)

Houston & Texas Central Railroad v. Texas, 177 U.S. 66 (1900)

State Bill of Attainder and State Ex Post Facto

No State shall…pass any Bill of Attainder, ex post facto Law….
(Article I, Section 10, Clause 1)

∾

The Framers regarded bills of attainder and ex post facto laws as so offensive to liberty that they prohibited their use by both Congress (Article I, Section 9, Clause 3) and the states. The Framers had observed the use of bills of attainder by Parliament, particularly in cases of treason, and they were determined to deny the national legislature any such power. As Justice Samuel Chase noted in *Calder v. Bull* (1798), the Framers applied the prohibition to the states "[t]o prevent such and similar acts of violence and injustice."

The issue of ex post facto laws was more nuanced. Many of the Founders regarded retroactive laws, both civil and criminal, as contrary to the principle of legality itself. Roman Law, as well as Henry de Bracton, Sir Edward Coke, and Sir William Blackstone in English law, and the influential Baron de Montesquieu condemned the practice. Thomas Jefferson noted in an 1813 letter to Isaac McPherson, "The sentiment that ex post facto laws are against natural right, is so strong in the United States, that few, if any, of the state constitutions have failed to proscribe them." At Philadelphia, some Framers, such as James Wilson, thought ex post facto laws so extra-legal that they were void ab initio; no textual prohibition was necessary. But a majority wanted the prohibition stated in express terms.

All seemed to agree that ex post facto criminal laws were forbidden, but there was more ambiguity as to the validity of ex post facto civil laws. Part of the issue lay in the difference between a new law that changed preexisting legal obligations, and one that merely impacted (albeit severely) preexisting legal relationships. When Rhode Island, for example, issued a massive amount of paper money, it vitiated creditors' holdings even though the legislature had not changed the terms of the contracts. Yet some observers termed the issuance of paper money an ex post facto law. Other states did change the terms of contracts, tolling the period for repayment. These kinds of measures constituted the "fluctuating policy" and "legislative interferences" that James Madison decried in *The Federalist* No. 44.

At the Constitutional Convention, George Mason moved to remove the ex post facto prohibition from the states precisely because he believed it would prevent some state retroactive legislation that he thought beneficial. In the ratifying conventions, Anti-Federalists such as Patrick Henry also feared the impact of ex post facto prohibition on state economic legislation. At the Convention, Elbridge Gerry supported Mason, but apparently only because he wanted the clause rewritten to apply specifically to civil cases. The motion was unanimously rejected.

After the Convention, most Federalists believed the prohibition applied only to criminal statutes, a view adopted by the Supreme Court beginning with *Calder v. Bull*. In *Calder*, Justice Samuel Chase noted that if the Ex Post

Facto Clause applied to retroactive civil legislation, then the impairment of contracts clause would have been superfluous. As Professor Robert Natelson has pointed out, the resulting prohibitions in the Constitution form a coherent pattern. The Ex Post Facto Clause prohibited retroactive criminal legislation, whereas the prohibition on the states from issuing paper money and from impairing the obligation of contracts covered the most objectionable forms of retroactive civil laws. Finally, the pattern was completed in the Fifth Amendment by the Takings Clause and the Due Process Clause, each of which limited the federal government's ability to enact certain kinds of retroactive civil laws.

The substantive legal content of the Bill of Attainder and the Ex Post Facto Clauses in Sections 9 and 10 of Article I are fundamentally the same. Consult the entries on Article I, Section 9, Clause 3.

David F. Forte

See Also

Article I, Section 9, Clause 3 (Bill of Attainder)
Article I, Section 9, Clause 3 (Ex Post Facto)
Article I, Section 10, Clause 1 (State Coinage)
Article I, Section 10, Clause 1 (Obligation of Contract)
Amendment V (Due Process Clause)
Amendment V (Takings Clause)

Suggestions for Further Research

Wayne A. Logan, *"Democratic Despotism" and Constitutional Constraint: An Empirical Analysis of Ex Post Facto Claims in State Courts*, 12 Wm. & Mary Bill Rts. J. 439 (2004)

Robert G. Natelson, *Statutory Retroactivity: The Founders' View*, 39 Idaho L. Rev. 439 (2003)

Daniel E. Troy, *When Does Retroactivity Cross the Line? Winstar, Eastern Enterprises and Beyond: Toward a Definition and Critique of Retroactivity*, 51 Ala. L. Rev. 1329 (2000)

Significant Cases

Calder v. Bull, 3 U.S. (3 Dall.) 386 (1798)
Eastern Enterprises v. Apfel, 524 U.S. 498 (1998)

Obligation of Contract

No State shall...pass any...Law impairing the Obligation of Contracts....
(Article I, Section 10, Clause 1)

~

*A*rticle I, Section 10, contains a list of prohibitions concerning the role of the states in political, monetary, and economic affairs. As the Constitutional Convention was completing its work on prohibiting states from issuing paper money as legal tender, Rufus King of Massachusetts rose to propose "a prohibition on the States to interfere in private contracts." King relied on a central provision of the Northwest Ordinance:

> [I]n the just preservation of rights and property, it is understood and declared, that no law ought ever to be made, or have force in the said territory, that shall, in any manner whatever, interfere with or affect private contracts or engagements, bona fide, and without fraud, previously formed.

The Obligation of Contract Clause thus had its origins in previous national policy by extending to the states a prohibition that was already in effect in the Northwest Territory. In the brief debate that followed, George Mason feared the prohibition would prevent the states from establishing time limits on when actions could be brought on state-issued bonds. James Wilson responded that the clause would prevent "retrospective interferences only," that is, impairment of contracts already made. These comments suggest that the Framers may well have intended to limit states in their impairment of private contracts already made. But the issue is not free from doubt. The words "previously formed" were not carried over to the Obligation of Contract Clause, so that the text reads as though it has some prospective application of uncertain extent. It is therefore conceivable to apply the Obligation of Contract Clause prospectively to allow the passage of statutes of limitations, by thinking of it as a rule that protects against both retroactive and selective impairments of future contracts that would have the effect of shifting the balance of advantage from one contracting party to another.

The twin protections found in Article I, Section 10, prohibited the state from issuing paper money and, to some extent at least, from regulating economic affairs. That one-two combination troubled the Anti-Federalists, who feared that the two clauses operating in tandem would prevent the states from assisting the debtor classes. The states could no longer debase the currency with new issues of paper tender; Luther Martin asserted that the states would no longer be able "to prevent the wealthy creditor and the monied man from totally destroying the poor though even industrious debtor." In response to the Anti-Federalists, James Madison declared in *The Federalist* No. 44 that the Obligation of Contract Clause was essential to "banish speculations on public measures, inspire a general prudence and industry, and give a regular course to the business of society." Debtor relief was regarded as undermining the long-term stability of commercial expectations.

Support for the Obligation of Contract Clause was found in other quarters. In the South Carolina ratifying convention, Charles Pinckney argued that these two limitations on the states would help cement the union by barring the states from discriminating against out-of-state commercial interests. Edmund Randolph, in the Virginia ratifying convention, declared that the Obligation of Contract Clause was essential to enforcing the provision in the peace treaty with Great Britain guaranteeing private British debts. The Obligation of Contract Clause, therefore, served a double duty: it afforded both a protection to individuals against their states and a limitation on the states that prevented them from intruding on essential federal interests.

The language of the clause reflects these historical concerns and ambiguities. In tone, the clause reads as a stern imperative. Unlike Section 10, Clauses 2 and 3 (which relate to such matters as the imposition of duties on imports and exports), Congress cannot override the prohibition by giving its consent to any state action that violates this provision. The brief terms of the clause, however, cover more than the endless round of debtor-relief statutes the Framers had in mind, for the clause covers all types of contracts, not just debt instruments. The Framers also sought to insulate commercial exchanges from the regulatory power of the state in order to reduce the burdens on interstate commerce, and thus to contribute to the formation of the United States as an extended commercial Republic. But again the correspondence is not perfect, because the Obligation of Contract Clause applies not only to those contracts with interstate connections, but also to all local contracts.

What is clear, however, is that in the antebellum period the Obligation of Contract Clause was the only open-ended federal constitutional guarantee that applied to the states. As such, the Obligation of Contract Clause came by default to be the focal point of litigation for those who sought to protect economic liberties against state intervention. The Supreme Court's interpretation of the clause, both before and after the Civil War, has been filled with odd turns and strange surprises.

Everyone conceded that the clause applied to ordinary contracts between private persons, including partnerships and corporations. That seemed to be the understanding at the Constitutional Convention. But did the Obligation of Contract Clause also reach actions by the state so as to prevent it from repudiating its own contracts, including those that granted legal title of state owned lands to private persons, *Fletcher v. Peck* (1810), or which sought to revoke state charters for private colleges, *Trustees of Dartmouth College v. Woodward* (1819)? In both of these cases, Chief Justice John Marshall opted strongly for the broader reading of the clause in order to restrain conduct by government—reneging on grants—that would be regarded as unacceptable if done by any private individual. In this instance, moreover, the broad reach of the Obligation of Contract Clause uneasily coexisted with the principle of sovereign immunity, which Alexander Hamilton had strongly defended in *The Federalist* Nos. 81 and 82. That principle prevented the state from being sued for breach of its own ordinary commercial contracts. But that immunity did not allow the state to undo its own contracts once their performance was completed. This reading fits so well with the general purpose of limited government that to this day no one has rejected the view that the Obligation of Contract Clause applies to state contracts. But there has been a spirited debate as to how much protection it supplies in light of the doctrine of sovereign immunity. Certainly much is to be said on behalf of the stability of titles to property obtained in grants from the states. But we cannot ignore the reciprocal problem: if the Obligation of Contract Clause is read so broadly so as to invite groups to lobby for sweetheart agreements, reformist governments would not be able to set such agreements aside.

Most of the interpretive questions regarding the clause, however, deal with the impact of the Obligation of Contract Clause on the state regulation of private agreements, where of course the issue of sovereign immunity does not arise. That issue, in turn, is divided into two parts. The first asks whether the Obligation of Contract Clause protects the rights that are vested in contracts that are *in existence* at the time the regulation is passed. The second asks whether the Obligation of Contract Clause imposes limitations on the power of the state to regulate contracts *not yet* established. The answer to the first question is relatively uncontroversial. The clause must apply to preexisting contracts, for otherwise it would be a dead letter. Hence, early decisions held that state insolvency laws could not order the discharge of contracts that were formed before the state statute was passed. *Sturges v. Crowninshield* (1819). The legislature could not flip the background rules of the legal system to the prejudice of individuals who had advanced money on the faith of earlier arrangements. The clause also applied to a wide range of debtor-relief laws, wherein individuals sought to escape or defer the payment of interest, or to avoid foreclosure of their mortgages in hard economic times. It was, however, one thing to say that the Obligation of Contract Clause applied, and quite another to say that all forms of debtor relief were regarded as beyond the power of the state. Many cases adopted the slippery distinction that the Obligation of Contract Clause preserved the *obligation* under contract, but did not prevent the state from limiting

one or another *remedy* otherwise available. Small erosions of contract rights were regarded as permissible, but large deviations were not, even though the clause speaks of all impairments (large or small) in the same breath. But in general, the prohibition against state intervention into existing contracts holds unless (as will be discussed later) the state offers some police-power justification for its actions.

The Court reached a much more definitive conclusion on the second question in 1827, by holding in *Ogden v Saunders* (4–3, with John Marshall and Joseph Story dissenting) that the Obligation of Contract Clause did not apply to those contracts that had not been formed as of the date of the passage of the legislation. In one sense, the decision is surely unexceptionable, for it would be odd if a revision of, say, the parol evidence rule in 2000 could not apply to any contracts signed before that date. The rule itself does not bias the case one way or another, but it is intended to improve the overall administration of justice. Individuals typically do not rely on these rules at formation, either. It would be contrary to its original design to read the Obligation of Contract Clause as blocking any improvements in the administration of commercial justice.

By the same token, the broad refusal to apply the Obligation of Contract Clause prospectively could go too far. For example, suppose a state just announced that from this day forward it reserved the right to nullify at will any contracts that were thereafter formed. At that point, it would take only a short generation after passage of this statute to gut the Obligation of Contract Clause. But if that stratagem is forbidden, then the clause must have *some* prospective application, notwithstanding intimations in the Convention that it only had retroactive application. At this point, one way to read the clause is to hold that its prohibitions are prospective but not absolute. The state may alter the rules governing future contracts only in ways that offer just compensation to all contracting parties in the form of greater security and stability in their contractual obligations. The three legislative reforms that arose most frequently in the early debates—a statute of frauds, a statute of limitations, and recording acts—are all measures that meet this standard.

By refusing to give the clause any prospective role, *Ogden* opened the gateway to partisan legislation that limited the ability of some parties to contract without imposing similar restrictions on their economic competitors. In practice, *Ogden* meant that all general state economic regulation lay outside the scope of constitutional limitation. That gap in the system of constitutional regulation remained until after the Civil War, at which time some protection against state interference with future contracts was supplied under the so-called dormant Commerce Clause (with respect to interstate agreements only) and under the doctrine of liberty of contract as it developed under the Due Process Clause, and, in certain limited cases, under the equal protection clauses. But since *Ogden*, the Obligation of Contract Clause has been an observer, not a central player, in the constitutional struggle to limit prospective state economic regulation.

The Obligation of Contract Clause does continue to have some traction with respect to contracts previously formed, but even in this context, two types of implied limitations on its use have been introduced: the just-compensation exception and the police-power exception. In principle, the initial question is why any implied terms should be read into any constitutional provision, when no mention of them is made by the Framers. Here the simplest answer is that the logic of individual rights and liberties requires that adjustment. The Constitution thus creates presumptions and leaves it open to interpretation as to how these should be qualified in ways that do not gut the original guarantee.

Consider first the question of property takings with just compensation. Suppose that A buys land from B, which the government then wishes to condemn with payment of just compensation. Surely the government's right to condemn is not blocked by A's declaration that he received absolute title to the property from B. The standard rule is that the power to take property for public use is "inherent in government," so that the condemnation can go forward. Should there be any difference when A buys the land from the government, instead of B, and now claims that the government cannot go back on its grant? As early as 1848, in *West River Bridge Co. v. Dix*, the

Supreme Court allowed the condemnation to go forward. The Obligation of Contract Clause has to be read subject to a just-compensation exception, for the condemnation does "impair" the contract right by denying the owner's right to hold out for an above-market price. Reading the just-compensation exception into the Obligation of Contract Clause does not do violence to a structure that already allows other private property to be taken for public use upon payment of just compensation.

The second set of exceptions to the Obligation of Contract Clause involves the police power. Again, this power is nowhere mentioned explicitly in the Constitution, but it is read in connection with every substantive guarantee that it supplies against federal or state power. The customary formulation allows the state to override (*without* compensation) private rights of property. It should, therefore, do so with ordinary contracts as well. Nonetheless, because no compensation is provided, logically, the class of justifications should be *more* stringent than the public-use requirement that allows the impairment of contracts *with* compensation. The canonical formulation defines the state police power as regulation in the name of safety, health, morals, and the general welfare. Stopping contracts to pollute, to bribe, or to fix prices has always been held to fall within the police-power exception. The New Deal constitutional transformation of 1937, however, greatly expanded the scope of the police power beyond these broadly libertarian objectives, so that it no longer was possible to distinguish between general welfare and special interests.

The great transitional case of *Home Building & Loan Ass'n v. Blaisdell* (1934) is notable for ushering in an era that allowed courts to multiply the police-power exceptions to the contractual guarantees offered by the Obligation of Contract Clause, even when no compensation was supplied. The actual decision, dealing with a state-imposed mortgage moratorium, could be explained in part as an effort to counter the ruinous effects of deflationary policies (which in effect increased, in constant dollars, the amount of the debts), but the decision itself was cast in broader terms and unleashed many other legislative initiatives that sought to neutralize the protections secured by individual contracts. Most notably, in *Exxon Corp. v. Eagerton* (1983), the Court found that a "broad societal interest" was sufficient to justify a decision to prevent a company from asserting its explicit contractual right to pass on any increased severance tax to its consumers.

At present, therefore, it is doubtful whether the Supreme Court will find a police-power justification for any piece of special legislation with interest-group support, thereby gutting the clause insofar as it applies to broad classes of existing contracts. Ironically, however, the Court has remained more suspicious of government's efforts to use legislation to extricate itself from its *own* covenants, noting the obvious risk of self-dealing that this behavior represents. It thus struck down efforts of the Port Authority of New York and New Jersey to nullify bond covenants that prohibited it from using bond proceeds to support mass transit. *United States Trust Co. v. New Jersey* (1977). And in *Allied Structural Steel Co. v. Spannaus* (1978), the Court refused to allow Minnesota to impose retroactively more-stringent financial obligations on an employer in the winding up of its pension plan. These limitations on state power notwithstanding, the modern age often finds little intellectual respect for freedom of contract or for the sanctity of contracts validly formed. More than any fine point of the law, that initial intellectual predilection explains the lukewarm reception that Obligation of Contract Clause claims receive in the current legal environment.

Richard A. Epstein

See Also
Amendment V (Takings Clause)

Suggestions for Further Research
William Winslow Crosskey, Politics and the Constitution in the History of the United States (1953)

Richard A. Epstein, *Toward the Revitalization of the Contract Clause*, 51 U. Chi. L. Rev. 703 (1984)

Robert L. Hale, *The Supreme Court and the Contract Clause: I, II, III*, 57 Harv. L. Rev. 512, 621, 852 (1944)

Stanley I. Kutler, Privilege and Creative Destruction: The Charles River Bridge Case (1971)

Michael W. McConnell, *Contract Rights and Property Rights: A Case Study in the Relationship Between Individual Liberties and Constitutional Structure*, 76 Cal. L. Rev. 267 (1988)

Samuel R. Olken, *Charles Evans Hughes and the Blaisdell Decision: A Historical Study of Contract Clause Jurisprudence*, 72 Or. L. Rev. 513 (1993)

Stuart Sterk, *The Continuity of Legislatures: Of Contracts and the Contract Clause*, 88 Colum. L. Rev. 647 (1988)

Benjamin Fletcher Wright, Jr., The Contract Clause of the Constitution (1938)

Significant Cases
Fletcher v. Peck, 10 U.S. (6 Cranch) 87 (1810)

Sturges v. Crowninshield, 17 U.S. (4 Wheat.) 122 (1819)

Trustees of Dartmouth College v. Woodward, 17 U.S. (4 Wheat.) 518 (1819)

Ogden v. Saunders, 25 U.S. (12 Wheat.) 213 (1827)

Charles River Bridge v. Warren Bridge, 36 U.S. (11 Pet.) 420 (1837)

West River Bridge Co. v. Dix, 47 U.S. (6 How.) 507 (1848)

Home Building & Loan Ass'n v. Blaisdell, 290 U.S. 398 (1934)

United States Trust Co. v. New Jersey, 431 U.S. 1 (1977)

Allied Structural Steel Co. v. Spannaus, 438 U.S. 234 (1978)

Energy Reserves Group v. Kansas Power & Light Co., 459 U.S. 400 (1983)

Exxon Corp. v. Eagerton, 462 U.S. 176 (1983)

State Title of Nobility

No State shall...grant any Title of Nobility.
(**Article I, Section 10, Clause 1**)

~

*L*ike the corresponding prohibition on federal titles of nobility in Article I, Section 9, Clause 8, the prohibition on state titles of nobility was designed to affirm and protect the republican character of the American government. Both provisions were carried forward from Article VI of the Articles of Confederation, which had forbidden "the United States in Congress assembled," as well as "any of them," to "grant any title of nobility."

Even before the Articles, states had renounced the power to grant titles. David Ramsey, the eighteenth-century historian of the American Revolution, reported that at the time of independence, the states "agreed in prohibiting all hereditary honours and distinctions of ranks" in order to provide "farther security for the continuance of republican principles in the American constitution." *The History of the American Revolution* (1789). American state legislatures, he further observed, were "miniature pictures of the community," representing persons of all stations and classes rather than confining their membership to persons of noble rank. James Madison also found in *The Federalist* No. 39 that "the general form and aspect" of American governments could only be "strictly republican": "[i]t is evident that no other form would be reconcilable with the genius of the people of America; with the fundamental principles of the Revolution; or with that honorable determination . . . to rest all our political experiments on the capacity of mankind for self-government." Given the social and political circumstances of the United States at the time of the Founding, therefore, it is not surprising that the Constitution's prohibition on state titles of nobility was uncontroversial: as Madison wrote tersely in *The Federalist* No. 44, the prohibition "needs no comment." What is perhaps surprising, then, is that it was thought necessary at all.

The answer may be that the Founders feared that, without adequate precautions, the republican venture might fail. "[W]ho can say," Madison asked in *The Federalist* No. 43, "what experiments may be produced by the caprice of particular States, by the ambition of enterprising leaders, or by the intrigues and influence of foreign powers?" Before the French Revolution, republican governments were rare: they existed only in such countries as Holland, Poland, or Venice, and even there only (as Madison argued in *The Federalist* No. 39) in attenuated or precarious forms. The existence of genuinely republican institutions, made possible by the absence of a hereditary aristocracy, was the hallmark of American exceptionalism. Conscious of that fact, the Founders sought to ensure, chiefly by the architectural features of the Constitution, but also by such minor clauses as the prohibitions on titles, that the American "political experiment on the capacity of mankind for self-government" would succeed.

Robert Delahunty

See Also
Article I, Section 9, Clause 8 (Emoluments Clause)

Import-Export Clause

No State shall, without the Consent of the Congress, lay any Imposts or Duties on Imports or Exports, except what may be absolutely necessary for executing its inspection Laws: and the net Produce of all Duties and Imposts, laid by any State on Imports and Exports, shall be for the Use of the Treasury of the United States; and all such Laws shall be subject to the Revision and Controul of the Congress.
(**ARTICLE I, SECTION 10, CLAUSE 2**)

～

A primary concern of the Framers of the Constitution was ending the interstate commercial depredations that had occurred during the Confederation period. Thus, the Constitution gave Congress the power to regulate interstate, foreign, and Indian commerce. The Framers also took care to place restrictions on state power under the new government. Often, the restrictions in Article I, Section 10, mirror the powers granted to Congress. Evidence from the Constitutional Convention and the ratification debates suggest that the Framers intended the Import-Export Clause to complement congressional power to raise revenue and regulate interstate commerce by restricting the states' ability to tax commerce entering and leaving their borders.

Indeed, the clause was likely understood originally to encompass domestic, as well as foreign, imports and exports. During the Convention, James Madison opposed allowing states to tax imports to protect native industries. Such protections would "[require] duties not only on imports directly from foreign Countries, but from the other States in the Union, which would revive all the mischiefs experienced from the want of a Gen[era]l Government over commerce." Opponents of ratification often complained of the restrictions placed on states by the new constitution and proposed that only their powers to tax and regulate foreign commerce be restricted.

The Supreme Court's early interpretations of the clause confirmed this interpretation. In *Brown v. Maryland* (1827), Chief Justice John Marshall assumed that the clause applied "equally to importations from a sister State" as well as to foreign imports. In *Almy v. California* (1861), the Court held that the clause prohibited California from taxing gold exported to New York. In *Woodruff v. Parham* (1869), however, the Court concluded that the "Imports or Exports" referred to in the clause referred only to foreign imports and exports. In reaching that conclusion, however, the Court made no analysis of the original understanding, and declared that Chief Justice John Marshall was in error in *Brown v. Maryland* (1827). In fact, the *Woodruff* opinion recharacterized Chief Justice Roger B. Taney's *Almy* opinion as a "dormant" Commerce Clause opinion, though it clearly was not.

Subsequent cases addressed when domestic goods became "Exports" or when foreign goods ceased being "Imports" and thus subject to state taxation. *See, e.g., Kosydar v. National Cash Register* (1974) (discussing when goods become "exports"); *Low v. Austin* (1872) (holding that goods cease to be "Imports" when no longer in "original package"). In *Michelin Tire Corp. v. Wages* (1976), the Supreme Court adopted a new analysis of the Import-Export Clause. A nondiscriminatory state tax would be invalidated only if it (1) prevented the federal gov-

ernment from regulating foreign commerce uniformly; (2) diverted import revenue from the federal government to the states; or (3) risked interstate disharmony like that seen under the Confederation. *See also Itel Containers Int'l Corp. v. Huddleston* (1993) (applying *Michelin Tire*).

More recently, *Woodruff v. Parham* has been questioned. In 1997, Justice Clarence Thomas argued that case was wrongly decided, that the historical evidence plainly showed that the Import-Export Clause *did* apply domestically, and that the clause should be substituted for the Court's dormant Commerce Clause doctrine, which infers limits on a state's ability to regulate interstate commerce from the Commerce Clause. *Camps Newfound/Owatonna, Inc. v. Town of Harrison* (1997) (Thomas, J., dissenting). In addition, Justice Thomas noted that since the Supreme Court's narrowing of the Import-Export Clause in *Michelin Tire*, the fear expressed in *Woodruff* that applying the clause to domestic imports would unfairly exempt out-of-state goods from taxation was no longer credible.

Brannon P. Denning

See Also

Article I, Section 8, Clause 1 (Spending Clause)

Article I, Section 8, Clause 3 (Commerce with Foreign Nations)

Article I, Section 8, Clause 3 (Commerce Among the States)

Article I, Section 9, Clause 6 (Port Preference Clause)

Article I, Section 10, Clause 3 (Compact Clause)

Suggestions for Further Research

Boris I. Bittker, Bittker on the Regulation of Interstate and Foreign Commerce §§ 12.01–12.09 (1999 & supp.)

Boris I. Bittker & Brannon P. Denning, *The Import-Export Clause*, 68 Miss. L.J. 521 (1998)

1 William Winslow Crosskey, Politics and the Constitution in the History of the United States 295–304, 316–317 (1953)

Brannon P. Denning, *Justice Thomas, the Import-Export Clause, and* Camps Newfound/Owatonna v. Harrison, 70 Colo. L. Rev. 155 (1999)

Walter Hellerstein, Michelin Tire Corp. v. Wages, *Enhanced State Power to Tax Imports*, 1976 Sup. Ct. Rev. 99 (1977)

Michael D. Ramsey, *The Power of the States in Foreign Affairs: The Original Understanding of Foreign Policy Federalism,* 75 Notre Dame L. Rev. 342 (1999)

Significant Cases

Brown v. Maryland, 25 U.S. (12 Wheat.) 419 (1827)

Almy v. California, 65 U.S. (24 How.) 169 (1861)

Woodruff v. Parham, 75 U.S. (8 Wall.) 123 (1869)

Low v. Austin, 80 U.S. (13 Wall.) 29 (1872)

Zschernig v. Miller, 389 U.S. 429 (1968)

Kosydar v. National Cash Register, 417 U.S. 62 (1974)

Michelin Tire Corp. v. Wages, 423 U.S. 276 (1976)

Itel Containers International Corp. v. Huddleston, 507 U.S. 60 (1993)

Camps Newfound/Owatonna, Inc. v. Town of Harrison, 520 U.S. 564 (1997) (Thomas, J., dissenting)

Compact Clause

> No State shall, without the Consent of Congress, lay any Duty of Tonnage, keep Troops, or Ships of War in time of Peace, enter into any Agreement or Compact with another State, or with a foreign Power, or engage in War, unless actually invaded, or in such imminent Danger as will not admit of delay.
>
> (ARTICLE I, SECTION 10, CLAUSE 3)

~

*T*he Framers of the Constitution had little difficulty seeing that combinations among the states, or any foreign-affairs activities undertaken by the states, were so fraught with danger to the union, that none should be allowed unless Congress consented. Comparable prohibitions had already been contained in the Articles of Confederation, but the Framers chose somewhat stronger language in the Constitution to assure national supremacy in foreign affairs and in relations among the states. The provisions caused no significant debate at the Constitu-

tional Convention, and James Madison described them in *The Federalist* No. 44 as "fall[ing] within reasonings which are so obvious, or have been so fully developed, that they may be passed over without remark."

The constitutional logic of the provisions reflects a profound insight. Fearing that "factions," or interest groups, operating at the state level would endanger the Union and the legitimate interests of sister-states, Madison urged the Convention to include a congressional "negative" of "state laws in all cases whatsoever." Under his plan, *no* state law could go into effect without prior congressional approval. The Convention rejected Madison's proposal as unduly nationalistic and, moreover, unnecessarily broad, on the theory that most state laws would have little if any effect on the union or sister-states. The Convention instead subjected state laws to the operation of the Supremacy Clause: state laws become and remain in effect unless they are inconsistent with federal law or the Constitution.

Courts, however, cannot always be relied upon, and constitutional obstacles—in particular, the difficulty of mobilizing concurrent majorities in both houses of Congress and the Executive's assent—may prevent Congress from counteracting dangerous state enactments. Thus, for classes of state activities that could be presumed to threaten the union or sister-states, the Convention supplemented federal supremacy with either an absolute prohibition on state action (*See* Article I, Section 10, Clause 1) or the Madisonian "negative" (*See* Article I, Section 10, Clauses 2 and 3). The congressional approval requirement ensures that each state will be informed of, and heard on, potentially threatening sister-state activities, thus reducing the states' costs in monitoring and countermanding such activities. Moreover, the requirement compels the *proponents* of presumptively problematic state activities to mobilize the requisite majorities at the federal level, thus affording an added measure of security.

Among the provisions of the clause, only the Compact Clause has played a significant role in constitutional litigation. (The last Supreme Court case concerning the tonnage clause, a subject of frequent litigation in the nineteenth century, was in 1935.) The Supreme Court has interpreted the clause from an explicitly nontextual, "functionalist" perspective. While the foreign Compact Clause applies (as a constitutional matter, if not always in practice) to a broad range of formal and informal agreements between a state and foreign countries, the Supreme Court has determined that the domestic Compact Clause applies only to a narrow class of state agreements (those that establish binding obligations and, typically, multistate administrative agencies). Moreover, in *United States Steel Corp. v. Multistate Tax Commission* (1978), the Supreme Court declared that state compacts require congressional approval only if they "encroach upon the supremacy of the United States." Because states may not encroach upon federal supremacy in any event, a broad reading of *United States Steel* effectively deprives the Compact Clause of any independent constitutional force.

While the Supreme Court has never found a state compact void for want of congressional approval, some contemporary unapproved interstate agreements (such as the 1998 tobacco settlement between attorneys general and man-ufacturers) establish tax and regulatory regimes of unprecedented complexity and consequence. It remains to be seen whether this emerging trend could prompt a reexamination and rediscovery of the forgotten Compact Clause.

Michael S. Greve

Suggestions for Further Research

David Engdahl, *Characterization of Interstate Arrangements: When Is a Compact Not a Compact?* 64 Mich. L. Rev. 63 (1965)

Felix Frankfurter & James Landis, *The Compact Clause of the Constitution: A Study in Interstate Adjustments*, 34 Yale L.J. 685 (1925)

Michael S. Greve, *Compacts, Cartels, and Congressional Consent*, 68 M. L. Rev. 285 (2003)

Larry D. Kramer, *Madison's Audience*, 112 Harv. L. Rev. 611 (1999)

Significant Cases

Virginia v. Tennessee, 148 U.S. 503 (1893)

U.S. Steel Corp. v. Multistate Tax Commission, 434 U.S. 452 (1978)

ARTICLE II

Executive Vesting Clause

The executive Power shall be vested in a President of the United States of America.

(**Article II, Section 1, Clause 1**)

~

*T*he Executive Vesting Clause (or "Vesting Clause") grants the President those authorities that were traditionally wielded by executives.

Accordingly, the President may control federal law execution by directing and removing executive officers. The clause also accords the President those foreign-affairs authorities not otherwise granted to Congress or shared with the Senate. Thus, the President can control the formation and communication of foreign policy and can direct America's diplomatic corps. Because the Constitution nowhere assigns or shares these foreign-affairs powers, they remain part of the executive power granted to the President by the Executive Vesting Clause.

The Articles of Confederation lacked an independent chief executive. Instead, the Continental Congress exercised the executive power, appointing and dominating the secretaries of the executive departments. Unfortunately, law execution under the direction of a distracted, plural executive was neither vigorous nor swift. Congress likewise proved a poor steward of foreign affairs, with American diplomats complaining that Congress could not act with the requisite speed or secrecy. Similar problems plagued state governors. Though state constitutions formally created separate executives, most state executives were nearly as weak as their federal counterparts, because state constitutions typically subordinated state executives to the state legislatures. For instance, some state constitutions explicitly made executive authority subject to legislative limitation. Other times, the executive power was shared with a council. In that era, legislatures routinely hamstrung or usurped executive powers.

Resolving to avoid the problems plaguing state and national executives, the Constitution's makers created an energetic, responsible, and unified executive. A single executive could demand vigorous law execution by subordinates and avoid the dissension that would arise from disagreements amongst plural chief executives. A unitary executive would also make it possible to hold the executive responsible, because all eyes would be drawn to the chief executive rather than to some plural executive, where each executive would attempt to claim all the credit and shift any blame. James Wilson spoke for most when he remarked that a "single magistrate" would supply the "most energy, dispatch, and responsibility" to the execution of the laws, a view echoed by Alexander Hamilton in *The Federalist* No. 70. Indeed, the Framers rejected both the idea of plural chief executives and the creation of an executive council, because either proposal would serve to weaken and shield the chief executive. The Anti-Federalists well understood the Framers' design and criticized the unitary executive, the lack of a council, and the manner of his election.

In discussing the need for a unitary executive, the Founders also confirmed the chief executive's primary law-enforcement power. In particular, delegates spoke of the President executing federal law himself and controlling the law execution of executive subordinates. Likewise, the delegates spoke of the President's principal foreign-affairs role, oftentimes referring to the Senate's role in treaty-making as a limited exception to the grant of foreign-affairs authority to the President. The President's residual control of foreign affairs is most clearly seen in the vigorous actions of the Washington administration. The Founders believed that law execution and a residual control of foreign affairs, the two most important executive branch functions, were best overseen by a single, responsible, independent chief executive.

The Executive Vesting Clause's general rule that the President enjoys those powers traditionally vested with executives (i.e., the executive power) is subject to two important limitations. First, the President lacks executive authority explicitly granted to Congress. Hence the President cannot declare war, grant letters of marque and reprisal, or regulate commerce, even though executives had often wielded such authority in the past. In these instances, Congress retained portions of the executive power that the Continental Congress had wielded under the Articles. Second, specific constitutional provisions may check customary executive authority. Notwithstanding his executive power, the President cannot make treaties or appointments without the advice and consent of the Senate. Likewise, the President's pardon power is limited to offenses against the United States and does not extend to impeachments or violations of state law.

Some statesmen and scholars have doubted whether the Executive Vesting Clause really grants any power at all. Some have claimed that the "executive Power" merely refers to those specific powers enumerated elsewhere in Article II. Others have argued that the Executive Vesting Clause does no more than designate the title and number of the apex of the executive branch. To claim more for the Executive Vesting Clause supposedly would make the rest of Article II redundant. There are reasons to reject such doubts. First, these arguments shunt aside the late-eighteenth-century understanding of executive power. The phrase "executive Power" was not used as an empty catchall meant to encompass any and all authority granted by a constitution to an executive. The phrase encompassed, at a minimum, law execution and foreign-affairs powers.

Second, traditional rules of statutory interpretation require us to take seriously the differences in phrasing across the three vesting clauses. Article I, Section 1 ("All legislative Powers herein granted shall be vested in a Congress of the United States....") makes clear that it vests no authorities separate from those enumerated in the rest of Article I. In contrast, Article III, Section 1 ("The judicial Power of the United States, shall be vested in one supreme Court, and in such inferior Courts as the Congress may...establish.") clearly vests the federal courts with judicial authority. The Executive Vesting Clause reads like its Article III counterpart, in sharp contrast to the Article I introductory clause.

Third, although the title and number theory attempts to avoid redundant readings, it fails on its own terms. Because the rest of Article II makes absolutely clear that there would be only one executive styled the "President" (provisions in Article II repeatedly mention a "President" and use the pronoun "he"), the title and number theory would render the Executive Vesting Clause itself redundant. If every reading of the clause yields some redundancy, then arguments about redundancy cannot supply a reason for preferring one reading over another.

While the Executive Vesting Clause is most often associated with law execution and foreign affairs, the clause may grant authority beyond these areas. For instance, many believe that the clause supports an executive privilege that enables the President to shield intra-executive communications from Congress and the judiciary. Others contend that the clause grants the President certain immunities in court, such as immunity from suits challenging his official actions. Perhaps the clause also

grants the President certain "emergency powers" to take extraordinary actions during national exigencies.

The clause has played a rather limited role in constitutional litigation. With some notable exceptions—such as Justice Robert H. Jackson's concurring opinion in *Youngstown Sheet & Tube Co. v. Sawyer* (1952)—the Supreme Court apparently has accepted the notion that the Executive Vesting Clause grants powers beyond those enumerated in the remainder of Article II. Most famously, in *Myers v. United States* (1926), the Court cited the Executive Vesting Clause as the source of removal and supervisory powers over executive officers. A more recent case, *Nixon v. Fitzgerald* (1982), cites the clause as a source of three powers (law enforcement, foreign affairs, and a supervisory power over the executive branch). Even *Morrison v. Olson* (1988), which upheld the constitutionality of the Independent Counsel Act, acknowledged that the Executive Vesting Clause granted the President control over prosecutions.

Yet despite the judicial willingness to accept that the clause grants power, judicial decisions have limited the clause's reach. Post-*Myers*, the Supreme Court essentially permitted the creation of a fourth branch of government by indirectly sanctioning the congressional creation of independent agencies that simultaneously exercise legislative, executive, and judicial power. Additionally, *Morrison* upheld the constitutionality of independent counsels because the Court concluded that the good-cause removal restriction at issue in the case did not "unduly trammel on executive authority." If *Morrison* is taken at face value, it suggests that while the Executive Vesting Clause grants substantive powers to the President, the Congress may create officers who can exercise such powers independent of the President.

In a case touching upon foreign affairs, the judiciary has recently affirmed that the executive power grants foreign-affairs authority to the President. *See American Insurance Ass'n v. Garamendi* (2003). This marks a departure from prior case law, which had grounded the executive's foreign-affairs powers not in any constitutional text, but in necessity and sovereignty. *See United States v. Curtiss-Wright Export Corp.* (1936).

Sai Prakash

See Also

Article I, Section 1 (Legislative Vesting Clause)
Article II, Section 2, Clause 1 (Commander in Chief)
Article II, Section 2, Clause 2 (Treaty Clause and Appointments Clauses)
Article II, Section 3, Clause 1 (Take Care Clause)
Article III, Section 1 (Judicial Vesting Clause)

Suggestions for Further Research

Steven G. Calabresi, *Some Normative Arguments for the Unitary Executive*, 48 ARK. L. REV. 23 (1995)

Steven G. Calabresi & Saikrishna Prakash, *The President's Power to Execute the Laws*, 104 YALE L.J. 541 (1994)

Steven G. Calabresi & Kevin H. Rhodes, *The Structural Constitution: Unitary Executive, Plural Judiciary*, 105 HARV. L. REV. 1153 (1992)

HAROLD HONGJU KOH, THE NATIONAL SECURITY CONSTITUTION: SHARING POWER AFTER THE IRAN-CONTRA AFFAIR (1990)

Lawrence Lessig & Cass R. Sunstein, *The President and the Administration*, 94 COLUM. L. REV. 1, 4 (1994)

H. Jefferson Powell, *The Founders and the President's Authority over Foreign Affairs*, 40 WM. & MARY L. REV. 1471 (1999)

Saikrishna Prakash, *The Essential Meaning of Executive Power*, 2003 U. ILL. L. REV. 701 (2003)

Saikrishna B. Prakash & Michael D. Ramsey, *The Executive Power over Foreign Affairs*, 111 YALE L.J. 231 (2001)

ABRAHAM D. SOFAER, WAR, FOREIGN AFFAIRS, AND CONSTITUTIONAL POWER (1984).

Significant Cases

Myers v. United States, 272 U.S. 52 (1926)
Humphrey's Executor v. United States, 295 U.S. 602 (1935)
United States v. Curtiss-Wright Corp., 299 U.S. 304 (1936)
Youngstown Sheet & Tube Co. v. Sawyer, 343 U.S. 579 (1952)
United States v. Nixon, 418 US 683 (1974)
Nixon v. Fitzgerald, 457 U.S. 731 (1982)

Morrison v. Olson, 487 U.S. 654 (1988)
Clinton v. Jones, 520 U.S. 681 (1997)
American Insurance Ass'n v. Garamendi, 123 S.Ct. 2374 (2003)

Presidential Term

[The President] shall hold his Office during the Term of four Years....
(ARTICLE II, SECTION 1, CLAUSE 1)

∼

*B*efore deciding on the length of the term of office for the President, the Framers debated whether, after a first term, the President was to be reappointed by the legislature or by the people. James Madison vehemently opposed reappointment by the legislature, arguing that the separation of powers was essential to the preservation of liberty: "The Executive could not be independent of the Legislature, if dependent on the pleasure of that branch for a re-appointment." If the President were thus beholden to the legislature, "tyrannical laws may be made that they may be executed in a tyrannical manner."

On the other hand, the proposal to allow "re-appointment by Legislature for good-behavior" struck George Mason as allowing for too long a tenure. "An Executive during good behavior is a softer name only for an executive for life." Others wanted to avoid "a temptation on the side of the executive to intrigue with the Legislature for a re-appointment." Some feared foreign intrigue in the reappointment of a President.

After deciding that a President would not be reappointed by the Legislature, the Framers debated whether a President should be eligible for a second term at all. Several of the Framers were in support of reeligibility after a first term. As Roger Sherman reasoned, there was no need of "throwing out of office the men best qualified to execute its duties." Gouverneur Morris argued that reeligibility would incite a President to merit public esteem with the hopes of reelection and would eliminate the risk of having a

President use his short time in office to garner wealth and provide for friends. Alexander Hamilton adamantly argued that one of the keys to a successful executive is administrative stability, which would be best supported by a longer duration in office and would encourage a President to "act his part well." After removing the exclusion to reeligibility after a first term, the Framers turned to determine how many years a given term would be (proposals ranged from three to twenty). Eventually, the Framers settled on four years. According to Justice Joseph Story in his *Commentaries on the Constitution of the United States*, the period of four years is not long enough to risk any harm to the public safety. Although some Anti-Federalists thought that four years was sufficient time "to ruin his country," Hamilton wrote in *The Federalist* No. 71 that duration in office is "requisite to the energy of the executive authority" and that a four-year term struck the proper balance, giving a President enough time "to make the community sensible of the propriety of the measures he might incline to pursue" and to not "justify any alarm for the public liberty."

David F. Forte

See Also
Article II, Section 1, Clause 3 (Electoral College)
Amendment XII (Electoral College)

Vice President

...and, together with the Vice President, chosen for the same Term....
(**Article II, Section 1, Clause 1**)

~

*I*n early September 1787, after the Constitutional Convention had received and debated the draft from the Committee of Detail, the delegates appointed a Committee of Eleven to resolve a number of issues that continued to stymie the Convention. Among the Committee's felicitous innovations was the office of Vice President. In this brief phrase, later approved by the Convention, the Committee of Eleven accomplished two signal results. First, the Vice President would be elected at the same time, for the same term, and by the same constituency as the President. The intent was to preserve the independence of the executive should the person who was Vice President succeed to the duties of the presidency. Second, by separating this phrase from the previous sentence, it is clear that the Vice President was not vested with any part of the constitutionally mandated executive power. There would be no plural executive.

The primary constitutional role of the Vice President was to be available to become President (or Acting President) should the office become vacant, or should a contingent election of a President fail in the House of Representatives. This is underscored by the original arrangement whereby presidential electors voted for two candidates; the one with the most votes (provided it constituted a majority of the electors) would be President and the individual with the next greatest number of votes would be Vice President. (Article II, Section 1, Clause 3.) Even when the Twelfth Amendment modified the method of electing a President and Vice President, the purpose of the Framers remained: the person who was to hold the office of President or Vice President should be chosen free of legislative control. Of course, should it happen that there was no person so chosen available to fill the presidency, the Constitution provides that Congress may by law provide for an officer to "act as President" until a President is elected. That contingency, however, has never occurred, and its need has been further obviated by the operation of the Twenty-fifth Amendment.

The other constitutional duty of the Vice President (*see* Article I, Section 3, Clause 4), to be President of the Senate, had implications for succession as well. George Mason objected to the mixing of executive and legislative powers; he preferred that an executive council be established, the president of which would serve as Vice President of the United States. But the Framers were opposed to an executive council. Further, were the Senate to have elected its own president, that person would almost certainly have been in line for succession. As James Madison stated, the question centered "on the appointment of the vice President [as] president of the Senate instead of making the President of the Senate the vice president, which seemed to be the alternative."

As it occurred, for 140 years, the primary role of the Vice President was legislative though without much influence. Jack Garner, former Speaker of the House and Vice President to Franklin D. Roosevelt, famously described the office (in a bowdlerized quote) as "not worth a bucket of warm spit." The Vice President did not begin to have executive responsibilities until the twentieth century. Vice President Thomas R. Marshall chaired some of Woodrow Wilson's Cabinet meetings when the President was absent. President Warren G. Harding had his Vice President, Calvin Coolidge, attend all Cabinet meetings, a practice that became institutionalized under Franklin D. Roosevelt, though Garner still felt excluded from any effective voice on policy. It was not until the 1950s, under President Dwight D. Eisenhower, that the Vice President, Richard M. Nixon, became a fully functioning executive official, attending 193 Cabinet meetings, 217 National Security Council sessions, and chairing important executive committees. Since that time, the extent of the executive role of the Vice President has depended upon his relationship with the President.

Nine Vice Presidents have filled the presidency upon the death or resignation of the President: John Tyler, Millard Fillmore, Andrew Johnson, Chester A. Arthur, Theodore Roosevelt, Calvin Coolidge, Harry S. Truman, Lyndon B. Johnson, and Gerald R. Ford (Roosevelt, Coolidge, Truman, and Lyndon Johnson were subsequently re-elected as President). Five other Vice Presidents have attained the presidency by election in their own right: John Adams, Thomas Jefferson, Martin Van Buren, Richard M. Nixon, and George H.W. Bush. Thus, although a candidate for President often chooses a running mate for electoral reasons, the person elected as Vice President has a significant chance to become President.

David F. Forte

See Also

Article I, Section 3, Clause 4 (Vice President as Presiding Officer)

Article II, Section 1, Clause 3 (Electoral College)

Article II, Section 1, Clause 6 (Presidential Succession)

Amendment XXII (Presidential Term Limit)

Amendment XXV (Presidential Succession)

Suggestions for Further Research

Mark O. Hatfield, Vice Presidents of the United States, 1789-1993 (1997)

Paul C. Light, Vice-Presidential Power: Advice and Influence in the White House (1984)

L. Edward Purcell, The Vice Presidents: A Biographical Dictionary (1998)

Harold C. Relyea, *The Vice-Presidency: Evolution of the Modern Office*, 1933-2001, Congressional Research Service (2001)

Presidential Electors

[The President] shall…together with the Vice President, chosen for the same Term, be elected, as follows: Each State shall appoint, in such Manner as the Legislature thereof may direct, a Number of Electors, equal to the whole Number of Senators and Representatives to which the State may be entitled in the Congress: but no Senator or Representative, or Person holding an Office of Trust or Profit under the United States, shall be appointed an Elector.

(Article II, Section 1, Clause 2)

～

*A*fter struggling with numerous proposals on the election of the President, the delegates to the Constitutional Convention settled on establishing a college of electors and apportioning the number according to the total of Representatives and Senators from each state. This method permitted the smaller states to have a somewhat greater proportionate share in the choosing of the President, though not as large an advantage as they had in the Senate. The Framers not only rejected the direct popular election of the President, but also left it to the state legislatures to determine how the states' electors were to be appointed.

This language in fact paralleled the provisions for state legislative appointment of congressional delegates in the Articles of Confederation, and of U.S. Senators under Article I of the Constitution. With political parties widely disdained, this process was designed to pick not the candidate from the most popular political faction, but the wisest and most virtuous leader. The Framers rejected direct popular election of the President (and of Senators), both because they believed that the populace would be ill-informed about national figures and because the Framers wanted to avoid interfering with state authority and underweighing small states. The Framers also rejected having Congress select the President because they feared that would make the President dependent on Congress. They hoped that the Electoral College would obviate these problems and would form a truly deliberative body on this single issue. The delegates to the Convention disagreed about whether electors should be popularly elected or appointed by state legislatures. They resolved that question by leaving the matter up to each state legislature.

Developments since then have changed much of the expected *practice*, but cases have confirmed the original understanding regarding electoral *powers* absent constitutional alteration. Our democratic ethos increasingly embraced popular elections, leading all state legislatures by 1880 to provide for popular election of presidential electors, and the Sixteenth Amendment in 1913 mandated the same for Senators. This development, and the growing view that political party politics reflected rather than undermined democratic choice, made the notion of electors exercising their own independent judgment seem dubious by the early 1800s. Current case law such as *Ray v. Blair* (1952) allows the states to present voters with ballots that list only the presidential candidates (even though the votes for a candidate are really for his party's slate of electors), and also per-

mits the states to pass laws requiring electors to pledge that, if chosen, they will vote for their party's candidate. Electors rarely do otherwise, though the enforceability of those pledges against a wayward elector remains unsettled.

Because the above ballot and pledge requirements were directed by state legislatures, they came within those legislatures' federal constitutional power to direct the manner of selecting presidential electors. Although the Framers appear not to have considered whether this state legislative power could be constricted by state constitutions, subsequent cases adjudicating the question held that it could not because the federal Constitution's text vests this authority directly in the state legislatures rather than in the states. Indeed, notwithstanding the fact that what a state legislature "is" might reasonably be thought to be determined by state constitutional procedures, *McPherson v. Blacker* (1892) stated that state legislatures need not (though they usually did) even follow normal state constitutional procedural requirements that legislatures vote bicamerally or present their decisions to the executive for possible veto. The Supreme Court's initial unanimous decision in the 2000 election dispute vacated the Florida Supreme Court's first decision for failing to take into account this doctrine prohibiting state constitutions from constricting state legislative directions about the appointment of presidential electors. *Bush v. Palm Beach County Canvassing Board* (2000).

State legislatures must, however, exercise their federal constitutional power to direct the manner of selecting presidential electors consistent with other provisions of the federal Constitution, including the First and Fourteenth Amendments. So have held a series of cases, from *McPherson*, *Williams v. Rhodes* (1968), and *Anderson v. Celebrezze* (1983), to the *Bush v. Gore* (2000) decision that invalidated a manual recount process for unconstitutionally giving election officials standardless discretion over how to count certain ballots. *McPherson* and *Williams* explicitly rejected the argument, sometimes cited by critics of *Bush v. Gore*, that the selection of presidential electors is a political question beyond any judicial review to assure compliance with the federal Constitution.

An unresolved question is whether a state legislature's determination that a state court deviated from state legislative directions would be judicially reviewable. This issue would have arisen had the Supreme Court not decided *Bush v. Gore* on December 12, 2000, because the Florida legislature was poised to complete its direct appointment of electors on December 13, citing its concern that the state supreme court had deviated from the state legislature's preelection directions and allowed the contest to exceed the federal statutory deadline for making contest determinations binding when Congress counted electoral votes. Had the Florida legislature proceeded with such a direct appointment, the courts might have concluded that such a state legislative decision was an unreviewable political question (as are state legislative ratifications of constitutional amendments) or that only Congress (when exercising its Twelfth Amendment counting powers) could review the validity of such state legislative action.

Einer Elhauge

See Also

Article I, Section 3, Clause 1 (Senate)
Article V
Amendment XII (Electoral College)
Amendment XVI (Income Tax)

Significant Cases

McPherson v. Blacker, 146 U.S. 1 (1892)
Ray v. Blair, 343 U.S. 214 (1952)
Williams v. Rhodes, 393 U.S. 23 (1968)
Anderson v. Celebrezze, 460 U.S. 780 (1983)
Bush v. Gore, 531 U.S. 98 (2000)
Bush v. Palm Beach County Canvassing Board, 531 U.S. 70 (2000)

Electoral College

The Electors shall meet in their respective States, and vote by Ballot for two Persons, of whom one at least shall not be an Inhabitant of the same State with themselves. And they shall make a List of all the Persons voted for, and of the Number of Votes for each; which List they shall sign and certify, and transmit sealed to the Seat of the Government of the United States, directed to the President of the Senate. The President of the Senate shall, in the Presence of the Senate and House of Representatives, open all the Certificates, and the Votes shall then be counted. The Person having the greatest Number of Votes shall be the President, if such Number be a Majority of the whole Number of Electors appointed; and if there be more than one who have such Majority, and have an equal Number of Votes, then the House of Representatives shall immediately chuse by Ballot one of them for President; and if no Person have a Majority, then from the five highest on the List the said House shall in like Manner chuse the President. But in chusing the President, the Votes shall be taken by States, the Representation from each State having one Vote; A quorum for this purpose shall consist of a Member or Members from two thirds of the States, and a Majority of all the States shall be necessary to a Choice. In every Case, after the Choice of the President, the Person having the greatest Number of Votes of the Electors shall be the Vice President. But if there should remain two or more who have equal Votes, the Senate shall chuse from them by Ballot the Vice President.

(ARTICLE II, SECTION 1, CLAUSE 3)

      ~

*A*t the Constitutional Convention in 1787, delegates had expressed concern that a meeting of a single body in the nation's capital to elect a

President opened the door to intrigue and undue influence by special interests, foreign governments, and political factions. Meeting in their home states, electors would find it difficult to collude or buy and sell votes.

A more difficult problem was how to structure the voting within the Electoral College. During the debates at the Constitutional Convention, some delegates argued that the diversity and dispersal of the people over an expansive territory militated against direct popular election, for voters would be unable to form a majority behind any one candidate. In response, James Madison proposed that every individual voter cast three votes for President, at least two for persons from a state other than his own. Madison's idea later resurfaced, and the Convention applied it in modified form to the presidential electors of the Electoral College. Requiring each elector to cast two votes for President increased the chances that electors could form a majority. Indeed, under the arithmetic, it was possible that as many as three candidates could have a majority of the votes of the electors. The provision did not prevent a New York elector from voting for two Virginians, but prohibited a Virginia elector from doing so. The Framers also accepted Madison's small but significant amendment to add the word "appointed" after the original text requiring a "Majority of the whole Number of Electors" for election. Thus the basis of what constitutes a majority changes if a state fails to appoint electors. As it turned out, in the first presidential election, New York failed to appoint electors, and George Washington won by the unanimous vote of the electors appointed.

If two or three persons received a majority vote and an equal vote, the House of Representatives must choose one of them for President. In deference to a suggestion by George Washington, the Convention gave this responsibility to the popularly elected House, not the Senate, but representatives had to vote as state delegations, each state having one vote. If no candidate received a majority of the electoral vote, the House would choose from among the top five candidates. Because each state had one vote, regardless of population, the procedure gave proportionately more influence to the smaller states. The choice of five also gave to smaller states a greater chance of having one of their residents elected by the House, a concession to them that balanced the advantage that large states had in the electoral vote. The contingency election process also reassured delegates who had favored congressional election of the President in the first instance. The Twelfth Amendment modified these provisions, following a crisis in 1800, when Thomas Jefferson and Aaron Burr each received an equal number of electoral votes.

The creation of the office of Vice President appears to have been directly related to the mode of choosing the President. The Constitution gives to the Vice President only two specific constitutional responsibilities: he is President of the Senate, and he receives and opens the electoral votes. In 1789, the Senate elected John Langdon as President of the Senate "for the sole purpose of opening and counting the votes for President of the United States" (there being no sitting Vice President). In 1793, the Vice President, John Adams, "opened, read, and delivered" the certificates and votes of the electors to the tellers appointed by the respective houses. The tellers "ascertained the votes." By 1797, Vice President Adams only opened and delivered the certificates and reports of the electors to the tellers who counted the votes. Practice has generally followed that precedent. The issue of who counts the votes was particularly sensitive in 1876, during the contested election between Rutherford B. Hayes and Samuel Tilden. There were disputes in South Carolina, Louisiana, Florida, and Oregon about which electors had been appointed. The President of the Senate, Thomas W. Ferry, was a Republican; the Democratic Party controlled the House and the Republicans controlled the Senate. The Congress invented a novel solution to the problem of who would count the votes by creating an electoral commission, composed of five Senators, five Representatives, and five Supreme Court Justices, to determine the results.

Finally, under this clause, whoever was runner-up in the electoral vote, with or without a majority vote, presumably a national figure competent to serve as President, became Vice President. Clearly, the Founders did not anticipate rival national political parties whose top candidates could be the top two vote recipients. In the 1796 election, Federalist John Adams became President and Republican Thomas Jefferson (Adams's bitter political opponent) became Vice President. Four years later, both Jefferson and his Vice-Presidential running mate, Aaron Burr, received an equal number of votes. The House ultimately voted in favor of Jefferson, but only after thirty-six ballots. Hence, the Twelfth Amendment, ratified in 1804, also changed this method of choosing the Vice President. In the contingency election for Vice President, the Senate makes the choice. Senators do not vote as state delegations; thus, disagreements between the two Senators from a state do not lead to a stalemate. Only one time in U.S. history, in 1836, did the Senate choose the Vice President, Richard M. Johnson, who served under Martin Van Buren.

Tadahisa Kuroda

See Also

Suggestions for Further Research

Joseph Jackson, Survey of the Electoral College in the Political System of the United States (1945)

Tadahisa Kuroda, The Origins of the Twelfth Amendment: The Electoral College in the Early Republic, 1787–1804 (1994)

David A. McKnight, The Electoral System of the United States (1878)

Jack N. Rakove, Original Meanings, Politics and Ideas in the Making of the Constitution (1996)

Shlomo Slonin, *The Electoral College at Philadelphia: The Evolution of an Ad Hoc Congress for the Selection of a President*, 73 J. Am. Hist. 35 (1986)

Presidential Vote

The Congress may determine the Time of chusing the Electors, and the Day on which they shall give their Votes; which Day shall be the same throughout the United States.
(**Article II, Section 1, Clause 4**)

~

*T*his clause requires that all electors vote on the same "Day" but allows Congress to set a multi-day range of "Time" for when states choose their electors. Congress has exercised this authority to set a uniform day (the Tuesday after the first Monday in November) for states to appoint electors. But Congress has also provided in the same statute that, if a state's election "has failed to make a choice" on that day, then the state legislature can afterward appoint electors in any manner it deems fit, thus effectively extending the "time" for choosing electors.

Unfortunately, the statutory text exercising this constitutional authority provides no criteria for deciding *when* an election "fails to make a choice" or *who* gets to decide when no choice was made. The historical record indicates that Congress thought this statutory language included cases where floods or inclement weather prevented "any considerable number" of voters from reaching the polls and that, in such cases, Congress wanted to confirm the power of the state's "legislature to authorize the continuance of the elections" past the congressionally prescribed election day. This legislative history indicates that an election might "fail to make a choice" even though there had been an election with a certifiable result, at least when that result was distorted by flooding or bad weather. It also makes clear that, at least in that circumstance, Congress contemplated that the state legislature was the entity that would decide whether the election had failed to make a choice. Unfortunately, the legislative history does not indicate what other circumstances Congress thought might mean an election failed to make a choice.

One interpretation is that Congress contemplated that each state legislature would have the power to decide when in its judgment other problems (including perhaps a state judicial failure to follow legislative directions or resolve election contests by congressional deadlines) meant the election failed to make a choice or was distorted. Alternatively, one might narrowly interpret the "failure to make a choice" language to prevent state legislatures from using dubious pretexts to reverse whatever presidential-election outcomes they disliked. Arguing against the alternative interpretation is the fact that state legislative decisions (unlike judicial decisions) are political actions ultimately reviewable by the state electorate, which would be displeased if a state legislature tried to alter that electorate's presidential choice on mere pretext. Further, allowing state legislatures to make such judgments could be coupled with (possibly deferential) federal judicial review as to whether the state legislatures acted pretextually and/or with congressional review when it exercises its constitutional power to decide which electoral votes to count.

Another unresolved issue is whether Congress's Twelfth Amendment power to "count" electoral votes gives it discretion to refuse to count the votes of electors whom the state legislature has properly appointed. Such congressional refusal would seem to violate Article II, Section 1, Clause 2. But the action might not be judicially reviewable, in which case only the national electorate would (at the next congressional election) be able to review any such congressional decision to exceed the proper scope of its counting power.

Einer Elhauge

See Also

Article I, Section 3, Clause 1 (Senate)
Article V

Amendment XII (Electoral College)
Amendment XVI (Income Tax)

Presidential Eligibility

No Person except a natural born Citizen, or a Citizen of the United States, at the time of the Adoption of this Constitution, shall be eligible to the Office of President; neither shall any Person be eligible to that Office who shall not have attained to the Age of thirty five Years, and been fourteen Years a Resident within the United States.
(**Article II, Section 1, Clause 5**)

~

*T*he Constitution imposes three eligibility requirements on the Presidency—based on the officeholder's age, residency, and citizenship—that must be satisfied at the time of taking office. By virtue of the Twelfth Amendment, the qualifications for Vice President are the same. The Framers established these qualifications in order to increase the chances of electing a person of patriotism, judgment, and civic virtue.

First, Presidents must be thirty-five years of age or older. In contrast, Senators must be at least thirty years old, and Representatives no less than twenty-five years old. As Justice Joseph Story has noted, the "character and talent" of a man in the middle age of life is "fully developed," and he has had the opportunity "for public service and for experience in the public councils."

Second, the President must have been a "Resident" of the United States for fourteen years. By contrast, to be a Member of Congress, one must be an "Inhabitant" of the State one is representing. During the Constitutional Convention, James Madison contended that "both [terms] were vague, but the latter ['Inhabitant'] least so in common acceptation, and would not exclude persons absent occasionally for a considerable time on public or private business."

Then as now, inhabitant meant being a legal domiciliary, but resident could mean either a domiciliary or a physical presence. Perhaps the Framers desired a person as President who had actually been present in the United States for the required period and had developed an attachment to and understanding of the country, rather than one who was legally an inhabitant, but who may have lived abroad for most of his life. On the other hand, the distinction may have been one of style rather than substance. As Justice Story later noted, "by 'residence,' in the constitution, is to be understood, not an absolute inhabitancy within the United States during the whole period; but such an inhabitancy, as includes a permanent domicil in the United States."

There is some evidence that the Framers believed the fourteen-year residency requirement could be satisfied cumulatively, rather than consecutively. An earlier version of the clause excluded individuals who have "not been *in the whole*, at least fourteen years a resident within the U.S." (emphasis added), and historical evidence suggests that deletion of the phrase "in the whole" was not intended to alter the provision's meaning. This might explain the election of Herbert Hoover, whose successful 1928 campaign for President came less than fourteen years after his return to the United States in 1917. Others may argue that Hoover had simply maintained a United States domicile throughout his tenure abroad.

The third qualification to be President is that one must be a "natural born Citizen" (or a citizen at the time of the adoption of the Constitution). Although any citizen may become a Member of Congress so long as he has held citizenship for the requisite time period, to be President, one must be "a natural born Citizen." Undivided loyalty to the United States was a prime concern. During the Constitutional Convention, John Jay wrote to George Washington, urging "a strong check to the admission of Foreigners into the administration of our national Government; and to declare expressly that the Commander in Chief of the American army shall not be given to nor devolve on, any but a natural born Citizen." Justice Story later noted that the natural-born–citizenship requirement "cuts off all chances for ambitious foreigners, who might otherwise be intriguing for the office."

Under the longstanding English common-law principle of *jus soli*, persons born within the territory of the sovereign (other than children of enemy aliens or foreign diplomats) are citizens from birth. Thus, those persons born within the United States are "natural born citizens" and eligible to be President. Much less certain, however, is whether children born abroad of United States citizens are "natural born citizens" eligible to serve as President. As early as 1350, the British Parliament approved statutes recognizing the rule of *jus sanguinis*, under which citizens may pass their citizenship by descent to their children at birth, regardless of place. Similarly, in its first naturalization statute, Congress declared that "the children of citizens of the United States, that may be born beyond the sea, or out of the limits of the United States, shall be considered as natural born citizens." 1 Stat. 104 (1790). The "natural born" terminology was dropped shortly thereafter. *See, e.g.*, 8 U.S.C. § 1401(c). But the question remains whether the term "natural born Citizen" used in Article II includes the parliamentary rule of *jus sanguinis* in addition to the common law principle of *jus soli*. In *United States v. Wong Kim Ark* (1898), the Supreme Court relied on English common law regarding *jus soli* to inform the meaning of "citizen" in the Fourteenth Amendment as well as the natural-born–citizenship requirement of Article II, and noted that any right to citizenship though *jus sanguinis* was available only by statute, and not through the Constitution. Notwithstanding the Supreme Court's discussion in *Wong Kim Ark*, a majority of commentators today argue that the Presidential Eligibility Clause incorporates both the common-law and English statutory principles, and that therefore, Michigan Governor George Romney, who was born to American parents outside of the United States, was eligible to seek the Presidency in 1968.

The Presidential Eligibility Clause does not explicitly cover those who serve merely as Acting President, a constitutionally distinct office. Although Congress has imposed by statute, 3 U.S.C. § 19(e), the same eligibility requirements for service as Acting President, that provision may not be required as a constitutional matter.

James C. Ho

See Also

Article I, Section 2, Clause 2 (Qualifications for Representatives)

Article I, Section 3, Clause 3 (Qualifications for Senators)

Article II, Section 1, Clause 6 (Presidential Succession)

Amendment XII (Electoral College)

Amendment XIV, Section 1 (Citizenship)

Amendment XXV (Presidential Succession)

Suggestions for Further Research

Charles Gordon, *Who Can Be President of the United States: The Unresolved Enigma*, 28 MD. L. REV. 1 (1968)

James C. Ho, *President Schwarzenegger—Or At Least Hughes?*, 7 GREEN BAG 2D 108 (2004)

James C. Ho, *Unnatural Born Citizens and Acting Presidents*, 17 CONST. COMMENT. 575 (2000)

Randall Kennedy, *A Natural Aristocracy?*, 12 CONST. COMMENT. 175 (1995)

Jordan Steiker, Sanford Levinson & J. M. Balkin, *Taking Text and Structure Really Seriously: Constitutional Interpretation and the Crisis of Presidential Eligibility*, 74 TEX. L. REV. 237 (1995)

Significant Cases

United States v. Wong Kim Ark, 169 U.S. 649 (1898)

United States *ex rel.* Guest v. Perkins, 17 F. Supp. 177 (D.D.C. 1936)

Presidential Succession

In Case of the Removal of the President from Office, or of his Death, Resignation, or Inability to discharge the Powers and Duties of the said Office, the Same shall devolve on the Vice President, and the Congress may by Law provide for the Case of Removal, Death, Resignation or Inability, both of the President and Vice President, declaring what Officer shall then act as President, and such Officer shall act accordingly, until the Disability be removed, or a President shall be elected.

(ARTICLE II, SECTION 1, CLAUSE 6)

∽

*T*his provision constitutes the anchor for presidential succession in the United States. It provides for the Vice President to take over in the event of the removal, death, resignation, or inability of the President. It also authorizes Congress to establish a line of succession beyond the vice presidency. Left unclear by the clause was whether the Vice President became President or simply acted as President in a case of succession.

Other ambiguities in the provision were noted at the Constitutional Convention of 1787 by John Dickinson of Delaware, who asked, "[W]hat is the extent of the term 'disability' & who is to be the judge of it?" James Madison expressed concern that the provision would prevent the filling of a presidential vacancy by a special election, and he therefore successfully inserted the expression "until the Disability be removed, or a President shall be elected." It is not clear whether this change was intended to apply when the Vice President succeeded or only when an officer designated by Congress was called upon to serve in the case of a double vacancy. In any event, there has never been a special election for President, although the provision allowing for its possibility was included in the country's early presidential succession laws.

Both the First and Second Congresses debated who should be in the line of succession. The Secretary of State, the Chief Justice, the President Pro Tempore, and the Speaker were all mentioned. On March 1, 1792, Congress resolved the issue by choosing the President Pro Tempore and Speaker, respectively, prompting criticism from Madison and others that the congressional officers were not within the contemplation of the succession provision. This law was never implemented.

In 1841, when President William Henry Harrison died in office, Vice President John Tyler assumed the presidency for the rest of the term. His claim of being President, not simply Vice President acting as President, drew criticism. The precedent he set, however, took and became the operating principle when other Presidents died in office. On the other hand, Tyler's example became a major obstacle for situations involving the temporary inability of a President because, under the wording of this clause, the status of a Vice President in a case of death would appear to be the same as in a case of inability or resignation or removal. As a consequence, on a number of occasions Vice Presidents declined to consider relieving a disabled President because of the Tyler precedent and also because of the ambiguities first raised by John Dickinson. This was the case in 1881 when President James A. Garfield lay dying and some suggested that Vice President Chester A. Arthur take charge, and again in 1919 after President Woodrow Wilson's stroke when Vice President Thomas R. Marshall was urged to do the same. In 1967, the adoption of the Twenty-fifth Amendment eliminated much of the remaining uncertainties regarding presidential succession.

John Feerick

See Also

Amendment XXV (Presidential Succession)

Suggestions for Further Research

Akhil R. Amar & Vikram David Amar, *Is the Presidential Succession Law Constitutional?*, 48 STAN. L. REV. 113 (1995)

Steven G. Calabresi, *The Political Question of Presidential Succession*, 48 STAN. L. REV. 155 (1995)

JOHN D. FEERICK, FROM FAILING HANDS: THE STORY OF PRESIDENTIAL SUCCESSION (1965)

RUTH C. SILVA, PRESIDENTIAL SUCCESSION (1968)

Compensation

The President shall, at stated Times, receive for his Services, a Compensation, which shall neither be increased nor diminished during the Period for which he shall have been elected, and he shall not receive within that Period any other Emolument from the United States, or any of them.

(ARTICLE II, SECTION 1, CLAUSE 7)

~

*T*his clause accomplishes two things: it establishes that the President is to receive a "Compensation" that is unalterable during the period "for which he shall have been elected;" and it prohibits him within that period from receiving "any other Emolument" from either the federal government or the states.

The proposition that the President was to receive a fixed compensation for his service in office seems to have been derived from the Massachusetts Constitution of 1780, which served as a model for the Framers in other respects as well. The Constitutional Convention hardly debated the issue, except to reject, politely but decisively, the elderly Benjamin Franklin's proposal that the President should receive no monetary compensation. Perhaps the Framers feared that if Franklin's proposal were accepted, only persons of great wealth would accept presidential office.

As Alexander Hamilton explained in *The Federalist* No. 73, the primary purpose of requiring that the President's compensation be fixed in advance of his service was to fortify the independence of the presidency, and thus to reinforce the larger constitutional design of separation of powers. "The Legislature, with a discretionary power over the salary and emoluments of the Chief Executive, could render him as obsequious to their will, as they might think proper to make him. They might in most cases either reduce him by famine, or tempt him by largesses, to surrender at discretion his judgment to their inclinations." For similar separation of powers reasons, Article III, Section 1, provides that federal judges "shall, at stated Times, receive for their Services, a Compensation" although that provision only forbids Congress from *diminishing* the judges' compensation, not from *increasing* it. The distinction, as Hamilton noted in *The Federalist* No. 79, "probably arose from the difference in the duration of the respective offices."

The prohibition on presidential "emoluments" is one of several constitutional provisions addressed to potential conflicts of interest. Further, the Compensation Clause eliminated one possible means of circumventing the requirement that the President's compensation be fixed: without this provision Congress might seek to augment the President's "Compensation" by providing him with (what would purportedly differ) additional "emoluments." Significantly, the prohibition on presidential emoluments also extends to the states. That requirement helps to ensure presidential impartiality among particular members or regions of the Union.

A modern problem arose when President Ronald Reagan continued to receive retirement benefits as a retired governor of California while he was in the White House. He had been receiving benefits since the expiration of his second term in 1975. In a 1981 opinion, the Justice Department's Office of Legal Counsel focused on the purpose of the Compensation Clause, which was in its view "to prevent Congress or any of the states from attempting to influence the President through financial rewards or penalties." Given that President Reagan's retirement benefits were a vested right under California law rather than a gratuity that the state could withhold, the purpose of the clause would not be furthered by preventing him from receiving them.

The meaning of the Compensation Clause also arose in the context of President Richard M. Nixon's papers. As authorized by the Presidential Recordings and Materials Preservation Act, the government had taken or seized President Nixon's papers after he had left office. President Nixon (succeeded by his estate) sued for compensation for the taking of what he alleged to be his property under the Takings Clause of the Fifth Amendment. The government argued that the Compensation Clause precluded payment of compensation on the theory that the presidential materials were the product of President Nixon's exercise of powers conferred on him by the United States, and that therefore he could not sell them for his personal profit, even after his presidency, without impermissibly receiving an "Emolument" over and above the fixed compensation to which he was entitled. The district court rejected the government's argument, relying in part on a prior appellate determination that President Nixon was the owner of the materials in question. It found that President Nixon's entitlement to just compensation had vested when the government took his property (i.e., after he had left office), and therefore that "the plain language of the Emoluments Clause would not be violated because Mr. Nixon would receive compensation subsequent to the expiration of his term of office." The government argued that such a finding necessarily implied that a sitting President could sell his papers for profit *during* his tenure of office—to which the court demurred that "those are not the facts in this case." The court also found, however, that the papers "were not transferred to [President Nixon] by the government as compensation for his service in office," perhaps implying that a President could indeed sell his papers during his term. *Griffin v. United States* (1995). Under the Presidential Records Act of 1978, however, Presidents no longer have title to their papers, 44 U.S.C. § 2202, and so cannot sell them, thus obviating the issue of whether such sales would be emoluments.

Robert Delahunty

See Also

Article I, Section 9, Clause 8 (Emoluments Clause)
Article III, Section 1 (Judicial Compensation Clause)

Suggestions for Further Research

The President and the Judges—Tax on Salaries of, 13 Op. Att'y Gen. 161 (1869)

President Reagan's Ability to Receive Retirement Benefits from the State of California, 5 Op. Off. Legal Counsel 187 (1981)

Significant Case

Griffin v. United States, 935 F. Supp. 1 (D.D.C. 1995)

Oath of Office

Before he enter on the Execution of his Office, he shall take the following Oath or Affirmation:—"I do solemnly swear (or affirm) that I will faithfully execute the Office of President of the United States, and will to the best of my Ability, preserve, protect and defend the Constitution of the United States."

(ARTICLE II, SECTION 1, CLAUSE 8)

～

*T*he Framers fittingly placed the Oath of Office Clause between preceding clauses that set forth the organization of the executive department and succeeding clauses that specify the contours of the President's executive power. The President takes the oath after he assumes the office but before he executes it.

The clause is one of several that employ the oath concept, but it is the only clause that actually specifies the language of an oath for a constitutional actor. The clause does not specify who shall administer the oath, though it has been the common, but not universal, practice for the Chief Justice to do so. While Article VI's Oaths Clause simply requires the persons specified therein to "be bound by Oath or Affirmation, to support this Constitution," the Presidential Oath Clause requires much more than this general oath of allegiance and fidelity. The clause, in notable part, enjoins the President to swear or affirm that he "will to the best of [his] Ability, preserve, protect and defend the Constitution of the United States."

The Framers undoubtedly drew upon similar provisions in a number of early state constitutions in drafting the clause, but they plainly believed that a special oath for the President was indispensable. At the Constitutional Convention, when George Mason and James Madison moved to add the "preserve, protect and defend" language, only James Wilson objected, on the ground that "the general provision for oaths of office, in a subsequent place, rendered the amendment unnecessary." The prospect of George Washington becoming President cannot

be discounted. The Framers perhaps desired an oath that would replicate the public values of the man who was presiding over the Convention. More significantly, because the presidency was singular, there were no available internal checks, as there were in the other branches, with their multiple members. A specially phrased internal check was therefore necessary, one that tied the President's duty to "preserve, protect and defend" to his obligations to God.

The location and phrasing of the Oath of Office Clause strongly suggest that it is not empowering, but that it is limiting—the clause limits how the President's "executive power" is to be exercised. One unanswered question is whether the President can even legally execute his powers should he intentionally refuse to take or affirm the oath. The clause shares a tight linkage with Article II's Take Care Clause, which requires that the President "shall take Care that the Laws be faithfully executed." The duty faithfully to execute the Constitution as supreme law might be thought to presuppose a power to interpret *what* is to be executed: "to say what the law is," to borrow a famous phrase from Chief Justice John Marshall. Indeed, some scholars—and Presidents—have seized upon the clause as the font of the President's power of "executive review"—the President's coordinate power to interpret the Constitution, even against conflicting interpretations by the legislative or judicial departments. The penultimate draft of the clause, referred by the Framers to the Committee of Style and Arrangement and reported by that committee, provides some support for this reading. That draft provided that the President act to the best of his "judgment and power," instead of to the best of his "Ability."

Finally, the "preserve, protect and defend" language of the Oath of Office Clause might be thought to place a special constitutional duty on the President to fight for the nation's survival, whether Congress has declared war or not. So thought President Abraham Lincoln during the Civil War. Similarly, President George W. Bush often declared that his primary duty was to "protect" the people of the United States.

Vasan Kesavan

See Also

Article II, Section 3 (Take Care Clause)

Article VI, Clause 3 (Oaths Clause)

Suggestions for Further Research

Scott E. Gant & Bruce G. Peabody, *Musings on a Constitutional Mystery: Missing Presidents and "Headless Monsters"?*, 14 Const. Comment. 83 (1997)

Joel K. Goldstein, *The Presidency and the Rule of Law: Some Preliminary Explorations*, 43 St. Louis U. L.J. 791 (1999)

Henry P. Monaghan, *The Protective Power of the Presidency*, 93 Colum. L. Rev. 1 (1993)

Michael Stokes Paulsen, *The Most Dangerous Branch: Executive Power to Say What the Law Is*, 83 Geo. L.J. 217 (1994)

Commander in Chief

The President shall be Commander in Chief of the Army and Navy of the United States....
(Article II, Section 2, Clause 1)

∼

*F*ew constitutional issues have been so consistently and heatedly debated by legal scholars and politicians in recent years as the distribution of war powers between Congress and the President. As a matter of history and policy, it is generally accepted that the executive takes the lead in the actual conduct of war. After all, a single, energetic actor is better able to prosecute war successfully than a committee; the enemy will not wait for deliberation and consensus. At the same time, the Founders plainly intended to establish congressional checks on the executive's war power. Between these guideposts is a question of considerable importance: Does the Constitution require the President to obtain specific authorization from Congress before initiating hostilities?

Article II, Section 1, Clause 1, vests the entirety of the "executive Power" in a single person, the President of the United States. By contrast, under Article I Congress enjoys only those legislative powers "herein granted." Scholars generally agree that this vesting of executive power confers upon the President broad authority to engage in foreign relations, including war, except in those areas in which the Constitution places authority in Congress. The debate, then, is over the extent of Congress's constitutional authority to check the President in matters of war.

Article II, Section 2, expressly designates the President as "Commander in Chief of the Army and Navy of the United States, and of the Militia of the several States, when called into the actual Service of the United States." Presidential power advocates argue that this provision confers substantive constitutional power upon the executive branch to engage military forces in hostilities. The executives throughout British history as well as in the colonial governments and several of the states prior to the Constitution generally enjoyed such power. In contrast, the Articles of Confederation did not provide for a separate executive branch and thus gave "the sole and exclusive right and power of determining on peace and war" to Congress.

The presumption of presidential initiative in war established by these two provisions of Article II appears to be bolstered by other constitutional provisions. Article I, Section 10, Clause 3, expressly prohibits states from "engag[ing] in War, unless actually invaded, or in such imminent Danger as will not admit of delay" unless they have obtained the "Consent of Congress." By contrast, no such limitation on engagement in war by the President can be found in Article II. Although Article II expressly authorizes the President to engage in other foreign relations powers (such as the making of treaties and the appointment of ambassadors) only with the consent of Congress, it imposes no such check with respect to the use of military force.

The lack of an express consent requirement for executive initiation of hostilities is particularly meaningful in light of preconstitutional American practice. America's earliest years were haunted by fear of executive tyranny, following the recent experience of living under British rule, and that fear was reflected in several of the legal charters preceding the United

States Constitution. Under the Articles of Confederation, the United States could not "engage in any war" absent the consent of nine states. The constitution of South Carolina expressly provided that the state's executive could neither "commence war" nor "conclude peace" without legislative approval. Other states limited executive war power differently through a variety of structural limitations, such as frequent election, term limits, and selection of the executive by the legislature. In one extreme example, Pennsylvania replaced its single governor with a twelve-person executive council. Problems arising out of weak executive authority soon brought about a reversal in the trend, however. New York established a strong executive, vested with the authority of commander in chief and free of term limits or consent requirements, and Massachusetts and New Hampshire soon followed suit. The text of the Constitution suggests a continuation of, rather than a departure from, this newer trend of enhancing executive authority.

Any power to initiate hostilities would be useless, of course, without the resources necessary to engage in hostilities. Under our Constitution, the power to provide those resources is unequivocally vested with Congress. Under Article I, it is Congress, not the President, that has the power to "lay and collect Taxes" and to "borrow Money," to make "Appropriations" and "provide for the common Defence," to "raise and support Armies" and "provide and maintain a Navy," and to "call[] forth the Militia." Thus the President may be Commander in Chief, but he has nothing to command except what Congress may provide. As a result of Congress's authority over the purse, the President is unable as a practical (if not constitutional) matter to engage in hostilities without Congress.

Based on these provisions of the Constitution, some originalist scholars have concluded that Congress's war power is limited to its control over funding and its power to impeach executive officers. They contend that the President is constitutionally empowered to engage in hostilities with whatever resources Congress has made available to the executive.

Advocates of stronger congressional war power, by contrast, contend that Congress not only has the power to deprive the executive of military resources, but also to control the President's authority to initiate hostilities. They typically locate the textual hook for their argument in Article I, Section 8, which vests the powers to "declare War" and to "grant Letters of Marque and Reprisal" in Congress, not the President. Congressionalists argue that these two powers exhaust the entire range of possible hostilities and that their vesting in Congress must mean that the President cannot initiate hostilities without prior congressional authorization.

Presidentialists contend that the power to "declare War" is only a power to alter international legal relationships. In their view, placing the power to *declare* war in Congress does not affect the President's domestic constitutional authority to engage in hostilities. Notably, Article I provides that states may not, "without the Consent of Congress, . . . *engage* in War," and Article III defines treason as "*levying* War" against the United States—suggesting that the power to "declare War" is a lesser power that does not include the ability to control the actual initiation and conduct of war. Presidentialists also argue that the Marque and Reprisal Clause vests Congress only with the power to authorize private citizens to engage in hostilities for private, commercial gain.

A final textual clue should be noted. Congressionalists generally contend that, although the President may not *initiate* hostilities, the Declaration of War Clause leaves the President with the authority as Commander in Chief to *repel* invasions without prior congressional approval. According to his own notes of the Constitutional Convention, James Madison successfully moved to replace the phrase "make" war with "declare" war, "leaving to the Executive the power to repel sudden attacks." Congressionalists read this power to repel attacks as exhaustive, rather than merely illustrative, of presidential authority. On the other hand, Article I expressly provides that *states* generally may not engage in war without congressional consent "unless actually invaded, or in such imminent Danger as will not admit of delay"; there is no such language, by contrast, governing the *President*. In addition, Article I vests authority with

Congress to "call[] forth the Militia to . . . suppress Insurrections and repel Invasions."

In summary, the argument for executive initiative rests on the background understanding that the vesting of "executive Power" and the "Commander in Chief" designation together constitute a substantive grant of authority to the President to conduct military operations. The argument also rests on the absence of explicit provision for congressional incursion into that power, other than through its express powers over funding and impeachment. Under this view, the contrary position—that congressional consent is required before the initiation of hostilities—suffers from a lack of strong textual support.

Accordingly, congressionalist scholars frequently turn to other authorities. First, they cite statements from various Founders, both before and after the Framing period, in support of broader congressional power. For example, they frequently quote James Wilson, who had urged limits on presidential power during the Constitutional Convention, and who argued during the Pennsylvania ratifying convention that "[t]his system will not hurry us into war; it is calculated against it. It will not be in the power of a single man, or a single body of men, to involve us in such distress; for the important power of declaring war is vested in the legislature at large: this declaration must be made with the concurrence of the House of Representatives: from this circumstance we may draw a certain conclusion that nothing but our national interest can draw us into a war."

Presidentialists respond that Wilson's statement must be placed in context. They claim that Wilson was simply responding to concerns that exercise of the treaty power alone could start a war. They further note that nowhere in Wilson's reference to declarations of war did he ever deny the President's authority to initiate hostilities without a declaration.

Presidentialists also focus attention on the ratification debates in the battleground state of Virginia, where Anti-Federalists launched a feverish campaign against, among other things, excessive executive power to wage war. Notably, the Federalist effort to ease concerns rested largely on congressional control of the purse—*not* the Declaration of War Clause. Presidentialists also cite James Madison's statement that "the sword is in the hands of the British King. The purse in the hands of the Parliament. It is so in America, as far as any analogy can exist."

Congressionalists and presidentialists also disagree about the proper interpretation of numerous post-ratification statements by Founders and later prominent American figures, as well as early American practice under the Constitution. For example, congressionalists cite the limited, defensive-oriented approach taken by President Thomas Jefferson during the Tripolitan War (1801–1805) and by others in the nation's earliest hostilities. Presidentialists respond by noting Alexander Hamilton's sharp criticisms of Jefferson as well as the broader theory of presidential power urged by Jefferson himself when he was Secretary of State. More generally, presidentialists note that, out of only five declarations of war in our nation's history, the first did not take place until the War of 1812. Presidentialists also contend that early Congresses exerted significant control over hostilities not by refusing to exercise its powers under the Declaration of War Clause, but by denying the President a large, peacetime, standing military force through its control of the purse. In their view, early references to presidential subservience to Congress merely reflected Congress's ability to deny funding to presidential initiatives, and little else. Finally, presidentialists generally criticize the usefulness of post-ratification statements as little more than the self-interested assertions of politicians caught in the heat of partisan conflict, and not as good faith endeavors to ascertain original meaning.

The modern debate over the allocation of war powers between Congress and the President was triggered largely by the establishment of a large United States peacetime military force in the wake of World War II.

United States intervention in Korea in 1950 began with congressional support but without a formal declaration of war. When the war stalemated, executive power was challenged. President Harry S. Truman responded by claiming independent constitutional authority to commit troops without congressional authorization. Presidents Lyndon B. Johnson and Richard M. Nixon undertook military operations of breathtaking breadth in Vietnam, armed with only the Gulf of Tonkin Resolution. Congressional criticism of that protracted campaign led not only to funding restrictions, but also to the 1973 enactment of the War Powers Resolution, over President Nixon's veto. The Resolution substantially limits the President's ability to engage U.S. forces in hostilities for more than sixty days, absent a declaration of war or specific congressional authorization, and requires the President to consult with Congress about military deployments.

The War Powers Resolution has proven largely impotent in practice. President James Earl Carter did not consult with Congress before attempting to rescue Iranian hostages. President Ronald Reagan refused formal compliance (instead claiming "consistency") with the terms of the Resolution when he deployed American military forces in Lebanon, Grenada, Libya, and the Persian Gulf. Before Desert Storm, President George H.W. Bush publicly declared that he had constitutional power to initiate war unilaterally. Congress responded by authorizing him to use force. President William Jefferson Clinton followed these precedents in Somalia, Haiti, Bosnia, the Middle East, and Kosovo.

Members of Congress have periodically filed suit to enforce the War Powers Resolution and the congressionalist interpretation of the Declaration of War Clause, but courts have generally avoided ruling on the merits by dismissing such cases on a variety of procedural grounds. In *Campbell v. Clinton* (2000), for example, the D.C. Circuit unanimously dismissed a congressional challenge to President Clinton's airstrikes campaign in the former Yugoslavia, albeit under a panoply of competing theories arising out of the legislative standing, mootness, and political question doctrines. In *O'Connor v. United States* (2003), the court dismissed a challenge to President George W. Bush's intention behind the war in Iraq because it posed a nonjusticiable political question and "there are no judicially discoverable standards that would permit a court to determine whether the intentions of the President in prosecuting a war are proper."

John Yoo and James C. Ho

See Also
Article I, Section 8, Clause 11 (Marque and Reprisal)
Article I, Section 8, Clause 12 (Army Clause)
Article I, Section 8, Clause 13 (Navy Clause)
Article I, Section 8, Clause 15 (Militia Clause)
Article I, Section 8, Clause 16 (Organizing the Militia)
Article II, Section 2, Clause 1 (Commander of Militia)

Suggestions for Further Research
Ellen C. Collier, Ed., Congressional Research Service, Instances of Use of United States Forces Abroad, 1798–1993 (1993)

Louis Fisher, Congressional Abdication on War & Spending (2000)

Louis Henkin, Foreign Affairs and the U.S. Constitution (2nd ed. 1996)

Louis Fisher, Presidential War Power (2d ed. 2004)

Harold Hongju Koh, The National Security Constitution: Sharing Power After the Iran-Contra Affair (1990)

Montgomery Kosma, Our First Real War, 2 Green Bag 2d 169 (1999)

H. Jefferson Powell, The President's Authority over Foreign Affairs: An Essay in Constitutional Interpretation (2002)

Michael D. Ramsey, *Textualism and War Powers*, 69 U. Chi. L. Rev. 1543 (2002)

John C. Yoo, *Clio at War: The Misuse of History in the War Powers Debate*, 70 U. Colo. L. Rev. 1169 (1999)

John C. Yoo, *The Continuation of Politics by Other Means: The Original Understanding of War Powers*, 84 Cal. L. Rev. 167 (1996)

John C. Yoo, *War and Constitutional Texts*, 69 U. Chi. L. Rev. 1639 (2002)

Significant Cases
Campbell v. Clinton, 203 F.3d 19 (D.C. Cir. 2000)
Doe v. Bush, 322 F.3d 109 (1st Cir. 2003)
O'Connor v. United States, 72 Fed. Appx. 768 (10th Cir. 2003)

Commander of Militia

The President shall be Commander in Chief...of the Militia of the several States, when called into the actual Service of the United States....

(ARTICLE II, SECTION 2, CLAUSE 1)

≈

*T*he Framers of the Constitution crafted a complex network of provisions dealing with the militia. They believed that there should be a national army, but that resources and politics dictated that the militia would provide the bulk of the forces needed to defend the country. Although they were sensitive to the fear of a standing army and the political concerns of the states, there was one principle on which they agreed: when the states' militias were needed to defend the country, the President, and not the governors, would be in charge. The phrasing of the President's power changed over the months in Philadelphia, but the exclusivity of the President's power was never questioned. The most significant change came from Roger Sherman, who moved the addition "and of the Militia of the several States, *when called into the actual service of the US.*" This assured that the President could not take the militia away from the states except when properly called forth by Congress under Article I, Section 8, Clause 15.

In 1792, Congress passed the Uniform Militia Act, also known as the "calling forth" act, permitting the President to call out the militia to put down insurrections or rebellions. This power was initially limited to those events that could not be handled by judicial proceedings or by marshals in the exercise of their duties. The act also required a district judge to certify that circumstances were beyond the control of lawful authority and required the President to alert the insurrectionists to end their activities before the militia could be called out. In the meantime, the government launched three major campaigns against the Indians in the Ohio Territory in 1790, 1791, and 1794. In each case, federal forces were supplemented by large numbers of militia volunteers. But it was the Whiskey Rebel-

lion in the summer of 1794 that impelled George Washington to issue the first formal call for the militia to put down the threatened insurrection. Washington took personal command of the force of 12,950 militiamen from Pennsylvania, New Jersey, Virginia, and Maryland. No President since Washington has taken personal control of the militia when called into the active service of the federal government.

In 1795, Congress passed another militia act, aimed at giving the President the power to call out the state forces in the event of insurrection. This law did away with the certification requirements (but retained the requirement of alerting the insurrectionists to disperse) of the 1792 law and granted the President the authority to call forth the militia when the nation was invaded, in imminent danger of invasion, or when faced with "combinations" against the nation. The key provision of that law was "That whenever it may be necessary, in the judgment of the President, to use the military force hereby directed to be called forth...."

During the War of 1812, when President James Madison called up the militias, the New England states, opposed to the war and threatening secession, objected to the President's powers. In response to a request by the governor of Massachusetts, the Supreme Judicial Court of Massachusetts issued an advisory opinion declaring that the governors or commanders in chief of the several states had the exclusive right to determine whether exigent circumstances existed for the militia to be called out. This decision effectively recognized a veto power of the governor over the use of their respective states' militias. It also stood the Constitution's enumerated powers on its head. Article I, Section 8, Clause 15, and Article II, Section 2, Clause 1, of the Constitution specifically granted to the Congress and the President, respectively, the power to call out and command the militia when needed in active service to the United States.

In response to the argument for state control of the militia, Secretary of State James Monroe argued that when the militia is called into the actual service of the United States, all state authority over that militia ends. The militia assumes a position within the regular standing army and is paid by the federal government. Its members become, effectively, United States soldiers. They are subject to the same control as regular army personnel, including command by regular army officers.

In 1827 the U.S. Supreme Court supported the Monroe position. In *Martin v. Mott*, Justice Joseph Story stated, "We are all of opinion, that the authority to decide whether the exigency has arisen, belongs exclusively to the President, and that his decision is conclusive upon all other persons." To cement further the right of the President to determine when to call forth the militia, Justice Roger B. Taney declared in *Luther v. Borden* (1849) that not only is a decision by a President to call out the militia in response to an exigency not subject to state executive approval, but the decision is not subject to judicial review either.

Gubernatorial resistance to the President's call for the militia reemerged during the Civil War. On April 15, 1861, President Abraham Lincoln called for 75,000 militia for three-month terms. The governors of Maryland, Kentucky, Missouri, Tennessee, Arkansas, and North Carolina (the last three states eventually seceded) refused, although volunteer units from all those states ultimately fought for the Union. As the war progressed, the bulk of the army came from requisitions from the states and the draft. The militias, relatively small and often not well trained, were marginal.

After the Civil War, the militia fell into desuetude (except for a brief and unsuccessful attempt to constitute a militia, based mostly on the freedmen in the reconstructed South) until it began a slow transition into the National Guard. The National Defense Act of 1916 made the National Guard a component of the regular army. During World War I, President Woodrow Wilson drafted members of the National Guard into the regular army.

In 1957, resisting a federal court order, Governor Orville Faubus ordered portions of the Arkansas National Guard to prevent the entrance of black students into Little Rock High School. In the first use of the Guard to maintain internal order since the Civil War, President Dwight Eisenhower placed the entire Arkansas National Guard under presidential control and ordered the Guard to obey the President and not the governor. The Arkansas National Guard complied.

In the 1980s, governors again resisted a presidential call for the militia (National Guard). Some of them objected to the deployment of their states' National Guard troops to Central America. Led by Minnesota governor Rudy Perpich, these governors withheld their consent to federally ordered National Guard active duty training, as was their prerogative under then current federal law. In response, Congress enacted the Montgomery Amendment, which prohibited governors from withholding consent for National Guard active duty service outside the United States. Perpich filed suit against the Department of Defense, arguing that the Montgomery Amendment was unconstitutional because it infringed on the militia training authority granted to the states under Article I, Section 8, Clause 16. Perpich also sought to enjoin the use of Minnesota National Guard troops in any training outside the United States that did not have the governor's consent. Ultimately, the Supreme Court upheld the supremacy of presidential control over the operations of the militia when called into actual service of the United States. Like James Monroe and Justice Joseph Story, the Court held that a state governor could not veto the use of a state militia when called upon by the nation in accordance with Congress's constitutional power and the President's constitutional authority.

Recent Presidents have made more use of the National Guard as a reserve, calling units up for long periods of duty abroad, in actions in the two Gulf Wars, Bosnia, and Afghanistan.

David F. Forte

See Also

Article II, Section 2, Clause 1 (Commander in Chief)

Amendment II (To Keep and Bear Arms)

Suggestions for Further Research

Jerry Cooper, The Militia and the National Guard in America Since Colonial Times: A Research Guide (1993)

Lawrence Delbert Cress, Citizens in Arms: The Army and Militia in American Society to the War of 1812 (1982)

John K. Mahon, History of the Militia and the National Guard (1983)

William H. Riker, Soldiers of the States: The Role of the National Guard in American Democracy (1957)

Otis A. Singletary, Negro Militia and Reconstruction (1957)

C. Edward Skeen, Citizen Soldiers in the War of 1812 (1999)

Significant Cases

Martin v. Mott, 25 U.S. (12 Wheat.) 19 (1827)

Luther v. Borden, 48 U.S. (7 How.) 1 (1849)

Dukakis v. Department of Defense, 686 F. Supp. 30 (D. Mass. 1988), *aff'd* 859 F.2d 1066 (1st Cir. 1988)

Perpich v. Department of Defense, 496 U.S. 334 (1990)

Opinion Clause

The President … may require the Opinion, in writing, of the principal Officer in each of the executive Departments, upon any Subject relating to the Duties of their respective Offices ….

(**Article II, Section 2, Clause 1**)

≈

*T*he Opinion Clause arose out of the debates at the Constitutional Convention regarding whether the American President would exercise executive authority singly or in concert with other officials or privy councilors. A brief review of English custom illuminates the choices made by the Framers. Formally, parliamentary "ministers" were ministers to the king. In addition, all British

citizens were "subjects" of the king, and the king could require any nobleman, judge, or Member of Parliament to serve in *his* Privy Council and provide him with personal or official advice. By the end of the eighteenth century, however, the ministerial offices had assumed such practical and administrative power that it diminished the king's responsibility for actions taken by the government. The king was expected to defer increasingly to his ministers' decisions. The state of the English executive at the time of the framing was this: legally, the king could do no wrong; politically, the king was responsible for no administrative wrong.

At various stages during the Convention, the Framers rejected proposals to divide or condition executive power. Their intent from contemporary records is clear: they wanted "[e]nergy in the executive," as Alexander Hamilton put it in *The Federalist* No. 70; and they wanted to maximize presidential responsibility for executive decisions. Some of the Framers, including James Madison, desired a single executive but supported a Council of Revision—composed of the President and judges—to exercise the veto power. Rufus King explained why the proposal was rejected: "If the Unity of the Executive was preferred for the sake of responsibility, the policy of it is as applicable to the revisionary [veto] as to the Executive power." Yet, vesting all executive power in one person was enough of a break with English tradition to cause unease. Several delegates supported a constitutional "Privy Council" or "Council of State," which could not bind the President but would provide him with advice.

One argument advanced against a privy council was that the department head most responsible for the matter put to the council might evade his special share of responsibility for the decision. The Opinion Clause was born of this concern. The original version assumed the President would have a privy council but that he could "require the written opinion of any one or more of the [relevant] members [of the council] … [and] every officer abovementioned shall be responsible for his opinion on the affairs relating to his particular Department." But the Framers rejected even a weak advisory council.

Charles Pinckney concluded that: "The President shd. be authorized to call for advice or not as he might chuse. Give him an able Council and it will thwart him; a weak one and he will shelter himself under their sanction." Later, a committee headed by Gouverneur Morris was tasked with further consideration of the matter. The committee also rejected the idea. Morris explained: "The Presidt. by persuading his Council to concur in his wrong measures, would acquire their protection for them."

Instead, Morris proposed language that formed the basis of the current Opinion Clause, merely authorizing the President "to call for the opinions of the Heads of Departments, in writing." To distinguish this proposal even further from that of a collegial council, the clause was later revised to specify that written opinions could be obtained "upon any Subject relating to the Duties of their respective Offices." Thus modified, the clause does not encourage the President to seek a consensus from all department heads on any matter.

As adopted, the Opinion Clause reinforces the authority and accountability of an executive who is bound by law. The President may demand written reports regarding his principal officers' performance of their duties (a typical management prerogative), but not concerning his personal business. The Framers' rejection of a formal cabinet independent of the President prevents department heads from exercising an independent sphere of influence over policy and denies them a forum in which to enlist others in debates over the President's policies. In addition, the Opinion Clause contains a negative inference reinforced by Article II, Section 3, which allows the President to recommend to Congress such measures "as he shall judge necessary and expedient." The two clauses reflect the Constitution's separation of powers structure by preventing Congress from requiring presidential appointees to report directly to Congress rather than to the President. As Chief Justice John Marshall noted in *Marbury v. Madison* (1803), "To aid [the President] in the performance of these duties, he is authorized to appoint certain officers, who act by his authority and in conformity with his orders." Congress can require reports from the

respective departments, but Congress cannot interfere with prior presidential review of those reports and presidential control over what is transmitted to Congress.

As a result of the debates over the Opinion Clause and a privy council, the Constitution nowhere requires a formal Cabinet. President George Washington found it prudent to organize his principal officers into a Cabinet, and it has been part of the executive branch structure ever since. Nevertheless, no "prime minister" deflects the political accountability of the President. Presidents have used Cabinet meetings of selected principal officers but to widely differing extents and for different purposes. Secretary of State William H. Seward and then Professor Woodrow Wilson advocated use of a parliamentary-style Cabinet government. But President Abraham Lincoln rebuffed Seward, and Woodrow Wilson would have none of it in his administration. Several twentieth-century Presidents made pledges to use their "cabinets" as deliberative bodies, but Eisenhower was one of the few who did so.

Recent Cabinets have grown unwieldy for effective deliberations with up to twenty-five members, including key White House staff in addition to department and agency heads. President Ronald Reagan formed seven subcabinet councils to review many policy issues, and subsequent Presidents have followed that practice. But most recent Presidents have met infrequently with their entire Cabinets. In an age when the President relies heavily on White House staff for immediate advice and assistance, Presidents often use Cabinet meetings to make the Cabinet members feel more a part of the President's inner circle or to increase their loyalty to the administration.

A Cabinet that has no constitutional blessing may actually make it a more valuable tool than one constrained by constitutional design. There is more flexibility in the President's choice of which officers and councilors should be included. Moreover, a Cabinet that meets at the pleasure of the President will naturally be more mindful to serve his interests rather than their own or those of their departments. Thus, the Framers increased the likelihood that the President will obtain useful advice from his principal officers by leaving the advice structure entirely to his discretion.

Todd Gaziano

See also

Article I, Section 7, Clause 3 (Presentment of Resolutions)

Article II, Section 1, Clause 1 (Executive Vesting Clause)

Article II, Section 1, Clause 1 (A Note on Administrative Agencies)

Article II, Section 2, Clause 2 (Appointments Clause)

Article II, Section 3 (Take Care Clause)

Suggestions for Further Research

Akhil R. Amar, *Some Opinions on the Opinion Clause*, 82 Va. L. Rev. 647 (1996)

Steven G. Calabresi & Kevin H. Rhodes, *The Structural Constitution: Unitary Executive, Plural Judiciary*, 105 Harv. L. Rev. 1153 (1992)

James P. Pfiffner, The Modern Presidency (3d ed. 2000)

Significant Cases

Marbury v. Madison, 5 U.S. (1 Cranch) 137 (1803)

United States v. Germaine, 99 U.S. 508 (1879)

Pardon Power

The President ... shall have Power to grant Reprieves and Pardons for Offences against the United States, except in Cases of Impeachment.
(Article II, Section 2, Clause 1)

⁓

The power to pardon is one of the least limited powers granted to the President in the Constitution. The only limits mentioned in the Constitution are that pardons are limited to offenses against the United States (i.e., not civil or state cases), and that they cannot affect an impeachment process. A reprieve is the commutation or lessening of a sentence already imposed; it does not affect the legal guilt of a person. A pardon, however, completely wipes out the legal effects of a conviction. A pardon can be issued from the time an offense is committed, and can even be issued after the full sentence has been served. It cannot, however, be granted before an offense has been committed, which would give the President the power to waive the laws.

The presidential power to pardon was derived from the royal English Prerogative of Kings, which dated from before the Norman invasion. The royal power was absolute, and the king often granted a pardon in exchange for money or military service. Parliament tried unsuccessfully to limit the king's pardon power, and finally it succeeded to some degree in 1701 when it passed the Act of Settlement, which exempted impeachment from the royal pardon power.

During the period of the Articles of Confederation, the state constitutions conferred pardon powers of varying scopes on their governors, but neither the New Jersey Plan nor the Virginia Plan presented at the Constitutional Convention included a pardon power for the chief executive. On May 29, 1787, Charles Pinckney introduced a proposal to give the chief executive the same pardon power as enjoyed by English monarchs, that is, complete power with the exception of impeachment. Some delegates argued that treason should be excluded from the pardon power. George Mason argued that the President's pardon power "may be sometimes exercised to screen from punishment those whom he had secretly instigated to commit the crime and thereby prevent a discovery of his own guilt." James Wilson answered that pardons for treason should be available and successfully argued that the power would be best used by the President. Impeachment was available if the President himself was involved in the treason. A proposal for Senate approval of presidential pardons was also defeated.

The development of the use of the pardon power reflects its several purposes. One purpose is to temper justice with mercy in appropriate cases, and to do justice if new or mitigating evidence comes to bear on a person who may have been wrongfully convicted. Alexander Hamilton reflects this in *The Federalist* No. 74, in which he argues that "humanity and good policy" require that "the benign prerogative of pardoning" was necessary to mitigate the harsh justice of the criminal code. The pardon power would provide for "exceptions in favor of unfortunate guilt."

Chief Justice John Marshall in *United States v. Wilson* (1833) also commented on the benign aspects of the pardon power: "A pardon is an act of grace, proceeding from the power entrusted with the execution of the laws, which exempts the individual, on whom it is bestowed from the punishment the law inflicts for a crime he has committed. It is the private, though official act of the executive magistrate . . . ." Another purpose of the pardon power focuses not on obtaining justice for the person pardoned, but rather on the public-policy purposes of the government. For instance, James Wilson argued during the Convention that "pardon before conviction might be necessary in order to obtain the testimony of accomplices." The public-policy purposes of the pardon were echoed by Justice Oliver Wendell Holmes in *Biddle v. Perovich* (1927): "A pardon in our days is not a private act of grace from an individual happening to possess power. It is a part of the constitutional scheme."

Pardons have also been used for the broader public-policy purpose of ensuring peace and tranquility in the case of uprisings and to bring peace after internal conflicts. Its use might be needed in such cases. As Alexander Hamilton argued in *The Federalist* No. 74, "in seasons of insurrection or rebellion there are often critical moments when a well-timed offer of pardon to the insurgents or rebels may restore the tranquility of the commonwealth; and which, if suffered to pass unimproved, it may never be possible afterwards to recall." Presidents have sought to use the pardon power to overcome or mitigate the effects of major crises that afflicted the polity. President George Washington granted an amnesty to those who participated in the Whiskey Rebellion; Presidents Abraham Lincoln and Andrew Johnson issued amnesties to those involved with the Confederates during the Civil War; and Presidents Gerald R. Ford and James Earl Carter granted amnesties to Vietnam-era draft evaders.

The scope of the pardon power remains quite broad, almost plenary. As Justice Stephen Field wrote in *Ex parte Garland* (1867), "If granted before conviction, it prevents any of the penalties and disabilities consequent upon conviction from attaching [thereto]; if granted after conviction, it removes the penalties and disabilities, and restores him to all his civil rights; it makes him, as it were, a new man, and gives him a new credit and capacity. . . . A pardon reaches both the punishment prescribed for the offence and the guilt of the offender. . . . so that in the eye of the law the offender is as innocent as if he had never committed the offence." A pardon is valid whether accepted or not, because its purposes are primarily public. It is an official act. According to *United States v. Klein* (1871), Congress cannot limit the President's grant of an amnesty or pardon, but it can grant other or further amnesties itself. Though pardons have been litigated, the Court has consistently refused to limit the President's discretion. Chief Justice Warren E. Burger, however, in *Schick v. Reed* (1974), seemed to limit the Court's restraint to pardons under "conditions which do not in themselves offend the Constitution."

The possibility of a President pardoning himself for a crime is not precluded by the explicit language of the Constitution, and, during the summer of 1974, some of President Richard M. Nixon's lawyers argued that it was constitutionally permissible. But a broader reading of the Constitution and the general principles of the traditions of United States law might lead to the conclusion that a self-pardon is constitutionally impermissible. It would seem to violate the principles that a man should not be a judge in his own case; that the rule of law is supreme and the United States is a nation of laws, not men; and that the President is not above the law.

The pardon power has been and will remain a powerful constitutional tool of the President. Its use has the potential to achieve much good for the polity or to increase political conflict. Only the wisdom of the President can ensure its appropriate use.

James Pfiffner

Suggestions for Further Research

David Gray Adler, *The President's Pardon Power*, in Inventing the American Presidency, Thomas E. Cronin, ed. (1989)

Edward S. Corwin, The President: Office and
  Powers (1940)

William Duker, *The President's Power to Pardon: A
  Constitutional History*, 18 Wm. & Mary L. Rev.
  475 (1977)

Brian C. Kalt, *Pardon Me? The Constitutional Case
  Against Presidential Self-Pardons*, 106 Yale L.J.
  779 (1996)

Significant Cases

United States v. Wilson, 32 U.S. (7 Pet.) 150 (1833)

Ex parte Garland, 71 U.S. (4 Wall.) 333 (1867)

United States v. Klein, 80 U.S. (13 Wall.) 128 (1871)

Biddle v. Perovich, 274 U.S. 480 (1927)

Schick v. Reed, 419 U.S. 256 (1974)

Treaty Clause

**The President ... shall have Power,
by and with the Advice and Consent of the Senate, to make Treaties,
provided two thirds of the Senators
present concur....**

(Article II, Section 2, Clause 2)

~

The Treaty Clause has a number of striking
features. It gives the Senate, in James Madison's
terms, a "partial agency" in the President's for-
eign-relations power. The clause requires a
supermajority (two-thirds) of the Senate for
approval of a treaty, but it gives the House of
Representatives, representing the "people," no
role in the process.

Midway through the Constitutional Convention, a working draft had assigned the treaty-
making power to the Senate, but the Framers,
apparently considering the traditional role of a
nation-state's executive in making treaties,
changed direction and gave the power to the
President, but with the proviso of the Senate's
"Advice and Consent." In a formal sense, then,
treaty-making became a mixture of executive
and legislative power. Most people of the time
recognized the actual conduct of diplomacy as
an executive function, but under Article VI

treaties were, like statutes, part of the "supreme
Law of the Land." Thus, as Alexander Hamilton
explained in *The Federalist* No. 75, the two
branches were appropriately combined:

> The qualities elsewhere detailed as indis-
> pensable in the management of foreign
> relations point out the executive as the
> most fit in those transactions; while the
> vast importance of the trust and the oper-
> ation of treaties as laws plead strongly for
> the participation of the whole or a por-
> tion of the legislative body in the office of
> making them.

Another reason for involving both President
and Senate was that the Framers thought American interests might be undermined by treaties
entered into without proper reflection. The
Framers believed that treaties should be strictly
honored, both as a matter of the law of nations
and as a practical matter, because the United
States could not afford to give the great powers
any cause for war. But this meant that the nation
should be doubly cautious in accepting treaty
obligations. As James Wilson said, "Neither the
President nor the Senate, solely, can complete a
treaty; they are checks upon each other, and are
so balanced as to produce security to the people."

The fear of disadvantageous treaties also
underlay the Framers' insistence on approval by
a two-thirds majority of the Senate. In particular, the Framers worried that one region or
interest within the nation, constituting a bare
majority, would make a treaty advantageous to
it but prejudicial to other parts of the country
and to the national interest. An episode just a
year before the start of the Convention had
highlighted the problem. The United States
desired a trade treaty with Spain, and sought
free access to the Mississippi River through
Spanish-controlled New Orleans. Spain offered
favorable trade terms, but only if the United
States would give up its demands on the Mississippi. The Northern states, which would have
benefited most from the trade treaty and cared
little about New Orleans, had a majority, but
not a supermajority, in the Continental Congress. Under the Articles of Confederation,

treaties required assent of a supermajority (nine out of thirteen) of the states, and the South was able to block the treaty. It was undoubtedly that experience that impelled the Framers to carry over the supermajority principle from the Articles of Confederation.

At the Convention, several prominent Framers argued unsuccessfully to have the House of Representatives included. But most delegates thought that the House had substantial disadvantages when it came to treaty-making. For example, as a large body, the House would have difficulty keeping secrets or acting quickly. The small states, wary of being disadvantaged, also preferred to keep the treaty-making power in the Senate, where they had proportionally greater power.

The ultimate purpose, then, of the Treaty Clause was to ensure that treaties would not be adopted unless most of the country stood to gain. True, treaties would be more difficult to adopt than statutes, but the Framers realized that an unwise statute could simply be repealed, but an unwise treaty remained a binding international commitment, which would not be so easy to unwind.

Other questions, however, remained. First, are the provisions of the clause exclusive—that is, does it provide the only way that the United States may enter into international obligations?

While the clause does not say, in so many words, that it is exclusive, its very purpose—not to have any treaty disadvantage one part of the nation—suggests that no other route was possible, whether it be the President acting alone, or the popularly elected House having a role. On the other hand, while the Treaty Clause was, in the original understanding, the exclusive way to make treaties, the Framers also apparently recognized a class of less-important international agreements, not rising to the level of "treaties," which could be approved in some other way. Article I, Section 10, in describing restrictions upon the states, speaks of "Treat[ies]" and "Agreement[s] ... with a foreign Power" as two distinct categories. Some scholars believe this shows that not all international agreements are treaties, and that these other agreements would not need to go through the procedures of the

Treaty Clause. Instead, the President, in the exercise of his executive power, could conclude such agreements on his own. Still, this exception for lesser agreements would have to be limited to "agreements" of minor importance, or else it would provide too great an avenue for evasion of the protections the Framers placed in the Treaty Clause.

A second question is how the President and Senate should interact in their joint exercise of the treaty power. Many Framers apparently thought that the President would oversee the actual conduct of diplomacy, but that the Senate would be involved from the outset as a sort of executive council advising the President. This was likely a reason that the Framers thought the smaller Senate was more suited than the House to play a key role in treaty-making. In the first effort at treaty-making under the Constitution, President George Washington attempted to operate in just this fashion. He went to the Senate in person to discuss a proposed treaty before he began negotiations. What is less clear, however, is whether the Constitution actually requires this process, or whether it is only what the Framers assumed would happen. The Senate, of course, is constitutionally authorized to offer "advice" to the President at any stage of the treaty-making process, but the President is not directed (in so many words) as to when advice must be solicited. As we shall see, this uncertainty has led, in modern practice, to a very different procedure than some Framers envisioned. It seems clear, however, that the Framers expected that the Senate's "advice and consent" would be a close review and not a mere formality, as they thought of it as an important check upon presidential power.

A third difficult question is whether the Treaty Clause implies a Senate power or role in treaty termination. Scholarly opinion is divided, and few Framers appear to have discussed the question directly. One view sees the power to make a treaty as distinct from the power of termination, with the latter being more akin to a power of implementation. Since the Constitution does not directly address the termination power, this view would give it to the President as part of the President's executive powers to conduct foreign affairs and to execute the laws.

When the termination question first arose in 1793, Washington and his Cabinet, which included Hamilton and Thomas Jefferson, embraced this view. All of them thought Washington could, on his own authority, terminate the treaty with France if necessary to keep the United States neutral.

A second view holds that, as a matter of the general eighteenth-century understanding of the legal process, the power to take an action (such as passing a statute or making a treaty) implies the power to undo the action. This view would require the consent of the President and a supermajority of the Senate to undo a treaty. There is, however, not much historical evidence that many Framers actually held this view of treaty termination, and it is inconsistent with the common interpretation of the Appointments Clause (under which Senate approval is required to appoint but not to remove executive officers).

The third view is that the Congress as a whole has the power to terminate treaties, based on an analogy between treaties and federal laws. When the United States first terminated a treaty in 1798 under John Adams, this procedure was adopted, but there was little discussion of the constitutional ramifications.

Finally, there is a question of the limits of the treaty power. A treaty presumably cannot alter the constitutional structure of government, and the Supreme Court has said that executive agreements—and so apparently treaties—are subject to the limits of the Bill of Rights just as ordinary laws are. *Reid v. Covert* (1957). In *Geofroy v. Riggs* (1890), the Supreme Court also declared that the treaty power extends only to topics that are "properly the subject of negotiation with a foreign country." However, at least in the modern world, one would think that few topics are so local that they could not, under some circumstances, be reached as part of the foreign-affairs interests of the nation. Some have argued that treaties are limited by the federalism interests of the states. The Supreme Court rejected a version of that argument in *State of Missouri v. Holland* (1920), holding that the subject matter of treaties is not limited to the enumerated powers of Congress. The revival

of interest in federalism limits on Congress in such areas as state sovereign immunity, *see Seminole Tribe of Florida v. Florida* (1996), and the Tenth Amendment, *see Printz v. United States* (1997), raises the question whether these limits also apply to the treaty power, but the Court has not yet taken up these matters.

Turning to modern practice, the Framers' vision of treaty-making has in some ways prevailed and in some ways been altered. First, it is not true—and has not been true since George Washington's administration—that the Senate serves as an executive council to advise the President in all stages of treaty-making. Rather, the usual modern course is that the President negotiates and signs treaties independently and then presents the proposed treaty to the Senate for its approval or disapproval. Washington himself found personal consultation with the Senate to be so awkward and unproductive that he abandoned it, and subsequent Presidents have followed his example.

Moreover, the Senate frequently approves treaties with conditions and has done so since the Washington administration. If the President makes clear to foreign nations that his signature on a treaty is only a preliminary commitment subject to serious Senate scrutiny, and if the Senate takes seriously its constitutional role of reviewing treaties (rather than merely deferring to the President), the check that the Framers sought to create remains in place. By going beyond a simple "up-or-down" vote, the Senate retains some of its power of "advice": the Senate not only disapproves the treaty proposed by the President but suggests how the President might craft a better treaty. As a practical matter, there is often much consultation between the executive and members of the Senate before treaties are crafted and signed. Thus modern practice captures the essence of the Framers' vision that the Senate would have some form of a participatory role in treaty-making.

A more substantial departure from the Framers' vision may arise from the practice of "executive agreements." According to the Restatement of Foreign Relations Law of the United States, the President may validly conclude executive agreements that (1) cover matters that are solely within his executive power, or (2) are made pursuant to a treaty, or (3) are made pursuant to a legitimate act of Congress. Examples of important executive agreements include the Potsdam and Yalta agreements of World War II, the General Agreement on Tariffs and Trade, which regulated international trade for decades, and the numerous status-of-forces agreements the United States has concluded with foreign governments.

Where the President acts pursuant to a prior treaty, there seems little tension with the Framers' vision, as Senate approval has, in effect, been secured in advance. Somewhat more troublesome is the modern practice of so-called congressional–executive agreements, by which some international agreements have been made by the President and approved (either in advance or after the fact) by a simple majority of both houses of Congress, rather than two-thirds of the Senate. Many of these agreements deal particularly with trade-related matters, which Congress has clear constitutional authority to regulate. Congressional–executive agreements, at least with respect to trade matters, are now well established, and recent court challenges have been unsuccessful. *Made in the USA Foundation v. United States* (2001). On the other hand, arguments for "complete interchangeability"—that is, claims that anything that can be done by treaty can be done by congressional–executive agreement—seem counter to the Framers' intent. The Framers carefully considered the supermajority rule for treaties and adopted it in response to specific threats to the Union; finding a complete alternative to the Treaty Clause would in effect eliminate the supermajority rule and make important international agreements easier to adopt than the Framers wished.

The third type of executive agreement is one adopted by the President without explicit approval of either the Senate or the Congress as a whole. The Supreme Court and modern practice embrace the idea that the President may under some circumstances make these so-called sole executive agreements. *United States v. Belmont* (1937); *United States v. Pink* (1942). But the scope of this independent presidential power remains a serious question. The *Pink*

and *Belmont* cases involved agreements relating to the recognition of a foreign government, a power closely tied to the President's textual power to receive ambassadors (Article II, Section 3). The courts have consistently permitted the President to settle foreign claims by sole executive agreement, but at the same time have emphasized that the Congress has acquiesced in the practice. *Dames & Moore v. Regan* (1981); *American Insurance Ass'n v. Garamendi* (2003). Beyond this, the modern limits of the President's ability to act independently in making international agreements have not been explored. With respect to treaty termination, modern practice allows the President to terminate treaties on his own. In recent times, President James Earl Carter terminated the U.S.–Taiwan Mutual Defense Treaty in 1977, and President George W. Bush terminated the ABM Treaty with Russia in 2001. The Senate objected sharply to President Carter's actions, but the Supreme Court rebuffed the Senate in *Goldwater v. Carter* (1979). President Bush's action was criticized in some academic quarters but received general acquiescence. In light of the consensus early in Washington's administration, it is probably fair to say that presidential termination does not obviously depart from the original understanding, inasmuch as the Framers were much more concerned about checks upon entering into treaties than they were about checks upon terminating them.

Michael D. Ramsey

See Also

Suggestions for Further Research
David Gray Adler, The Constitution and the Termination of Treaties (1986)

Arthur Bestor, *Respective Roles of the Senate and President in the Making and Abrogation of Treaties—The Original Intent of the Framers of the Constitution Historically Examined*, 55 Wash. L. Rev. 1 (1979)

Curtis Bradley, *The Treaty Power and American Federalism*, 97 Mich. L. Rev. 390 (1998)

Curtis Bradley & Jack Goldsmith, *Treaties, Human Rights, and Conditional Consent*, 149 U. Pa. L. Rev. 399 (2000)

David F. Forte, *The Foreign Affairs Power: The Dames & Moore Case*, 31 Cleveland St. L. Rev. 43 (1982)

David Golove, *Treaty-Making and the Nation: The Historical Foundations of the Nationalist Conception of the Treaty Power*, 98 Mich. L. Rev. 1075 (2000)

John O. McGinnis & Michael B. Rappaport, *Our Supermajority Constitution*, 80 Tex. L. Rev. 703 (2002)

Saikrishna B. Prakash & Michael D. Ramsey, *The Executive Power over Foreign Affairs*, 111 Yale L.J. 231 (2001)

Jack N. Rakove, *Solving a Constitutional Puzzle: The Treatymaking Clause as a Case Study,* Persp. Am. Hist. (N.S.), 233–281 (1984)

Michael D. Ramsey, *Executive Agreements and the (Non)Treaty Power,* 77 N.C. L. Rev. 133 (1998)

Peter J. Spiro, *Treaties, Executive Agreements, and Constitutional Method,* 79 Tex. L. Rev. 961 (2001)

Edward T. Swaine, *Does Federalism Constrain the Treaty Power?,* 103 Colum. L. Rev. 403 (2003)

Significant Cases

Geofroy v. Riggs, 133 U.S. 258 (1890)

State of Missouri v. Holland, 252 U.S. 416 (1920)

United States v. Belmont, 301 U.S. 324 (1937)

United States v. Pink, 315 U.S. 203 (1942)

Reid v. Covert, 354 U.S. 1 (1957)

Goldwater v. Carter, 444 U.S. 996 (1979)

Dames & Moore v. Regan, 453 U.S. 654 (1981)

Seminole Tribe of Florida v. Florida, 517 U.S. 44 (1996)

Printz v. United States, 521 U.S. 898 (1997)

Made in the USA Foundation v. United States, 242 F.3d 1300 (11th Cir. 2001)

American Insurance Ass'n v. Garamendi, 123 S. Ct. 2374 (2003)

Appointments Clause

The President...shall nominate, and by and with the Advice and Consent of the Senate, shall appoint Ambassadors, other pub-

lic Ministers and Consuls, Judges of the supreme Court, and all other Officers of the United States, whose Appointments are not herein otherwise provided for, and which shall be established by Law....
(**ARTICLE II, SECTION 2, CLAUSE 2**)

~

*T*his clause contemplates three sequential acts for the appointment of principal officers—the nomination of the President, the advice and consent of the Senate, and the Appointment of the Official by the President. This clause applies to principal officers in contradistinction to inferior officers, whose appointment is addressed in the next portion of the clause. Although the Senate must confirm principal officers, including Ambassadors and Supreme Court Justices, Congress may choose to require that any officers whose office is "established by Law" be confirmed by the Senate, whether they be inferior or not.

The important questions for principal officers and their confirmation are, first, whether the President has plenary power of nomination or whether the Constitution limits this power by requiring the President to seek prenomination advice; second, whether the President must nominate only those who meet qualifications set by Congress; and, third, whether the Senate has plenary power to reject nominees or whether that power is circumscribed by some standard.

Both the debates among the Framers and subsequent practice confirm that the President has plenary power to nominate. He is not obliged to take advice from the Senate on the identity of those he will nominate, nor does the Congress have authority to set qualifications for principal officers. The Senate possesses the plenary authority to reject or confirm the nominee, although its weaker structural position means that it is likely to confirm most nominees, absent compelling reasons to reject them.

The very grammar of the clause is telling: the act of nomination is separated from the act of appointment by a comma and a conjunction.

Only the latter act is qualified by the phrase "advice and consent." Furthermore, it is not at all anomalous to use the word *advice* with respect to the action of the Senate in confirming an appointment. The Senate's consent is advisory because confirmation does not bind the President to commission and empower the confirmed nominee. Instead, after receiving the Senate's advice and consent, the President may deliberate again before appointing the nominee.

The purpose of dividing the act of nomination from that of appointment also refutes the permissibility of any statutory restriction on the individuals the President may nominate. The principal concern of the Framers regarding the Appointments Clause, as in many of the other separation of powers provisions of the Constitution, was to ensure accountability while avoiding tyranny. Hence, following the suggestion of Nathaniel Gorham of New Hampshire and the example of the Massachusetts Constitution drafted by John Adams, the Framers gave the power of nomination to the President so that the initiative of choice would be a single individual's responsibility but provided the check of advice and consent to forestall the possibility of abuse of this power. Gouverneur Morris described the advantages of this multistage process: "As the President was to nominate, there would be responsibility, and as the Senate was to concur, there would be security."

The Federalist similarly understands the power of nomination to be an exclusively presidential prerogative. In fact, Alexander Hamilton answered critics who would have preferred the whole power of appointment to be lodged in the President by asserting that the assignment of the power of nomination to the President alone assures sufficient accountability:

[I]t is easy to show that every advantage to be expected from such an arrangement would, in substance, be derived from the power of nomination which is proposed to be conferred upon him; while several disadvantages which might attend the absolute power of appointment in the hands of that officer would be avoided. In

the act of nomination, his judgment alone would be exercised; and as it would be his sole duty to point out the man who, with the approbation of the Senate, should fill an office, his responsibility would be as complete as if he were to make the final appointment. *The Federalist* No. 76.

Chief Justice John Marshall in *Marbury v. Madison*, Justice Joseph Story in his *Commentaries on the Constitution of the United States*, and the modern Supreme Court in *Edmond v. United States* (1997) all confirm that understanding.

Congress establishes offices, and the President, at least in regard to principal officers, nominates office holders. Under the Necessary and Proper Clause (Article I, Section 8, Clause 8), Congress has often established qualifications for those who can serve in the offices it has created, thereby limiting the range of those the President can nominate. Andrew Jackson protested that such acts were an unconstitutional infringement of his appointing power, but Congress has continued the practice to this day. The Supreme Court has held that Congress may not provide itself with the power to make appointments, *Buckley v. Valeo* (1976), but it is unclear how far Congress may go in setting qualifications for principal officers without contravening the Framers' interest in assuring the President's accountability for the initial choice. President James Monroe declared that Congress had no right to intrude upon the President's appointing power. In *Myers v. United States* (1926), Chief Justice Taft declared that the qualifications set by Congress may not "so limit selection and so trench upon executive choice as to be in effect legislative designation." In *Public Citizen v. U.S. Department of Justice* (1989), Justice Anthony Kennedy, concurring, opined that the President's appointing power was exclusive, and that only the Incompatibility Clause (Article I, Section 6, Clause 2) limits the range of his choice. The Court, however, has yet to make a definitive statement on the issue.

Closely related to the Framers' interest in assuring accountability was their interest in avoiding an appointment that would be the result of secret deals. In defending the clause's structure of presidential nomination and public confirmation, Hamilton contrasted it with the appointments process by a multimember council in his own state of New York. Such a council acting in secret would be "a conclave in which cabal and intrigue will have their full scope.... [T]he desire of mutual gratification will beget a scandalous bartering of votes and bargaining for places." Delegates to the Constitutional Convention had expressed similar concerns. If the Senate had a formal prenomination advisory role, the Senate leaders and the President might well be tempted to make a deal that would serve their parochial interests and then be insulated from all but pro forma scrutiny. Other contemporaneous commentary on the Appointments Clause repudiates any special constitutional prenomination role for the Senate. James Iredell, a leading proponent of ratification in North Carolina and subsequently a Supreme Court Justice, observed at his state's ratifying convention: "As to offices, the Senate has no other influence but a restraint on improper appointments. The President proposes such a man for such an office. The Senate has to consider upon it. If they think him improper, the President must nominate another, whose appointment ultimately again depends upon the Senate."

The practice of the first President and Senate supported the construction of the Appointments Clause that reserves the act of nomination exclusively to the President. In requesting confirmation of his first nominee, President Washington sent the Senate this message: "I nominate William Short, Esquire, and request your advice on the propriety of appointing him." The Senate then notified the President of Short's confirmation, which showed that they too regarded "advice" as a postnomination rather than a prenomination function: "Resolved, that the President of the United States be informed, that the Senate advise and consent to his appointment of William Short Esquire...." The Senate has continued to use this formulation to the present day. Washington wrote in his diary that Thomas Jefferson and John Jay agreed with him that the Senate's pow-

ers "extend no farther than to an approbation or disapprobation of the person nominated by the President, all the rest being Executive and vested in the President by the Constitution." Washington's construction of the Appointments Clause has been embraced by his successors. Some Presidents have consulted with key Senators and a few with the Senate leadership, but they have done so out of comity or political prudence and never with the understanding that they were constitutionally obliged to do so. A law setting qualifications would not only invade the power of the President, it would also undermine the authority of the Senate as the sole authority to decide whether a principal officer should be confirmed.

The other principal controversy arising from the Appointments Clause has concerned the authority of the Senate to reject nominees. The Senate has independent authority in that it may constitutionally refuse to confirm a nominee for any reason. While ideology and jurisprudential "point of view" were not among the kinds of concerns listed by the Framers as justifying the requirement of advice and consent, nothing in the text of the clause appears to limit the kind of considerations the Senate can take up. It is thus reasonable to infer that the Framers located the process of advice and consent in the Senate as a check to prevent the President from appointing people who have unsound principles as well as blemished characters. As the President has complete discretion in the use of his veto power, the Senate has complete and final discretion in whether to accept or approve a nomination.

Given that the Senate was not to exercise choice itself, it appeared to Alexander Hamilton that a nominee should be rejected only for "special and strong reasons." The President's power of repeated nomination provides a check on the Senate's ability to reject a nominee on something less than an articulable weighty reason. In fact, Hamilton argued that if the Senate fails to make that case and rejects the nominee for a pretextual reason, the President would generally be in a position to find a second candidate without these putative defects who generally shares the President's point of view. It is rare, however, for a President to renominate a person to a position once the Senate has declined to accept the nomination.

The President does possess an advantage in the unitary nature of the executive office as compared to the diffuse and variegated nature of the Senate—even when it is controlled by the opposition party. The President is a single individual, whereas the Senate is a body composed of many individuals with a wide range of views, including members with views like that of the President. When the President has a substantial basis of party support in the Senate and thus a nucleus of probable supporters, he has leverage for confirmation. Thus, the image of a divided government as a government in any sense equally divided when it comes to an analysis of the Appointments Clause and the confirmation process is a fundamentally false image, as George Mason recognized: "Notwithstanding the form of the proposition by which the appointment seemed to be divided between the Executive & Senate, the appointment was substantially vested in the former alone." Moreover, the President's advantage in the process is a considered feature of the Framers' design: they knew how to create a process by which the power of the executive and the Senate would be rendered more equal. Unlike the approval of treaties, it does not take a supermajority to approve a presidential nominee.

Because the President has the initiative of choice in the appointments to the executive branch and the judiciary, the views of his prospective appointees are more likely to become a presidential campaign issue than in senatorial campaigns. Since he possesses the greatest discretion, the political process fastens upon him the greatest accountability. However, when a substantial number of Senators assert that there are strong and compelling political reasons to reject a nominee (as opposed to rejecting one because of a flawed character), the Constitution's structure ensures a confirmation battle. As such, the Constitution contains mechanisms designed to contain conflict within the republican process in order to protect against the degeneration of the Republic's original ideals and thus ensure the Republic's stability. The Appointments Clause is a prime example of such a mechanism. It structures the confirmation process so that when two of the Republic's national governing branches are in fundamental disagreement, there will be a struggle to persuade the people of the correctness of their respective positions. In the case of a struggle over constitutional interpretation as in a Supreme Court nomination, the public will be forced to consider the first principles of the Republic—in this case, the role of the judiciary and the proper method of interpreting its governing document. Citizens will thus vicariously enjoy some measure of the experience of the Framing of the Constitution, thus contributing to the Republic's self-regeneration.

John McGinnis

See Also

Article I, Section 6, Clause 2 (Incompatibility Clause)

Article II, Section 2, Clause 2 (Inferior Officers)

Article II, Section 2, Clause 3 (Recess Appointments Clause)

Article II, Section 3 (Commissions)

Suggestions for Further Research

Michael Gerhardt, The Federal Appointments Process: A Constitutional and Historical Analysis (2000)

John O. McGinnis, *The President, the Senate, the Constitution and the Confirmation Process: A Reply to Professors Strauss and Sunstein*, 71 Tex. L. Rev. 633 (1993)

David A. Strauss & Cass R. Sunstein, *The Senate, the Constitution and the Confirmation Process*, 101 Yale L.J. 1491 (1993)

Significant Cases

Marbury v. Madison, 5 U.S. (1 Cranch) 137 (1803)

Myers v. United States, 272 U.S. 52 (1926)

Buckley v. Valeo, 424 U.S. 1 (1976)

Morrison v. Olson, 487 U.S. 654 (1988)

Public Citizen v. U.S. Department of Justice, 491 U.S. 440 (1989)

Weiss v. United States, 510 U.S. 163 (1994)

Edmond v. United States, 520 U.S. 651 (1997)

Inferior Officers

...the Congress may by Law vest the Appointment of such inferior Officers, as they think proper, in the President alone, in the Courts of Law, or in the Heads of Departments.

(ARTICLE II, SECTION 2, CLAUSE 2)

∾

*T*he appointment power has become one of the chief powers of the President. The "by Law" language concerning inferior officers—sometimes known as the Excepting Clause—authorizes the President in certain cases to exercise the appointment power alone, or through the heads of departments who are themselves his appointees. That mechanism greatly expands the scope of the appointment power beyond the restrictions of Senate consent.

The Appointments Clause (Article II, Section 2, Clause 2) divides constitutional officers into two classes: principal officers, who must be appointed through the advice and consent mechanism; and inferior officers, who may be appointed through advice and consent of the Senate, but whose appointment Congress may place instead in any of the "three repositories of the appointment power" in the Excepting Clause. *See Freytag v. Commissioner of Internal Revenue* (1991); *United States v. Germaine* (1879). These two methods are the only means of appointing government officers under the Constitution. Most officers are considered inferior officers.

Significantly, Congress itself may not exercise the appointment power; its functions are limited to the Senate's role in advice and consent, and to deciding whether to vest a direct appointment power over a given office in the President, a Head of Department, or the Courts of Law. The Framers were particularly concerned that Congress might seek to exercise the appointment power and fill offices with their supporters, to the derogation of the President's control over the executive branch. The Appointments Clause thus functions as a restraint on Congress and as an important structural element in the separation of powers. Attempts by Congress to circumvent the Appointments Clause, either by making appointments directly, or through devices such as "unilaterally appointing an incumbent to a new and distinct office" under the guise of legislating new duties for an existing office, have been rebuffed by the courts. *Buckley v. Valeo* (1976); *Weiss v. United States* (1994).

The final "by Law" language emerged at the end of the Constitutional Convention, as a late addendum to the compromise over the device of presidential nomination and Senate advice and consent for principal officers. The language occasioned little debate. An earlier version of the language would have given the President a broader power to "appoint officers in all cases not otherwise provided for by this Constitution," but some delegates worried that this language would permit the President to create offices as well as to fill them, a classic case of institutional corruption. The requirement that the President can appoint inferior officers only when Congress has "by Law vest[ed]" that power in the President apparently sought to preclude that possibility.

Although separation of powers values lay behind the language of the Appointments Clause, early judicial interpretations struck a more practical note. Chief Justice John Marshall, sitting as a circuit justice, opined that the "by Law" language was the Framers' means to ensure "that they had provided for all cases of offices." *United States v. Maurice* (1823). The Supreme Court in *United States v. Germaine* (1879) gave its explanation of the Framers' intent behind the "by Law" language as anticipating that "when offices became numerous, and sudden removals necessary," the advice and consent process might prove too "inconvenient."

Two chief questions recur under the "by Law" language: (1) who are "inferior Officers," not subject to the requirement of advice and consent; and (2) what constitutes a "Department," when Congress seeks to place the appointment power away from the President?

As an initial matter, most government employees are not officers and thus are not subject to the Appointments Clause. In *Buckley v. Valeo*, the Supreme Court held that only those appointees "exercising significant authority pursuant to the laws of the United States" are "Officers of the United States," and consequently it is only those who exercise such "significant authority" who must be appointed by a mechanism set forth in the Appointments Clause.

The Framers did not define the line between principal officers and inferior officers, and the Court has been content to approach the analysis on a case-by-case basis rather than through a definitive test. *See Morrison v. Olson* (1988). In *Morrison,* the Court listed certain factors as hallmarks of "inferior Officer" status, such as removability by a higher executive branch official other than the President, and limitations on the officer's duties, jurisdiction, and tenure. In *Edmond v. United States* (1997), the Court, while continuing to deny that it had recognized any definitive test, stated that "'inferior Officers' are officers whose work is directed and supervised at some level by others who were appointed by Presidential nomination with the advice and consent of the Senate." Among those officers recognized as "inferior" are district court clerks, federal supervisors of elections, the Watergate Special Prosecutor, and an Independent Counsel appointed under the Ethics in Government Act of 1978.

The phrase "Heads of Departments" also has not been precisely defined by the Court. On the one hand, judicial interpretations of the phrase refer to the heads of departments that are within the executive branch, "or at least have some connection with that branch." *Buckley v. Valeo.* Under this view, the heads of all agencies and departments exercising executive power under the President would seem to qualify as "Heads of Departments." *See also Printz v. United States* (1997). Similarly, in *Freytag v. Commissioner of Internal Revenue* (1991), the Court interpreted "Heads of Departments" to refer "to executive divisions like the Cabinet-level departments." The use of the phrase "*like* the Cabinet-level departments" could mean that, in addition to the Cabinet departments, other entities within the executive branch that are sufficiently analogous to the Cabinet departments may qualify as "Departments" for purposes of the Appointments Clause.

On the other hand, the *Freytag* Court itself seemed unclear what it meant by the phrase "like the Cabinet-level departments," and certainly stepped back from any bright-line test. The *Freytag* Court sought to harmonize its analysis with the interpretation given the different term "executive Departments" in the Opinion Clause (which has been interpreted to refer only to Cabinet departments) and with earlier cases that suggested that only the Cabinet Secretaries qualified as "Heads of Departments." Ultimately, the *Freytag* Court seems to have reserved the question whether the heads of non-Cabinet executive-branch agencies could be deemed to be "Heads of Departments" for purposes of the Appointments Clause. Perhaps the phrase "like the Cabinet-level departments" was included in *Freytag* as an indication that the Court would not necessarily be inflexible about requiring Cabinet status in future cases. If that is so, then "Heads of Departments" would appear to include (as Justice Antonin Scalia reasons in his concurrence in *Freytag*) the heads of the Cabinet Departments and also the heads of "all independent executive establishments."

Douglas Cox

See Also

Article I, Section 6, Clause 2 (Sinecure Clause)

Article II, Section 1, Clause 1 (Executive Vesting Clause)

Article II, Section 2, Clause 1 (Opinion Clause)

Article II, Section 2, Clause 3 (Recess Appointments Clause)

Suggestions for Further Research

Theodore Y. Blumoff, *Separation of Powers and the Origins of the Appointments Clause*, 37 Syracuse L. Rev. 1037 (1987)

Michael J. Gerhardt, *Toward a Comprehensive Understanding of the Federal Appointments Process*, 21 Harv. J.L. & Pub. Pol'y 479 (1998)

Edward Susolik, *Separation of Powers and Liberty: The Appointments Clause*, Morrison v. Olson, *and the Rule of Law*, 63 S. Cal. L. Rev. 1515 (1990)

Significant Cases

United States v. Maurice, 26 F. Cas. 1211 (C.C.D. Va. 1823)

United States v. Germaine, 99 U.S. 508 (1879)

Buckley v. Valeo, 424 U.S. 1 (1976)

Morrison v. Olson, 487 U.S. 654 (1988)

Freytag v. Commissioner of Internal Revenue, 501 U.S. 868 (1991)

Weiss v. United States, 510 U.S. 163 (1994)

Edmond v. United States, 520 U.S. 651 (1997)

Printz v. United States, 521 U.S. 898 (1997)

Recess Appointments Clause

The President shall have Power to fill up all Vacancies that may happen during the Recess of the Senate, by granting Commissions which shall expire at the End of their next Session.

(Article II, Section 2, Clause 3)

∽

*T*he Framers adopted the Recess Appointments Clause, without debate, to prevent governmental paralysis. Early sessions of the Senate lasted only three to six months, with Senators dispersing throughout the country during the six-to-nine-month recesses. During these periods, they were unable to provide their advice and consent to executive nominations for positions that fell open when officeholders died or resigned. The clause thus served as a "supplement" to the vigorously debated appointment power, which was necessary so that the Senate was not required "to be continually in session for the appointment of officers." *The Federalist* No. 67 (Alexander Hamilton).

The recess appointment power, like the appointment power (Article II, Section 2, Clause 2), applies to "Officers of the United States." Recess appointments to the judiciary have generated significant concern because unconfirmed judges lack the life tenure and guaranteed salary required by Article III. More than 300 judges have received recess appointments, including Supreme Court Justices William J. Brennan, Jr., Potter Stewart, and Earl Warren (all appointed by President Dwight D.

Eisenhower). Since 1980, however, only three judges have received recess appointments: Roger L. Gregory (appointed by President William Jefferson Clinton to the Fourth Circuit), Charles W. Pickering, Sr. (appointed by President George W. Bush to the Fifth Circuit), and William H. Pryor (appointed by President George W. Bush to the Eleventh Circuit).

Presidents have used the Recess Appointments Clause to fill not only vacancies that occur during recesses, but also those that initially arose when the Senate was in session. In certain cases, however, a federal statute, 5 U.S.C. § 5503, prohibits the payment of salaries to the latter appointees. Another relevant issue, on which courts have taken varied positions, is whether there is a vacancy when the position is occupied by a "holdover" who remains in office after the expiration of his term.

Presidents have used the clause during both intersession recesses, which occur between two sessions of a Senate, and intrasession recesses, which occur within a Senate session. For the first 150 years of the nation's history, Presidents made recess appointments almost exclusively during intersession recesses. In the post-World War II era, however, and especially since the mid-1980s, Presidents have made recess appointments during intrasession recesses, including recesses of less than two weeks. Some commentators have concluded that the text and intent of the Framers suggest that Presidents can make recess appointments only during intersession recesses of the Senate. Others contend that the text of the clause does not differentiate between types of recesses and that historical practice allows intrasession recess appointments.

A recess appointment lasts until the end of the "next Session" of the Senate. Since sessions in the early twenty-first century typically last ten to twelve months, an appointment made during an intersession recess would last approximately one year, until the end of the following session. On the other hand, an intrasession appointment could last as long as two years, through the end of the *succeeding* session.

Presidents in recent years have more frequently utilized the recess appointment power, often to avoid the Senate's role in the confirmation process. Despite this trend, the threat of governmental paralysis present at the time of the Framers is drastically reduced today, due to shorter recesses, improvements in transportation and communication, Senate activity taking place during recesses, and statutory succession and holdover provisions that provide for the temporary filling of vacancies.

Michael A. Carrier

See Also

Article I, Section 3, Clause 2 (Senatorial Classes and Vacancies Clause)

Article I, Section 7, Clause 2 (Pocket Veto)

Article II, Section 2, Clause 2 (Appointments Clause)

Suggestions for Further Research

1 Op. Att'y Gen. 631 (1823)

13 Op. Off. Legal Counsel 314 (1979)

16 Op. Off. Legal Counsel 15 (1992)

23 Op. Att'y Gen. 599 (1901)

33 Op. Att'y Gen. 20 (1921)

Michael A. Carrier, *When Is the Senate in Recess for Purposes of the Recess Appointments Clause?*, 92 Mich. L. Rev. 2204 (1994)

Stuart J. Chanen, *Constitutional Restrictions on the President's Power to Make Recess Appointments*, 79 Nw. U. L. Rev. 191 (1984)

Thomas A. Curtis, *Recess Appointments to Article III Courts: The Use of Historical Practice in Constitutional Interpretations*, 84 Colum. L. Rev. 1758 (1984)

Note, *Recess Appointments to the Supreme Court—Constitutional but Unwise?*, 10 Stan. L. Rev. 124 (1957)

Michael B. Rappaport, The Original Meaning of the Recess Appointments Clause (2004)

Virginia L. Richards, *Temporary Appointments to the Federal Judiciary: Article II Judges?*, 60 N.Y.U. L. Rev. 702 (1985)

Significant Cases

United States v. Allocco, 305 F.2d 704 (2d Cir. 1962)

Staebler v. Carter, 464 F. Supp. 585 (D.D.C. 1979)

United States v. Woodley, 751 F.2d 1008 (9th Cir. 1985)

Mackie v. Clinton, 827 F. Supp. 56 (D.D.C. 1993), *vacated in part as moot*, 1994 WL 163761 (D.C. Cir. 1994)

Swan v. Clinton, 100 F.3d 973 (D.C. Cir. 1996)

Wilkinson v. Legal Services Corp., 865 F. Supp. 891 (D.D.C. 1994), *rev'd on other grounds*, 80 F.3d 535 (D.C. Cir. 1996)

Evans v. Stephens, 387 F.3d 1220 (11th Cir. 2004)

State of the Union

[The President] shall from time to time give to the Congress Information of the State of the Union....
(Article II, Section 3)

〜

*A*s Chief Justice John Marshall pointed out in *Marbury v. Madison* (1803), much of the power of the executive is, in its nature, discretionary. Not so with the President's obligation to provide Congress with a report on the state of the Union. In his *Commentaries on the Constitution of the United States*, Justice Joseph Story observed that because the President has more information of the complex workings of the government, "[t]here is great wisdom, therefore, in not merely allowing, but in requiring, the president to lay before congress all facts and information, which may assist their deliberations; and in enabling him at once to point out the evil, and to suggest the remedy." Only the President—with his unique knowledge of military operations, foreign affairs, and the day-to-day execution of the laws, as well as being the only national representative of the whole people—can give a comprehensive assessment of the overall state of the nation and its relations with the world.

The Framers fastened this duty upon the President as a means of transparency and accountability. Justice Story noted, "He is thus justly made responsible, not merely for a due administration of the existing systems, but for due diligence and examination into the means of improving them." Other constitutionally defined communications, such as the President's veto message to Congress, his recommendation of measures to Congress, and the Senate's advice and consent of presidential nominations, represent James Madison's examples of the "partial agency" (*The Federalist*

No. 47) of one department in the workings of another department. But like the Oath of Office Clause, the State of the Union Clause requires the President to respect the legislative role of the Congress at the same time that it accounts for executive discretion in the fulfillment of the duty.

Unlike the British model of a "speech from the throne" to Parliament, which represents the sovereign "king in parliament" basis of the British constitution, the American version speaks to the separation of powers and the ultimate accountability of each branch of government to the sovereign people. Thus, the State of the Union Clause respects and upholds the separation of powers doctrine just as it acknowledges the nature of presidential unity and decisiveness, key "ingredients which constitute energy in the executive," as Alexander Hamilton wrote in *The Federalist* No. 70.

The provenance of the clause derived from the example of early state constitutions, as well as Hamilton's unadopted draft language:

> The President at the beginning of every meeting of the Legislature as soon as they shall be ready to proceed to business, shall convene them together at the place where the Senate shall sit, and shall communicate to them all such matters as may be necessary for their information, or as may require their consideration.

George Washington gave the first "Annual Message" in the Senate chamber in January 1790, after the Congress had met for the first time in 1789 but two months before its second session in March 1790. Subsequent messages came shortly after the convening of Congress, fulfilling the intended purpose of the Framers that the occasion was not for pomp but for practical content. Congress, for its part, does not need to respond, although it did so early in the Republic through a formal resolution of each House and, in more recent times, by a reply by a Member of the opposition party.

Historically, annual messages mostly focused on foreign relations, and introduced the reports and recommendations of department heads. It was not until the twentieth century, with the ease of communications and access to information, as well as the President's increased public presence and role as political party leader, that the State of the Union became less reporting and assessment and more policy advocacy and political persuasion. Although it is not a requirement, there was an expectation that the message would be delivered orally by the President (as was done by Washington and John Adams). Thomas Jefferson thought the practice too royal and refused to do so personally; he had clerks read it to Congress. Woodrow Wilson revived the oral tradition in 1913, a practice that has been followed by every President since Franklin D. Roosevelt. With the advent of radio (first used by Calvin Coolidge in 1923) and television (first used by Harry S. Truman in 1947), the State of the Union address has become an important occasion for speaking directly to the American people.

Matthew Spalding

See Also

Article I, Section 7, Clause 2 (Pocket Veto Power)
Article II, Section 2, Clause 2 (Appointments Clause)
Article II, Section 3 (Recommendations Clause)
Article II, Section 3 (Take Care Clause)

Suggestions for Further Research

Edward Corwin, The President: Office and Powers, 1787–1984 (5th ed., rev'd 1984)
Vasan Kesavan & J. Gregory Sidak, *The Legislator-in-Chief*, 44 Wm. & Mary L. Rev. 1 (2002)

Recommendations Clause

> [The President] shall from time to time ... recommend to their Consideration such Measures as he shall judge necessary and expedient ....
> (ARTICLE II, SECTION 3)

~

*D*espite the Article I provision that "All legislative Powers herein granted shall be vested in a Congress of the United States," the Constitution gives the President, as James Madison put it in *The Federalist* No. 47, a significant "partial agency" in the legislative process. Among his most important legislative functions is the duty to recommend measures to the Congress. Through this provision, the President has come to play an important, and often primary, role in the legislative process, though it took more than a century for the implications of the Recommendations Clause to be fully developed. One reading of the Constitution is that Congress proposes legislation, then the President signs or vetoes the bill. In practice, Congress often waits for the President to propose legislation, and it is common for legislators to criticize him if he does not make such proposals.

At the Constitutional Convention, the clause originally contained the word "Matters," but the Framers changed it to "Measures," indicating that the President was to recommend specific legislation (including the improvement of existing legislation) and not simply put forth general ideas. On the motion of Gouverneur Morris, the Convention also changed the word "may" to "shall," as Morris stated, "in order to make it the duty of the President to recommend, & thence prevent umbrage or cavil at his doing it." Beyond those changes, there was little discussion. In *The Federalist* No. 77, Alexander Hamilton listed the provision among several minor presidential powers, commenting that "no objection has been made to this class of authorities; nor could they possibly admit of any."

Explicitly, the clause imposes a duty, but its performance rests solely with the President. Congress possesses no power to compel the President to recommend, as he alone is the "judge" of what is "necessary and expedient." Unlike the Necessary and Proper Clause of Article I, which limits Congress's discretion to effectuating only its delegated powers, the phrase "necessary and expedient" implies wider range of discretion for the President. Because this is a political question, there has been little judicial involvement with the President's actions under the clause as long as Presidents have not tried to extend their legislative powers. In *Youngstown Sheet & Tube Co. v. Sawyer*

(1952), the Court noted that the Recommendations Clause serves as a reminder that the President cannot make law by himself: "The power to recommend legislation, granted to the President, serves only to emphasize that it is his function to recommend and that it is the function of the Congress to legislate." The Court made a similar point in striking down the line-item veto. *Clinton v. City of New York* (1998). When President William Jefferson Clinton attempted to shield the records of the President's Task Force on Health Care Reform as essential to his functions under the Recommendations Clause, a federal circuit court rejected the argument and noted, "[T]he Recommendation Clause is less an obligation than a right. The President has the undisputed authority to recommend legislation, but he need not exercise that authority with respect to any particular subject or, for that matter, any subject." *Ass'n of American Physicians & Surgeons v. Clinton* (1993).

The phrase "recommend to their Consideration" signifies the republican nature of the process. The President's recommendations are not royal edicts. They are suggestions to the people's and the states' representatives. His election is from a different constituency from either the House or the Senate, and his recommendations consequently provide a more national perspective for the Congress to consider. Combined with the later addition of the Freedom of Assembly and Petition Clause (in the First Amendment), the Recommendations Clause serves as an additional conduit for mediated public influence on the legislative process.

Except in times of emergency or war, early Presidents were not actively involved in trying to influence Congress. Washington sent only three proposals to Congress, and though Thomas Jefferson actively influenced the legislative process, he preferred to act behind the scenes rather than through formal recommendations. John Adams was more aloof than either. But as the national government became more involved in the economy (after the Interstate Commerce Act of 1887 and the development of the Industrial Revolution), Presidents began to try to affect congressional action.

Active presidential involvement in pressing for legislation began with Theodore Roosevelt and expanded during the presidency of Woodrow Wilson. With the approach of World War I, the executive branch drafted legislation before working with Congress. With the return of Republican Presidents in the 1920s, presidential activism decreased. The breakthrough of the modern presidency with respect to the legislative process came with Franklin D. Roosevelt's legendary Hundred Days. After calling the Seventy-Third Congress into special session on March 9, 1933, shortly after his inauguration, Roosevelt sent to Congress over the next 100 days a flurry of proposed laws intended to help the nation cope with the economic disaster of the Great Depression. Most of the laws were actually drafted in the White House, and the Democrat-controlled Congress passed most without hearings or any careful legislative scrutiny.

After FDR, presidentially inspired programs became a mainstay of the legislative process. Though reluctant at first, Dwight Eisenhower established the Office of Congressional Relations to assist him in dealing with Congress. The subsequent record of presidential administrations has been varied.

Vasan Kesavan, James Pfiffner,
and J. Gregory Sidak

See Also

Article I, Section 1 (Legislative Vesting Clause)
Article I, Section 7, Clause 2 (Pocket Veto Clause)
Article II, Section 2, Clause 2 (Treaty Clause)
Article II, Section 2, Clause 2 (Appointments Clause)
Article II, Section 3 (State of the Union)

Suggestions for Further Research

Edward Corwin, The President: Office and Powers, 1787–1984 (5th ed., rev'd 1984)
George C. Edwards, At the Margins (1989)
Vasan Kesavan & J. Gregory Sidak, *The Legislator-in-Chief*, 44 Wm. & Mary L. Rev. 1 (2002)
J. Gregory Sidak, *The Recommendation Clause*, 77 Geo. L.J. 2079 (1989)
James Sundquist, The Decline and Resurgence of Congress (1985)

Stephen J. Wayne, The Legislative Presidency (1978)

Significant Cases

Youngstown Sheet & Tube Co. v. Sawyer, 343 U.S. 579 (1952)
Ass'n of American Physicians & Surgeons v. Clinton, 997 F.2d 898 (D.C. Cir. 1993)
Clinton v. City of New York, 524 U.S. 417 (1998)

Convening of Congress

[The President] may, on extraordinary Occasions, convene both Houses, or either of them, and in Case of Disagreement between them, with Respect to the Time of Adjournment, he may adjourn them to such Time as he shall think proper....

(Article II, Section 3)

~

*U*nder British practice, the king could convene or dissolve Parliament at will. In the Declaration of Independence, it was one of the grounds for separation from England:

He has called together legislative bodies at places, unusual, uncomfortable, and distant from the repository of the public records; that he had dissolved representative bodies, for opposing his invasions of the rights of the people; and after such dissolutions, he had refused to reassemble them for a long period of time.

The Framers of the Constitution insisted, therefore, that Congress's right to convene must be independent of the will of the executive. Article I, Section 4, Clause 2. "Each house," Thomas Jefferson wrote in 1790, had a "natural right to meet when and where it should think best."

Nonetheless, the Framers also understood that the government must be able to meet exigent circumstances and therefore gave the President the very limited power to convene Congress "on extraordinary occasions." Justice Joseph Story indicated in his *Commentaries on the Constitution of the United States* that the President's need to conduct foreign relations effectively would be the primary motive for convening Congress. He gave as examples the need "to repel foreign aggressions, depredations, and direct hostilities; to provide adequate means to mitigate, or overcome unexpected calamities; to suppress insurrections; and to provide for innumerable other important exigencies, arising out of the intercourse and revolutions among nations."

Beginning with John Adams in 1797, the President has convened both the House and the Senate twenty-seven times, normally for crises such as war, economic emergency, or critical legislation. In addition, the President has called the Senate to meet to confirm nominations. With the ratification of the Twentieth Amendment, which brought forward the date on which Congress convenes, and with the practice of Congress to remain in session twelve months out of the year, there is practically no need for the President to call extraordinary sessions anymore. President Harry S. Truman called the last special session on July 15, 1948.

Even more important to the Framers was limiting the power of the executive to dissolve the legislature. They understood that that power was among the quickest routes to tyranny. Under the Constitution, therefore, "the President can only adjourn the national Legislature in the single case of disagreement about the time of adjournment." *The Federalist* No. 69 (Alexander Hamilton). It is only an administrative power, one that the President has never had to exercise.

David F. Forte

See Also

Ambassadors

[The President] shall receive Ambassadors and other public Ministers....

(**ARTICLE II, SECTION 3**)

≈

*I*n the Articles of Confederation, the powers "of sending and receiving ambassadors" were vested in Congress, though they could be delegated to the Committee of the States when Congress was not in session (Article IX). In the Constitutional Convention, the delegates at first followed the example of the Articles by vesting the appointment of American ambassadors as well as the treaty power in the Senate without executive participation. The Committee of Detail adopted Edmund Randolph's suggestion that the President be given the power to "receive" ambassadors. The Committee of Eleven later transferred to the President the treaty and appointment powers (subject to Senate approval), joining them to the independent power to receive ambassadors and other public ministers, such as consuls and other diplomats accredited to the United States by any foreign state. The Convention approved the changes. In this light, it is difficult to say that the power to receive ambassadors was initially thought to be part of any larger executive-branch responsibility for foreign affairs. In *The Federalist* No. 69, in fact, Alexander Hamilton described the President's power to receive ambassadors as merely the most "convenient" expedient, compared to the "necessity of convening the legislature" whenever a new ambassador arrived in the American capital.

Does the power to receive ambassadors necessarily imply a power to refuse their reception? And if it does, what degree of presidential control of foreign relations follows from such a power? In his 1829 *View on the Constitution*, William Rawle declared, "Under the expression, *he is to receive ambassadors*, the president is charged with all transactions between the United States and foreign nations." Ministerially, the President will refuse to receive putative ambassadors whose credentials are in serious doubt.

Where no such doubt exists, however, a refusal to receive an ambassador amounts to a decision not to "recognize" a foreign government, or at least not to carry on diplomatic relations with it, with all the consequences in international law and diplomacy that may follow from such a rupture.

From an early date, the federal courts have held that the clause raises only "political questions" to be decided by the other branches, not by the judiciary. Credentials as an ambassador may matter greatly in certain legal cases, but the courts will not inquire further than to assure themselves that the President has or has not received an ambassador as representing his government. *United States v. Ortega* (1825); *In re Baiz* (1890).

The historical debate over the deeper implications of the clause—namely, whether it accords the President an unfettered right to "recognize" another nation for diplomatic purposes—has accordingly taken place in the political arena. Alexander Hamilton (as "Pacificus") and James Madison (as "Helvidius") first discussed the question in their debate over President Washington's Neutrality Proclamation of 1793. Madison characterized the power of reception as merely ministerial, carrying no discretion to accept or reject the legitimacy of a foreign government—a discretion he would have lodged in Congress. Hamilton, altering the position he expressed in *The Federalist*, held that the power "includes that of judging, in the case of a Revolution of Government in a foreign Country, whether the new rulers are competent organs of the National Will and ought to be recognised or not." He concluded that the clause touched on "an important instance of the right of the Executive to decide the obligations of the Nation with regard to foreign Nations."

As a practical matter, Hamilton's argument of 1793 has prevailed historically. As then Representative John Marshall put it in 1800, "[t]he President is the sole organ of the nation in its external relations, and its sole representative with foreign nations. Of consequence the demand of a foreign nation can only be made on him." Should a would-be ambassador arrive in the capital and be refused reception by the President, there is nowhere else under the Constitution that he can turn. Likewise, it is difficult to see how the reception of an ambassador, and the consequent opening of diplomatic relations with a previously unrecognized government, can be undone by the action of another branch of government. *United States v. Belmont* (1937). Congress possesses other formal powers over foreign affairs, but this clause has come to be widely understood as giving the President one of his considerable advantages in the conduct of American foreign policy.

Matthew Franck

See Also

Article I, Section 8, Clause 3 (Commerce with Foreign Nations)
Article I, Section 8, Clause 11 (Declare War)
Article I, Section 10, Clause 1
Article II, Section 2, Clause 2 (Treaty Clause)
Article II, Section 2, Clause 2 (Appointments Clause)
Article III, Section 2, Clause 1
Article III, Section 2, Clause 2

Suggestions for Further Research

Edward S. Corwin, The President: Office and Powers 1787–1957, 177 (4th ed. 1957)
Alexander Hamilton, Pacificus no. 1 (29 June 1793), *in* 15 The Papers of Alexander Hamilton 33 (Harold C. Syrett et al. eds. 1969)
Louis Henkin, Foreign Affairs and the United States Constitution, 35 (2d ed.1996)
James Madison, Helvidius no. 3 (7 September 1793), *in* 15 The Papers of James Madison 95 (William T. Hutchinson et al. eds., 1985)

Significant Cases

United States v. Ortega, 27 F. Cas. 359 (C.C.E.D. Pa. 1825) (No. 15,971)
In re Baiz, 135 U.S. 403 (1890)
United States v. Belmont, 301 U.S. 324 (1937)
Guaranty Trust Co. of New York v. United States, 304 U.S. 126 (1938)
United States v. Pink, 315 U.S. 203 (1942)
Goldwater v. Carter, 444 U.S. 996 (1979)

Take Care Clause

[The President] shall take Care that
the Laws be faithfully executed....
(ARTICLE II, SECTION 3)

∾

$\mathcal{T}$he Take Care Clause (also known as the Faithful Execution Clause) is best read as a duty that qualifies the President's executive power. By virtue of his executive power, the President may execute the lawful and control the lawful execution of others. Under the Take Care Clause, however, the President must exercise his law-execution power to "take Care that the Laws be *faithfully* executed."

Though the clause's antecedents can be traced as far back as the late seventeenth century, its more immediate predecessors were found in the 1776 Pennsylvania Constitution and the 1777 New York Constitution. Both Constitutions granted their respective executives the "executive power" and also required them to execute the laws faithfully. Accordingly, the Pennsylvania and New York state executives understood that it was they, and not others, who were to see that the laws were faithfully executed.

The ratifying debates repeatedly evince the notion that the President had a duty to execute the law faithfully. Addressing the North Carolina ratifying convention, William Maclaine declared that the Faithful Execution Clause was "one of the [Constitution's] best provisions." If the President "takes care to see the laws faithfully executed, it will be more than is done in any government on the continent; for I will venture to say that our government, and those of the other states, are, with respect to the execution of the laws, in many respects mere ciphers." Not surprisingly, President George Washington clearly read the clause as imposing on him a unique duty to ensure the execution of federal law. Discussing a tax rebellion, Washington observed, "it is my duty to see the Laws executed: to permit them to be trampled upon with impunity would be repugnant to" that duty.

To be sure, the extent of the faithful-execution duty is rather unclear. Plainly, the President need not enforce every law to its fullest extent. Common sense suggests that the President may enjoy some discretion in order to gauge the costs and benefits of investigation, apprehension, and prosecution. Moreover, the pardon power (*see* Article II, Section 2, Clause 1) supplies a constitutional reason for concluding that the President need not enforce the law every time he feels there is a violation, for, notwithstanding his faithful-execution duty, the President may pardon an offense even before a trial or conviction. It is also possible that the clause does nothing more than incorporate the English Bill of Rights provisions that forbade the Crown from dispensing or suspending the law. Under this reading of the clause, the President can neither authorize violations of the law (he cannot issue dispensations) nor can he nullify a law (he cannot suspend its operation). He has, nonetheless, very wide discretion in enforcing the criminal law.

Those opposed to a strong executive have offered alternative ways of construing the Take Care Clause. On one view, the clause merely requires that the President oversee those statutorily charged with executing law, and does not assume that the President may control law execution. In other words, rather than controlling law execution, the President is limited to the narrow power of ensuring faithful law execution by others. A more extreme construction suggests that the President must obey even those statutes that forbid him from overseeing law execution. Thus, if a tax statute bars presidential oversight with respect to its execution, the President must take care to heed that statutory constraint on presidential power.

Each of these alternate readings of the clause is problematic. The first reading runs afoul of historical evidence. Both English and American experience support reading the Executive Vesting Clause (Article II, Section 1, Clause 1) as enabling the President to execute the law and to control the law execution of others. Given this understanding of the Executive Vesting Clause, the Take Care Clause should not be read to limit the President to the role of an aloof overseer of law execution. Consistent with this view, contemporaneous discussions of the Take Care

Clause emphasize the President's power over law execution; they do not support the claim that the President's law-execution role is one limited to ensuring faithful execution by others. Furthermore, there is no historical evidence supporting the notion that Congress can use the faithful-execution duty as a means by which it may strip away any presidential prerogative, let alone the executive's essential task of executing the laws. Such a reading would make the Constitution's Executive Vesting Clause surplusage and would undermine the Constitution's separation of powers.

The Take Care Clause has played a limited role in constitutional litigation. In 1831, the Supreme Court observed that in faithfully executing the law, "[the President] is bound to avail himself of every appropriate means not forbidden by law." *United States v. Tingey*. And from time to time, the Supreme Court will cite the clause in passing when discussing the President's duties and powers. Since the New Deal, however, the Supreme Court has sanctioned the creation of independent agencies, which operate as a fourth branch of government. Among other things, these independent agencies execute various federal laws (communications, banking, securities) by investigating and arranging for the prosecution of alleged lawbreakers. Restrictions on removal, and a tradition of independence, often make it impossible for the President to ensure that the independent agencies faithfully execute the law. Hence, with respect to the laws that the independent agencies execute, the President *does not* take care that such laws are faithfully executed.

As noted earlier, the President possesses wide discretion in deciding how and even when to enforce laws. He also has a range of interpretive discretion in deciding the meaning of laws he must execute. When an appropriation provides discretion, the President can gauge when and how appropriated moneys can be spent most efficiently. However, the President may not prevent a member of the executive branch from performing a ministerial duty lawfully imposed upon him by Congress. *Marbury v. Madison* (1803); *Kendall v. United States ex rel. Stokes* (1838). Nor may the President take an action

not authorized either by the Constitution or by a lawful statute. *Youngstown Sheet & Tube Co. v. Sawyer* (1952). Finally, the President may not refuse to enforce a constitutional law, or "cancel" certain appropriations, for that would amount to an extra-constitutional veto or suspension power.

With respect to congressional appropriations, presidents from Thomas Jefferson onward have asserted a power to impound funds. In Jefferson's case, he refused to spend money on purchasing gunboats, saying that they were not immediately needed, and that he was awaiting a better design. Beginning with President Franklin D. Roosevelt, however, the executive began to withhold spending for some objects altogether. President Richard M. Nixon expanded that practice to the fullest, refusing to spend on many programs for budgetary and fiscal reasons. Sometimes the executive branch has argued that this impoundment power flows from the Executive Vesting and/or Take Care Clauses. Other times, it has claimed that the appropriation statutes themselves granted the President the discretion to impound sums appropriated. Impoundment opponents have often cited the Take Care Clause as a reason why impoundments are unconstitutional, at least where Congress has made it clear that it expects the entire sums appropriated to be expended. In the wake of the impoundment controversies of the 1970s when federal courts struck down President Nixon's attempt to impound funds, *see Train v. City of New York* (1975), Congress enacted a more restrictive impoundment framework. To date, no President has argued that the framework amounts to an unconstitutional limitation on a broader impoundment power arising out of the Constitution.

In modern times, the Take Care Clause has been cited most frequently (sometimes in dissent) as a reason for strictly enforcing Article III's case or controversy requirement. To the extent that the judiciary allows plaintiffs without "standing" to prosecute allegedly illegal activity, the judiciary may be usurping the President's Take Care duty. Unlike the executive, the judiciary does not have a roving commission to ensure faithful law execution. Accordingly, some members of the Court have claimed that the Take Care Clause has negative implications for the judiciary's role in law execution; that is, while the executive has a general commission to execute the laws, the judiciary may only vindicate the laws when there is a proper case or controversy before them.

Sai Prakash

See Also
Article II, Section 1, Clause 1 (Executive Vesting Clause)
Article II, Section 2, Clause 1 (Pardon Power)
Article III, Section 1 (Judicial Vesting Clause)

Suggestions for Further Research
Steven G. Calabresi & Saikrishna Prakash, *The President's Power to Execute the Laws*, 104 YALE L.J. 541 (1994)

Steven G. Calabresi & Kevin H. Rhodes, *The Structural Constitution: Unitary Executive, Plural Judiciary*, 105 HARV. L. REV. 1153 (1992)

Gary Lawson & Christopher Moore. *The Executive Power of Constitutional Interpretation*, 81 IOWA L. REV. 1267 (1996)

Lawrence Lessig & Cass R. Sunstein, *The President and the Administration*, 94 COLUM. L. REV. 1, 4 (1994)

CHRISTOPHER N. MAY, PRESIDENTIAL DEFIANCE OF "UNCONSTITUTIONAL" LAWS: REVIVING THE ROYAL PREROGATIVE (1998)

Saikrishna B. Prakash, *The Essential Meaning of Executive Power*, 2003 U. ILL. L. REV. 701

Peter L. Strauss, *Presidential Rulemaking*, 72 CHI.-KENT L. REV. 965 (1997)

Significant Cases
Marbury v. Madison, 5 U.S. (1 Cranch) 137 (1803)
United States v. Tingey, 30 U.S. (5 Pet.) 115 (1831)
Kendall v. United States *ex rel.* Stokes, 37 U.S. (12 Pet.) 524 (1838)
United States *ex rel.* Goodrich v. Guthrie, 58 U.S. (17 How.) 284 (1854)
Mississippi v. Johnson, 71 U.S. (4 Wall.)475 (1866)
Cunningham v. Neagle, 135 U.S. 1 (1890)
Myers v. United States, 272 U.S. 52 (1926)
Youngstown Sheet & Tube Co. v. Sawyer, 343 U.S. 579 (1952)

Train v. City of New York, 420 U.S. 35 (1975)
Lujan v. Defenders of Wildlife, 504 U.S. 555 (1992)

Commissions

[The President] shall Commission all the Officers of the United States.
(ARTICLE II, SECTION 3)

∼

*A*t the time of the Framing, every officer of the English government was an officer of the Crown, commissioned in the king's name. In feudal Britain, the sovereign enjoyed an absolute prerogative to create and bestow fiefs, packages of rights and responsibilities that included titles, land grants, and offices. The grant of a fief would often be evidenced by a gift, which might be a banner, a sword, or a more formal charter. As the feudal system faded, the authority to create offices and commission officers remained an attribute of monarchical power. Indeed, the Declaration of Independence complains, "He [the king] has erected a multitude of New Offices, and sent hither swarms of Officers to harass our people, and eat out their substance." Many Americans considered the English system inherently flawed, consolidating too much power with the executive and thus begetting cronyism and abuse.

In the years following independence, the new state and national governments experimented with decentralized methods of selecting and empowering officials. The Articles of Confederation granted Congress the power to appoint civil officers and split the power to appoint military officers between Congress and the state legislatures. Regardless of the mode of selection, Congress was to commission "all officers whatever in the service of the United States." The states experimented with numerous other mechanisms.

The delegates at the Constitutional Convention vigorously debated the appointment power, eventually arriving at the system described in Article II, Section 2. But the Commissions Clause was never subject to debate; the Framers apparently accepted that granting commissions was a natural duty for the executive. When the Committee of Detail issued the first draft of the Constitution, the clause was already in its present form. The one person vested with the executive power would commission every officer of the national government.

The Framers structured the appointment power as follows. Congress creates the office (except for those solely under the President in his exercise of the foreign affairs power). The President "appoints" (actually nominates) principal officers, but Congress may by law vest the appointment of inferior officers in other persons or departments but not in Congress itself. The Senate approves the nominee, and the President completes the appointment by commissioning the officer. Delivery of the commission is not necessary to effectuate the appointment. *Marbury v. Madison* (1803).

Where the President has either constitutional or statutory authority to appoint (nominate) an officer, and the Senate has approved the nomination, the President may still decide not to commission the officer, which effectually kills the appointment. On the other hand, when an inferior officer has been appointed by someone other than the President, the President's duty is then ministerial: he is obliged to commission that person once the nomination has been approved.

While Justice Robert H. Jackson once called this duty "trifling," Chief Justice John Marshall pointed out in *Marbury* that granting a commission is the distinct act, done in the name of the President, which empowers an officer. Marshall also noted the important evidentiary value of commissions to officers in asserting their authority to citizens and in courts of law.

The placement of the Commissions Clause is also instructive. Rather than being nestled in the discussion on appointments in Article II, Section 2, the clause is attached with a comma to the Take Care Clause. The two together contemplate that the President will supervise others in their enforcement of the law. Solicitor General James Beck, successfully defending the President's removal power in *Myers v. United States* (1926), argued that "the commission of every high federal official comes to him not from Congress, which created the office, but from the President."

Although the executive power is vested in the President alone, he necessarily exercises this power through government officers, and thus the clause focuses accountability for the execution of the laws in the unitary executive. Beck argued that the President can only "take Care that the Laws be faithfully executed" if he is responsible for (and can remove) the officers who exercise his executive authority.

Trent England

See Also

Article I, Section 6, Clause 2 (Incompatibility Clause)
Article II, Section 2, Clause 2
Article II, Section 2, Clause 3 (Recess Appointments Clause)

Suggestion for Further Research

Peter L. Strauss, *The Constitution Under Clinton: The President and Choices Not to Enforce*, 63 L. & Contemp. Probs. 107 (2000)

Significant Cases

Marbury v. Madison, 5 U.S. (1 Cranch) 137 (1803)
Myers v. United States, 272 U.S. 52 (1926)
Youngstown Sheet & Tube Co. v. Sawyer, 343 U.S. 579 (1952)
Buckley v. Valeo, 424 U.S. 1 (1976)

Standards for Impeachment

The President, Vice President and all civil Officers of the United States, shall be removed from Office on Impeachment for, and Conviction of, Treason, Bribery, or other high Crimes and Misdemeanors.

(Article II, Section 4)

∽

*I*mpeachment is the constitutionally specified means by which an official of the executive or judicial branch may be removed from office for misconduct. There has been considerable controversy about what constitutes an impeachable offense. At the Constitutional Convention, the delegates early on voted for "mal-practice and neglect of duty" as grounds for impeachment, but the Committee of Detail narrowed the basis to treason, bribery, and corruption, then deleting the last point. George Mason, who wanted the grounds much broader and similar to the earlier formulation, suggested "maladministration," but James Madison pointed out that this would destroy the President's independence and make him dependent on the Senate. Mason then suggested "high Crimes and Misdemeanors," which the Convention accepted.

Because "high Crimes and Misdemeanors" was a term of art used in English impeachments, a plausible reading supported by many scholars is that the grounds for impeachment can be not only the defined crimes of treason and bribery, but also other criminal or even noncriminal behavior amounting to a serious dereliction of duty. That interpretation is disputed, but it is agreed by virtually all that the impeachment remedy was to be used in only the most extreme situations, a position confirmed by the relatively few instances in which Congress has used the device.

The word "impeachment" is popularly used to indicate both the bringing of charges in the House and the Senate vote on removal from office. In the Constitution, however, the term refers only to the former. At the Convention, the delegates experimented with differing impeachment proceedings. As finally agreed, a majority vote of the House of Representatives is required to bring impeachment charges (Article I, Section 2, Clause 5), which are then tried before the Senate (Article I, Section 3, Clause 6). Two-thirds of the Senate must vote to convict before an official can be removed. The President may not pardon a person who has been impeached (Article II, Section 2, Clause 1). If an official is impeached by the House and convicted by the requisite vote in the Senate, then Article I, Section 3, Clause 7, provides that the person convicted is further barred from any "Office of honor, Trust or Profit under the United States." The convicted official also loses any possible federal pensions. With a

few exceptions, those impeached and removed have generally faded into obscurity.

In *The Federalist* No. 64, John Jay argued that the threat of impeachment would encourage executive officers to perform their duties with honor, and, used as a last resort, impeachment itself would be effective to remove those who betray the interests of their country. Like the limitations on the offense of treason, the Framers placed particular grounds of impeachment in the Constitution because they wished to prevent impeachment from becoming a politicized offense, as it had been in England. Nonetheless, Alexander Hamilton, in *The Federalist* No. 65, also warned that during impeachment proceedings, it would be difficult for Congress to act solely in the interests of the nation and resist political pressure to remove a popular official. The Framers believed that the Senate, elected by the state legislatures, would have the requisite independence needed to try impeachments. The Framers also mandated a supermajority requirement to militate against impeachments brought by the House for purely political reasons.

There have been several impeachment proceedings initiated since the adoption of the Constitution, principally against judges in the lower federal courts. The most important impeachments were those brought against United States Associate Justice Samuel Chase in 1805, against President Andrew Johnson in 1867, and against President William Jefferson Clinton in 1999. None of these three resulted in removal from office, and all three stand for the principle that impeachment should not be perceived as a device simply to remove a political opponent. In that regard, the caution of the Framers has been fulfilled.

President George Washington appointed Samuel Chase to the Supreme Court in 1796. Washington had been warned of Chase's mercurial behavior, but Chase had written the President that, if he were appointed, he would do nothing to embarrass the administration. In his early years on the Court, Chase kept his pledge and did render some fine decisions clarifying the powers of the federal government. In the election of 1800, however, when Thomas Jefferson ran against Washington's Vice President and successor John

Adams, Chase earned the ire of Jefferson's emerging Republican party. For one thing, Chase actively took to the hustings to campaign for Adams (a move rare for sitting judges even then). What finally brought President Jefferson to approve of efforts by his party's representatives in Congress to remove the judge was a grand-jury charge Chase made in Baltimore in 1803. There Chase lamented the Jeffersonian restructuring of the federal judiciary in order to abolish the Circuit Court judgeships that the Adams administration had created, and the Maryland Jeffersonians' abolishing a state court and establishing universal male suffrage in Maryland. Chase argued that all of this was plunging the country into "mobocracy." Chase voiced sentiments common to a wing of the party of Washington and Adams, but Jefferson and his men believed that to have a federal judge publicly articulating such views was harmful to the government, and they moved against Chase. In addition to citing his behavior in Baltimore, the impeachment charges included several counts based on Chase's conduct during controversial trials in 1800 against Jeffersonian writers who had been prosecuted under the Alien and Sedition Act of 1798 (a temporary measure that punished libels against the government).

The proceeding against Chase was part of a broader Jeffersonian assault on the judiciary, and it was widely believed, at least among Federalists, that if it were successful, Chief Justice John Marshall might be the next target. None of the specifications brought against Chase charged him with any criminal conduct, and their thrust seemed to be that his legal rulings were simply not in accordance with Jeffersonian theory on how trials ought to be conducted or how juries should function. There was substantial legal precedent behind each of Chase's rulings, however, and although he may have been guilty of having a hair-trigger temper, it was also clear that to permit his removal would seriously, perhaps permanently, compromise the independence of the judiciary. The requisite two-thirds majority of Senators could not be cobbled together to remove Chase, and, in fact, members of Jefferson's own party even voted for acquittal. From that time to this, the Chase acquittal has been understood to bar the removal of a Supreme Court Justice on the ground of his political preferences. Subsequently, there have been several attempts to begin impeachment proceedings against particular Justices, but none has ever prevailed in the House.

Andrew Johnson, who succeeded to the presidency following Abraham Lincoln's assassination in 1865, was impeached because of his failure to follow procedures specified in federal legislation (passed over his veto) that prohibited the firing of Cabinet officials without the permission of Congress. The legislation, known as the Tenure of Office Act, was arguably unconstitutional because it compromised the independence of the executive. Nevertheless, the radical Republicans, who then controlled Congress and who recoiled at President Johnson's active hostility to their plans to protect the newly freed slaves, sought to keep the sympathetic members of Abraham Lincoln's Cabinet in office. When Johnson fired Secretary of War Edwin Stanton, the gauntlet was thrown down, and impeachment was voted by the House. Though just as political as the Chase impeachment proceedings, there was some support for the Tenure of Office Act (Alexander Hamilton, writing in the *The Federalist* No. 77, had suggested that the consent of the Senate would be necessary "to displace as well as to appoint" officials). As it turned out, the conviction of Johnson failed in the Senate by only one vote.

The administration of President William Jefferson Clinton was beset by assorted scandals, many of which resulted in the appointment of special federal prosecutors, and several of which resulted in the convictions of lesser officials. One of the special prosecutors, Kenneth Starr, recommended to the Congress in 1998 that it consider evidence that the President had obstructed justice, tampered with witnesses, lied to a grand jury, and sought to conceal evidence in connection with a civil proceeding brought against him involving claims of sexual harassment. President Clinton denied the charges, but the Arkansas federal judge who presided in that civil proceeding eventually cited and fined Clinton for contempt based on his untruthful testimony.

A majority of the Republican-controlled House of Representatives voted in early 1999 to impeach the President based upon Judge Starr's referral. The House managers argued that what the President had done was inconsistent with his sworn duty to take care that the laws of the nation be faithfully executed. When the matter was tried in the Senate, in February 1999, however, the President's defenders prevailed, and no more than fifty Senators (all Republicans) could be found to vote for conviction on any of the charges.

The only other time a President came close to being impeached was the case of Richard M. Nixon. He resigned from office in 1974, after a House Committee had voted to put before the full House a number of impeachment charges, the most serious of which was that he had wrongly used the FBI and the CIA in order to conceal evidence that persons connected to the White House had participated in a burglary at the Democratic Party's offices at the Watergate apartment complex. Nixon avoided impeachment, though not disgrace.

There is no authoritative pronouncement, other than the text of the Constitution itself, regarding what constitutes an impeachable offense, and what meaning to accord to the phrase "other high Crimes and Misdemeanors." When he was a Congressman, Gerald R. Ford advocated the ultimately unsuccessful impeachment of a Supreme Court Justice by defining an impeachable offense as anything on which a majority of the House of Representatives can agree. As impeachment is understood to be a political question, Ford's statement correctly centers responsibility for the definition of "high Crimes and Misdemeanors" in the House. The federal courts have thus far treated appeals from impeachment convictions to be nonjusticiable. *Nixon v. United States* (1993). Even if the issue of impeachment is nonjusticiable, it does not mean that there are no appropriate standards that the House should observe.

Some scholarly commentary at the time of the Nixon impeachment proceedings argued that the actual commission of a crime was necessary to serve as a basis for an impeachment proceeding. However, the historical record of impeachments in England, which furnished the Constitution's Framers with the term "high Crimes and Misdemeanors," does not support such a limitation; at that time, the word "Misdemeanors" meant simply "misdeeds," rather than "petty crimes," as it now does. The issue was revisited at the time of the Clinton impeachment, when those who sought to remove the President from office, basing their arguments principally on the English experience and *The Federalist* No. 64, claimed that a President could be removed for any misconduct that indicated that he did not possess the requisite honor, integrity, and character to be trusted to carry out his functions in a manner free from corruption. As James Iredell (later Associate Justice of the Supreme Court) opined in the North Carolina ratifying convention, impeachment should be used to remedy harm "arising from acts of great injury to the community."

On the other hand, some have argued that a President should not be impeached unless he has actually engaged in a major abuse of power flowing from his office as President (although judges, who serve during "good behavior," have been impeached for conduct occurring outside of their official duties). In the end, because it is unlikely that a Court would ever exercise judicial review over impeachment and removal proceedings, the definitional responsibility to carry them out with fidelity to the Constitution's text remains that of the House of Representatives and the Senate.

Stephen B. Presser

See Also

Suggestions for Further Research

Raoul Berger, Impeachment: The Constitutional Problems (1974)

Michael J. Gerhardt, The Federal Impeachment Process: A Constitutional and Historical Analysis (2d ed. 2000)

Peter Charles Hoffer and N.E.H. Hull, Impeachment in America, 1635–1805 (1984)

STANLEY I. KUTLER, THE WARS OF WATERGATE: THE
   LAST CRISIS OF RICHARD NIXON (1990)

RICHARD POSNER, AN AFFAIR OF STATE: THE INVES-
   TIGATION, IMPEACHMENT AND TRIAL OF PRESI-
   DENT CLINTON (1999)

Stephen B. Presser, *Would George Washington Have
   Wanted Bill Clinton Impeached?*, 67 GEO. WASH.
   L. REV. 666 (1999)

WILLIAM H. REHNQUIST, GRAND INQUESTS: THE
   HISTORIC IMPEACHMENTS OF JUSTICE SAMUEL
   CHASE AND PRESIDENT ANDREW JOHNSON (1992)

Cass R. Sunstein, *Impeachment and Stability*, 67 GEO.
   WASH. L. REV. 699 (1999)

KEITH E. WHITTINGTON, CONSTITUTIONAL CON-
   STRUCTION: DIVIDED POWERS AND CONSTITU-
   TIONAL MEANING (1999)

Significant Cases

United States v. Nixon, 418 U.S. 683 (1974)

Nixon v. United States, 506 U.S. 224 (1993)

Clinton v. Jones, 520 U.S. 681 (1997)

A Note on Administrative Agencies

≈

*A*dministrative agencies, the hallmark institutions of the modern regulatory state, vary by form and function in accordance with the tasks they are asked to perform. Some are relatively small entities that execute narrowly specified duties; others are sizeable bureaucracies with large budgets and broad discretionary authority. Some are subunits of executive departments; others are free-standing. The latter, in turn, fall into two categories: executive agencies (so called because they are ultimately accountable to the President) and "independent" agencies (which are wholly accountable neither to the President nor to Congress).

The legal status, powers, and purpose of administrative agencies are prescribed by acts of Congress and vary enormously in the breadth and detail of their delegated authority. Many agencies exercise legislative, executive, and judicial powers. They can issue regulations having the same force and effect as statutes, impose fines and penalties for violations of their regulations, and conduct trial-type proceedings that affect the rights and interests of particular parties. Unless otherwise specified in their enabling acts or subsequent legislation, agency operations are governed by the 1946 Administrative Procedure Act (APA), which authorizes a variety of different proceedings, sets rules for each, and establishes criteria for obtaining judicial review following final agency action.

Administrative agencies are usually justified in terms of their ability to redress perceived or actual market failures: for example, controlling monopoly power, "windfall" profits, or "excessive" competition; or compensating for externalities, inadequate information, or unequal bargaining power. Whatever might be said by way of praise or criticism about the mission or behavior of particular agencies, their number and variety testify to the growth of the federal government. Indeed, few subjects are now considered to be beyond the pale of federal regulation.

Although public officials have long since accommodated themselves to administrative agencies as a necessary adjunct of contemporary government, the nature and reach of agency powers remains controversial. This is especially true of independent agencies, comprising the so-called "headless fourth branch of government," which from their very inception have been a constitutional anomaly. In theory, independent agencies are subject to the authority of the constitutional branches in the sense that the President appoints agency leadership (subject to senatorial confirmation), Congress authorizes agency expenditures and conducts legislative oversight, and judicial review ensures agency compliance with statutory and constitutional requirements. But these controls, precisely because they are remote, indirect, and incomplete, tend to mock the principle of accountability that informs the separation of powers.

The anomalous constitutional character of independent agencies has prompted efforts by the political branches to exert greater political control over their behavior. President Franklin D. Roosevelt, for example, unsuccessfully sought to subject independent agency heads to the presidential removal power. *Humphrey's Executor v.*

United States (1935). Congress, in turn, has tried and failed to assert its own authority over both the appointment and removal of agency officers. *Buckley v. Valeo* (1976); *Bowsher v. Synar* (1986).

Executive-congressional competition of this sort reflects unresolved ambiguities about the modern administrative state. In a complex society, Congress cannot specify every detail of legislative policy. Room must be left for the exercise of discretionary judgment, which means that legislative delegation is inevitable if Congress decides to regulate many subjects extensively. The separation-of-powers principle, however, necessarily limits the extent to which Congress may delegate its legislative authority. What are the constitutional standards that distinguish valid and invalid delegations? When Congress delegates, does discretion then vest automatically and entirely in the executive? Once it delegates authority, may Congress nevertheless retain control over certain details of policy and, if so, how much and by what means? What happens when congressional efforts to control details run up against the constitutional power of the President to execute the law?

These questions are difficult enough when applied to executive agencies, but they are particularly nettlesome when applied to independent agencies, which by their nature are neither congressional fish nor presidential fowl. As it began to construct the administrative state, Congress slowly acknowledged a growing political dilemma: being unwilling or unable to oversee the fine details of legislative policy, Congress was prepared to delegate broad rule-making authority. At the same time, it was reluctant to vest all discretionary control over details in the executive. Presidents, for their part, initially sought to maximize their own authority over administrative agencies, but yielded over time to the palpable reality of congressional power. After much political experimentation and compromise over many decades, as qualified from time to time by the instruction of the Supreme Court, independent agencies as we know them today came into being. They are, at bottom, the institutional embodiment of a congressional desire to delegate the details of governance and retain authority at the same time. The short and recent history of the administrative state is a story of more or less continual struggle

between the political branches for control of agency discretion, with the judiciary playing the occasional role of referee. Prior to the 1930s, the Court sustained piecemeal delegations of legislative authority on varying grounds, *Field v. Clark* (1892), *United States v. Grimaud* (1911), and *J.W. Hampton, Jr. & Co. v. United States* (1928), but later efforts to invest administrative agencies with essentially open-ended authority to make and enforce rules gave the Court pause. Accordingly, it invalidated a number of New Deal regulatory schemes, either because they lacked intelligible standards necessarily implied by the separation of powers (the nondelegation doctrine) or because they failed to comport with requisite due-process requirements. *A. L. A. Schechter Poultry Corp. v. United States* (1935); *Panama Refining Co. v. Ryan* (1935); *Carter v. Carter Coal Co.* (1936).

Although the Justices eventually relaxed their opposition beginning in the late 1930s, their reservations about improperly delegated legislative authority have retained a certain purchase. The enactment of the APA in 1946 quieted many procedural concerns, but the substantive scope of administrative discretion (whether exercised by executive or independent agencies) remains a matter of continuing controversy. As to rule-making, the judiciary at first allowed agencies great leeway in interpreting their own statutory authority. The courts later began to second-guess the interpretative license it had previously granted to agencies, only to revert to a modified version of the older rule. *See Chevron U.S.A. Inc. v. Natural Resources Defense Council, Inc.* (1984). The Justices also seem to be of two minds concerning congressional delegation generally. In some cases, they have upheld extraordinarily broad delegations, but in others they have sought to rein Congress in. *Compare Industrial Union Department, AFL-CIO v. American Petroleum Institute* (1980); *Mistretta v. United States* (1989); and *Whitman v. American Trucking Ass'ns, Inc.* (2001). This oscillation may very well reflect the Court's continuing ambivalence about the constitutionality of delegation.

Although administrative agencies are a given of modern industrial society, the political branches continue to battle for control of agency action. In the 1960s and 1970s, in an effort to curb the executive generally and to tighten its own authority over regulation, Congress imposed various forms of legislative veto, all of which the Supreme Court invalidated in *I.N.S. v. Chadha* (1983). Presidential efforts to inhibit excessive regulation have been more successful. In 1981, President Ronald Reagan issued an executive order (E.O. 12291) requiring executive agencies to apply cost-benefit analysis to proposed major rules and authorizing the Office of Management and Budget to police their efforts. Despite criticism by certain Members of Congress and interest groups, this approach has been continued with relatively minor modification by Reagan's successors in office.

Michael Uhlmann

Suggestions for Further Research

STEPHEN BREYER, REGULATION AND ITS REFORM (1982)

JAMES O. FREEDMAN, CRISIS AND LEGITIMACY (1978)

GARY LAWSON, FEDERAL ADMINISTRATIVE LAW (3d ed. 2004)

Gary Lawson, *The Rise and Rise of the Administrative State*, 107 HARV. L. REV. 1231 (1994)

Robert L. Rabin, *Federal Regulation in Historical Perspective*, 38 STAN. L. REV. 1189 (1986)

Significant Cases

Field v. Clark, 143 U.S. 649 (1892)

United States v. Grimaud, 220 U.S. 506 (1911)

J.W. Hampton, Jr. & Co. v. United States, 276 U.S. 394 (1928)

A. L. A. Schechter Poultry Corp. v. United States, 295 U.S. 495 (1935)

Humphrey's Executor v. United States, 295 U.S. 602 (1935)

Panama Refining Co. v. Ryan, 293 U.S. 388 (1935)

Carter v. Carter Coal Co., 298 U.S. 238 (1936)

Buckley v. Valeo, 424 U.S. 1 (1976)

Industrial Union Department, AFL-CIO v. American Petroleum Institute, 448 U.S. 607 (1980)

I.N.S. v. Chadha, 462 U.S. 919 (1983)

Chevron U.S.A. Inc. v. Natural Resources Defense Council, Inc., 467 U.S. 837 (1984)

Bowsher v. Synar, 478 U.S. 714 (1986)

Mistretta v. United States, 488 U.S. 361 (1989)

Whitman v. American Trucking Ass'ns, Inc., 531 U.S. 457 (2001)

ARTICLE III

Judicial Vesting Clause

The judicial Power of the United States shall be vested in one supreme Court, and in such inferior Courts as the Congress may from time to time ordain and establish.

(ARTICLE III, SECTION 1)

*T*he Constitution's first three Articles contain symmetrical introductory language. Each pro-

vides that a basic type of governmental "power"—"legislative" (making laws), "executive" (administering the laws), and "judicial" (expounding laws to decide particular cases)— "shall be vested" in a corresponding institution: "Congress," the "President," and "Courts," respectively. As originally conceived, the Constitution embodied the sovereign will of "We the People," who delegated power to three independent yet coordinate branches of government.

This separation-of-powers structure incorporated two novel Federalist ideas. First, "judicial

Power" became a distinct part of government, whereas in England it had been treated as an aspect of executive authority (although the English recognized adjudication as a discrete function). Second, like Congress and the President, federal judges ultimately derived their power from "the People," even though they were unelected and given tenure and salary guarantees to ensure their impartiality and prestige. This separate and independent judiciary consisted of a Supreme Court and any lower federal tribunals Congress chose to create. The powers of federal courts can most usefully be divided into three components: judicial review, justiciability, and equitable authority.

Since 1787, the central meaning of "judicial Power" has remained remarkably consistent: neutrally deciding a case by interpreting the law and applying it to the facts, then rendering a final and binding judgment. The most important cases in Article III are those "arising under th[e] Constitution [and] Laws of the United States." This clause complements Article VI, which provides that "[t]his Constitution, and the Laws of the United States which shall be made in pursuance thereof...shall be the supreme Law of the Land." There was a general understanding that this language, and the very nature of a written Constitution ordained by "the People," authorized judicial review of the constitutional validity of government actions. For example, in *The Federalist* No. 78, Alexander Hamilton reasoned as follows: (1) courts have a duty to resolve cases impartially according to the law; (2) the Constitution is the fundamental and supreme law in which "the People" explicitly limited the political branches; and (3) therefore, judges must follow the Constitution instead of a clearly contrary ordinary law. Hamilton's Anti-Federalist rival "Brutus," however, expressed the fear that federal judges would naturally aggrandize power to themselves and to the central government. "In their decisions," he said, "they will not confine themselves to any fixed or established rules." "This power," he concluded, "will enable them to mold the government into almost any shape they please."

The early Supreme Court operated on a restricted notion of judicial review, although it did not strike down any statute until *Marbury v. Madison* (1803). In that case, Chief Justice John Marshall repeated Hamilton's analysis and then held that Congress, by forcing the Court to assume original jurisdiction over an action involving a writ of mandamus (an order compelling action by an executive official), had plainly violated limitations on such jurisdiction prescribed in Article III. The Court expressly cabined its power to examining "judicial" issues of law rather than "political" questions committed by the Constitution to the executive branch's discretion.

This relatively constrained view of the judicial function continued until 1857, when the Court next invalidated a federal law—the critical and politically delicate Missouri Compromise—in *Dred Scott v. Sandford*. This disastrous attempt to transform judicial review into a mandate to substitute the Justices' policy preferences on slavery for those of political officials crippled the Court's prestige for a generation.

By the late nineteenth century, however, the Court began to interpret the judicial power as allowing it to overturn legislation that did not transgress any explicit constitutional command. Most famously, in *Lochner v. New York* (1905), it held that a state law restricting workers' hours violated the Fourteenth Amendment by depriving employers and employees of "liberty" and "property" without "due process of law." The Court construed this language, which originally had been intended to guarantee procedural protections, as creating a substantive right to contract freely. In 1937, the Court abandoned this approach and announced that *economic* legislation would be upheld if it had any rational basis. Subsequently, however, the Court has not shown similar deference to *social* legislation. Instead, it has struck down laws dealing with issues like education, crime, voting, and abortion—areas previously thought to have been left by the Constitution to the political process.

Judicial review can be exercised only over cases that are "justiciable" (i.e., presented in a form suitable for judicial resolution). The Supreme Court has developed many justiciability doctrines, which reflect both Article III requirements and self-imposed prudential limitations.

The Federalist Justices swiftly established three bedrock justiciability rules. First, federal court judgments expounding the law are final and cannot be reexamined or revised by Congress or the President. Second, judges will not render legal advice to political officials outside the context of a contested case. Third, even if a federal court possesses Article III jurisdiction over a case, it will decline to issue a decision if the underlying question presented is "political" in the sense of being entrusted by the Constitution exclusively to the President or Congress. Long-recognized examples of such political questions include the conduct of war and foreign affairs and the appointment of executive and judicial officials.

Gradually, several other justiciability doctrines evolved. Most importantly, a plaintiff must establish "standing" to sue by demonstrating the existence of an individualized injury caused by an adverse defendant. Furthermore, courts avoid premature adjudication, especially challenges to administrative agency proceedings, by insisting that claims be "ripe" for review (i.e., sufficiently developed both factually and legally). Finally, cases are usually dismissed as "moot" if the parties' dispute has ended.

Although the Court has never deviated from its bans on nonfinal judgments and advisory opinions, it has not taken a similarly consistent approach to standing, ripeness, mootness, and the political question doctrine during the modern era. The Justices appointed by Franklin D. Roosevelt strengthened all of these doctrines to minimize litigation attacking regulatory and social welfare legislation, which mushroomed during the New Deal. By contrast, the Warren Court relaxed justiciability requirements to broaden access to the federal judiciary, particularly where necessary to vindicate constitutional rights. Perhaps most significantly, the Court interpreted the Constitution as allowing judicial review of several questions formerly viewed as "political," such as the apportionment of state legislatures, *Baker v. Carr* (1962), and Congress's power to judge the qualifications of its Members, *Powell v. McCormack* (1969).

The Burger and Rehnquist Courts likewise have rejected "political question" defenses in controversial cases involving gerrymandering, the apportionment of congressional districts, procedures for enacting statutes, Indian tribal affairs, assertions of executive privilege, the 2000 presidential election deadlock, and executive branch determinations regarding treaty compliance. Indeed, since the *Baker* decision, only two issues, impeachment and military training, have been deemed beyond the scope of judicial review. Although the Burger and Rehnquist Courts have continued the loose approach to the political question doctrine, they generally have strengthened rules of standing, ripeness, and mootness.

In short, the justiciability doctrines have changed over the years and have been employed with varying degrees of rigor. Nonetheless, their purpose has remained constant: to assure the appropriate exercise of judicial power, especially the decision of constitutional cases.

Article III has long been construed as implicitly conferring all auxiliary "inherent" authority necessary for courts to exercise judicial power competently. For instance, because adjudication depends on finding accurate and relevant facts, federal judges inherently have the ability to manage pretrial discovery, make evidentiary rulings, compel witnesses to testify, and appoint experts. Similarly, issuing a judgment is a key component of judicial power, and therefore courts can independently enter and correct their judgments. Finally, courts by their very nature must be able to maintain their authority and supervise the judicial process—for example, by sanctioning disobedience of their orders and courtroom misconduct. Over the past century, the scope of inherent judicial powers has grown dramatically to cope with the vast increase in the amount and complexity of litigation.

Likewise, the judiciary's equitable discretion has expanded greatly since *Brown v. Board of Education* (1954), which countenanced broad decrees to remedy unconstitutional discrimination in public schools. *Brown* and other desegregation cases encouraged federal courts to fashion complex remedies in other major public policy areas, such as prison reform. Congress, however, can limit the range of the federal judiciary's injunctive powers.

In sum, Article III's introductory language has always been read as granting federal courts the "judicial Power" of deciding cases and any inherent and equitable authority needed to do so properly. The Court has continually adapted the contours of judicial power, however, to address broader legal and political changes.

Robert J. Pushaw, Jr.

See Also

Preamble

Article I, Section 1 (Legislative Vesting Clause)

Article I, Section 8, Clause 9 (Inferior Courts)

Article II, Section 1, Clause 1 (Executive Vesting Clause)

Article II, Section 2, Clause 2 (Appointments Clause)

Article VI, Clause 2 (Supremacy Clause)

Suggestions for Further Research

Evan Caminker, *Allocating the Judicial Power in a "Unified Judiciary,"* 78 Tex. L. Rev. 1513 (2000)

Letter from the Justices of the Supreme Court to President George Washington (Aug. 8, 1793), *reprinted in* Stewart Jay, Most Humble Servants: The Advisory Role of Early Judges, at 179–180 (1997)

James S. Liebman & William F. Ryan, *"Some Effectual Power": The Quantity and Quality of Decision-making Required of Article III Courts*, 98 Colum. L. Rev. 696 (1998)

Robert J. Pushaw, Jr., *The Inherent Powers of Federal Courts and the Structural Constitution*, 86 Iowa L. Rev. 735 (2001)

Robert J. Pushaw, Jr., *Justiciability and Separation of Powers: A Neo-Federalist Approach*, 81 Cornell L. Rev. 393 (1996)

Significant Cases

Hayburn's Case, 2 U.S. (2 Dall.) 409 (1792)

Marbury v. Madison, 5 U.S. (1 Cranch) 137 (1803)

United States v. Hudson & Goodwin, 11 U.S. (7 Cranch) 32 (1812)

Martin v. Hunter's Lessee, 14 U.S. (1 Wheat.) 304 (1816)

Cohens v. Virginia, 19 U.S. (6 Wheat.) 264 (1821)

Osborn v. Bank of the United States, 22 U.S. (9 Wheat.) 738 (1824)

Wayman v. Southard, 23 U.S. (10 Wheat.) 1 (1825)

Dred Scott v. Sandford, 60 U.S. (19 How.) 393 (1857)

United States v. Klein, 80 U.S. (13 Wall.) 128 (1871)

Murdock v. City of Memphis, 87 U.S. 590 (1875)

Lochner v. New York, 198 U.S. 45 (1905)

West Coast Hotel Co. v. Parrish, 300 U.S. 379 (1937)

Coleman v. Miller, 307 U.S. 433 (1939)

Brown v. Board of Education, 347 U.S. 483 (1954)

Baker v. Carr, 369 U.S. 186 (1962)

United Mine Workers of America v. Gibbs, 383 U.S. 715 (1966)

Abbott Laboratories v. Gardner, 387 U.S. 136 (1967)

Powell v. McCormack, 395 U.S. 486 (1969)

United States Parole Commission v. Geraghty, 445 U.S. 388 (1980)

Lujan v. Defenders of Wildlife, 504 U.S. 555 (1992)

Bush v. Gore, 531 U.S. 98 (2000)

Supreme Court

The judicial Power of the United States shall be vested in one supreme Court....

(ARTICLE III, SECTION 1)

~

*W*hen the Constitutional Convention opened in Philadelphia, the very existence of a national judiciary was at issue. Delegates who favored state power argued that national laws could be enforced by state courts, whereas others, such as James Madison, foresaw the need for national judicial power. The "one supreme Court" created by the Constitution reflected ambivalence over the nature and scope of this power, and the Framers left to Congress significant discretion to determine the number of Supreme Court Justices; the establishment, structure and jurisdiction of a lower federal judiciary; and the ability to make exceptions to the Court's appellate jurisdiction.

While considering the question of a unitary executive, the delegates to the Constitutional Convention concluded that the judiciary was to be a legal rather than a political body. The Convention rejected the notion that the judicial branch should be any part of a proposed "Council of Revision," which would have overseen the executive power to exercise a veto or to revise laws. Elbridge Gerry remarked that it was foreign to the nature of the judicial office to judge the policy of public measures. Rufus King argued that judges have to consider laws afresh, without having participated in making them.

Following the implicit command of the Constitution, Congress created a Supreme Court in the Judiciary Act of 1789 and set the number of Justices at six. The Judiciary Act also established a subordinate federal judicial structure of several district and three circuit courts, each of the latter including two "riding" Supreme Court Justices (reduced to one in 1793). The act also gave the Supreme Court appellate jurisdiction over federal questions growing out of litigation in state courts, thus cementing national power, while at the same time allowing state courts to make determinations on federal questions prior to final appeal. However, the act also confined the Supreme Court to questions of law rather than fact—an appellate limitation unusual for the time. This innovation was aimed at calming residual fears of national judicial power overturning local jury findings.

The first Chief Justice, John Jay, confirmed the intention of the Framers by insisting on the legal, rather than political, function of the Court and its Justices. In *Hayburn's Case* (1792), he wrote on circuit that Congress could only assign properly judicial tasks to the judiciary, thus upholding federal judges' refusal to act as pensions claims adjudicators. Jay, speaking for the Court in a letter to President George Washington, also declined to render an advisory opinion Washington had requested concerning treaty interpretation.

In *Marbury v. Madison* (1803), Chief Justice John Marshall deftly reinforced both federal judicial power and the notion of the Court as a legal body. He did so by refusing to enter into a political dispute on the grounds that Congress could not constitutionally grant to the Court powers not authorized by the Constitution—in this case, the power to issue a writ of mandamus. Underlying Marshall's reasoning is the idea that the Constitution itself is a law to be interpreted by courts, and that courts cannot decide "questions in their nature political," or force coequal branches to perform political or discretionary acts.

The Federalist Congress reduced the number of Justices sitting on the Supreme Court to five by the Judiciary Act of 1801, hoping to prevent incoming President Thomas Jefferson from appointing a Justice when the sixth sitting Justice retired. The 1801 Act also established separate Circuit Court judgeships, obviating the need for Supreme Court Justices to ride circuit. But such riding—and a Supreme Court of six—were quickly reinstituted under President Jefferson, who was suspicious of national judicial power and desirous of keeping Justices in contact with local mores. As the nation expanded, so did the number of circuits and the number of Supreme Court Justices to sit on them. The number of Justices also expanded and contracted due to the politics of the Civil War and its aftermath, first from nine to ten to support President Abraham Lincoln's war policies, then to seven to deprive President Andrew Johnson of several appointments. Since 1869, Congress has set the number of Justices at nine, despite a threat by President Franklin D. Roosevelt to increase the Court's size to suit his political agenda.

Bradley C. S. Watson

See Also

Article I, Section 8, Clause 9 (Inferior Courts)
Article III, Section 1 (Judicial Vesting Clause)

Suggestions for Further Research

David P. Currie, The Constitution in the Supreme Court: The First Hundred Years, 1789–1888 (1985)

1 Julius Goebel, Jr., History of the Supreme Court of the United States: Antecedents and Beginnings to 1801 (1971)

Maeva Marcus et al., eds., The Documentary History of the Supreme Court of the United States, 1789–1800 (1985)

Maeva Marcus, ed., Origins of the Federal Judiciary: Essays on the Judiciary Act of 1789 (1992)

Charles Warren, *New Light on the History of the Federal Judiciary Act of 1789*, 37 Harv. L. Rev. 49 (1923)

Significant Cases

Hayburn's Case, 2 U.S. (2 Dall.) 409 (1792)
Marbury v. Madison, 5 U.S. (1 Cranch) 137 (1803)

Inferior Courts

The judicial Power of the United States shall be vested in one supreme Court, and in such inferior Courts as the Congress may from time to time ordain and establish.

(**Article III, Section 1**)

∾

This clause is discussed in David Engdahl's essay on the Inferior Courts Clause (Article I, Section 8, Clause 9) on page 123.

Good Behavior Clause

The Judges, both of the supreme and inferior Courts, shall hold their Offices during good Behaviour....

(**Article III, Section 1**)

∾

$\mathcal{T}$he Good Behavior Clause of Article III is the foundation stone for the independent judiciary in the American tripartite system of government. In a system designed to protect against tyranny of both the majority and the minority, the clause is a constitutional contract with those men and women who serve in the judiciary—a contract that can be rescinded only through an act of impeachment.

In recent years, the Good Behavior Clause has been the subject of considerable academic debate due to its close association with the impeachment standard in Article II. When the clause was drafted, however, there was little discussion of its meaning. The Good Behavior Clause affirmed the life-tenure guarantee of federal judges—a fundamental requirement for the separation-of-powers doctrine that underlies the Constitution.

Although judges in England were given the protection under a good-behavior provision in the 1701 Act of Settlement, colonial judges were given no such guarantee and served at the whim of the Crown. This deficit led to some of the stated grievances in the Declaration of Independence, including the charge that the king "has made Judges dependent on his Will alone, for the tenure of their offices...." Thus, the Good Behavior Clause was an English import, put to a slightly different American use. As Alexander Hamilton explained in *The Federalist* No. 78:

> In a monarchy [the good behavior standard] is an excellent barrier to the despotism of the prince; in a republic it is a no less excellent barrier to the encroachments and oppressions of the representative body.... [I]t is the best expedient which can be devised in any government to secure a steady, upright, and impartial administration of the laws.

In the records of the Constitutional Convention, it is clear that the Good Behavior Clause was viewed simply as an expression of life tenure as opposed to a distinct standard for removal. The only effort to change this language reflects this understanding. On August 27, 1787, John Dickinson of Delaware moved to add, after the words "good Behaviour," the words "provided that they may be removed by the Executive on the application [by] the Senate and House of Representatives." The Dickinson amendment was voted down by a vote of 7–1. The Dickinson amendment is interesting because it would have effectively created a different standard and system of removal for federal judges. Notably, Gouverneur Morris of Pennsylvania objected that such a change would defeat the intent of creating an independent judiciary. He noted that it would be a "contradiction in terms to say that the Judges hold their offices during good behavior, and yet be removable without a trial." Morris's reference to a "trial" indicates an understanding that such a proceeding is addressed elsewhere in the Constitution. (The debate over the impeachment standard would occur only two weeks later on September 8, 1787.)

This limited exchange hardly answers the question conclusively that good behavior was never intended as a distinct standard for removal. However, it strongly reinforces the view that, had this been the intention of the Framers, a more rigorous debate would have occurred over the language, given the importance of judicial independence to the constitutional scheme.

The meaning of the Good Behavior Clause has periodically been raised in the context of impeachment cases, where it is a natural starting point in any removal effort. In some cases, there is a powerful temptation to look to the Good Behavior Clause as a convenient device to remove a judge who is obnoxious or embarrassing but not necessarily guilty of a "high crime and misdemeanor." Frustration with the latter standard was expressed most famously by Thomas Jefferson when he denounced it as a "bungling way of removing Judges...an impracticable thing—a mere scarecrow." The Good Behavior Clause serves as a cautionary note for Congress that the intent of the Framers was to protect judicial officers from what James Wilson described in the debates as "every gust of faction which might prevail in the two branches of our [government]." The protection against factional attacks on the judiciary is found in the process and standard for impeachment under Article II.

While comparatively small in number, impeached judges have been removed for a variety of misdeeds. The first judge removed was John Pickering in 1804, whose "free and intemperate use of intoxicating liquors" led to a litany of "high misdemeanors." While Pickering's counsel argued an insanity defense to rebut any intentional misdemeanors, the Senate convicted him. In a more recent case, Judge

Alcee Hastings argued that his acquittal on federal charges of conspiracy and bribery should shield him from impeachment in 1989. The House and Senate, however, disagreed. After a formal referral of the case from the Judicial Conference, Hastings was impeached and removed from the bench.

The issue surfaced again during the impeachment and trial of former President William Jefferson Clinton. Some judicial cases clearly established that the alleged criminal conduct by Clinton did fall within the past interpretation given "other high Crimes and Misdemeanors." Though not directly relevant to the charge against an executive officer, it was nonetheless asserted in both the House and the Senate proceedings that the Good Behavior Clause created a lower standard that was neither material nor analogous to the standard governing the removal of a President.

Still, both the language and the weight of historical evidence indicate that the Good Behavior Clause was intended to refer to life tenure rather than to a distinct standard for removal. However, just as the Good Behavior Clause reminds the other branches that the judiciary is truly independent, it also reminds judges that life tenure is not a license for the wanton or the corrupt. It is in this sense both a shield and a sword—an affirmation of judicial independence and a reservation for judicial removal.

Jonathan Turley

See Also

Suggestions for Further Research

Ronald D. Rotunda, *An Essay on the Constitutional Parameters of Federal Impeachment*, 76 Ky. L. Rev. 707 (1988)

Jonathan Turley, *The Executive Function Theory, The Hamilton Affair and Other Constitutional Mythologies*, 77 N.C. L. Rev. 1791 (1999)

Judicial Compensation Clause

The Judges, both of the supreme and inferior Courts…shall, at stated Times, receive for their Services a Compensation, which shall not be diminished during their Continuance in Office.

(ARTICLE III, SECTION 1)

≈

*T*he Judicial Compensation Clause of Article III, Section 1, Clause 1, would appear to be the dream of a textualist interpretation. The clause clearly and unambiguously states that the compensation of federal judges cannot be diminished during their service. Yet this clause has produced some of the most direct confrontations between the judicial and legislative branches.

The Judicial Compensation Clause is literally and conceptually tied to the Good Behavior Clause. (*See* Article III, Section 1.) The guarantee of life tenure would only afford judges independence if they could not be made dependent through their salaries and benefits. This was an issue of particular interest to the Framers because the compensation of colonial judges had been a heated point of contention with the Crown.

The necessity of increases in judicial compensation was the subject of division during the Constitutional Convention. James Madison believed that allowing increases during a judge's service would create a dependence on the legislative branch. He wanted the Judicial Compensation Clause to read "no increase or diminution shall be made" to a judge's salary. On July 18, 1787, the issue came to a head when delegates argued for the prohibition on increases to be struck from the clause. Gouverneur Morris insisted that Congress should be given the ability to raise salaries "as circumstances might require." Other Framers, such as Benjamin Franklin, agreed with Morris, for the Framers had had intimate experience with the effects of inflation during and after the Revolution. Madison lost, and the Framers removed the language banning judicial salary increases.

Unlike the President, whose salary under Article II, Section 1, Clause 7, could neither be decreased nor increased, judges had lifetime appointments and would have grievously suffered from inflation. Thus, it was resolved that Congress could not diminish judicial salaries, but could increase them.

Given the clarity of the language on any direct diminishment of judicial salaries, most of the controversy under this clause concerns forms of indirect or collateral diminishment. In 2001, for example, Justice Antonin Scalia argued in his opinion concurring in part and dissenting in part in *United States v. Hatter* (2001) that the repeal of an exemption of judges from Medicare taxes violated the Judicial Compensation Clause. In that case the majority held that the Judicial Compensation Clause did not forbid Congress from applying a "generally applicable, nondiscriminatory tax" to the salaries of federal judges, whether or not they were appointed before enactment of the tax. However, the Court said, the Judicial Compensation Clause did prevent the government from collecting Social Security taxes, but not Medicare taxes, from federal judges who held office before Congress extended those taxes to federal employees. The Court also concluded that the Judicial Compensation Clause violation, with respect to Social Security taxes, was not cured by subsequent pay increases for federal judges in amounts greater than newly imposed Social Security taxes. In 2002, in *Williams v. United States*, judges challenged the denial of annual cost-of-living adjustments (COLAs) for judicial salaries. The Ethics Reform Act of 1989 protected federal judges against reductions in their compensation due to inflation. However, in 1995, 1996, and 1997, Congress acted to block these salary adjustments for federal judges. A district court judge and three Supreme Court Justices found considerable merit in the arguments of the judges challenging Congress. However, the Court declined to review the case by one vote and let stand an appellate-court opinion that denied the challenge.

There is no question that the Framers were concerned about collateral reductions. Although not known as COLAs in the 1700s, the concept of inflation adjustment was not unfamiliar to the Framers. For example, Alexander Hamilton specifically addressed the effect of "fluctuations in the value of money" on judicial salaries. However, in the language of the Constitution such adjustments were to be left to the discretion of Congress.

Jonathan Turley

See Also
Article III, Section 1 (Good Behavior Clause)

Suggestion for Further Research
Adrian Vermeule, *The Constitutional Rule of Official Compensation*, 102 COLUM. L. REV. 501 (2002)

Significant Cases
United States v. Will, 449 U.S. 200 (1980)
United States v. Hatter, 532 U.S. 557 (2001)
Williams v. United States, 535 U.S. 911 (2002)

A Note on Non-Article III Courts

~

There are at least three categories of adjudication that occur under the federal Constitution. First, under Article III, life-tenured judges exercise the judicial power of the United States as defined in Article III. Supreme Court Justices are the only Article III judges established in the Constitution. All other Article III judgeships are created by statute. The second category is made up of Article I judges and courts. These judges are appointed and confirmed in the same manner as Article III judges and Article II Cabinet secretaries. The four national Article I courts derive their power from the powers given by Article I to the Congress: the payment of money owed by the United States, taxation, regulation of the armed forces, and the governance of the District of Columbia and the territories. Most Article I judges have a statutory equivalent of life tenure and salary protection.

The third category of adjudicators is career employees of the executive branch. This is by far the largest group, consisting of around 4,000 individuals organized into hundreds of categories. Some have special career tenure protection. Others have no tenure protection other than civil service. And some are political appointees with no career protection. Most of these executive-branch adjudicators are subject to review by political appointees, either in departments or by independent regulatory commissions. In turn, the political appointees' decisions can be reviewed in Article I or Article III courts.

Judges in federal territories are created under Congress's Article IV power to govern federal territory, and judges in the District of Columbia are created pursuant to Congress's Article I power to govern the federal capital. These judges have never had life tenure or salary guarantees. William Marbury, for instance, held his commission as a Justice of the Peace for the District of Columbia under a five-year term of office; and judges today in Guam and the Virgin Islands have ten-year terms of office and no constitutional salary guarantees. (Judges in American Samoa have indefinite terms of office.) Although a lower court in 1803 held unconstitutional the absence of salary guarantees for these judges, the Supreme Court, in *American Insurance Co. v. 356 Bales of Cotton* (1828), broadly approved the use of non-Article III tribunals in federally governed territory on the ground that their jurisdiction "is not a part of the judicial power" described in Article III. Accordingly, tribunals in federal territories may determine all kinds of cases, including criminal cases, without necessarily conforming to the requirements of Article III.

Military courts-martial also exercise essentially criminal jurisdiction, though in a limited sphere. The members of courts-martial need not have Article III tenure and salary guarantees; their authority stems instead from the President's Article II executive power as commander in chief and from Congress's Article I powers to "make Rules for the Government and Regulation of the land and naval Forces" and to "provide for...disciplining, the Militia." As the Supreme Court held in 1857 in *Dynes v. Hoover*,

> [t]hese provisions show that Congress has the power to provide for the trial and punishment of military and naval offences in the manner then and now practiced by civilized nations; and that the power to do so is given without any connection between it and the 3d article of the Constitution defining the judicial power....

Sovereign immunity provided the rationale for the first major creation of a non-Article III court under Congress's Article I powers: the Court of Claims. For the first seventy-nine years of the Republic, there was no remedy against the federal government for takings of property, breaches of contract, or governmental torts. Relief against virtually any legal wrong, except imprisonment, was at the whim of the federal government. The only remedy was to implore Congress for a private bill of relief. By the 1850s, over 20,000 such bills were pending. Few were dealt with, and corruption in the passage of some resulted in scandal. In 1855, the Congress created the Court of Claims to deal with the claims that had led to private bills. In 1887, Congress enacted the Tucker Act, creating a life-tenured panel of five judges that heard any claim for money against the United States based on the Constitution, statute, regulation, or contract. Only tort claims were left to congressional discretion. This limitation ended in 1947, when the Congress waived sovereign immunity for torts and gave to Article III courts jurisdiction over tort claims subject to limitations, the most significant of which was the denial of a jury trial.

Modern statutes permit tax-refund actions, tort actions, and some contract or takings claims involving small amounts to be brought in Article III courts, but many statutory waivers of sovereign immunity require suit to be brought in non-Article III tribunals. Because Congress does not have to permit suit at all, it can set conditions on those suits to which it has consented. *United States v. Sherwood* (1941).

Today, the principal non-Article III tribunals that hear such cases include the Court of Federal Claims, which adjudicates claims against the United States founded in contracts, statutes, regulations, or takings; the Tax Court, which allows taxpayers to challenge their tax liability without first paying the tax and then filing for a refund; and the Court of Veterans Appeals, which determines claims by veterans under relevant benefits statutes. The United States Court of Appeals for the Armed Forces was established to provide a civilian court for the review of court-martial criminal sentences.

All of the national Article I courts are subject to Article III appellate review. The Court of Federal Claims and the Court of Veterans Appeals are subject to appellate review by the Court of Appeals for the Federal Circuit. The Tax Court is subject to appellate review by the circuit in which the taxpayer resides. The United States Court of Appeals for the Armed Forces is subject to Supreme Court review. All Article I judges are appointed by the President with Senate confirmation. They are thus officers of the United States, unlike administrative judges. Their salaries are statutorily tied to district or circuit judge salaries. They all have lengthy tenure by statute, as well as senior status systems, which in the case of the Tax Court and Court of Federal Claims are similar to those of Article III judges.

The most sweeping rationale for non-Article III tribunals is the so-called public rights doctrine. This doctrine originated in 1856 in *Murray's Lessee v. Hoboken Land & Improvement Co.*, in which the Supreme Court permitted the government to adjudicate deficiencies against its own tax collectors without full judicial process. "Public rights" in that context meant rights of the public against certain government officials. Modern cases, however, have permitted ordinary administrative agencies to adjudicate even purely private common-law rights on the theory that such rights are "public" whenever they are ancillary to a regulatory scheme. Thus, for example, the Commodity Futures Exchange Commission has been allowed to adjudicate common-law counterclaims resulting from transactions within its enforcement jurisdiction. *Commodity*

Futures Trading Commission v. Schor (1986). This rationale obviously validates as well ordinary agency adjudication in the administration of regulatory programs. The limits, if any, of Congress's power to entrust adjudication to non-Article III decision-makers is uncertain. Nor is it clear to what extent decisions of non-Article III tribunals must be subject to appellate review in Article III courts, although Congress by statute has generally made such review available.

As a matter of original understanding, executive adjudication may seem problematic, but not all adjudication (understood as the application of legal standards to particular facts) requires an exercise of the judicial power. Many exercises of Article II "executive Power" are functionally indistinguishable from exercises of the "judicial Power," which is not surprising given the close historical and conceptual connections between executive and judicial power. So long as a particular exercise of power, such as a court-martial or a benefit determination, meets the constitutional definition of "executive Power," it need not be performed by an Article III judge, even if could be performed by such a judge. There can be areas of overlap between the executive and judicial powers, which gives Congress a measure of freedom as to which department to charge with particular adjudicative tasks. The task of figuring out which adjudicative functions, if any, must be performed only by Article III courts has perplexed originalists and nonoriginalists alike for more than two centuries.

Loren Smith and Gary Lawson

Suggestions for Further Research

Richard H. Fallon, Jr., *Of Legislative Courts, Administrative Agencies, and Article III*, 101 Harv. L. Rev. 915 (1988)

Gary Lawson & Guy Seidman, The Constitution of Empire: Territorial Expansion and the American Legal History, 139–150 (2004)

Martin H. Redish, *Legislative Courts, Administrative Agencies, and the Northern Pipeline Decision*, 1983 Duke L.J. 197 (1983)

Craig A. Stern, *What's a Constitution Among Friends?—Unbalancing Article III*, 146 U. Penn. L. Rev. 1043 (1998)

Significant Cases

United States v. More, 7 U.S. (3 Cranch) 159 (1805)

American Insurance Co. v. 356 Bales of Cotton, 26 U.S. (1 Pet.) 511 (1828)

Murray's Lessee v. Hoboken Land & Improvement Co., 59 U.S. (18 How.) 272 (1856)

Dynes v. Hoover, 61 U.S. (20 How.) 65 (1857)

United States v. Sherwood, 312 U.S. 584 (1941)

Palmore v. United States, 411 U.S. 389 (1973)

Northern Pipeline Construction Co. v. Marathon Pipe Line Co., 458 U.S. 50 (1982)

Commodity Futures Trading Commission v. Schor, 478 U.S. 833 (1986)

Judicial Power

The judicial Power shall extend to all Cases, in Law and Equity, arising under this Constitution, the Laws of the United States....
(Article III, Section 2, Clause 1)

~

*A*rticle III, Section 2, delineates the scope of the federal judicial power by listing nine kinds of "Cases" and "Controversies" to which the "judicial Power" of the United States may extend. By far the most important is the category encompassing "all Cases, in Law and Equity, arising under this Constitution, the Laws of the United States, and Treaties made, or which shall be made, under their Authority." This is often referred to as the "federal question" jurisdiction, and, although that is something of a misnomer, it is a convenient label.

From the beginning, the Framers intended the scope of the jurisdiction to be broad. The federal question jurisdiction made its first appearance at the Constitutional Convention in the Virginia Plan, which would have authorized federal courts to hear "questions which may involve the national peace and harmony." By the time the Committee of Detail began its work, the Convention had added to this language a grant of jurisdiction over "Cases arising under the Laws passed by the general Legislature." When the Committee of Detail reported to the Convention, the reference to "national peace and harmony" had disappeared, but the "arising under" language remained.

There was little discussion of this provision at the Convention. In the course of a single day, the Convention deleted the reference to "the general Legislature" and extended the judicial power to cases arising under the Constitution and treaties in addition to the cases arising under federal laws. When the Committee of Style reported to the Convention in September, the provision read substantially as it does today: the federal judicial power extends "to all cases, both in law and equity, arising under this constitution, the laws of the United States, and treaties made, or which shall be made, under their authority."

The potential breadth of this language prompted criticism by opponents of the proposed constitution during the debates over ratification in the key state of Virginia. George Mason, for example, could find no "limitation whatsoever, with respect to the nature or jurisdiction of [the federal] courts." James Madison, a supporter of ratification, did not dispute this assertion; rather, he asserted that "the judicial power [of the national government] should correspond with the legislative."

When does a case "arise under" federal law, so that it falls within the judicial power of the United States? The authoritative answer to this question is found largely in two decisions by Chief Justice John Marshall in the early years of the Republic.

The better-known of the two decisions is *Osborn v. Bank of the United States* (1824). Marshall's delineation of the constitutional scope of the jurisdictional grant proceeds in two steps. First, he declares that a "question" is "federal" if "the title or right set up by the party may be defeated by one construction of the Constitution or law of the United States, and sustained by the opposite construction, provided the facts necessary to support the action be made out."

In other words, a federal question is a question whose answer depends in some way on federal law. Marshall then says that a case "arises under" the Constitution or laws of the United States if a federal question "forms an ingredient of the original cause"—that is, is an element of the plaintiff's claim.

The breadth of this definition is made clear by a companion case in which the Court upheld federal jurisdiction over a suit by the Bank of the United States to recover on negotiable notes issued by a state bank. *Bank of the United States v. Planters' Bank of Georgia* (1824). The liability of the defendant bank would appear to have depended solely on state law. How, then, could Marshall have concluded that a federal question formed an element of the "original cause"? Marshall's answer is that questions like the bank's capacity to sue necessarily exist in every case brought by the bank, even though the particular proposition is not questioned. *Osborn* thus establishes that, so long as a proposition of federal law is a *logical antecedent* of the plaintiff's claim, it is sufficient as a constitutional matter to support federal judicial power over the case.

Three years before *Osborn*, in *Cohens v. Virginia* (1821), the Court considered a challenge to its own authority to exercise appellate jurisdiction over a case originating in state court. The defendants, convicted of a crime under state law, invoked what we would today call a defense of preemption: they "claimed the protection of an act of Congress." They also asserted that the Supreme Court could consider their appeal because it was a case "arising under" federal law. The state of Virginia disagreed, taking the position that that a case could "arise under" the federal constitution or federal law only if the constitution or law was the basis for the claim of the party who had initiated the lawsuit.

The state's interpretation is a plausible reading of the language of Article III, but the Supreme Court rejected it as "too narrow." The Court said that cases are defined by the rights of *both parties*, and a case "may truly be said to arise under the constitution or law of the United States whenever its correct decision depends on the construction of either." The *Cohens* definition thus supports the Supreme Court's jurisdiction to hear appeals from state courts when those courts have decided federal questions.

Capacious though they are, neither the *Osborn* definition nor the one in *Cohens* would necessarily cover all of the cases in which Congress has authorized the *removal* of actions from state to federal court. But in a series of nineteenth-century decisions the Court made plain that Article III authorizes removal of any case in which a defense under federal law has been invoked, even though the federal issue may prove not to be dispositive.

The Supreme Court's decisions have thus established that Congress can authorize federal courts to hear cases in which a federal question is (1) a logical antecedent of the plaintiff's claim (whether or not contested); or (2) the basis of a defense actually raised (even though it may not be dispositive); or (3) the basis of the decision actually made (typically by a state court). The area of uncertainty involves Congress's power to authorize jurisdiction over cases in which a federal question is an element neither of the original cause nor of the defense, but in which a *litigant* is a member of a class that Congress seeks to protect (e.g., federal employees sued in state court) or the *area* is one in which Congress has taken an interest under an Article I grant of power (e.g., consumer protection or nuclear accidents).

Until recently, Supreme Court case law cast little doubt on the breadth of Congress's authority to vest federal question jurisdiction in federal courts. However, the decision in *Mesa v. California* (1989) makes clear that the power is not unlimited. In *Mesa*, the Court construed the statute that allows removal to federal court of suits brought against federal officers for acts done under color of their federal office. The Court held that the statute allows removal only if the officer alleges a federal defense to the state-law claim. The Court explained that if the statute were construed to allow grant of district-court jurisdiction simply because a federal officer is a defendant, it would "necessarily present grave constitutional problems." The opinion thus implies that to support "arising under" jurisdiction, a federal question must be present somewhere in the case. However, the Court did not rule out the possibility that, under some circumstances, Congress might be able to vest "arising under" jurisdiction to protect federal interests even in the absence of a federal question.

It is important to emphasize that the broad construction of the "arising under" language of Article III has no bearing on the scope of the statutory grant of federal question jurisdiction, even though the statute uses language identical to that of the Constitution. The Court has read the statutory jurisdiction not to extend as far as it could under the Constitution. Full discussion is beyond the scope of this encyclopedia; it is sufficient to note that neither a federal defense (as in *Cohens*) nor a "logical antecedent" provides a basis for district court jurisdiction under 28 U.S.C. § 1331. Rather, the federal question must be, at a minimum, a necessary element of a "well pleaded complaint"—the plaintiff's claim for relief.

Finally, it should be made clear that federal jurisdiction extends to cases, not issues. When a federal court has jurisdiction over a case that arises under federal law, the jurisdiction extends to the whole case, and the court will often have power to consider other issues in the case whether state or federal.

Arthur Hellman

See Also

Article III, Section 2

Suggestions for Further Research

Ray Forrester, *The Nature of a "Federal Question,"* 16 TULANE L. REV. 362 (1942)

Paul Mishkin, *The Federal "Question" in the District Courts*, 53 COLUM. L. REV. 157 (1953)

G. EDWARD WHITE, THE MARSHALL COURT AND CULTURAL CHANGE 1814–1835, CH. VIII (Oxford 1991)

Significant Cases

Cohens v. Virginia, 19 U.S. (6 Wheat.) 264 (1821)

Bank of the United States v. Planters' Bank of Georgia, 22 U.S. (9 Wheat.) 904 (1824)

Osborn v. Bank of the United States, 22 U.S. (9 Wheat.) 738 (1824)

Mesa v. California, 489 U.S. 121 (1989)

Treaties

The judicial Power shall extend to all Cases, in Law and Equity, arising under this Constitution, the Laws of the United States, and Treaties made, or which shall be made, under their Authority....

(ARTICLE III, SECTION 2, CLAUSE 1)

~

*T*hroughout the Constitutional Convention, the Framers consistently expressed the desire that a national judiciary have jurisdiction over legal issues arising from the nation's international rights and obligations. The proposition was part of both the Virginia and New Jersey Plans, and the delegates put forward numerous formulations throughout the Convention. They wanted, in Edmund Randolph's words, to protect "the security of foreigners" and "the harmony of states and the citizens thereof." It was not, however, until August 27, while the delegates were refining the Committee of Detail's jurisdictional language, that John Rutledge from South Carolina rose and moved to include the words "and treaties made or which shall be made under their authority" after the "United States" in the Treaties Clause of what would become Article III. The language succinctly granted the federal judiciary jurisdiction over all treaties entered into by the United States from the moment of its independence. The proposal was unanimously approved. During ratification, Alexander Hamilton explained the provision in *The Federalist* No. 80, stating that the federal judicial authority should extend "to all those [cases] which involve the peace of the confederacy, whether they relate to the intercourse between the United States and foreign nations, or to that between the States themselves," including treaties.

In the Judiciary Act of 1789, the First Congress granted limited jurisdiction to the newly created federal court system, and limited rights of appeal. The Supreme Court, however, refused to offer advisory opinions on the construction of treaties when asked to do so by President George Washington in 1793. It had similarly refused a request by Congress for it to review veterans' pension claims, on the grounds that it was not a judicial function and was contrary to the separation of powers.

The Court would only hear cases properly brought before it. In Section 25 of the Judiciary Act, Congress allowed appeals to the Supreme Court from the highest state court's "decisions against the validity of a...treaty,...or against any title, right, privilege, or exemption set up or claimed under any...treaty." In *Owings v. Norwood's Lessee* (1809), Chief Justice John Marshall explained the scope of the Court's jurisdiction under the Treaties Clause:

The reason for inserting that clause in the constitution was, that all persons who have real claims under a treaty should have their causes decided by the national tribunals. It was to avoid the apprehension as well as the danger of state prejudices....Each treaty stipulates something respecting the citizens of the two nations, and gives them rights. Whenever a right grows out of, or is protected by, a treaty, it is sanctioned against all the laws and judicial decisions of the States; and whoever may have this right, it is to be protected. But if the person's title is not affected by the treaty, if he claims nothing under a treaty, his title cannot be protected by the treaty.

In *Martin v. Hunter's Lessee* (1816), Justice Story noted that the claimant must have relied on a treaty to his detriment and that the error must be evident from the record. However, Story declared that the record need not refer to the disputed interpretation of a treaty in specific terms, for "[t]he treaty of peace was not necessary to have been stated, for it was the supreme law of the law, of which all courts must take notice." On the other hand, the Supreme

Court later noted that if neither the state nor the claimant disputes the claimant's rights under a treaty, then the Supreme Court has no jurisdiction under the Judiciary Act to review the case. *Gill v. Oliver's Executors* (1850).

Over its history, the Court has crafted a number of prudential rules in its interpretation of treaties. It will rely on clarifications, interpretations, and understandings of a treaty formulated by the executive branch. The courts will not infer an obligation from a treaty that has not been articulated in clear terms. *Society for the Propagation of the Gospel in Foreign Parts v. New Haven* (1823). They will follow the evident meaning of the text; and "where a provision of a treaty fairly admits of two constructions, one restricting, the other enlarging, rights which may be claimed under it, the more liberal interpretation is to be preferred." *Bacardi Corp. of America v. Domenech* (1940). Under the political-question doctrine, the courts will not determine whether a treaty obligation with another nation has been broken. *Clark v. Allen* (1947).

Traditionally, the courts were less likely to accord the legislative branches a say in the interpretation of a treaty. *Jones v. Meehan* (1899). The text would govern, *Maximov v. United States* (1963), unless an ambiguity caused recourse to ratification history for clarification. *See Air France v. Saks* (1985). However, in *Sumitomo Shoji America, Inc. v. Avagliano* (1982), the Court suggested that the parties' intent would control even over the text, a proposition Justice Antonin Scalia vigorously objected to in *United States v. Stuart* (1989), where the majority limited its investigation of treaty intent to Senate floor debates. Scalia condemned the "unprecedented" use of such materials: "The question before us in a treaty case is what the two or more sovereigns agreed to, rather than what a single one of them, or the legislature of a single one of them, thought it agreed to."

Finally, a court will only recognize the legal validity of a treaty if it has been "executed" into federal law. "Self-executing treaties" become part of the law of the United States directly, but the courts will not enforce "non-self-executing treaties" until they are carried into law by an act of Congress. (*See* Article VI, Clause 2). A federal statute and a properly executed treaty have equal status in law, the latter in time taking precedence. Therefore, if Congress passes a law that contradicts earlier treaty obligations of the United States, the courts will enforce the law over the treaty. In order to avoid such a conflict, however, the courts will construe a law not to be in conflict with extant treaty obligations if such a construction is at all reasonable.

The jurisdictional statute regulating treaty review is currently 28 U.S.C. § 1257. It allows appeal by writ of certiorari to the Supreme Court if the validity of a treaty or of a state statute under a treaty is questioned, or if "any right, privilege, or immunity is specially set up or claimed" under a treaty. Furthermore, under 28 U.S.C. § 1331 "district courts shall have original jurisdiction of all civil actions arising under... treaties of the United States." District courts may also take jurisdiction over cases brought in state court involving treaties under the complicated rules of pendent jurisdiction.

Dennis W. Arrow

See Also

Article I, Section 10, Clause 1 (State Treaties)
Article II, Section 2, Clause 2 (Treaty Clause)
Article VI, Clause 2 (Supremacy Clause)

Suggestions for Further Research

Martin S. Flaherty, *History Right? Historical Scholarship, Original Understanding, and Treaties as "Supreme Law of the Land,"* 99 Colum. L. Rev. 2095 (1999)

John Norton Moore, *Treaty Interpretation, the Constitution and the Rule of Law*, 42 Va. J. Int'l. L. 163 (2001)

Michael P. Van Alstine, *The Judicial Power and Treaty Delegation*, 90 Cal. L. Rev. 1305 (2002)

John C. Yoo, *Globalism and the Constitution: Treaties, Non-Self-Execution, and the Original Understanding*, 99 Colum. L. Rev. 2218 (1999)

John C. Yoo, *Treaty Interpretation and the False Sirens of Delegation*, 90 Cal. L. Rev. 1305 (2002)

Significant Cases

Owings v. Norwood's Lessee, 9 U.S. (5 Cranch) 344 (1809)

Smith v. Maryland, 10 U.S. (6 Cranch) 286 (1810)

Martin v. Hunter's Lessee, 14 U.S. (1 Wheat.) 304 (1816)

Society for the Propagation of the Gospel in Foreign Parts v. New Haven, 21 U.S. (8 Wheat.) 464 (1823)

United States v. Arredondo, 31 U.S. (6 Pet.) 691 (1832)

Gill v. Oliver's Executors, 52 U.S. (11 How.) 529 (1850)

Geofroy v. Riggs, 133 U.S. 258 (1890)

New York Indians v. United States, 170 U.S. 1 (1898)

Jones v. Meehan, 175 U.S. 1 (1899)

Bacardi Corp. of America v. Domenech, 311 U.S. 150 (1940)

Clark v. Allen, 331 U.S. 503 (1947)

Maximov v. United States, 373 U.S. 49, 54 (1963)

Sumitomo Shoji America, Inc. v. Avagliano, 457 U.S. 176 (1982)

Air France v. Saks, 470 U.S. 392 (1985)

United States v. Stuart, 489 U.S. 353 (1989)

Ambassadors

The judicial Power shall extend to ...all Cases affecting Ambassadors, other public Ministers and Consuls....

(**ARTICLE III, SECTION 2, CLAUSE 1**)

~

*A*t the Constitutional Convention, William Paterson put forward the New Jersey Plan designed to counter the more nationalist plan set out by Virginia. Despite its focus on the rights of the states, Paterson's plan nonetheless acknowledged the necessity of national competency and supremacy in a number of areas. It proposed to authorize, for example, the federal judiciary to hear appeals from state courts in "all cases touching the rights of Ambassadors." The provision excited no discussion, and the Committee of Detail penned the final version, including placing the subject within the original jurisdiction of the Supreme Court. (*See* Article III, Section 2, Clause 2.)

All, including the Anti-Federalist Brutus, seemed to agree with the sentiments of Alexander Hamilton that placing the jurisdiction of cases dealing with foreign ministers had "an evident connection with the preservation of the national peace." *The Federalist* No. 80. Justice Joseph Story in his *Commentaries on the Constitution of the United States* thought that every question involving the "rights, powers, duties, and privileges" of public ministers was "so intimately connected with the public peace, and policy, and diplomacy of the nation, and touches the dignity and interest of the sovereigns of the ministers connected so deeply, that it would be unsafe, that they should be submitted to any other, then the highest judicature of the nation."

In *Osborn v. Bank of the United States* (1824), the Supreme Court declared that the foreign diplomat need not be a party to the case to trigger federal jurisdiction, although original jurisdiction is not mandated when the diplomat is merely a victim of a crime. *United States v. Ortega* (1826). Federal jurisdiction under this clause does not apply to United States diplomats, *Ex parte Gruber* (1925), nor to divorce suits involving foreign diplomats, *Ohio ex rel. Popovici v. Agler* (1930), nor to suits involving former foreign diplomatic agents or those whose tours of duty in the United States have ended. *Farnsworth v. Sanford* (1940). Furthermore, although the Ambassador Clause speaks of "Ambassadors, other public Ministers and Consuls," under modern practice consuls are not normally regarded as diplomatic agents and hence are not subject to this provision. Finally, the fact that the Constitution lodges these cases in the federal judiciary does not preclude the foreign diplomatic agent from pleading sovereign immunity.

David F. Forte

See Also

Article III, Section 2, Clause 2 (Appellate Jurisdiction Clause)

Significant Cases

Osborn v. Bank of the United States, 22 U.S. (9 Wheat.) 67 (1824)

United States v. Ortega, 24 U.S. (11 Wheat.) 67 (1826)

Ex parte Gruber, 269 U.S. 302 (1925)

Ohio *ex rel.* Popovici v. Agler, 280 U.S. 379 (1930)

Farnsworth v. Sanford, 115 F.2d 375 (5th Cir. 1940), *cert. denied*, 313 U.S. 586 (1940)

Admiralty

The judicial Power shall extend to ...all Cases of admiralty and maritime Jurisdiction....
(ARTICLE III, SECTION 2, CLAUSE 1)

~

*I*n England, a long-established separate system of courts, beginning with Edward III, dealt with maritime and admiralty issues. According to Sir William Blackstone in *Commentaries on the Laws of England*, these courts had jurisdiction "to determine all maritime injuries, arising upon the seas, or in parts out of the reach of the common law." During the Revolution, state prize courts often violated international law by condemning prizes belonging to sister states, or nations that were neutral or even allies of the United States. Consequently, after Independence, both the Articles of Confederation and the Constitution gave the national government exclusive admiralty and maritime jurisdiction. In Philadelphia, the only debate among the Framers of the Constitution was whether to lodge admiralty questions in a separate court or, as they finally decided, in the federal judiciary. There was unanimity, even among the Anti-Federalists, that this power should be national.

Congress, under the Judiciary Act of 1789, gave the district courts exclusive jurisdiction over admiralty and maritime cases, now codified in 28 U.S.C. § 1333. The clause also accords exclusive federal jurisdiction to captures and prize cases, codified in 28 U.S.C. § 1333(2). *See Glass v. The Sloop Betsey* (1794); *The Paquete Habana* (1900). Further, Congress possesses broad power to alter traditional admiralty and maritime rules, though it cannot delegate such power to the states. *Knickerbocker Ice Co. v. Stewart* (1920).

According to Justice Joseph Story in his *Commentaries on the Constitution of the United States*, admiralty and maritime jurisdiction "extends to all acts and torts done upon the high seas, and within the ebb and flow of the sea, and to all maritime contracts, that is to all contracts touching trade, navigation, or business upon the sea, or the waters of the sea within the ebb and flow of the tide." *See DeLovio v. Boit* (1815); *United States v. Wiltberger* (1820); *Waring v. Clarke* (1847). In 1845, breaking from English precedent, Congress extended admiralty jurisdiction to include inland navigable lakes and rivers. In 1948, Congress further expanded jurisdiction to "include all cases of damage or injury, to person or property, caused by a vessel on navigable water, notwithstanding that such damage or injury be done or consummated on land." At first, the Court, in *Gutierrez v. Waterman Steamship Corp.* (1963), held that this act covered injuries that occur to a person while on a dock loading or unloading a vessel; but in *Victory Carriers, Inc. v. Law* (1971), the Court limited *Gutierrez* to situations where the injury is "caused by appurtenance of a ship."

In addition to tort claims under admiralty law, the Court has dealt with federal jurisdiction over maritime contracts. In Justice Joseph Story's lengthy and influential opinion in *DeLovio*, the Court stated that maritime jurisdiction covers "all contracts, (wheresoever they may be made or executed, or whatsoever may be the form of the stipulations) which relate to the navigation, business, or commerce of the sea." In that case, the Court broke new ground by extending maritime jurisdiction to maritime insurance contracts. Whether a contract is "purely maritime" has been a cornerstone of maritime jurisdiction. For example, in *People's Ferry Co. v. Beers* (1858), the Court held that a construction contract to build a ship, as opposed to a repair contract, was not covered under maritime jurisdiction.

Generally, the federal judiciary has exclusive jurisdiction over admiralty and maritime issues. The Judiciary Act of 1789, however, created an exception known as the savings clause, which states: "saving to suitors, in all cases, the right of a common law remedy, where the common law is competent to give it." It is currently codified in 28 U.S.C. § 1333(1). In *Waring v. Clarke*, the

Court stated that the purpose behind the savings clause was to preserve a right to trial by jury whenever possible (admiralty and maritime cases typically involve bench trials). In *The Moses Taylor* (1866), the Court made the distinction that federal courts have exclusive jurisdiction over *in rem* suits and concurrent jurisdiction with the states over *in personam* suits insofar as *in personam* jurisdiction is part of the state's traditional common-law jurisdiction. A state even has jurisdiction over an *in rem* proceeding if the state is seeking the common-law remedy of forfeiture. *C. J. Hendry Co. v. Moore* (1943).

A state's concurrent jurisdiction over *in personam* suits is not without limits, however. The scope of those limits has been a highly disputed subject in the Supreme Court's jurisprudence. For many decades, the Supreme Court held, for example, that state workers'-compensation laws as applied to maritime injuries invaded the exclusive jurisdiction of Congress. *Southern Pacific Co. v. Jensen* (1917). Nor would the Court permit Congress to delegate such authority to the states. *Knickerbocker Ice Co. v. Stewart* (1920). Finally, Congress itself passed the Longshoremen's and Harbor Workers' Compensation Act in 1927, but reserved application of the act only after state law had been held to be inapplicable. The post-1938 Court upheld the act. *Parker v. Motor Boat Sales, Inc.* (1941). But Congress's attempt to protect the concurrent jurisdiction of the states was dealt a blow by the Court in *Calbeck v. Travelers Insurance Co.* (1962). Justice William J. Brennan, Jr., writing for the majority, essentially deleted recourse to state jurisdiction from the statute. As a result, the federal statute now applies regardless of whether an appropriate state remedy is available. Justices Potter Stewart and John M. Harlan dissented on the ground that the majority was rewriting the clear language and undoing the legislative history of the statute. Since that time, both Congress and the Court have continued to try to define the appropriate limits to state jurisdiction in statutes and cases. *See United States v. Locke* (2000); *Lewis v. Lewis & Clark Marine, Inc.* (2001).

Prior to 1875, the Supreme Court was able to exercise appellate review over both the facts

and the law in admiralty and maritime suits. In fact, Justice Joseph Story has argued that the real goal of the controversial Appellate Jurisdiction Clause (Article III, Section 2, Clause 2) "was to retain the power of reviewing the fact, as well as the law, in cases of admiralty and maritime jurisdiction." In an effort to relieve the Supreme Court of a rather cumbersome caseload, Congress limited appellate review over admiralty and maritime disputes to issues of law.

David F. Forte

See Also

Article III, Section 2, Clause 2 (Appellate Jurisdiction Clause)

Amendment XI (Suits Against a State)

Suggestions for Further Research

David J. Bederman, *Admiralty and the Eleventh Amendment*, 72 Notre Dame L. Rev. 935 (1997)

Henry J. Bourguignon, *The First Federal Court: The Federal Appellate Prize Court of the American Revolution, 1775-1787* (1977)

William R. Casto, *The Origins of Federal Admiralty Jurisdiction in an Age of Privateers, Smugglers, and Pirates*, 37 Am. J. Legal Hist. 117 (1993)

Jonathan M. Gutoff, *Original Understandings and the Private Law Origins of the Federal Admiralty Jurisdiction: A Reply to Professor Casto*, 30 J. Mar. L. & Com. 361 (1999)

Matthew J. Harrington, *The Legacy of the Colonial Vice-Admiralty Courts*, 26 J. Mar. L. & Com. 581 (1995) and 27 J. Mar. L. & Com. 323 (1996)

Gerald J. Mangone, United States Admiralty Law (1997)

Thomas J. Schoenbaum, Admiralty and Maritime Law (2004)

Significant Cases

Chisholm v. Georgia, 2 U.S. (2 Dall.) 419 (1793)

Glass v. The Sloop Betsey, 3 U.S. (3 Dall.) 6 (1794)

United States v. McGill, 4 U.S. (4 Dall.) 426 (C.C.D. Pa. 1806)

De Lovio v. Boit, 7 F. Cas. 418 (C.C.D. Mass. 1815) (No. 3776)

United States v. Wiltberger, 18 U.S. (5 Wheat.) 76 (1820)

Waring v. Clarke, 46 U.S. (6 How.) 441 (1847)

New Jersey Steam Nav. Co. v. Merchants' Bank of Boston, 47 U.S. (6 How.) 344 (1848)

Genesee Chief v. Fitzhugh, 53 U.S. (12 How.) 443 (1852)

People's Ferry Co. v. Beers, 61 U.S. (20 How.) 393 (1858)

The Moses Taylor, 71 U.S. (4 Wall.) 411 (1866)

The Daniel Ball, 77 U.S. (10 Wall.) 557 (1870)

The Lottawanna, 88 U.S. (21 Wall.) 558 (1874)

Ex parte Easton, 95 U.S. 68 (1877)

The Abbotsford, 98 U.S. 440 (1878)

The Paquete Habana, 175 U.S. 677 (1900)

Martin v. West, 222 U.S. 191 (1911)

Southern Pacific Co. v. Jensen, 244 U.S. 205 (1917)

North Pacific Steamship Co. v. Hall Bros. Marine Railway & Shipbuilding Co., 249 U.S. 119 (1919)

Knickerbocker Ice Co. v. Stewart, 253 U.S. 149 (1920)

Western Fuel Co. v. Garcia, 257 U.S. 233 (1921)

Grant Smith-Porter Ship Co. v. Rohde, 257 U.S. 469 (1922)

Panama R. Co. v. Johnson, 264 U.S. 375 (1924)

Red Cross Line v. Atlantic Fruit Co., 264 U.S. 109 (1924)

Washington v. W. C. Dawson & Co., 264 U.S. 219 (1924)

Langnes v. Green, 282 U.S. 532 (1931)

Marine Transit Corp. v. Dreyfus, 284 U.S. 263 (1932)

United States v. Flores, 289 U.S. 137 (1933)

Parker v. Motor Boat Sales, Inc., 314 U.S. 244 (1941)

Davis v. Department of Labor & Industries, 317 U.S. 249 (1942)

C. J. Hendry Co. v. Moore, 318 U.S. 133 (1943)

O'Donnell v. Great Lakes Dredge & Dock Co., 318 U.S. 36 (1943)

Madruga v. Superior Court of California, 346 U.S. 556 (1954)

Romero v. International Terminal Operating Co., 358 U.S. 354 (1959)

Kossick v. United Fruit Co., 365 U.S. 731 (1961)

Calbeck v. Travelers Insurance Co., 370 U.S. 114 (1962)

Gutierrez v. Waterman Steamship Corp., 373 U.S. 206 (1963)

Nacirema Operating Co. v. Johnson, 396 U.S. 212 (1969)

Victory Carriers, Inc. v. Law, 404 U.S. 202 (1971)

Executive Jet Aviation, Inc. v. Cleveland, 409 U.S. 249 (1972)

Sun Ship v. Pennsylvania, 447 U.S. 715 (1980)

Foremost Insurance Co. v. Richardson, 457 U.S. 668 (1982)

Sisson v. Ruby, 497 U.S. 358 (1990)

Exxon Corp. v. Central Gulf Lines, 500 U.S. 603 (1991)

American Dredging Co. v. Miller, 510 U.S. 443 (1994)

Jerome B. Grubart, Inc. v. Great Lakes Dredge & Dock Co., 513 U.S. 527 (1995)

United States v. Locke, 529 U.S. 89 (2000)

Lewis v. Lewis & Clark Marine, Inc., 531 U.S. 438 (2001)

Federal Party

The judicial Power shall extend to ...Controversies to which the United States shall be a Party....
(ARTICLE III, SECTION 2, CLAUSE 1)

∼

*A*mong the numerous jurisdictional grants to the new federal court system, one of the least controversial was the proposition that the new federal courts should have jurisdiction over any case to which the new United States was a party. The provision for jurisdiction over cases to which the United States is a party was a comparatively late addition to the Constitution, adopted long after the Committee of Detail had completed its work. It seemed to reflect nothing more than a correction of an oversight. As Alexander Hamilton said of this jurisdictional grant: "any other plan would be contrary to reason." *The Federalist* No. 80. Even the Constitution's most vigorous opponents in the Anti-Federalist camp acknowledged the logic of this position. Later, Chief Justice John Jay noted in *Calder v. Bull* (1798) that federal jurisdiction over cases involving the United States was necessary "because in cases in which the whole people are interested, it would not be equal, or wise, to let any one state decide, and measure out the justice due others."

Today, the interesting legal questions about this clause involve determinations of precisely what entity is the "United States" and when the United States has consented to be a party to a lawsuit.

The text of the Federal Party Clause, of course, allows for jurisdiction when the United

States acts as a plaintiff, but that circumstance (in which the affirmative act of filing a suit is, effectively, also a consent to the jurisdiction of the court) is far less problematic or controversial than when the United States has been named as a party defendant. The Supreme Court early on held that the United States, as a legal entity, had an inherent right to bring suit without authorization from Congress, *Dugan v. United States* (1818), although the Judiciary Act of 1789 channeled civil suits brought by the United States to federal district courts.

The more difficult issue relates to the United States's status as a defendant in a suit. The clause, while providing for federal jurisdiction over suits to which the United States is a party, does not specify the situations in which such suits are in fact permitted. When the United States is named as a defendant, the general rule has become that, absent a waiver, sovereign immunity shields the federal government and its agencies from suit. As Alexander Hamilton said: "It is inherent in the nature of sovereignty not to be amenable to the suit of an individual without its consent." *The Federalist* No. 81. Early Supreme Courts cases affirmed the doctrine. *Cohens v. Virginia* (1821); *United States v. Clarke* (1834). Consent can only be manifested when Congress passes a statute expressly waiving the United States's claim of sovereign immunity from suit for a particular case or class of cases.

Many examples of these waivers exist in the law today. Agencies, such as the Federal Deposit Insurance Corporation, are often created with the power to "sue or be sued." And the United States frequently consents to subject itself to generally applicable laws, as it has done in permitting itself to be sued by private parties for alleged environmental violations. A most frequent source of suits against the United States, however, is the Federal Tort Claims Act, which waives the sovereign immunity of the United States for certain torts committed by federal employees "under circumstances where the United States, if a private person, would be liable to the claimant in accordance with the law of the place where the act or omission occurred." This provision captures a large host of conduct, ranging from medical malpractice of Army doctors to traffic accidents of federal employees. Finally, in 1976, an amendment to the Administrative Procedure Act waived sovereign immunity for suits against the United States that do not involve monetary damages. As a result of these various waivers, the Federal Party Clause has become a significant source of litigation in the federal courts.

Finally, it bears noting that the United States, as a distinct entity, may in many circumstances be distinguished from either federal officers acting in their official capacity or distinct federal entities and instrumentalities. The law regarding this distinction is complex. In some instances, for example, the United States may be substituted as a party for a federal official sued in his official capacity. In that situation the suit becomes grounded in the constitutional grant of jurisdiction over "controversies to which the United States is a party." In other cases, the official or the instrumentality stands apart from the United States, and suits in federal court must rely on different jurisdictional grants, such as the statutory grant of federal-question jurisdiction.

Paul Rosenzweig

Significant Cases

Calder v. Bull, 3 U.S. (3 Dall.) 386 (1798)

Dugan v. United States, 16 U.S. (3 Wheat.) 172 (1818)

Cohens v. Virginia, 19 U.S. (6 Wheat.) 264 (1821)

United States v. Clarke, 33 U.S. (8 Pet.) 436, 444 (1834)

Federal Housing Administration v. Burr, 309 U.S. 244 (1940)

United States v. Sherwood, 312 U.S. 584 (1941)

Interstate Disputes

The judicial Power shall extend to . . . Controversies between two or more States. . . .
(ARTICLE III, SECTION 2, CLAUSE 1)

∼

*T*hough of modest jurisprudential importance today, the clause providing for federal-court jurisdiction over disputes between two states is emblematic of the issues at the heart of the constitutional Founding. The movement to adopt a Constitution grew out of substantial dissatisfaction with the operation of the Articles of Confederation, including the Confederation's difficulty in settling disputes between states over economic policies and territorial claims. Establishing federal jurisdiction to resolve such disputes reflects the political sea change involved in the movement from a confederation to a federal union.

Under Article IX of the Articles of Confederation, disputes between the states (which mostly involved the settlement of land claims to the west) were settled in a convoluted manner: Congress would name thirty-nine individuals (three from each state) as potential commissioners to resolve the dispute. The opposing states would then each alternately strike names from the list until thirteen names remained, from which seven or nine names would be drawn by lot. Those selected were to determine the dispute. This process had some success. Article IX courts, advancing the conception that the states could be subjected to a higher authority, resolved a few land disputes between states. However, as might be imagined, this cumbersome process often proved to be an impediment to dispute resolution.

Initially, the Committee of Detail retained this method for adjudicating interstate disputes in the draft of the Constitution. After further consideration, the Framers provided for federal-court jurisdiction over interstate disputes generally, but retained the Confederation Article IX method for resolving territorial and jurisdictional questions. It was not until rather late in the process, on August 24, that the Convention chose to adopt the simpler system of federal-court jurisdiction for arbitrating all disputes between two or more states. As John Rutledge of South Carolina said in making the proposal, the provision of a national judiciary made the Article IX-type provisions for resolving interstate disputes "unnecessary."

As the Supreme Court noted in the modern case of *New York v. United States* (1992), "In the end, the Convention opted for a Constitution in which Congress would exercise its legislative authority directly over individuals rather than over States." Nonetheless, providing for federal jurisdiction to monitor disputes *between* states is, as James Madison admitted, an "unavoidable" exception to that general principle. *The Federalist* No. 39. As Alexander Hamilton more fully explained, "The reasonableness of the agency of the national courts in cases in which the State tribunals cannot be supposed to be impartial, speaks for itself. No man ought certainly to be a judge in his own cause, or in any cause in respect to which he has the least interest or bias." *The Federalist* No. 80.

The logic of this position was such that even Anti-Federalists, such as Brutus, conceded the utility of the provision, and there is little or no recorded opposition to this grant of federal jurisdiction in the ratifying debates. Thus, the Convention had come to the view that, as Justice Joseph Story later summarized in his *Commentaries on the Constitution of the United States*, federal jurisdiction over interstate disputes was appropriate "because domestic tranquility requires, that the contentions of states should be peaceably terminated by a common judicatory; and, because, in a free country, justice ought not to depend on the *will* of either litigant."

The Constitution neither compels nor limits the Supreme Court in deciding what kinds of disputes between states it will hear. *Rhode Island v. Massachusetts* (1838). In the early years of the Republic, boundary cases constituted the principal source of disputes that states brought before the Supreme Court, but subsequently the Court has heard, among others, cases dealing with water rights, natural gas, and contractual and other financial conflicts. The predominant contemporary application of this clause is that, in conjunction with the original-jurisdiction provisions of Clause 2 (*see* Article III, Section 2, Clause 2), it provides a mechanism for resolving border and water-resource disputes between neighboring states. Two recent examples of such suits are the dispute between New York and New Jersey to settle title to Ellis Island, *New Jersey v. New York* (1998), and the dispute among several states allocating the water flowing in the North Platte River. *Nebraska v. Wyoming and*

Colorado (2001). Typically, such cases are resolved by the Supreme Court directly, after extensive factual inquiry and a report from an appointed Special Master.

Paul Rosenzweig

See Also

Article I, Section 10, Clause 3 (Compact Clause)
Article III, Section 2, Clause 2 (Original Jurisdiction)

Suggestion for Further Research

Vincent L. McKusick, *Discretionary Gatekeeping: The Supreme Court's Management of its Original Jurisdiction Docket*, 45 Me. L. Rev. 185 (1993)

Significant Cases

Martin v. Hunter's Lessee, 14 U.S. (1 Wheat.) 304 (1816)
Rhode Island v. Massachusetts, 37 U.S. (12 Pet.) 657 (1838)
State of New Jersey v. People of State of New York, 30 U.S. (5 Pet.) 284 (1931)
New York v. United States, 505 U.S. 144 (1992)
New Jersey v. New York, 523 U.S. 767 (1998)
Nebraska v. Wyoming and Colorado, 534 U.S. 40 (2001)

Citizen-State Diversity

The judicial Power shall extend to … Controversies … between a State and Citizens of another State … and between a State … and foreign States, Citizens or Subjects.

(**Article III, Section 2, Clause 1**)

~

*A*rticle III's provisions extending the federal judicial power "to Controversies between a State and Citizens of another State" and "between a State … and foreign States, Citizens or Subjects" are generally known as the Citizen-State Diversity Clauses. Although these clauses have a variety of applications, they have played a primary role in enduring controversies over the scope of state sovereign immunity in suits by private parties.

The Founding generation seems generally to have accepted the notion that the states enjoyed some form of sovereign immunity, derived from the common law, that shielded them against suits by private individuals. Article III's express provision for federal court jurisdiction over suits between individuals and state governments thus raised the possibility that ratification of the Constitution would override this common-law immunity. Some Framers, such as Edmund Randolph and James Wilson, seemed to embrace this possibility as a means for ensuring that state governments would honor their debts; Randolph, for example, asked, "Are we to say that we shall discard this government because it would make us all honest?" Anti-Federalists, on the other hand, opposed Article III based on the same expectation. George Mason stressed the threat of private lawsuits to a state's dignity, inquiring: "Is this state to be brought to the bar of justice like a delinquent individual?" Others stressed the practical consequences of state suability, given the financially precarious position of the states following the Revolutionary War. In particular, many feared that suits by private parties to enforce the states' war debts in federal courts might bankrupt the nascent state governments. The Anti-Federalist writer Brutus, for example, warned that Article III would "produce the utmost confusion, and in its progress, will crush the states beneath its weight."

James Madison, Alexander Hamilton, and other Federalists reacted to these concerns by insisting that Article III left the states' preexisting immunities intact. Madison explained that the Citizen-State Diversity Clauses were designed to allow state governments to come into federal court as plaintiffs, not to allow private citizens to overcome a state's immunity as defendant. And Hamilton acknowledged the states' fundamental immunity from such suits in *The Federalist* No. 81, stating that "[i]t is inherent in the nature of sovereignty not to be amenable to the suit of an individual without its consent…. [T]he exemption…is now enjoyed by the government of every State in the

Union. Unless, therefore, there is a surrender of this immunity in the plan of the convention, it will remain with the States."

The Supreme Court rejected Madison's and Hamilton's reading, however, in *Chisholm v. Georgia* (1793). That case involved a suit by a South Carolina citizen to recover Revolutionary War debts owed by the State of Georgia. The State of Georgia insisted that it was immune from such suits, but the Court upheld its jurisdiction. While Justice Wilson rejected the very notion of state sovereign immunity on the broad ground that it was antithetical to republican government, Justices John Jay, John Blair, and William Cushing relied primarily on the Citizen-State Diversity Clauses. They argued that those clauses had in fact done precisely what the Anti-Federalists feared—that is, overridden the common-law immunity that the states would otherwise have enjoyed in a suit by a private individual. Only Justice James Iredell dissented, primarily on the ground that Congress had not passed any statute that clearly authorized private suits against state governments in the federal courts.

The Court would later say, in *Hans v. State of Louisiana* (1890), that *Chisholm* "created such a shock of surprise throughout the country that, at the first meeting of Congress thereafter, the Eleventh Amendment to the Constitution was almost unanimously proposed, and was in due course adopted by the legislatures of the States." That Amendment provided that "[t]he Judicial power of the United States shall not be construed to extend to any suit in law or equity, commenced or prosecuted against one of the United States by Citizens of another State, or by Citizens or Subjects of any Foreign State." Several commentators have noted the extent to which the latter part of the amendment tracks the language of the Citizen-State Diversity Clause; the "diversity theory" of the amendment thus infers that it was intended simply to "repeal" the Citizen-State Diversity Clauses in all cases in which a nonconsenting state is the defendant. Others have advanced somewhat different interpretations of the amendment's text and intent; the important point for present purposes is simply that the proper reading of the Eleventh Amendment—and the scope of state sovereign immunity generally—remains bound up with disputes about what the Framers intended to accomplish with the Citizen-State Diversity Clauses.

Ernest A. Young

See Also
Amendment XI (Suits Against a State)

Suggestions for Further Research
William Fletcher, *A Historical Interpretation of the Eleventh Amendment: A Narrow Construction of an Affirmative Grant of Jurisdiction Rather than a Prohibition Against Jurisdiction*, 35 STAN. L. REV. 1033 (1983)

CLYDE JACOBS, THE ELEVENTH AMENDMENT AND SOVEREIGN IMMUNITY (1972)

Significant Cases
Chisholm v. Georgia, 2 U.S. (2 Dall.) 419 (1793)

Cohens v. Virginia, 19 U.S. (6 Wheat.) 264 (1821)

Hans v. State of Louisiana, 134 U.S. 1 (1890)

Atascadero State Hospital v. Scanlon, 473 U.S. 234 (1985)

Seminole Tribe of Florida v. Florida, 517 U.S. 44 (1996)

Alden v. Maine, 527 U.S. 706 (1999)

Diversity Clause

The judicial Power shall extend to ...Controversies...between Citizens of different States....
(ARTICLE III, SECTION 2, CLAUSE 1)

∽

*T*he clause authorizing diversity of citizenship jurisdiction was intended to protect out-of-state litigants from local bias in state courts. The records of the Constitutional Convention contain surprisingly little discussion of the clause. The reason for this silence, however, may have been that most delegates shared Alexander

Hamilton's belief that "the reasonableness of the agency of the national courts in cases in which the state tribunals cannot be supposed to be impartial, speaks for itself." *The Federalist* No. 80. Some of the Framers appear to have been less worried about state-court partiality. In the Virginia ratification debates, James Madison is said to have conceded that diversity jurisdiction might well have been left to the state courts; and Chief Justice John Marshall is reported to have given only half-hearted support to the Diversity Clause. But as Marshall later remarked in the classic statement of the purpose of the clause, however impartial the state courts may be in fact, "the Constitution itself either entertains apprehensions on this subject, or views with such indulgence the possible fears and apprehensions" of potential out-of-state litigants that it authorizes the extension of the federal judicial power to controversies between citizens of different states. *Bank of the United States v. Deveaux* (1809).

Although the Diversity Clause authorizes such extension, the actual grant of power to try diversity cases is conferred by statute. Congress has never conferred this power to the full extent authorized by the clause. For example, it has always limited the federal courts' jurisdiction over diversity cases to those in which the amount in controversy between the parties exceeds a certain sum; and it has refused to allow a defendant to invoke diversity jurisdiction for the purpose of removing a case from a state court to the federal system when the defendant is a citizen of the state in which the suit was brought (and when, consequently, he would generally have nothing to fear from any local bias on the part of a state court).

Chief Justice Marshall interpreted the clause as not applying to residents of the District of Columbia, *Hepburn v. Ellzey* (1805), but Congress later extended federal diversity jurisdiction to the District's residents by statute. Similarly, Marshall excluded corporations from qualifying as parties under the clause, *Bank of the United States v. Deveaux* (1809), but later Court decisions allowed corporations to be parties under the fiction that their shareholders were citizens of the state of incorporation. *See Marshall v. Baltimore & Ohio Railroad Co.* (1853).

The Supreme Court has recognized additional limitations on the federal courts' diversity jurisdiction. Most importantly, the Court has required (with a few exceptions) that parties to a lawsuit based on diversity jurisdiction be "completely" diverse: that is, no party on one side of the dispute may be a citizen of the same state as any party on the other side. To qualify under the clause, the parties must be domiciled in different states. Differential residency is not sufficient. For class actions, however, only the named parties, not all the members of the class, must be domiciled in different states.

For many years, the substantive law that federal courts applied in diversity cases was its own federal common law. *Swift v. Tyson* (1842). Through statute, however, the courts utilized the procedural law of the state in which the court sat. That formula was reversed in *Erie Railroad Co. v. Tompkins* (1938). Subsequently, a complex body of law has developed governing which law the federal court will apply. In the main, a federal court will apply the substantive law of the state in which the court sits, including the state's conflict-of-laws rules; but the federal court will follow federal procedural practice, unless the state's procedure would be material in determining the outcome of the case. *See Guaranty Trust Co. v. York* (1945). In most cases, the federal court is bound to apply state law as determined by the state's highest court. Although drastically reduced by the *Erie* decision, federal common law still governs in some areas of peculiar federal concern, such as relations with other nations. *Banco Nacional de Cuba v. Sabbatino* (1964).

Many today believe that diversity jurisdiction should be further curtailed or abolished. They argue that it is anachronistic because there is little danger today of bias against out-of-state litigants; that it encourages forum-shopping; and that it results in an inefficient use of judicial resources. On the other side, a widespread belief that federal judges are better qualified than their state-court counterparts leads many practitioners to oppose further restrictions. Moreover, many insist that local bias persists, especially in rural areas (where state courts are somewhat more likely to be located); and they counsel against departing from the precaution of the Framers.

Terence Pell

See Also

Article IV, Section 2, Clause 1 (Privileges and Immunities Clause)

Suggestion for Further Research

Henry J. Friendly, *The Historical Basis of Diversity Jurisdiction*, 16 HARV. L. REV. 483 (1928)

Significant Cases

Hepburn v. Ellzey, 6 U.S. (2 Cranch) 445 (1805)
Strawbridge v. Curtiss, 7 U.S. (3 Cranch) 267 (1806)
Bank of the United States v. Deveaux, 9 U.S. (5 Cranch) 61 (1809)
Swift v. Tyson, 41 U.S. (16 Pet.) 1 (1842)
Marshall v. Baltimore & Ohio Railroad Co., 57 U.S. (16 How.) 314 (1853)
Dodge v. Woolsey, 59 U.S. (18 How.) 331 (1856)
Erie Railroad Co. v. Tompkins, 304 U.S. 64 (1938)
Klaxon Co. v. Stentor Manufacturing Co., 313 U.S. 487 (1941)
Guaranty Trust Co. v. York, 326 U.S. 99 (1945)
Lumberman's Mutual Casualty Co. v. Elbert, 348 U.S. 48 (1954)
Banco Nacional de Cuba v. Sabbatino, 376 U.S. 398 (1964)
Carden v. Arkoma Ass'n, 494 U.S. 185 (1990)

Land Grant Jurisdiction Clause

The judicial Power shall extend to ... Controversies ... between Citizens of the same State claiming Lands under Grants of different States ....
(ARTICLE III, SECTION 2, CLAUSE 1)

~

$\mathcal{D}$erived from Article IX of the Articles of Confederation, the Framers included the Land Grant Jurisdiction Clause along with the Citizen-State Diversity Clause in order to promote "peace and harmony" among the states by providing, as Justice Joseph Story described, an impartial federal tribunal in matters where "a state tribunal might not stand indifferent in a controversy where the claims of its own sovereign were in conflict with those of another sovereign." *Town of Pawlet v. Clark* (1815).

The Framers were mindful of the possibility of serious disputes over the western lands among the states and between citizens of the several states and of the same state. It was the same concern that had led to the predecessor clause in the Articles of Confederation. Maryland refused to ratify the Articles of Confederation until 1781—four years after the Continental Congress had approved the document—because of conflicting land claims. Maryland's primary concern was that Virginia would be able to dominate the national congress should it prevail in its extensive claim to all the lands west "to the South Sea," as conveyed in its initial royal charter. Moreover, several other states—Massachusetts, Connecticut, North Carolina, South Carolina, and Georgia—had similar, overlapping claims, derived from their own royal charters, and New York, as "suzerain of the Iroquois Indians," also laid claim to vast expanses of land west of the Delaware River. These conflicting claims threatened to embroil the states in a series of border disputes that were significant enough to place the new union itself at risk.

Virginia's cession of the lands northwest of the Ohio River in 1783, the parallel cessions of the western lands by the other states over the following decade, and the passage of the Northwest Ordinance while the Constitutional Convention was meeting all defused much potential conflict. These often-overlooked cessions demonstrated the commitment and the sacrifice that the states made for the sake of the future stability of the union. Nonetheless, boundary disputes among ten of the states convinced the Framers of the need of a federal forum to settle such conflicts. The Convention rejected a proposal to lodge jurisdiction in the Senate in favor of making it a judicial concern. Further agreements and compromises by the states have largely rendered the Land Grant Jurisdiction Clause obsolete.

A few minor border disputes have occasionally arisen involving citizens of the same state. *Schroeder v. Freeland* (1951) dealt with a private dispute over ownership of land between Iowa and Nebraska affected by accretion of the Missouri River. The more serious land disputes, over which the Supreme Court has original jurisdiction, typically involve the states themselves. In 1998, the Supreme Court resolved a dispute over portions of Ellis Island in favor of New Jersey over New York. *New Jersey v. New York* (1998).

The clause is currently implemented by 28 U.S.C. § 1354, which gives federal district courts jurisdiction without regard to the amount in controversy, *United States v. Sayward* (1895), but only for citizens of the same state. Citizens of different states, claiming land under grants from different states, can have their cause heard in federal court only under the Citizen-State Diversity Clause. *Stevenson v. Fain* (1904). Nevertheless, the Land Grant Jurisdiction Clause stands for two important propositions: the federal courts should decide cases in which the state courts would have an apparent bias; and too great a geographic imbalance between members of the union was a threat to the body politic.

John C. Eastman

See Also
Article III, Section 2, Clause 1 (Citizen-State Diversity)

Suggestions for Further Research
Charles Moore, The Northwest Under Three Flags: 1635–1796 (1900, repr. 1989)

Shosuke Sato, History of the Land Question in the United States (1886)

Payson Jackson Treat, The National Land System, 1785–1820 (1910)

Significant Cases
Town of Pawlet v. Clark, 13 U.S. (9 Cranch) 292 (1815)

United States v. Sayward, 160 U.S. 493 (1895)

Stevenson v. Fain, 195 U.S. 165 (1904)

Schroeder v. Freeland, 188 F.2d 517 (8th Cir. 1951)

Port of Portland v. Tri-Club Islands, Inc., 315 F. Supp. 1160 (D. Ore. 1970)

New Jersey v. New York, 523 U.S. 767 (1998)

Citizen-State Diversity

The judicial Power shall extend to all Cases...between a State, or the Citizens thereof, and foreign States, Citizens or Subjects.
(Article III, Section 2, Clause 1)

~

This clause is discussed in Ernest A. Young's essay on the Citizen-State Diversity Clause on page 252.

Original Jurisdiction

In all Cases affecting Ambassadors, other public Ministers and Consuls, and those in which a State shall be Party, the supreme Court shall have original Jurisdiction.
(Article III, Section 2, Clause 2)

~

*T*he Supreme Court's original jurisdiction is limited to a narrow but important range of cases. The grant of appellate jurisdiction under Article III is far broader, although under the Appellate Jurisdiction, Congress has at least some discretion to modify it. The Court has been assiduous in protecting the Constitution's core grant of original jurisdiction from congressional expansion. The Court explicitly declared in *Marbury v. Madison* (1803) that Congress cannot add to the Supreme Court's original jurisdiction. Under Section 13 of the Judiciary Act of 1789, Congress had granted the Court mandamus power (the power to order lower courts or executive officials to perform duties required by law). In *Marbury*, Chief Justice John Marshall held that the mandamus power as applied to executive officials was actually a grant of original jurisdiction, and that Congress could not constitutionally expand the original jurisdiction of the Supreme Court. Writing for the Court, the Chief Justice declared Section 13 unconstitutional and denied the relief sought. Marshall's carefully crafted opinion reinforced the significance of original jurisdiction in two ways: (1) by limiting its scope to the categories of cases contained in the text; and, as a consequence, (2) by shifting its focus from executive matters to suits between states.

The Original Jurisdiction Clause has both theoretical and practical importance. Although Marshall's opinion emphasized the principle of textual interpretation, it also made practical sense that Article III should be read to limit the power of Congress to add to the Court's original jurisdiction. If Congress could have expanded the Court's original docket, citizens would have been forced to litigate in the national capital, which was often inconvenient and distant. But even as narrowly written and construed, in state-versus-state cases original jurisdiction still played an indispensable role in eliminating the bias and parochialism of state courts and lower federal courts (where judges were likely to be drawn from the same pool of local lawyers). The need for original federal power in state-versus-state cases had been a concern of the Constitution's drafters: "Whatever practices may have a tendency to disturb the harmony between the States are proper objects of federal superintendence and control." *The Federalist* No. 80.

While Congress cannot add to the Supreme Court's original jurisdiction, the Court has accepted a reduction of the power through Congress's creation of concurrent jurisdiction with lower federal courts over some kinds of original matters cases (suits against ambassadors and consuls and suits between the United States and a state, for example). Parochial biases are less prevalent in these cases and, in any event, when filed in the lower federal courts, these cases can later be transferred to the Court's appellate docket. The current jurisdictional statute, 28 U.S.C. § 1251, makes controversies between two or more states exclusive and provides for concurrent jurisdiction over all other categories of original cases.

From the beginning, the most important kinds of suits between states involved disputes over boundaries. These were precisely the situations where the forces of provincialism and self-interest were most likely to compromise a state or lower federal court. Between 1790 and 1900, the only suits between states the Court heard on its original docket concerned boundary disputes. By the twentieth century, the category of original disputes began to include other important matters, such as water-rights cases and Commerce Clause claims (related to the use of state economic, regulatory, or tax powers). These kinds of cases continue to this day. *See, e.g., Maryland v. Louisiana* (1981), which deals with Louisiana's severance tax on natural gas. On occasion, when purely legal and urgent constitutional challenges are raised, the Court has also permitted suits to be filed on an original basis by states against the United States. *See South Carolina v. Katzenbach* (1966) (the Voting Rights Act of 1964).

Original cases are not heard as of right before the Supreme Court even though its jurisdiction is exclusive. Original cases are commenced by a petition for leave to file a complaint. Such petitions are frequently denied, sometimes because the Court believes that a matter between states is too trivial (e.g., whether state universities breached a contract to play football) or, conversely, when the Court considers that the matters sought to be reviewed are too broad or unmanageable (e.g., issues of interstate water or air pollution) or simply because the Court is not ready to hear the matter.

Once the Court grants the states' petitions to file a complaint, it usually appoints a Special Master to make factual and legal recommendations. The Special Master, in turn, holds hearings and takes testimony, subject in a general way to the Federal Rules of Evidence. Unlike appeals of district court decisions under the Federal Rules of Civil Procedure, the Master is given no formal deference on findings of fact by the Supreme Court, although such findings are often accepted by the Court. The parties also present briefs, arguments, and proposed recommendations, after which the Special Master issues a final report. The parties then can take exceptions to that report to the Supreme Court, where it is briefed and argued and proceeds much like a traditional appellate or certiorari case.

There have been fewer than two hundred state-versus-state original cases in the history of the Republic, less than one per year of constitutional life. There have been only two original cases under the "affecting Ambassadors" section of the clause. Despite these relatively modest numbers, original jurisdiction continues to serve an indispensable purpose in resolving matters of high moment between states. No forum other than the Supreme Court can act with the authority and dignity necessary to resolve what are in effect diplomatic encounters between contending sovereigns under our constitutional system.

Paul Verkuil

Suggestions for Further Research

Vincent L. McKusick, *Discretionary Gatekeeping: The Supreme Court's Management of Its Original Jurisdiction Docket Since 1961*, 138 Am. Phil. Soc'y 195 (1994)

James E. Pfander, *Marbury, Original Jurisdiction, and the Supreme Court's Supervisory Powers*, 101 Colum. L. Rev. 1515 (2001)

Significant Cases

Cohens v. Virginia, 19 U.S. (6 Wheat.) 264 (1821)

Ames v. Kansas *ex rel.* Johnston, 111 U.S. 449 (1884)

Kansas v. Colorado, 185 U.S. 125 (1902)

South Carolina v. Katzenbach, 383 U.S. 301 (1966)

Maryland v. Louisiana, 451 U.S. 725 (1981)

New Jersey v. New York, 523 U.S. 767 (1998)

Nebraska v. Wyoming and Colorado, 534 U.S. 40 (2001)

Appellate Jurisdiction Clause

In all the other Cases before mentioned, the supreme Court shall have appellate Jurisdiction, both as to Law and Fact, with such Exceptions, and under such Regulations as the Congress shall make.

(Article III, Section 2, Clause 2)

~

The phrase in the Appellate Jurisdiction Clause that raised the most serious concerns was the grant to the Supreme Court of appellate jurisdiction "both as to Law and Fact." The Anti-Federalist opposition was certain it meant the end of the civil jury and allowed a second trial of those criminally charged at the appellate level.

The Anti-Federalist Brutus argued:

Who are the supreme court? Does it not consist of the judges? and they are to have the same jurisdiction of the fact as they are to have of the law. They will therefore have the same authority to determine the fact as they will have to determine the law, and no room is left for a jury on appeals to the supreme court.

Alexander Hamilton responded in *The Federalist* No. 81, arguing that for common-law cases "revision of the law only" would be proper for the Supreme Court, but for civil law cases, such as prize cases, review of facts "might be essential to the preservation of the public peace." Hamilton added that the grant of appellate jurisdiction would not abolish the right to trial by jury and that Congress possessed the power to restrict the Supreme Court in this area: "The legislature of the United States would certainly have full power to provide that in appeals to the Supreme Court there should be no re-examination of facts where they had been tried in the original causes by juries."

Following Hamilton's lead, Justice Joseph Story suggested in his *Commentaries on the Constitution of the United States* that the object of the clause's reference to jurisdiction over "Law and Fact" was to allow for the review of law and fact in cases of admiralty and maritime jurisdiction. Ultimately, the Seventh Amendment and the Double Jeopardy Clause of the Fifth Amendment mollified the Anti-Federalists' concerns by removing jury findings of fact from appellate review.

The Appellate Jurisdiction Clause also seemingly grants Congress unbounded authority to make "Exceptions" to the appellate jurisdiction. The Convention delegates at first rejected a clause providing that "the Judicial power shall be exercised in such manner as the Legislature shall direct"; but later, after the judicial power was defined in what eventually became Article III, the Framers appended this clause, permitting, as Federalists like John Marshall claimed, a broad power of Congress to regulate the appeals process to the Supreme Court. Justice Story later opined that Congress possessed "the utmost latitude" in limiting classes of cases that could reach the Supreme Court, so long as "the whole judicial power" was "vested either in an original or appellate form, in some courts created under [Congress's] authority." *Martin v. Hunter's Lessee* (1816).

Early on, Chief Justice Oliver Ellsworth had gone further and suggested that "If Congress has provided no rule to regulate our proceedings, we cannot exercise an appellate jurisdiction." *Wiscart v. D'Auchy* (1796). In dissent, Justice James Wilson maintained that the Supreme Court's appellate jurisdiction flowed directly from the Constitution until Congress took steps to make exceptions to it. Justice Wilson's dissenting view in *Wiscart* garnered a majority vote in *DuRousseau v. United States* (1810). Chief Justice John Marshall's unanimous majority opinion recognized that the appellate jurisdiction is created by the Constitution, not by the Judiciary Act of 1789. Nevertheless, utilizing standard rules for statutory interpretation, the *DuRousseau* Court explained that Congress had described particular aspects of the Court's jurisdiction in that statute, "and this affirmative description has been understood to imply a negative of the exercise of such appellate power as is not comprehended within it." In other words, by providing for certain classes of appeals to reach the Supreme Court, Congress tacitly intended to "except" all others from Supreme Court review.

In *Martin v. Hunter's Lessee* and *Ableman v. Booth* (1859), Justice Story and Chief Justice Roger B. Taney, respectively, described the need to provide for Supreme Court review of decisions of the states' highest courts, in order, as Chief Justice Taney put it, "to secure the independence and supremacy of the General Government in the sphere of action assigned to it; [and] to make the Constitution and laws of the United States uniform, and the same in every State."

The seminal decision on jurisdiction-stripping statutes under the Appellate Jurisdiction Clause came shortly after the Civil War. *Ex parte McCardle* (1869) involved a newspaper editor in military custody, who had appealed a lower federal court's denial of habeas corpus relief to the United States Supreme Court, pursuant to the Habeas Corpus Act of 1867. After the Supreme Court heard oral argument, Congress repealed the provisions of the statute that had authorized Supreme Court review. The Court concluded that, pursuant to Congress's power under the Appellate Jurisdiction Clause, it had no jurisdiction to decide the case. The Court also expressed a deferential view toward legislative acts in this context, noting: "We are not at liberty to inquire into the motives of the legislature. We can only examine into its power under the Constitution; and the power to make exceptions to the appellate jurisdiction of this court is given in express words."

Shortly thereafter, the Supreme Court found that a different jurisdiction-stripping statute did not fall within the Congress's Appellate Jurisdiction Clause power. In *United States v. Klein* (1871), Congress had enacted a statute which provided that persons whose property had been seized during the Civil War could recover proceeds of their property if they proved they had not given aid to the rebellion during the War. The Supreme Court had previously held that a presidential pardon for such activities was proof that a person had not given aid to the rebellion. *United States v. Padelford* (1870). In *Klein*, the claimant had succeeded in the lower court, but the government had appealed. While the case was pending in the Supreme Court, Congress passed a law that attempted to reverse the holding in *Padelford*. The new law *required* courts to treat the pardon as proof of disloyalty, and on proof of such pardon, the jurisdiction of the court would cease and the suit be dismissed.

The *Klein* Court noted that, if Congress had "simply denied the right of appeal in a particular class of cases," the act would have been a valid exercise of legislative power under the Appellate Jurisdiction Clause. However, the Court determined that the statute withheld jurisdiction only as a means to an end, and that its purpose was to negate the Supreme Court's interpretation of the effect of a presidential pardon. Congress did have the power, the Court averred, to change underlying substantive law upon which the claim had been litigated, *Pennsylvania v. Wheeling & Belmont Bridge Co.* (1856), but Congress could not do so by invading the President's power to pardon, nor to direct a particular decision in a pending case.

Klein was a rare case. Although it showed that Congress cannot use its powers over jurisdiction to override a constitutional provision (such as the President's pardon power, or, by extension, a provision of the bill of rights), the Supreme Court has affirmed Congress's broad power to make exceptions to its jurisdiction, *The Francis Wright* (1881), and its equally broad power to change underlying substantive law even if that change affects the outcome in a pending case. *Robertson v. Seattle Audubon Society* (1992). Congress, however, may not by legislation reopen a case already decided and finalized, that is, when the time for appeal has passed. *Plaut v. Spendthrift Farm, Inc.* (1995).

Recent debate over the Appellate Jurisdiction Clause has centered on proposals for legislation that would remove existing Supreme Court jurisdiction. Constitutional scholars strongly disagree as to how far Congress may go in removing Supreme Court jurisdiction under the clause. The traditional view, exemplified by Gerald Gunther, is that the text gives Congress power to remove the Supreme Court's appellate jurisdiction with little or no internal Article III limitation. Gunther and Ronald Rotunda argue that extrinsic restraints, such as those found in the Bill of Rights and

elsewhere in the Constitution, could be applied. However, Gunther notes that under *McCardle*, the Court may still avoid looking into Congress's "motivations" except where the extrinsic restraint so requires.

Henry Hart and others have suggested that the Appellate Jurisdiction Clause may not be used to "destroy the essential role of the Supreme Court in the constitutional plan." As Gunther noted, however, there is no "essential functions" limit on the face of the Appellate Jurisdiction Clause, and *McCardle* provides precedent for judicial deference to congressional limitations of appellate jurisdiction.

Ira Mickenberg and Robert Clinton distinguish between the words "Exceptions" and "Regulations" in the Constitution. Clinton argues that the phrase "such Exceptions" referred to the class of cases assigned to the original jurisdiction of the Supreme Court under Article III. Mickenberg suggests that an "Exception" could not abolish all appellate jurisdiction, and supports limits to the exception power as a matter of original intent. David Engdahl doubts that the Framers would have imperatively granted jurisdiction to the federal courts in Article III only to allow Congress "to take it all away." He suggests that the power is more properly lodged in the Necessary and Proper Clause. Paul Bator recognizes Congress's power to strip the Court of its appellate jurisdiction, but, as a matter of policy and in light of intended constitutional structure, argues that such an act would violate "the spirit of the Constitution."

Lawrence Sager takes the view that although Congress has broad authority to regulate appellate jurisdiction, Congress cannot remove jurisdiction with regard to a federal constitutional question from both the lower courts and the Supreme Court. In a variation, Akhil Amar has argued that Article III provides for two tiers of jurisdiction. Those grants of jurisdiction phrased with the emphatic "shall" must be left somewhere in the federal judicial system; the remaining grants may be removed or excepted by Congress. Justice Joseph Story, in dictum, has made a similar claim in *Martin v. Hunter's Lessee*. John Harrison disputes

Amar's thesis on the basis of a careful textual analysis of Article III.

The Supreme Court has remained aloof from the scholarly contest, leaving its precedents to stand for broad congressional authority to limit the appellate jurisdiction of the Supreme Court. Thus far, the Court has followed the lead of John Marshall, who stated in the Virginia ratifying convention: "Congress is empowered to make exceptions to the appellate jurisdiction, as to law and fact, of the Supreme Court. These exceptions certainly go as far as the legislature may think proper for the interest and liberty of the people."

Andrew S. Gold

See Also

Article III, Section 2, Clause 1 (Judicial Power)
Amendment V (Double Jeopardy)
Amendment VII (Reexamination Clause)

Suggestions for Further Research

Akhil R. Amar, *A Neo-Federalist View of Article III: Separating the Two Tiers of Federal Jurisdiction*, 65 B.U. L. Rev. 205 (1985)

Paul M. Bator, *Congressional Power over the Jurisdiction of the Inferior Federal Courts*, 27 Villanova L. Rev. 1030 (1981-1982)

Robert N. Clinton, *A Mandatory View of Federal Court Jurisdiction: A Guided Quest for the Original Understanding of Article III*, 132 U. Pa. L. Rev. 741 (1984)

David. E. Engdahl, *Intrinsic Limits of Congress' Power Regarding the Judicial Branch*, 1999 BYU L. Rev. 75 (1999)

Gerald Gunther, *Congressional Power to Curtail Federal Court Jurisdiction: An Opinionated Guide to the Ongoing Debate*, 36 Stan. L. Rev. 895 (1984)

John Harrison, *The Power of Congress to Limit the Jurisdiction of Federal Courts and the Text of Article III*, 64 U. Chi. L. Rev. 203 (1997)

Henry Hart, *The Power of Congress to Limit the Jurisdiction of Federal Courts: An Exercise in Dialectic*, 66 Harv. L. Rev. 1362 (1953)

Ira Mickenberg, *Abusing the Exceptions and Regulations Clause: Legislative Attempts to Divest the Supreme Court of Appellate Jurisdiction*, 32 Am. U. L. Rev. 497 (1983)

Martin Redish, *Constitutional Limitations on Congressional Power to Control Federal Jurisdiction: A Reaction to Professor Sager*, 77 Nw. U. L. Rev. 143 (1982)

Ronald Rotunda, *Congressional Power to Restrict the Jurisdiction of the Lower Federal Courts and the Problem of School Busing*, 64 Geo. U. L.J. 839 (1976)

Lawrence Sager, *Constitutional Limitations on Congress' Authority to Regulate the Jurisdiction of the Federal Courts*, 95 Harv. L. Rev. 17 (1981)

Mark Strasser, *Taking Exception to Traditional Exceptions Clause Jurisprudence: On Congress's Power to Limit the Court's Jurisdiction*, 2001 Utah L. Rev. 125 (2001)

William Van Alstyne, *A Critical Guide to Ex Parte McCardle*, 15 Ariz. L. Rev. 229 (1973)

Julian Velaso, *Congressional Control over Federal Court Jurisdiction: A Defense of the Traditional View*, 46 Cath. U. L. Rev. 971 (1997)

Significant Cases

Wiscart v. D'Auchy, 3 U.S. (3 Dall.) 321 (1796)
United States v. More, 7 U.S. (3 Cranch) 159 (1805)
DuRousseau v. United States, 10 U.S. (6 Cranch) 307 (1810)
Martin v. Hunter's Lessee, 14 U.S. (1 Wheat.) 304 (1816)
Pennsylvania v. Wheeling & Belmont Bridge Co., 59 U.S. (18 How.) 421 (1856)
Ableman v. Booth, 62 U.S. (21 How.) 506 (1859)
Ex parte McCardle, 74 U.S. (7 Wall.) 506 (1869)
Ex parte Yerger, 75 U.S. (8 Wall.) 85 (1869)
United States v. Padelford, 76 U.S. (9 Wall.) 531 (1870)
United States v. Klein, 80 U.S. (13 Wall.) 128 (1871)
The Francis Wright, 105 U.S. 381 (1881)
United States v. Sioux Nation of Indians, 448 U.S. 371 (1980)
Robertson v. Seattle Audubon Society, 503 U.S. 429 (1992)
Plaut v. Spendthrift Farm, Inc., 514 U.S. 211 (1995)

Criminal Trials

The Trial of all Crimes, except in Cases of Impeachment, shall be by Jury; and such Trial shall be held in the State where the said Crimes shall have been committed; but

when not committed within any
State, the Trial shall be at such
Place or Places as the Congress may
by Law have directed.
(ARTICLE III, SECTION 2, CLAUSE 3)

∼

*T*he American right to a trial by a jury of one's
peers traces its lineage back to 1297 and the
Magna Carta. By the mid-sixteenth century,
the jury had already taken on the form it
retains to this day in federal courts and some
state courts—twelve citizens were summoned
to sit in sworn judgment of the criminal alle-
gations against one of their peers.

The English practice of using juries continued in America from the very first settlements. The Charter of the Virginia Company
in 1606 declared that the colonists who were
to settle there would enjoy all the rights of
Englishmen, which included the right to jury
trial. Juries played a vital role in the mid-eighteenth century in resisting English authority
in the contest that ultimately led up to the
American Revolution. The most noted of the
colonial cases was the trial of John Peter
Zenger, a New York printer whom the jury
acquitted on charges of seditious libel, forty-
one years before the drafting of the Declaration of Independence.

King George III responded to such jury nullification of English laws by expanding the
jurisdiction of non-jury courts, such as the
Admiralty courts, and increasingly using those
courts as the vehicles for enforcement. Thus it
was that in 1776 the Declaration of Independence listed as a grievance against George III
his "depriving us . . . of the benefits of trial by
jury." As a consequence, Article III—the portion of the Constitution governing the role of
the judiciary—makes clear that judges are not
the only judicial actors of constitutional significance. It provides a crucial role for the jury.

There was little debate about this portion of
the Constitution, because the need for the
criminal jury was one of the few subjects of
agreement between Federalists and Anti-Federalists. Alexander Hamilton observed in *The
Federalist* No. 83 that "[t]he friends and adver-

saries of the plan of the convention, if they
agree in nothing else, concur at least in the
value they set upon the trial by jury." The only
distinction to be drawn, in his view, was
between the Federalist view that it is "a valuable safeguard to liberty" and the Anti-Federalist view that it is "the very palladium of free
government."

Indeed, Thomas Jefferson believed so
strongly in the jury that he noted, "[w]ere I
called upon to decide whether the people had
best be omitted in the Legislative or Judiciary
department, I would say it is better to leave
them out of the Legislative." John Adams
shared Jefferson's praise of the jury, observing
that "the common people . . . should have as
complete a control, as decisive a negative, in
every judgment of a court of judicature" as
they have in the legislature.

Because judges themselves were part of the
government, many Framers feared they would
not be an adequate check on government
abuse of the criminal process. The jury, therefore, was made part of the original structure of
government in order to provide a mechanism
for ensuring that individuals would not lose
their liberty under a criminal law until the
people themselves concurred.

In many criminal cases in the nation's early
history, the jury not only applied the law to the
facts it found, but decided questions of law
themselves. Thus, many judges refused to tell
jurors that they were obliged to accept the
judge's view of the law, and lawyers argued
questions of law before the jury in some cases.

Over time, however, this power eroded. In
1895, the Supreme Court concluded in *Sparf
and Hansen v. United States* that the jury did
not have the "right" to decide legal questions.
As a result, today judges can—and do—
instruct juries that they must accept the judge's
view of the law, and lawyers are no longer
allowed to argue the merits of the law to the
jury. Because the jury possesses authority to
issue an unreviewable general verdict of
acquittal, the jury nevertheless retains the raw
power to check general laws with which it disagrees in individual cases. But because the trial
judge does not instruct the jury that it has this

authority, the jurors may not know that they have it. In addition, even if the jurors are aware of this power, they must exercise it knowing it is contrary to the judge's instructions. Hence, there will be cases in which the jury does not exercise that power and instead follows the judge's instructions, even when the jury itself disagrees with the law in question, with the judge's interpretation of the law, or with the law's application in the case before it.

The jury's power has eroded in a second respect. Prior to 1930, jury trials in federal court, like jurisdictional provisions, could not be waived, reflecting the mandatory language in Article III that the trial of all crimes "shall" be by jury. In *Patton v. United States* (1930), however, the Supreme Court concluded that a defendant could waive a jury trial in favor of a bench trial. Nonetheless, the prosecutor may still insist upon, and the court must grant, a jury trial.

There are two additional trends in criminal justice that have further diminished the jury's ability to check the government in criminal cases. First, the vast majority of cases never reaches the jury because of the increase in the number of cases resolved by plea bargain.

The second major trend involves the changing nature of sentencing. Congress and many state legislatures have shifted from a model that vested broad sentencing discretion with judges to a regime in which the legislature (or a sentencing commission) specifies in generally applicable laws how particular findings of fact must affect the defendant's sentence. Thus, these laws are indistinguishable from other criminal laws: they identify blameworthy behavior and specify the criminal punishment for that behavior. But there is a crucial exception: the legislature insists that judges, not juries, apply these laws.

In *Apprendi v. New Jersey* (2000), the Supreme Court held that the legislature does not have unbounded authority to label criminally blameworthy facts as sentencing factors instead of offense elements, because such authority could undercut the jury's constitutional role. The Court in *Apprendi* therefore held that it is unconstitutional for the legislature to remove from the jury the assessment of facts (other than recidivism) that increase the statutorily prescribed range of penalties to which a defendant is exposed. The Court has not yet extended this rule to apply to the penalties prescribed by the Federal Sentencing Guidelines.

Article III (and the Sixth Amendment) also contain provisions relating to venue, the place where a case is to be tried, and vicinage, the place from which the members of the jury pool trying the case are to be drawn. The Declaration of Independence condemned the English practice of transporting colonial defendants overseas to England for trial by juries of Englishmen. In response, the Constitution guarantees a criminal defendant both the right to be tried in the state where his alleged crime was committed and by a jury drawn from the population of the state and district where the alleged crime occurred.

Rachel E. Barkow

See Also

Amendment V (Double Jeopardy)
Amendment VI (Jury Trial)
Amendment VII (Right to Jury in Civil Cases)

Suggestions for Further Research

Jeffrey Abramson, We, the Jury: The Jury System and the Ideal of Democracy (1994).

Albert W. Alschuler & Andrew G. Deiss, *A Brief History of Criminal Jury Trial in the United States*, 61 U. Chi. L. Rev. 867 (1994)

Andrew Joseph Gildea, *The Right to Trial by Jury*, 26 Am. Crim. L. Rev. 1507 (1989)

Matthew P. Harrington, *The Law-Finding Function of the American Jury*, 1999 Wisc. L. Rev. 377

Mark DeWolfe Howe, *Juries as Judges of Criminal Law*, 52 Harv. L. Rev. 582 (1939)

Stanton D. Krauss, *An Inquiry into the Right of Criminal Juries To Determine the Law in Colonial America*, 89 J. Crim. L. & Criminology 111, 123 (1998)

Significant Cases

Sparf and Hansen v. United States, 156 U.S. 51 (1895)
Patton v. United States, 281 U.S. 276 (1930)

Duncan v. Louisiana, 391 U.S. 145 (1968)
Apprendi v. New Jersey, 530 U.S. 466 (2000)

Treason

Treason against the United States, shall consist only in levying War against them, or in adhering to their Enemies, giving them Aid and Comfort. No Person shall be convicted of Treason unless on the Testimony of two Witnesses to the same overt Act, or on Confession in open Court.

(ARTICLE III, SECTION 3, CLAUSE 1)

~

*T*he word *treason*, as transmitted to the English language from the Latin through the French, means "giving or delivering up." The common law understood treason as treachery or breach of faith. It was therefore a crime committed between parties who enjoyed an established relationship of mutual benefit and trust. *Petit treason* referred to a wife killing her husband, or a servant or ecclesiastic killing his lord or master. *High treason* involved a breach between subject and sovereign, a betrayal of (or neglect of duty or renunciation of allegiance to, in word or deed) a sovereign to whom a subject owes allegiance by birth or residence. Sir Edward Coke, Baron de Montesquieu, Sir Matthew Hale, and Sir William Blackstone considered treason the highest of crimes and declared that it must be precisely defined to prevent its abuse by governmental authorities. In England, commencing during the reign of Edward III, Parliament narrowed the definition of treason but later widened it according to political exigencies.

The laws of the American colonies reflected the broad outlines of the common law of England, both as to breadth of the offense and severity of punishment, though sometimes the definitions of treason in the colonies were broader than those in England. By the eigh-

teenth century, laws began more consistently to reflect the English law of treason, and eventually, during the revolutionary period, came to require more precise definitions, more exacting standards of proof, and more lenient punishments. During the Revolution, many states adopted language recommended by the Continental Congress and its "Committee on Spies," defining treason as adherence to the king of Great Britain (including accepting commissions from him) or to other "Enemies," giving them "Aid and Comfort."

Reflecting the American Founders' concern with protecting individual rights and their fear of arbitrary governmental power, the Framers of the Constitution sought a precise and permanent definition of treason, the permissible means of proving it, and the limitations on the punishment for it. The drafters of the Constitution reached back (as had the Continental Congress) to language in the statute of 25 Edward III (1350), which limited treason, among other things, to compassing or imagining the death of the king, levying war against the king, or adhering to the king's enemies, giving them aid and comfort. But the Framers' work was even narrower. They did not include the language of "compassing or imagining," which had been the basis of the English doctrine of "constructive treason," an effective and easily abused method for dealing with political opponents. Thus, in the Constitution, treason consists only in levying war against the United States or adhering to its enemies by giving them aid and comfort. It may be proved only by confession in open court, or on the testimony of no fewer than two witnesses to the same overt act.

The debates in the Constitutional Convention show an awareness of English common law and legislative history. James Madison suggested that the proposed definition reported by the Committee of Detail—limiting treason to the levying of war and adherence to enemies—was imprudently narrow and would effectively disallow the wisdom of experience. Others, such as John Dickinson, argued in favor of narrow wording. In the end, the phrase "giving them Aid and Comfort" was added to restrict even further the definition of the crime, and evidentiary requirements were tightened by the addition of the phrase "overt Act." Furthermore, as James Wilson noted in his 1791 *Lectures on Law*, treason requires generalized grievances and aims against the United States or its government as a whole, rather than particularized, essentially private grievances or aims. Respecting the federal nature of the union, the constitutional definition leaves open the possibility of concurrent state laws for treasons against them in their respective sovereign capacities.

When it came time to defend the Constitution, Madison left behind his earlier aversion to a narrow definition of treason and, in *The Federalist* No. 43, lauded the Convention's wisdom as raising a constitutional bar to "new-fangled and artificial treasons" (understood as the results and instruments of faction), and as limiting the consequences of guilt. In *The Federalist* No. 84, Alexander Hamilton mentions the definition of treason as one of the guarantors of rights that make a separate bill of rights unnecessary.

The Supreme Court has had occasion to pronounce on treason, albeit infrequently. In *Ex parte Bollman* (1807), Chief Justice John Marshall rejected the idea of "constructive treason" and held that for treason to be established on the ground of levying war against the United States, an accused must be part of an actual assemblage of men for a treasonable purpose. Conspiracy short of the actual levying of war is insufficient. But in the related case of *United States v. Burr* (1807), Marshall tacked slightly. He again rejected constructive treason, but did so by holding that Aaron Burr, if not physically present in an assemblage of men, could still be convicted of treason on the testimony of two witnesses that he actively helped effect or aid such an assemblage—in effect, aided in the levying of war. Together, these cases made a treason conviction exceedingly difficult for anything other than manifest participation in a treasonable act.

After *Burr*, the leading treason cases grew out of World War II, for adherence to enemies. In *Cramer v. United States* (1945), the Supreme Court held that a specific intent—adherence to the enemy, and therefore to harm the United States—is necessary, rather than the simple rendition of aid. Further, the majority came close

to holding that such adherence requires proof, not just of an act that on its face is "commonplace" (such as a meeting) but a manifestly treasonable overt act, evidenced by the testimony of at least two witnesses. But in *Haupt v. United States* (1947)—the Court's first affirmation of a treason conviction—the Court effectively relaxed *Cramer's* standard of proof by holding that the testimony of two witnesses to overt acts might be supported by other evidence as to the accused's treasonable intent, including out-of-court confessions and admissions. In a concurring opinion, Justice William O. Douglas (who dissented in *Cramer*) affirmed that the separate elements of intent and overt act are amenable to different modes of proof, and only the latter triggers the constitutional requirement of testimony by two witnesses.

In *Kawakita v. United States* (1952), the Supreme Court held that dual citizenship does not diminish a citizen's allegiance to the United States, and, in a treason prosecution, whether someone intends to renounce American citizenship hinges on particular facts and may be a question for a jury.

Lower courts have had occasion to enter verdicts of treason, commencing with the Whiskey Rebellion, some of them arguably on broader grounds than what the Supreme Court would later countenance. For example, courts held that armed resistance to the collection of taxes constituted constructive treason. A number of cases arising out of the Civil War also suggested, without directly interpreting the Constitution, that Confederate activities amounted to treason (although the general amnesty of December 25, 1868, pardoned all Confederates). Because of the particular and high constitutional standards associated with the definition and proof of treason, hostile or subversive acts falling short of treason but directed toward the whole polity have been prosecuted under various laws of Congress, including those dealing with espionage (for example, the conviction and execution of Ethel and Julius Rosenberg in 1953) and, more recently, terrorism. The exercise of federal prosecutorial discretion has also led to the prosecution on other grounds of individuals for acts that arguably amount to treason (for example,

John Walker Lindh captured in Afghanistan in 2001), or to failure to prosecute at all.

Bradley C. S. Watson

Suggestions for Further Research

Henry Mark Holzer, *Why Not Call It Treason? From Korea to Afghanistan*, 29 S.U. L. Rev. 181 (2002)

James Willard Hurst, The Law of Treason in the United States: Collected Essays (1971)

Significant Cases

Ex parte Bollman, 8 U.S. (4 Cranch) 75 (1807)

United States v. Burr, 25 F. Cas. 55 (C.C. Va. 1807) (No. 14,693)

Cramer v. United States, 325 U.S. 1 (1945)

Haupt v. United States, 330 U.S. 631 (1947)

Kawakita v. United States, 343 U.S. 717 (1952)

Punishment of Treason

The Congress shall have Power to declare the Punishment of Treason, but no Attainder of Treason shall work Corruption of Blood, or Forfeiture except during the Life of the Person attainted.

(Article III, Section 3, Clause 2)

～

*U*nder common law, punishment for treason generally included drawing, hanging, beheading, and quartering. As with other crimes carrying sentence of death, those adjudged guilty of treason and finally sentenced were considered *attaint*, or stained, meaning dead in the eyes of the law—even before execution. Once attainder was established, the attainted forfeited his real estate to the Crown—a requirement symbolizing lack of entitlement to the benefits of society. Attainder also worked corruption of blood, preventing the attainted from inheriting or transmitting property and preventing any person from deriving title through the attainted. Forfeitures and corruption of blood worked

hardship on dependents and relatives in order to provide maximum deterrence. Eventually, Parliament modified the laws of forfeiture and corruption of blood to protect the innocent.

According to the Constitution, punishment can be set by Congress, but not to include corruption of blood or forfeiture extending beyond the offender's life. Quite apart from this limitation, Justice Joseph Story notes the explicit grant of congressional power over punishment was intended as a leniency, to preclude the assumption of the common-law punishment's harshest elements. The First Congress used its constitutional power of declaring the punishment for treason by establishing the penalty of death, with seven years' imprisonment for misprision of treason.

The actual punishments for those convicted of the federal crime of treason have generally been more lenient than the statutory maximums. Those convicted for their part in the Whiskey Rebellion were pardoned by President George Washington. The United States government regarded Confederate activity as a levying of war, but all Confederates were pardoned by presidential amnesty. Max Haupt, convicted for giving aid and comfort to his alien son, was spared death and sentenced to life imprisonment. (His son Herbert was convicted by a military tribunal for his role as saboteur, and executed.) Tomoyo Kawakita, convicted of treason for abusing American prisoners of war, was sentenced to death but had his sentence commuted to life imprisonment by President Dwight D. Eisenhower. By contrast, the Rosenbergs' espionage convictions brought death sentences.

Of the two successful prosecutions for treason at the state level—Thomas Dorr in Rhode Island in 1844 and John Brown in Virginia in 1859—only Brown was executed. Dorr was pardoned, and elements of the political agitations for which he was convicted were soon adopted into law in Rhode Island.

Bradley C. S. Watson

See Also
Article I, Section 9, Clause 3 (Bill of Attainder)

ARTICLE IV

Full Faith and Credit Clause

Full Faith and Credit shall be given in each State to the public Acts, Records, and judicial Proceedings of every other State. And the Congress may by general Laws prescribe the Manner in which such Acts, Records and Proceedings shall be proved, and the Effect thereof.

(ARTICLE IV, SECTION 1)

*A*n essential purpose of the Full Faith and Credit Clause is to assure that the courts of one state will honor the judgments of the courts of another state without the need to retry the whole cause of action. It was an essential mechanism for creating a "union" out of multiple sovereigns. The first sentence of the Full Faith and Credit Clause appeared almost verbatim in Article IV of the Articles of Confederation, which read: "Full faith and credit shall be given in each of these States to the records, acts and judicial proceedings of the courts and magistrates of every other State." At the Constitutional Convention, the originally proposed article also specifically required each state to enforce the other states' judgments regarding debts, but that portion was dropped. There was little discussion of the constitutional provision during the Convention and ratifying period, but it was commonly assumed that the clause was at least in part intended to ensure that debtors could not escape their creditors by crossing into other states. Moreover, the "public Acts" requirement was apparently added to force state courts to enforce each other's insolvency laws.

Because the clause was drawn from the Articles of Confederation, there is very little discussion of it in the *The Federalist*, although James Madison asserted in No. 42 that its clarity was a great improvement over the version in the Articles. He listed the clause as one of several that "provide for the harmony and proper intercourse among the States."

The Supreme Court has invoked the clause to police state-court proceedings in three contexts: (1) determining when a state must take jurisdiction over claims that arise in other states; (2) limiting the application of local state law over another state's law in multistate disputes; and (3) recognizing and enforcing judgments rendered in sister-state courts.

First, the Court has used the clause to oblige state courts to hear claims that arise under sister-state laws. Thus, the Court has stated that a court cannot categorically refuse to hear claims that arise under another state's laws, at least where the courts recognize the equivalent claim based on local law. *Hughes v. Fetter* (1951). Nor may a state attempt to monopolize litigation by requiring that enforcement actions be heard solely in local courts. *Tennessee Coal, Iron & Railroad Co. v. George* (1914); *Crider v. Zurich Insurance Co.* (1965).

Second, the Supreme Court has also restricted state courts' ability to apply their own laws to multistate disputes. State courts may almost always apply their own procedural rules, including their own statutes of limitations, but there are times when a state's substantive law should give way to the substantive law of another state. It was Justice Joseph Story who first seriously explored this issue in 1834, and the first Supreme Court cases did not appear until the early twentieth century. Initially, the Court required the states to adhere to the traditional territorial principles for the choice of law to apply. That is, if particular legally designated events of a dispute happened in a particular state, say Massachusetts, but if the dispute came to trial in Pennsylvania, the Pennsylvania court had to apply Massachusetts law. *Western Union Telegraph Co. v. Brown* (1914); *New York Life Insurance Co. v. Dodge* (1918). Later, the Court allowed a state to apply its own substantive law whenever it had a legitimate interest in the outcome of the case. *Pacific Employers Insurance Co. v. Industrial Accident Commission* (1939). The most recent Supreme Court cases have collapsed the Due Process and Full Faith and Credit Clause inquiries into a single requirement for the application of forum law: "that state must have a significant contact or significant aggregation of contacts, creating state interests, such that choice of its law is neither arbitrary nor fundamentally unfair." *Allstate Insurance Co. v. Hague* (1981).

With this shift in tests, the Court has backed away from constitutional scrutiny of state-court choice-of-law decisions. In fact, the Court has allowed one state to sue another state in the first state's courts despite the defendant state's sovereign-immunity laws. *State of Nevada v. Hall* (1979); *Franchise Tax Board of California v. Hyatt* (2003). Moreover, the Court has only once in the last fifty years limited a state's ability to apply its own law. *Phillips Petroleum Co. v. Shutts* (1985).

Third, although the Court has largely backed away from policing state choice-of-law decisions, it has imposed stringent requirements regarding recognition and enforcement of sister-state judgments. Practical interests usually require each state to recognize and enforce almost all final court judgments rendered by sister states, even those that offend the public policy of the enforcing state. Pursuant to Congress's implementing statute, the enforcing state's courts must give judgments at least as much effect as the rendering state would. Nonetheless, states can still apply their own statutes of limitations when enforcing judgments by other states' courts, and state administrative decisions that are not reviewed by a court are not entitled to respect in other states.

The Court has recognized a few relatively narrow policy-based exceptions to the states' obligations to enforce the judgments of other states' courts. First, a defendant who did not appear in the first proceeding can collaterally attack a judgment against him on the grounds that the first state's courts lacked personal jurisdiction over the defendant. Second, states are not permitted directly to affect land titles in other states by, for example, issuing a deed to land located in another state. Third, judgments based on purely penal claims (i.e., criminal or administrative fines) need not be enforced by other states. To fall into this penal exception, the judgment must be for the purpose of punishment rather than compensation, and the recovery must be in favor of the state, not a private individual. But tax judgments, judgments for punitive damages in favor of private plaintiffs, and compensatory tort judgments in favor of the state all fail to qualify for this penal exception. Fourth, states can apply their own evidentiary rules. For example, the enforcing state may accept testimony that would have been illegal under the rendering state's law. Finally, if a state court issues a divorce decree in an *ex parte* proceeding (where only one spouse appears), the absent spouse can collaterally attack the validity of the present spouse's domicile within the rendering state.

Congress has invoked its full faith and credit authority in certain specific contexts related to marriage, divorce, and children. A state court may modify a sister-state court's child-custody and support orders to suit "the best interests of the child." The Parental Kidnapping Prevention Act (28 U.S.C. § 1738a) attempts to fix jurisdiction over child-custody determinations and requires states that lack jurisdiction under the Act to enforce valid custody orders. The Full Faith and Credit for Child Support Orders Act (28 U.S.C. § 1738b) allocates jurisdiction over the rendering of child-support orders and specifies states' enforcement obligations. When it appeared that Hawaii was recognizing the validity of same-sex marriages, Congress responded with the Defense of Marriage Act (DOMA) (28 U.S.C. § 1738c). DOMA enables each state to refuse to recognize other states' acts, records, and judicial proceedings purporting to validate same-sex marriages. Moreover, the Act specifically enables each state to deny rights and claims arising from same-sex marriages created in other states. These congressional acts presumably work to displace Supreme Court Full Faith and Credit Clause precedent in these areas.

Erin O'Hara

See Also
Amendment XIV, Section 1 (Due Process Clause)

Suggestions for Further Research
Robert H. Jackson, *Full Faith and Credit—The Lawyer's Clause of the Constitution*, 45 COLUM. L. REV. 1 (1945)

Frederic L. Kirgis, Jr., *The Role of Due Process and Full Faith and Credit in Choice of Law*, 62 CORNELL L. REV. 94 (1976)

James R. Pielemeier, *Why We Should Worry About Full Faith and Credit to Laws*, 60 S. CAL. L. REV. 1299 (1987)

Polly J. Price, *Full Faith and Credit and the Equity Conflict*, 84 VA. L. REV. 747 (1998)

William L. Reynolds, *The Iron Law of Full Faith and Credit*, 53 MD. L. REV. 412 (1994)

Stewart E. Sterk, *The Muddy Boundaries Between Res Judicata and Full Faith and Credit*, 58 WASH. & LEE L. REV. 47 (2001)

Russell J. Weintraub, *Due Process and Full Faith and Credit Limitations on a State's Choice of Law*, 44 IOWA L. REV. 449 (1959)

Ralph U. Whitten, *The Constitutional Limits on State Choice of Law: Full Faith and Credit*, 12 MEM. ST. U. L. REV. 1 (1981)

Ralph U. Whitten, *The Original Understanding of the Full Faith and Credit Clause and the Defense of Marriage Act*, 32 CREIGHTON L. REV. 255 (1998)

Significant Cases
Huntington v. Attrill, 146 U.S. 657 (1892)

Fauntleroy v. Lum, 210 U.S. 230 (1908)

Fall v. Eastin, 215 U.S. 1 (1909)

Tennessee Coal, Iron & Railroad Co. v. George, 233 U.S. 354 (1914)

Western Union Telegraph Co. v. Brown, 234 U.S. 542 (1914)

New York Life Insurance Co. v. Dodge, 246 U.S. 357 (1918)

Pacific Employers Insurance Co. v. Industrial Accident Commission, 306 U.S. 493 (1939)

Williams v. North Carolina, 325 U.S. 226 (1945)

Hughes v. Fetter, 341 U.S. 609 (1951)

Crider v. Zurich Insurance Co., 380 U.S. 39 (1965)

State of Nevada v. Hall, 440 U.S. 410 (1979)

Allstate Insurance Co. v. Hague, 449 U.S. 302 (1981)

Phillips Petroleum Co. v. Shutts, 472 U.S. 797 (1985)

University of Tennessee v. Elliot, 478 U.S. 788 (1986)

Sun Oil v. Wortman, 486 U.S. 717 (1988)

Baker v. General Motors Corp., 522 U.S. 222 (1998)

Franchise Tax Board of California v. Hyatt, 123 S. Ct. 1683 (2003)

Privileges and Immunities Clause

The Citizens of each State shall be entitled to all Privileges and Immunities of Citizens in the several States.

(**ARTICLE IV, SECTION 2, CLAUSE 1**)

"Privileges and immunities" constituted a summary of ancient rights of Englishmen that the colonists fought to maintain during the struggle against the mother country. Founding documents, such as the Declarations and Resolves of the First Continental Congress and the Articles of Confederation, championed these rights. In Philadelphia, when the Committee of Detail proposed the Privileges and Immunities Clause, the Framers approved it with no debate.

In many of the charters of the original colonies, the Crown guaranteed some variation of franchises, privileges, immunities, or liberties to "free and natural subjects...as if they and every of them were born within the realm of England." Ultimately deriving from the emancipation of the serfs in the Middle Ages, the privileges, immunities, franchises, and liberties summed up the legal rights of freemen, which were inestimably greater than those afforded to the serf, the indentured servant, or the foreigner. The Crown granted them to the colonists in the New World to the same extent as to freemen in England itself, thereby creating a common subject status among free-born Englishmen.

The package of rights granted to the colonists had distinct components. "Liberties" were not rights of individuals, but the right of a corporation, or manor, or abbot, to make and enforce laws within their respective jurisdictions. A formal grant of liberty from the king was a "franchise." Thus, when the king allowed a colony the right "from Time to Time to Make, Ordain, and Establish all manner of wholesome and reasonable Laws, Statutes, Ordinances, Directions, and Instructions, not Contrary to the Laws of this Realm of England," the king was legally granting a franchise to the colonists to exercise the liberty of self-governance. The phrase "to exercise the franchise," meaning to vote, ultimate derives from this older notion of the "liberty" to make laws.

"Liberties" and "franchises" constituted the power of a governing unit to make rules. In contrast, "immunities" were exceptions that the king granted from the force of the law. Immunities gave individuals, towns, or other entities freedom from having to abide by a legal obligation. The king frequently gave villages immunity from having to pay tolls on merchandise produced within their precincts. He also granted certain individuals immunity from compulsory public service.

The courts enforced privileges, which included: trial by jury; the initiation of suits against freemen by summons, not arrest; freedom from civil process while a witness or an attorney was at court, or while a clergyman was performing divine service; the exclusion of essential personal property, like ploughs or the tools of one's trade, from distraint; the benefit of clergy in capital cases; the rights of possession and inheritance of land; the right to use deadly force to defend one's abode; the privilege of members of Parliament to be free from arrest while on duty; and the right of merchants in certain towns to trade freely.

In America, there were specific practical effects to the guarantees of privileges and immunities. First, despite the significant differences among the colonies, the granting of common privileges and immunities made all colonists common subjects under a single Crown. Second, any freeman had the right to travel and take up residence within any of the English colonies. No colonist could be held to be a foreigner in any other colony. Benjamin Franklin, born in Boston, became a Pennsylvanian simply by moving to Philadelphia. Third, as has been described, privileges and immunities referred to a specific set of legal entitlements, individual as well as communitarian.

Finally, the grants of privileges and immunities operated as a kind of equal-protection guarantee, particularly for merchants. It meant that temporary travelers in a colony, not just those who moved in to take up residence, could buy and sell and have the protection of the law without the need for a special grant or charter from the host colony. Even under the umbrella of mercantilism, then, common privileges and immunities allowed for a robust exchange of goods and commercial paper.

The privilege to be free from economic discrimination was based on the underlying right to carry on a lawful trade. The government could pass generally applicable laws and commercial regulations, but it could not discriminate against visitors in their lawful mercantile activities. Corporations, as creations of the state, were a special case; but if a governmental agent prevented a freeman from participating in mercantile endeavors on equal legal grounds with others, the freeman could justly claim a violation of his rights as a free-born English subject. As a corollary, many regarded monopolies as "odious" and violative of the right to a lawful calling. The prohibition of monopolies, however, never quite gelled into a fundamental privilege.

In sum, the colonial experience of privileges and immunities meant: (1) membership in a common political community, (2) a right to travel, (3) a series of particularly defined rights centering around access to the courts, and (4) equal protection of the laws for commercial activities based upon the right of every freeman to a lawful calling.

Along the path to independence, "Privileges and Immunities" began to be set alongside ideas of natural rights as mutual supports for the patriot cause. Yet the notion of privileges and immunities still referred to a set of historically obtained rights and not to general natural rights, though the two categories were seen to be in utter harmony. The First Continental Congress made that distinction in its Declaration and Resolves of 1774. The delegates asserted some rights as natural, that is, that the colonists "are entitled to life, liberty, and property, and they have never ceded to any sovereign power whatever, a right to dispose of either without their consent." But when the delegates came to describing the privileges and immunities of the colonists, they pointed to specific English grants: "That these, His Majesty's Colonies, are likewise entitled to all the immunities and privileges granted and confirmed to them by royal charters, or secured by their several codes of provincial laws."

After independence, a clause protecting privileges and immunities went through a number of drafts before its final formulation in the Articles of Confederation. What is clear from the various formulations, however, is that the drafters based the guarantee of privileges and immunities on the same principles as were in the colonial charters. As finally approved, Article IV of the Articles (including a full faith and credit clause) sought to create a common citizenship, a right to travel, and equal protection for commercial activities.

James Madison believed that the privileges and immunities clause in the Articles of Confederation was repetitive and confusing, and stood in the way of Congress's power to regulate naturalization. As a result, the Constitution's Article IV became simpler and direct. It created a common citizenship, but Congress would determine who could become citizens. It prohibited states from discriminating against residents of other states in judicial process and in economic activities. The clause was self-executing. Congress possesses no independent power to enforce the clause. *United States v. Harris* (1883). As Alexander Hamilton noted in *The Federalist* No. 80, the federal courts would be the agency of enforcement.

The clause did not refer to a set of independent natural rights; many of the new state constitutions distinguished between natural rights and privileges and immunities. Privileges and immunities remained positive, not natural, rights and subject to the tradition of liberty as self-govern-

ment. Consequently, after the Revolution, the states stood in the place that Parliament had occupied in the 1760s: privileges and immunities existed, and some certainly were fundamental, but the "people" through their legislature could alter them. Despite the expected common corpus of privileges and immunities, Article IV of the Constitution does not compel a state to provide for the privileges and immunities of its own citizens, but only to treat out-of-state residents equally in the enjoyment of whatever privileges and immunities obtained within the state.

Thus, a state could revise or repeal a traditional privilege or immunity, and the nonresident had no right to claim it for himself. In 1821, William Cranch, Chief Judge of the Circuit Court of the District of Columbia, was called upon to decide the constitutionality of a federal law prohibiting free blacks from residing in the District without first obtaining a surety from a white person guaranteeing their good behavior. The purpose of the act was to prevent poor blacks from immigrating into the District and burdening the distribution of services under the poor laws. Gaining a white surety was expected to be impossible.

William Cranch found no obstacle to the law in the Privileges and Immunities Clause of Article IV (which treats the District of Columbia as a state). "A citizen of one state," he wrote, "coming into another state, can claim only those privileges and immunities which belong to citizens of the latter state, in like circumstances." *Costin v. Corp. of Washington* (1821). Free blacks lost the effective right to travel to the District of Columbia, and Article IV afforded them no protection.

Two years later, however, a judge equated privileges and immunities with natural rights. In *Corfield v. Coryell* (1823), Justice Bushrod Washington, on circuit, declared,

> The inquiry is, what are the privileges and immunities of citizens in the several states? We feel no hesitation in confining these expressions to those privileges and immunities which are, in their nature, fundamental; which belong, of right, to the citizens of all free governments; and which have, at all times, been

enjoyed by the citizens of the several states which compose this Union, from their time of becoming free, independent, and sovereign.

Bushrod Washington's statement was dictum. In the actual holding, he decided that New Jersey could discriminate against out-of-state citizens in the harvesting of oysters because the citizens of New Jersey "owned" oysters as a natural resource. A number of courts cited *Corfield v. Coryell* before the Civil War, but only for its holding and never for its dictum.

The Supreme Court rejected a natural-rights content to Article IV's Privileges and Immunities Clause in *Paul v. Virginia* (1869). Thus, although Justice Samuel F. Miller confusingly quoted Justice Washington's dictum in the famous *Slaughter-House Cases* (1873), his summary of the meaning of the clause was correct as a matter of law: the "sole purpose" of Article IV's Privileges and Immunities Clause, he declared,

> was to declare to the several States that whatever those rights, as you grant or establish them to your own citizens, or as you limit or qualify, or impose restrictions on their exercise, the same, neither more nor less, shall be the measure of the rights of citizens of other States within your jurisdiction.

Bushrod Washington's dictum, however, had taken on a life of its own. It figured in abolitionist ideology and had much to do with the debate over the Privileges or Immunities Clause of the Fourteenth Amendment. But the Supreme Court continued to reject it as defining the Privileges and Immunities Clause of Article IV. *See McKane v. Durston* (1894).

The application of most of the procedural protections of the Bill of Rights to the states by way of the Fourteenth Amendment limited the traditional scope of the Privileges and Immunities Clause of Article IV to access to courts, travel, and equal treatment for nonresidents. The courts have affirmed a right of the nonresident to have "reasonable and adequate" access to the courts of a host state. *Canadian Northern Ry. Co.*

v. Eggen (1920). The Supreme Court has recognized a right to travel, but it has had difficulty in finding a secure constitutional locus for the right. Most recently in *Saenz v. Roe* (1999), the Court asserted that the right to travel emanates from the Privileges or Immunities Clause of the Fourteenth Amendment.

In terms of equal treatment for visitors, however, the modern Court's application of the Privileges and Immunities Clause of Article IV has been generally consistent with legal tradition and the views of the Framers. The clause protects nonresident citizens, not corporations. *Bank of Augusta v. Earle* (1839); *Paul v. Virginia*. The clause protects visitors only in regard to their enjoyment of a "fundamental right," which is almost invariably defined as a right to a lawful or common calling, which, in turn, can be regulated by generally applicable legislation by the host state.

Lawful callings include the practice of law, *Supreme Court of New Hampshire v. Piper* (1985); fishing (the Court has abandoned the fiction that a state's citizens own its natural resources), *Toomer v. Witsell* (1948); construction work, *United Building & Construction Trades Council v. Mayor and Council of Camden* (1984); and merchant activities, *Ward v. Maryland* (1870); but not recreational hunting, *Baldwin v. Fish and Game Commission* (1978).

Once the Court determines that there is a lawful calling, it applies a form of intermediate scrutiny: (1) whether "noncitizens constitute a peculiar source of the evil at which the [discriminatory] statute is aimed"; and (2) whether there is a "reasonable relationship between the danger represented by noncitizens, as a class, and the . . . discrimination practice upon them." *Hicklin v. Orbeck* (1978).

The Court has also applied the clause to discriminatory taxation, *Lunding v. New York Tax Appeals Tribunal* (1998), but found that the clause was not violated when a state requires a higher tuition at a state university for nonresident students. *Vlandis v. Kline* (1973). Justice Antonin Scalia would substitute the nondiscriminatory imperative of the Privileges and Immunities Clause for the Court's traditional use of the dormant commerce power, even though the Privileges and Immunities Clause does not apply to corporations. *Tyler Pipe Industries v. Department of Revenue* (1987). Finally, the suspicion against monopolies is treated as it was historically: not as a fundamental immunity, but as an activity regulated by legislation.

David F. Forte and Ronald Rotunda

See Also

Article I, Section 8, Clause 3 (Commerce Among the States)
Article I, Section 8, Clause 4 (Naturalization)
Amendment XIV, Section 1 (Privileges or Immunities)
Amendment XIV, Section 1 (Due Process Clause)

Suggestions for Further Research

David S. Bogen, *The Privileges and Immunities Clause of Article IV*, 37 CASE W. RES. L. REV. 794 (1987)

Michael Conant, *Antimonopoly Tradition under the Ninth and Fourteenth Amendments: Slaughter-House Cases Re-examined*, 31 EMORY L.J. 785 (1982)

Douglas G. Smith, *Natural Law, Article IV, and Section One of the Fourteenth Amendment*, 47 AM. U. L. REV. 351 (1997)

Significant Cases

Costin v. Corp. of Washington, 6 F. Cas. 612 (C.C.D.C. 1821) (No. 3266)
Corfield v. Coryell, 6 F. Cas. 546 (C.C.E.D. Pa. 1823) (No. 3230)
Bank of Augusta v. Earle, 38 U.S. (13 Pet.) 519 (1839)
Paul v. Virginia, 75 U.S. (8 Wall.) 168 (1869)
Ward v. Maryland, 79 U.S. (12 Wall.) 418 (1870)
Slaughter-House Cases, 83 U.S. (16 Wall.) 36 (1873)
United States v. Harris, 106 U.S. 629 (1883)
McKane v. Durston, 153 U.S. 684 (1894)
Canadian Northern Railway Co. v. Eggen, 252 U.S. 553 (1920)
Toomer v. Witsell, 334 U.S. 385 (1948)
Mullaney v. Anderson, 342 U.S. 415 (1952)
Vlandis v. Kline, 412 U.S. 441 (1973)
Baldwin v. Fish and Game Commission, 436 U.S. 371 (1978)
Hicklin v. Orbeck, 437 U.S. 518 (1978)
United Building & Construction Trades Council v. Mayor and Council of Camden, 465 U.S. 208 (1984)
Supreme Court of New Hampshire v. Piper, 470 U.S. 274 (1985)

Tyler Pipe Industries v. Department of Revenue, 483 U.S. 232 (1987)
Supreme Court of Virginia v. Friedman, 487 U.S. 59 (1988)
Barnard v. Thorstenn, 489 U.S. 546 (1989)
Lunding v. New York Tax Appeals Tribunal, 522 U.S. 287 (1998)
Saenz v. Roe, 526 U.S. 489 (1999)

Interstate Rendition Clause

A Person charged in any State with Treason, Felony, or other Crime, who shall flee from Justice, and be found in another State, shall on Demand of the executive Authority of the State from which he fled, be delivered up, to be removed to the State having Jurisdiction of the Crime.

(**ARTICLE IV, SECTION 2, CLAUSE 2**)

∽

*T*he Extradition or Interstate Rendition Clause derives from similar language in the Articles of Confederation, but the principle of extradition between governments dates to antiquity. The Framers' purpose was to foster comity between states and to prevent criminals from evading law enforcement. Despite its classical roots, the Framers regarded interstate rendition as distinct from international extradition. In 1793, Congress passed the first rendition act—today, 18 U.S.C. § 3182—for fear that the clause was not self-executing. The statute governed rendition from territories as well as states. Although there is no express power granted to Congress to govern rendition, Justice Joseph Story regarded it as implied from the moral duty of Congress to carry into execution the duties imposed on the federal government by the Constitution. *Prigg v. Pennsylvania* (1842).

On its face, the clause requires (1) a facially valid criminal charge in a demanding state, (2) a flight to an asylum state, and (3) an executive demand for return. The Framers specified the words "Treason" and "Felony" to show that political crimes warrant rendition, as well as "other Crimes" to comprehend all crimes, regardless of gravity. *Taylor v. Taintor* (1872); *Kentucky v. Dennison* (1860). Exempted from the scope of the clause are civil liabilities and private debts. As to what constitutes a criminal charge, the 1793 act requires indictment or affidavit, but does not mention the criminal information. This omission arguably was deliberate, as such information was a known device abused by the British. The meaning of "charged" remains unresolved in this respect.

The clause suggests that deliberate flight is required. Thus, early scholars speculated, for example, that a person involuntarily removed from one state to a second state could not be rendered back or rendered forward to a third state. But consistently with the clause's law-enforcement purpose, flight has been construed without regard to intent, requiring only that the person sought be alleged to have been physically present in the demanding state so as to commit an overt act in furtherance of a crime there. *Strassheim v. Daily* (1911); *Appleyard v. Massachusetts* (1906). The fact that a fugitive is present in an asylum state before the indictment is issued does not insulate him from rendition. *Roberts v. Reilly* (1885).

In the antebellum period, a crisis of executive demands and compliance arose, as some Northern governors refused to return fugitives charged with slavery-related crimes to Southern states. Since the Civil War, the Supreme Court has clarified and limited the scope of the executive power in the asylum state to decline rendition. That executive may determine only whether the person sought is charged with a crime under the demanding state's law, and whether that person is a fugitive, that is, was present in the demanding state when the alleged overt act occurred. *Munsey v. Clough* (1905). A court may inquire similarly upon a habeas corpus petition. *Michigan v. Doran* (1978). But other questions—of, for example, guilt or innocence, sufficiency of evidence, construction of state law, or adequacy of justice in the demanding state—are triable only in the demanding state. *New Mexico ex rel. Ortiz v.*

Reed (1998); *Lascelles v. Georgia* (1893). In 1987, the Supreme Court resolved the last vestige of antebellum indecision, ruling in *Puerto Rico v. Branstad* (1987) that federal courts may compel state executives to render fugitives properly demanded.

Rendition particulars today are controlled chiefly by the Uniform Extradition and Rendition Act, adopted in some form in every state. State rendition laws have been upheld insofar as they are consistent with the Constitution and federal statute. Furthermore, states today provide for rendition outside the scope of the clause. For example, states may agree to render subpoenaed witnesses and charged persons who were never present in the demanding state. It is unclear whether these ancillary agreements in any way offend the original conception of the Interstate Rendition Clause as an exclusive process. For example, an agreement between two states to allow rendition even if there are procedural deficiencies in the demand for rendition may contravene the Due Process Clause of the Fourteenth Amendment.

Richard Peltz

See Also

Article IV, Section 1 (Full Faith and Credit Clause)

Article IV, Section 2, Clause 1 (Privileges and Immunities Clause)

Article IV, Section 2, Clause 3 (Fugitive Slave Clause)

Article IV, Section 3, Clause 2 (Property Clause)

Amendment X (Reserved Powers of the States)

Amendment XIV, Section 1 (Due Process Clause)

Suggestions for Further Research

Leslie W. Abramson, *Extradition in America: Of Uniform Acts and Governmental Discretion*, 33 Baylor L. Rev. 793 (1981)

John G. Hawley, Inter-State Extradition (1890)

Rollin C. Hurd, A Treatise on the Right of Personal Liberty, and on the Writ of Habeas Corpus (1858)

2 John Bassett Moore, A Treatise on Extradition and Interstate Rendition (1891)

John J Murphy, *Revising Domestic Extradition Law*, 131 U. Pa. L. Rev. 1063 (1983)

James Scott, The Law of Interstate Rendition (1917)

Dale Patrick Smith, *Dissertation: Interstate Extradition: A Case Study in Constitutional Interpretation* (1984)

Samuel T. Spear, The Law of Extradition, International and Inter-State (3d ed. 1885)

Significant Cases

Prigg v. Pennsylvania, 41 U.S. (16 Pet.) 539 (1842)

Kentucky v. Dennison, 65 U.S. (24 How.) 66 (1860)

Taylor v. Taintor, 83 U.S. (16 Wall.) 366 (1872)

Roberts v. Reilly, 116 U.S. 80 (1885)

Lascelles v. Georgia, 148 U.S. 537 (1893)

Munsey v. Clough, 196 U.S. 364 (1905)

Appleyard v. Massachusetts, 203 U.S. 222 (1906)

Strassheim v. Daily, 221 U.S. 280 (1911)

Michigan v. Doran, 439 U.S. 282 (1978)

Puerto Rico v. Branstad, 483 U.S. 219 (1987)

New Mexico *ex rel.* Ortiz v. Reed, 524 U.S. 151 (1998)

Fugitive Slave Clause

No Person held to Service or Labour in one State, under the Laws thereof, escaping into another, shall, in Consequence of any Law or Regulation therein, be discharged from such Service or Labour, but shall be delivered up on Claim of the Party to whom such Service or Labour may be due. (Article IV, Section 2, Clause 3)

~

Toward the end of the Constitutional Convention, during the debate over the Privileges and Immunities Clause (Article IV, Section 2, Clause 1), Charles Pinckney of South Carolina remarked that "some provision should be included in favor of property in slaves." Thereafter, he and his fellow South Carolinian, Pierce Butler, moved "to require fugitive slaves and servants to be delivered up like criminals." The motion was withdrawn after James Wilson and Roger Sherman objected, but the next day it was renewed as a formal addition to what would become Article IV. It passed unanimously and without debate. This was probably because there was a strong precedent in the Northwest Ordinance of 1787 (passed six weeks earlier by Congress), which included a fugitive-slave provision along with its declaration (presaging the Thirteenth Amendment) that "neither slavery nor involuntary servitude" would exist in the territory.

A model of circumlocution, the resulting clause is the closest of the so-called Slave Clauses (Article I, Section 2, Clause 3; Article I, Section 9, Clause 1; and Article V) to recognizing slavery as a protected institution. It also became the most controversial of the clauses and was at the center of many constitutional disputes in the 1840s and 1850s.

As initially proposed in the Convention, the language spoke of persons "bound to service or labor" being delivered up to the person "justly claiming their service or labor." This was revised by the Committee of Style to refer to persons "legally held to service or labour" being delivered up to "the party to whom such service or labour may be due," thereby making the law the arbiter and removing the recognition of "just" claims to slave property. In contrast, for instance, the previous clause (Article IV, Section 2, Clause 2) speaks of those charged with crimes "who shall flee from Justice."

At the last moment, the phrase "Person legally held to Service or Labour in one state" was amended to read "Person held to Service or Labour in one state, under the Laws thereof" to make the clause comply, according to James Madison's notes, "with the wish of some who thought the term legal equivocal, and favoring the idea that slavery was legal in a moral view." This revision emphasized as well that slaves were held according to the laws of individual states, and that slaveholding was not based either upon natural law or the common law, avoiding the implication that the Constitution itself legally sanctioned the practice. The section also leaves a clear implication, contrary to the holding in *Dred Scott v. Sandford* (1857), that the slave owner's property claim did not apply in federal territories, if Congress chose to prohibit slavery there. Indeed, according to the legal requirements of the clause, an escaped slave would have ceased to be a slave as soon as he had entered a state that did not recognize slavery under its own law.

Of the other three sections in Article IV, two grant powers to Congress and one vests power in the United States generally. Written in the passive voice, Section 2 confers no powers on the federal government but limits state authority, giving rise to the argument that the clause is simply declaratory. In 1793, however, Congress passed legislation to enforce the clause. In its first decision on the issue, the Supreme Court held (in a decision written by Justice Joseph Story) that Congress had exercised powers that were necessary and proper to carry out the provision and that a state law that penalized the seizure of fugitive slaves was unconstitutional. *Prigg v. Pennsylvania* (1842). Story did note, in an obiter dictum, that the federal government could not compel state officials to enforce the act. This led to numerous states passing personal-liberty laws (prohibiting state officials from enforcing the federal statute) and then to a new federal Fugitive Slave Act enacted as part of the Compromise of 1850. In *Moore v. Illinois* (1852), the Supreme Court held that states could impose penalties on their citizens for harboring fugitive slaves. Later, when the Wisconsin Supreme Court supported resistance to the Fugitive Slave Act by declaring it unconstitutional, the United States Supreme Court unanimously reversed. *Ableman v. Booth* (1859).

In *Dred Scott v. Sandford*, Chief Justice Roger B. Taney attempted to use this clause, along with the so-called Slave Trade Clause (Article I, Section 9, Clause 1), as evidence that slaves were not citizens but were to be considered property according to the Constitution. By this clause, Taney argued, "the States pledge themselves to each other to maintain the right of property of the master, by delivering up to him any slave who may have escaped from his service."

The more generally accepted interpretation, however, is that this clause did not speak to the issue of citizenship at all, but was a necessary accommodation to existing slavery interests in particular states, required for the sake of establishing the Constitution—"scaffolding to the magnificent structure," Frederick Douglass called it, "to be removed as soon as the building was completed." This point is underscored by the fact that, although slavery was abolished by constitutional amendment (*see* the Thirteenth Amendment), not one word of the original text had to be amended or deleted.

Matthew Spalding

See Also

Article I, Section 2, Clause 3 (Three-Fifths Clause)

Article I, Section 8, Clause 3 (Commerce Among the States)

Article I, Section 9, Clause 1 (Slave Trade Clause)

Article V (Prohibition on Amendment: Slave Trade)

Suggestions for Further Research

Don E. Fehrenbacher, The Slaveholding Republic: An Account of the United States Government's Relations to Slavery (2001)

Donald L. Robinson, Slavery in the Structure of American Politics, 1765–1820 (1971)

Herbert J. Storing, *Slavery and the Moral Foundations of the American Republic, in* Robert H. Horwitz, The Moral Foundations of the American Republic (1986)

Significant Cases

Prigg v. Pennsylvania, 41 U.S. (16 Pet.) 539 (1842)

Moore v. Illinois, 55 U.S. (14 How.) 13 (1852)

Dred Scott v. Sandford, 60 U.S. (19 How.) 393 (1857)

Ableman v. Booth, 62 U.S. (21 How.) 506 (1859)

New States Clause

New States may be admitted by the Congress into this Union; but no new States shall be formed or erected within the Jurisdiction of any other State; nor any State be formed by the Junction of two or more States, or Parts of States, without the Consent of the Legislatures of

the States concerned as well as of
the Congress.
(ARTICLE IV, SECTION 3, CLAUSE 1)

∼

*A*t the Constitutional Convention, the Committee of Detail proposed that "new States shall
be admitted on the same terms with the original States." That proposal would have taken the
policy behind the Northwest Ordinance of 1787
and made it a constitutional imperative. But
Gouverneur Morris wanted the equality of
admitted states to be struck because he feared
the political power of the Western states would
"overwhelm" the East. Over the objections of
James Madison, his motion to strike out the
requirement of equality won 7-2. He then
moved to make sure that no state could be
formed out of a previous state without the consent of the previous state as well as the "general
legislature" (i.e., Congress). In this case as well,
he wanted the Eastern states that still had claims
to Western lands (e.g., Virginia, North Carolina) to have a veto over whether their western
counties (which eventually became Kentucky
and Tennessee) could become states. This
motion passed 6-5. Like the question of the
establishment of lower federal courts, the Convention effectively passed the issue of the status
of newly admitted states over to the political
process.

Once the new Constitution went into effect,
however, Congress admitted Vermont and Kentucky on equal terms and thereafter formalized
the condition in its acts of admission for subsequent states, declaring that the new state enters
"on an equal footing with the original States in
all respects whatever." Thus the Congress, utilizing the discretion allowed by the Framers,
adopted a policy of equal status for newly
admitted states.

A number of observers, however, including
Gouverneur Morris, contended that Congress
could only admit states from territory that the
United States possessed at the time of the Constitution's formation. That position was echoed
by New England Federalists upset with Thomas
Jefferson over the purchase of Louisiana. There
is no indication of any such limitation, however, in the text or in the view of most of the
Framers. Further, time and the admission of
new states have made that argument irrelevant.
Utilizing its discretion, Congress admitted new
states from newly acquired territory and opted
to give equal status to each.

The Supreme Court, however, chose to
impose the very constitutional requirement that
the Framers had rejected. With the growth of
states' rights advocacy during the antebellum
period, the Court asserted that the Constitution
mandated admission of new states on the basis
of equality. *Lessee of Pollard v. Hagan* (1845).
The doctrine remains constant to this day and
has engendered problems in construing the
legal effect of conditions that Congress has
placed on the admission of a number of states.

According to traditional historic practice,
Congress passes an enabling act prescribing the
process by which the people of a United States
territory may draft and adopt a state constitution. Texas is the exception: it was an independent republic, and, under the Resolution of
Annexation, has the option of creating up to
four additional states out of its territory. Many
enabling acts contain restrictions, such as the
prohibition of bigamy in the Utah, Arizona,
New Mexico, and Oklahoma acts. The applicant
state then submits its proposed constitution to
Congress, which either accepts it or requires
changes. For example, in 1866, Congress refused
the proposed Nebraska constitution because it
limited suffrage to white males. Upon approval
of the new state constitution, Congress may
direct the President to issue a proclamation certifying the entry of the new state into the United States. A number of states, however, drafted
constitutions for submission to Congress absent
enabling acts and were subsequently admitted.

Although the enabling act becomes a "fundamental law" of the state, its provisions must
give way to the "equal footing" rights once the
new state becomes a member of the Union. In
Lessee of Pollard v. Hagan, the Supreme Court
held that an enabling act could not divest Alabama of its sovereign ownership rights to land
under internal navigable waters; and in *Coyle v.
Smith* (1911), the Court invalidated a provision
in Oklahoma's enabling act that constrained

where the state could place its capital. The rule the Court has fashioned is that Congress can regulate the state through the enabling act only insofar as Congress could do so under one of its enumerated powers. Thus, under its power to regulate territories, Congress could, in its enabling act, require Utah to deny the franchise to women in voting for delegates to the state's constitutional convention, but that restriction could not bind Utah once it had become a state. *Anderson v. Tyree* (1895). More typically, enforceable provisions in enabling acts have included exemption of federal property from state taxation, the method of regulating public lands, and the rules of commerce among the Indians.

Finally, despite the ambiguous second semicolon in the clause, new states may be formed out of an existing state provided all parties consent: the new state, the existing state, and the Congress. In that way, Kentucky, Tennessee, Maine, West Virginia, and arguably Vermont came into the Union.

David F. Forte

See Also

Article IV, Section 3, Clause 2 (Property Clause)

Suggestions for Further Research

Frank DiCastri, *Are All States Really Equal? The "Equal Footing" Doctrine and Indian Claims to Submerged Lands*, 1997 Wis. L. Rev. 179 (1997)

Vasan Kesavan & Michael Stokes Paulsen, *Is West Virginia Unconstitutional?*, 90 Cal. L. Rev. 291 (2002)

Carolyn Landever, *Whose Home on the Range? Equal Footing, the New Federalism and State Jurisdiction on Federal Lands*, 47 Fla. L. Rev. 557 (1995)

Gary Lawson & Guy Seidman, The Constitution of Empire: Territorial Expansion and the American Legal History (2004)

Significant Cases

Lessee of Pollard v. Hagan, 44 U.S. (3 How.) 212 (1845)

Anderson v. Tyree, 12 Utah 129, 42 P. 201 (1895)

Stearns v. Minnesota, 179 U.S. 223 (1900)

Coyle v. Smith, 221 U.S. 559 (1911)

United States v. Sandoval, 231 U.S. 28 (1913)

Property Clause

The Congress shall have Power to dispose of and make all needful Rules and Regulations respecting the Territory or other Property belonging to the United States....
(Article IV, Section 3, Clause 2)

The federal government owns or controls about thirty percent of the land in the United States. These holdings include national parks, national forests, recreation areas, wildlife refuges, vast tracts of range and wasteland managed by the Bureau of Land Management, reservations held in trust for Native American tribes, military bases, and ordinary federal buildings and installations. Although federal property can be found in every state, the largest concentrations are in the west, where, for example, the federal government owns over eighty percent of the land within Nevada.

The primary constitutional authority for the management and control of this vast real-estate empire is the Property Clause. The exact scope of this clause has long been a matter of debate. Broadly speaking, three different theories have been advanced.

The narrowest conception, which can be called the *proprietary theory*, maintains that the Property Clause simply allows Congress to act as an ordinary owner of land. It can set policy regarding whether such lands will be sold or retained and, if they are retained, who may enter these lands and for what purposes. Under this conception, the clause confers no political sovereignty over federal landholdings. Unless one of the enumerated powers of Article I applies, such as the power to raise armies or establish a post office, political sovereignty over federal lands remains with the several states in which the land is located.

The broadest conception, which can be called the *police-power theory*, regards the clause as conferring not only the powers of ownership but also general sovereign authority to regulate private conduct that occurs on federal land or that affects federal land. In default of any federal rule, state law applies. But if Congress determines that a federal rule "respecting" federal land is "needful," it may adopt federal legislation that supersedes state law. Thus, the Property Clause gives Congress the authority to adopt any type of legislation for federal lands, including codes of criminal law, family law, and exemptions from state taxation for persons residing on federal lands.

Although most commentators have polarized around the proprietary and police-power theories, there is also an intermediate conception of the Property Clause, which can be labeled the *protective theory*. This conception would go beyond the proprietary theory in regarding the clause as a partial source of sovereign authority. But it would stop short of the police-power theory by limiting that authority to legislation designed to protect the proprietary interests of the United States. Under this intermediate conception, for example, the clause would permit Congress to pass federal legislation regulating the sale of federal land, protecting federal land from trespasses and nuisances, or exempting federal land from state taxation. On the other hand, the clause would not permit Congress to enact a general code of criminal law or family law, nor would it permit Congress to exempt persons residing on federal land from general rules of state taxation.

It is not certain which of these three theories corresponds with the original understanding of the Framers, inasmuch as the debates from the Constitutional Convention and the ratification process have little to say about the Property Clause. One clue is provided by the structure of the Constitution. Article I, which sets forth the enumerated powers of Congress, includes a specific grant of power over the governance of federal property. Article I, Section 8, Clause 17, known as the Enclave Clause, is plainly a grant of sovereign authority—indeed, exclusive sovereign authority—over the District of Columbia and other federal enclaves acquired with the consent of the state in which they are located.

Article I is the place where one would expect to find a grant of power to Congress to exercise political sovereignty over federal lands. Article IV, in contrast, which generally deals with issues of state-to-state relations (i.e., full faith and credit, privileges and immunities, extradition, repatriation of slaves, creation of new states, protection of states against invasion) would be an odd place to put such a power. Moreover, it is inconsistent with the careful drafting of the Constitution to assume that the Framers included two overlapping grants of sovereign political authority over federal lands. These structural considerations make it doubtful that the broad police-power theory is consistent with the original understanding.

Another important piece of evidence is the Northwest Ordinance, which Congress, under the Articles of Confederation, enacted as the Constitutional Convention was meeting, and which the First Congress reenacted after the Constitution was ratified. This statute established the territorial government for the land comprising what is today the states of Ohio, Indiana, Michigan, Illinois, and Wisconsin. James Madison and other leaders at the Convention thought that the Articles of Confederation did not contain an adequate source of power to sustain the Northwest Ordinance. The Property Clause was designed to remedy that defect. This suggests that the Framers intended the Property Clause to be broad enough at least to constitutionalize the provisions of the Northwest Ordinance.

The Northwest Ordinance included a number of provisions respecting the governance of the new territory that would have to be described as pure police-power measures. These include clauses preserving the freedom of religion, prohibiting uncompensated takings of property, and outlawing slavery. Other provisions of the Ordinance addressed the status of federal land once new states were formed from the territory and admitted to the Union. Such states were prospectively prohibited from interfering with the disposal of lands by the United States or with regulations adopted by Congress to secure title to bona fide purchasers, and they were barred from imposing any tax on federal lands.

Taking the structural and historical evidence together, we can infer what may plausibly have been the original understanding of the Property Clause. The Property Clause authorized Congress to exercise a general police power within the territories before they were formed into states. Once states were admitted to the union, however, Congress could exercise full police powers over federal land located in a state only in accordance with the Enclave Clause, that is, only when the land was acquired with the consent of the state in question. As to what "needful Rules and Regulations" Congress could enact respecting federal lands in a state not located in an enclave, the Northwest Ordinance suggests that at least some preemptive federal legislation was contemplated, but only if designed to protect the proprietary interests of the United States. In short, the Framers intended that the police-power theory would apply to federal land located in territories, but that the protective theory would apply to non-enclave federal land located in states.

A leading nineteenth-century exposition of the constitutional authority of the federal government over federal lands, *Fort Leavenworth Railroad Co. v. Lowe* (1885), is generally consistent with this conclusion. There, Justice Stephen J. Field wrote that the authority of the federal government over territories is "necessarily paramount." But once a territory is organized as a state and admitted to the union on equal footing with other states, the state government assumes general sovereignty over federal lands, and the federal government has the rights only of an "individual proprietor." The federal government can exercise rights of general sovereignty over property only if there has been a formal cession of sovereignty by the state under the Enclave Clause. Justice Field qualified this vision of separated sovereignty, however, by noting that if the federal government acquires land outside the Enclave Clause, any federal forts, buildings, or other installations erected on such land "will be free from any such interference and jurisdiction of the State as would destroy or impair their effective use for the purposes designed."

The judicial vision of how much power the Property Clause confers on the federal government has hardly remained constant. To the contrary, it has evolved significantly over time. In the first half of the nineteenth century, the clause was understood to be primarily a source of authority for establishing territorial governments. Once new states were admitted to the Union, the federal government became a mere

trustee of any remaining federal lands, holding and protecting them, pending their sale to private persons. *Lessee of Pollard v. Hagan* (1845). With the infamous decision of *Dred Scott v. Sandford* (1857) the Court went further, holding that the Property Clause does not permit the exercise of police powers by the federal government in territory acquired after the Founding, and in particular that it does not permit the federal government to prohibit slavery in such territory. *Dred Scott v. Sandford*. Because the Northwest Ordinance had included a similar prohibition, and the Property Clause was designed to constitutionalize the Northwest Ordinance, *Dred Scott* is contrary to the original understanding in this respect.

By the end of the nineteenth century, the interpretation of the clause shifted decisively toward the protective theory, as intimated in *Fort Leavenworth*. In one pivotal decision, the Court held that Congress could prohibit persons from putting up fences on private land if this would block access to public lands. *Camfield v. United States* (1897). The Court said:

> While we do not undertake to say that Congress has the unlimited power to legislate against nuisances within a State, which it would have within a Territory, we do not think the admission of a Territory as a State deprives it of the power of legislating for the protection of the public lands, though it may thereby involve the exercise of what is ordinarily known as the police power, so long as such power is directed solely to its own protection. A different rule would place the public domain of the United States completely at the mercy of state legislation.

Shortly thereafter, the Court upheld the reservation of vast tracts of land such as national forests, indicating that these lands were held in trust for the people of the whole country, and that it was for Congress, not the courts, to say how that trust should be administered. *Light v. United States* (1911).

The leading modern decision, *Kleppe v. New Mexico* (1976), reflects a further evolution in judicial understanding, as it in effect embraces the full-blown police-power theory. At issue was the constitutionality of the Wild, Free-Roaming Horses and Burros Act, which prohibits capturing, killing, or harassing wild horses and burros that range on public lands. Writing for the Court, Justice Thurgood Marshall specifically rejected the contention that the Property Clause includes only "(1) the power to dispose of and make incidental rules regarding the use of federal property; and (2) the power to protect federal property." He concluded that "Congress exercises the powers both of a proprietor and of a legislature over the public domain." Thus, without regard to whether wild animals are the property of the United States, or whether the act could be justified as a form of protection of the public lands, Congress was held to have sufficient power under the Property Clause to adopt regulatory legislation protecting wild animals that enter upon federal lands.

To date, Congress has not attempted to exploit the new "enumerated power" conferred by the Court in *Kleppe v. New Mexico*. Although one can imagine how *Kleppe v. New Mexico* could be elaborated in new ways, any effort to use the Property Clause to sustain legislation that goes beyond protecting federal proprietary interests would seemingly be inconsistent with the original design of the Constitution.

Thomas W. Merrill

See Also

Article I, Section 8, Clause 3 (Commerce Among the States)

Article I, Section 8, Clause 17 (Enclave Clause)

Suggestions for Further Research

Peter A. Appel, *The Power of Congress "Without Limitation": The Property Clause and Federal Regulation of Private Property*, 86 MINN. L. REV. 1 (2001)

David E. Engdahl, *State and Federal Power over Federal Property*, 18 ARIZ. L. REV. 283 (1976)

Significant Cases

Lessee of Pollard v. Hagan, 44 U.S. (3 How.) 212 (1845)

Dred Scott v. Sandford, 60 U.S. (19 How.) 393 (1857)

Fort Leavenworth Railroad Co. v. Lowe, 114 U.S. 525 (1885)

Camfield v. United States, 167 U.S. 518 (1897)

Light v. United States, 220 U.S. 523 (1911)

Kleppe v. New Mexico, 426 U.S. 529 (1976)

Claims

...nothing in this Constitution shall be so construed as to Prejudice any Claims of the United States, or of any particular State.
(ARTICLE IV, SECTION 3, CLAUSE 2)

~

$\mathcal{S}$hortly after the Constitutional Convention had adopted a constitutional provision that required the consent of affected state legislatures if Congress tried to create a state out of the territory of any existing ones (Article IV, Section 3, Clause 1), the Framers faced a potentially divisive problem that arose from that provision. The Framers feared that states might weaken federal power by preventing Congress from making "needful Rules and Regulations" for admission to the union of western territory ceded to the United States during and after the American Revolution. The western land claims of many states were still unresolved, and the Convention had adopted a provision that required the consent of state legislatures in order to create new states out of existing states; for these reasons, the Framers feared that some states might argue that any territory for which Congress would try to make "needful Rules and Regulations" was in fact their territory and so could not be prepared for admission to the union by the United States.

To prevent such a misconstruction and protect the legitimate claims of the new federal government, Daniel Carroll of Maryland proposed at the Convention that "nothing in this Constitution shall be construed to affect the claim of the U.S. to vacant lands ceded to them by the Treaty of peace." While holding that states were not sovereign nations and thus could not in principle claim land ceded by one nation (Britain) to another, James Madison recognized (as Justice Joseph Story later wrote in his *Commentaries on the Constitution of the United States*) that the question of "to whom of right belonged the vacant territory appertaining to the crown at the time of the revolution, whether to the states, within whose charter territory it was situated, or to the Union in its federative capacity" was "a subject of long and ardent controversy, and . . . threatened to disturb the peace, if not to overthrow the government of the Union." To avert a potential crisis, Madison successfully proposed that the Convention should be "neutral and fair" and "ought to go farther and declare that the claims of particular States also should not be affected."

Since its adoption in the Constitution, this clause has spawned very little constitutional controversy and has functioned largely as its author hoped: by giving the same protection to both state and federal land claims, it diffused potential conflict over whose claims in the western territories would have constitutional preeminence. Potential conflicts were put over for decision by the political branches, which successfully handled the disposition of the western territories.

Jeffrey Sikkenga

See Also

Article IV, Section 3, Clause 1 (New States Clause)
Article IV, Section 3, Clause 2 (Property Clause)

Suggestion for Further Research

Dale van Every, Ark of Empire: The American Frontier, 1784–1803 (1963)

Guarantee Clause

The United States shall guarantee to every State in this Union a Republican Form of Government, and shall protect each of them against Invasion; and on Applica-

tion of the Legislature, or of the Executive (when the Legislature cannot be convened), against domestic Violence.

(**Article IV, Section 4**)

∼

*T*his section is called the Guarantee Clause, because by its terms the federal government makes certain guarantees to the states. One of these—protection from foreign invasion—continued Congress's prior obligation under the Articles of Confederation. This guarantee is a part of the larger doctrine, reflected in both the Articles and the Constitution, that although the federation may be decentralized internally, it is to have a common foreign policy and present a unified face to the outside world.

The other principal guarantee in Article IV, Section 4, is that the federal government will assure the states "a Republican Form of Government." The guarantee of protection from domestic violence may be treated as part of the republican guarantee. The assurance of a republican form did not appear in the Articles of Confederation. Participants in the Constitutional debate of 1787–1788 expressed varying views over exactly what constituted the "Republican Form" of government. However, there was a consensus as to three criteria of republicanism, the lack of any of which would render a government un-republican.

The first of these criteria was popular rule. The Founders believed that for government to be republican, political decisions had to be made by a majority (or in some cases, a plurality) of voting citizens. The citizenry might act either directly or through elected representatives. Either way, republican government was government accountable to the citizenry. To a generation immersed in Latin learning and looking to pre-imperial Rome for inspiration, a republic was very much *res publica*—the people's affair.

The second required element of republican government was that there be no monarch. The participants in the constitutional debates believed that monarchy, even constitutional monarchy, was inconsistent with republican government. In fact, when Alexander Hamilton proposed a President with lifetime tenure, the delegates so disagreed that they did not even take the time to respond.

The third criterion for a republic was the rule of law. Ex post facto laws, bills of attainder, extreme debtor-relief measures—most kinds of retroactive legislation, for example, were deemed inconsistent with the rule of law, and therefore un-republican.

Many participants in the post-Convention debates (such as James Iredell of North Carolina) suggested an additional criterion of republicanism: absence of a titled aristocracy. This criterion was not part of the consensus; other participants observed that some previous republics (e.g., pre-imperial Rome) and some contemporary republics (e.g., Holland) featured titled aristocracies. Indeed, the most influential contemporary foreign political writer, Baron de Montesquieu, had divided republics into aristocratic and democratic varieties. To assure, therefore, that the American states remained more purely democratic republics, the drafters of the Constitution inserted Article I, Section 10, which forbids states from conferring titles of nobility.

It is sometimes claimed that the Founders wanted American governments to be "republics rather than democracies," but this claim is not quite accurate. In their linguistic usage, the Founders employed the terms "democracy" and "republic" with overlapping or even interchangeable meanings. Only one species of democracy was deemed inconsistent with republicanism. This was "pure democracy" or "simple and perfect democracy," a theoretical constitution identified by Aristotle and mentioned by John Adams and James Madison, among others. A pure democracy had no magistrates, because the "mob" made all decisions, including all executive and judicial decisions. The Founders saw this kind of democracy as inconsistent with republicanism, because it did not honor the rule of law. The Guarantee Clause's protection against domestic violence assures orderly government and the rule of law, and protects the states' legitimate magistracy against mob rule.

The primary purpose of the Guarantee Clause, however, was not protection against pure democracy but against monarchy. Based on precedents in ancient Greece, the drafters feared that kings in one or more states would attempt to expand their power in ways that would destabilize the entire federation. Having republican government in each state was deemed necessary to protect republican government throughout the United States.

There is not much federal case law on the Guarantee Clause, primarily because in the 1849 case of *Luther v. Borden*, the Supreme Court declared in dictum that enforcement of the clause is a political question for Congress and not a justiciable issue for the courts. With one minor deviation, the Supreme Court has continued to adhere to this doctrine. Examples are the Court's decisions in *Pacific States Telephone & Telegraph Co. v. Oregon* (1912) and *Baker v. Carr* (1962). Thus, citizens of a state who believe their state's government is no longer republican should apply to Congress for relief rather than to the courts. It has been established, however, that congressional admission of a state to the union legally implies that the state's then-existing constitution satisfies the Guarantee Clause. Yet the clause does not freeze that state constitution into place, but allows states wide latitude to innovate, so long as they retain the three basic elements of the republican form.

There has been somewhat more Guarantee Clause activity in state courts. Most have arisen when opponents of direct citizen lawmaking (initiative and referendum) argue that it violates the "republican form" for voters to legislate directly rather than through representatives, even though early in our history states often passed resolutions instructing their representatives on how to vote on certain issues. The Delaware Supreme Court accepted that argument in *Rice v. Foster* (1847). However, numerous citations from the Founding era indicate that this argument is erroneous, and it has been rejected entirely or in part by all other state courts considering the issue. Examples include the supreme courts of Oregon, *Kadderly v. City of Portland* (1903), of Colorado, *Bernzen v. City of Boulder* (1974) and other cases, and of Washington, *Hartig v. City of Seattle* (1909).

The other portion of the clause declaring that the United States shall protect each state "against Invasion" was designed by the Framers to prevent a sectional president from refusing to defend certain parts of the nation from foreign attack. As St. George Tucker noted, the provision guarded against "the possibility of an undue partiality in the federal government in affording it's [sic] protection to one part of the union in preference to another, which may be invaded at the same time." There has been, however, no occasion when that section has been invoked.

Robert G. Natelson

See Also

Article I, Section 10, Clause 1 (State Title of Nobility)

Suggestions for Further Research

George M. Dennison, The Dore War: Republicanism on Trial (1976)

Robert G. Natelson, *A Republic Not a Democracy? Initiative, Referendum, and the Constitution's Guaranty Clause*, 80 Tex. L. Rev. 807 (2002)

M.N.S. Sellers, The Sacred Fire of Liberty: Republicanism, Liberalism and the Law (1998)

St. George Tucker, Blackstone's Commentaries (1803)

William M. Wiecek, The Guarantee Clause of the U.S. Constitution (1972)

Significant Cases

Rice v. Foster, 4 Harr. (Del.) 479 (1847)

Luther v. Borden, 48 U.S. (7 How.) 1 (1849)

Minor v. Happersett, 88 U.S. (21 Wall.) 162 (1874)

Kadderly v. City of Portland, 44 Or. 118, 74 P. 710 (1903)

Hartig v. City of Seattle, 53 Wash. 432, 102 P. 408 (1909)

Pacific States Telephone & Telegraph Co. v. Oregon, 223 U.S. 118 (1912)

Baker v. Carr, 369 U.S. 186 (1962)

Bernzen v. City of Boulder, 186 Colo. 81, 525 P.2d 416 (1974)

ARTICLE V

Amendments

The Congress, whenever two thirds of both Houses shall deem it necessary, shall propose Amendments to this Constitution, or, on the Application of the Legislatures of two thirds of the several States, shall call a Convention for proposing Amendments, which, in either Case, shall be valid to all Intents and Purposes, as Part of this Constitution, when ratified by the Legislatures of three fourths of the several States, or by Conventions in three fourths thereof, as the one or the other Mode of Ratification may be proposed by the Congress.…

(Article V)

*T*he process of amendment developed with the emergence of written constitutions that established popular government. The charters granted by William Penn in 1682 and 1683 provided for amending, as did eight of the state constitutions in effect in 1787. Three state constitutions provided for amendment through the legislature, and the other five gave the power to specially elected conventions.

The Articles of Confederation provided for amendments to be proposed by Congress and ratified by the unanimous vote of all thirteen state legislatures. This proved to be a major flaw in the Articles, as it created an insuperable obstacle to constitutional reform. The amendment process in the Constitution, as James Madison explained in *The Federalist* No. 43, was meant to establish a balance between the excesses of constant change and inflexibility: "It guards equally against that extreme facility which would render the Constitution too mutable; and that extreme difficulty which might perpetuate its discovered faults."

In his *Commentaries on the Constitution of the United States*, Justice Joseph Story wrote that a government that provides

> no means of change, but assumes to be fixed and unalterable, must, after a while, become wholly unsuited to the circumstances of the nation; and it will either degenerate into a despotism, or by the pressure of its inequalities bring on a revolution . . . . The great principle to be sought is to make the changes practicable, but not too easy; to secure due deliberation, and caution; and to follow experience, rather than to open a way for experiments, suggested by mere speculation or theory.

The Virginia Plan at the start of the Constitutional Convention called for amendment "whensoever it shall seem necessary." The Committee of Detail proposed a process whereby Congress would call for a constitutional convention on the request of two-thirds of the state legislatures. After further debate, the delegates passed language proposed by Madison (and seconded by Alexander Hamilton) that the national legislature shall propose amendments when two-thirds of each House deems it necessary, or on the application of two-thirds of the state legislatures, to be ratified by three-fourths of the states in their legislatures or by state convention.

The Convention made two specific exceptions to the Amendments Clause, concerning the slave trade (Article V, Clause 2) and equal state suffrage in the Senate (Article V, Clause 2), but defeated a motion to prevent amendments that affected internal police powers in the states. Just before the end of the Convention, George Mason objected that the amendment plan gave too much power to Congress, and thus the provision was added requiring Congress to call a convention on the application of two-thirds of the states. The careful consideration of the amending power demonstrates that the Framers would have been astonished by more recent theories claiming the right of the Supreme Court to superintend a "living" or "evolving" Constitution outside of the amendment process. More significantly, the double supermajority requirements—two-thirds of both Houses of Congress and three-quarters of the states—create extensive deliberation and stability in the amendment process and restrain factions and special interests. It helps keep the Constitution as a "constitution," and not an assemblage of legislative enactments.

The advantage of the Amendments Clause was immediately apparent. The lack of a bill of rights—the Convention had considered and rejected this option—became a rallying cry during the ratification debate. Partly to head off an attempt to call for another general convention, but mostly to legitimize the Constitution among patriots who were Anti-Federalists, the advocates of the Constitution (led by Madison) agreed to add amendments in the first session of Congress. North Carolina and Rhode Island acceded to the Constitution, and further disagreements were cabined within the constitutional structure.

Madison had wanted the amendments that became the Bill of Rights to be interwoven into the relevant sections of the Constitution. More for stylistic rather than substantive reasons, though, Congress proposed (and set the precedent for) amendments appended separately at the end of the document. Some have argued that this method makes amendments more susceptible to an activist interpretation than they would be otherwise.

Since 1789, over 5,000 bills proposing to amend the Constitution have been introduced in Congress; thirty-three amendments have been sent to the states for ratification. No attempt by the states to call a convention has ever succeeded, though some have come within one or two states of the requisite two-thirds. The movement favoring direct election of Senators was just one state away from an amending convention when Congress proposed the Seventeenth Amendment.

Because no amending convention has ever occurred, an important question is whether a convention can be limited in scope, either to a particular proposal or within a particular subject. While most calls for amending conventions in the nineteenth century were general, the modern trend is to call for limited conventions. Some scholars maintain that such attempts violate Article V and are therefore void. Other questions include the practical aspects of how an amending convention would operate and whether any aspects of such a convention would be subject to judicial review.

Much greater certainty exists as to the power of Congress to propose amendments. In a challenge to the Eleventh Amendment, the Supreme Court waved aside the suggestion that amendments proposed by Congress must be submitted to the President according to the Presentment Clause (Article I, Section 7, Clause 2). *Hollingsworth v. Virginia* (1798). In the *National Prohibition Cases* (1920), the Court held that the "two-thirds of both Houses" requirement applies to a present quorum, not the total membership of each body. One year later, in *Dillon v. Gloss* (1921), the Court allowed Congress, when proposing an amendment, to set a reasonable time limit for ratification by the states.

Since 1924, no amendment has been proposed without a ratification time limit, although the Twenty-seventh Amendment, proposed by Madison in the First Congress more than two hundred years ago, was finally ratified in 1992. Regardless of how an amendment is proposed, Article V gives Congress authority to direct the mode of ratification. *United States v. Sprague* (1931). Of the ratified amendments, all but the Twenty-first Amendment, which was ratified by state conventions, have been ratified by state legislatures. In *Hawke v. Smith* (1920), the Court struck down an attempt by Ohio to make that state's ratification of constitutional amendments subject to a vote of the people, holding that where Article V gives authority to state legislatures, these bodies are exercising a federal function.

Although some scholars have asserted that certain kinds of constitutional amendments might be "unconstitutional," actual substantive challenges to amendments have been unsuccessful. *National Prohibition Cases* (1920); *Leser v. Garnett* (1922). The Supreme Court's consideration of procedural challenges thus far does not extend beyond the 1939 decision of *Coleman v. Miller*, dealing with Kansas's ratification of a child labor amendment. The Court split on whether state ratification disputes are nonjusticiable political questions, but then held that Congress, "in controlling the promulgation of the adoption of constitutional amendment[s]," should have final authority over ratification controversies.

In the end, the Framers believed that the amendment process would protect the Constitution from undue change at the same time that it would strengthen the authority of the Constitution with the people. "The basis of our political systems is the right of the people to make and to alter their Constitutions of Government," George Washington wrote in his Farewell Address of 1796. "But the Constitution which at any time exists, 'till changed by an explicit and authentic act of the whole People, is sacredly obligatory upon all."

Trent England and Matthew Spalding

See Also

Article I, Section 7, Clause 2 (Presentment Clause)
Article V (Prohibition on Amendment: Slave Trade)
Article V (Prohibition on Amendment: Equal Suffrage in the Senate)

Suggestions for Further Research

RICHARD B. BERNSTEIN, AMENDING AMERICA: IF WE LOVE THE CONSTITUTION SO MUCH, WHY DO WE KEEP TRYING TO CHANGE IT? (1993)

Richard B. Bernstein, *The Sleeper Wakes: The History and Legacy of the Twenty-seventh Amendment*, 61 FORDHAM L. REV. 497 (1992)

ROBERT A. GOLDWIN, FROM PARCHMENT TO POWER: HOW JAMES MADISON USED THE BILL OF RIGHTS TO SAVE THE CONSTITUTION (1997)

Edward Harnett, *A "Uniform and Entire" Constitution; or, What if Madison Had Won?*, 15 CONST. COMMENT. 251 (1998)

John O. McGinnis & Michael B. Rappaport, *Our Supermajoritarian Constitution*, 80 Tex. L. Rev. 703 (2002)

Henry P. Monaghan, *We the People[s], Original Understanding, and Constitutional Amendment*, 96 Colum. L. Rev. 121 (1996)

Seth Barrett Tillman, *A Textualist Defense of Article I, Section 7, Clause:* Why Hollingsworth v. Virginia *Was Rightly Decided, and Why* I.N.S. v. Chadha *Was Wrongly Resolved*, 83 Tex. L. Rev. 1373 (2005)

John R. Vile, The Constitutional Amending Process in American Political Thought (1992)

Significant Cases

Hollingsworth v. Virginia, 3 U.S. (3 Dall.) 378 (1798)

Hawke v. Smith, 253 U.S. 221 (1920)

National Prohibition Cases, 253 U.S. 350 (1920)

Dillon v. Gloss, 256 U.S. 368 (1921)

Leser v. Garnett, 258 U.S. 130 (1922)

United States v. Sprague, 282 U.S. 716 (1931)

Coleman v. Miller, 307 U.S. 433 (1939)

Prohibition on Amendment: Slave Trade

...no Amendment which may be made prior to the Year One thousand eight hundred and eight shall in any Manner affect the first and fourth Clauses in the Ninth Section of the first Article....

(Article V)

~

Toward the end of the Constitutional Convention, after previous clauses concerning slavery had been settled, and in the midst of the discussion about the process of amending the Constitution, John Rutledge of South Carolina said that "he never could agree to give a power by which the articles relating to slaves might be altered by the States not interested in that property and prejudiced against it." An addition to the clause was immediately agreed to that forbade amending the so-called Slave Trade Clause (Article I,

Section 9, Clause 1) and the Direct Taxes Clause (Article I, Section 9, Clause 4) prior to 1808, after which Congress could regulate the slave trade.

This provision calls attention to the delicacy and precariousness of the compromises involved in these two clauses. Protecting the Slave Trade Clause revealed Southern concerns about the strength of antislavery opinion (which was focused on stopping the slave trade) and the fact that outside of a few states, it would be hard to prevent a coalition of Northern and upper Southern states from changing the Constitution on this question by amendment. Likewise, shielding the Direct Taxes Clause was an indirect way to emphasize the "Three-fifths Compromise" (Article I, Section 2, Clause 3) concerning the apportionment of direct taxes, as well as adding "other taxes" to that ratio, reflecting significant fears that the power to tax could be used to undermine the institution of slavery. Underscoring the temporary nature of the compromise, language in Article V ties the Direct Taxes Clause to the clause's "implied invitation" to legislate on the slave trade after 1808. In fact, Congress accepted the invitation and, although the law underwent several modifications in subsequent years, passed a federal prohibition of the slave trade, effective January 1, 1808.

Interestingly, reference to the Fugitive Slave Clause (Article IV, Section 2, Clause 3) is not included here among the clauses protected from amendment. By omission, this signifies the broad consensus supporting the Fugitive Slave Clause and the fact that it was not at the time thought to be controversial.

Matthew Spalding

See Also

Article I, Section 2, Clause 3 (Three-fifths Clause)

Article I, Section 9, Clause 1 (Slave Trade)

Article I, Section 9, Clause 4 (Direct Taxes)

Article IV, Section 2, Clause 3 (Fugitive Slave Clause)

Suggestions for Further Research

Henry P. Monaghan, *We the People[s], Original Understanding, and Constitutional Amendment*, 96 Colum. L. Rev. 121 (1996)

Prohibition on Amendment: Equal Suffrage in the Senate

...no State, without its consent, shall be deprived of its equal Suffrage in the Senate.

(ARTICLE V)

～

*A*rticle V specifies the means by which the Constitution of the United States can be amended. It ends by forbidding amendments that would repeal the language in Article I, Section 9, which prohibits a ban on the importation of slaves prior to 1808, or the language in Article I, Section 3, which provides for equal representation of the states in the Senate. These are the only textually entrenched provisions of the Constitution. The first prohibition was absolute but of limited duration—it was to be in force for only twenty years; the second was less absolute—"no state, without its consent, shall be deprived of its equal Suffrage in the Senate"—but permanent.

The first unamendable provision of the Constitution was part of what Frederick Douglass called the "scaffolding" necessary for the construction and adoption of the Constitution's "magnificent structure, to be removed as soon as the building was completed." The second unamendable provision shows how seriously the smaller states were committed to protecting the "original federal design." Its sponsor was Roger Sherman of Connecticut, architect of what is often called the Connecticut Compromise or "the Great Compromise," whereby states were to be represented proportionately in the House and equally in the Senate. Two days before the Convention ended, on September 15, Sherman "expressed his fears that three fourths of the States might be brought to do things fatal to particular States, as abolishing them altogether or depriving them of their equality in the Senate." He therefore proposed language barring amending the Constitution to deprive states of their equal suffrage. When his motion failed, Sherman indicated how profoundly concerned he was by proposing the elimination of Article V altogether. This motion also failed, but it prompted Gouverneur Morris to propose the language ultimately adopted by the Constitutional Convention. As James Madison wrote in his notes, "This motion being dictated by the circulating murmurs of the small States was agreed to without debate, no one opposing it, or on the question saying no."

The provision does more than protect the equal representation of small states. As Madison noted in *The Federalist* No. 39, it ensures a polity of mixed sovereignty, one in which the states are an integral part of the federal government. This, of course, is precisely why those who do not think the Constitution "democratic" enough would wish to remove that portion of the Constitution. They argue variously that Article V can be amended through the convention mechanism; or by the people as a whole as stated in the Preamble; or, more brazenly, by first amending out the provision of the Fifth Amendment, and then requiring the Senate to be apportioned by population. Professor Henry Monaghan points out that such proposals are inconsistent with the vision of the Framers and would undermine the structural plan of the Constitution. That plan was an integrated and dynamic federalism.

As Chief Justice Salmon Chase declared in *Texas v. White* (1869):

Not only, therefore, can there be no loss of separate and independent autonomy to the States, through their union under the Constitution, but it may be not unreasonably said that the preservation of the States, and the maintenance of their governments, are as much within the design and care of the Constitution as the preservation of the Union and the maintenance of the National government. The Constitution, in all its provisions, looks to an indestructible Union, composed of indestructible States.

Denying the states their intended role in the federal government by abolishing their equality in the Senate would destroy the grounding of the Union: "without the States in union, there could be no such political body as the United States," *Texas v. White*, citing *Lane County v. Oregon* (1869). Moreover, as the text itself stands, at most the provision could only technically be voided by the unanimous consent of all the states.

This provision has been seldom invoked. Most recently, it has been employed by those opposed to proposed constitutional amendments that would give the District of Columbia full representation in the Congress. Their argument is that an amendment that would allow the District—a nonstate—to have two Senators would deprive the states of their equal suffrage in the Senate and would therefore require unanimous ratification by all the states. Others have suggested that the provision would void a constitutional amendment requiring a supermajority to pass tax increases.

Ralph Rossum

See Also

Article V

Suggestions for Further Research

Akhil R. Amar, *The Consent of the Governed: Constitutional Amendment Outside Article V*, 94 Colum. L. Rev. 457 (1994)

Lynn A. Baker, *New Frontiers of Federalism: Federalism: The Argument from Article V*, 13 Ga. St. U. L. Rev. 923 (1997)

Henry P. Monaghan, *We the Peoples, Original Understanding, and Constitutional Amendment*, 96 Colum. L. Rev. 121 (1996)

Eric A. Posner & Adrian Vermeule, *Legislative Entrenchment: A Reappraisal*, 111 Yale L.J. 1665 (2002)

Stuart Sierk, *Retrenchment on Entrenchment*, 71 Geo. Wash. L. Rev. 231 (2003)

Significant Cases

Lane County v. Oregon, 74 U.S. (7 Wall.) 71 (1869)

Texas v. White, 74 U.S. (7 Wall.) 700 (1869)

ARTICLE VI

Debt Assumption

All Debts contracted and Engagements entered into, before the Adoption of this Constitution, shall be as valid against the United States under this Constitution, as under the Confederation.

(**Article VI, Clause 1**)

$\sim$

To finance the War of Independence, the American states and the Continental Congress sold millions of dollars in public bonds to soldiers, ordinary Americans, and investors both within America and abroad. The Constitutional Convention first addressed the debt issue during its debates on the proposed powers of Congress. On August 21, 1787, the Convention considered this proposal: "The Legislature of the U.S. shall have the power to fulfil the engagements which have been entered into by Congress, and to discharge as well the debts of the U-S: as the debts incurred by the several States during the late war, for the common defence and general welfare."

Whether Congress could discharge the state debts was left unsettled because the ensuing debate centered on a different question: Would the new federal government necessarily inherit the debt obligations of the old Continental and Confederation Congresses? There was precedent for such an action in Article XII of the Articles of Confederation, which declared that the Articles Congress was liable for "monies borrowed and debts contracted by" the old Continental Congress.

Nor was this the only support. Writers on the law of nations, such as Hugo Grotius, held that the various forms of government were only different means by which political societies achieved the same basic ends. In their view, political societies existed prior to and separate from their particular forms of government (e.g., monarchy or aristocracy), and they could change that form without destroying their existence or altering their fundamental obligations to other countries.

Elbridge Gerry objected that the August 21 proposal only gave the new Congress the "power" rather than the *obligation* to pay back the debt. He feared that this wording would allow Congress to neglect the rightful return on bonds due to the creditor "class of citizens." To Oliver Ellsworth and Roger Sherman, such a concern was misplaced because the "U-S heretofore entered into Engagements" by Congresses "who were their agents" and "will hereafter be bound to fulfil them by their new agents."

While Edmund Randolph agreed that the United States was still liable for its obligations, he maintained that the "new Govt" was one of enumerated powers and thus would have only the power given to it by the Constitution. Without an explicit grant of constitutional power, the federal government would be in the strange position of not having the authority to pay off the debts still owed by the country. Unlike Randolph, James Madison held that the obligation to pay debts necessarily conferred the power to pay debts whether or not the Constitution gave the new government such a specific power. Madison argued that the new federal government would receive its constitutional power in domestic matters through enumerated grants from the people of the states; but the states themselves "never possessed the essential rights of sovereignty," which were "war, peace, treaties," and other powers over external affairs. Thus, in matters relating to

repayment of debts to foreign bondholders, the new national government would inherit its powers directly from the Articles. Thus, Congress did not need an explicit grant of power from the new Constitution. In defending the clause against Anti-Federalist criticism, Madison maintained that its insertion was not a legal or constitutional necessity but was done only "for the satisfaction of the foreign creditors of the United States." *The Federalist* No. 43.

Following a motion by Gouverneur Morris on August 25, the Convention changed the clause from a grant of power to Congress to an obligation of the United States. The change was then accepted by the Convention, which split the power to "pay the Debts," leaving it in Article I, Section 8, from the obligation to uphold "debts" and "Engagements," moving the latter to Article VI. A few commentators later thought that "engagements" also referred to the central government's obligations to the people of the Northwest Territory under the Northwest Ordinance (1787), but none of the Framers in Philadelphia made that connection while debating the clause.

After some political struggles in the early 1790s, the new federal government made good on the bond obligations inherited from the Articles of Confederation, thus vitiating the possibility for serious constitutional controversy. Subsequently, early Supreme Court cases like *Ware v. Hylton* (1796) and *Terrett v. Taylor* (1815) settled constitutional issues of contracts and property rights from the pre-Constitution era, not by interpreting the Debt Assumption Clause, but by invoking the Supremacy Clause of Article VI.

Jeffrey Sikkenga

See Also
Article I, Section 8, Clause 1 (Spending Clause)

Suggestions for Further Research
David P. Currie, *The Constitution in Congress: Substantive Issues in the First Congress, 1989–1791*, 61 U. Chi. L. Rev. 775 (1994)

Peter Onuf, Statehood and Union: A History of the Northwest Ordinance (1987)

Significant Cases

Ware v. Hylton, 3 U.S. (3 Dall.) 199 (1796)

Terrett v. Taylor, 13 U.S. (9 Cranch) 43 (1815)

Supremacy Clause

This Constitution, and the Laws of the United States which shall be made in Pursuance thereof; and all Treaties made, or which shall be made, under the Authority of the United States, shall be the supreme Law of the Land; and the Judges in every State shall be bound thereby, any Thing in the Constitution or Laws of any State to the Contrary notwithstanding.

(ARTICLE VI, CLAUSE 2)

~

*A*ny federal system needs a strategy for dealing with potential conflicts between the national and local governments. There are at least three strategies available. First, each government could be given exclusive jurisdiction over its respective sphere, which would, at least in theory, avoid altogether the possibility of direct conflict. Second, the governments could have concurrent jurisdiction, but one government could be given power to veto actions of the other, either in the event of actual conflict or in general classes of cases. Third, both governments could be allowed to act without mutual interference, but one government's acts could be given primacy over the other's acts in the event of actual conflict.

The Supremacy Clause embodies the third strategy. It is a conflict-of-laws rule specifying that certain national acts take priority over any state acts that conflict with national law. In this respect, the Supremacy Clause follows the lead of Article XIII of the Articles of Confederation, which provided that "[e]very state shall abide by the determinations of the united states in congress assembled, on all questions which by this confederation are submitted to them."

Federal statutes and other federal laws are, of course, "supreme" only if made in pursuance of the Constitution, and Chief Justice John Marshall used this language in *Marbury v. Madison* (1803) to support his argument that the Constitution contemplates judicial review. Thus, the Supremacy Clause does not grant power to any federal actor, such as Congress. It deals with resolving a conflict between the federal and state governments once federal power has been validly exercised. It is a straightforward interpretative rule that is addressed to *all* legal interpreters, including Members of Congress, federal executive officials, federal judges, state-court judges, or other state officials. It does not preclude other strategies for dealing with potential national and state conflict, nor does it allocate power between the national and state governments. Other parts of the Constitution do that.

There was support at the Constitutional Convention for a supremacy clause that would adopt other conflict-resolving strategies. James Madison, among others, favored a direct congressional power to veto state laws, and he even seconded the strong proposal of Charles Pinckney "that the National Legislature shd. have authority to negative all [state] Laws which they shd. judge to be improper." The Convention repeatedly rejected all such proposals for a federal veto power over state laws. The objective of the Framers throughout was to devise strategies that would reduce occasions for national and state conflict.

The Supremacy Clause in its final form was adopted by the Convention without serious dissent. Indeed, the essence of its final form was proposed by the Anti-Federalist Luther Martin. While some Anti-Federalists subsequently objected in broad terms to the prospect of federal supremacy, nothing in those debates negated the general understanding that the Supremacy Clause was a straightforward conflict-of-laws rule designed to resolve conflicts between state and federal law touching on the same subject.

The clause's language, context, and history leave some important questions unanswered. For example, what constitutes a conflict? Must it be literally impossible to comply with both the state and federal rules, or is it enough that a state's law will in some fashion alter or stand as an obstacle to the operation of the federal rule? Properly applied as a conflict-of-laws provision, the Supremacy Clause would lead a common-law court to acknowledge that a conflict does not always occur simply because two sovereigns have legislated on a common subject; both Congress and the courts recognize that principle today.

Consequently, the modern Court has fashioned subsidiary rules to try to determine when there is a genuine conflict between a state and federal law on the same subject, or, in modern parlance, whether the federal law has "preempted" the state law. Modern doctrine generally holds that preemption occurs whenever it is intended by Congress. That intent, of course, can most directly be demonstrated by an express provision in a federal statute declaring the statute's preemptive effect. Even in the absence of an express preemption provision, however, state law is preempted "[w]hen Congress intends federal law to 'occupy the field'" or "to the extent of any conflict with a federal statute." *Crosby v. National Foreign Trade Council* (2000). Conflicts can also result either when it is literally impossible to comply with both state and federal law or, much more commonly, when a state law "stands as an obstacle to the accomplishment and execution of the full purposes and objectives of Congress." *Hines v. Davidowitz* (1941). Determining whether a state law sufficiently obstructs federal purposes and is thus preempted "is a matter of judgment, to be informed by examining the federal statute as a whole and identifying its purpose and intended effects." *Crosby*. There is, however, an interpretative presumption against preemption in areas of traditional state concern. As the Court stated in *Rice v. Santa Fe Elevator Corp.* (1947), "[W]e start with the assumption that the historic police powers of the States were not to be superseded by the Federal Act unless that was the clear and manifest purpose of Congress."

The preemption doctrine in its current form is a twentieth-century development. No state statute was invalidated for anything other than a straightforward conflict with a specific federal regulation until 1912, and the focus on congressional intent as the touchstone of preemption did not emerge until the New Deal when the locus of reformist legislation shifted from the states to the federal government. However, in *Cooley v. Board of Wardens* (1851) the Court first invalidated a state law using what today we would call a "dormant Commerce Clause" analysis, which treats the state law as preempted by the intent of Congress to have no law, state or federal, governing the commercial matter in question.

In addition to serving a central role in preemption analysis, the Supremacy Clause is often seen as the source of the principle that states cannot regulate, interfere with, or control federal instrumentalities. This principle is generally traced to *McCulloch v. Maryland* (1819), in which the Court held that Maryland could not constitutionally tax the operations of the Bank of the United States. Chief Justice John Marshall declared in *McCulloch* that

> [i]t is of the very essence of supremacy, to remove all obstacles to its action within its own sphere, and so to modify every power vested in subordinate governments, as to exempt its own operations from their influence. This effect need not be stated in terms. It is so involved in the declaration of supremacy, so necessarily implied in it, that the expression of it could not make it more certain.

Modern law has to some extent qualified the broadest implications of this early formulation of the supremacy principle. If federal supremacy indeed "remove[s] all obstacles" to federal action that might be posed by state regulation, states could be constitutionally forbidden even from taxing the salaries of federal employees. The Court indeed embraced such an idea for some time before specifically rejecting it in 1939 in *Graves v. New York ex rel. O'Keefe*. Modern law maintains instead that "[a] state regulation is invalid only if it regulates the United States directly or discriminates against the Federal Government or those with whom it deals." *North Dakota v. United States* (1990) (plurality opinion).

While the federal government can prevent states from interfering with federal operations, whether through taxes or otherwise, that does not necessarily mean that the Supremacy Clause is the basis upon which Congress exercises its power to protect federal operations. The valid exercise of any one of Congress's enumerated powers can constitute the constitutional source of a statute that effectively preempts a state law. In particular, the Necessary and Proper Clause would be a vehicle for a statute that explicitly disables state law from operating in an area of federal concern. Thus, for an explicitly preemptive statute to be constitutional, it must be "necessary and proper for carrying into Execution" some enumerated federal power, subject, of course, to the constitutional limits of the Necessary and Proper Clause itself.

For example, Congress could decide (explicitly or implicitly) that it alone should regulate the radiological-safety aspects involved in the construction and operation of a nuclear plant, and thus preempt the field from any state regulation of nuclear power safety. *Pacific Gas & Electric v. Energy Resources Commission* (1983). Congress could decide (explicitly or implicitly) that it wanted to gradually phase in passive restraints in automobiles, thus preempting a local tort law that required airbags to be installed in all new cars. *Geier v. American Honda Motor Co., Inc.* (2000). Congress might decide that it wanted an area in interstate commerce to be regulated only by the free market and not by the states, thus precluding state legislation in this particular area altogether.

Inasmuch as any state statute that regulates federal activities in ways forbidden by a congressional statute would conflict with valid federal law, Congress is thus logically free to *permit* state regulation of federal instrumentalities through a sufficient expression of intent. For example, the Supreme Court has allowed Congress either to authorize or to limit state taxation of federal banks. *Carson v. Roane-Anderson Co.* (1952).

Under this approach, Congress is the arbiter of the scope and nature of federal immunity. Courts would merely interpret existing congressional statutes and apply conflict-resolving Supremacy Clause principles. On the other hand, if the Supremacy Clause is seen as a source—even a defeasible source—of immunity, as John Marshall asserted, then it falls to courts in the first instance to determine the scope of national immunity. The approaches are not necessarily in conflict. At times, the Supreme Court is called upon to determine if there is a conflict between state and federal laws, even when Congress has not explicitly decided to preempt state action in the field. Nonetheless, the sequence seems clear. Congress, under its delegated powers, or a state, under its police power, may establish legal rules dealing with the same subject. It then falls to the courts to determine, under the Supremacy Clause, whether the state and federal rules are in conflict.

Article VI, Section 2, treats treaties differently from laws. There is a textual distinction in the clause between laws "made in pursuance [of the Constitution]" and treaties "made under the authority of the United States." *See State of Missouri v. Holland* (1920). The effectiveness of national treaties was a special concern of the Founding generation. This language ensured that treaties entered into by the United States prior to ratification of the Constitution—most notably, the 1783 treaty of peace with Great Britain and its guarantees against confiscations of Loyalist property—took precedence over conflicting state laws. The phrasing does not in any way imply that treaties are "supreme" even if they are not made in pursuance of the Constitution. The Supreme Court has declared that neither a treaty approved by the Senate nor an executive agreement made under the President's authority can create obligations that violate constitutional guarantees such as found in the Bill of Rights. *Reid v. Covert* (1957).

Like federal statutes, treaties are "supreme" only when they are effective as domestic law. Thus, the manner in which treaties become legally effective is important. "Self-executing treaties" become part of the law of the United States directly. On the other hand, the courts will not enforce "non-self-executing treaties" until they are carried into law by an act of Congress. Determining whether a treaty is self-executing or non-self-executing is a complex and confusing task, as lower courts have readily averred. In general, the courts will treat a treaty as non-self-executing if it requires any governmental funding to accomplish its purposes, or if there is any expressed intent by the terms of the treaty, the President, the Senate, or even the record of negotiation that indicates that the government desired that the treaty be non-self-executing.

In addition, there is a vigorous debate among scholars over what was the Framers' original understanding on this point. One group holds that the Framers intended that most treaties, with few exceptions, were to be self-executing (unless the terms of the treaty indicate otherwise). Another group of commentators argues that any treaty that impinges upon Congress's Article I powers is non-self-executing. Otherwise, the Framers' careful system of protecting the people from onerous legislation through the separation of powers could be outflanked by the President and the Senate alone.

Howsoever a treaty becomes part of the law of the United States, it is on a par with other federal laws and can be repealed by Congress, though the United States' obligations under international law remain. Under Supreme Court precedents, the last expression of the sovereign will controls, so an act of Congress that is in conflict with a treaty will control if the act became law after the Senate ratified the treaty, and vice versa. To avoid such conflicts, the courts have fashioned a prudential rule whereby laws will be interpreted to be in harmony with United States treaty obligations if at all possible.

Gary Lawson

Suggestions for Further Research

David E. Engdahl, Constitutional Federalism (1987)

Stephen A. Gardbaum, *The Nature of Preemption*, 79 Cornell L. Rev. 767 (1994)

Stephen A. Gardbaum, *Rethinking Constitutional Federalism*, 74 Tex. L. Rev. 795 (1996)

S. Candice Hoke, *Preemption Pathologies and Civil Republican Values*, 71 B.U. L. Rev. 685 (1991)

S. Candice Hoke, *Transcending Conventional Supremacy: A Reconstruction of the Supremacy Clause*, 24 Conn. L. Rev. 829 (1992)

Caleb Nelson, *Preemption*, 86 Va. L. Rev. 225 (2000)

Jordan Paust, *Self-Executing Treaties*, 82 Am. J. Int'l L. 760 (1988)

John C. Yoo, *Globalism and the Constitution: Treaties, Non-Self-Execution, and the Original Understanding*, 99 Colum. L. Rev. 2218 (1999)

Significant Cases

Marbury v. Madison, 5 U.S. (1 Cranch) 137 (1803)
McCulloch v. Maryland, 17 U.S. (4 Wheat.) 316 (1819)
Gibbons v. Ogden, 22 U.S. (9 Wheat.) 1 (1824)
Cooley v. Board of Wardens 53 U.S. (12 How.) 299 (1851)
Collector v. Day, 78 U.S. (11 Wall.) 113 (1871)
State of Missouri v. Holland, 252 U.S. 416 (1920)
Graves v. New York *ex rel.* O'Keefe, 306 U.S. 466 (1939)
Hines v. Davidowitz, 312 U.S. 52 (1941)
Rice v. Santa Fe Elevator Corp., 331 U.S. 218 (1947)
Carson v. Roane-Anderson Co., 342 U.S. 232 (1952)
Reid v. Covert, 354 U.S. 1 (1957)
Pacific Gas & Electric v. Energy Resources Commission, 461 U.S. 190 (1983)
North Dakota v. United States, 495 U.S. 423 (1990)
Printz v. United States, 521 U.S. 898 (1997)
Crosby v. National Foreign Trade Council, 530 U.S. 363 (2000)
Geier v. American Honda Motor Co., Inc. 529 U.S 861 (2000)

Oaths Clause

The Senators and Representatives before mentioned, and the Members of the several State Legislatures, and all executive and judicial Officers, both of the United States and of the several States, shall be bound by Oath or Affirmation, to support this Constitution....

(Article VI, Clause 3)

～

*A*lthough the practical application of the Constitution is largely in the hands of state judges, the primacy of the Constitution ultimately depends on officers of the law—in particular, officers of each branch of government—being equally bound to its support. In this sense, the Oaths Clause is the completion of the Supremacy Clause.

In England, subjects were required to swear loyalty to the reigning monarch; many early American documents included oaths of allegiance to the British king. During the American

Revolution, General George Washington required all officers to subscribe to an oath renouncing any allegiance to King George III and pledging their fidelity to the United States. Most of the new state constitutions included elaborate oaths that tied allegiance to and provided a summary of the basic constitutional principles animating American constitutionalism. There was no oath in the Articles of Confederation.

At the Constitutional Convention, Edmund Randolph proposed, as part of the Virginia Plan, "that the Legislative Executive & Judiciary powers within the several States ought to be bound by oath to support the articles of Union." When it was objected that this would unnecessarily intrude on state jurisdiction, Randolph responded that he

> considered it as necessary to prevent that competition between the National Constitution & laws & those of the particular States, which had already been felt. The officers of the States are already under oath to the States. To preserve a due impartiality they ought to be equally bound to the Natl. Govt. The Natl. authority needs every support we can give it.

The Oaths Clause helps to fulfill the Framers' plan to integrate the states into the electoral, policy-making, and executory functions of the federal union, subject to the limits of the Tenth Amendment. For example, the Supreme Court has held that Congress may not "conscript" the legislatures or executive officers of a state directly into federal service. *New York v. United States* (1992); *Printz v. United States* (1997). In *The Federalist* No. 27, Alexander Hamilton offered a careful and nuanced description of the Oaths Clause: "thus, the legislatures, courts, and magistrates, of the respective members, will be incorporated into the operations of the national government as far as its just and constitutional authority extends; and it will be rendered auxiliary to the enforcement of its laws."

For the sake of consistency and unity, the delegates amended the Oaths Clause to cover officers of the national government as well. Later, the delegates added the words "or affir-

mation" (to oblige the Quakers, who were circumspect of taking oaths, as a matter of religious doctrine) as well as the ban on federal religious tests (in the next clause).

The simple declaration to "support the Constitution" has constitutional significance at all levels of government. An opinion of the Attorney General in 1875 declared that Members of Congress do not assume office until the completion of the oath, but that a state may not question a state representative's motives and refuse to allow him to take the oath and his seat. *Bond v. Floyd* (1966). The oath was at the heart of John Marshall's opinion in *Marbury v. Madison* (1803) obliging judges to give priority to the Constitution over ordinary legislative acts. Justice Joseph Story likewise stated in his *Commentaries on the Constitution of the United States* that officers sworn to support the Constitution are "conscientiously bound to abstain from all acts inconsistent with it," and that in cases of doubt they must "decide each for himself, whether, consistently with the Constitution, the act can be done." But taking the oath does not relieve a judge from obedience to higher judicial authority, even if he thinks the higher court was acting contrary to the Constitution. *Glassroth v. Moore* (2003). Beyond the mechanism of the separation of powers, the Oaths Clause places an independent obligation on officeholders to observe the limits of their authority. The Framers included a specific oath for the President in Article II, Section 1, Clause 8.

The Framers' general understanding was that proscribing religious tests did not necessarily remove the religious significance of the general oath. "The Constitution enjoins an oath upon all the officers of the United States," Oliver Wolcott noted at the Connecticut ratifying convention. "This is a direct appeal to that God who is the avenger of perjury." Customarily, officeholders add the words "so help me God" at the completion of their oaths.

The very first law passed by the first session of the House of Representatives was "An Act to regulate the Time and Manner of administering certain Oaths." Two days later, the Chief Justice of New York administered to the Representatives an oath to "solemnly swear or affirm (as the case may be) that I will support the Constitution of the

United States." The Senate amended the legislation to apply to state officers, who are also subject to Article VI. When Representative Elbridge Gerry objected that Congress had no authority to specify the oath of state officers, the response was that Congress was implicitly authorized by Article VI itself, if not by the Necessary and Proper Clause, to prescribe oaths. This broad interpretation of implied congressional power was used as a precedent to justify the Fugitive Slave Act in 1793, later upheld on similar grounds by the Supreme Court in *Prigg v. Commonwealth of Pennsylvania* (1842).

During the Civil War, Congress promulgated an oath to require civil servants and military officers to not only swear allegiance to the United States but also affirm that they had not engaged in any previous disloyal conduct. Congress repealed the latter condition in 1884, leaving wording that is nearly identical to the current oath taken by Members and federal employees.

Under current law any individual elected or appointed to an office of honor or profit in the civil service or uniformed services, except the President, shall take the following oath: "I, [name], do solemnly swear (or affirm) that I will support and defend the Constitution of the United States against all enemies, foreign and domestic; that I will bear true faith and allegiance to the same; that I take this obligation freely, without any mental reservation or purpose of evasion; and that I will well and faithfully discharge the duties of the office on which I am about to enter." (33 U.S.C. § 3331.) By federal statute, all state officers shall take an oath in the simple form first promulgated in 1789. (4 U.S.C. § 101.)

Matthew Spalding

See Also

Article I, Section 3, Clause 6 (Trial of Impeachment)
Article II, Section 1, Clause 8 (Oath of Office)
Article VI, Clause 2 (Supremacy Clause)
Article VI, Clause 3 (Religious Test)

Suggestions for Further Research

14 Op. Att'y Gen. 406 (U.S. 1 AG 1875)
Patrick O. Gudridge, *The Office of the Oath*, 20 Const. Comment. 387 (2003)

Harold M. Hyman, To Try Men's Souls: Loyalty Tests in American History (1981)

Nash E. Long, *The "Constitutional Remand": Judicial Review of Constitutionally Dubious Statutes*, 14 J. L. & Pol. 667 (1998)

Mathew A. Pauley, I Do Solemnly Swear: The President's Constitutional Oath (1999)

Vic Snyder, *You've Taken an Oath to Support the Constitution, Now What? The Constitutional Requirement for a Congressional Oath of Office*, 23 U. Ark. Little Rock L. Rev. 897 (2001)

Significant Cases

Marbury v. Madison, 5 U.S. (1 Cranch) 137 (1803)
Prigg v. Pennsylvania, 41 U.S. (16 Pet.) 539 (1842)
Bond v. Floyd, 385 U.S. 116 (1966)
New York v. United States, 505 U.S. 144 (1992)
Printz v. United States, 521 U.S. 898 (1997)
Glassroth v. Moore, 335 F.3d 1282 (11th Cir. 2003)

Religious Test

...no religious Test shall ever be required as a Qualification to any Office or public Trust under the United States.

(Article VI, Clause 3)

~

*T*he original, unamended Constitution contains one explicit reference to religion: the Article VI ban on religious tests for "any office or public trust under the United States." Despite much litigation over the constitutional border between church and state, there have been no judicial decisions involving the religious test ban. The clause has been entirely self-executing. We do not know whether the Framers intended the clause to apply to every federal officeholder, howsoever minor; but no federal official has ever been subjected to a formal religious test for holding office.

By its plain terms, the ban extended only to federal officeholders. States were free at the time of the Founding to impose religious tests as they saw fit. All of them did. State tests limited public offices to Christians or, in some states, only to Protestants. The national government, on the other hand, could not impose any religious test whatsoever. National offices were open to everyone.

The surviving accounts of the Constitutional Convention indicate that the Article VI ban "was adopted by a great majority of the convention, and without much debate." We know that North Carolina opposed the prohibition; the Connecticut and Maryland delegations were divided. All the other delegates were in favor. But even some "nay" votes were not necessarily in favor of religious tests. Connecticut's Roger Sherman, for example, thought the ban unnecessary, "the prevailing liberality" being sufficient security against restrictive tests.

Of course the "prevailing liberality" was not very liberal. The clause was hotly disputed in some states during the 1788–1789 struggle over ratification of the Constitution. The objection was simple: "Jews," "Turks," "infidels," "heathens," and even "Roman Catholics" might hold national office under the proposed Constitution. As more soberly expressed by Pennsylvanian Benjamin Rush: "many pious people wish the name of the Supreme Being had been introduced somewhere in the new Constitution." The Religious Test Clause was thus a focal point for reservations about the Constitution's entirely secular language.

Some defenders of the Constitution argued, in response, that a belief in God and a future state of reward and punishment could, notwithstanding the test ban, be required of public officers. On this interpretation, Article VI banned only *sectarian* tests, such as would exclude *some* Christians from office. Others asserted that the requirement that officers take an oath to support and defend the Constitution necessarily implied a religious commitment. (*See* Oaths Clause, Article VI, Clause 3.)

In the ratification debates, the defenders of the Constitution put forward two reasons for the religious test ban. First, various Christian sects feared that, if any test were permitted, one might be designed to their disadvantage. No single sect could hope to dominate national councils. But any sect could imagine itself the victim of a combination of the others. Oliver Ellsworth noted that if a religious oath "were in favour of either congregationalists, presbyteri-

ans, episcopalions, baptists, or quakers, it would incapacitate more than three-fourths of the American citizens for any publick office; and thus degrade them from the rank of freemen." More importantly, the Framers sought a structure that would not exclude some of the best minds and the least parochial personalities to serve the national government. In his 1787 pamphlet, "An Examination of the Constitution," Tench Coxe wrote of the salubriousness of the religious test ban: "The people may employ any wise or good citizen in the execution of the various duties of the government."

The limitation to federal officeholders was mooted by the Supreme Court in the 1961 case, *Torcaso v. Watkins*. Relying upon the First Amendment religion clauses, the Court struck down religious tests for any public office in the United States. Not even a simple profession of belief in God—as was required of Roy Torcaso, an aspiring notary public—may now be required. *Torcaso* thus totally eclipses the Religious Test Clause of Article VI. The scope of an individual's immunity from disqualification from office on religious bases now depends upon the meaning of the Establishment and Free Exercise of Religion Clauses, not upon Article VI. Because the First Amendment's breadth is as wide as all government activity, questions about the precise meaning of "office of public trust" are also moot. Whether the Religious Test Clause by itself extends to Members of Congress or all the way down to postal workers no longer matters—save perhaps to historians.

Gerard V. Bradley

See Also

Amendment I

Suggestions for Further Research

Morton Borden, Jews, Turks, and Infidels (1984)

Gerard Bradley, *The No Religious Test Clause and the Constitution of Religious Liberty: A Machine That Has Gone of Itself*, 37 Case W. Res. L. Rev. 674 (1987)

Significant Case

Torcaso v. Watkins, 367 U.S. 488 (1961)

ARTICLE VII

Ratification Clause

The Ratification of the Conventions of nine States, shall be sufficient for the Establishment of this Constitution between the States so ratifying the Same.

(ARTICLE VII, CLAUSE 1)

This laconic sentence, the last and shortest of the Constitution's articles, was the key to the legal and political process that replaced the Articles of Confederation with the Constitution of the United States. In one stroke, Article VII expressed the Constitution's view of the Union and echoed the Declaration of Independence's view of the relation between positive and natural law. Seldom has so much political import been conveyed in so few words.

Behind the provision lay the delicate political problem confronting the Framers of the new Constitution: what to do about the Articles of Confederation. In 1786, the abortive Annapolis convention had issued a summons (drafted by Alexander Hamilton) requesting a new meeting of the states to consider all measures that would "render the constitution of the Federal Government adequate to the exigencies of the Union." The Confederation Congress had renewed but narrowed that call, charging the delegates to the Constitutional Convention with "the sole and express purpose of revising the Articles of Confederation and reporting to Congress and the state legislatures such alterations and provisions therein as shall . . . render the federal constitution adequate to the exigencies of Government & the preservation of the Union." Eight of the twelve state delegations to the Convention arrived under the former terms, and four under the latter, less elastic ones.

But now the Convention was proposing to replace, not renovate, the Articles. And it was appealing not to "Congress and the state legislatures," but over and around their heads to special ratification conventions to be elected by the people in each state. And to add insult to injury, the Framers were setting the threshold for ratification at nine states, not the thirteen necessary for constitutional revision under the Articles.

Article VII thus announced a bold new ratification procedure. It was needed because there was no chance that the one specified in the Articles would result in the Constitution's passage. The Confederation Congress, which under the Articles had to approve amendments before sending them to the state legislatures, could not be expected to rejoice at its own extinction. The state legislatures, which would be stripped of considerable powers by the proposed plan of government (*see* Article I, Section 10), could not be expected to concur in their own diminishment. Experience supported these conjectures: no amendment, however minor its attempt to strengthen the general government, had ever survived the ratification process dictated by the Articles.

It was not that Article VII's procedures were wholly unheard of: The Massachusetts Constitution of 1780, largely written by John Adams, had already pioneered the use of the popularly elected ratifying convention. Nor did Article VII entirely bypass Congress and the state legislatures. The Constitutional Convention sent its handiwork to the Confederation Congress and, in a separate resolution, requested (1) that Congress forward the proposed Constitution to the state legislatures and (2) that the legislatures call special elections for the ratifying conventions. Congress unanimously went along and the thirteen legislatures eventually complied, and their actions, historian Forrest McDonald has argued, constituted in effect "an amendment to the Articles' amending process," thus serving to legalize or at least regularize the Constitution's departures from the Articles' writ. Nevertheless, the Framers went out of their way to remove any suggestion from Article VII that the Congress (never mentioned therein) was being asked to give its approbation to the Constitution, much less that it and the legislatures were invited to debate it line-by-line. On the contrary, the implication was that the Congress and the state legislatures were middlemen, intended to transmit the plan to the real authorities, the popular conventions.

The political necessity of circumventing the established procedure was apparent to almost everyone. The Virginia Plan at the Constitutional Convention had called for the ultimate decision on ratification to be made by popular conventions, not by the state legislatures. James Wilson, early in the Convention, had urged that a "partial union" of consenting states not be held hostage to "the inconsiderate or selfish opposition" of a few states. Nonetheless, the plan's opponents objected, in Elbridge Gerry's words, to "the indecency and pernicious tendency of dissolving in so slight a manner, the solemn obligations of the Articles of Confederation."

Yet the case for superseding the Articles' strictures was not so "slight." There were important republican principles at stake. As James Madison argued in *The Federalist* No. 40, "in all great changes of established governments forms ought to give way to substance" because "a rigid adherence...to the former would render nominal and nugatory the transcendent and precious right of the people to 'abolish or alter their governments as to them shall seem most likely to effect their safety and happiness....'" In *The Federalist* No. 43, Madison noted that the Framers were recurring

> to the absolute necessity of the case; to the great principle of self-preservation; to the transcendent law of nature and of nature's God, which declares that the safety and happiness of society are the objects at which all political institutions aim, and to which all such institutions must be sacrificed.

In short, to save the Revolution and its principles, and to vindicate the Declaration of Independence, it was necessary to set aside the Articles of Confederation. The way from a flawed confederation to "a more perfect Union" involved a return to first principles. This was the very sort of return and renewal—of "revolution," in the sense of coming back around to the starting point—contemplated in the Virginia and Massachusetts bills of rights. During the ratification debates, the Constitution's advocates focused their arguments, therefore, on the defects of the Confederation. The more numerous and deep-seated its flaws, the less it deserved the veneration it was manifestly not receiving.

Among its shortcomings, none was more telling than its departure from the republican standard in respect of its own ratification. In many states, the Articles had been ratified by the legislature only; the people themselves had not been consulted. In conflicts between acts of the states and the Congress, the republican presumption thus often went to the former. To repeat the mistake by asking the state legislatures to ratify the proposed Constitution would vitiate the new government before it had begun. At the Convention, James Madison admitted that the new plan would make "essential inroads on the State Constitutions," but pointed out that asking state legislatures to ratify the new Constitution would in effect promulgate "a novel and dangerous doctrine" that a *legislature* could change the *constitution* "under which it held its existence."

To the Anti-Federalists, these objections were beside the point. In their view, the Articles had not needed full-blown popular ratification because they were precisely not a constitution. The Articles were more like a treaty among sovereign powers. The Federalists regarded this point as a confession of the Confederation's "imbecillity." Madison, in a striking passage at the Convention, explained that "the difference between a system founded on the Legislatures only, and one founded on the people, [is] the true difference between a *league* or *treaty*, and a *Constitution*." In the former, there were no real questions of constitutionality; only in the latter case, when a law violated "a constitution established by the people themselves," would judges consider an "unwise or perfidious" measure "null & void."

In a treaty under the law of nations, Madison continued, "a breach of any one article by any of the parties, frees the other parties from their engagements." He implied that the state governments' frequent violations of their obligations to the Confederation had already come close to dissolving (in the Articles' words) their "firm league of friendship," and with it the obligation to abide scrupulously by its amendment provisions. In "a union of people under one Constitution," by contrast, "the nature of the pact always has been understood to exclude such an interpretation." As the supreme law of the land, ordained and established by "We the People," the Constitution would be obligatory on the states.

Article VII's bold dismissal of the Confederation's rule of unanimity emphasized the break still further. The number nine had been proposed in the Convention by Edmund Randolph. It was, he said, a "respectable majority of the whole" and had the advantage of being familiar from "the constitution of the existing Congress," which required nine votes (a traditional supermajority of two-thirds, rounded up) in order to approve any important question. Other numbers had been considered, but anything short of thirteen signified the same thing, that the United States was no longer a treaty organization of sovereign or virtually sovereign states, but a people with a government in which constitutional majorities would be empowered actually to govern. The republican cause would be rescued from embarrassment and paralysis: twelve states could no longer be denied by a thirteenth, the majority would not be ruled by the minority, and the virtuous would not be beholden to the vicious.

At the same time, however, the Constitution's ratification by conventions in at least nine states would establish the new government only "between the states so ratifying the Same." There were limits to the nationalism contemplated by the plan. The people of the United States could not compel constitutional change on the states choosing to be disunited. In this respect, as in others, the Constitution recognized and granted to the states considerable

sovereignty or jurisdiction in their own spheres. Once the people of a state agreed to ratify the Constitution, it agreed in effect to amend its own state constitution to align it with the supreme law's new distribution of powers and duties, and henceforth to subordinate itself to that supreme law. The best description of the new arrangement is probably Madison's, who in *The Federalist* No. 39 famously pronounced it "neither a national nor a federal Constitution, but a composition of both."

In the event, New Hampshire became the ninth state to ratify, and the Confederation Congress, still very much in existence, began to take steps to put the new Constitution into operation. This was in keeping with the resolutions of the Constitutional Convention that had accompanied the proposed Constitution to Congress. Virginia and New York quickly ratified as well, creating a union of eleven states. In September 1788, the Congress passed a resolution authorizing the appointment of presidential electors in the ratifying states by January 1789, the first presidential vote by the electors in February, and the commencement of proceedings under the new Constitution on March 4, 1789. North Carolina rejected the Constitution and did not reverse itself until November 1789. Rhode Island, which did not participate in the Constitutional Convention and refused at first to call a ratifying convention, held out until May 1790.

One effect of Article VII, which allowed the Constitution to proceed despite the holdout states, was to induce those states to come aboard. They, least of all, wished to confront the delicate question of what would become of them if they remained permanently outside the Union. In its wake, Article VII left a minor controversy over when exactly the Articles of Confederation had expired, which question was addressed by the Supreme Court in *Owings v. Speed* (1820). The Court ruled that Congress had effectively dissolved "by the successive disappearance of its members" in November 1788, and that, legally speaking, it had breathed its last on March 2, 1789, the day before the new Congress had been directed to assemble.

Unlike the old Congress, essentially the meeting place of a league based on states' rights, the new Congress was a creature of the Constitution, based on what Madison called "the supreme authority of the people themselves." That is the ultimate significance of Article VII.

Charles Kesler

See Also

Preamble

Article I, Section 10

Significant Case

Owings v. Speed, 18 U.S. (5 Wheat.) 420 (1820)

Attestation Clause

Done in Convention by the Unanimous Consent of the States present the Seventeenth Day of September in the Year of our Lord one thousand seven hundred and Eighty seven and of the Independence of the United States of America the Twelfth In witness whereof We have hereunto subscribed our Names....

(**Article VII, Clause 2**)

⁓

Two days before the end of the Constitutional Convention, just before the final vote on the completed document, three delegates voiced objections to the new Constitution. Edmund Randolph of Virginia (who had introduced the Virginia Plan) thought the Constitution was not sufficiently republican, and moved that there should be another convention to address amendments to be proposed by the states. George Mason, also of Virginia, seconded the motion, arguing that without significant changes the new government would end in either monarchy or a tyrannical aristocracy. Elbridge Gerry of Massachusetts feared the powers of Congress were too broad; he thought the best that could be done was to provide for a

second general convention. When the two questions were put to a vote, the eleven states present (Rhode Island had not sent a delegation, and New York's had left) all voted against a second convention and then all voted in favor of the final text of the Constitution. The document was then ordered engrossed, or formally written, in preparation for endorsement.

When the Convention reconvened on September 17, after the final reading of the document, Benjamin Franklin delivered an address (read by James Wilson) strongly endorsing the Constitution despite any perceived imperfections. Hoping to gain the support of critics and create a sense of common accord, Franklin then proposed, and the Convention agreed, that the Constitution be signed by the delegates as individual witnesses of "the *unanimous* consent of the *states present.*"

Thus the signers subscribed their names "In witness" to what was "Done in Convention," and, with the exception of George Washington, who signed first and separately (as President and deputy from Virginia), the names are grouped by state. As a result, the document suggests the unanimity of the Declaration of Independence: delegates did not sign "on the part and behalf of" particular states, as they had in the Articles of Confederation. The states are listed (as in Article I, Section 2, and the draft of the Preamble, as well as in the Declaration of Independence and the Articles of Confederation) in geographical order, from New Hampshire in the north to Georgia in the south.

In the end, Randolph, Mason, and Elbridge Gerry did not sign the Constitution; as Madison wrote in his notes, they "declined to give it the sanction of their names." The arrangement did allow Alexander Hamilton to sign as a witness for New York, even though the rest of his delegation had already departed.

At least sixty-five individuals had received appointments to the Convention, fifty-five attended at various times over the course of the sessions, and thirty-nine delegates signed the final document. George Read of Delaware signed twice: once for himself, then again for John Dickinson (who had left due to illness, and had authorized Read to sign his name).

Although he was not a delegate, William Jackson, the secretary of the Convention, signed to attest, or authenticate, the delegates' signatures.

Also of note is the method by which the Constitution is dated: "the Seventeenth Day of September in the Year of our Lord" 1787, and "of the Independence of the United States of America the Twelfth." Dating documents to "the Year of our Lord" had become more unusual; the Declaration of Independence, for instance, simply states "In Congress, July 4, 1776." Dating important documents in American political history to the Declaration of Independence was at that point relatively frequent. The dual reference can be found in only two other national documents: the Articles of Confederation and the Northwest Ordinance (considered, along with the Declaration, to be the "organic documents" of the nation). The language here is neither insignificant nor unintentional: these dates serve to place the document in the context of the religious traditions of Western civilization and, at the same time, to link it to the regime principles proclaimed in the Declaration of Independence, the Constitution having been written in the twelfth year after July 1776. The usage stands in contrast to both the contemporary British tradition, in which documents were dated to the reign of the sitting monarch (*see* the Magna Carta of 1215 and the Petition of Right of 1628), and the French decision in 1793 to reject the Gregorian calendar altogether and begin measuring time starting with the French Revolution.

Matthew Spalding

AMENDMENTS

Establishment of Religion

Congress shall make no law respecting an establishment of religion....
(AMENDMENT I)

~

*I*n recent years the Supreme Court has placed the Establishment and the Free Exercise of Religion Clauses in mutual tension, but it was not so for the Framers. None of the Framers believed that a governmental connection to religion was an evil in itself. Rather, many (though not all) opposed an established church because they believed that it was a threat to the free exercise of religion. Their primary goal was to protect free exercise. That was the main thrust of James Madison's famous *Memorial and Remonstrance* (1785), in which he argued that the state of Virginia ought not to pay the salaries of the Anglican clergy because that practice was an impediment to a person's free connection to whatever religion his conscience directed him.

Nor did most of the Founding generation believe that government ought to be "untainted" by religion, or ought not to take an interest in furthering the people's connection to religion. The Northwest Ordinance (1787), which the First Congress reenacted, stated: "Religion, morality, and knowledge, being necessary to good government and the happiness of mankind, schools and the means of education shall forever be encouraged." As President, George Washington's practice concretized the understanding of most of his contemporaries. In his first inaugural address, Washington declared as his "first official act" his "fervent supplications to that Almighty Being who rules over the universe" that He might bless the new government. Directing his words to his compatriots, Washington said:

> In tendering this homage to the Great Author of every public and private good, I assure myself that it expresses your sentiments not less than my own; nor those of my fellow citizens at large less than either. No people can be bound to acknowledge and adore the invisible hand which conducts the affairs of men more than those of the United States.

Washington bracketed his years as President with similar sentiments in his Farewell Address (1796):

> Of all the dispositions and habits which lead to political prosperity, Religion and morality are indispensable supports. In vain would that man claim the tribute of Patriotism, who should labour to subvert these great Pillars of human happiness, these firmest props of the duties of Men and citizens. The mere Politician, equally with the pious man, ought to respect and to cherish them.

And he added: "And let us with caution indulge the supposition, that morality can be maintained without religion."

There is nothing in the drafting history of the First Amendment that contradicts Washington's understanding of the appropriate relation between government and religion. In the First Congress, the committee proposal in the House read, "no religion shall be established by law, nor shall the equal rights of conscience be infringed." But some evinced concern that the phrase might put in doubt the legitimacy of some of the states' own religious establishments. Six of the original thirteen states had established churches. James Madison believed modifying the phrasing to prohibit a "national religion" would be sufficient to allay that concern and would make clear that the new gov-

ernment was not to impinge on the rights of conscience by establishing a governmental connection to a church. Representative Samuel Livermore of New Hampshire suggested that "Congress shall make no laws touching religion or the rights of conscience." The House finally settled on this language: "Congress shall make no law establishing religion, or prohibiting the free exercise thereof, nor shall the rights of Conscience be infringed." The Senate preferred the formula "Congress shall make no law establishing articles of faith, or a mode of worship, or prohibiting the free exercise of religion," which likely would have permitted direct financial support to a sect. In the end, the conference between the House and the Senate agreed on the current version: "Congress shall make no law respecting an establishment of religion, or prohibiting the free exercise thereof." The addition of the word "respecting" is significant. It prohibits Congress from legislating either to establish a national religion or to disestablish a state religion. As Laurence Tribe has written, "[a] growing body of evidence suggests that the Framers principally intended the Establishment of Religion Clause to perform two functions: to protect state religious establishments from national displacement, and to prevent the national government from aiding some, but not all, religions."

Leaving the question of establishment to the states does not entail the absence of religious liberty. Even before the incorporation of the religion clauses and without intervention by the federal courts, religious freedom and tolerance had spread throughout the United States. To be sure, religious conflicts occurred at the local level where discrimination, particularly against Catholics and Jews existed. The framework established by the Constitution, however, made it possible for religious minorities to gain protection through political representation.

Contemporaneous history strongly indicates that most Framers supported religion because it increased virtue among the people, a necessary element for the maintenance of a free republic. Nonetheless, when it came time to speak upon the matter, the Supreme Court preferred to base its conception of the original understanding of the clause on its interpretation of a phrase from a letter by Thomas Jefferson to the Danbury Baptist Association of Connecticut (1802). Although he had been in France during the Constitutional Convention, Jefferson's metaphor of a "wall of separation" was interpreted by the Court as the authoritative statement of a "high and impregnable" barrier between church and state, even though this was itself an expansion beyond Jefferson's own meaning and practice. *Everson v. Board of Education of Ewing* (1947); *see also Reynolds v. United States* (1879).

The modern view of the Establishment of Religion Clause began with *Everson v. Board of Education of Ewing* in 1947, where the Court initiated the current separationist approach to the Establishment of Religion Clause. On the way to reaching its decision, the Supreme Court held that the Due Process Clause of the Fourteenth Amendment applied the First Amendment's proscriptions against establishment to the states. Although there is vigorous debate as to whether the provisions of the Fourteenth Amendment "incorporate," or replicate, the guarantees of the Bill of Rights and fastens them on the states, most commentators opine that the Establishment of Religion Clause is the least likely candidate for incorporation. The Establishment of Religion Clause was designed as a protection of the states against the federal government. It seems anomalous to many scholars, even to some who support incorporation generally, that the Establishment of Religion Clause could be called an individual right for purposes of the Fourteenth Amendment.

Notwithstanding the historians' doubts, the Supreme Court has firmly adhered to the incorporation of the Establishment of Religion Clause against the states. As a result of the incorporation of the Religion Clause into the Fourteenth Amendment, almost all of the federal cases compelling "separation of church and state" have been applied against state laws.

The contradictory decisions of the Supreme Court on the Establishment of Religion Clause render the area inchoate if not incoherent. A "moment of silence for meditation and prayer" in school is contrary to the Constitution (only

if the *motive* is religious), *Wallace v. Jaffree* (1985), but a paid chaplain in Congress or state legislatures is not, *Marsh v. Chambers* (1983). Religious schools may not receive funds for maintenance expenses, *Committee for Public Education & Religious Liberty v. Nyquist* (1973), but places of worship can enjoy a tax exemption, *Walz v. Tax Commision of City of New York* (1970). Prayers at high school football games are invalid, *Santa Fe Independent School District v. Doe* (2000), but the bailiff's call, "God Save this Honorable Court," may be heard within the chambers of the Supreme Court.

Since *Everson*, the Supreme Court has developed three different and conflicting views regarding the Establishment of Religion Clause: (1) separationism, (2) coercion, and (3) endorsement.

The separationist view of *Everson* led to the banning of prayer and Bible reading from public schools. *Engel v. Vitale* (1962); *School District of Abington Township v. Schempp* (1963). To enforce separationism, the Court settled on a three-part test in *Lemon v. Kurtzman* (1971). The *Lemon* test requires courts to consider whether the law in question has (1) a secular purpose, (2) a primary effect that neither advances nor inhibits religion, and (3) does not create excessive entanglement with religion. Subsequently, the entanglement element was subsumed into the primary effect inquiry. *Agostini v. Felton* (1997). The strict separationists on the Court did allow for a few exceptions to the *Lemon* test under the rubric of "ceremonial deism," whereby particular customary practices may be protected from Establishment Clause scrutiny if "they have lost through rote repetition any significant religious content." *Lynch v. Donnelly* (1984).

A major historical challenge to the separationist position emerged in the dissent written by (then) Justice William H. Rehnquist in *Wallace v. Jaffree* in 1985. Rehnquist argued that the original meaning of the Establishment of Religion Clause only "forbade establishment of a national religion, and forbade preference among religious sects or denominations." In defending this "no denominational preference" position and criticizing strict separationism,

Rehnquist observed that Thomas Jefferson is "a less than ideal source of contemporary history as to the meaning of the Religion Clauses of the First Amendment." Absent from the country when the Bill of Rights was written, Jefferson was not involved in the legislative drafting of the First Amendment. Earlier, Jefferson had figured prominently, along with Madison, in the struggle over religious liberty in Virginia; they shared similar views on these matters and had cooperated during this debate. Nevertheless, in considering Madison's actions in the Congress, as the Rehnquist opinion states, it "is totally incorrect [to] suggest that Madison carried these views onto the floor of the United States House of Representatives when he proposed the language which would ultimately become the Bill of Rights."

Rehnquist offered several other pieces of evidence to contradict the "wall of separation" metaphor, including numerous Thanksgiving proclamations and other actions by Presidents and the Congress, as well as the Northwest Ordinance, which Congress took up on the same day the Bill of Rights was introduced. The Northwest Ordinance is generally known for providing land grants for public schools in the new states and territories, but it also allowed grants for religious schools until Congress limited grants to nonsectarian institutions in 1845.

Although these various pieces of historical evidence support the proposition that the Establishment of Religion Clause merely requires "no preference between denominations," others criticize that view on originalist grounds. For instance, Douglas Laycock has noted that the Congress that drafted the First Amendment rejected several preliminary drafts that would have clearly stated the "no preference" principle—for example, one draft stated that "Congress shall make no law establishing One Religious Sect or Society in preference to others." Instead, the Congress adopted the arguably broader language forbidding any law "respecting an establishment of religion." The "no preference" position, whatever its originalist merits, has not figured in Supreme Court opinions since the 1985 Rehnquist dissent in *Wallace v. Jaffree*.

As another alternative to separationism, some Justices assert that the Establishment of Religion Clause was originally meant only to prohibit the government from coercing individuals to practice religion or support it. It is often associated with Justices who believe the government has the power to "accommodate" the diverse religious practices of the people. This principle, to which the Court has given attention in decisions such as *Lee v. Weisman* (1992), would allow government to support religion in ways that do not coerce individuals. For example, states could permit the erection of religious symbols in public places or issue proclamations of thanksgiving to God. This position likewise finds some support in Founding-era statements, such as James Madison's 1789 explanation to the House that the goal was to prevent a sect or combination of sects from "establish[ing] a religion to which they would compel others to conform," or from "enforc[ing] the legal observation of it by law." The "no coercion" principle likewise is consistent with the long line of religious expressions by government, running from the Founding period to the present; government may express religious sentiments as long as it does not force anyone to agree with such expressions or participate in such ceremonies. As applied by the Court, however, particularly in the opinions of Justice Anthony Kennedy, the "no coercion principle" is broad enough to prohibit even student-led nonsectarian prayers at school assemblies such as graduations or sporting events if the state, in some way, is selecting the student for that purpose.

Finally, Justice Sandra Day O'Connor has offered an alternative to both the strict separationist view (usually articulated in the *Lemon* test) and the "no coercion" principle. According to Justice O'Connor, the Establishment of Religion Clause prohibits a state from "endorsing" a religion. She defines the test for "endorsement" as whether an objective, reasonable observer would see the state action as sending "a message to nonadherents that they are not full members of the political community." *Lynch v. Donnelly* (1984). Justice Antonin Scalia has criticized the test, though some of the strict separationists have adopted Justice O'Connor's wording as supporting their interpretation of the Establishment of Religion Clause. *See County of Allegheny v. American Civil Liberties Union, Greater Pittsburgh Chapter* (1989).

Establishment of Religion Clause jurisprudence remains unsettled as Justices form shifting majorities around one or the other of the three tests. Recently the coercion test has been the basis of invalidating prayers in public school settings, *Lee v. Weisman*; *Santa Fe Independent School District v. Doe* (2000). Concerning the question whether the phrase "under God" can be part of the Pledge of Allegiance public-school children are allowed (but not required) to recite, the Supreme Court refused to rule in a recent case because the plaintiff lacked standing (and was not directly injured by the practice). *Elk Grove Unified School District v. Newdow* (2004).

The *Lemon* test, or a form of it, was invoked to invalidate the teaching of creationism, *Edwards v. Aquillard* (1987), and state-sponsored posting of the Ten Commandments, *Stone v. Graham* (1980). (The Supreme Court has recently granted a writ of certiorari in two Ten Commandments cases, *Van Orden v. Perry* and *McCreary County, Kentucky v. ACLU of Kentucky*.) The endorsement test has provided the formula that a number of Justices have used to decide the constitutionality of religious displays on public property, such as a Nativity scene, *County of Allegheny v. American Civil Liberties Union, Greater Pittsburgh Chapter* and a cross, *Capitol Square Review and Advisory Board v. Pinette* (1995). More frequently, the Court has approved religious practice or symbols on public property as protected by the Freedom of Speech Clause of the First Amendment, *Good News Club v. Milford Central School* (2001).

After a long series of cases dealing with aid to religious schools, a majority of the Court has embraced the principle that there is no Establishment of Religion Clause violation if the state gives tuition aid (e.g., tuition vouchers) directly to the parents who can decide which schools their children will attend, whether religiously affiliated or not, rather than giving the aid directly to the religious school. *Zelman v. Simmons-Harris* (2002). Finally, the Court has approved "exceptions"

based on tradition, such as tax exemptions, *Walz v. Tax Commission of City of New York* (1970), and legislative chaplains, *Marsh v. Chambers* (1983), even though the Framers of the Establishment of Religion Clause did not find a provision of a chaplain to be an "exception" but in harmony with a governmental policy of encouraging religious expression and exercise.

John Baker

[Editors' Note: In 2005, the Supreme Court continued to maintain doctrinal confusion in two closely divided opinions. The Court, per Justice Stephen G. Breyer, struck down the placement of copies of the Ten Commandments in court houses as violative of the *Lemon* test, *McCreary County v. ACLU of Kentucky*, but, in a plurality opinion by Chief Justice William H. Rehnquist, upheld a monument of the Ten Commandments on the Texas State House grounds as a "passive" display recognizing the role of religion in the life of the country, *Van Orden v. Perry*.]

See Also

Article VI, Clause 3 (Oaths Clause)
Amendment I (Free Exercise of Religion)

Suggestions for Further Research

John S. Baker, Jr., *The Establishment Clause as Intended: No Preference among Sects and Pluralism in a Large Commercial Republic, in* THE BILL OF RIGHTS: ORIGINAL MEANING AND CURRENT UNDERSTANDING (Eugene W. Hickok, Jr., ed., 1991)

GERARD BRADLEY, CHURCH-STATE RELATIONSHIPS IN AMERICA (1987)

DANIEL L. DREISBACH, THOMAS JEFFERSON AND THE WALL OF SEPARATION BETWEEN CHURCH AND STATE (2002)

PHILIP HAMBURGER, SEPARATION OF CHURCH AND STATE (2002)

Douglas Laycock, *"Nonpreferential" Aid to Religion: A False Claim About Original Intent*, 27 WM. & MARY L. REV. 875 (1986)

Douglas Laycock, *The Underlying Unity of Separation and Neutrality*, 46 EMORY L.J. 43 (1997)

Michael W. McConnell, *Establishment and Disestablishment at The Founding, Part I: Establishment of Religion*, 44 Wm. & Mary L. Rev. 2105 (2003)

Significant Cases

Reynolds v. United States, 98 U.S. 145 (1879)

Everson v. Board of Education of Ewing, 330 U.S. 1 (1947)

Illinois *ex rel.* McCollum v. Board of Education, 333 U.S. 203 (1948)

Zorach v. Clauson, 343 U.S. 306 (1952)

Engel v. Vitale, 370 U.S. 421 (1962)

School District of Abington Township v. Schempp, 374 U.S. 203 (1963)

Epperson v. Arkansas, 393 U.S. 97 (1968)

Walz v. Tax Commission of City of New York, 397 U.S. 664 (1970)

Lemon v. Kurtzman, 403 U.S. 602 (1971)

Committee for Public Education & Religious Liberty v. Nyquist, 413 U.S. 756 (1973)

Stone v. Graham, 449 U.S. 39 (1980)

Marsh v. Chambers, 463 U.S. 783 (1983)

Mueller v. Allen, 463 U.S. 388 (1983)

Lynch v. Donnelly, 465 U.S. 668 (1984)

Wallace v. Jaffree, 472 U.S. 38 (1985)

Witters v. Washington Department of Services for Blind, 474 U.S. 481 (1986)

Edwards v. Aquillard, 482 U.S. 578 (1987)

Bowen v. Kendrick, 487 U.S. 589 (1988)

County of Allegheny v. American Civil Liberties Union, Greater Pittsburgh Chapter, 492 U.S. 573 (1989)

Lee v. Weisman, 505 U.S. 577 (1992)

Zobrest v. Catalina Foothills School District, 509 U.S. 1 (1993)

Capitol Square Review and Advisory Board v. Pinette, 515 U.S. 753 (1995)

Rosenberger v. Rector and Visitors of the University of Virginia, 515 U.S. 819 (1995)

Agostini v. Felton, 521 U.S. 203 (1997)

Santa Fe Independent School District v. Doe, 530 U.S. 290 (2000)

Good News Club v. Milford Central School, 533 U.S. 98 (2001)

Zelman v. Simmons-Harris, 536 U.S. 639 (2002)

Elk Grove Unified School District v. Newdow, 124 S. Ct. 2301 (2004)

McCreary County v. ACLU of Kentucky, 2005 WL 1498988, 2005 U.S. LEXIS 5211 (2005)

Van Orden v. Perry, 2005 WL 1500276, 2005 U.S. LEXIS 5215 (2005)

Free Exercise of Religion

Congress shall make no law respecting an establishment of religion, or prohibiting the free exercise thereof....

(**Amendment I**)

~

$\mathcal{E}$stablishing freedom of religion as both constitutional principle and social reality is among America's greatest contributions to the world. Nevertheless, the concept of free exercise of religion is not self-defining. The boundaries of free exercise, like those of other rights, must be delineated as against the claims of society and of other individuals. The history of the Free Exercise of Religion Clause, in both its original understanding and modern interpretations, reveals two recurring impulses, one giving free exercise a broad scope, the other a narrow scope. The narrower view sometimes collapses free exercise into other constitutional rights—for example, treating religious activity as no more than a variety of speech or expression—whereas the broader view sees the right of choice in religious practice as independently valuable. The tension between broad and narrow rights has played out in four sets of issues under the Free Exercise of Religion Clause.

One key issue concerns the meaning of the protected "exercise" of religion: Does it encompass only the belief and profession of a religion, or does it also protect conduct that stems from religious tenets or motivations; for example, wearing a head covering or religious garb, or refusing to accept blood transfusions or other medical treatment?

The weight of the original understanding controverts the narrowest interpretation of the right, that belief alone is protected. At the Founding, as today, "exercise" connoted action, not just internal belief. Thomas Jefferson, in his famous 1802 "wall of separation" letter to the Danbury Baptist Association, did draw a sharp distinction between protected belief and unprotected action: "the legislative powers of government reach actions only, and not opinions, [and] [m]an has no natural right in opposition to his social duties." But a number of statements from other leading figures support the broader view—from James Madison's statement that religion includes "the manner of discharging" duties to God, to William Penn's statement that "liberty of conscience [means] not only a meer liberty of the mind, in believing or disbelieving... but the exercise of ourselves in a visible way of worship."

The significance of the Free Exercise of Religion Clause lay less in its legal effect than in its affirmation of the value of religion in American culture. Until the middle of the twentieth century, the Free Exercise of Religion Clause applied only to actions by the federal government. In 1940, however, in *Cantwell v. State of Connecticut*, the Court "incorporated" the Free Exercise of Religion Clause into the Due Process Clause of the Fourteenth Amendment and applied it to the states. Subsequently, most contests over free exercise have involved state statutes.

In its first interpretation of the Free Exercise of Religion Clause, *Reynolds v. United States* (1879), the Supreme Court confronted a federal law banning polygamy in the territories, thereby limiting the practice then required by the Mormon religion. The Court adopted the narrower reading of the right, protecting belief only and not action, relying on Jefferson's letter to the Danbury Baptists. Since then, however, the Court has ruled more frequently in line with the original meaning, protecting religiously motivated actions such as proselytization, *Cantwell*, refusing work on one's sabbath, *Sherbert v. Verner* (1963), choosing the education of one's children, *Wisconsin v. Yoder* (1972), and sacrificing animals at a worship service, *Church of Lukumi Babalu Aye v. City of Hialeah* (1993).

Because it is now accepted that the Free Exercise of Religion Clause protects religiously motivated conduct as well as belief, the most important modern issue has been whether the protection only runs against laws that target religion itself for restriction, or, more broadly, whether the clause sometimes requires an exemption from a generally applicable law. To take just one of many examples, must an Orthodox Jewish military officer, who is religiously obligated to wear a yarmulke, be exempted from a general rule forbidding all servicemen to wear anything other than official headgear?

The text of the clause can support either the narrow or the broad reading on this issue. A law could well be said to be "prohibiting the free exercise [of religion]" if it in fact prohibits a religious practice, even if it does so incidentally, rather than overtly or intentionally. On the other hand, one might argue that the legislature does not "make [a] law prohibiting the free exercise" unless the prohibition or restriction on religion is part of the law's very terms or is the legislature's intent, as opposed to simply the effect of the law in a particular application.

This issue therefore requires examination of the legal background and the Founding generation's attitude toward conflicts between law and religious conscience. By 1789, all but one of the states had free-exercise–type provisions in their constitutions, many with very similar phrasing. Many of these state grants of religious freedom included provisos that such freedom would not justify, or could be denied for, practices that "disturb[ed] the public peace" or were "inconsistent with the peace and safety of the State." In the leading modern discussion of the original understanding, Michael McConnell has argued that the provisos reflect the broader, pro-exemptions conception of free exercise, because if religious practices were subject to all general laws, there would be no reason to identify a subset of laws that that protected the peace of the state. In response, Philip Hamburger has asserted that the provisos stated the conditions, not for denying freedom to particular religious practices, but for denying religious freedom altogether to persons or groups engaging in such practices. Thus, a congregation whose members handled poisonous snakes at certain worship services could presumably have their worship services outlawed altogether. Hamburger's second and more significant argument is that in eighteenth-century legal terminology, "every breach of law [was] against the peace [of the state]," so that the provisos would have been triggered by any secular law of general applicability.

The legal background also includes accommodations made by colonial and state legislatures for specific religious practices. Virtually all states by 1789 allowed Quakers to testify or vote by an affirmation rather than an oath; several colonies had exempted Quakers and Mennonites from service in the militia; and there was a patchwork of other exemptions throughout the states. Supporters of the narrower view of the Free Exercise of Religion Clause, such as Professor Hamburger, argue that these examples imply only that specific statutory exemptions may be granted by legislative grace. But advocates of the broader interpretation, such as Professor McConnell, infer that the Founding generation thought that exemption from the law was the appropriate response to conflicts between legal and religious duties, that is, that exemption was part of the meaning of "free exercise" so long as the religious activity did not harm public peace or others' rights.

Even more deeply, the question of exemptions from generally applicable laws implicates ideological differences over the relationship between civil government and religion. One important philosophical influence on the Founders, the Enlightenment liberalism stemming from the writings of John Locke, does not lend itself easily to exempting religious practice from general secular laws. In his famous *Letter Concerning Toleration* (1689), Locke argued that the proper domains of government and religion were largely separate; "the power of civil government... is confined to the care of this world," whereas "churches have [no] jurisdiction in worldly matters." Although this limit on government control over belief and doctrine was liberal for its time, just as central to Locke's understanding was the limit on religion's role in worldly matters. And in those cases where both religion and government claimed jurisdiction—that is where religious duties clashed with general laws, and an exemption is sought— Locke gave the nod to the government on the ground that "the private judgment of any per-son concerning a law enacted in political matters... does not take away the obligation of that law, nor deserve a dispensation."

The Enlightenment view, however, was not the dominant, or even the most important, impetus for religious freedom in America. Popular support for religious freedom came heavily from the newer evangelical Protestant sects, especially the Baptists and Presbyterians. These religious "enthusiasts," who helped defeat religious taxes in Virginia and elect James Madison to Congress, began from a different premise: that religion was a matter of duties to God, and that God, in the words of Massachusetts Baptist leader Isaac Backus, "is to be obeyed rather than any man." Madison echoed these ideas in his *Memorial and Remonstrance Against Religious Assessments* (1785), arguing that the duty to the Creator "is precedent, both in order of time and in degree of obligation, to the claims of Civil Society." Everyone who joins a civil society must "do it with a saving of his allegiance to the Universal Sovereign." This view logically suggests that the proper governmental response to conflicts between legal and religious duties is, at least sometimes, exemption from legal duties. Whether the governmental response should be legislatively enacted exemptions, or judicial-enforced prohibitions against the government, remains the problem.

Whether religious exemptions from generally applicable laws are ever mandated by the free exercise concept has been the central question in this area for many years. After rejecting constitutionally mandated exemptions for many years, the Supreme Court switched course and exempted religious claimants from generally applicable laws in *Sherbert v. Verner* and *Wisconsin v. Yoder*. In *Sherbert*, the Court struck down a state law that denied unemployment benefits to a Seventh-Day Adventist whose religion forbade her from working or being available for work on Saturday. In *Yoder*, the Court held that the Free Exercise of Religion Clause protected members of the Amish faith from having to abide by a compulsory school attendance law.

The pro-exemptions approach, however, was often applied half-heartedly in the next two decades, and in *Employment Division, Oregon*

Department of Human Resources v. Smith (1990), the Court declared that the Free Exercise of Religion Clause did not grant an exemption from generally applicable drug law to members of a Native American religion that used peyote in its religious services. The Court abandoned the pro-exemptions approach in most cases, holding that exemptions are not required from a "neutral law of general applicability." Because most restrictions on religious conduct today come from the application of general laws rather than from laws targeting religion, *Smith* potentially could greatly shrink the protections accorded religiously motivated actions.

In response to *Smith*, Congress passed the Religious Freedom Restoration Act of 1993 (RFRA), reinstating the *Sherbert-Yoder* test that laws that "substantially burden" religion, even if they are generally applicable, must be justified as the "least restrictive means" of achieving a "compelling governmental interest." Nonetheless in *City of Boerne v. Flores* (1997), the Supreme Court struck down RFRA as applied to state and local laws, on the ground that Congress exceeded its power in attempting to define the constitutional parameters of the Free Exercise of Religion Clause. RFRA may remain applicable to federal laws, and a number of states have passed their own versions of RFRA. Thus, the rule concerning exemptions from general laws remains divided under modern law, just as there is division and ambivalence in the original understanding of the Free Exercise of Religion Clause.

Related to the question whether religious exercise should be exempted from generally applicable laws is the question whether the exercise "of religion" extends to behavior motivated by norms of secular conscience, as opposed to beliefs in God or other traditional features of religion. For example, should the exemption from school-attendance laws for the Amish in *Yoder* extend to followers of Henry Thoreau who rejected traditional schooling for their children?

The word "religion" might be understood in direct contrast to a broader idea of "conscience" that includes secular-based norms. Both terms were used during the Founding period—indeed, during the debates on the language of the First Amendment, which began with Madison's proposal to protect "the full and equal rights of conscience" but eventually changed to "the free exercise of religion." The change may have meant little substantively, because during the Founding period "conscience" was often used as synonymous with "religion." Or possibly the change may have meant a narrowing from all deep moral convictions to theistic ones.

In a pair of cases involving challenges to military conscription during the Vietnam War, the Supreme Court read the statutory phrase "religious training and belief" to encompass objections based on any secular conscientious belief "which occupies in the life of its possessor a place parallel to that filled by the God of those" who are traditionally religious. *United States v. Seeger* (1965); *Welsh v. United States* (1970). Those expansive cases, however, were decided under the language of the draft-exemption statute. The Court has been more cautious in construing "religion" under the Free Exercise of Religion Clause itself.

The final question to bedevil courts in Free Exercise of Religion Clause cases has been just what sort of effect on religious exercise triggers protection. Are Free Exercise rights violated only when one is put in jail or fined for religious practice, or are some less serious burdens also unconstitutional?

The term "prohibiting" in the Free Exercise of Religion Clause may suggest the narrower scope of the right, covering only the affirmative imposition of sanctions such as imprisonment or a fine. Indeed, "prohibiting" might be contrasted directly with "infringing," the term used in an earlier draft, and with its broader counterpart in other First Amendment Clauses: "no law *abridging*" the freedom of speech, press, assembly, or petition. Madison rejected a parallel argument during the 1798 debate over the Alien and Sedition Acts. In response to the claim that Congress could regulate freedom of the press without "abridging" it, he argued against such a semantic distinction because "the liberty of conscience and the freedom of the press were equally and completely exempted from all [congressional] authority whatever."

In *Sherbert*, the Court adopted a broad understanding of unconstitutional "burdens" on religion, holding that the state violated Free Exercise by withholding unemployment benefits on the basis of the claimant's religiously motivated refusal to work on Saturdays. Later, however, the Court took a more narrow approach, pointing to the term "prohibiting" in holding that the government did not violate Free Exercise by building a road that disrupted forest areas sacred to Native American believers, because the project did not "coerce individuals into acting contrary to their religious beliefs." *Lyng v. Northwest Indian Cemetery Protective Ass'n* (1988). *Sherbert*, however, though now limited in its application, has never been directly overruled by the Court. The Court has never questioned *Sherbert*'s holding that the government can "prohibit" free exercise by withholding important benefits from the individual because of a religious practice, not only by imprisoning or fining him.

Thomas Berg

Suggestions for Further Research

Walter Berns, The First Amendment and the Future of American Democracy (1983)

Philip A. Hamburger, *A Constitutional Right of Religious Exemption: An Historical Overview*, 60 Geo. Wash. L. Rev. 915 (1992)

Kurt T. Lash, *The Second Adoption of the Free Exercise Clause: Religious Exemptions and the Fourteenth Amendment*, 88 Nw. U. L. Rev. 1106 (1994)

Ira C. Lupu, *Where Rights Begin: The Problem of Burdens on the Free Exercise of Religion*, 102 Harv. L. Rev. 933 (1989)

Michael Malbin, Religion and Politics: The Intentions of the Authors of the First Amendment (1978)

Michael W. McConnell, *The Origins and Historical Understanding of Free Exercise of Religion*, 103 Harv. L. Rev. 1409 (1990)

John Witte, Jr., *The Essential Rights and Liberties of Religion in the American Constitutional Experiment*, 71 Notre Dame L. Rev. 371 (1996)

Significant Cases

Reynolds v. United States, 98 U.S. 145 (1879)
Cantwell v. State of Connecticut, 310 U.S. 296 (1940)

Sherbert v. Verner, 374 U.S. 398 (1963)
United States v. Seeger, 380 U.S. 163 (1965)
Welsh v. United States, 398 U.S. 333 (1970)
Wisconsin v. Yoder, 406 U.S. 205 (1972)
Lyng v. Northwest Indian Cemetery Protective Ass'n, 485 U.S. 439 (1988)
Employment Division, Oregon Department of Human Resources v. Smith, 494 U.S. 872 (1990)
Church of Lukumi Babalu Aye v. City of Hialeah, 508 U.S. 520 (1993)
City of Boerne v. Flores, 521 U.S. 507 (1997)
Cutter v. Wilkinson, 125 S. Ct. 2113 (2005)

Freedom of Speech and of the Press

> Congress shall make no law... abridging the freedom of speech, or of the press....
>
> (Amendment I)

$\sim$

$\mathcal{W}$hat exactly did the Framers mean by "freedom of speech, or of the press"? Surprisingly, there is little definitively known about the subject. The debates in the First Congress, which proposed the Bill of Rights, are brief and unilluminating. Early state constitutions generally included similar provisions, but there is no record of detailed debate about what those state provisions meant. The Framers cared a good deal about the freedom of the press, as the *Appeal to the Inhabitants of Quebec*, written by the First Continental Congress in 1774, shows:

> The last right we shall mention regards the freedom of the press. The importance of this consists, besides the advancement of truth, science, morality, and arts in general, in its diffusion of liberal sentiments on the administration of Government, its ready communication of thoughts between subjects, and its consequential promotion of union among them, whereby oppressive officers are shamed or intimidated into

more honorable and just modes of conducting affairs.

The statement mentions some of the values that the Founders saw as inherent in the principle of freedom of the press: the search and attainment of truth, scientific progress, cultural development, the increase of virtue among the people, the holding of governmental officials to republican values, the strengthening of community, and a check upon self-aggrandizing politicians. But broad statements such as this may tell us less than we would like to know about what "the freedom of the press" meant to the Founders as a rule of law, when the freedom would yield to competing concerns, or whether the freedom prohibited only prior restraints or also subsequent punishments.

There were very few reported Founding-era court cases interpreting the federal and state Freedom of Speech and of the Press Clause, and very few Founding-era political controversies that would have excited some detailed discussion of what the clauses meant. The governments of the time were quite small, and the statute books thin. There were few laws restricting commercial advertising. There was only one state law banning pornography, and that appears to have been unenforced until 1821. There were a few state blasphemy laws, but they were largely unenforced from the early 1700s until the 1810s. There were no bans on flag-burning, campaign spending, or anonymous speech. This may but does not necessarily mean that such speech was broadly believed to be constitutionally protected; then as today, the government did not ban all that it had the power to ban. But the paucity of such bans meant that few people in that era really had occasion to define what the constitutional boundaries of speech and press protection might be. The only speech restriction that was broadly enforced was traditional libel law. Defaming another person was understood to be constitutionally unprotected.

In fact, the most prominent free press debate of the years immediately following the Framing—the Sedition Act controversy—illustrated that there was little consensus on even as central an issue as whether the free press guarantee only prohibited prior restraints on publications critical of the government, or whether it also forbade punishment for "seditious" speech once it was made. In 1798, the country was fighting the Quasi War with France. The Federalist Party controlled all three branches of the federal government, and its members suspected many Republican party stalwarts of sympathizing with France and the French Revolution and thus of fomenting disloyalty. Congress consequently made it a crime to publish "any false, scandalous and malicious writing or writings . . . with intent to defame" the government, the Congress, or the President, "or to stir up sedition within the United States, or to excite any unlawful combinations . . . for opposing or resisting any law of the United States, . . . or to aid, encourage or abet any hostile designs of any foreign nation against the United States, their people or government." Notably, malicious falsehoods about the Vice President—Thomas Jefferson, who was a leading Republican—were not covered by the law, and the law was scheduled to expire on March 3, 1801, the day before Federalist President John Adams's term was to end. Several publishers were in fact convicted under the law, often under rather biased applications of the falsity requirement.

Then Federalist Congressman John Marshall, although doubtful that the Sedition Act was wise, nonetheless argued that the free press guarantee meant only "liberty to publish, free from previous restraint"—free of requirements that printers be licensed, or that their material be approved before publication. Under this view, which echoed the British law as expounded by Sir William Blackstone, criminal punishment after publication was constitutional. Others, such as James Madison, the principal drafter of the Bill of Rights, argued the opposite: "[T]his idea of the freedom of the press can never be admitted to be the American idea of it; since a law inflicting penalties on printed publications would have a similar effect with a law authorizing a previous restraint on them."

Likewise, Marshall and other Federalists argued that the freedom of the press must necessarily be limited, because "government cannot be . . . secured, if by falsehood and malicious slander, it is to be deprived of the confidence and affection of the people." Not so, reasoned Madison and other Republicans: even speech that creates "a contempt, a disrepute, or hatred [of the government] among the people" should be tolerated because the only way of determining whether such contempt is justified is "by a free examination [of the government's actions], and a free communication among the people thereon." It was as if half the country read the constitutional guarantee one way, and the other half, the other way.

The Founding generation undoubtedly believed deeply in the freedom of speech and of the press, but then, as now, these general terms were understood quite differently by different people. Many people did not think about their precise meanings until a concrete controversy arose; and when a controversy did arise, the analysis was often influenced by people's political interests as much as by their honest constitutional understanding.

A 1995 Supreme Court case, *McIntyre v. Ohio Elections Commission*, illustrates the continuing debate over the original meaning of the clause. The question in *McIntyre* was whether the government could outlaw anonymous electioneering. The majority dealt with the question based on the Court's twentieth-century case law and twentieth-century First Amendment theories. Justices Clarence Thomas and Antonin Scalia, the Court's most devoted originalists, however, did focus on the original meaning discussion but reached different results.

Both Justices recognized that there was "no record of discussions of anonymous political expression in the First Congress, which drafted the Bill of Rights, or in the state ratifying conventions." They both recognized that much political speech in the time of the Framers (such as *The Federalist* itself) was anonymous. Indeed, much political speech justifying resistance to Parliament before the Revolution was also anonymous. To Justice Thomas, the experience of the Founders in their own use of anonymous speech was dispositive of what they would have regarded as a vital part of the freedom of speech, particularly where political speech was at issue. Justice Scalia, however, who has a narrower view of what can be accepted as evidence of original

intent apart from the text of the provision itself, argued that "to prove that anonymous electioneering was used frequently is not to establish that it is a constitutional right"—perhaps the legislatures simply chose not to prohibit the speech, even though they had the constitutional power to do so. Justice Thomas did produce evidence that some Founding-era commentators saw anonymity as constitutionally protected, Justice Scalia replied that many of these were mere "partisan cr[ies]" that said little about any generally accepted understanding. Justice Thomas found the evidence sufficient to justify reading the First Amendment as protecting anonymous speech. Justice Scalia did not think the historical evidence of what people did necessarily showed much about what people were seen as having a constitutional right to do. Instead, Scalia turned to American practices of the 1800s and the 1900s, a source that he considers authoritative where the original meaning is uncertain. A consensus on the original meaning on this subject thus remains elusive.

Despite the originalist debate between Justices Thomas and Scalia, today's free speech and free press law is not much influenced by original meaning. It is mostly the creature of the experience and thinking of the twentieth century, as the Court first began to hear a wide range of free speech cases only in the late 1910s. This approach has produced the following free speech rules:

1. As with all of the Bill of Rights, the free speech/press guarantee restricts only *government* action, not action by private employers, property owners, householders, churches, universities, and the like.

2. As with most of the Bill of Rights, the free speech/press guarantee applies equally to *federal and state governments*, which includes local governments as well as all branches of each government. In particular, the civil courts are subject to the First Amendment, which is why libel law and other tort law rules must comply with free speech/press principles. *New York Times Co. v. Sullivan* (1964).

3. The free speech and the free press clauses have been read as providing essentially equal protection to *speakers and writers*, whether or

not they are members of the institutional press, and largely regardless of the medium—books, newspapers, movies, the Internet—in which they communicate. Newspapers enjoy no more and no fewer constitutional rights than individuals. The one exception is over-the-airwaves radio and television broadcasting, which has for historical reasons been given less constitutional protection. *Reno v. ACLU* (1997).

4. The free speech/press guarantee also extends to any conduct that is *conventionally understood as expressive*—for instance, waving a flag, wearing an armband, or burning a flag. It also extends to conduct that is necessary in order to speak effectively, as, for example, using money to buy a public address system or to buy advertising. Restrictions on independent campaign expenditures, for instance, raise First Amendment problems because restricting the use of money for speech purposes is a speech restriction. *Stromberg v. California* (1931); *Buckley v. Valeo* (1976); *McConnell v. Federal Election Commission* (2003).

5. The free speech/press guarantee extends not just to political speech but also to speech about *religion, science, morality, social conditions, and daily life,* as well as to *art and entertainment.* In the words of a 1948 case, "The line between the informing and the entertaining is too elusive for the protection of that basic right. Everyone is familiar with instances of propaganda through fiction. What is one man's amusement, teaches another's doctrine." And the guarantee extends to low-brow expression (such as jokes or even profanity) as well as high-brow expression. *Winters v. New York* (1948); *Cohen v. California* (1971).

6. The free speech/press guarantee extends to all viewpoints, good or evil. There is no exception, for instance, for Communism, Nazism, Islamic radicalism, sexist speech, or "hate speech," whatever that rather vague term may mean. "Under the First Amendment there is no such thing as a false idea. However pernicious an opinion may seem, we depend for its correction not on the conscience of judges and juries but on the competition of other ideas." *Gertz v. Robert Welch, Inc.* (1974); *New York Times Co. v. Sullivan* (1964).

7. There is, however, a small set of rather narrow *exceptions* to free speech protection:

a. *Incitement:* Speech may be restricted if it is (i) *intended* to persuade people to engage in (ii) *imminent* unlawful conduct, *and* is (iii) *likely* to cause such imminent unlawful conduct. Outside this narrow zone, even speech that advocates lawbreaking is constitutionally protected. *Brandenburg v. Ohio* (1969).

b. *False statements of fact:* False statements of fact may generally be punished if they are *knowing lies,* though generally not if they are honest mistakes (even unreasonable mistakes). There are, however, some situations where even honest mistakes can be punished, and a few where even intentional lies are protected. *Gertz v. Robert Welch, Inc.* (1974).

c. *Obscenity:* Hard-core pornography is punishable if (i) the average person, applying contemporary community standards, would find that the work, taken as a whole, appeals to a shameful or morbid interest in sex or excretion; (ii) the work depicts or describes, in a way that is patently offensive under contemporary community standards, sexual conduct specifically defined by the applicable state law; *and* (iii) the work, taken as a whole, lacks serious literary, artistic, political, or scientific value. *Miller v. California* (1973).

d. *Child pornography:* Sexually themed live performances, photographs, and movies that were made *using actual children* may be punished even if they do not fit within the obscenity test. This does not cover digitized pictures, drawings, or text materials, which are constitutionally protected unless they are obscene. The Court has reasoned that child pornography is unprotected because it hurts the children involved in its making, so the exception only covers cases where actual children were indeed involved. *Ashcroft v. Free Speech Coalition* (2002).

e. *Threats:* Speech that is reasonably perceived as a threat of violence (and not just rhetorical hyperbole) can be punished. *Virginia v. Black* (2003).

f. *Fighting words:* Face-to-face insults that are addressed to a particular person and are likely to cause an imminent fight can be punished. More generalized offensive speech that is not addressed to a particular person cannot be punished even if it is profane or deeply insulting. *Cohen v. California* (1971).

g. *Speech owned by others:* Intellectual property laws, such as copyright law, may restrict people from using particular *expression* that is owned by someone else; but the law may not let anyone monopolize *facts* or *ideas. Harper & Row Publishers, Inc. v. Nation Enterprises* (1985).

h. *Commercial advertising:* Commercial advertising is constitutionally protected, but less so than other speech (political, scientific, artistic, and the like). Misleading commercial advertising may be barred, whereas misleading political speech cannot be. Commercial advertising may also be required to include *disclaimers* to keep it from being misleading; such disclaimers can't be required for political speech. It is an open question whether commercial advertising may be restricted for paternalistic reasons, because of a fear that people will learn accurate information but will do bad things based on that information—for example, buy more alcohol, smoke more, or use more electricity when there is a shortage. This exception applies only to speech that *proposes a commercial transaction* between the speaker and the listener; it does not apply to speech that is merely sold in commerce, such as books, videos, and databases. *44 Liquormart, Inc. v. Rhode Island* (1996).

8. All of the preceding rules apply to restrictions that relate to what the speech communicates—to the tendency of the speech to persuade people, offend them, or make them feel unsafe. *Content-neutral* restrictions that relate to the noncommunicative impact of speech—for instance, noise, obstruction of traffic, and so on—are easier to justify. The test for content-neutral restrictions is complicated, but the key point is that the government may generally impose content-neutral "time, place, and manner restrictions" so long as those restrictions leave open *ample alternative channels* for communication. All such restrictions, however, must be neutral as to content: if they treat speech differently based on content, they are generally unconstitutional even if they focus only on the time, place, and manner of the speech. *Ward v. Rock Against Racism* (1989).

9. Finally, all of the preceding rules apply to restrictions that are imposed by the government *acting as sovereign* and backed by the threat of jail terms, fines, or civil liability. They also apply to the government controlling what is said in "traditional public fora," such as parks, streets, sidewalks, or the post office. But when the government is acting as, for instance, (a) employer, (b) K–12 educator, (c) proprietor of government property other than traditional public fora, (d) subsidizer, (e) speaker, or (f) regulator of the airwaves, it has broader (though not unlimited) authority. The rules for that, unfortunately, are too elaborate to set forth here. *Connick v. Myers* (1983); *Tinker v. Des Moines Independent Community School District* (1969); *ISKCON v. Lee* (1992); *Rosenberger v. Rector and Visitors of the University of Virginia* (1995); *FCC v. League of Women Voters of California* (1984).

Free speech/press law is sometimes called the tax code of constitutional law. The discussion above suggests how complex the law is, but while some of the complexity may be needless, much of it is inevitable. Communication is in many ways the most complicated of human activities, and no simple rule can properly deal with all the different kinds of harms that it can cause—or all the different kinds of harms that restricting communication can cause.

Eugene Volokh

See Also

Article I, Section 6, Clause I (Speech and Debate Clause)

Suggestions for Further Research

Michael Kent Curtis, Free Speech, "The People's Darling Privilege" (2000)

Leonard Levy, Emergence of a Free Press (1995)

David Rabban, Free Speech in Its Forgotten Years, 1870–1920 (1997)

Rodney A. Smolla, Smolla and Nimmer on Freedom of Speech (1996)

Thomas G. West, *Freedom of Speech in the American Founding and in Modern Liberalism*, Social Philosophy and Policy 21:2 (Summer 2004): 310–384

Significant Cases

Stromberg v. California, 283 U.S. 359 (1931)

Winters v. New York, 333 U.S. 507 (1948)

New York Times Co. v. Sullivan, 376 U.S. 254 (1964)

Brandenburg v. Ohio, 395 U.S. 444 (1969)

Tinker v. Des Moines Independent Community School District, 393 U.S. 503 (1969)

Cohen v. California, 403 U.S. 15 (1971)

Miller v. California, 413 U.S. 15 (1973)

Gertz v. Robert Welch, Inc., 418 U.S. 323 (1974)

Buckley v. Valeo, 424 U.S. 1 (1976)

Connick v. Myers, 461 U.S. 138 (1983)

FCC v. League of Women Voters of California, 468 U.S. 364 (1984)

Harper & Row Publishers, Inc. v. Nation Enterprises, 471 U.S. 539 (1985)

Ward v. Rock Against Racism, 491 U.S. 781 (1989)

ISKCON v. Lee, 505 U.S. 672 (1992)

McIntyre v. Ohio Elections Commission, 514 U.S. 334 (1995)

Rosenberger v. Rector and Visitors of the University of Virginia, 515 U.S. 819 (1995)

44 Liquormart, Inc. v. Rhode Island, 517 U.S. 484 (1996)

Reno v. ACLU, 521 U.S. 844 (1997)

Ashcroft v. Free Speech Coalition, 535 U.S. 234 (2002)

McConnell v. Federal Election Commission, 540 U.S. 93 (2003)

Virginia v. Black, 538 U. S. 343 (2003)

Johanns v. Livestock Marketing Ass'n, 125 S. Ct. 2055 (2005)

Freedom of Assembly and Petition

> Congress shall make no law... abridging... the right of the people peaceably to assemble, and to petition the Government for a redress of grievances.
>
> (Amendment I)

∼

*U*nder modern Supreme Court jurisprudence, the right to petition and the right of peaceable assembly have been almost completely collapsed into freedom of speech. Yet an analysis of the text and background of the First Amendment suggests that the petition and assembly rights have independent scope.

Before it was explicitly recognized in the Constitution, the right to petition had a long-standing Anglo-American pedigree as a right independent of general free speech and press rights. The Magna Carta first formally recognized the right to petition the king. Initially, the right applied only to certain nobles. Later, Parliament claimed the right to petition as a quid pro quo for its approval of royal requests for new taxes. In 1669, Parliament recognized the right of every British subject to petition Parliament, and in 1689, the Declaration of Rights established that not only is it "the right of the subjects to petition the king," but also that "all commitments and prosecutions for such petitioning is illegal." At a time when the king was considered above the law, petitions were the only method short of revolt to seek redress for illegal royal action.

By the late seventeenth century, petitions were the public's primary means of communicating with government officials and were directed to all levels of government, including the royal bureaucracy and parliament. Moreover, the king and Parliament generally treated petitions seriously and worked to resolve legitimate grievances raised by petitions. Much of the legislation passed by Parliament over a period of centuries was introduced in response to petitions from the public.

Petitioning naturally spread to the American colonies. In 1642, the Massachusetts Body of Liberties became the first colonial charter to provide explicit protection for the right to petition. By the time of the American Revolution, five other colonies—Delaware, New Hampshire, North Carolina, Pennsylvania, and Vermont—had followed suit. The other colonies recognized the right informally. Throughout British North America, petitioning was an important way for individuals to express their views to the local governing bodies, especially colonial assemblies. The assemblies, following English tradition, treated petitions seriously and often referred them to committees for further action. Petitions were not always granted, but they were always answered.

In 1774, the Declaration and Resolves of the First Continental Congress proclaimed that the colonists "have a right peaceably to assemble, consider of their grievances, and petition the King; and that all prosecutions, prohibitory proclamations, and commitments for the same, are illegal." The emphasis on the government's lack of power to punish a citizen for petitioning made the right to petition more robust in the revolutionary era than the more general right to freedom of speech. Colonial governments generally recognized the right to freedom of speech, but this typically meant only that laws could not create prior restraints on speech. The right to petition, however, had a full legal pedigree.

When considering the Bill of Rights, Congress approved the right to petition with little controversy. The right to assembly was somewhat more controversial. Four of the original thirteen states expressly guaranteed the right of assembly in their constitutions or charters in 1789. This right, however, was considered more of an adjunct to other rights than an independent right. Representative Theodore Sedgwick moved to strike the words "to assemble and" from what became the First Amendment. He believed the words to be unnecessary surplusage. He argued, "If people freely converse together, they must assemble for that purpose; it is a self-evident, unalienable right which the people possess; it is certainly a thing that never would be called in question." Sedgwick lost, however, in part because many believed that the right of the people to assemble encompassed the right to assemble in a constitutional convention and change the structure of government, a right in fact established in the Constitution itself in Article V.

The right to petition only guarantees that citizens can communicate with the sovereign through petitions. It does not guarantee that the sovereign will respond in any particular way, or indeed, at all. Parliament and colonial legislatures nevertheless felt obligated to respond to every petition, because those bodies had judicial as well as legislative functions. In the American constitutional scheme, judicial power rests solely in the judicial branch, and the judiciary is the only branch of government that is always obligated to consider and respond to petitions submitted to it. The executive branch (including for these purposes the independent regulatory agencies) may arguably have the obligation to respond to petitions when, in the modern administrative era, it is exercising judicial-like functions.

Congress initially took petitions very seriously, following the tradition of its colonial forebears. The House of Representatives scheduled time into its regular business in order to hear petitions on the floor. Typically, the Representative of the petitioner's state would assume the role of referring the petition to a special committee for consideration. The committee considered petitions and reported to Congress, resulting either in a consideration of a bill or rejection of the petition. The exception was in petitions regarding slavery. A pattern developed by which Congress responded to petitions by sending them to committee, where they ultimately died without being answered, rejected, or denied. In 1836, the House adopted a rule that "all petitions relating ... to the subject of slavery or the abolition of slavery shall, without being either printed or referred, be laid upon the table and that no further action whatever be had thereon." In 1840, the House ruled that it would not receive abolitionist petitions at all. After a fierce debate over the right to petition, led in part by Congressman (and former President) John Quincy Adams, the House repealed the "gag rule" in 1844, but thereafter antislavery petitions simply died in committee as before. Unlike those from the abolitionist movement, petitions regarding such issues as the National Bank, expulsion of Cherokees from Georgia, and the Alien and Sedition Acts, among many others, were duly considered by Congress.

The right to petition, along with the right to peaceable assembly, became less important as modern democratic politics gradually replaced petitioning and public protests as the primary means for constituents to express their views to their representatives. Today, Congress treats most petitions in a pro forma way. A Representative may present a petition on behalf of a private party to the Clerk of the House, who enters it in the Journal.

Although the right to petition is somewhat anachronistic in modern times and has largely been subsumed in the right to freedom of speech, it continues to have some independent weight. Most importantly, under the *Noerr-Pennington* doctrine, an effort to influence the exercise of government power, even for the purpose of gaining an anticompetitive advantage, does not create liability under the antitrust laws. *Eastern Railroad Presidents Conference v. Noerr Motor Freight, Inc.* (1961); *United Mine Workers of America v. Pennington* (1965). The Supreme Court initially adopted this doctrine under the guise of freedom of speech, but it more precisely finds its constitutional home in the right to petition. Unlike speech, which can often be punished in the antitrust context, as when corporate officers verbally agree to collude, the right to petition confers absolute immunity on efforts to influence government policy in a noncorrupt way. *Noerr-Pennington* has been expanded beyond its original antitrust context to all situations in which plaintiffs attempt to use a defendant's lobbying activity or filing of a lawsuit (provided the lawsuit was not a sham) as evidence of illegal conduct. For example, trade associations cannot be held liable in tort for lobbying the government for lenient safety standards for their industry.

The Supreme Court confronted the right to petition and its cognate, the right of assembly, in *United States v. Cruikshank* (1876), declaring that the right was "an attribute of national citizenship." In *Hague v. CIO* (1939), members of the Court debated whether the right as applied against states resided in the Fourteenth Amendment's Privileges or Immunities Clause or, as later cases concluded, in the amendment's Due Process Clause. The rights to petition and to peaceable assembly were also crucial in persuading the Supreme Court to hold that the First Amendment implicitly contains a right to expressive association, that is, a right to associate to engage in the activities protected by the First Amendment. The right of expressive association protected civil rights protesters from hostile state action in the 1950s and 1960s, and, after the Court's 2000 decision in *Boy Scouts of America v. Dale*, also protects private groups that wish to promote traditional ideals and values. To a large extent, then, the rights to petition and peaceable assembly have found their modern home in the right to expressive association.

David Bernstein

See Also

Article V

Amendment I (Freedom of Speech and of the Press)

Suggestions for Further Research

M. Glenn Abernathy, The Right of Assembly and Association (2d ed. 1961)

Akhil Amar, The Bill of Rights: Creation and Reconstruction (1998)

Gary Lawson & Guy Seidman, *Downsizing the Right to Petition*, 93 Nw. U. L. Rev. 739 (1996)

Gregory A. Mark, *The Vestigial Constitution: The History and Significance of the Right to Petition*, 66 Fordham L. Rev. 2153 (1998)

Jason Mazzone, *Freedom's Associations*, 77 Wash. L. Rev. 639 (2002)

Don L. Smith, The Right to Petition for the Redress of Grievances: Constitutional Development and Interpretations (1971)

Significant Cases

United States v. Cruikshank, 92 U.S. 542 (1876)

Hague v. CIO, 307 U.S. 496 (1939)

Eastern Railroad Presidents Conference v. Noerr Motor Freight, Inc., 365 U.S. 127 (1961)

United Mine Workers of America v. Pennington, 381 U.S. 657 (1965)

Boy Scouts of America v. Dale, 530 U.S. 640 (2000)

Clingman v. Beaver, 125 S. Ct. 2029 (2005)

To Keep and Bear Arms

A well regulated Militia, being necessary to the security of a free State, the right of the people to keep and bear Arms, shall not be infringed.

(Amendment II)

～

*M*odern debates about the meaning of the Second Amendment have focused on whether it protects a right of individuals to keep and bear arms or, instead, a right of the states to maintain militia organizations like the National Guard. This question, however, was apparently never even discussed for a long time after the

Bill of Rights was framed. The early discussions took the basic meaning of the amendment largely for granted and focused instead on whether it actually added anything significant to the original Constitution. The debate has shifted primarily because of subsequent developments in the Constitution and in constitutional law.

The Founding generation mistrusted standing armies. Many Americans believed, on the basis of English history and their colonial experience, that central governments are prone to use armies to oppress the people. One way to reduce that danger would be to permit the government to raise armies (consisting of full-time paid troops) only when needed to fight foreign adversaries. For other purposes, such as responding to sudden invasions or similar emergencies, the government might be restricted to using a militia, consisting of ordinary civilians who supply their own weapons and receive a bit of part-time, unpaid military training.

Using a militia as an alternative to standing armies had deep roots in English history, and possessed considerable appeal, but it also had some serious problems. Alexander Hamilton, for example, thought the militia system could not serve its purpose effectively, primarily because it violated the basic economic principle of the division of labor. And even those who treasured the militia recognized that it was fragile. The reason it was fragile was the same reason that made Hamilton disparage it: citizens were always going to resist undergoing unpaid military training, and governments were always going to want more professional—and therefore more efficient and tractable—forces.

This led to a dilemma at the Constitutional Convention. Experience during the Revolutionary War had demonstrated convincingly that militia forces could not be relied on for national defense, and the occasions requiring a defense of the nation might not always be foreseen very far in advance. The Convention therefore decided to give the federal government almost unfettered authority to establish armies, including peacetime standing armies. But that decision created a threat to liberty, especially in light of the fact that the proposed Constitution also for-bade the states from keeping troops without the consent of Congress.

One solution might have been to *require* Congress to establish and maintain a well-disciplined militia, which would have to comprise a very large percentage of the population (in order to prevent it from becoming in effect a professional army under another name, like our modern National Guard organizations). This would have deprived the federal government of the excuse that it needed peacetime standing armies, and it would have established a meaningful counterweight to any rogue army that the federal government might create. That possibility was never taken seriously, and for good reason. How could a constitution define a well-regulated or well-disciplined militia with the requisite precision and detail and with the necessary regard for changes in future circumstances and national needs? It would almost certainly have been impossible.

Another solution might have been to forbid Congress from interfering with state control over the militia. This might have been possible, but it would have been self-defeating. Fragmented control over the militia would inevitably have resulted in an absence of uniformity in training, equipment, and command, and no really effective fighting force could have been created.

Thus, the choice was between a variety of militias controlled by the individual states, which would likely be too weak and divided to protect the nation, and a unified militia under federal control, which almost by definition could not be expected to prevent federal tyranny. This conundrum could not be solved, and the Convention did not purport to solve it. Instead, the Convention presumed that a militia would exist, but it gave Congress almost unfettered authority to regulate that militia, just as it gave the new federal government almost unfettered authority over the army and navy.

This massive shift of power from the states to the federal government generated one of the chief objections to the proposed Constitution. Anti-Federalists argued that federal control over the militia would take away from the states their principal means of defense against federal oppression and usurpation, and that European history demonstrated how serious the danger was. James Madison, for one, responded that such fears of federal oppression were overblown, in part because the new federal government was structured differently from European governments. But he also pointed out a decisive difference between America and Europe: the American people were armed and would therefore be almost impossible to subdue through military force, even if one assumed that the federal government would try to use an army to do so. In *The Federalist* No. 46, he wrote:

> Besides the advantage of being armed, which the Americans possess over the people of almost every other nation, the existence of subordinate governments, to which the people are attached and by which the militia officers are appointed, forms a barrier against the enterprises of ambition, more insurmountable than any which a simple government of any form can admit of. Notwithstanding the military establishments in the several kingdoms of Europe, which are carried as far as the public resources will bear, the governments are afraid to trust the people with arms. And it is not certain that with this aid alone they would not be able to shake off their yokes.

Implicit in the debate between the Federalists and Anti-Federalists were two *shared* assumptions: first, that the proposed new constitution gave the federal government almost total legal authority over the army and the militia; and second, that the federal government should not have any authority at all to disarm the citizenry. The disagreement between Federalists and Anti-Federalists was only over the narrower question of how effective an armed population could be in protecting liberty.

The Second Amendment left that disagreement unresolved, and it therefore did not satisfy the Anti-Federalist desire to preserve the military superiority of the states over the federal government. But that inadequacy also prevented the Second Amendment from generating any

opposition. Attempting to satisfy the Anti-Federalists' desire would have been hugely controversial, and it would have entailed amending the original Constitution. Nobody suggested that the Second Amendment could have any such effect, but neither did anyone suggest that the federal government needed or rightfully possessed the power to disarm American citizens.

As a political gesture to the Anti-Federalists, a gesture highlighted by the Second Amendment's prefatory reference to the value of a well-regulated militia, express recognition of the right to arms was something of a sop. But the provision was easily accepted because *everyone* agreed that the federal government should not have the power to infringe the right of the people to keep and bear arms, any more than it should have the power to abridge the freedom of speech or prohibit the free exercise of religion.

A great deal has changed since the Second Amendment was adopted. The traditional militia fairly quickly fell into desuetude, and the state-based militia organizations were eventually incorporated into the federal military structure. For its part, the federal military establishment has become enormously powerful in comparison with eighteenth-century armies, and Americans have largely lost their fear that the federal government will use its power to oppress them politically. And whereas eighteenth-century civilians routinely kept at home the very same weapons that they would need if called to war, modern soldiers are equipped with weapons that differ significantly from those that are commonly thought appropriate for civilian uses. These changes have raised questions about the value of an armed citizenry, and many people today reject the assumptions that almost everybody accepted when the Second Amendment was adopted.

The law has also changed. Perhaps most significantly, the Fourteenth Amendment has been interpreted to make most provisions of the Bill of Rights applicable to the states. When it was enacted, the Second Amendment applied only to the federal government, which left the states free to regulate firearms in whatever ways they saw fit. The Supreme Court has not yet decided, one way or the other, whether the Second Amendment will be added to the list of provisions that apply to the state governments. If the Court does extend its reach to the states, that decision will generate a great many questions about the appropriate balance between public safety and private liberty that the Framers of the Second Amendment had no reason at all to consider.

Apart from the potentially important effects of the Fourteenth Amendment, a rather small but significant body of Second Amendment case law has developed. In *United States v. Miller* (1939), the Supreme Court issued what is still its only important decision interpreting the scope of the right to keep and bear arms. In that case, the Court upheld a federal statute that regulated the interstate transportation of machine guns and short-barreled shotguns. For better or worse, the Court's opinion is so ambiguous that advocates for almost every conceivable interpretation of the Second Amendment have been able to claim that it supports their view.

Initially, however, the lower federal courts were unanimous in their interpretation of *Miller*. Every court that considered the question concluded that the Second Amendment does not protect any meaningful individual right to keep or bear arms. One line of cases in the lower courts read *Miller* to endorse the proposition that the Second Amendment merely guarantees a right of the states to maintain their own military organizations. Another line of cases arrived at much the same result by concluding that individuals can only exercise their Second Amendment rights by joining a state militia organization. Under either line of reasoning, the Second Amendment effectively becomes a nullity because it places virtually no limits on government's power to disarm American citizens.

The view of the Second Amendment reflected in these lower-court decisions was subjected to sustained and powerful criticism by academic commentators during the last few years of the twentieth century. Eventually, these critics saw their views accepted by the United States Court of Appeals for the Fifth Circuit, in the case of *United States v. Emerson* (2001). The *Emerson* court issued a lengthy and scholarly opinion

that rejected the states'-rights interpretation adopted over the years by all of the other courts of appeals that had ruled on the issue. According to the *Emerson* court:

> the Second Amendment protects the right of individuals to privately keep and bear their own firearms that are suitable as individual, personal weapons and are not of the general kind or type excluded by *Miller*, regardless of whether the particular individual is then actually a member of a militia.

Although the court upheld the somewhat complicated federal regulation at issue in the case, it also indicated that the law barely passed constitutional muster and strongly signaled that there are sharp limits on the federal government's authority to disarm individual Americans.

The *Emerson* decision unsettled a long-standing judicial consensus, and it quickly provoked a counterattack from the Ninth Circuit. This debate among the lower courts invites the Supreme Court to give the Second Amendment the kind of serious consideration that it has never received. But that may not happen soon. One reason is that the *Emerson* court did uphold the statute at issue in the case. Thus, notwithstanding the fundamental difference between the Fifth Circuit's interpretation of the Constitution and that of other lower courts, the statute will continue to be applied throughout the country. Without a real, practical discrepancy in the way that the law applies in various sections of the nation, the Supreme Court may not feel the need to resolve what is an essentially theoretical disagreement among the lower courts.

No court has yet held that the Fourteenth Amendment makes the Second Amendment applicable to the state governments, which have been the source of almost all of the most restrictive regulations on guns. Except in the District of Columbia, federal law has created relatively few serious obstacles to civilian possession and use of firearms. Thus, unless Congress enacts new laws, or the D.C. Circuit joins the Fifth Circuit in adopting the individual-right interpretation, the actual application of federal law may not be affected by *Emerson*, and the Supreme Court may see no need to resolve the debate that *Emerson* initiated.

Emerson's significance could prove limited for another reason. Even if the Supreme Court accepts the individual-right interpretation adopted by the Fifth Circuit, the Court could easily create a legal test under which almost any conceivable gun-control regulation would pass constitutional muster. One possibility would be an adaptation of the so-called rational basis test that is used to uphold virtually all economic regulations against challenges under the Due Process and Equal Protection Clauses. Under that test, any firearm regulation would be upheld so long as it was not so completely arbitrary that no rational legislature could believe that it served any legitimate governmental purpose. Because the prevention of death and injuries to innocent people is certainly a legitimate purpose, almost any gun-control statute would survive this test, whether or not it was actually or even plausibly effective in achieving such a purpose.

It is also possible, of course, that the Court will choose to adopt a much more stringent legal test, perhaps along the lines of those used to put meaningful restrictions on the government's power to abridge the freedom of speech or the free exercise of religion. This approach, which *Emerson* appeared to adopt, could lead to truly significant developments in constitutional law, especially if the Supreme Court were also to apply the Second Amendment to the states through the Fourteenth Amendment.

Thus, in the end, the future role of the Second Amendment in constitutional law is likely to depend less on the debate between the individual-right and states'-rights interpretations, and more on whether the Justices of the Supreme Court recognize a high constitutional value in the preservation of an armed citizenry. Whether they will do so in a case that really matters is a question to which we cannot yet know the answer.

Nelson Lund

See Also

Suggestions for Further Research

Michael C. Dorf, *What Does the Second Amendment Mean Today?*, 76 Chi.-Kent L. Rev. 291 (2000)

Don B. Kates, Jr., *Handgun Prohibition and the Original Meaning of the Second Amendment*, 82 Mich. L. Rev. 204 (1983)

David B. Kopel, *The Second Amendment in the Nineteenth Century*, 1998 BYU L. Rev. 1359

Leonard W. Levy, Origins of the Bill of Rights (1999)

Nelson Lund, *The Ends of Second Amendment Jurisprudence: Firearms Disabilities and Domestic Violence Restraining Orders*, 4 Tex. Rev. L. & Pol. 157 (1999)

Nelson Lund, *The Past and Future of the Individual's Right to Arms*, 31 Ga. L. Rev. 1 (1996)

L. A. Powe, Jr., *Guns, Words, and Constitutional Interpretation*, 38 Wm. & Mary L. Rev. 1311 (1997)

Glenn Harlan Reynolds, *A Critical Guide to the Second Amendment*, 62 Tenn. L. Rev. 461 (1995)

Significant Cases

United States v. Miller, 307 U.S. 174 (1939)
United States v. Emerson, 270 F.3d 203 (5th Cir. 2001)
Silveira v. Lockyer, 312 F.3d 1052 (9th Cir. 2002)

Quartering of Troops

No Soldier shall, in time of peace be quartered in any house, without the consent of the Owner, nor in time of war, but in a manner prescribed by law.

(Amendment III)

~

*T*he Third Amendment combines a straightforward ban on nonconsensual, peacetime quartering of soldiers in citizens' houses with a requirement that wartime quartering be done by means approved by the legislature. The brief congressional debates on the text make clear that the amendment reflects an effort to balance private property rights and the potential wartime need for military quarters.

The Anti-Federalists used the absence of a ban on quartering as an argument against ratification. Once the concept of a Bill of Rights was agreed upon, however, there was little controversy over the inclusion of a ban on quartering. Six of the original thirteen states also adopted constitutional provisions banning the quartering of soldiers.

The British practice of quartering soldiers in America grew out of the lack of regular army bases, unclear legislative authority for British army quartering in America, and the need to move large bodies of troops about the country during conflicts with the French and Indians. Although there were numerous conflicts over quartering in both Britain and America before the 1770s, the most significant episodes concerned the British quartering of soldiers in private homes to punish the people of Boston under the Intolerable Acts of 1774.

Because of its clear text, there have been few court opinions discussing the Third Amendment. The quartering problem has largely been solved today by paying communities to host military bases. When the Supreme Court has cited the Third Amendment, it has been as part of nonoriginalist interpretations that list it as one of the sources of "penumbras, formed by emanations" that create a zone of privacy in no specific clause of the Constitution. For example, the Court cited it in the name of marital privacy as support for constitutional restrictions on state governments' abilities to regulate the sale of contraceptives in *Griswold v. Connecticut* (1965).

Andrew P. Morriss

See Also
Declaration of Independence, para. 16 (including quartering among the grievances against the king)

Suggestions for Further Research
Tom W. Bell, *The Third Amendment: Forgotten but Not Gone*, 2 Wm. & Mary Bill Rts. J. 117 (1993)

Andrew P. Morriss and Richard L. Stroup, *Quartering Species: The 'Living Constitution,' the Third Amendment, and the Endangered Species Act*, 30 Envtl. L. 769 (2000)

Significant Case
Griswold v. Connecticut, 381 U.S. 479 (1965)

Searches and Seizures

The right of the people to be secure in their persons, houses, papers, and effects, against unreasonable searches and seizures, shall not be violated....

(AMENDMENT IV)

~

*T*he Fourth Amendment is the most prolific source of constitutional litigation in American history, particularly with application to the states after its incorporation through the Due Process Clause of the Fourteenth Amendment. *Mapp v. Ohio* (1961). Its reach is indescribably broad: every one of the millions of arrests made annually is a Fourth Amendment event. So too is every search of every person or private area by a public official, whether a police officer, schoolteacher, probation officer, airport security agent, or corner crossing guard. The Fourth Amendment is the constitutional sentry whenever someone's privacy is diminished by a governmental search or seizure. It protects a person's "legitimate expectation of privacy." *Katz v. United States* (1967). "Legitimate," the Court declares, means an actual expectation of privacy that society is prepared to recognize as "reasonable." In defining that phrase, the reasonableness clause of the Fourth Amendment has spawned a vast amount of litigation.

The Founders' interest in protecting Americans against unreasonable searches and seizures (and in requiring particularized warrants, as the subsequent Warrant Clause of the Fourth Amendment mandates) arises out of a trio of famous eighteenth-century cases, two from

England and one from the colonies. The English cases, *Entick v. Carrington* (1765) and *Wilkes v. Wood* (1763), involved pamphleteers who were critics of the government. Both were arrested and all their books and papers seized (and, in Wilkes's case, all the papers of forty-nine of his friends) using warrants that named neither the suspects nor the places to be searched. Both defendants sued the seizing agents for trespass and won judgments in their favor.

In the case with which the Framers of the Constitution would have been most familiar, James Otis defended several colonial smugglers against seizures made through the use of "writs of assistance," which permitted the customs agents to search any place in which smuggled goods might be concealed, even if there was no particular suspicion the goods were there. Though Otis lost the case, no less an authority than John Adams saw the dispute as the spark of the American Revolution: "Then and there was the child 'Independence' born."

The Searches and Seizures Clause may have independent meaning from that of the Warrant Clause. When Congress first considered the Bill of Rights, the text had no mention of "reasonableness." Representative Elbridge Gerry of Massachusetts said that he "presumed there was a mistake in the wording of this clause; it ought to be 'the right of the people to be secure in their persons, houses, papers, and effects, against unreasonable seizures and searches.'" Thus, the Searches and Seizures Clause can be thought of as an independent prohibition on the acts of governmental agents.

On the other hand, considerable historical evidence supports a different hypothesis about original intent. Based upon their experiences with British "general warrants," the Framers outlawed such devices in the Warrant Clause. By requiring probable cause and a particular description of the place to be searched and the things to be seized, the Framers prohibited rambling intrusions and rummages into people's belongings. Because courts were in the business of issuing warrants, they would naturally take charge of enforcing this provision, gauging the adequacy of the "probable cause" alleged and the particularity described.

On this view, the first part of the Fourth Amendment—the Searches and Seizures Clause—did not authorize courts to do anything. It was a statement of political moral principle, understood by the Founders to be merely declaratory, an explanation or justification for the Warrant Clause, which followed it. On this view no broad "common law" of search and seizure was invited or envisioned by those who enacted the Fourth Amendment. "The right of the people" was a collective right of the political community, not an individual's immunity against intrusion by agents of that community.

Fourth Amendment events governed by the reasonableness rule are subject to a body of law crafted by our nation's courts, both state and federal. The result has been an enormous judicial corpus of law resting on these categorical distinctions:

1. In the criminal context, a showing of individualized probable cause is necessary. Before the police may search a place or arrest an individual, they must demonstrate to a neutral magistrate that there is probable cause that a crime has occurred or that evidence of a crime may be found in the particular location described. Any search pursuant to a warrant issued by a magistrate is deemed "reasonable." *Illinois v. Gates* (1983).

2. Many circumstances exist in which law enforcement may dispense with the requirement to secure a warrant, so long as their conduct is otherwise objectively reasonable. For example, they may conduct a search when exigent circumstances demand it. *Mincey v. Arizona* (1978). They may seize that which is in "plain view." *Horton v. California* (1990). And, when mere regulatory interests are implicated, a lower level of individualized suspicion is generally sufficient to permit regulatory agencies to conduct unannounced inspections of industrial sites without probable cause. *Donovan v. Dewey* (1981).

3. Police encounters with citizens that fall short of an actual arrest—a brief, investigative stop for questioning, for example—are permitted if the police officer has some reasonable suspicion of criminality. *Terry v. Ohio* (1968).

4. Occasionally, the government's need to deal with potentially dangerous or disruptive hidden

conditions justifies random, suspicionless intrusions. Examples in this last category include airports, *Florida v. Royer* (1983), and certain public school settings, such as athlete drug testing. *Vernonia School District 47J v. Acton* (1995).

The primary mechanism for enforcing the Searches and Seizures Clause is the exclusionary rule: evidence seized illegally may not be used against the one whose privacy was invaded, at least where there is a criminal trial against him, and there only in the prosecutor's case-in-chief. Apart perhaps from the required *Miranda* warning (*see* the Fifth Amendment's Self-Incrimination Clause), the exclusionary rule is the most criticized Warren Court criminal justice innovation. In 1961, in the case of *Mapp v. Ohio*, the Court, incorporating the Fourth Amendment through the Due Process Clause of the Fourteenth Amendment, declared that exclusion was constitutionally required in all state and federal courts. Before *Mapp*, states were free to enforce the Fourth Amendment by means other than exclusion.

Did the Framers intend the exclusionary rule? Even the rule's most ardent supporters admit that they did not. Virtually no one doubts that, until the twentieth century, criminals did not go free, as Judge (later Justice) Benjamin N. Cardozo put it, "because the constable blundered." *People v. Defore* (1926). The criminal would have been convicted, and the offending constable would have been liable as a tort-feasor for trespassing upon a person's privacy without proper authority or cause.

The central argument in favor of exclusion is that it is necessary to give the Fourth Amendment real, as opposed to theoretical, meaning. If police officers were allowed to offend the Constitution with impunity (which, it is alleged, they would if a defendant could be convicted on tainted evidence), the Fourth Amendment would be a "mere form of words." This argument presupposes that illegal searches and seizures are deterred by the prospect of exclusion. If the evidence cannot be used at trial, what is the point of seizing it?

The predominant view of judges and commentators is consistent with this understanding of the deterrent effect of the exclusionary rule. The trend since the mid-1970s has been to limit the exclusionary rule to the prosecutor's case-in-chief. The reason for the limitation is that it is thought that any additional deterrent effect gained by exclusion—from the grand-jury or civil trials—is negligible, or clearly outweighed by the adverse effect upon the integrity of fact-finding proceedings.

Gerard V. Bradley

See Also

Amendment IV (Warrant Clause)
Amendment V (Self-Incrimination Clause)

Suggestions for Further Research

Akhil Amar, The Constitution and Criminal Procedure: First Principles (1997)

Gerard Bradley, *The Constitutional Theory of the Fourth Amendment*, 38 DePaul L. Rev. 817 (1988)

Gerard Bradley, *Present at the Creation? A Critical Guide to* Weeks v. United States *and Its Progeny*, 30 St. Louis L.J. 1031 (1986)

Thomas Y. Davies, *Recovering the Original Fourth Amendment*, 98 Mich. L. Rev. 549 (1999)

Donald Dripps, *The Case for the Contingent Exclusionary Rule*, 38 Am. Crim. L. Rev. 1 (2001)

Walter LaFave, Search and Seizure: A Treatise on the Fourth Amendment (3d ed. 1996)

William Stuntz, *Privacy's Problem and the Law of Criminal Procedure*, 93 Mich. L. Rev. 1016 (1996)

William Stuntz, *The Uneasy Relationship Between Criminal Procedure and Criminal Justice*, 107 Yale L.J. 1 (1997)

Significant Cases

Wilkes v. Wood, 19 How. St. Tr. 1153 (C.P. 1763)
Entick v. Carrington, 19 How. St. Tr. 1029 (C.P. 1765)
People v. Defore, 242 N.Y. 13, 21 N.E. 585 (1926)
Mapp v. Ohio, 367 U.S. 643 (1961)
Katz v. United States, 389 U.S. 347 (1967)
Terry v. Ohio, 392 U.S. 1 (1968)
Mincey v. Arizona, 437 U.S. 385 (1978)
Donovan v. Dewey, 452 U.S. 594 (1981)
Florida v. Royer, 460 U.S. 491 (1983)
Illinois v. Gates, 462 U.S. 213 (1983)
Horton v. California, 496 U.S. 128 (1990)
Vernonia School District 47J v. Acton, 515 U.S. 646 (1995)

Warrant Clause

...no Warrants shall issue, but upon probable cause, supported by Oath or affirmation, and particularly describing the place to be searched, and the persons or things to be seized.

(Amendment IV)

~

*T*he first half of the Fourth Amendment's text bans "unreasonable searches and seizures." The second half, known as the Warrant Clause, states a set of basic requirements for search warrants—that they must be supported by an affidavit that establishes probable cause, and that they must describe both the location and objects of the search.

On its face, the Warrant Clause would appear to be one of the most clearly written clauses in our Constitution. It requires that warrants be supported by probable cause, that the police officer seeking the warrant swear to the truth of the facts used to support his application, and that, once issued, the warrant describe where the search is to take place and what the officer is allowed to look for. All this is plain from the text. Perhaps because they are so plain, the rules just described have not been the subject of much litigation.

There are, though, two important questions the text does not answer, or at least does not answer clearly. Those questions have been the subject of a great deal of litigation and commentary: What does "probable cause" mean? The Fourth Amendment's text does not say. And, a trickier question, are officers ever *required* to obtain warrants in order to carry out a search or make an arrest? Again the text leaves the question open, though it implies that the answer is no: the phrasing of the Warrant Clause limits warrants but does not mandate their use.

The first of these questions can be quickly answered. In *Brinegar v. United States* (1949), the Supreme Court defined "probable cause" as information that would lead "a man of reasonable caution" to believe "that an offense has been or is being committed." In *Illinois v. Gates*

(1983), the Court put it more succinctly, describing probable cause as "a fair probability." Those definitions may sound too vague to be useful, but in practice the standard seems clear enough. In most cases "probable cause" means what the ordinary definition of "probable" would suggest: more likely than not. That "51 percent" standard does not always apply: in practice, courts seem to give the police a little more leeway when the crime being investigated is especially serious, and a little less when the crime seems minor. As with any vague standard, the phrase "probable cause" has occasioned a great deal of litigation and commentary, but the contested territory is small. All sides agree that the phrase means more than just a possibility, and less than a near-certainty. A clearer definition than that may be impossible.

The second question, whether warrants are ever required, is more complex. At first blush the question seems nonsensical. Of course, warrants are sometimes required; otherwise, why would the Fourth Amendment mention them? When the Fourth Amendment was written, the sole remedy for an illegal search or seizure was a lawsuit for money damages. Government officials used warrants as a defense against such lawsuits. Today a warrant seems the police officer's foe—one more hoop to jump through—but at the time of the Founding, it was the constable's friend, a legal defense against any subsequent claim. Thus it was perfectly reasonable to specify limits on warrants (probable cause, particular description of the places to be searched and the things to be seized) but never to require their use.

That is probably (though not clearly—some historians disagree) how the clause was understood when it was written. Like the state constitutional provisions on which it was modeled, the Fourth Amendment arose as a response to three famous cases decided in the 1760s. In each of those three cases, agents of the Crown conducted very broad searches; in each, the agents had warrants authorizing the searches; finally, in none of the three searches did those warrants meet the requirements that were later spelled out in the Fourth Amendment's text. The point of the text was to forbid the kind of behavior seen in the three cases—not to require warrants, but to prevent the government from using them to justify overly broad searches.

The first of the three cases was *Wilkes v. Wood* (1763). Wilkes was a London pamphleteer critical of the king's ministers; he was also a Member of Parliament and perhaps the most popular man in England. One of the king's secretaries issued a sweeping warrant, ordering the arrest of Wilkes and those associated with a pamphlet he had authored and the seizure of all Wilkes's books and papers. Wilkes sued, and he won the then-staggering total of five thousand pounds. *Wilkes v. Wood* was a famous and celebrated case in the colonies, so much so that several towns were named after John Wilkes (as was Abraham Lincoln's assassin).

The second case, *Entick v. Carrington* (1765), was similar. Like Wilkes, John Entick wrote pamphlets criticizing the government. As with Wilkes, one of the king's underlings issued a warrant, commanding officers to seize Entick and all his papers. As with Wilkes, the warrant extended to *all* Entick's papers, not merely to those that might offer evidence of crime. Entick likewise sued and won; the case was likewise famous in the colonies, prompting local officials to name several towns after the judge in Entick's case—Lord Camden.

The third case is the famous *Writs of Assistance Case* (1761) in Boston. The warrant in that case authorized the search of any place in which the Crown's agents thought smuggled goods might be hidden. The things to be seized were described, but the places to be searched were not. A number of Boston merchants challenged these "writs of assistance." James Otis, representing the merchants, argued that the common law banned such "general warrants." Otis lost his case, but his argument was popular in the increasingly rebellious colonies.

Historians generally agree that the Warrant Clause was written to adopt the decisions in *Wilkes* and *Entick* and the losing argument in the *Writs of Assistance Case*. General warrants, meaning both warrants not supported by probable cause and warrants that failed to describe the places or objects of the search, were banned. But the police (at that time, constables) were probably free to not use warrants at all. The rea-

son that the last point is not entirely clear is that no one seems to have thought much about the question. When the Fourth Amendment was adopted, police forces did not yet exist (they arose in America beginning in the 1830s). A good deal of criminal investigation was conducted by private parties, with evidence turned over to the local constable or magistrate after the suspect was charged. Constables became involved only when it was time to make an arrest (and sometimes not even then), at which time they typically searched the arrestee's person and home. It is clear that those actions did not require a warrant in 1791.

Thus the original understanding of the Warrant Clause was in one sense clear, and in one sense not. It was clear what the conditions were for a valid warrant—those conditions are spelled out in the Fourth Amendment's text. It was not clear whether warrants were ever required (though they probably were not), because the issue had not arisen with any regularity.

Today's Warrant Clause doctrine differs from the historical understanding in some important respects. That doctrine can be divided into two parts. The first deals with the conditions of a valid warrant. The second deals with when warrants are required.

The conditions of a valid warrant are straightforward: with two qualifications, Warrant Clause doctrine tracks the Fourth Amendment's text. Probable cause and particular description are required, as the text says. So is something not mentioned in the text: early on, American courts decided that warrants should be issued only by judicial officers (in most jurisdictions, that means magistrates) and not by anyone in the prosecutor's office or the executive branch of government more generally. The other qualification concerns probable cause. The Supreme Court has approved warrants not based on probable cause in some regulatory settings. Thus, in *Camara v. Municipal Court* (1967), housing inspectors were allowed to use what the Court called "administrative warrants"—orders authorizing the random selection of some buildings for code inspection. Such administrative warrants are sometimes used, as in *Camara*, to enforce building and fire codes, but not for much else.

The police are not allowed to use administrative warrants when enforcing criminal law. The justification of this state of affairs is that police officers investigating crime tend to have more power than other government officials: the police can break down doors, use force (even deadly force) to subdue suspects, and, in some cases, they may destroy suspects' property if that is a necessary consequence of the search for evidence. Other government officials tend not to have those powers. Consequently ordinary citizens tend not to find a building code inspection as frightening as a police search or arrest. The distinct legal requirements reflect those differences in official power and in the fear that such power inspires.

The second issue, when are warrants required, is more complicated. In summary, warrants are required when the police search a home or an office, unless the search must happen immediately, and there is no opportunity to obtain a warrant. Warrants are also required for wiretaps—a special category covered (along with most computer searches) by federal statute. Outside those categories warrants are almost never required.

There is a slightly more elaborate way to put the point. Until recently the Supreme Court said that warrants were required for all searches and seizures, save those that fell within some exception to that requirement. The classic statement of this rule, and the classic defense of a broad warrant requirement, was penned by Justice Robert H. Jackson in *Johnson v. United States* (1948). Today, the Court uses different language, emphasizing not the second half of the Fourth Amendment's text, but the first (the ban on "unreasonable searches and seizures"). *See Indianapolis v. Edmond* (2000). Notwithstanding this change in legal rhetoric, the old categories, a warrant requirement with a list of exceptions, still exist. The scope of the requirement is defined by the many exceptions to it. The major ones are these:

1. *Exigent circumstances.* The police need not get a warrant when doing so is practically impossible.

2. *Arrests outside the home.* The police must have probable cause to justify the arrest, but they need not have a warrant.

3. *Searches incident to arrest.* This means a search of the arrestee's person and any baggage he or she may be carrying; if the person is in a car when arrested, the officer may search the passenger compartment of the car (though not the trunk).

4. *Inventory searches.* The police may seize any belongings the arrestee has in his possession at the time of arrest (including his car), bring those items back to the police station, and make a record of them and their contents.

5. *Automobiles.* Cars, including their trunks, may be searched without warrants, as long as the searching officers have probable cause.

6. *Street stops and frisks.* Officers are allowed to detain a suspect for a brief period, and to frisk him for weapons, given reasonable suspicion of criminal activity.

In addition to these exceptions, there are several categories of searches that involve government officials other than police officers (e.g., searches of lockers by school principals, and government employers searching employees' file cabinets), or government interests separate from the interest in criminal law enforcement (e.g., searches of vehicles at the nation's borders, searches of baggage at airports). Such searches generally do not require warrants.

That list of exceptions and special categories aside, other searches and seizures do require warrants. Notice, however, that the major categories of searches and seizures that do not appear on the above list are searches of homes, arrests within homes, searches of private offices or other privately owned buildings (other than for fire inspection and the like), and wiretaps. The overwhelming majority of search and arrest warrants are issued in such cases because, apart from such cases, warrants are almost never required.

A generation ago those propositions were widely contested; the scope of the warrant requirement was the subject of a great deal of litigation, including a number of Supreme Court decisions. That is no longer the case. Today Fourth Amendment litigation focuses on warrant*less* searches and seizures. The Searches and Seizures Clause—the first half of the Fourth Amendment's text—is now the primary source of Fourth Amendment litigation and commentary.

William J. Stuntz

See Also

Amendment IV (Searches and Seizures)

Suggestions for Further Research

Thomas Y. Davies, *Recovering the Original Fourth Amendment*, 98 Mich. L. Rev. 549 (1999)

Wayne R. LaFave, Search and Seizure: A Treatise on the Fourth Amendment (1986)

Maurice H. Smith, The Writs of Assistance Case (1978)

Carol S. Steiker, *Second Thoughts About First Principles*, 107 Harv. L. Rev. 820 (1994)

William J. Stuntz, *The Substantive Origins of Criminal Procedure*, 105 Yale L. J. 393 (1995)

William J. Stuntz, *Warrants and Fourth Amendment Remedies*, 77 Va. L. Rev. 881 (1991)

Telford Taylor, Two Studies in Constitutional Interpretation (1969)

Significant Cases

Writs of Assistance Case, Quincy 51 (Mass. 1761)

Wilkes v. Wood, 19 How. St. Tr. 1153 (C.P. 1763)

Entick v. Carrington, 19 How. St. Tr. 1029 (C.P. 1765)

Johnson v. United States, 333 U.S. 10 (1948)

Brinegar v. United States, 338 U.S. 160 (1949)

Camara v. Municipal Court, 387 U.S. 523 (1967)

Illinois v. Gates, 462 U.S. 213 (1983)

Indianapolis v. Edmond, 531 U.S. 32 (2000)

Grand Jury Requirement

No person shall be held to answer for a capital, or otherwise infamous crime, unless on a presentment or indictment of a Grand Jury....

(Amendment V)

∼

Grand juries have historically served two functions: accusatory and protective. The accusatory function has roots in the English common law. The Founders' motivation for adding this provision to the Constitution was principally to protect those accused of crimes from prosecutorial overreach. Contemporary practice, however, limits the extent to which grand juries are capable of performing that aspect of their traditional role.

A typical federal grand jury consists of twenty-three citizens drawn from the community. The jurors meet in a closed courtroom, with no judge, no accused, no press, and no lawyer but the prosecutor present. The prosecution presents evidence that a particular suspect committed a crime; the prosecutor is then excused, and the jurors deliberate and vote on whether there is enough evidence to justify the filing of criminal charges against this suspect and sending the case forward to trial. If a majority of jurors believe that there is sufficient evidence, the jurors return a "true bill," which when signed by the prosecutor becomes the indictment: the formal criminal charge that the government must prove beyond a reasonable doubt at trial.

Grand juries originated in England, probably in the twelfth century, and began as an effort to increase the king's power. Their original purpose was strictly accusatory; grand jurors were expected to bring to the proceedings any information or suspicions they had about their neighbors and criminal activity. By the mid-seventeenth century, the jurors also assumed the responsibility to investigate and protect citizens against unfounded charges. This dual role of accuser and protector of the accused was the model that settlers brought with them to this country. The first grand-jury session was held in Virginia in 1625, and the practice soon spread to the other English colonies.

Prior to the American Revolution, the grand jury's role as a shield for the accused took on increasing importance. The most famous such case involved John Peter Zenger, accused of seditious libel in 1734 for publishing material that was critical of the governor of New York. The evidence against Zenger was strong, but three grand juries refused to indict, impressing on colonists their power to frustrate the enforcement of unpopular laws. As the Revolution drew closer, royal prosecutors who tried to enforce

English tax and import laws also found themselves stymied by local grand juries, who at times refused to let even meritorious cases go forward to trial. These experiences, coupled with the writings of influential legal thinkers (particularly Sir William Blackstone, Henry Care, and John Adams), convinced the colonists of the need for grand-jury review as a restraint on government power. When there was no mention of grand juries in the original Constitution, the criticism was swift; so in December 1791, the Fifth Amendment to the Constitution, containing the Grand Jury Requirement Clause, was ratified.

The Supreme Court has concluded that, unlike nearly all of the other provisions of the Bill of Rights, the Grand Jury Requirement Clause is not "incorporated" against the states, that is, the federal Constitution does not require that states use grand juries at all. If they do, they are not required to follow the federal procedures. *Hurtado v. California* (1884). The result is that many states use grand juries sparingly, and, if they do, use significantly different procedures from those that are required in federal criminal cases. Given that states are still the primary enforcers of the criminal law, this interpretation severely limits the importance of this part of the Fifth Amendment.

The current state of the law restricts the ability of a grand jury to serve as a significant shield against prosecutorial overreach. There are several reasons for this. First, the Supreme Court has greatly limited the ability of criminal suspects to challenge federal grand-jury procedures. The proceedings are secret, and thus a suspect has no way of knowing if the evidence presented by the prosecution is complete or accurate. Even if a suspect can ascertain what evidence the jury hears, his ability to attack the indictment based on this information is small. Federal courts have not required prosecutors to disclose evidence to the grand jurors that is favorable to the accused. *See United States v. Williams* (1992). In addition, the Supreme Court has held that a suspect has no ability to challenge an indictment even if the jurors only considered evidence (such as hearsay) that would not be admissible in a later trial; "[a]n indictment returned by a legally constituted and unbiased grand jury," the Court has said, "if valid on its face, is enough to call for a trial of the charge on the merits. The Fifth Amendment requires nothing more." *Costello v. United States* (1956).

Second, criminal law enforcement has changed dramatically since the Bill of Rights was ratified. Prosecutors are now highly professional and specialized, and federal criminal laws have become more complex. One result of this change is that grand jurors lack the realistic ability to decide whether the prosecutor has presented "enough" evidence to justify an indictment. The question that jurors are asked is ultimately a legal one concerning the sufficiency of the evidence, a question that is posed after the only lawyer in the room—the prosecutor—has recommended that the defendant be indicted. Because the prosecutor has complete control over the evidence the grand jurors hear, and because the jurors have no benchmark against which to measure that evidence, it is rare for jurors to second-guess a prosecutor's recommendation. Consequently, grand jurors agree with the prosecutor's recommendation and return a true bill in nearly every case where they are asked to do so.

So despite the original purpose of the Fifth Amendment, most observers now agree that the grand jury has returned to its accusatory roots and is now used as an investigative tool that is much more of a benefit to the prosecutor than to criminal suspects. Grand juries today have broad subpoena power, which enables them to gather an extraordinary amount of evidence in criminal investigations. Suspects often waive the right to grand-jury review of their case; they may prefer to forgo the minimal protection that comes from this review and avoid the potential for a more searching investigation of their conduct.

Andrew Leipold

See Also

Suggestions for Further Research
Sara Sun Beale et al., Grand Jury Law and Practice (2d ed. 1997)

R. Michael Cassidy, *Toward a More Independent Grand Jury: Recasting and Enforcing the Prosecutor's Duty to Disclose Exculpatory Evidence*, 13 GEO. J. LEGAL ETHICS 361 (2000)

Mark Kadish, *Behind the Locked Door of an American Grand Jury: Its History, Its Secrecy, and Its Process*, 24 FLA. ST. U. L. REV. 1 (1996)

WAYNE R. LaFAVE, JEROLD H. ISRAEL, & NANCY J. KING, CRIMINAL PROCEDURE, 8.1–8.15, 15.1–15.7 (2 ed. 1999)

Andrew D. Leipold, *Why Grand Juries Do Not (and Cannot) Protect the Accused*, 80 CORNELL L. REV. 260 (1995)

Ric Simmons, *Re-Examining the Grand Jury: Is There Room for Democracy in the Criminal Justice System?*, 82 B.U. L. REV. 1 (2002)

Thomas P. Sullivan & Robert D. Nachman, *If It Ain't Broke, Don't Fix It: Why the Grand Jury's Accusatory Function Should Not Be Changed*, 75 J. CRIM. L. & CRIMINOLOGY 1047 (1984)

RICHARD D. YOUNGER, THE PEOPLE'S PANEL: THE GRAND JURY IN THE UNITED STATES 1634–1941 (1963)

Significant Cases

Hurtado v. California, 110 U.S. 516 (1884)
Costello v. United States, 350 U.S. 359 (1956)
United States v. Williams, 504 U.S. 36 (1992)

Grand Jury Exception

No person shall be held to answer for a capital, or otherwise infamous crime, unless on a presentment or indictment of a Grand Jury, except in cases arising in the land or naval forces, or in the Militia, when in actual service in time of War or public danger....

(AMENDMENT V)

∽

Since the time of the drafting of the Fifth Amendment, there has been a debate over which constitutional protections are applicable to courts-martial. The text of the amendment exempts only the requirement of a grand-jury indictment. Though it was universally understood at the time of the Founding that jury trials did not apply to courts-martial, there is no such textual exception in the Sixth Amendment. An earlier draft presented to Congress did specifically exclude military trials from the jury guarantee, but that version was rejected. Perhaps the Framers believed that the exemption to jury trials was so universally recognized, it would have been redundant to have specified it.

During the Virginia ratifying convention, Anti-Federalists Patrick Henry and George Mason feared that the lack of a bill of rights would permit Congress, as Henry stated, to "inflict the most cruel and ignominious punishments on the militia," implying that it might be a device to establish a national standing army. But it does not necessarily follow that the Fifth Amendment was intended to apply to military defendants. Nonetheless, in contemporaneous British practice, the protections against double jeopardy and self-incrimination were accorded to defendants in military trials. Early in the eighteenth century, Sir Matthew Hale even declared that the military should not be subject to courts-martial during peacetime. How much of British practice should be carried over into the legal obligations of the American Constitution is difficult to discern. The Framers are virtually silent on the matter.

It seems clear enough that the Framers intended Congress to have plenary authority to define the rules regulating the armed forces (Article I, Section 8, Clause 14) at least in relation to the executive, and perhaps to the judiciary as well.

Subsequent to the ratification of the Fifth Amendment, the courts left it to Congress to define offenses against the military and the manner of their being adjudicated. Judicial review of decisions of military tribunals was very limited. In 1950, the Supreme Court, in *Johnson v. Eisentrager*, held German nationals, confined in U.S. Army custody in Germany after their conviction by military commission of violating the laws of war, had no right to the writ of habeas corpus to test the legality of their detention. In the course of reaching that conclusion, the majority reasoned that enemy aliens have no greater rights than Americans and that "American citizens conscripted into the military service are thereby stripped of their Fifth Amendment rights and as members of the military establishment are subject to its discipline, including military trials for offenses against aliens or Americans." The Court further emphasized that the military has "well-established...power...to exercise jurisdiction over members of the armed forces...." If the military tribunals acquire "lawful authority to hear, decide and condemn, [then] their action is not subject to judicial review merely because they have made a wrong decision on disputed facts." On the other hand, the Uniform Code of Military Justice (1950), supplemented by the *Manual for Courts-Martial*, affirmatively grants due-process rights essentially comparable to those in a civilian court, such as the guarantee of counsel, protection from self-incrimination and double jeopardy, and being advised of rights before interrogation; and the Court of Military Appeals (renamed the United States Court of Appeals for the Armed Forces in 1994) has held that service members are entitled to all constitutional rights except those that are expressly or by implication inapplicable to the military. *United States v. Clay* (1951); *United States v. Jacoby* (1960).

The only Article III court appeal permitted by the Uniform Code of Military Justice is to the Supreme Court by writ of certiorari from decision of the United States Court of Appeals for the Armed Forces. Nonetheless, federal courts will review cases collaterally, primarily through the writ of habeas corpus. Until 1953, such collateral review centered on the question of whether the military tribunal possessed proper jurisdiction. *Hiatt v. Brown* (1950). Review remained highly deferential. For the civilian courts to entertain a petition on a writ of habeas corpus, the petitioner must be in actual military custody, and he must have exhausted all available legal remedies within the military justice system.

In 1953, the Supreme Court opened a new avenue of appeal. In *Burns v. Wilson* (1953), a decision that remains highly controversial, a plurality of the Justices declared that military courts had the same responsibility as civilian courts "to protect a person from the violation of his constitutional rights." But the Justices also stated that the requirements of military discipline may result in an application of constitutional rights different from those accorded to civilian defendants. Finally, the Justices stated that civilian courts could review claims de novo, but only if the military courts had "manifestly refused to consider" the petitioners' assertions of error.

Subsequently, *Rasul v. Bush* (2004), relying on *Burns* and other cases, read *Eisentrager* narrowly and held that the federal habeas statute now confers federal district court jurisdiction to hear challenges of alien detainees held at Guantanamo Bay. However, the Court explicitly did not decide the substance of those rights and limited the habeas extraterritorial reach to Guantanamo Bay, which it said had a unique relationship to the United States. At the same time, in *Rumsfeld v. Padilla* (2004), the Court, on jurisdictional grounds, avoided ruling on the extent of the President's power to keep a U.S. citizen in military custody as an enemy combatant; but in *Hamdi v. Rumsfeld* (2004) the Court decided, without a majority opinion, that the government must give a U.S. citizen held in the United States some type of hearing at which he can contest the facts on which the government decided to treat him as an enemy combatant.

Since *Burns*, federal courts have applied its positions in differing ways. Some courts are not deferential to the military courts' findings on issues of constitutional law and will review such claims. Others will only review claims that were not given full and fair consideration by the military justice system. In sum, either through the Uniform Code of Military Justice, or court decisions on collateral review, the law now grants persons within the military system of justice their basic due process rights.

David F. Forte

See Also

Article I, Section 8, Clause 11
Article I, Section 8, Clause 12 (Army Clause)

Article I, Section 8, Clause 14 (Military Regulations)

Article I, Section 8, Clause 15 (Militia Clause)

Article I, Section 8, Clause 16 (Organizing the Militia)

Article II, Section 2, Clause 1 (Commander in Chief)

Amendment VI (Jury Trial)

Suggestion for Further Research

Gordon D. Henderson, *Courts-Martial and the Constitution: The Original Understanding*, 71 Harv. L. Rev. 293 (1957)

Jonathan Lurie, *The Role of the Federal Judiciary in the Governance of the American Military: The United States Supreme Court and Civil Rights and Supervision Over the Armed Forces*, in Richard Kohn ed., The United States Military Under the Constitution of the United States, 1789–1989 (1991)

Significant Cases

Hiatt v. Brown, 339 U.S. 103 (1950)

Johnson v. Eisentrager, 339 U.S. 763 (1950)

United States v. Clay, 1 C.M.R. 74 (1951)

Burns v. Wilson, 346 U.S. 137 (1953)

United States v. Jacoby, 29 C.M.R. 244 (1960)

Hamdi v. Rumsfeld, 124 S. Ct. 2633 (2004)

Rasul v. Bush, 124 S. Ct. 2686 (2004)

Rumsfeld v. Padilla, 124 S. Ct. 2711 (2004)

Double Jeopardy

> ... nor shall any person be subject for the same offence to be twice put in jeopardy of life or limb....
>
> (AMENDMENT V)

～

*A*lthough the principle can be found in Greek, Roman, and canon law, the prohibition against double jeopardy came into the United States Constitution from English common law. According to Sir William Blackstone's *Commentaries on the Laws of England*, it was a "universal maxim of the common law of England, that no man is to be brought into jeopardy more than once of the same offence." A defendant to a criminal charge could plead either a former conviction or a former acquittal to the same offense and have the charges dismissed.

All state constitutions drafted prior to the Bill of Rights contained a double-jeopardy provision. The principle was so universal that when James Madison proposed on the floor of the First Congress that "No person shall be subject, except in cases of impeachment, to more than one punishment, or trial for the same offence," Members rose to object that the language was not strong enough. Representatives Egbert Benson and Sherman declared that the wording would prevent a new trial for a person who had been improperly convicted. Others argued that it should stand as drafted, because it was merely "declaratory of the law as it now stood." The House defeated an attempt to remove the words "or trial," but the Senate revised the language to its present form, which the House accepted.

The history of the interpretation of the Double Jeopardy Clause by the Supreme Court is complex, and, as the Court itself confessed, it is not a "model of consistency and clarity." *Burks v. United States* (1978). Over time, however, the Court identified the clause as embodying three protections of the individual against the government: (1) no second prosecution for the same offense after an acquittal; (2) no second prosecution for the same offense after a guilty verdict; and (3) no multiple punishments for the same offense. *See Monge v. California* (1998). The Court recognized early on that the clause could not be read literally; it refers only to "jeopardy of life or limb," a reference that made sense when most serious offenses were sanctioned by capital punishment but hardly makes sense today, when most sanctions are merely a fine or imprisonment. Despite the wording of the clause, the Court applies it to any indictment or information charging a person with any statutory or common-law felony or misdemeanor sanctioned by death, imprisonment, or fine. Of course, the Double Jeopardy Clause originally applied only to the federal government, *Palko v. State of Connecticut* (1937), but in *Benton v. Maryland* (1969), the Court held that the Double Jeopardy Clause of the Fifth Amendment applied to the states as well as to the federal government.

Current double-jeopardy jurisprudence falls under five basic headings: (1) sovereign, (2) sanction, (3) trial, (4) retrial, and (5) offense.

First, the Court reads the Double Jeopardy Clause as a protection against conduct by the same "sovereign." Accordingly, as the federal government is, as is each state, a separate "sovereign," the Double Jeopardy Clause does not prohibit a federal prosecution after a state prosecution. Despite the doctrine, the federal government as a matter of policy will not prosecute a matter first prosecuted at the state level, absent unusual circumstances. Nor does the clause prohibit a state prosecution following a federal prosecution. Nor does it prohibit successive state prosecutions. But it does prohibit successive prosecutions by the state and a local government or two local governments, because each derives its sovereignty from a common source, the state constitution. Indian entities are treated as separate sovereigns.

Second, a sanction counts for double-jeopardy purposes only if it is a criminal "punishment." What counts as a punishment for double-jeopardy purposes depends on the nature of the sanction imposed. Based on identical conduct, a civil forfeiture of property may follow a criminal acquittal of the owner of the property. Civil fines are not a form of criminal punishment. But a tax may not be specially imposed on criminal conduct. A sexual predator may be retained in civil confinement after his criminal term of imprisonment ends; the Court holds that the confinement is punishment under neither the Double Jeopardy nor the Ex Post Facto Clauses of the Constitution.

Third, determining when a "lawful trial" begins and ends is crucial to the application of the concept of double jeopardy. Accordingly, the court must have jurisdiction over the offense. Jeopardy attaches in a bench trial when the first witness is sworn; it begins in a jury trial when the jury is sworn. Finally, the trial ends with an acquittal, that is, a decision of not guilty on the facts, whether the decision is legally right or legally wrong, even if the acquittal is "based upon an egregiously erroneous foundation." An appellate court may also grant an acquittal.

Fourth, the Double Jeopardy Clause does not absolutely prohibit retrials. The clause is no bar to a new trial when the defendant successfully appeals his conviction, but a successful appeal of a lesser charge (manslaughter) by a defendant precludes a retrial on a greater charge (murder). Nor may a new trial be held if an appellate court finds that the conviction was not based on sufficient evidence. On the other hand, retrials may be held when a defendant requests a mistrial or when a "manifest necessity" is present. Manifest necessity is present, for example, if the jury deadlocks or is unduly influenced by the misconduct of the defense counsel.

Fifth, a crucial issue turns on the definition of "offense." Modern criminal law is characterized by "specificity in draftsmanship"; it is also characterized, as a result, by an "extraordinary proliferation of overlapping and related statutory offenses." Double-jeopardy protections depend, therefore, on a careful ascertaining of what constitutes an "offense," that is, what is the "allowable unit of prosecution." However, few limits, if any, are imposed by the Double Jeopardy Clause on the legislative power to define offenses. But once a legislature defines that proscription, it "determines the scope of protection afforded by a prior conviction or acquittal." To ascertain whether two statutory offenses constitute two "offenses" for double jeopardy, which would prohibit successive prosecutions, the Court follows a multiple-element test to determine whether each "offense" contains an element that is not common to the other. *Blockburger v. United States* (1932). Under the *Blockburger* test, the Double Jeopardy Clause prevents successive prosecutions for both greater and lesser included offenses. The focus of the test is on statutory elements rather than evidence or conduct. Nevertheless, a prosecution of a lesser offense (e.g., assault and battery) does not preclude the prosecution of a greater offense (murder) if all of the elements of the greater offense (e.g., death) were not present at the time of the prosecution of the lesser offense. On the other hand, a distinction is drawn between successive prosecutions and multiple punishments. Even if individual offenses are not separate under the *Blockburger* test, the Double Jeopardy Clause does not prevent multiple punishments for them when they are tried together, when the legislature intended the higher level of punishment.

G. Robert Blakey

See Also

Amendment XIV (Due Process Clause)

Suggestions for Further Research

Roscoe Pound, The Development of Constitutional Guarantees of Liberty (1957)

Thirty-First Annual Review of Criminal Procedure, 90 Geo. L.J. 1087 (2002)

Significant Cases

United States v. Perez, 22 U.S. (9 Wheat.) 579 (1824)

Ex parte Lange, 85 U.S. (18 Wall.) 163 (1874)

United States v. Ball, 163 U.S. 662 (1896)

Blockburger v. United States, 284 U.S. 299 (1932)

Palko v. State of Connecticut, 302 U.S. 319 (1937)

United States v. Green, 355 U.S. 184 (1957)

Petite v. United States, 361 U.S. 529 (1960)

Fong Foo v. United States, 369 U.S. 141 (1962)

Benton v. Maryland, 395 U.S. 784 (1969)

Waller v. Florida, 397 U.S. 387 (1970)

Brown v. Ohio, 432 U.S. 161 (1977)

Burks v. United States, 437 U.S. 1 (1978)

Sanabria v. United States, 437 U.S. 54 (1978)

Missouri v. Hunter, 459 U.S. 359 (1983)

Heath v. Alabama, 474 U.S. 82 (1985)

Kansas v. Hendricks, 521 U.S. 346 (1997)

Monge v. California, 524 U.S. 721 (1998)

Smith v. Massachusetts, 125 S. Ct. 1129 (2005)

Self-Incrimination

No person ... shall be compelled in any criminal case to be a witness against himself....

(Amendment V)

~

*S*cholars such as John Wigmore and Leonard Levy have suggested that the privilege against self-incrimination reflects the Framers' antipathy to two specific abuses. One abuse was the European practice of judicial torture, and the other was the questioning of witnesses sworn to the oath ex officio before the notorious courts of the High Commission and the Star Chamber in England. The oath ex officio pledged the witness to answer any and all questions truthfully, without any indication of the subject matter. The oath was used to persecute political and religious dissenters and had the obnoxious effect of forcing devout individuals to choose between admitting offenses, to be followed by hanging, or denying offenses, to be followed by damnation. Some recent scholarship has offered an alternative to this account. It suggests that the privilege against self-incrimination arose mainly from American practice rather than as a reaction against European or English royal abuses.

In America the privilege arose because of the particular practice of self-representation by defendants. Consistent with the practice of English common law, the accused could not be forced to be sworn as a witness in the late eighteenth and early nineteenth centuries in America. The reason for the rule was fear that the guilty would be tempted to swear falsely and be damned by God. The accused representing himself, therefore, literally could not be called to be a witness against himself. This rule was also congenial with a law, which prevailed in England well into the nineteenth century, that parties to the litigation were themselves incompetent to testify, either on their own behalf or if examined by their adversaries. In effect, the Fifth Amendment codified this practice.

The defendant typically represented himself and could speak for himself throughout the trial, both by making unsworn statements heard by the jury and by examining witnesses. Such statements were, of course, voluntary. On the other hand, early American practice involved pretrial questioning of the accused by a magistrate or justice of the peace where the defendant could be pressed to admit wrongdoing.

The Founders, then, regarded the privilege as valuable enough to include in the Constitution, but their own practice put considerable pressure on defendants to surrender incriminating information before trial. The assertion of the privilege at trial became more common as the advent of modern police forces had the effect of replacing pretrial judicial questioning with custodial interrogation by the police, particularly when defendants availed themselves of professional attorneys.

Judicial interpretations of the Self-Incrimination Clause were slow in coming. John Marshall, both in *Marbury v. Madison* (1803) and in the treason trial of Aaron Burr (1807), permitted third-party witnesses to claim the privilege. The federal government prosecuted relatively few cases, and the Court held that the privilege, like the rest of the Bill of Rights, did not apply to the states, a situation that did not change until after the Civil War, when the Supreme Court, over a period of many years, read the Due Process Clause of the Fourteenth Amendment to incorporate most of the Bill of Rights.

In the 1880s, the Supreme Court took the view that the privilege protected private books and papers. With antecedents in the common law, the privilege protected an individual against a subpoena demanding incriminating private documents. Indeed, even if the government obtained the papers without a subpoena, the use of private papers as evidence against their owner was equated with compelled testimony. During this same period, the Supreme Court upheld a congressional statute providing for compelled testimony under the grant of transactional immunity, but rejected the claim that corporations could assert the privilege.

In 1964, the Supreme Court held that the privilege applies against the states as a matter of Fourteenth Amendment due process, and that testimony compelled in state court could not be used against the witness in a federal prosecution (and vice versa). *Malloy v. Hogan*; *Murphy v. Waterfront Commission*. Subsequently, Fifth Amendment doctrine changed significantly. The most dramatic change was the decision in *Miranda v. Arizona* (1966), holding that information received from the interrogation of arrested persons by the police was presumptively the product of unconstitutional compulsion in the absence of the specific warnings. The *Miranda* doctrine prohibits custodial interro-

gation absent a knowing and voluntary waiver of the rights to silence and counsel.

Subsequent cases have developed in detail the meaning of custody, interrogation, waiver, and the consequences of invoking silence and/or counsel. For example, the Court ruled that if the defendant elects to testify at trial, statements tainted by *Miranda* violations may be admitted to impeach. The *Miranda* exclusionary rule is also more limited with respect to derivative evidence than the Fourth Amendment exclusionary rule. In 2000, in *Dickerson v. United States*, the Supreme Court reaffirmed *Miranda* and struck down a congressional statute that had purported to return to pre-*Miranda* practice, although the majority appeared to concede that the Constitution itself did not require the *Miranda* rule.

Outside the police-interrogation context, the privilege protects against compelled testimonial evidence tending to incriminate the witness. Compulsion is not limited to court order, but includes such pressures as the threatened loss of government employment or public contracts, or an inference of guilt from silence at a criminal trial. Testimonial evidence means a communication of information from the target's memory or knowledge. Thus fingerprints, tissue samples, and physical evidence are not testimonial: the government can compel their production. In a reversal of its earlier position, the modern Court has held that the Fifth Amendment does not protect physical evidence like private papers unless official compulsion forced the defendant to create the document. In the case of private papers, the Fourth Amendment and not the Fifth Amendment normally governs the government's power to seize papers, just like the Fourth Amendment limits the government's powers to seize conversations by wiretap. The privilege applies when the evidence sought is incriminating, that is, it provides a link in a chain of proof that might be useful, and the risk of prosecution is more than fanciful. Where a violation of the Self-Incrimination Clause is the product of a directly coerced or compelled confession, the government may not use in a later case that confession or any evidence that is the fruit of such coercion. If, however, the original illegality is a violation of the *Miranda* rule, rather than actual coercion, the government may use in a later prosecution evidence that was discovered as a fruit of the *Miranda*-violative confession.

Evidence is not incriminating, however, and the privilege cannot be asserted if it is produced under an immunity order by the court, that is, a promise not to use the compelled information against the defendant. The government may grant the witness "transactional immunity," or "use and derivative use immunity." Transactional immunity bars any prosecution for the conduct to which the testimony relates. Use and derivative use immunity, the only type of immunity constitutionally required, permits the government to prosecute the witness, but only after proving that it, the prosecution, has made no use of the compelled testimony or any evidence derived from it. Typically, the prosecution will exhaust all other avenues of investigation before applying for a use immunity order, and the supporting affidavit will describe in detail all of the evidence the prosecution has prior to the compelled testimony. Nonetheless, the risk that immunized testimony may aid the prosecution indirectly is thought sufficiently serious that many states still authorize only transactional immunity above and beyond the Fifth Amendment's protections.

Leaving the *Miranda* situation aside, the witness must claim the privilege, or it will be deemed waived. Of course, direct police physical or psychological coercion or compulsion that produces a "confession" is inadmissible whether or not a "waiver" is asserted by the police. In addition, the government may not coercively obtain a waiver by, for example, threatening the loss of public employment or government contracts. A criminal defendant who elects to take the stand waives the privilege with respect to questions asked on cross-examination that are reasonably related to the direct examination.

Donald Dripps

See Also

Amendment IV (Searches and Seizures)
Amendment XIV, Section 1 (Due Process Clause)

Suggestions for Further Research

R. H. Helmholz, ed., The Privilege Against Self-Incrimination: Its Origins and Development (1997)

Wayne R. LaFave, Jerold H. Israel, & Nancy J. King, Criminal Procedure (2d ed.1999)

Leonard W. Levy, Origins of the Fifth Amendment (1968)

Leonard W. Levy, *Origins of the Fifth Amendment and Its Critics*, 19 Cardozo L. Rev. 821 (1997)

John Henry Wigmore, A Treatise on the System of Evidence in Trials at Common Law 2250 (1904)

Significant Cases

Marbury v. Madison, 5 U.S. (1 Cranch) 137 (1803)
Malloy v. Hogan, 378 U.S. 1 (1964)
Murphy v. Waterfront Commission, 378 U.S. 52 (1964)
Miranda v. Arizona, 384 U.S. 436 (1966)
Schmerber v. California, 384 U.S. 757 (1966)
Kastigar v. United States, 406 U.S. 441 (1972)
Pennsylvania v. Muniz, 496 U.S. 582 (1990)
Dickerson v. United States, 530 U.S. 428 (2000)

Due Process Clause

No person shall... be deprived of life, liberty, or property, without due process of law....

(Amendment V)

~

*A*rticle Thirty-nine of the Magna Carta (1215) proclaimed that "no free man shall be taken or imprisoned or disseised or outlawed or exiled or in any way ruined, nor will we go or send against him, except by the lawful judgment of his peers or by the law of the land." This "law of the land" requirement, which is often called the *principle of legality*, prohibited unilateral, arbitrary action by the king against certain protected private interests.

The phrase "due process of law" made its first appearance in a statute of 1354 concerning court procedures. "Due process of law" meant that judgments could only issue when the defendant was personally given the opportunity to appear in court pursuant to an appropriate writ (i.e., was served process). The phrase retained this technical meaning in English law into the eighteenth century.

At the time of the drafting of the Bill of Rights, at least eight state constitutions contained clauses restraining government from depriving persons of life, liberty, or property except pursuant to the law of the land. The Fifth Amendment, which otherwise tracked the form of these state provisions, used the phrase "due process of law" instead of "law of the land." The reasons for this change in terminology are uncertain, but it is likely that the Founding generation was misled by some seventeenth-century statements of Sir Edward Coke (familiar to virtually all the Founders), who had declared— wrongly, in the judgment of modern historians—that the phrases "law of the land" and "due process of law" were essentially equivalent. Accordingly, the constitutional meaning of "due process of law" almost certainly refers to the principle of legality rather than to pleading technicalities.

Until very close to the time of the Framing, the judicial power was generally viewed as an aspect of executive power. Thus, the essence of the eighteenth-century American understanding of the phrase "without due process of law" meant something like "executive or judicial action taken without lawful authorization and/or not in accordance with traditional forms of justice." The Supreme Court extended the principle to Congress in *Murray's Lessee v. Hoboken Land & Improvement Co.* (1856). There, the Court determined that the Due Process Clause limited the power of Congress to authorize novel forms of adjudication. The case involved a constitutional challenge to a statutory procedure in which the government collected deficiencies from tax collectors without first having a court determine whether the tax collector really owed the money to the government. The Court found that the clause "is a restraint on the legislative as well as on the executive and judicial powers of the government, and cannot be so construed as to leave congress free to make any process 'due process of law,' by its mere will." In order to determine whether legislatively prescribed forms of adjudication violated due process of law, the Court looked to "those settled usages and modes of proceeding existing in the common and statute law of England." The Court found a long tradition in English and American law of auditing tax collectors without prior hearings and accordingly upheld the practice.

The Due Process Clause requires that deprivations of "life, liberty, or property" be accompanied by due process of law. The deprivation of other interests that do not fall within this enumeration need not be accompanied by due process of law. When the Due Process Clause was ratified in 1791, the meaning of "liberty" as a personal right was clear. Sir William Blackstone, whose influence on the Founding generation was enormous, wrote in his *Commentaries on the Laws of England* that the right to liberty meant "the power of locomotion, of changing situation, or removing one's person to whatsoever place one's own inclination may direct; without imprisonment or restraint, unless by due course of law." That definition excludes such matters as bodily integrity. Those interests, however, were encompassed by Blackstone's definition of life, which referred to an array of rights lumped together under the general heading of personal security: "a person's legal and uninterrupted enjoyment of his life, his limbs, his body, his health, and his reputation." The term "property" in 1791 was more ambiguous. It could have referred to land, to land plus chattels, to anything of exchangeable value, or (what seems most likely) to whatever interests common-law courts would have recognized as property entitled to legal protection. None of these understandings would include as property future enjoyment of government benefits, such as jobs or licenses. The law sharply distinguished between property rights and mere privileges that the government could continue or terminate at its pleasure.

The eighteenth-century lawyer trying to define the phrase "life, liberty, or property" would have had to face a very sticky problem that could not be answered by reference to Blackstone, tradition, or any other authoritative source of meaning: Do these terms draw their meaning from federal law, state law, or both? Does the Constitution contain its own internal definitions of those terms, so that the Constitution itself determines whether a particular interest is property? Are they defined by reference to the laws of the states, so that a particular interest might be constitutional "property" in Pennsylvania but not in New York? Or must the universe of constitutionally protected interests be determined by some combination of federal and state law?

Perhaps the best answer, though it is impossible to prove this claim decisively, is that federal law sets the outer boundaries of "life, liberty, and property" and state law fixes the details. Surely the Constitution does not itself determine whether a particular estate in land, such as a surface estate on mining land, is or is not "property" for purposes of the Due Process Clause; either answer is permissible and, accordingly, can vary from one jurisdiction to another. But if a state decided that land was henceforth no longer to be considered "property," that would pass the boundaries of acceptability. Federal law thus establishes for each term a "core" of meaning that no jurisdiction can alter, but beyond that core, governments are free to expand or contract the range of constitutionally protected interests.

Modern doctrine has significantly modified the original understanding of how one determines compliance with "due process of law." Instead of reference to traditionally accepted procedural forms, contemporary law, dating back a century, has judged the adequacy of procedures by a mélange of practical factors that resist easy reduction. As Justice Frankfurter summarized matters in a famous concurring opinion in *Joint Anti-Fascist Refugee Committee v. McGrath* in 1951: "'[D]ue process' is compounded of history, reason, the past course of decisions, and stout confidence in the strength of the democratic faith which we profess.... It is a delicate process of judgment by those whom the Constitution entrusted with the unfolding of the process."

In *Matthews v. Eldridge* (1976), the Court attempted to clarify its case law by requiring consideration of

first, the [significance of the] private interest that will be affected by the official action; second, the risk of an erroneous deprivation of such interest through the procedures used, and the probable value, if any, of additional or substitute procedural safeguards; and finally, the [weight of the] Government's interest, including the function involved and the fiscal and administrative burdens that the additional or substitute procedural requirement would entail.

This balancing-of-factors approach is universally decried as unpredictable. Many observers also object to the Court's optimistic goal of accurate decision-making, and there is considerable disagreement about which other possible goals of procedure should be factored into the mix.

In addition, one of the trickiest questions in modern law concerns the *timing* of procedures: which procedures (if any) must come *before* the government deprives people of protected interests? The law in this area remains unsettled in many important respects and defies simple description.

The most dramatic transformations in modern due process have concerned the range of interests encompassed by the phrase "life, liberty, or property." As late as 1950, the original meaning still largely held sway, though Blackstone's broad understanding of "life" mysteriously vanished in favor of a much narrower meaning. No doubt this development, which was never expressly acknowledged, put pressure on the other terms in the enumeration to include such worthy interests as physical integrity and reputation. More importantly, the rise of the post-New Deal administrative state vastly expanded the range of circumstances under which official action could affect people's lives, and the concomitant expansion of government benefits, jobs, and licenses raised the stakes of excluding such interests from procedural protection. By the early 1960s, a majority of the Court was prepared to treat the phrase "life, liberty, or property" as a convenient shorthand for "any interest whose loss would be grievous" rather than as a list of three distinct terms with distinct, ascertainable meanings—a development that some commentators half-jokingly described as "lifelibertyproperty." On this new understanding, government benefits could easily constitute interests whose loss would be grievous.

In 1970, the Court formalized this understanding in *Goldberg v. Kelly*, where the State of New York, in its argument to the Supreme Court concerning the need for elaborate pretermination hearings prior to termination of benefits under the Aid to Families with Dependent Children Act, did not even argue that expected future receipt of AFDC benefits was not a constitutionally protected interest. Subsequent cases quickly extended constitutional protection to such interests as government licenses and reputation.

In 1972, the Supreme Court established the framework of modern law in *Board of Regents of State Colleges v. Roth*. That case reestablished some differentiations among the three protected interests. The Court held that "liberty" and "property" were distinct terms with ascertainable meanings, though "life" continues to be conspicuously absent from modern recitations of the range of protected interests. The Court explicitly stated, however, that these terms would not be construed in accordance with their original meaning, but would have to be construed to include the extended range of interests recognized in prior case law, including government benefits.

Accordingly, the Court has expanded the definition of the term "liberty," beginning with *Meyer v. State of Nebraska* (1923), in which it declared that "liberty" includes "not merely freedom from bodily restraint but also the right of the individual to contract, to engage in any of the common occupations of life, to acquire useful knowledge, to marry, establish a home and bring up children, to worship God according to the dictates of his own conscience, and generally to enjoy those privileges long recognized...as essential to the orderly pursuit of happiness by free men." It is true that the term has been held not to include (at least under some circumstances) a right to government employment, an interest in reputation, or many

interests claimed by prisoners. The government is free, however, to *construct* these excluded interests to be constitutionally protected through statutes and regulations by specifying a clear causal connection between satisfaction of criteria of eligibility and receipt of a benefit, but they are not automatically protected as a matter of constitutional command. Nonetheless, the Court's extraordinary expansion of the concept of "liberty" reached its apogee in the famous (some critics say infamous) declaration by Justice Anthony Kennedy: "At the heart of liberty is the right to define one's own concept of existence, of meaning, of the universe, and of the mystery of human life." *Planned Parenthood of Southeastern Pennsylvania v. Casey* (1992).

It is state law today that primarily defines the term "property." Interests within the traditional understanding of property are generally still considered to be property. Interests beyond the traditional understanding, such as government benefits and licenses, are constitutionally protected if statutory or regulatory provisions draw a clear causal line from the satisfaction of eligibility criteria to the receipt of benefits. The case law distinguishes the substance of the created interest from the procedures for its termination. The latter is what the Due Process Clause protects. Within the zone beyond the constitutional core of "liberty" and "property," government can determine which substantive interests shall receive due-process protection, but once that substantive decision is made, the constitutional law of due process assesses the adequacy of the procedures. In other words, the government may not make acceptance of "unconstitutional" termination procedures a condition of receiving government benefits.

If an interest does not fall within the meaning of the phrase "life, liberty, or property," the Due Process Clause does not mandate any particular procedures for its deprivation. Other sources of law, whether constitutional or statutory, may well do so, but the Due Process Clause is, so to speak, "turned off." There are several other "on-off switches" that determine the applicability of the Due Process Clause.

First, the clause only applies to government action; private entities are not bound by the

Fifth Amendment or, indeed, by anything in the Constitution except the Thirteenth Amendment. This can pose difficult questions when the acting entity is nominally private but is involved in some fashion with the government. *See* "State Action" in the Fourteenth Amendment, Section 1. Second, modern law holds that the word "deprived" in the Due Process Clause means an *intentional* (or, at a minimum, a *reckless*) taking of a protected interest. Losses inflicted by government negligence do not implicate the Due Process Clause.

Third, and most importantly, administrative agencies are responsible for the vast bulk of governmental actions that work deprivations of interests within the compass of the Due Process Clause. Those agencies engage in two forms of official action: *rule-making*, which strongly resembles in form and function the promulgation of a statute by the legislature, and *adjudication*, which strongly resembles in form and function the decision of a case by a court. The Due Process Clause has never been understood to impose procedural requirements on legislatures (though it does, under modern understandings, regulate the content of legislation that authorizes executive or judicial procedures). For almost a century, courts have held that agency rule-making shares in this legislative immunity from due-process analysis; agency rule-making is subject to no constitutional procedural requirements. Agency adjudication, however, is subject to due-process analysis, but agencies do not stand in the same shoes as courts. Procedures that would be obviously inadequate in judicial proceedings are considered constitutionally adequate for agency adjudication. The size of the gap is uncertain, which typifies the complexity of the modern law of procedural due process.

Gary Lawson

See Also

Amendment XIV, Section 1 (State Action)

Suggestions for Further Research

Frank Easterbrook, *Substance and Due Process*, 1982 SUP. CT. REV. 85 (1982)

John Harrison, *Substantive Due Process and the Constitutional Text*, 83 VA. L. REV. 493 (1997)

Keith Jurow, *Untimely Thoughts: A Reconsideration of the Origins of Due Process of Law*, 19 AM. J. LEGAL HIST. 265 (1975)

GARY LAWSON, FEDERAL ADMINISTRATIVE LAW 357–498 (2d ed. 2001)

JERRY L. MASHAW, DUE PROCESS IN THE ADMINISTRATIVE STATE (1985)

Significant Cases

Murray's Lessee v. Hoboken Land & Improvement Co., 59 U.S. (18 How.) 272 (1856)

Meyer v. State of Nebraska, 262 U.S. 390 (1923)

Pierce v. Society of Sisters, 268 U.S. 510 (1925)

Joint Anti-Fascist Refugee Committee v. McGrath, 341 U.S. 123 (1951)

Goldberg v. Kelly, 397 U.S. 254 (1970)

Board of Regents of State Colleges v. Roth, 408 U.S. 564 (1972)

Matthews v. Eldridge, 424 U.S. 319 (1976)

Planned Parenthood of Southeastern Pennsylvania v. Casey, 505 U.S. 833 (1992)

Takings Clause

...nor shall private property be taken for public use, without just compensation.

(AMENDMENT V)

~

*T*he drafter of this clause, James Madison, opined: "A Government is instituted to protect property of every sort...This being the end of government, that alone is *a just* government, which *impartially* secures to every man, whatever is his *own*." Against the proposition that the singular purpose of our government is the protection of property, there is the curiosity that the original Constitution scarcely mentions the term. Although at least two states demanded every other provision that we know today as the Bill of Rights, not one requested the Takings Clause. What explains the anomaly?

The beginning of an answer can be found in Alexander Hamilton's observation that "the true protection of men's rights are to be found not among old parchments, or musty records. They are written...in the whole *volume* of human nature...and can never be erased or obscured." Alexander Hamilton was, of course, referring to the natural law, which is one of the doctrinal foundations of the United States set out in the Declaration of Independence.

As a matter of original understanding, the American Founders viewed the natural right to acquire or possess property as embedded in the common law, which they regarded as the natural law applied to specific facts. Thus, the Framers thought that there was little need to create a "parchment protection" against the states, which were, after all, carrying on the common-law tradition. Many early colonial and state charters had explicitly protected "the means of acquiring and possessing property" as part of the common-law rights of Englishmen brought over at the time of the first settlements. Nonetheless, Madison apparently believed that the federal government, which, of course, had no long-standing tradition of supporting property rights, should be explicitly restricted to follow the common-law form. It was not until the late nineteenth century that the clause would be judicially applied to the states through the Due Process Clause of the Fourteenth Amendment. *Chicago, Burlington & Quincey Railroad Co.* (1897).

Property is not, however, entirely a natural right. The Founders understood that it would need to be further defined in statute. Particular rights of sale or use might well vary from place to place. For example, Thomas Jefferson introduced legislation in Virginia that would abolish landed estates (so-called entails) that were inheritable only through limited bloodlines. Similar restrictions were present in the common law through the rule against perpetuities, which prevents an owner from leaving property with ultimate ownership uncertain for too long a period after his death.

Because the Fifth Amendment places a restriction on the ability and manner of taking property by the federal government, this begs a central question: what is the source of the federal government's power of eminent domain in the first place? The states clearly had that power through their longstanding common-law tradition. How did the new federal government come to possess it as well? Two answers have been proposed. The first suggests that the power to take property is inherent in any sovereign. *Jones v. United States* (1883); *Mississippi & Rum River Boom Co. v. Patterson* (1878). Although Hugo Grotius, who coined the phrase "eminent domain" in 1625, disagreed, a sovereign in certain very limited—usually war-time—situations, has been allowed to take property without the obligation to compensate. In another rare circumstance, where property is physically taken, if the taking results in no net loss to the owner, compensation is not due. *Brown v. Legal Foundation of Washington* (2003). Putting these rarities aside, it is frequently said that the very institution of the federal government brings with it the power of eminent domain.

A second answer is that the federal power of eminent domain resides in, and is limited by, the Necessary and Proper Clause (Article I, Section 8, Clause 18), or by Congress's implied powers as confirmed by the Necessary and Proper Clause. *McCulloch v. Maryland* (1819); *United States v. Gettysburg Electric Railway Co.* (1896). Under this perspective, Congress may exercise the power of eminent domain only in order to effectuate one of its delegated powers. Similarly, the executive is limited to property takings allowable only under Article II executive powers, but they are far more restricted. *Youngstown Sheet & Tube Co. v. Sawyer* (1952). Inasmuch as James Madison came to support and propose a Bill of Rights because he realized the range of congressional power under the Necessary and Proper Clause, and inasmuch as the Takings Clause is primarily his offering, such a reading has historical credence.

What changes to the definition of property, then, can the federal government—and since incorporation of the Fifth Amendment, a state or local government—legislate without offending the natural right to property that underlies the common law? Justice Oliver Wendell Holmes initially opined that regulation must not go "too far": a judicial limit, but not a very formidable one. *Pennsylvania Coal Co. v. Mahon* (1922). Worse, the test actually looked at the wrong question. It focused on whether the regulation diminished the value of the property, rather than asking whether the regulation actually was consistent with common-law limitations on the use of property. The confusion between restrictions on use and diminution of value continues to affect the judicial interpretation of the clause.

So what limits have the modern cases placed on the regulation of property? In other words, what is "too far"? The Supreme Court easily determined that a regulation that authorizes the physical occupation of property was a taking. *Loretto v. Teleprompter Manhattan CATV Corp.* (1982). This categorical protection of the right to exclude emerged from the ancient protection against trespass. But *Loretto*'s significance was not great as a practical matter, because few regulations have the brazenness, short of formal condemnation, to authorize third parties to station themselves on other's property. Occasionally, regulation comes close to outright physical occupation, by conditioning the grant of a governmental permit upon some forfeiture of a property interest. For example, one homeowner was told that he could expand his home, but only if he provided a beach easement to the public. *Nollan v. California Coastal Commission* (1987). Another was told that she could enlarge a retail plumbing store if she set aside property for a bike path. *Dolan v. City of Tigard* (1994).

In these cases, the Court has held that the Takings Clause prohibits the regulating agencies from using the permit process to leverage their governmental power to achieve what they wish without cost. To survive review, regulatory conditions must "substantially advance" a legitimate governmental interest and be reasonably "proportionate" to the external effects likely to be caused by the property owner's proposal. In *Nollan*, the landowner was freed of the beach-easement requirement because it was unnecessary to the government's stated purposes. In *Dolan*, the store owner did not have to facilitate the bike path, because, however desirable that might be, the need for it was not caused by the activity being regulated (the expansion of a plumbing store).

The Court has also applied the Takings Clause to invalidate regulations that deprive property of all of its economic use. *Lucas v. South Carolina Coastal Council* (1992). This, too, is a taking unless the regulation parallels the limitations in the background principles of the state's law of property and nuisance. In *Lucas*, the desired property use was for residential construction, and the regulating state could not show that the common-law nuisance principles prohibited that use of the property.

The significance of the common-law/natural-right backdrop of property continues to shape constitutional doctrine. But what happens if modern regulation does not just mimic the common law but imposes far greater restrictions, based perhaps on modern environmental considerations? Recent judicial pronouncements indicate that the courts would regard at least a certain amount of environmental restriction as a reasonable extension of the common-law principle. But if one knowingly purchases land in a jurisdiction with an expansive environmental regime, the landowner is not automatically precluded from a takings claim. Rather, that knowledge is only one additional factor for the court to consider in judging whether the regulation can justifiably be considered a taking. *Palazzolo v. Rhode Island* (2001).

Other factual matters do play a significant role in keeping most takings cases out of court. State administrative and judicial determinations regarding the final application of regulations to individual parcels and the availability of compensation to owners are prolonged and expensive. Until these processes are completed, a "ripeness doctrine" prevents owners from seeking relief in federal court. *Williamson County Regional Planning Commission v. Hamilton Bank* (1985). The Court has occasionally expressed frustration with the bureaucratic games that result in protracted litigation, *Monterey v. Del Monte Dunes at Monterey, Ltd.* (1999), but most often property owners are turned away from the courts and told to keep working through the prescribed processes.

The most difficult Takings Clause cases are the most common ones. In these, the regulation has not physically invaded or precipitated a total loss, or even been employed to gain undue leverage. Rather, regulation reduces, often significantly but not totally, the economic prospects for property, and an owner asks to be compensated. The governing case here remains *Penn Central Transportation Co. v. City of New York* (1978). In *Penn Central*, which dealt with an ordinance that preserved a historic landmark by imposing a large loss on the property owner by forbidding construction of an office tower above it, the Court admitted that the takings issue was "a problem of considerable difficulty." "There was," said the Court, "no 'set formula' for determining when 'justice and fairness' require that economic injuries caused by public action be compensated by the government, rather than remain disproportionately concentrated on a few persons." The Court admitted that in the typical case it would apply an ad hoc balancing test that would consider (1) the economic impact on the property owner, (2) the extent to which the regulation interfered with investment-backed expectations, and (3) the character or extent of the government action.

In the weighing of these factors, most property owners have lost their claims for compensation. A few have prevailed by recharacterizing the portion taken as a complete deprivation of a part, rather than a partial deprivation of a whole. The Court has said that, where there is a regulation that is terminated after a court has concluded that it constituted a taking, the owner's deprivation during the temporary period in which the regulation was effective is compensable. *First English Evangelical Lutheran Church of Glendale v. County of Los Angeles* (1987). However, whether a planned moratorium (even if it lasts for years) constitutes a taking must be determined by using the *Penn Central* multifactor test. *Tahoe-Sierra Preservation Council, Inc. v. Tahoe Regional Planning Agency* (2002).

Despite the frustration and cost of litigation of enforcing the Takings Clause, property owners remain indefatigable, and they are especially so when they perceive regulation to exceed a reasonable scope and invade that which may fairly be thought to be one of the natural rights of ownership. The ultimate purpose of the Takings Clause was well described by the Court more than forty years ago as "designed to bar Government from forcing some people alone to bear public burdens which, in all fairness and justice, should be borne by the public as a whole." *Armstrong v. United States* (1960). That is the central principle that prompted the Framers to add the Takings Clause to the Bill of Rights.

Douglas W. Kmiec

[Editors' Note: In *Kelo v. City of New London* (2005) the city of New London planned to use eminent domain to acquire property for a redevelopment project that would replace existing private homes in good condition with private office space and parking lots. The property owners argued that the taking was not "for [a] public use," and thus violated the Fifth Amendment. In a 5–4 opinion, the Court upheld the taking, holding that where a government presents a "comprehensive development plan" with "public benefits" that are not merely "incidental or pretextual," the Court will apply a deferential, rational-basis–like standard to determine whether the asserted public benefit of the taking satisfies the public use requirement. In dissent, Justice Sandra Day O'Connor argued that taking of a private property for the benefit of another private party does not constitute public use, unless there is a direct public benefit, such as the elimination of a blighted area.]

See Also

Article I, Section 10, Clause 1 (Obligation of Contract Clause)

Amendment V (Due Process Clause)

Amendment XIV, Section 1 (Due Process Clause)

Suggestions for Further Research

James W. Ely, Jr., Property Rights in American History (1997)

Richard A. Epstein, Takings: Private Property and the Power of Eminent Domain, 289–293 (1985)

Matthew P. Harrington, *"Public Use" and the Original Understanding of the So-Called "Takings" Clause*, 53 HASTINGS L. J. 1245 (2002)

Douglas W. Kmiec, *At Last, the Supreme Court Solves the Takings Puzzle*, 19 HARV. J.L. & PUB. POL'Y 147 (1995)

Douglas W. Kmiec, *Inserting the Last Remaining Pieces into the Takings Puzzle*, 38 WM. & MARY L. REV. 995 (1997)

DOUGLAS W. KMIEC, LAND USE AND ZONING LAW (annually supplemented)

Douglas W. Kmiec, *The Original Understanding of the Taking Clause Is Neither Weak nor Obtuse*, 88 COLUM. L. REV. 1630 (1988)

THOMAS G. ROBERTS, TAKING SIDES ON THE TAKING ISSUE (2002)

BERNARD H. SIEGAN, PROPERTY AND FREEDOM (1997)

William Michael Treanor, *The Original Understanding of the Takings Clause and the Political Process*, 95 COLUM. L. REV. 782 (1995)

Significant Cases

McCulloch v. Maryland, 17 U.S. (4 Wheat.) 316 (1819)

Mississippi & Rum River Boom Co. v. Patterson, 98 U.S. 403 (1878)

Jones v. United States, 109 U.S. 513 (1883)

United States v. Gettysburg Electric Railway Co., 160 U.S. 668 (1896)

Chicago, Burlington & Quincey Railroad Co. v. City of Chicago, 166 U.S. 226 (1897)

Pennsylvania Coal Co. v. Mahon, 260 U.S. 393 (1922)

Youngstown Sheet & Tube Co. v. Sawyer, 343 U.S. 579 (1952)

Armstrong v. United States, 364 U.S. 40 (1960)

Penn Central Transportation Co. v. City of New York, 438 U.S. 104 (1978)

Loretto v. Teleprompter Manhattan CATV Corp., 458 U.S. 419 (1982)

Williamson County Regional Planning Commission v. Hamilton Bank of Johnson City, 473 U.S. 172 (1985)

First English Evangelical Lutheran Church of Glendale v. County of Los Angeles, 482 U.S. 304 (1987)

Nollan v. California Coastal Commission, 483 U.S. 825 (1987)

Lucas v. South Carolina Coastal Council, 505 U.S. 1003 (1992)

Dolan v. City of Tigard, 512 U.S. 374 (1994)

Monterey v. Del Monte Dunes at Monterey, Ltd., 526 U.S. 687 (1999)

Palazzolo v. Rhode Island, 533 U.S. 606 (2001)

Tahoe-Sierra Preservation Council, Inc. v. Tahoe Regional Planning Agency, 535 U.S. 302 (2002)

Brown v. Legal Foundation of Washington, 538 U.S. 216 (2003)

Lingle v. Chevron, 125 S. Ct. 2074 (2005)

Kelo v. City of New London, 2005 WL 1469529, 2005 U.S. LEXIS 5011

Speedy Trial Clause

In all criminal prosecutions, the accused shall enjoy the right to a speedy... trial....

(AMENDMENT VI)

~

$\mathscr{F}$rom the time of the Assize of Clarendon (1166) and the Magna Carta (1215), the common law created protections in response to English monarchs who imprisoned enemies of the Crown without permitting them access to courts. By 1642, Sir Edward Coke was able to conclude that English judges "have not suffered the prisoner to be long detained, but... have given the prisoner full and speedy justice...." The evil to be avoided was lengthy pretrial detention. The English Habeas Corpus Act of 1679, for example, required timely hearings while the accused was on bail.

The Framers of the Constitution understood that a speedy trial was part of the essence of the rights of Englishmen. When the First Congress drafted the Bill of Rights, it approved without discussion the right to a speedy trial. At that time, the rights to habeas corpus (Article I, Section 9, Clause 2), to nonexcessive bail (Eighth Amendment), and to a speedy trial were seen as interrelated. Under common-law practice, judges would grant a habeas corpus petition and dismiss the indictment if a defendant was detained too long prior to trial. Once the defendant was free, the harm of pretrial detention ceased, and the speedy-trial requirement was moot. The state could, if it wished, reindict later so long as the statute of limitations was not a bar. Early American cases sometimes decided the issue of pretrial detention simply through the application of state habeas corpus without even referring to the right to a speedy trial. *See, e.g., Logan v. State* (1814).

As with most of the other provisions of the Bill of Rights, the Supreme Court has incorporated the Speedy Trial Clause into the Fourteenth Amendment and applied it to the states. *Klopfer v. North Carolina* (1967). The modern Court, moreover, views the right to a speedy trial as preventing not only the harm of pretrial detention, but also harm to the defense caused by delay—for example, fading memories or the deaths of witnesses. Thus, release on bail no longer stops the speedy-trial "clock," and a violation can occur simply because of harm to the defense. On the other hand, the failure of the defense to move to dismiss the case counts against a defendant who later asserts a right to a speedy trial, because the Court views this defendant as acquiescing in the delay.

One's right to a speedy trial in most instances begins from the time of arrest or indictment, not from the moment an investigation begins. It is left to statutes of limitations to cure the abuse of too long an investigation. At present, the Federal Speedy Trial Act (1974) defines the time limits for criminal actions to begin. Generally speaking, an indictment or information must be filed within thirty days of arrest, and a trial should occur within seventy days of the filing.

Most constitutional violations are cured by ordering a trial that is free of the error. But the harm that delay would normally cause the defense cannot be remedied by a new trial. The Court's response to this conundrum is to require that the indictment be dismissed, or the conviction vacated, without possibility of retrial. *Strunk v. United States* (1973).

To make a conviction impossible to obtain when the trial is held too late is logical but extreme. As a result, courts are loath to find violations of the speedy-trial right. Furthermore, the speedy-trial test the Supreme Court has adopted gives lower courts great discretion in deciding speedy-trial claims. *Barker v. Wingo* (1972) held that courts should consider (1)

whether and how the defendant asserts his right to a speedy trial; (2) the length of the delay; (3) the reason the State offers to excuse the delay; and (4) the prejudice that the defendant suffered (pretrial deprivation of liberty as well as harm to the defense caused by the delay). The facts of *Barker* itself demonstrate how much discretion courts have to decide whether a trial is speedy. Willie Barker stood convicted of the brutal murder of an elderly couple. Even though the trial occurred more than five years after indictment, the Court unanimously held that it did not violate the defendant's right to a speedy trial.

George Thomas

See Also

Article I, Section 9, Clause 2 (Habeas Corpus)
Amendment V (Due Process Clause)
Amendment VIII (Cruel and Unusual Punishment)
Amendment XIV, Section 1 (Due Process Clause)

Suggestions for Further Research

Akhil R. Amar, *Sixth Amendment First Principles*, 85 Geo. L.J. 641 (1996)

Anthony G. Amsterdam, *Speedy Trial Rights and Remedies*, 27 Stan. L. Rev. 525 (1975)

Annual Review of Criminal Procedure: Speedy Trial, 90 Geo. L.J. 1454 (2002)

Brian P. Brooks, Comment, *A New Speedy Trial Standard for* Barker v. Wingo: *Reviving a Constitutional Remedy in an Age of Statutes*, 61 U. Chi. L. Rev. 587 (1994)

Alfredo Garcia, *Speedy Trial Swift Justice: Full-Fledged Citizenship or a Second-Class Citizen?*, 21 Sw. U. L. Rev. 31 (1992)

H. Richard Uviller, Barker v. Wingo: *Speedy Trial Gets a Fast Shuffle*, 72 Colum. L. Rev. 1376 (1972)

Significant Cases

Logan v. State, 7 S.C.L. (2 Tread.) 493 (S.C. Ct. App. 1814)

Beavers v. Haubert, 198 U.S. 77 (1905)

Klopfer v. North Carolina, 386 U.S. 213 (1967)

Barker v. Wingo, 407 U.S. 514 (1972)

Strunk v. United States, 412 U.S. 434 (1973)

United States v. MacDonald, 456 U.S. 1 (1982)

United States v. Loud Hawk, 474 U.S. 302 (1986)

Doggett v. United States, 505 U.S. 647 (1992)

Cutter v. Wilkinson, 125 S. Ct. 2113 (2005)

Public Trial

In all criminal prosecutions, the accused shall enjoy the right to a ... public trial ....

(AMENDMENT VI)

~

The public-trial right in the Sixth Amendment is deeply rooted in Anglo-American history, tradition, and values. It reflects, among other things, the Founders' hostility toward secret proceedings reaching back to the Star Chamber, which pre-dated the Glorious Revolution in England (1688). There was widespread agreement with Sir Edward Coke's view that a trial is almost by definition open and public. Thus, Justice Joseph Story, in his *Commentaries on the Constitution of the United States*, emphasized that, in "the established course of the common law ... trials for crimes" are "always public." The Supreme Court has echoed this view, stating that "[b]y immemorial usage, wherever the common law prevails, all trials are in open court, to which spectators are admitted." *In re Oliver* (1948).

Like most other provisions of the Bill of Rights, the public-trial guarantee has been construed by the Supreme Court to constrain both federal and state governments. Although deeply rooted and fundamental, the public-trial right is not absolute. Although the Sixth Amendment's public-trial right belongs to the criminal defendant, the public and the press also have a First Amendment interest in open proceedings. Therefore, "a defendant can, under some circumstances, waive his constitutional right to a public trial, [but] he has no absolute right to compel a private trial." *Singer v. United States* (1965). In addition, when the "dignity, order and decorum" that are and must be "hallmarks of criminal justice proceedings" are flagrantly disregarded, *Illinois v. Allen* (1970), the proceedings

may, if necessary, be closed temporarily. *Waller v. Georgia* (1984). For example, judges will occasionally close portions of trials to protect minor victims in sex-offense trials or when necessary to preserve the confidentiality of sensitive information, such as the identity of undercover witnesses. Though the Sixth Amendment's guarantee of a public "trial" includes the impaneling of the jury and return of the verdict, as well as certain pretrial proceedings, it does not require that all stages and phases of criminal prosecutions be open to the public. Grand jury proceedings, for example, are secret. *United States v. Procter & Gamble Co.* (1958).

For individual defendants, as Justice Hugo L. Black observed in the *Oliver* case, a public trial serves as a "safeguard against any attempt to employ our courts as instruments of persecution." As Justice John M. Harlan later put it, "the public-trial guarantee embodies a view of human nature, true as a general rule, that judges, lawyers, witnesses, and jurors will perform their respective functions more responsibly in an open court than in secret proceedings." *Estes v. Texas* (1965). Professor Wayne LaFave has noted that public trials also make proceedings known to potential witnesses and help to deter untruthful testimony. As Sir William Blackstone wrote in his *Commentaries on the Laws of England*, the "open examination of witnesses ... in the presence of all mankind, is much more conducive to the clearing up of truth, than private and secret examination ....[A] witness may frequently depose that in private which he will be ashamed to testify in a public and solemn tribunal."

Thus, any closure of a criminal trial implicates not only the defendant's Sixth Amendment rights, but also the First Amendment freedoms of the press and citizens generally. Open trials not only protect the innocent from wrongful conviction, they also serve the public interest in maintaining confidence in the criminal-justice system and its officers. As the Supreme Court has observed, "the First Amendment right of access to criminal trials" reflects the "common understanding" that "a major purpose of that Amendment was to protect the free discussion of governmental affairs." *Globe*

Newspaper Co. v. Superior Court (1982). Our constitutionalized preference for open trials, in other words, reflects our democratic commitment to "the ultimate right of the public to change policy and policymakers." *Gannett Co. v. DePasquale* (1979). The Court has also relied upon the First Amendment to guarantee a presumption of public trials in civil cases. *Richmond Newspapers, Inc. v. Virginia* (1980). A lawyer, however, may be disciplined for statements to the press about a pending case he is involved in for "speech that is substantially likely to have a materially prejudicial effect." *Gentile v. State Bar of Nevada* (1991).

Richard W. Garnett

See Also

Amendment I (Freedom of Speech and of the Press)
Amendment VI (Jury Trial)
Amendment VI (Confrontation Clause)

Suggestions for Further Research

Akhil R. Amar, *Sixth Amendment First Principles*, 84 Geo. L.J. 641 (1996)

Annual Review of Criminal Procedure: Sixth Amendment at Trial, 91 Geo. L.J. 584 (2003)

Thomas M. Fleming, Annotation, *Exclusion of Public from State Criminal Trial in Order to Prevent Disturbance by Spectators or Defendant*, 55 A.L.R. 4th 1170 (1987)

Alfredo Garcia, *Clash of the Titans: The Difficult Reconciliation of a Fair Trial and a Free Press in Modern American Society*, 32 Santa Clara L. Rev. 1107 (1992)

John H. Langbein, *Shaping the Eighteenth Century Criminal Trial: A View from the Ryder Sources*, 50 U. Chi. L. Rev. 1 (1983).

Thomas F. Liotti, *Closing the Courtroom to the Public: Whose Rights Are Violated?*, 63 Brook. L. Rev. 501 (1997)

Max Radin, *The Right to a Public Trial*, 6 Temp. L.Q. 381 (1932)

Significant Cases

In re Oliver, 333 U.S. 257 (1948)
United States v. Procter & Gamble Co., 356 U.S. 677 (1958)

Estes v. Texas, 381 U.S. 532 (1965)
Singer v. United States, 380 U.S. 24 (1965)
Illinois v. Allen, 397 U.S. 337 (1970)
Gannett Co. v. DePasquale, 443 U.S. 368 (1979)
Richmond Newspapers, Inc. v. Virginia, 448 U.S. 555 (1980)
Globe Newspaper Co. v. Superior Court, 457 U.S. 596 (1982)
Press-Enterprise Co. v. Superior Court of California, 464 U.S. 501 (1984)
Waller v. Georgia, 467 U.S. 39 (1984)
Press-Enterprise Co. v. Superior Court of California, 478 U.S. 1 (1986)
Arizona v. Fulminante, 499 U.S. 279 (1991)
Gentile v. State Bar of Nevada, 501 U.S. 1030 (1991)

Jury Trial

In all criminal prosecutions, the accused shall enjoy the right to a ... trial, by an impartial jury of the State and district wherein the crime shall have been committed, which district shall have been previously ascertained by law....

(Amendment VI)

~

*T*he Framers of the Constitution of 1789 and of the Bill of Rights revered trial by jury—a right that Sir William Blackstone had described as "the palladium of English liberty." By the time of the Framing, common-law juries had a more than five-century history in England. They had been part of the American experience from the start. Although juries then were considerably less representative of the adult population than they are today, they were the most democratic of the governmental institutions in the colonies. Most Americans cheered their resistance to repressive colonial measures, especially British revenue laws and seditious libel laws.

In some colonies, juries had the power to judge questions of law as well as fact. They consisted of twelve people who always acted by unanimous vote. In felony cases, nonjury trials were unknown, and guilty pleas infrequent. Trials were expeditious and routine.

The period since the Framing has seen notable changes in the general understanding of the right to jury trial.

As originally understood, the Sixth Amendment guaranteed the right to jury trial only in the federal courts, and the ratification of the Fourteenth Amendment in 1868 did not alter this understanding. One hundred years after the approval of the Fourteenth Amendment, however, the Supreme Court held in *Duncan v. Louisiana* (1968) that the amendment's Due Process Clause "incorporated" the right to jury trial and made it applicable to the states. The Court said that although juries were not essential to fairness in every legal system, they were essential to the U.S. system. It wrote, "Providing an accused with the right to be tried by a jury of his peers gave him an inestimable safeguard against the corrupt or overzealous prosecutor and against the compliant, biased, or eccentric judge."

The federal courts initially followed the jury selection rules of the states in which they sat, and all of the states limited jury service to men. All of them except Vermont also limited jury service to property owners or taxpayers. Blacks were formally disqualified in only a few states.

The Sixth Amendment was not thought to preclude expansion of the right to serve on juries, but it also was not thought to *require* any expansion. Moreover, the Fourteenth Amendment's Equal Protection Clause was not initially thought to extend "political" rights, including the right to serve on juries, to either African-Americans or women.

In 1879, however, the Supreme Court held in *Strauder v. West Virginia* that a statute disqualifying blacks from jury service violated the equal protection rights of black *litigants*. It was only in 1991 that the Court concluded that the Equal Protection Clause protected prospective jurors themselves from discrimination.

The Court has read the Sixth Amendment as well as the Equal Protection Clause to eliminate jury disqualifications of the sort the Framers approved. It held in 1975 that a "fair cross-section requirement" implicit in the amendment precluded the "systematic" exclusion of a "distinctive group in the community." Because "systematic" exclusion need not be purposeful, the Sixth Amendment prohibits some forms of discrimination in jury selection the Equal Protection Clause does not reach. Racial minorities and women qualify as "distinctive groups." As currently understood, moreover, the Sixth Amendment also probably precludes property qualifications of the sort the Framers accepted.

At the time of the Framing, litigants could challenge a limited number of prospective jurors peremptorily. In a series of cases beginning in 1986, however, the Court held that litigants may not use peremptory challenges to discriminate on the basis of race, gender, or other suspect classification.

Although the Supreme Court previously had said that the Sixth Amendment required juries of twelve (a number that had 700 years of history behind it), the Court concluded in 1970 that the amendment allows juries of six. In 1978, however, it held five-person juries impermissible. A great many states now use six-person juries, especially in misdemeanor cases.

In *Apodaca v. Oregon* in 1972, four Supreme Court Justices concluded that conviction by a vote of 10–2 did not violate the Sixth Amendment. Four Justices dissented, arguing that the amendment preserved the historic requirement of unanimity. The remaining Justice agreed with the dissenters on the construction of the Sixth Amendment but rejected the view that "all of the elements of jury trial within the meaning of the Sixth Amendment are necessarily embodied in or incorporated into the Due Process Clause of the Fourteenth." As a result, nonunanimous verdicts are permissible in state but not federal courts. In a companion case, the Court upheld a state-court conviction by a 9–3 vote. Later, the Court held conviction by a vote of 5–1 unconstitutional; convictions by six-person juries must be unanimous.

Although juries sometimes disregarded the legal instructions of judges in England, they never acquired formal authority to do so. As early as 1628, Chief Justice Coke declared that judges do not decide questions of fact and juries do not decide issues of law.

The American practice, however, was different. In 1735 in New York, Andrew Hamilton told the court trying his client, publisher John Peter Zenger, that the authority of juries "to determine both the law and the fact" was "beyond all dispute." The jury's acquittal of Zenger, despite his apparent guilt of seditious libel, helped shape the American understanding of the role and duties of jurors. Some, but not all, American colonies permitted juries to decide issues of law, and in 1771 John Adams called it "an Absurdity to suppose that the Law would oblige [jurors] to find a Verdict according to the Direction of the Court, against their own Opinion, Judgment, and Conscience."

The authority of juries to decide issues of law was contested throughout the nineteenth century, but the opponents of jury authority gained the clear upper hand in the century's second half. Although three state constitutions still declare that juries may decide legal issues, the Supreme Court's 1895 decision in *Sparf and Hansen v. United States* effectively ended the battle and held that federal juries may not decide questions of law.

In the late 1960s and early 1970s, defendants charged with unlawful resistance to the war in Vietnam sought to revive the issue. They argued that judges should inform jurors of their right to acquit whenever conviction would be unjust (or at least permit defense attorneys to argue in favor of jury nullification). Although appellate courts rejected the defendants' arguments, the courts did not deny in all circumstances the appropriateness of jury nullification. If, as a matter of conscience, jurors decided to disregard the court's instruction, their disobedience might be justified. More recently, however, courts have denied the legitimacy of nullification altogether. In 1997, a federal Court of Appeals held that, even after jury deliberations had begun, a trial judge could remove a juror who had revealed "beyond doubt" an intention to violate the court's instructions on the law.

The Anti-Federalists who opposed ratification of the Constitution protested that the right to jury trial guaranteed by Article III was inadequate. Their objections led to the Sixth Amendment's requirement that juries must be drawn from "the State and district wherein the crime shall have been committed." Although the Sixth Amendment also declared that juries must be impartial, the requirement of impartiality did not imply that jurors should arrive at the courtroom unaware of the circumstances of the case before them. George Mason and Patrick Henry insisted that local juries would protect the defendant's right to be judged on the basis of "his character and reputation." Courts now voice greater concern about information obtained prior to trial, especially in cases of widespread pretrial publicity. The Supreme Court has said that although a juror need not "be totally ignorant of the facts and issues," he must be able to "lay aside his impression or opinion and render a verdict based on the evidence presented in court." *Irvin v. Dowd* (1961).

At the time of the Sixth Amendment, all trials in serious criminal cases were jury trials. In 1874, the Supreme Court declared that a defendant could not "be tried in any other manner than by a jury of twelve men, although he consent in open court to be tried by a jury of eleven men." *Home Insurance Co. of New York v. Morse* (1874). Nevertheless, the Court held in *Patton v. United States* (1930) that a defendant could waive the right to jury trial and agree to be tried by the court alone.

Today nearly half of the convictions in the felony cases tried are the products of trials before judges sitting without juries. Moreover, only a small minority of felony cases go to trial. Ninety-four percent of the felony convictions in both state and federal courts are by guilty plea, and behind this figure lies the practice of bargaining with defendants to waive the Sixth Amendment right to jury trial.

Far from encouraging guilty pleas in felony cases, courts at the time of the Bill of Rights actively discouraged them. Sir William Blackstone's *Commentaries on the Laws of England* observed that courts were "very backward in receiving and recording [a guilty plea] . . . and will generally advise the prisoner to retract it," and similar statements appeared in American treatises throughout the nineteenth century. When instances of plea bargaining began to appear in appellate reports in the decades following the

Civil War, lower courts generally denounced the practice and often declared it unconstitutional. The Supreme Court did not uphold the constitutionality of plea-bargained waivers of the right to jury trial until 1970.

When jury trial was routine, it was a reasonably summary procedure. As recently as the 1890s, a felony court apparently could conduct a half-dozen jury trials in a single day. The intervening century has seen a proliferation of procedures in contested cases and, as a result, an inability to contest many cases. Prolonged jury-selection procedures, cumbersome rules of evidence, repetitive cross-examination of witnesses, courtroom battles of experts, jury instructions that many empirical studies tell us jurors do not understand, and other complications have made trials inaccessible for all but a small minority of defendants. Only a shadow of the communitarian institution the Framers wished to preserve has survived into the twenty-first century. Although the Sixth Amendment declares, "In all criminal prosecutions, the accused shall enjoy the right to a speedy and public trial, by an impartial jury," one commentator has said that Americans could replace the word "all" in this Amendment with the words "virtually none."

Albert W. Alschuler

[Editors' Note: In June 2004, in *Blakely v. Washington*, and in January 2005 in *United States v. Booker* (consolidated with *United States v. Fanfan*), the Supreme Court construed the right to a jury trial in a manner that collaterally limited the lawful sentences that could be imposed on a convicted defendant. It held that a defendant could not mandatorily be sentenced to a term of imprisonment that exceeded the maximum authorized by the facts determined by the jury. As a consequence, the mandatory aspects of the Federal sentencing guidelines system (and those of several states) were deemed in violation of the jury trial right. The Court concluded, however, that the right to a jury trial did not limit the authority of a sentencing judge to discretionarily sentence a defendant above a guideline range so long as the sentence stayed within the statutorily authorized maximum.]

See Also

Article III, Section 2, Clause 3 (Criminal Trials)
Amendment VII (Right to Jury in Civil Cases)

Suggestions for Further Research

Jeffrey Abramson, We, the Jury: The Jury System and the Ideal of Democracy (1994)

Steven Adler, The Jury: Trial and Error in the American Courtroom (1994)

Albert W. Alschuler, *Plea Bargaining and Its History*, 79 Colum. L. Rev. 1 (1979)

Albert W. Alschuler, *The Supreme Court and the Jury: Voir Dire, Peremptory Challenges and the Review of Jury Verdicts*, 56 U. Chi. L. Rev. 153 (1989)

Albert W. Alschuler & Andrew G. Deiss, *A Brief History of the Criminal Jury in the United States*, 61 U. Chi. L. Rev. 867 (1994)

Harry Kalven, Jr. & Hans Zeisel, The American Jury (1966)

Linda K. Kerber, No Constitutional Right to Be Ladies: Women and the Obligations of Citizenship (1998)

Benno C. Schmidt, *Juries, Jurisdiction, and Race Discrimination: The Lost Promise of* Strauder v. West Virginia, 61 Tex. L. Rev. 1401 (1983)

Significant Cases

Home Insurance Co. of New York v. Morse, 87 U.S. (20 Wall.) 445 (1874)

Strauder v. West Virginia, 100 U.S. 303 (1879)

Sparf and Hansen v. United States, 156 U.S. 51 (1895)

Patton v. United States, 281 U.S. 276 (1930)

Hoyt v. Florida, 368 U.S. 57 (1961)

Irvin v. Dowd, 366 U.S. 717 (1961)

Swain v. Alabama, 380 U.S. 202 (1965)

Duncan v. Louisiana, 391 U.S. 145 (1968)

Williams v. Florida, 399 U.S. 78 (1970)

Apodaca v. Oregon, 406 U.S. 404 (1972)

Johnson v. Louisiana, 406 U.S. 356 (1972)

United States v. Dougherty, 473 F.2d 1113 (D.C. Cir. 1972)

Taylor v. Louisiana, 419 U.S. 522 (1975)

Ballew v. Georgia, 435 U.S. 223 (1978)

Burch v. Louisiana, 441 U.S. 130 (1979)

Duren v. Missouri, 439 U.S. 357 (1979)

Batson v. Kentucky, 476 U.S. 79 (1986)

Tanner v. United States, 483 U.S. 107 (1987)

Powers v. Ohio, 499 U.S. 400 (1991)

Georgia v. McCollum, 505 U.S. 42 (1992)

J.E.B. v. Alabama *ex rel.* T.B., 511 U.S. 127 (1994)

United States v. Thomas, 116 F.3d 606 (2d Cir. 1997)

Blakely v. Washington, 125 S. Ct. 21 (2004)

United States v. Booker, 125 S. Ct. 738 (2005)

Arraignment Clause

In all criminal prosecutions, the accused shall enjoy the right to ... be informed of the nature and cause of the accusation....
(AMENDMENT VI)

$\sim$

*T*he Constitution requires that an accused criminal defendant be informed of the nature of the charges against him. As Justice Hugo L. Black has written:

> No principle of procedural due process is more clearly established than that notice of the specific charge, and a chance to be heard in a trial of the issues raised by that charge, if desired, are among the constitutional rights of every accused in a criminal proceeding in all courts, state or federal. *Cole v. Arkansas* (1948).

The requirement of fair notice derives from early English common law; it was a matter of well-accepted agreement at the time of the adoption of the Constitution; and it is, today, largely a ministerial matter of routine criminal procedure.

The accused's right to be informed of the charges against him traces its origin at least as far back as twelfth-century England. Anglo-Saxon law required a precise and properly substantiated accusation, initiated either by individual complaint (called an appeal) or by an accusing jury (the predecessor of our grand jury), and specifying particular charges. However, at that time

England had a dual judicial system, and, in contrast to the accusatorial system of the common law, the ecclesiastical judicial system used an inquisitorial process. For example, one could be called to answer charges of heresy upon the mere unsworn suggestion of "ill fame" without the need for greater specificity.

In 1164, King Henry II began a process of ecclesiastical reform, requiring the ecclesiastical courts to identify a definite accusation before calling the accused to answer. The Magna Carta (1215) incorporated the trend towards an accusatorial system requiring specific charges:

> none shall be taken by petition or suggestion made to our lord the King, or to his Council, unless it be by indictment or presentation of good and lawful people of the same neighborhood where such deeds be done, in due manner, or by process made by writ original at the common law.

The effort to force the ecclesiastical courts to adhere to the common-law rule of precision in accusation foundered in the sixteenth century, as the inquisitorial system of justice returned to prominence. The High Commission and Star Chamber revived the practice of questioning a citizen without specifying the nature of the accusation against him. As a result, the practice of refusing to inform one being questioned of the nature of the charges against him became intertwined with the related right (now embodied in the Fifth Amendment) against self-incrimination (which the English courts of this era applied only prior to the presentation of formal charges). Those called to answer in the Star Chamber refused to do so on the dual ground that they did not know what they were accused of and that they could not be compelled to answer, thereby condemning themselves from their own mouths.

Thus in 1637, when Freeborn John Lilburne, a Puritan, was examined by the Star Chamber on unspecified charges, his response was twofold:

> I am not willing to answer you to any more of these questions, because I see you

go about by this examination to ensnare me; for, seeing the things for which I am imprisoned cannot be proved against me, you will get other matter out of my examination; and therefore, if you will not ask me about the thing laid to my charge, I shall answer no more.

It is unsurprising, then, that the American legal tradition, born of the English common law and informed by the history of religious persecution that motivated many Englishmen to emigrate, reflects an early and consistent adoption of the common-law accusatorial requirement for specificity. Requirements that an accused be informed of the nature of the charges against him can be found, for example, in the Virginia Declaration of Rights and in the constitutions of many (though not all) of the original states.

When the Bill of Rights was drafted in 1789, the right to be informed of the nature and cause of the accusation was included in James Madison's draft and, without recorded comment, became a part of the Sixth Amendment.

Initially, the function of the constitutional requirement was to provide the accused with adequate notice of the charges against him so that he could prepare a defense. As the concept of double jeopardy developed, the notice requirement came to serve the secondary purpose of allowing the accused to plead a prior acquittal as a bar to a second prosecution for the "same offense." It also came to serve as a means of informing the court of the nature of the charges so that the court might determine their legal sufficiency. One illustration of the early enforcement of this requirement was *United States v. Cruikshank* (1876), where the Supreme Court concluded that an indictment charging a defendant with having hindered certain citizens in their "free exercise and enjoyment . . . of the several rights and privileges granted and secured to them by the constitution," was insufficiently specific to satisfy the constitutional standard.

In contemporary American law, the notice and specificity requirement has taken on a largely ministerial character. Although indictments are required to state clearly the statutory offense being charged, the courts routinely refuse to enforce the requirement by requiring hypertechnical specificity. Generally, a charging instrument will be sufficient if it recites the offense in the terms of the statute allegedly violated (including all the elements of the crime) and identifies the date of the offense and the individuals alleged to have violated the law. *Hamling v. United States* (1974).

Thus, though no longer a practical basis for a defendant's challenge to his indictment, the clause continues to have enduring practical day-to-day effects on the administration of justice. It is the constitutional foundation, for example, of the continuing requirement that every defendant be arraigned on charges and have the indictment read to him; it lies behind every defendant's request for a bill of particulars, providing more specification for the charges; and it is the underlying basis for every challenge to the sufficiency of an indictment as vague or containing multiple charges in a single count. Thus, the constitutional requirement to be "informed of the nature and cause of the accusation" has become internalized by the judicial system and is interwoven into the fabric of daily procedure.

Paul Rosenzweig

Suggestions for Further Research

Laurence A. Brenner, *Requiem for Miranda: The Rehnquist Court's Voluntariness Doctrine in Historical Perspective*, 67 Wash. U. L.Q. 59 (1988)

Leonard W. Levy, The Origins of the Fifth Amendment (1968)

Frederick Pollock & Frederic William Maitland, The History of English Law (2d ed. 1951)

James Fitzgerald Stephen, A History of the Criminal Law of England (1883)

Significant Cases

United States v. Cruikshank, 92 U.S. 542 (1876)

Hagner v. United States, 285 U.S. 427 (1932)

Seven Cases v. United States, 239 U.S. 510 (1916)

Cole v. Arkansas, 333 U.S. 196 (1948)

Hamling v. United States, 419 U.S. 885 (1974)

Confrontation Clause

In all criminal prosecutions, the accused shall enjoy the right to... be confronted with the witnesses against him....

(AMENDMENT VI)

~

*T*he Confrontation Clause guarantees an essential element of the adversarial trial process. The clause envisions a trial where the accused sees and hears prosecution witnesses testify in person, in open court, in his presence, and subject to cross-examination. But that basic starting point still leaves difficult questions about the scope and limits of these rights. Is face-to-face confrontation always required? Or, given modern technology, can we substitute a rough equivalent, via video camera for example, where necessary to obtain a witness's testimony? What limits can a court place on cross-examination? And when does the clause allow prosecutors to use hearsay?

The text of the clause suggests some basic limits, and some ambiguity. On the one hand, it is clear that the clause applies only to an "accused" in a "prosecution," not during investigation before any formal charge is filed. The verb "confront" has always been understood to mean more than just a right to see and listen. It includes the right to challenge the witness and to test his credibility through cross-examination. The clause applies to "witnesses against" the accused; but defining that term has proved elusive. Clearly it includes someone called by the prosecution to testify at trial. Whether it includes a hearsay declarant—a person whose out-of-court statement is offered in evidence against the accused, though that person never appears in court to testify (and thus is not subject to cross-examination)—is a question that continues to perplex the courts.

There is no record of any debate over the Confrontation Clause in the First Congress. Nevertheless, history offers some guidance to understanding the purpose of the clause. Long before the American Constitution, trials featuring live testimony in open court subject to cross-examination were typical in the English common-law courts. Those who adopted the Sixth Amendment probably had

that model in mind, especially in light of the abuses the American colonists knew of or had experienced. The Framers likely were familiar with the history of early seventeenth-century "State Trials," where British prosecutors or examining magistrates obtained affidavits or depositions in private, then presented them as evidence in trials for treason against the Crown. Defendants typically, and futilely, demanded to have their accusers brought before them face-to-face. The American colonists themselves faced similar abuses in the 1760s, when Parliament allowed the colonial vice-admiralty courts to try certain offenses using a "civil law" model of trial based on written interrogatories instead of live testimony. Both George Mason and John Adams publicly condemned that practice. As the Supreme Court declared in its first major Confrontation Clause opinion, "The primary object of [the clause] was to prevent depositions or *ex parte* affidavits, such as were sometimes admitted in civil cases, being used against the prisoner in lieu of a personal examination and cross-examination of the witness." *Mattox v. United States* (1895).

Under the current state of the law, in most circumstances, basic confrontation rights are well settled. The clause gives a defendant the right to be present in the courtroom when prosecution witnesses testify. *Kentucky v. Stincer* (1987). The clause guarantees an "adequate opportunity" for "effective" cross-examination. *Pointer v. Texas* (1965).

Applying these basic principles has proved especially difficult in two circumstances:

1. *Confrontation and Hearsay.* When a witness at trial merely repeats "hearsay," a statement made out of court by someone else (the declarant), and when that declarant is dead, unavailable, or refuses to testify at trial, the defendant cannot "confront" or cross-examine him. Yet, recognizing that British and American courts admitted some forms of hearsay both before and after 1791, the Court has not gone so far as to hold that all incriminating hearsay is inadmissible when the declarant cannot be confronted. In *Crawford v. Washington* (2004), the Court held that the prosecutor's use of "testimonial" hearsay violates the Confrontation Clause unless the declarant is unavailable and the defendant had a prior opportunity to cross-exam-

ine the declarant. Drawing primarily on history, the Court found that the principal concern of the Confrontation Clause was the use of *ex parte* "testimony"—such as depositions, affidavits, or statements made by witnesses under government interrogation—against an accused. Thus, the Court held, such "testimonial" hearsay is inadmissible against a criminal defendant who has no opportunity to confront and cross-examine the declarant. Whether the Confrontation Clause applies at all to "nontestimonial" hearsay—such as excited utterances, business records and statements for purposes of medical diagnosis—remains unsettled after *Crawford*.

2. *Child Witnesses and Face-to-Face Confrontation*. The Court has limited the right to face-to-face confrontation in extraordinary cases. In *Maryland v. Craig* (1990), the Court allowed a child witness to testify via closed-circuit television without physically entering the courtroom because the child was emotionally unable to testify in the defendant's presence. The Court found that the process nevertheless satisfied the Confrontation Clause because it allowed for cross-examination and for the jury, defendant, and counsel to observe the demeanor of the child while she testified.

In sum, the Confrontation Clause prescribes an adversarial trial process that is designed to get at the truth by allowing defendants to challenge prosecution witnesses through face-to-face testimony and cross-examination. In order to accommodate some hearsay, and to allow for extraordinary cases where witnesses are incapable of testifying in the normal court setting, the Court has allowed exceptions to the basic rule, but only where the Court finds the resulting evidence sufficiently "reliable" in the absence of confrontation.

John G. Douglass

See Also
Amendment VI (Compulsory Process Clause)

Suggestions for Further Research
Akhil R. Amar, *Foreward: Sixth Amendment First Principles*, 84 Geo. L.J. 641 (1996)

Margaret A. Berger, *The Deconstitutionalization of the Confrontation Clause: A Proposal for a Prosecutorial Restraint Model*, 76 Minn. L. Rev. 557 (1992)

John G. Douglass, *Beyond Admissibility: Real Confrontation, Virtual Cross-Examination, and the Right to Confront Hearsay*, 67 Geo. Wash. L. Rev. 191 (1999)

John G. Douglass, *Confronting the Reluctant Accomplice*, 101 Colum. L. Rev. 1797 (2001)

Richard D. Friedman, *Confrontation: The Search for Basic Principles*, 68 Geo. L.J. 1011 (1998)

Randolph N. Jonakait, *Restoring the Confrontation Clause to the Sixth Amendment*, 35 UCLA L. Rev. 557 (1988)

Graham C. Lilly, *Notes on the Confrontation Clause and* Ohio v. Roberts, 36 U. Fla. L. Rev. 207 (1984)

Peter Westen, *Confrontation and Compulsory Process: A Unified Theory of Evidence for Criminal Cases*, 91 Harv. L. Rev. 567 (1978)

Significant Cases
Mattox v. United States, 156 U.S. 237 (1895)
Pointer v. Texas, 380 U.S. 400 (1965)
Bruton v. United States, 391 U.S. 123 (1968)
Davis v. Alaska, 415 U.S. 308 (1974)
Ohio v. Roberts, 448 U.S. 56 (1980)
Delaware v. Fensterer, 474 U.S. 15 (1985)
Kentucky v. Stincer, 482 U.S. 730 (1987)
Maryland v. Craig, 497 U.S. 836 (1990)
White v. Illinois, 502 U.S. 346 (1992)
Lilly v. Virginia, 527 U.S. 116 (1999) (concurring opinions)
Crawford v. Washington, 124 S. Ct. 1354 (2004)

Compulsory Process Clause

In all criminal prosecutions, the accused shall enjoy the right to ... have compulsory process for obtaining witnesses in his favor....

(Amendment VI)

~

*F*or centuries, Britons had struggled against the common-law rule that forbade an accused from calling witnesses in his defense in cases of treason or felony, or, even when allowed, not to permit the defense witness to be sworn under oath. The common-law rule survived in the American colonies even after England had abolished it by statute. After the Revolution, however, a number of state constitutions established in one form or another the right to call defense witnesses. When the First Congress considered the Compulsory Process Clause, there was little debate over its value, and it became part of the Sixth Amendment without opposition. The clause assured that the accused in a criminal case was guaranteed not only the right to call witnesses but also a process to obtain witnesses, so that defense evidence could be evaluated by a jury or, in a nonjury criminal case, by a judge. It was, in sum, an essential part of the right of an accused to present a defense.

The Supreme Court had little opportunity to interpret the Compulsory Process Clause and explain its meaning prior to 1967, when the Court ruled in *Washington v. Texas* that the clause was so fundamental to a fair trial that it was part of the Fourteenth Amendment's Due Process Clause and therefore binding on the states as well as on the federal government. *Washington v. Texas* also expanded the reach of the clause by holding unconstitutional a Texas penal statute that permitted the government to offer the testimony of one charged as a principal, accomplice, or accessory, but barred a defendant from calling the same person unless that person had been previously acquitted of the charges. The rationale for the disadvantage imposed upon defendants was that defendants would attempt to exculpate each other, and thus their testimony would be inherently biased and untrustworthy. The Supreme Court had upheld a similar rule in federal trials in *United States v. Reid* (1852), before changing its mind and rejecting the rule for federal trials in *Rosen v. United States* (1918). Although *Rosen* was not a constitutional ruling, the Court adopted its position in *Washington v. Texas* as binding under the Compulsory Process Clause, reasoning that "it could hardly be argued that a State would not violate the clause if it made all defense testimony inadmissible as a matter of procedural law." Furthermore, the Court

declared that "[i]t is difficult to see how the Constitution is any less violated by arbitrary rules that prevent whole categories of defense witnesses from testifying on the basis of *a priori* categories that presume them unworthy of belief."

The Court has had few occasions since to deal with the clause. *Green v. Georgia* (1979) held that it was an error for a state court to exclude a codefendant's confession offered by a defendant in a capital sentencing proceeding where the prosecution had relied on a codefendant's confession at his own trial. In *United States v. Valenzuela-Bernal* (1982), the defendant complained that the government had violated his rights under the clause when it deported potential alien witnesses; the Court ruled that the defendant must show that the testimony of the deported aliens would have been favorable and material. In *Rock v. Arkansas* (1987), the Court held that a per se rule excluding all hypnotically refreshed testimony impermissibly infringed on a criminal defendant's right to testify on her own behalf.

Unlike other Sixth Amendment guarantees, the right to call witnesses is totally at the defendant's initiative. It is not unlimited, but subject to reasonable restrictions. *Taylor v. Illinois* (1988). The ordinary rules of evidence apply to the exercise of the right. The Compulsory Process Clause, for example, does not guarantee a defendant the right to use polygraph evidence in a jurisdiction that forbids such evidence. *United States v. Scheffer* (1998).

Stephen Saltzburg

See Also
Amendment XIV, Section 1 (Due Process Clause)

Suggestions for Further Research
Robert N. Clinton, *The Right to Present a Defense, An Emergent Constitutional Guarantee in Criminal Trials*, 9 IND. L. REV. 713 (1976)

Peter Westen, *The Compulsory Process Clause*, 73 MICH. L. REV. 71 (1974)

Peter Westen, *Compulsory Process II*, 74 MICH. L. REV. 191 (1974)

Peter Westen, *Confrontation and Compulsory Process: A Unified Theory of Evidence for Criminal Cases*, 91 HARV. L. REV. 567 (1978)

Significant Cases

United States v. Reid, 53 U.S. (12 How.) 361 (1852)
Rosen v. United States, 245 U.S. 467 (1918)
Washington v. Texas, 388 U.S. 14 (1967)
Green v. Georgia, 442 U.S. 95 (1979)
United States v. Valenzuela-Bernal, 458 U.S. 858 (1982)
Rock v. Arkansas, 483 U.S. 44 (1987)
Taylor v. Illinois, 484 U.S. 400 (1988)
United States v. Scheffer, 523 U.S. 303 (1998)

Right-to-Counsel Clause

In all criminal prosecutions, the accused shall enjoy the right . . . to have the Assistance of Counsel for his defence.

(AMENDMENT VI)

～

*B*y affording a right to assistance of counsel, the Founders specifically meant to reject the English practice of prohibiting felony defendants from appearing through counsel except upon debatable points of law that arose during trial. After the Glorious Revolution in England (1688), Parliament passed a statute allowing those accused of treason to appear through counsel. The Framers clearly meant to extend the right to be heard through counsel to cases of felony as well as treason.

History does not speak so clearly to the related but distinct question of whether a defendant who is too poor to retain private counsel has the right to a lawyer paid at public expense. Self-representation appears to have been common at the time of the Founding, but representation by professional lawyers became more frequent during the first half of the nineteenth century. Some of the nineteenth-century treatise writers assumed that the legal profession would not permit poverty to deny legal assistance to defendants in serious cases. There were some instances of litigation over the question of whether volunteer lawyers for the poor would have an action for fees against the public authorities. The common practice thus seems to have been that members of the bar would represent indigent criminal defendants, motivated by public spirit, a thirst for trial experience, or the attendant publicity. In some places such lawyers were compensated at public expense.

While there can be no doubt that the Framers valued the right to counsel, their primary purpose lay in removing legal obstacles to representation by lawyers privately retained by defendants who could afford lawyers. Not until 1938 did the Supreme Court hold that the Sixth Amendment required court-appointed counsel for defendants too poor to afford private counsel, or a knowing and intelligent waiver of court-appointed counsel by the accused. *Johnson v. Zerbst* (1938). The Sixth Amendment, however, applied only in federal cases. As late as 1963, several poorer states, all in the South, refused to provide appointed counsel for all indigent felony defendants, many, if not most, of whom were black. Prior to 1963, the Supreme Court had addressed the question of counsel for the indigent accused persons in state cases under the Due Process Clause of the Fourteenth Amendment, rather than under the Sixth Amendment, which deals specifically with the right to counsel. In the state cases, beginning with *Powell v. State of Alabama* in 1932, the Court read due process to require appointed counsel in capital cases, and in felony cases when they presented special needs for legal advice.

The modern law interpreting the Right-to-Counsel Clause really begins with the 1963 decision in *Gideon v. Wainwright*, holding that the Fourteenth Amendment incorporates the right-to-counsel guarantee of the Sixth Amendment, making it applicable in state as well as federal cases. *Gideon* left open at least three important questions. First, when does the right to counsel arise? Second, are there offenses so minor that the government need not provide appointed counsel? Third, how competently must defense counsel perform to satisfy constitutional standards?

In the years since *Gideon*, the Court has held that the right to counsel arises with the institution of formal proceedings by way of indictment, information, complaint, or arraignment. Thus, whatever rights to counsel a suspect enjoys after arrest but before the filing of the charge (a timing decision largely within the control of the authorities) come, not from the Sixth Amendment, but from other sources, such as the *Miranda* rights derived from the Fifth Amendment Self-Incrimination Clause. Once the Sixth Amendment right to counsel has attached, the accused has the right to the presence of counsel during all subsequent critical stages of the case, including the preliminary hearing, pretrial motions, interrogation, plea negotiations, and of course the trial itself. The right to counsel ends with a final judgment of the trial court. The Supreme Court has declared that the right to counsel on appeal arises from the Equal Protection Clause, not the Sixth Amendment.

As to the level of criminal charge that triggers the right to counsel, the courts have never complied with the literal meaning of the Sixth Amendment. In this instance, at least, "all" does not mean "all criminal prosecutions": it means some. Petty offenses have been adjudicated without counsel from the time of the Founding to this day. The traditional understanding of petty offenses included misdemeanors punishable by less than six months in jail. The modern Supreme Court has held that no offense can be deemed petty for purposes of the exception to the right to counsel if the accused does in fact receive a sentence that includes incarceration, howsoever brief.

As for the standard of representation, the Supreme Court in *Strickland v. Washington* (1984) adopted a two-step test for ineffective assistance of counsel claims. To set aside a plea, verdict, or sentence on account of defective lawyering, the defendant must show that defense counsel's performance fell outside the range of professional competence and that counsel's performance prejudiced the defendant so as to call the reliability of the proceedings into question. In the first prong of the test, the courts indulge a presumption of competence; many vital decisions (e.g., whether to accept a plea bargain, whether to call the defendant as a witness) are so problematic that they are classified as unreviewable tactical choices. In the second prong, the burden lies on the defendant to show that, but for counsel's unprofessional errors, there is a fair probability that the results of the proceedings might have been different. Prejudice against the right to effective assistance of counsel is presumed only from the actual or constructive denial of counsel, an actual conflict of interest that impairs counsel's performance, or arbitrary interference by court ruling or statute with counsel's presentation of the defense. Lack of sufficient resources for indigent defense, in and of itself, does not constitute a violation of the Sixth Amendment. That question is left to Congress and the state legislatures to address.

Donald Dripps

Suggestions for Further Research

William M. Beaney, The Right to Counsel in American Courts (1955)

Richard Klein & Robert Spangenberg, The Indigent Defense Crisis (1993)

Wayne R. LaFave, Jerold H. Israel, & Nancy J. King, Criminal Procedure (2d ed. 1999)

Anthony Lewis, Gideon's Trumpet (1964)

Significant Cases

Powell v. State of Alabama, 287 U.S. 45 (1932)

Johnson v. Zerbst, 304 U.S. 458 (1938)

Gideon v. Wainwright, 372 U.S. 335 (1963)

Strickland v. Washington, 466 U.S. 668 (1984)

Alabama v. Shelton, 535 U.S. 654 (2002)

Right to Jury in Civil Cases

In Suits at common law, where the value in controversy shall exceed twenty dollars, the right of trial by jury shall be preserved....

(Amendment VII)

∼

*T*oward the end of the Constitutional Convention, Hugh Williamson of North Carolina noted that "no provision was yet made for juries in civil cases and suggested the necessity of it." Elbridge Gerry agreed, while George Mason further argued that the omission demonstrated that the Constitution needed a Bill of Rights. Nathaniel Gorham responded that the question should be left to Congress because of complexities in determining what kind of civil cases should be given to a jury. A few days later, when Gerry and Pinckney moved to insert "And a trial by jury shall be preserved as usual in civil cases," Gorham argued that there was no usual form, because the structure of civil juries varied among the states. Apparently sensing the difficulty in phrasing the guarantee, the Convention unanimously defeated the motion.

It was a costly oversight, for the omission of a guarantee of civil juries occasioned the greatest opposition to the Constitution in the ratifying conventions, as Alexander Hamilton candidly admitted in *The Federalist* No. 83. Hamilton tried to minimize the differences by arguing that the only difference between the supporters and detractors of the Constitution on this issue was that "the former regard it as a valuable safeguard to liberty; the latter represent it as the very palladium of free government." Mason and Gerry had themselves refused to sign the Constitution, citing the absence of the guarantee among their other concerns. In the ratification debates, the Anti-Federalists argued that the provision in the Constitution for juries in criminal cases necessarily implied their abolition in civil cases. The Anti-Federalists tied this argument to their objections to the power of the Supreme Court in Article III to hear appeals "both as to law and fact," suggesting that the Constitution would effectively abolish juries in the states as well.

In response, the Federalists continued to argue that defining in the Constitution the appropriate cases for civil juries was too difficult a task and that the Congress could be trusted to make provision for civil juries. This was a weak argument, as twelve of the states themselves protected civil juries in their constitutions. Of the six ratifying conventions that proposed amendments to the Constitution, five included a right to a jury in civil cases.

The history of the revolutionary struggle also counted against the Federalists. The colonists had had no objection to trials without juries in traditional admiralty and maritime cases. But when Parliament extended the jurisdiction of the admiralty courts to other cases, the colonists' opposition to England crystallized around the deprivation of their right to trial by jury. In the *Declaration of the Causes of Taking up Arms* (1775), the Second Continental Congress declared: "[S]tatutes have been passed for extending the jurisdiction of courts of Admiralty and Vice-Admiralty beyond their ancient limits; for depriving us of the accustomed and inestimable privilege of trial by jury, in cases affecting both life and property." The complaint was also among the bill of particulars in the Declaration of Independence.

The Seventh Amendment, passed by the First Congress without debate, cured the omission by declaring that the right to a jury trial shall be preserved in common-law cases, thus leaving the traditional distinction between cases at law and those in equity or admiralty, where there normally was no jury. The implied distinction parallels the explicit division of federal judicial authority in Article III to cases (1) in law, (2) in equity, and (3) in admiralty and maritime jurisdiction. The contemporaneously passed Judiciary Act of 1789 similarly provided that "the trial of issues of fact, in the district courts, in all causes except civil causes of admiralty and maritime jurisdiction, shall be by jury." As Justice Joseph Story later explained in *Parsons v. Bedford* (1830): "In a just sense, the amendment then may well be construed to embrace all suits which are not of equity and admiralty jurisdiction, whatever may be the peculiar form which they may assume to settle legal rights."

The Supreme Court has, however, arrived at a more limited interpretation. It applies the amendment's guarantee to the kinds of cases that "existed under the English common law when the amendment was adopted," *Baltimore & Carolina Line v. Redman* (1935), or to newly developed rights that can be analogized to what existed at that time, *Luria v. United States* (1913), *Curtis v. Loether* (1974). Accordingly, in a series of decisions in the second half of the twentieth century, the Supreme Court ruled that the Seventh Amendment guarantees the right to trial by jury in procedurally novel settings, like declaratory judgment actions, *Beacon Theatres v. Westover* (1959), and shareholder derivative suits, *Ross v. Bernhard* (1970). The Court also applied the amendment to cases adjudicating newly created statutory rights, *Curtis v. Loether, Pernell v. Southall Realty* (1974). In addition, the Supreme Court has ruled unanimously that when factually overlapping "legal" and "equitable" claims are joined together in the same action, the Seventh Amendment requires that the former be adjudicated first (by a jury); and that when legal claims triable to a jury are erroneously dismissed, relitigation of the entire action is "essential to vindicating [the plaintiff's] Seventh Amendment rights." *Lytle v. Household Manufacturing, Inc.* (1990).

The right to trial by jury is not constitutionally guaranteed in certain classes of civil cases that are concededly "suits at common law," particularly when "public" or governmental rights are at issue and if one cannot find eighteenth-century precedent for jury participation in those cases. *Atlas Roofing Co. v. Occupational Safety & Health Review Commission* (1977). Thus, Congress can lodge personal and property claims against the United States in non-Article III courts with no jury component. In addition, where practice as it existed in 1791 "provides no clear answer," the rule is that "[o]nly those incidents which are regarded as fundamental, as inherent in and of the essence of the system of trial by jury, are placed beyond the reach of the legislature." *Markman v. Westview Instruments* (1996). In those situations, too, the Seventh Amendment does not restrain congressional choice.

In contrast to the near-universal support for the civil jury trial in the eighteenth and early nineteenth centuries, modern jurists consider civil jury trial neither "implicit in the concept of ordered liberty," *Palko v. State of Connecticut* (1937), nor "fundamental to the American scheme of justice," *Duncan v. Louisiana* (1968). Accordingly, in company with only the Second Amendment and the Grand Jury Clause of the Fifth Amendment, the Seventh Amendment is not "incorporated" against the states; it applies only in the federal courts. In the federal courts, the parties can waive the right, but there is no longer a requirement, as there was in 1791, that civil juries be composed of twelve persons and must reach a unanimous verdict. *Colgrove v. Battin* (1973).

Eric Grant

See Also
Article III, Section 2, Clause 1 (Federal Party)
Article III, Section 2, Clause 2 (Original Jurisdiction)
Amendment VI (Jury Trial)

Suggestions for Further Research
George E. Butler II, *Compensable Liberty: A Historical and Political Model of the Seventh Amendment Public Law Jury*, 1 Notre Dame J.L. Ethics & Pub. Pol'y 595 (1985)

Eric Grant, *A Revolutionary View of the Seventh Amendment and the Just Compensation Clause*, 91 Nw. U. L. Rev. 144 (1996)

Stanton D. Krauss, *The Original Understanding of the Seventh Amendment Right to Jury Trial*, 33 U. Rich. L. Rev. 407 (1999)

1 John Phillip Reid, *Constitutional History of the American Revolution: The Authority of Rights* (1986)

Charles W. Wolfram, *The Constitutional History of the Seventh Amendment*, 57 Minn. L. Rev. 639 (1973)

Significant Cases
Parsons v. Bedford, 28 U.S. (3 Pet.) 433 (1830)
Kohl v. United States, 91 U.S. 367 (1876)
Luria v. United States, 231 U.S. 9 (1913)
Baltimore & Carolina Line v. Redman, 295 U.S. 654 (1935)
Palko v. State of Connecticut, 302 U.S. 319 (1937)
Beacon Theatres v. Westover, 359 U.S. 500 (1959)
Duncan v. Louisiana, 391 U.S. 145 (1968)
Ross v. Bernhard, 396 U.S. 531 (1970)
Colgrove v. Battin, 413 U.S. 149 (1973)
Curtis v. Loether, 415 U.S. 189 (1974)
Pernell v. Southall Realty, 416 U.S. 363 (1974)
Atlas Roofing Co. v. Occupational Safety & Health Review Commission, 430 U.S. 442 (1977)
Tull v. United States, 481 U.S. 412 (1987)

Granfinanciera, S.A. v. Nordberg, 492 U.S. 33 (1989)

Lytle v. Household Manufacturing, Inc., 494 U.S. 545 (1990)

Markman v. Westview Instruments, 517 U.S. 370 (1996)

Monterey v. Del Monte Dunes at Monterey, Ltd., 526 U.S. 687 (1999)

Reexamination Clause

In Suits at common law...no fact tried by a jury, shall be otherwise re-examined in any Court of the United States, than according to the rules of the common law....

(**AMENDMENT VII**)

~

*T*he principle that juries determine questions of fact is a fundamental underpinning of our legal system. The Seventh Amendment was drafted in response to complaints raised during the ratification process that the Constitution failed to protect the institution of the civil jury. The Reexamination Clause, in particular, answered the chorus of objections in the ratifying conventions that the Supreme Court's appellate power "both as to Law and Fact" would effectively abolish the civil jury by allowing the Supreme Court to retry facts on appeal. It is for this reason that Justice Joseph Story characterized the Reexamination Clause as "more important" than the initial phrase of the amendment guaranteeing juries in civil trials. *Parsons v. Bedford* (1830).

The "law and facts" provision in Article III, combined with the lack of express protection for civil juries in the Constitution, caused Anti-Federalists to fear that the right to juries in civil matters would be abolished upon the Constitution's ratification. Both George Mason and Richard Henry Lee of Virginia argued that the Constitution abolished juries in all civil cases. Lee noted: "By Article 3, section 2,...the Supreme Court shall have appellate jurisdiction, both as to law and fact.... By court is

understood a court consisting of judges; and the idea of a jury is excluded."

In *The Federalist* No. 83, Alexander Hamilton denied that the Constitution's silence regarding civil juries amounted to an abolition of civil juries. Reexaminations of facts, he said, would only result in a remand for another jury trial. He declared that under the Constitution, Congress had the power to protect the right to a jury trial in civil cases. Hamilton's disclaimer did not silence the Anti-Federalist demands for constitutional guarantees, and the ratifying conventions of New York, Virginia, Massachusetts, and New Hampshire proposed adding a protection for civil juries in the Constitution. Thus, although the Anti-Federalists were unsuccessful in preventing the ratification of the Constitution, they made it clear that their demand for a right to a civil jury trial would have to be acceded to.

The Seventh Amendment's Reexamination Clause prohibits reviewing courts from reexamining any fact tried by a jury in any manner other than according to the common law. Juries are not required in equitable or admiralty actions. Congress codified the distinction in the Judiciary Act of 1789, prior to the ratification of the Seventh Amendment. Under common law, appellate courts could review judgments only on writ of error, which limited review to questions of law. For example, in *Parsons v. Bedford*, Justice Story held that reviewing courts have no power to grant new trials based on a reexamination of the facts tried by a jury. The court can consider only those facts that "bear upon any question of law arising at the trial," and if there is error, the reviewing court's only option is to grant a new trial. Earlier, while on circuit in *United States v. Wonson* (1812), Story noted that a writ of error allows examination of "general errors of law only," and appellate courts "never can retry the issues already settled by a jury, where the judgment of the inferior court is affirmed." Trial courts could order a new trial for good cause, but reviewing courts could only examine alleged errors of law. Story's opinion encapsulates the traditional meaning of the Reexamination Clause.

The advent of the Federal Rules of Civil Procedure, along with other procedural devices allowing courts to weigh evidence, has cut into the traditional interpretation of the Reexamination Clause. Specifically, procedures such as summary judgment and directed verdicts, which greatly affect the substantive power enjoyed by juries, seriously question the traditional view that appellate courts are only allowed to review questions of law, not fact. Dissenting in *Parklane Hosiery Co. v. Shore* (1979), Justice William H. Rehnquist declared, "[T]o sanction creation of procedural devices which limit the province of the jury to a greater degree than permitted at common law in 1791 is in direct contravention of the Seventh Amendment."

Reflecting this trend, the Supreme Court had, up until recently, consistently held that the allowable amount of damages, including punitive damages, "involves only a question of fact." *St. Louis, Iron Mountain & Southern Ry. Co. v. Craft* (1915); *Barry v. Edmunds* (1886). However, in *Cooper Industries, Inc. v. Leatherman Tool Group, Inc.* (2001), the Court characterized punitive damages as a question of law, permitting an appeals court de novo review of excessive jury verdicts under the Cruel and Unusual Punishment Clause of the Eighth Amendment and therefore outside of the limitations of the Reexamination Clause.

A parallel trend is present in the handling of ordinary or compensable damages. The Court's decision in *Gasperini v. Center for Humanities, Inc.* (1996) specifically rejected the common-law standard of review in place in 1791 and validated review of the jury's fact-finding power by permitting appellate consideration of a jury award on the ground of excessiveness. The Court in *Gasperini* validated the previous practice, in which federal appellate courts had set aside jury verdicts only for "gross error," or if the result "shocked the conscience" or, later, if there was an "abuse of discretion" by the jury. None of these, the Court held, was contrary to the Reexamination Clause. It characterized such actions as "questions of law." In dissent, Justice Antonin Scalia stated, "It is not for us, much less for the Courts of Appeals, to decide that the Seventh Amendment's restriction on federal-court review of jury findings has outlived its usefulness."

Similarly, in *Weisgram v. Marly Co.* (2000), the Supreme Court rejected the argument that a reviewing court's striking of evidence from the record required remand to the lower court to consider whether a new trial was warranted. Instead, the Court found that a federal appellate court can direct the entry of judgment as a matter of law when, after "excis[ing] testimony erroneously admitted, there remains insufficient evidence to support the jury's verdict." The continuing erosion of the jury function exemplified in *Gasperini* and *Weisgram* seems to confirm what the Anti-Federalists sought to avoid and what the Framers of the Seventh Amendment provided against: the purpose of the Reexamination Clause was to insulate jury findings from judicial reexamination.

David F. Forte

See Also
Article III, Section 2, Clause 2 (Appellate Jurisdiction Clause)
Amendment VII (Right to Jury in Civil Cases)

Suggestions for Further Research
Debra Lyn Bassett, *"I Lost at Trial—In the Court of Appeals!": The Expanding Power of the Federal Appellate Courts to Reexamine Facts*, 38 Hous. L. Rev. 1129 (2001)

Ellen E. Sward, *The Seventh Amendment and the Alchemy of Fact and Law*, 33 Seton Hall L. Rev. 573 (2003)

Rachael E. Swartz, *"Everything Depends on How You Draw the Lines": An Alternative Interpretation of the Seventh Amendment*, 6 Seton Hall Const. L.J. 599 (1996)

Patrick Woolley, *Mass Tort Litigation and the Seventh Amendment Reexamination Clause*, 83 Iowa L. Rev. 499 (1998)

Significant Cases
United States v. Wonson, 28 F. Cas. 745 (C.C.D. Mass. 1812) (No. 16,750)
Blunt v. Little, 3 F. Cas. 760 (C.C.D. Mass. 1822) (No. 1578)
Parsons v. Bedford, 28 U.S. (3 Pet.) 433 (1830)
Barry v. Edmunds, 116 U.S. 550 (1886)

Metropolitan Railway Co. v. Moore, 121 U.S. 558 (1887)

Aetna Life Insurance Co. v. Ward, 140 U.S. 76 (1891)

St. Louis, Iron Mountain & Southern Railway Co. v. Craft, 237 U.S. 648 (1915)

United States v. Jefferson Electric Manufacturing Co., 291 U.S. 386 (1934)

Parklane Hosiery Co. v. Shore, 439 U.S. 322 (1979)

Pullman-Standard v. Swint, 456 U.S. 273 (1982)

Gasperini v. Center for Humanities, Inc., 518 U.S. 415 (1996)

Weisgram v. Marley Co., 528 U.S. 440 (2000)

Cooper Industries, Inc. v. Leatherman Tool Group, Inc., 532 U.S. 424 (2001)

Cruel and Unusual Punishment

Excessive bail shall not be required, nor excessive fines imposed, nor cruel and unusual punishment inflicted.

(AMENDMENT VIII)

〜

*T*he text of the Eighth Amendment derives from the 1689 English Bill of Rights, redacted in the Virginia Declaration of Rights and recommended by the Virginia ratifying convention. The English version used the words "bail ought not be required" as opposed to the amendment's "bail shall not be required," the latter reflecting James Madison's insistence that the amendments be legally enforceable and not mere hortatory statements. When considering the amendment, one Member of Congress thought the wording unclear. Nevertheless, Congress approved the language by a strong majority, perhaps because its phrasing had such a solid pedigree.

The Excessive Bail Clause of the 1689 English Bill of Rights was a response to the practice of some judges who set bails high to avoid having to release defendants on writs of habeas corpus (*see* Article I, Section 9, Clause 2). In both English and American practice, the level of bail is determined on a case-by-case basis to ensure the defendant's presence at trial. The court often takes into account the character of the charged offense and the previous behavior of the defendant. The Supreme Court has declared that a bail amount would be "excessive" under the Eighth Amendment if it were "a figure higher than is reasonably calculated" to ensure the defendant's appearance at trial. *Stack v. Boyle* (1951); *see also United States v. Salerno* (1987). Procedurally, the defendant must file a motion for reduction in order to contest a bail as excessive.

The Cruel and Unusual Punishment Clause seems to point to a preexisting right to bail. In fact, absent weighty circumstances, American courts have always presumed that each defendant has a right to liberty pending trial by payment of bail. Nevertheless, the courts have been deferential to legislative exceptions to the right to bail. *Carlson v. Landon* (1952). In British practice, most serious crimes were nonbailable. *See Hunt v. Roth* (C.A. Neb. 1981). In America, many colonial charters and state constitutions, as well as the Northwest Ordinance of 1787 and the Judiciary Act of 1789, guaranteed a right to bail but made exception for capital offenses. More recently, the Supreme Court has approved a state statute allowing pretrial detention of some juveniles, *Schall v. Martin* (1984). In *United States v. Salerno* (1987), the Court upheld the pretrial detention provisions in the Bail Reform Act of 1984 that applied to persons who were arrested for serious crimes and who might pose a danger to the community. Based on the Bail Reform Act, a federal district court has upheld detention without bail of persons with alleged terrorist connections. *United States v. Goba* (2003).

Scholars have debated the extent to which the clause restricts Congress as well as the judiciary. In *Salerno*, the Court declared that the government may pursue particular "compelling interests through regulation of pre-trial release," but it expressly left open the question of "whether the Cruel and Unusual Punishment Clause speaks at all to Congress's power to define the classes of criminal arrestees who shall be admitted to bail." The Supreme Court has not authoritatively applied the prohibitions on excessive bail to the states through the Due

Process Clause of the Fourteenth Amendment, although in *Schilb v. Kuebel* (1971), Justice Harry Blackmun for the majority noted that the Court has "assumed" that the prohibition has been incorporated.

The English Bill of Rights of 1689 also sought to undo the practice of the judges who, favoring the Stuarts, levied fines against the king's enemies, thus allowing them to be jailed for nonpayment. At the time of the drafting of the Eighth Amendment, a majority of states included the prohibition in their constitutions, and the provision induced no debate on the floor of Congress.

In *United States v. Bajakajian* (1998), the Supreme Court found little in the history of the clause to determine what would constitute an "excessive" fine. It declared that, within the context of judicial deference to the legislature's power to set punishments, a fine would not offend the Eighth Amendment unless it were "grossly disproportional to the gravity of a defendant's offense." Applying the standard, the Court, through Justice Clarence Thomas, found that a $357,144 civil forfeiture penalty for failing to report a currency transfer of more than $10,000 was grossly disproportionate to the fine for conviction, which would have been only $5,000. In dissent, Justice Anthony Kennedy found the scale of forfeiture quite common and would have deferred to Congress's determination of the need for and the appropriateness of the forfeiture.

Although the Court had held in *Austin v. United States* (1993) that a *civil forfeiture* penalty was included within the excessive fines provision, it had also declared that a *punitive damage* award in a purely civil case is not covered by the excessive fines clause, holding that "there must be a payment to a sovereign as punishment for some offense" for the clause to apply. *Browning-Ferris Industries v. Kelco Disposal, Inc.* (1989). The Court, in some highly contested decisions, now reviews punitive damage awards under the Due Process Clause of the Fourteenth Amendment. *See, e.g., BMW of North America v. Gore* (1996).

There has been much debate over the categories of punishments covered by the Cruel and Unusual Punishment Clause. Possible categories at issue are (1) punishments not prescribed by the legislature, (2) torturous punishments, and (3) disproportionate and excessive punishments. Although the issue is disputed, the weight of scholarly opinion indicates that the ban on cruel and unusual punishment in the 1689 English Bill of Rights applied only to punishments not authorized by Parliament. The American colonial understanding, on the other hand, was that the ban applied to torturous punishments such as pillorying, disemboweling, decapitation, and drawing and quartering. Inasmuch as such punishments were virtually absent in colonial America, Justice Joseph Story in his *Commentaries on the Constitution of the United States* believed that "[t]he provision would seem wholly unnecessary in a free government, since it is scarcely possible, that any department of such government should authorize, or justify such atrocious conduct."

Early Supreme Court interpretations subscribed to the view that the clause only curbed tortuous punishments as defined at the time of the amendment's ratification. *See Pervear v. Commonwealth* (1866). The Court subsequently upheld execution by public shooting, *Wilkerson v. Utah* (1878), and electrocution, *In re Kemmler* (1890). The third possible meaning of the clause, that is, prohibiting disproportionate or excessive punishments, was raised in dissent in *O'Neil v. Vermont* (1892). The Court adopted the dissent's view in *Weems v. United States* (1910) and reconfirmed that holding in *Louisiana ex rel. Francis v. Resweber* (1947). In *Trop v. Dulles* (1954), Chief Justice Earl Warren rejected reliance on the original understanding as the appropriate standard in favor of the "evolving standards of decency that mark the progress of a maturing society." Since that time, the Supreme Court's views on the amendment have been confused, and the current Court appears divided and unable to agree on a common interpretive standard.

In *Furman v. Georgia* (1972), the Court held in a 5–4 decision that the Eighth Amendment banned the arbitrary infliction of the death penalty, requiring states to rewrite their laws to give judges and juries standards according to which the penalty could be imposed. In the majority, three Justices opined that the intent of the clause was to ban arbitrary punishments. Two other Justices rejected an originalist approach to reach the same result. In the main, the majority believed that the penalty had been applied in a discriminatory or arbitrary manner. In dissent, Chief Justice Warren E. Burger declared that the Framers meant to ban only punishments not prescribed by law as well as tortuous punishments. In *Gregg v. Georgia* (1976), the Court held that the death penalty was not a per se violation of the Eighth Amendment. The majority opinion agreed with Chief Justice Burger's historical view of the original intent of the Eighth Amendment but nonetheless adopted Chief Justice Warren's "evolving standards of decency" standard. The decision requires separate phases in a trial for the determination of guilt and the imposition of the death sentence. In *Woodson v. North Carolina* (1976), the Court held that any law leaving the jury without discretion was unconstitutional.

The meandering history of Supreme Court opinions continued. In *Solem v. Helm* (1983), Justice Lewis F. Powell's majority opinion held that the ban on disproportionate punishments was part of the 1689 English Bill of Rights, even if the Framers' view was different. *Harmelin v. Michigan* (1991), however, reversed *Solem*, and Chief Justice Rehnquist rejected Justice Powell's analysis. Chief Justice Rehnquist and Justice Scalia reiterated that the primary purpose of the amendment was to void judge-imposed punishments that were not prescribed in the law. Concurring, Justice Kennedy argued that disproportionality is forbidden by the amendment. Justice Kennedy's views were accepted by the majority in *Atkins v. Virginia* (2001) in an opinion written by Justice John Paul Stevens. Nonetheless, Stevens refused to base his decision on the original meaning and relied on Warren's "evolving standards of decency" to hold that it is cruel and unusual to execute the mentally ill. Generally speaking, there is now a proportionality requirement at least in the Court's death-penalty cases.

In back-to-back cases, *Ewing v. California* (2003) and *Lockyer v. Andrade* (2003), the Court continued to advocate Justice Kennedy's interpretation of the Eighth Amendment but held that the life sentence in California's three-strikes law did not offend the principle of proportionality. Justice Scalia, joined by Justice Thomas, concurred on the ground that the clause lacks a proportionality requirement.

Over the past few decades, the Court has held that rape may not be punished by death, *Coker v. Georgia* (1977), because the state should not be able to take away the perpetrator's life if he did not take away the life of his victim. In line with this argument, the Court later held that only major accomplices in a felony murder conviction may be sentenced to death. *Enmund v. Florida* (1982), *Tison v. Arizona* (1987). The Court has also held that Congress may not take away a person's citizenship for desertion from the army. *Trop v. Dulles* (1958). Nor are inhumane prison conditions permissible under the Eighth Amendment, *Estelle v. Gamble* (1976), *Rhodes v. Chapman* (1981). Further, the amendment forbids serious or malicious harm caused by prison officials. *Wilson v. Seiter* (1991), *Hudson v. McMillian* (1992). Nor may a state execute a person under eighteen years of age, *Roper v. Simmons* (2005). A state may not punish a person for a "status offense," such as being a drug addict, *Robinson v. California* (1962), though the amendment does not, of course, bar prosecution for the buying and selling of drugs. The amendment, however, does not prohibit corporal punishment in public schools, *Ingraham v. Wright* (1977). In addition, a mandatory life sentence after three convictions is constitutional. *Rummel v. Estelle* (1980). In *Gherebi v. Bush* (2003), the federal appeals court did not reach the merits of the assertion by plaintiffs that the detention of persons at Guantanamo Bay was a violation of the Cruel and Unusual Punishment Clause.

David F. Forte

See Also

Suggestions for Further Research

William F. Duker, *The Right to Bail: A Historical Inquiry*, 42 ALA. L. REV. 33 (1977)

Barry L. Johnson, *Purging the Cruel and Unusual: The Autonomous Excessive Fines Clause and Desert-Based Constitutional Limits on Forfeiture after United States v. Bajakajian*, 2000 U. ILL. L. REV. 461 (2000)

Calvin R. Massey, *The Excessive Fines Clause and Punitive Damages: Some Lessons from History*, 40 VAND. L. REV. 1233 (1987)

Hermine Herta Meyer, *Constitutionality of Pretrial Detention*, 60 GEO. L.J. 1139 (1972)

Significant Cases

Pervear v. Commonwealth, 72 U.S. 475 (1866)
Wilkerson v. Utah, 99 U.S. 130 (1878)
In re Kemmler, 136 U.S. 436 (1890)
O'Neil v. Vermont, 144 U.S. 323 (1892)
Weems v. United States, 217 U.S. 349 (1910)
Louisiana *ex rel.* Francis v. Resweber, 329 U.S. 459 (1947)
Stack v. Boyle, 342 U.S. 1 (1951)
Carlson v. Landon, 342 U.S. 524 (1952)
Trop v. Dulles, 356 U.S. 86 (1958)
Robinson v. California, 370 U.S. 660 (1962)
Schilb v. Kuebel, 404 U.S. 357 (1971)
Furman v. Georgia, 408 U.S. 238 (1972)
Estelle v. Gamble, 429 U.S. 97 (1976)
Gregg v. Georgia, 428 U.S. 153 (1976)
Woodson v. North Carolina, 428 U.S. 280 (1976)
Coker v. Georgia, 433 U.S. 584 (1977)
Ingraham v. Wright, 430 U.S. 651 (1977)
Lockett v. Ohio, 438 U.S. 586 (1978)
Rummel v. Estelle, 445 U.S. 263 (1980)
Hunt v. Roth, 648 F.2d 1148 (1981)
Rhodes v. Chapman, 452 U.S. 337 (1981)
Enmund v. Florida, 458 U.S. 782 (1982)
Solem v. Helm, 463 U.S. 277 (1983)
Schall v. Martin, 467 U.S. 253 (1984)
Ford v. Wainwright, 477 U.S. 399 (1986)
Tison v. Arizona, 481 U.S. 137 (1987)
United States v. Salerno, 481 U.S. 739 (1987)
Thompson v. Oklahoma, 487 U.S. 815 (1988)
Browning-Ferris Industries v. Kelco Disposal, Inc., 492 U.S. 257 (1989)
Penry v. Lynaugh, 492 U.S. 302 (1989)
Stanford v. Kentucky, 492 U.S. 361 (1989)
Harmelin v. Michigan, 501 U.S. 957 (1991)

Wilson v. Seiter, 501 U.S. 294 (1991)
Hudson v. McMillian, 503 U.S. 1 (1992)
Austin v. United States, 509 U.S. 602 (1993)
BMW of North America, Inc. v. Gore, 517 U.S. 559 (1996)
United States v. Bajakajian, 524 U.S. 321 (1998)
Atkins v. Virginia, 533 U.S. 976 (2001)
Ewing v. California, 538 U.S. 11 (2003)
Lockyer v. Andrade, 538 U.S. 63 (2003)
Gherebi v. Bush, 352 F.3d 1278 (9th Cir. 2003)
United States v. Goba, 240 F. Supp. 2d 242 (W.D.N.Y. 2003)
Roper v. Simmons, 125 S. Ct. 1183 (2005)

Rights Retained by the People

The enumeration in the Constitution, of certain rights, shall not be construed to deny or disparage others retained by the people.

(AMENDMENT IX)

~

*O*ver the past few decades, a number of scholars and Justices, sometimes called noninterpretivists, have defined the "rights retained by the people" of the Ninth Amendment by various formulas such as "the traditions of the people," "ordered liberty," social justice, or current notions of autonomy. Originalists take a different perspective. Yet, even among originalists, there are differences in interpretation. At present there are three very different originalist theories of the Ninth Amendment's place in the constitutional structure.

The view traditionally held among most originalist scholars, as well as jurists and judges at least until recently, distinguishes between the purposes and functions of the Ninth and the Tenth Amendments, finding them complementary but not redundant.

The Tenth Amendment—reserving to the states or to the people of the several states the powers not delegated to the United States government—was designed to confirm the separate juridical competency of the respective states in relation to a federal government of limited powers. The Framers of the amendment drew some of its language from Article II of the Articles of Confederation, though they carefully retained legislative scope for congressional power under the Necessary and Proper Clause. *McCulloch v. Maryland* (1819).

According to the traditional view, the Ninth Amendment was written to accomplish a different set of objectives: (1) to prevent the application of the statutory rule of interpretation, *inclusio unius est exclusio alterius* (the inclusion of one thing necessarily excludes all others); (2) to permit the Federalists to save face by affirming the argument they had made against the necessity of a bill of rights; and (3) to confirm the republican principles, espoused by Federalists and Anti-Federalists alike, that the people retain their communal right of self-governance.

A well-known rule of interpretation concerned the Framers. During the ratifying conventions, many Anti-Federalists demanded a bill of rights. In answer, the defenders of the Constitution asserted that a bill of rights was not only unnecessary, but also dangerous. At the North Carolina ratifying convention, James Iredell (later Justice of the Supreme Court) declared:

> If we had formed a general legislature, with undefined powers, a bill of rights would not only have been proper, but necessary; and it would have then operated as an exception to the legislative authority in such particulars. It has this effect in respect to some of the American constitutions, where the powers of legislation are general. But where they are powers of a particular nature, and expressly defined, as in the case of the federal Constitution before us, I think, for the reasons I have given, a bill of rights is not only unnecessary, but would be absurd and dangerous.

In *The Federalist* No. 84, Alexander Hamilton asserted that a bill of rights would "contain various exceptions to powers which are not granted" and that this "would afford a colourable pretext to claim more than were granted." James Wilson had declared: "If we attempt an enumeration, every thing that is not enumerated is presumed to be given. The consequence is, that an imperfect enumeration would throw all implied power into the scale of the government, and the rights of the people would be rendered incomplete." When James Madison introduced his resolutions for the bill of rights to the House, including what would become the Ninth Amendment, he said:

> It has been objected also against a bill of rights, that, by enumerating particular exceptions to the grant of power, it would disparage those rights which were not placed in that enumeration; and it might follow by implication, that those rights which were not singled out, were intended to be assigned into the hands of the General Government, and were consequently insecure. This is one of the most plausible arguments I have ever heard against the admission of a bill of rights into this system; but, I conceive, that it may be guarded against.

Madison was, in other words, guarding against the well-understood rule of *inclusio unius est exclusio alterius*, whereby the very listing of certain rights as immune from congressional regulation would necessarily imply a grant of general legislative power in Congress to legislate over all others.

Madison's proposed amendment, then, was an attempt to avoid the result feared by James Wilson, who contended that a bill of rights "would imply that whatever is not expressed was given, which is not the principle of the proposed Constitution." That Wilson believed that the people's fundamental rights were secured by the Constitution's grant of limited, enumerated powers, is powerfully illustrated by his frank admission that a freedom of the press guarantee would have been essential had Congress been granted the power to regulate literary publications. Indeed, Wilson concluded that a free press guarantee would be essential in the District of Columbia, where the power of legislation would be "general," rather than limited and enumerated.

When the Virginia assembly debated the proposed amendment, Edmund Randolph wondered at the phrasing of the Ninth Amendment. He stated that he would rather have "a provision against extending the powers of Congress" than one giving "protection to rights reducible to no definitive certainty." In a letter to George Washington, Madison wrote that he thought Randolph's proposed distinction between preventing unenumerated powers and securing unenumerated rights was "altogether fanciful." He went on: "If a line can be drawn between the powers granted and the rights retained, it would seem to be the same thing, whether the latter be secured by declaring that they shall not be abridged, or that the former shall not be extended."

An additional, and directly related, purpose of the Ninth Amendment was to provide cover for the Federalists' most embarrassing gaffe during the ratification debates. As noted above, the Federalists had argued that the danger of a bill of rights was that by listing certain rights, it would change Congress into a legislature with general legislative powers, permitting it to rule on anything and everything not specifically prohibited to it. The Anti-Federalists responded that some prohibitions, such as the right of habeas corpus and trial by jury in criminal cases, had already been included. The Federalists had no credible response and were forced to accede to the demand for a bill of rights. But when it came time to draft the amendments, they crafted the Ninth to legitimate the argument they had made all along: the listing of certain rights does not give Congress the authority to legislate over every subject not listed.

Finally, according to the traditional view, the amendment confirmed the republican nature of the Constitution and the federal government. The "residual rights" retained by the people were not a set of particularized rights that somehow escaped the listing of the Bill of Rights. Rather, they were rights that eighteenth-century Americans thought of as inalienable, natural, communal, and political. Residual rights included the right held most dear by all segments of American opinion from James Otis to George Wash-

ington and beyond: the right of self-government. In sum, the Ninth Amendment protected the very liberty for which the Revolution was fought. Otherwise it could plausibly be argued that the listing of a few traditional rights was all the people possessed, and that by ratifying the Constitution, they had thereby given everything else over to the government.

The scholars affirming the traditional view hold that the Ninth Amendment was written by Federalists to accomplish Federalist aims: to legitimize the interpretive arguments they had made during the ratification debates and to affirm their belief, shared by the Anti-Federalists, in the sovereign authority of the people. The traditionalists believe that some modern conceptions that regard "rights retained by the people" as an unenumerated list of particular rights judicially discoverable and enforceable is an anachronistic projection of modern theories of rights, or worse, of political policies, into the text of the Ninth Amendment. Rather, in their view, the Ninth Amendment simply reinforces the integrity of the constitutional structure and the underlying sovereign authority of the people. The amendment provides no independent basis for judicial enforcement.

There is, however, a very different perception of the Ninth Amendment among some modern scholars. Generally of a libertarian point of view, this group of originalists, such as Randy Barnett, have argued that the Ninth Amendment does indeed point to a set of judicially enforceable unenumerated rights, often calling them "natural rights," rights that no government can legitimately deny. They argue that the Framers intended that such rights be protected, and they point out that the amendment has only become relevant recently because of its application to the states through the Fourteenth Amendment and because of the great expansion of government intrusion at all levels into the lives of individuals.

These scholars point to the acknowledged fact that, although the Constitution limited Congress to a set of enumerated powers, the means available to Congress, through the Necessary and Proper Clause, could permit it to trench upon the rights of the people. Madison, in particular, saw the danger, and it was one of the main reasons he changed his mind and vigorously pressed for a bill of rights in the First Congress. Madison placed the text of what would be the Ninth Amendment at the end of the list of specific rights in order to demonstrate that those rights were but a partial listing of all the rights retained by the people against governmental infringement. In the same letter (quoted earlier) from Madison to Washington, which the traditionalists believe supports their view, Barnett asserts that Madison was *distinguishing* between the mechanisms of limiting powers and of securing rights to the same end. Barnett contends that the same understanding was repeated in the work of an early interpreter of the Constitution, St. George Tucker.

This originalist interpretation of the Ninth Amendment differs from another latitudinarian view espoused by modern noninterpretivists who do not limit their understanding of "rights retained by the people" to the conceptions of the Framers. On the contrary, libertarian originalist proponents of natural rights do not believe in an "evolving Constitution," but in one that has the same force today as it did in 1791.

The originalist libertarians also reject that idea that the "rights retained by the people" are not judicially enforceable, for that would leave Congress or the state legislatures in the position of defining the extent of those rights. The more principled strategy would be for the Court to assume its appropriate position in enforcing all of the Bill of Rights, including the Ninth Amendment, by historical inquiry as to what those liberties were that the Framers sought to ensure. Some libertarian originalists assert that the "liberty" so protected would include economic or contractual rights, which the Court once enforced, but no longer does.

Lastly, a new, third version of the meaning of the Ninth Amendment has surfaced. In reviewing the Ninth Amendment's history, Kurt Lash finds that Madison drafted it in specific response to a number of state ratifying conventions' demands for a protection against construing the new federal government's delegated powers too broadly. Throughout the ratification debates, the consistent Anti-Federalist plaint

from writers such as Brutus and the Federal Farmer was that there were two enormous holes in the Federalists' assurance of the limited nature of federal power: the Necessary and Proper Clause and the Supreme Court. The former allowed Congress to invade areas left to the states in furtherance of executing its delegated powers. The latter allowed an organ of the federal government, the Supreme Court, to construe Congress's delegated powers as broadly as possible.

Many states, including Virginia, drafted resolutions for a bill of rights that sought to correct those two deficiencies. In response, Madison and the Congress drafted the Tenth Amendment to affirm that the states retained all powers not delegated to the federal government. But the Tenth Amendment would be ineffective if the Congress and the Court construed the federal government's delegated powers broadly enough to undo residual state authority. Consequently, the Ninth Amendment was drafted to plug that hole: it mandates that the delegated powers of Congress not be given a latitudinarian interpretation to the prejudice of the states.

Most recent scholarly interpretations of the Ninth Amendment dwell on the "rights retained by the people" language. The key words, however, are "shall not be construed." Following the urgings of the Virginia ratifying convention, Madison's draft of what would become the Ninth Amendment read:

> The exceptions, here or elsewhere in the constitution, made in favor of particular rights, shall not be construed as to diminish the just importance of other rights retained by the people, or as to enlarge the powers delegated by the constitution; but either as actual limitations of such powers, or as inserted merely for greater caution.

The Select Committee distilled Madison's language to the text that was sent to the states for ratification:

> The enumeration in this constitution of certain rights shall not be construed to

deny or disparage others retained by the people.

In the Virginia House of Representatives, Edmund Randolph objected to the new phrasing and preferred wording that would have limited "extending the powers of Congress" rather than protecting rights "retained by the people." But Madison saw no difference in the effect of each phrase and thus affirmed that the reason for the Ninth Amendment was not to expand the power of the Court to find new rights, but rather to restrict the ability of the Court to expand the legislative powers of Congress. Madison continued to maintain that that was the central meaning of the Ninth Amendment throughout his life, and his interpretation was seconded by most commentators of the time.

The courts have not had much occasion to construe the Ninth Amendment, but it seems clear that from the time of its ratification until the New Deal, the Ninth Amendment was understood as a principle limiting the construction of federal power to the detriment of the states. Nevertheless, it was not clear how much bite the Ninth Amendment's interpretive rule had. In some important cases, such as *McCulloch v. Maryland* (1819), the Court ignored the Ninth Amendment altogether. And in the *Legal Tender Cases* (1871), the Court openly declared that the limited nature of the Bill of Rights demonstrated that Congress had unenumerated powers, a position directly at odds with what every commentator affirms the Ninth Amendment was at the very least designed to prevent.

After 1937, the Supreme Court abandoned the effort to keep Congress within the bounds of its delegated powers, and even as a background principle protecting the traditional powers of the states and the people of the states, the Ninth Amendment fell into desuetude. In 1965, however, in *Griswold v. Connecticut*, several Justices of the Court revived the amendment, not in its traditional sense, but rather as a source for an "unenumerated rights" doctrine. The current judicial view of the Ninth Amendment is in some ways closer to the libertarian interpretation than to the traditional view, as when the Court protects the right to an abor-

tion or to same-sex relations under an "autonomy" rationale, *Planned Parenthood of Southeastern Pennsylvania v. Casey* (1992), *Lawrence v. Texas* (2003), even though the Court has not enforced the economic rights that libertarians believe the Ninth Amendment was designed originally to protect.

Opposing the use of the Ninth Amendment as an invitation for the Court to find new rights, a number of Justices, such as Justice Antonin Scalia, adhere to the traditional interpretation, reading the Ninth Amendment as designed to prevent the expansion of federal power seemingly implied by the listing of prohibitions within the Bill of Rights.

Thomas McAffee

See Also

Article I, Section 8, Clause 18 (Necessary and Proper Clause)

Article VI, Clause 2 (Supremacy Clause)

Amendment X (Reserved Powers of the States)

Suggestions for Further Research

Randy E. Barnett, Restoring the Lost Constitution: The Presumption of Liberty (2004)

Randy E. Barnett, The Rights Retained by the People: The History and Meaning of the Ninth Amendment (1989)

Raoul Berger, *The Ninth Amendment*, 66 Cornell L. Rev. 1 (1980)

Kurt T. Lash, *The Lost Jurisprudence of the Ninth Amendment*, 83 Tex. L. Rev. 597 (2005)

Kurt T. Lash, *The Lost Original Meaning of the Ninth Amendment*, 83 Tex. L. Rev. 331 (2004)

Calvin R. Massey, Silent Rights: The Ninth Amendment and the Constitution's Unenumerated Rights (1995)

Thomas B. McAffee, Inherent Rights, the Written Constitution, and Popular Sovereignty: The Founders' Understanding (2000)

Thomas B. McAffee, *The Original Meaning of the Ninth Amendment*, 90 Colum. L. Rev. 1215 (1990)

Thomas B. McAffee, *A Critical Guide to the Ninth Amendment*, 69 Temp. L. Rev. 61 (1996)

Susanna Sherry, *The Founders' Unwritten Constitution*, 54 U. Chi. L. Rev. 1127 (1987)

John C. Yoo, *Our Declaratory Ninth Amendment*, 42
　　EMORY L.J. 967 (1993)

Significant Cases

McCulloch v. Maryland, 17 U.S. (4 Wheat.) 316 (1819)
Houston v. Moore, 18 U.S. (5 Wheat.) 1 (1820)
Legal Tender Cases, 79 U.S. (12 Wall.) 457 (1871)
Griswold v. Connecticut, 381 U.S. 479 (1965)
Planned Parenthood of Southeastern Pennsylvania v.
　　Casey, 505 U.S. 833 (1992)
Lawrence v. Texas, 539 U.S. 558 (2003)

Reserved Powers of the States

**The powers not delegated to the
United States by the Constitution,
nor prohibited by it to the States,
are reserved to the States respectively, or to the people.**

（**AMENDMENT X**）

～

*T*he Tenth Amendment expresses the principle that undergirds the entire plan of the original Constitution: the national government possesses only those powers delegated to it. The
Framers of the Tenth Amendment had two purposes in mind when they drafted it. The first was
a necessary rule of construction. The second
was to reaffirm the nature of the federal system.

Because the Constitution created a government of limited and enumerated powers, the
Framers initially believed that a bill of rights was
not only unnecessary, but also potentially dangerous. State constitutions recognized a general
legislative power in the state governments;
hence, limits in the form of state bills of rights
were necessary to guard individual rights
against the excess of governmental power. The
Constitution, however, conferred only the limited powers that were listed or enumerated in
the federal Constitution. Because the *federal*
government could not reach objects not granted to it, the Federalists originally argued, there
was no need for a *federal* bill of rights. Further,
the Federalists insisted that, under the normal

rules of statutory construction, by forbidding
the government from acting in certain areas, a
bill of rights necessarily implied that the government could act in all other areas not forbidden to it. That would change the federal government from one of limited powers to one, like
the states, of general legislative powers.

The Federalists relented and passed the Bill
of Rights in the First Congress only after making certain that no such implication could arise
from the prohibitions of the Bill of Rights.
Hence, the Tenth Amendment—a rule of construction that warns against interpreting the
other amendments in the Bill of Rights to imply
powers in the national government that were
not granted by the original document.

That interpretative rule was vital because
some of the provisions of the Bill of Rights purport to limit federal powers that are not actually granted by the original Constitution and thus
might give rise to a (faulty) inference that the
Bill of Rights implied the existence of such powers. The First Amendment, for instance, states
that "Congress shall make no law...abridging
the freedom of speech, or of the press." Did that
mean that the original Constitution had therefore granted Congress power to abridge those
freedoms? The Federalists did not think so,
which is why they initially opposed inclusion of
a bill of rights. As Alexander Hamilton observed
of the unamended constitutional text in *The
Federalist* No. 84: "Here, in strictness, the people surrender nothing; and as they retain everything they have no need for particular reservations.... Why, for instance, should it be said
that the liberty of the press shall not be
restrained, when no power is given by which
restrictions may be imposed?" Numerous other
important figures made similar statements during the ratification debates. Obviously, the
nation chose to include the Bill of Rights, but
only with the Tenth Amendment as a bulwark
against implying any alteration in the original
scheme of enumerated powers. If Congress was
not originally delegated power to regulate
speech or the press, no such power is granted or
implied by adoption of the Bill of Rights.

Despite the Framers' concerns and the clear
text of the Tenth Amendment, the Supreme

Court indulged precisely this form of reasoning. In the *Legal Tender Cases* in 1871, declining to locate the power to issue paper money in any enumerated power, the Court wrote:

And, that important powers were understood by the people who adopted the Constitution to have been created by it, powers not enumerated, and not included incidentally in any one of those enumerated, is shown by the amendments.... They tend plainly to show that, in the judgment of those who adopted the Constitution, there were powers created by it, neither expressly specified nor deducible from any one specified power, or ancillary to it alone, but which grew out of the aggregate of powers conferred upon the government, or out of the sovereignty instituted. Most of these amendments are denials of power which had not been expressly granted, and which cannot be said to have been necessary and proper for carrying into execution any other powers. Such, for example, is the prohibition of any laws respecting the establishment of religion, prohibiting the free exercise thereof, or abridging the freedom of speech or of the press.

This is the precisely the kind of reasoning that the Tenth Amendment was designed to prohibit.

While providing a rule of construction for the relationship between the Bill of Rights and the scheme of enumerated powers, the Tenth Amendment also affirms the Constitution's basic scheme of defining the relationship between the national and state governments. The Founders were wary of centralized government. At the same time, the failure of the Articles of Confederation revealed the necessity of vesting some authority independent of the states in a national government. The Constitution therefore created a novel system of mixed sovereignty. Each government possessed direct authority over citizens: the states generally over their citizens, and the federal government under its assigned powers. In addition, the states qua states were made a constituency within the national government's structure. The state legislatures chose Senators, determined how presidential electors should be chosen, and defined who would be eligible to vote for Members of the House of Representatives. As noted in *The Federalist* No. 39, the new government was "in strictness, neither a national nor a federal Constitution, but a composition of both." Critical to this mixed system was the scheme of enumerated federal powers, which allows the federal government to operate only within defined spheres of jurisdiction where it is acknowledged to be supreme.

As James Madison wrote in *The Federalist* No. 45:

The powers delegated by the proposed Constitution to the Federal Government are few and defined. Those which are to remain in the State Governments are numerous and indefinite. The former will be exercised principally on external objects, as war, peace negotiation, and foreign commerce;...The powers reserved to the several states will extend to all the objects, which, in the ordinary course of affairs, concern the lives, liberties and properties of the people, and the internal order, improvement, and prosperity of the state.

Chief Justice John Marshall wrote in *Marbury v. Madison* (1803), "the powers of the [national] legislature are defined, and limited; and that those limits may not be mistaken or forgotten, the constitution is written." Alexander Hamilton, urging ratification in New York, recognized in *The Federalist* No. 33 that a congressional act beyond its enumerated powers is "merely [an] act of usurpation" which "deserves to be treated as such." The Tenth Amendment memorialized this constitutional solution of carefully enumerated, and thus limited, federal powers.

The Tenth Amendment had limited judicial application in the nation's first half century. No decision turned upon it, and in *McCulloch v. Maryland* (1819), Chief Justice Marshall declined an invitation to use it as a vehicle for narrowly construing federal powers. In the middle of the nineteenth century, the Tenth Amendment was connected to the later rejected states' rights doctrine of "dual federalism," which maintained that the national and state governments were "separate and distinct sovereignties, acting separately and independently of each other, within their respective spheres." *Tarble's Case* (1872). In contrast, the Framers' conception of the government was not one of "distinct sovereignties," but rather of a mixed sovereignty in which states were an integral and vital part. Beginning with the New Deal Court, the Supreme Court has countenanced an expansion of federal powers far beyond the expectations of those who framed and ratified the Constitution. The extent to which those developments are consistent with the Constitution depends on the construction of the various enumerated powers. Because the Tenth Amendment is a textual reaffirmation of the scheme of enumerated powers, the modern expansion of the federal government's role in national life has shaped, and perhaps altered, the role of the Tenth Amendment in modern jurisprudence.

Modern Supreme Court decisions recognize few limits to the scope of Congress's enumerated powers. Under current law, Congress may regulate, among other things, manufacturing, agriculture, labor relations, and many other purely intrastate activities and transactions. Indeed, in one case the Supreme Court upheld the power of Congress to regulate a single farmer's production of wheat intended for consumption at his own table. *Wickard v. Filburn* (1942). That expansion has generated federal–state conflicts that were not contemplated by the Founding generation, such as federal regulation of state-government employment relations, federal use of state officials to enforce federal regulatory regimes, direct federal commands to state agencies or legislatures, and extensive control of state policy through conditions on federal spending for states. These conflicts call for interpretation of the relevant grants of federal power, most significantly the Commerce Clause, the Spending Clause, and the Necessary and Proper Clause (*see* Article I, Section 8). If

the Constitution grants such power to Congress, the Tenth Amendment's terms are satisfied; if it does not, the Tenth Amendment is violated. That is the meaning of the oft-repeated statement of Chief Justice Harlan F. Stone in *United States v. Darby* (1941) that the Tenth Amendment is "but a truism that all is retained which has not been surrendered."

In *National League of Cities v. Usery* (1976), however, the Supreme Court indicated that the Tenth Amendment carries some substantive protection of the states. In that case, the Court invoked the Tenth Amendment to prevent application of the Fair Labor Standards Act to state employees. Justice William H. Rehnquist's opinion barred the federal government from transgressing upon the "functions essential to [a state's] separate and independent existence," activities taken as state qua state, which he regarded as protected by the Tenth Amendment's reservation of powers to the states. *National League of Cities* overruled *Maryland v. Wirtz* (1968), an earlier case in which Justice William O. Douglas, joined by Justice Potter Stewart, had dissented because "what is done here is nonetheless such a serious invasion of state sovereignty protected by the Tenth Amendment that it is in my view not consistent with our constitutional federalism."

The Court, in *National League of Cities*, embraced Justice William O. Douglas's earlier dissent, but nine years later, in *Garcia v. San Antonio Metropolitan Transit Authority* (1985), the Court overruled *National League of Cities*. The language and reasoning of *Garcia* led many observers to think that the federal judiciary would no longer entertain federalism challenges to congressional exercises of power and that the states' participation in the national political process would be their only protection against federal encroachments.

In recent years, that perception has changed somewhat, as the Supreme Court has revived the Tenth Amendment to enforce discrete limits on congressional attempts to extend enumerated powers to state operations. The Rehnquist Court, for example, has repeatedly curtailed Congress's ability to "commandeer" the machinery of state government. In *New York v.*

United States (1992), the Court prevented Congress from requiring a state legislature either to take care of a problem that Congress did not itself wish to deal with under its own enumerated powers (disposal of low-level radioactive wastes) or to take title to these hazardous waste materials and be responsible for their safe disposal. In *Gregory v. Ashcroft* (1991), the Court noted the serious Tenth Amendment implications that would be raised by a congressional attempt to regulate the employment of state judges. And in *Printz v. United States* (1997), the Court barred Congress from requiring state executive officials to implement a federal scheme of firearms regulation. Outside of this context of direct federal control of state operations, however, the Court has made little direct use of the Tenth Amendment.

Several other recent cases limit federal power without expressly relying upon the Tenth Amendment. *United States v. Lopez* (1995) and *United States v. Morrison* (2000) both struck down federal laws premised on an expansive application of the Commerce Clause—the regulation of guns in school zones (*Lopez*) and the creation of a federal civil remedy for gender-motivated violence (*Morrison*). To the extent that the Tenth Amendment is a codification of the principle of enumerated federal power, those decisions implicate the Tenth Amendment, as does every decision involving the scope of federal power.

The recent decisions employing the Tenth Amendment to limit congressional power have been enormously controversial, both among those who think those decisions go too far by applying nebulous, nontextual theories of federalism and among those who think that they do not go far enough by refusing to tackle head-on the modern expansion of enumerated federal powers. But the Court itself remains unsure as to precisely what role the Tenth Amendment plays in its constitutional analyses. Prohibiting the commandeering of state instrumentalities, for instance, may be a straightforward construction of the limits of congressional discretion under its enumerated powers; or it may be that such laws are not "necessary and proper for carrying into Execu-

tion" federal powers and are therefore beyond the powers delegated to Congress.

On the other hand, the Tenth Amendment may itself pose a substantive limit on assumedly granted powers. Even if modern developments permit (or require) expansion of congressional authority well beyond its eighteenth-century limits, such expansion cannot extinguish the "retained" role of the states as limited but independent sovereigns. The Tenth Amendment thus may function as a sort of "fail-safe" mechanism: Congress has broad power to regulate, and even to subject states to generally applicable federal laws, but the power ends when it reaches too far into the retained dominion of state autonomy.

Charles Cooper

See Also

Article I, Section 8, Clause 1 (Spending Clause)
Article I, Section 8, Clause 3 (Commerce Among the States)
Article I, Section 8, Clause 18 (Necessary and Proper Clause)
Article VI, Clause 2 (Supremacy Clause)
Amendment IX (Rights Retained by the People)
Amendment XI (Suits Against a State)
Amendment XIV, Section 1 (State Action)

Suggestions for Further Research

ADVISORY COMMISSION ON INTERGOVERNMENTAL RELATIONS: INTERGOVERNMENTAL PERSPECTIVE, Vol. 17, No. 4 (Fall 1991)

ROBERT H. BORK, THE TEMPTING OF AMERICA: THE POLITICAL SEDUCTION OF THE LAW (1990)

ALEXIS DE TOQUEVILLE, DEMOCRACY IN AMERICA (1832)

Significant Cases

Marbury v. Madison, 5 U.S. (1 Cranch) 137 (1803)
McCulloch v. Maryland, 17 U.S. (4 Wheat.) 316 (1819)
Collector v. Day, 78 U.S. (11 Wall.) 113 (1871)
Legal Tender Cases, 79 U.S. (12 Wall.) 457 (1871)
Tarble's Case, 80 U.S. (13 Wall.) 397 (1872)
United States v. Darby, 312 U.S. 100 (1941)
Wickard v. Filburn, 317 U.S. 111 (1942)
Maryland v. Wirtz, 392 U.S. 183 (1968)

National League of Cities v. Usery, 426 U.S. 833 (1976)

Garcia v. San Antonio Metropolitan Transit Authority, 469 U.S. 528 (1985)

Gregory v. Ashcroft, 501 U.S. 452 (1991)

New York v. United States, 505 U.S. 144 (1992)

United States v. Lopez, 514 U.S. 549 (1995)

Printz v. United States, 521 U.S. 898 (1997)

United States v. Morrison, 529 U.S 598 (2000)

Suits Against a State

The Judicial power of the United States shall not be construed to extend to any suit in law or equity, commenced or prosecuted against one of the United States by Citizens of another State, or by Citizens or Subjects of any Foreign State.

(AMENDMENT XI)

~

The Eleventh Amendment was ratified in 1795 as a response to the Supreme Court's decision in *Chisholm v. Georgia* (1793). *Chisholm* had held that the federal courts could hear suits by individuals against state governments for money damages, notwithstanding the sovereign immunity that the states had traditionally enjoyed. The resulting furor—based largely on concerns that the states would be held accountable for their Revolutionary War debts—gave rise in 1795 to the ratification of the Eleventh Amendment, which established a fairly narrow textual bar to jurisdiction in cases like *Chisholm* itself. *Chisholm* was the first major constitutional decision of the new Court, and the Eleventh Amendment reversed it, eight years before *Marbury v. Madison* (1803).

The notion of sovereign immunity predates the Eleventh Amendment, having its origins in the English common law as well as from political theorists such as Thomas Hobbes and Jean Bodin. The Framers were clearly aware of the traditional doctrine that the states were immune from private lawsuits as sovereign entities, and some Anti-Federalists feared that Article III, Section 1, of the Constitution—which declares that the federal judicial power extends to suits "between a State and Citizens of another State"—would override that doctrine. Several key Framers—including Alexander Hamilton, James Madison, and John Marshall—are on record denying that the Constitution would, of its own force, deprive the states of this immunity. The more difficult questions are ones that the Framers did not confront directly: Did the states' immunity apply in suits based on federal law, as opposed to the state common-law claim relied upon in *Chisholm*? And was that immunity *constitutional* in stature, or could Congress abrogate it?

The Court answered the first question in the 1890 case of *Hans v. State of Louisiana*, holding that the Eleventh Amendment bars private suits against the states even where federal jurisdiction is based on a federal question rather than diversity. The Court reached this conclusion despite the fact the amendment's text appears to bar jurisdiction only in suits "by Citizens of another State, or by Citizens or Subjects of any Foreign State." The Court reasoned that to allow Hans—a Louisiana native—to sue in circumstances where out-of-staters would be barred would be anomalous. The best explanation of this holding, relied upon in more recent cases, is that the sovereign immunity enjoyed by the states at the Founding was broadly applicable to all sorts of suits, and the Eleventh Amendment was intended only to "patch" the hole in that preexisting immunity created by the Court's decision in *Chisholm*. After *Hans*, the Court extended the states' immunity in a number of other ways inconsistent with the amendment's text, holding that the immunity applies in admiralty (notwithstanding the textual limitation to "suit[s] in law or equity") and in suits by foreign sovereigns and Indian tribes (notwithstanding the textual limitation to "*Citizens*" of a "State" or "Foreign State").

The second question—whether Congress may abrogate the states' sovereign immunity—has preoccupied the Court more recently. There is little doubt that the states enjoyed, at the Founding, the sort of sovereign immunity recognized in common law. Most common-law doctrines, however, are subject to legislative override. Debates at the Constitutional and ratification conventions focused on whether Article III was *itself* intended to override this traditional immunity; they did not address, however, whether Congress could do so by later legislative enactment. The Court's 1996 decision in *Seminole Tribe of Florida v. Florida* held that Congress may *not* abrogate state sovereign immunity, at least when it acts pursuant to its enumerated powers in Article I of the Constitution. *Seminole Tribe* determined that the states' traditional immunity was not a mere holdover from the common law but rather a basic principle of the constitutional structure.

Three years later, in *Alden v. Maine* (1999), the Court held that, notwithstanding the amendment's limited application to "[t]he Judicial power of the United States," Congress also lacked power to override state sovereign immunity for suits in *state* court. *Alden* frankly acknowledged that no such principle could be gleaned from the amendment's text; the Court relied, however, on a structural principle that predated the text and applied much more broadly. The phrase "Eleventh Amendment immunity," Justice Anthony Kennedy said, "is something of a misnomer.... Sovereign immunity derives not from the Eleventh Amendment but from the structure of the original Constitution itself."

Notwithstanding *Seminole Tribe* and *Alden*, however, Congress retains power to abrogate state sovereign immunity when it acts pursuant to its power to enforce the Reconstruction Amendments (i.e., the Thirteenth, Fourteenth, and Fifteenth). Several reasons have been given for this: those amendments postdate the Eleventh; they were designed by the Civil War victors to cut back on state sovereignty; and their textual grant of power to Congress to "enforce" their provisions may be interpreted to extend to subjecting the states to monetary remedies for violations. Although the Court decided the leading case on the enforcement power—*Fitzpatrick v. Bitzer*—in 1976, its more recent decisions have all reaffirmed that precedent.

In order to use the *Fitzpatrick* exception, Congress and private litigants have sought to rethink a number of federal statutory schemes, originally enacted under the Commerce Clause, as efforts to enforce the Fourteenth Amendment. The *Florida Prepaid Postsecondary Education Expense Board v. College Savings Bank* (1999) decision rejected Congress's attempt to use Section 5 of the Fourteenth Amendment to abrogate state sovereign immunity in patent and false-advertising suits as a means of preventing deprivations of property without due process of law. More recently, *Kimel v. Florida Board of Regents* (2000) and *Board of Trustees of the University of Alabama v. Garrett* (2001) rejected claims that state liability under the Age Discrimination in Employment Act (ADEA) and Americans with Disabilities Act (ADA) would validly remedy violations of the Equal Protection Clause. Nonetheless, abrogation under the enforcement power is appropriate when a high proportion of statutory violations are also constitutional violations of rights protected by Section 1 of the Fourteenth Amendment. Thus, *Nevada Department of Human Resources v. Hibbs* (2003) held that Congress may subject a state to suits for money damages by state employees in the event of the state's failure to comply with the family-care provision of the Family and Medical Leave Act (FMLA). *Hibbs* suggests that narrowly drawn abrogation statutes can pass muster under Section 5, particularly where the rights being enforced call for heightened judicial scrutiny.

In addition to abrogating state immunities under Section 5, Congress retains other important tools for holding state actors accountable for violations of federal law. Congress can, for example, require the states to waive their immunities as a condition for receipt of federal grants under the Spending Clause (Article I, Section 8, Clause 1). Furthermore, state sovereign immunity has never been understood to bar suits by the United States itself. Federal enforcement agencies thus may continue to enforce the ADEA and ADA against state governments. Nor does state immunity bar claims against state officers for injunctive relief or (when the officer is sued in his personal capacity) for money damages. So long as these options exist, the sovereign immunity embodied in the Eleventh Amendment and its extra-textual background principles will tend to force suits against the states into certain channels without entirely eliminating the possibility of relief.

Ernest A. Young

See Also

Article III, Section 2, Clause 1 (Citizen-State Diversity Clause)

Amendment XIV, Section 5 (Enforcement Clause)

Suggestions for Further Research

William Fletcher, *A Historical Interpretation of the Eleventh Amendment: A Narrow Construction of an Affirmative Grant of Jurisdiction Rather than a Prohibition Against Jurisdiction*, 35 STAN. L. REV. 1033 (1983)

Alfred Hill, *In Defense of Our Law of Sovereign Immunity*, 42 B.C. L. REV. 485 (2001)

Daniel J. Meltzer, *The Seminole Decision and State Sovereign Immunity*, 1996 SUP. CT. REV. 1

John E. Nowak, *The Scope of Congressional Power to Create Cause of Action Against State Governments and the History of the Eleventh and Fourteenth Amendments*, 75 COLUM. L. REV. 1413 (1975)

Ronald D. Rotunda, *The Eleventh Amendment, Garrett, and Protection for Civil Rights*, 55 ALA. L. REV. 1183 (2002)

Ernest A. Young, *State Sovereign Immunity and the Future of Federalism*, 1999 SUP. CT. REV. 1

Significant Cases

Chisholm v. Georgia, 2 U.S. (2 Dall.) 419 (1793)

Marbury v. Madison, 5 U.S. (1 Cranch) 137 (1803)

Cohens v. Virginia, 19 U.S. (6 Wheat.) 264 (1821)

Hans v. State of Louisiana, 134 U.S. 1 (1890)

Ex parte Young, 209 U.S. 123 (1908)

Edelman v. Jordan, 415 U.S. 651 (1974)

Fitzpatrick v. Bitzer, 427 U.S. 445 (1976)

Pennhurst State School & Hospital v. Halderman, 465 U.S. 89 (1984)

Seminole Tribe of Florida v. Florida, 517 U.S. 44 (1996)

Alden v. Maine, 527 U.S. 706 (1999)

College Savings Bank v. Florida Prepaid Postsecondary Education Expense Board, 527 U.S. 666 (1999)

Florida Prepaid Postsecondary Education Expense Board v. College Savings Bank, 527 U.S. 627 (1999)

Kimel v. Florida Board of Regents, 528 U.S. 62 (2000)

Board of Trustees of the University of Alabama v. Garrett, 531 U.S. 356 (2001)

Nevada Department of Human Resources v. Hibbs, 538 U.S. 721 (2003)

Electoral College

The Electors shall meet in their respective states and vote by ballot for President and Vice-President, one of whom, at least, shall not be an inhabitant of the same state with themselves; they shall name in their ballots the person voted for as President, and in distinct ballots the person voted for as Vice-President, and they shall make distinct lists of all persons voted for as President, and of all persons voted for as Vice-President, and of the number of votes for each, which lists they shall sign and certify, and transmit sealed to the seat of the government of the United States, directed to the President of the Senate; — the President of the Senate shall, in the presence of the Senate and House of Representatives, open all the certificates and the votes shall then be counted; — The person having the greatest number of votes for President, shall be the President, if such number be a majority of the whole number of Electors appointed; and if no person have such majority, then from the persons having the highest numbers not exceeding three on the list of those voted for as President, the House of Representatives shall choose immediately, by ballot, the President. But in choosing the President, the votes shall be taken by states, the representation from each state having one vote; a quorum for this purpose shall consist of a member or members from two-thirds of the states, and a majority of all the states shall be necessary to a choice. And if the House of Representatives shall not choose a President whenever the right of choice shall devolve upon them, before the fourth day of March next following, then the Vice-President shall act as President, as in case of the death or other constitutional disability of the President. — The person having the greatest number of votes as Vice-President, shall be the Vice-President, if such number be a majority of the whole number of Electors appointed, and if no person have a majority, then from the two highest numbers on the list, the Senate shall choose the Vice-President; a quorum for the purpose shall consist of two-thirds of the whole number of Senators, and a majority of the whole number shall be necessary to a choice. But no person constitutionally ineligible to the office of President shall be eligible to that of Vice-President of the United States.

(Amendment XII)

~

*T*he Twelfth Amendment sets out the procedures for the election of the President and Vice President: Electors cast one vote for each office in their respective states, and the candidate having the majority of votes cast for a particular office is elected. If no person has a majority for President, the House of Representatives votes from among the top three candidates, with each state delegation casting one vote. In the case of a failure of any vice presidential candidate to gain a majority of electoral votes, the Senate chooses between the top two candidates. The procedure for choosing the Presi-

dent and Vice President is set out in Article II, Section 1, Clauses 2–6, of the Constitution. This amendment replaces the third clause of that section, which had called for only a single set of votes for President and Vice President, so that the vice presidency would go to the presidential runner-up. In the unamended Constitution, the choice in the case of a non-majority in the Electoral College fell to the House of Representatives, as it does under the amendment, and the runner-up there would be chosen as Vice President.

The Twelfth Amendment, the last to be proposed by the Founding generation, was proposed for ratification in December 1803 and was ratified in 1804, in time for the presidential election that year. The previous system had yielded, in the election of 1796, Federalist John Adams's election as President, while his bitter rival and sometimes-close friend, Republican Thomas Jefferson, was elected Vice President. In the election of 1800, Republican electors, though they clearly preferred Jefferson, sought to guarantee that Republicans won both offices, and cast seventy-three electoral votes for both Thomas Jefferson and Aaron Burr. This threw the election into the House of Representatives, where it was only resolved (in Jefferson's favor) on the thirty-sixth ballot. The hardening of party lines and concomitant voting by party slates (which the Framers had not contemplated) and some dissatisfaction with the way in which electors were chosen in the states led to proposals for change, including a proposal that electors be chosen in separate electoral districts in each state. However, the only change successfully accomplished was that of separate voting for President and Vice President.

Although it remains theoretically possible for the Vice President to be someone other than the person designated by the President and his party, the Adams-Jefferson scenario under which the top two presidential candidates must together form a partnership in the executive branch is now much more unlikely. In fact, Jefferson refused to assist Adams in his administration and actively sought to frustrate the President's policies. In *Ray v. Blair* (1952), the Supreme Court held that a state could constitutionally impose a pledge from elector candidates to vote for their party's nominees in the Electoral College. However, electors have defected from time to time. In 1988, one elector voted for Lloyd Bentsen as President rather than Democratic presidential candidate Michael Dukakis. In 2000, Al Gore electors from the District of Columbia did not cast a vote, in protest of the fact that the District is not treated as a state under the Constitution. The extent to which the electors are bound to vote for the candidate of the party under whose designation they were elected as electors, and whether all electors from a state are bound to vote as a bloc, remains a matter for each state to determine "in such manner as the legislature thereof shall direct." Article II, Section 1, Clause 2. Electors in all but two states (Maine and Nebraska) do vote as a bloc, effectively ensuring a two-party system.

Most presidential elections have not generated Twelfth Amendment controversy. However, the provisions of the Amendment have surfaced from time to time, most commonly when a third-party candidate threatens to take a substantial percentage of the vote. In 1824, the failure of either Andrew Jackson or John Quincy Adams to garner a majority of electoral votes threw the election into the House of Representatives, where Adams won the presidency despite having fewer electoral votes than Jackson. In 1876, similar circumstances were resolved differently, when neither Rutherford B. Hayes nor Samuel Tilden received a majority of electoral votes, due to disputed votes in three Southern states. In that instance, Hayes won the presidency when a congressional commission awarded him all disputed electoral votes (and thus a one-vote majority).

The Twelfth Amendment also effected a less significant change by providing that if the House does not complete its selection by Inauguration Day, the Vice President shall act as President. The Constitution had already set out in Article II, Section 1, Clause 6, as was repeated in the amendment, that the powers and duties of the presidency would devolve on the Vice President in case of the President's death or disability. The procedure to be followed in the event of a failure to designate a President and related matters are now regulated by the Twentieth and Twenty-fifth Amendments.

The procedures for the selection of the President and Vice President set out in this Amendment have been more closely specified by 3 U.S.C. §§ 1–21. These provisions address the certification, delivery, and counting of the electoral ballots and the procedure to be followed if that count does not result in clear winners. Those procedures, as when there is controversy about the certification of Electoral College votes, are complex and their constitutionality has never been tested. They were the subject of considerable discussion in *Bush v. Gore* (2000), although the decision in that case did not turn upon them.

Charles Fried

Suggestions for Further Research

David P. Currie, The Constitution in Congress: The Jeffersonians, 1801–1829 (2001)

William Josephson & Beverly J. Ross, *Repairing the Electoral College*, 22 J. Legis. 145 (1996)

Tadahisa Kuroda, The Origins of the Twelfth Amendment: The Electoral College in the Early Republic, 1787–1804 (1994)

Sanford Levinson & Ernest A. Young, *Who's Afraid of the Twelfth Amendment?*, 29 Fla. St. U. L. Rev. 925 (2001)

Note: *Rethinking the Electoral College Debate: The Framers, Federalism, and One Person, One Vote*, 114 Harv. L. Rev. 2526 (2001)

Neal R. Pierce & Lawrence D. Longley, The People's President: The Electoral College in American History and the Direct Vote Alternative (1981)

Victor Williams & Alison M. Macdonald, *Rethinking Article II, Section 1 and its Twelfth Amendment Restatement: Challenging Our Nation's Malapportioned, Undemocratic Presidential Election Systems*, 77 Marq. L. Rev. 201 (1994)

Significant Cases

Ray v. Blair, 343 U.S. 214 (1952)

Bush v. Gore, 531 U.S. 98 (2000)

Abolition of Slavery

Section 1. Neither slavery nor involuntary servitude, except as a punishment for crime whereof the party shall have been duly convicted, shall exist within the United States, or any place subject to their jurisdiction.

Section 2. Congress shall have power to enforce this article by appropriate legislation.

(AMENDMENT XIII)

～

The Thirteenth Amendment was intended to complete the destruction of slavery begun by the U.S. government during the Civil War in its policy of military emancipation. The official aim of the war was to preserve the Union and the Constitution against the attempt of eleven Southern states to secede from the Union by armed force. In an attempt to keep the peace and prevent further secession, Congress proposed a constitutional amendment on March 2, 1861, stating that the Constitution should never be amended to give Congress power to abolish or interfere with slavery within any state. Once the South had seceded, the status of slavery in the rebellious states was subject to change. Union policy recognized that emancipation of slaves employed in support of the rebellion was a legitimate war measure. The Emancipation Proclamation, issued by President Abraham Lincoln on January 1, 1863, signaled the transformation of an expedient military strategy into a settled executive policy for maintaining the freedom of slaves, emancipated by military means or through enforcement of confiscation and treason statutes enacted by Congress.

On the assumption that slavery was a state rather than national institution, antislavery advocates at first anticipated that military defeat of the Confederacy would result in its abolition through amendment of state constitutions. The Emancipation Proclamation shifted the focus of antislavery strategy to the national government. Lincoln's proclamation stated that "the

Executive government of the United States, including the military and naval authorities thereof, will recognize and maintain the freedom" of emancipated slaves. The legal effect of the executive order on individual slaves was uncertain, however, and it was generally agreed that the proclamation did not repeal state constitutions and laws establishing slavery. To place slave emancipation on a secure constitutional footing, Congress proposed on January 31, 1865, to abolish slavery by constitutional amendment. Ratification of the Thirteenth Amendment, including approval by reconstructed governments in the former Confederate states, was completed on December 6, 1865.

The text of the Thirteenth Amendment reflects its historic character as the culmination of a movement that began during the American Revolution. Eschewing originality, the authors of the amendment relied on the language of the Northwest Ordinance of 1787, intended to keep slavery from being taken into national territory, to abolish it in lands where it had been established for over two centuries. This demonstration of textual fidelity to historic antislavery purpose expressed the desire of Congress to complete the Founders' system of constitutional liberty by making the personal liberty of individuals the concern of the national government.

The Thirteenth Amendment was intended to establish a positive guarantee of personal liberty, expressed in the negative form of a proscription of slavery or involuntary servitude. Viewed in historical context and in the tradition of American political thought, the amendment is an affirmation of the idea that liberty, in the most fundamental sense, consists in the right of individuals not to be interfered with in the exercise of their natural rights. As a guarantee of personal liberty for all persons in the United States, the amendment established a minimum national standard of equality.

The Thirteenth Amendment is libertarian in its nature and purpose, however, rather than egalitarian. The libertarian characteristic of the amendment was made clear in congressional debate in 1864. Congress rejected a more far-reaching proposal, which stated: "All persons are equal before the law, so that no person can hold another as a slave; and the Congress shall have the power to make all laws necessary and proper to carry this declaration into effect everywhere within the United States."

By conferring power on Congress to enforce the prohibition of slavery throughout the United States, the Thirteenth Amendment altered the relationship between the states and the federal government. State power to recognize or establish slavery as a legal institution was withdrawn; to that extent, at least, state authority to regulate the personal liberty and civil rights of individuals within their jurisdiction was restricted beyond the limits imposed by the original Constitution. Unlike most other parts of the Constitution, which are designed only to limit governmental action, enforcement of the Thirteenth Amendment is not limited by the requirement that it apply only to actions by states or state officials. The amendment establishes a rule of action for private individuals as well as for state governments. In the language of constitutional law, enforcement of the amendment is not limited by the requirement that the amendment's prohibitions apply only to state action. The U.S. Constitution, for the most part, does not apply to individuals except when they act under color of law (e.g., the policeman who searches your house). The Thirteenth Amendment is different because it applies to private individuals acting in their private capacities. A person violates the Thirteenth Amendment if he keeps a slave. Where the fundamental right of personal liberty is concerned, the distinction between public and private spheres, which otherwise serves as a limitation on government power in the United States, is not recognized under the Thirteenth Amendment.

In the view of its congressional framers, the comprehensive sweep of the abolition amendment was balanced by its libertarian purpose. The scope of the enforcement power delegated to Congress thus depends on the meaning of slavery and involuntary servitude. Explicit definition of these terms in the text of the Thirteenth Amendment was considered unnecessary because slavery was universally understood, and legally defined, as the right of a person to hold another human being as chattel. Slavery was

appropriating the work of another person by irresistible power and not by his consent.

In legislative debate there was disagreement over the anticipated force and effect of the prohibition of slavery. The most narrow interpretation of the amendment viewed it as conferring only an individual right not to be held as the property of another. Except for this limitation, states otherwise retained authority to regulate the civil rights of persons within their jurisdiction, and private individuals enjoyed freedom of association, including the right to discriminate as they pleased in commercial and social interactions. This ultra-restrictive view of the abolition amendment was challenged by its congressional authors. They believed that prohibition of slavery and involuntary servitude necessarily implied the conferral of basic civil rights reasonably required to exercise the right of personal liberty guaranteed by the Thirteenth Amendment. Preeminent in their view were the rights to labor and enjoy the fruits thereof; to enter into marriage and establish family relationships; to make and enforce contracts; to bring suit and testify in court; and generally to receive the benefit of common-law protections of person and property. Content to rely on the Northwest Ordinance and reluctant further to engage the contentious issue of the effect of the abolition of slavery on the federal system, congressional authors refrained from writing specific civil rights guarantees into the text of the Thirteenth Amendment.

A year later, faced with restrictive laws (the "Black Codes") enacted by reconstructed state governments regulating the status and rights of blacks within their jurisdictions, Congress enacted civil rights protections that it believed necessary to vindicate the right of personal liberty conferred by the Thirteenth Amendment. This legislative response forms an important part of the framing of the Amendment because it can be viewed as an authoritative congressional construction of the national government's enforcement power.

The Civil Rights Act of 1866 declared that all persons born in the United States, except Indians not taxed, were citizens of the United States. Regardless of race, color, or previous condition of servitude, citizens had the same right to make and enforce contracts; to sue, be parties, and give evidence in court; to inherit, lease, or own property; and to have the full and equal benefit of all laws for the security of person and property as was enjoyed by white persons. The Civil Rights Act authorized the courts to protect persons denied the enumerated rights because of their race against anyone acting under color of state authority.

The constitutional basis for national civil rights legislation of this magnitude was a matter of dispute. Many Members of Congress were convinced that the classification and unequal treatment of black citizens under state laws in the reconstructed South were an infringement of liberty and a badge of servitude subject to legislative correction by Congress under Section 2 of the Thirteenth Amendment. Other lawmakers, objecting to the "Black Codes," doubted that the abolition amendment gave Congress power to displace the states in civil rights matters and impose criminal sanctions on their officers in the manner of the Civil Rights Act. To supply any supposed defect in constitutional authority to legislate on civil rights under the Thirteenth Amendment, Congress therefore proposed a constitutional amendment that expressly authorized national legislation against state civil rights infringement. Affirming the rule of citizenship adopted by the Civil Rights Act, the Fourteenth Amendment prohibited states from abridging the privileges and immunities of citizens of the United States, depriving persons of life, liberty, and property without due process of law, or denying persons equal protection of the laws.

Judicial and legislative construction has, in substantial measure, conformed to the original understanding of the Thirteenth Amendment. Slavery and involuntary servitude have been defined in personal libertarian terms with respect to conditions of enforced compulsory service, rather than in social egalitarian terms based on a subjective and metaphorical view of slavery that focuses on social and cultural systems of dominance and subordination.

The most serious challenge to the Thirteenth Amendment was presented by labor arrangements in the post-Reconstruction South intended to restrict the mobility of black citizens. In the first half of the twentieth century, the Supreme Court invalidated as forms of involuntary servitude state laws restricting employment and contract liberty and authorizing compulsory labor for indebtedness. *Bailey v. State of Alabama* (1911), *United States v. Reynolds* (1914), *Taylor v. State of Georgia* (1942), *Pollock v. Williams* (1944). In a wide variety of cases concerning, among other things, military conscription, public work laws, discrimination in contracts, social security benefits, deportation of aliens, treatment of the criminally insane, labor union activities, and duties required of public school students, courts generally rejected claims of involuntary servitude in violation of the Thirteenth Amendment.

In these cases the judiciary addressed the question of the meaning and unaided force and effect of the prohibitions in Section 1 of the amendment. In a second line of cases, dealing with the enforcement power of Congress under Section 2, a broader interpretation appears that suggests a more social egalitarian view of the Thirteenth Amendment.

In the *Civil Rights Cases* (1883), the Supreme Court stated that Congress's enforcement authority under Section 2 extended to the "badges and incidents of slavery." However, the Court adopted a narrow view of this concept, rejecting a claim that exclusion of black citizens from privately operated places of public accommodation was a badge of slavery. The Court declared that "compulsory service of the slave for the benefit of the master, restraint of his movements except by the master's will, disability to hold property, to make contracts, to have a standing in court, to be a witness against a white person, and such like burdens and incapacities, were the inseparable incidents of slavery."

Through most of the twentieth century, the Thirteenth Amendment was not utilized to try to dismantle state-sponsored racial discrimination. Federal civil rights enforcement policy in the 1950s and 1960s was principally based on the Fourteenth and Fifteenth Amendments. In 1968, however, the Supreme Court approved a dramatic expansion of the meaning of the "badges and incidents" of slavery in *Jones v. Alfred H. Mayer, Co.* The Supreme Court decided that racial discrimination in the sale of housing, in the form of a property owner's refusal to sell to a Negro buyer, was a "relic of slavery" prohibited under the Civil Rights Act of 1866. Avoiding the requirements of the state-action doctrine under the Fourteenth Amendment, which made prohibition of private discrimination problematic, the Court relied on the antislavery amendment and permitted Congress to define for itself what the "badges and incidents" of slavery were. The Court declared: "Surely Congress has the power under the Thirteenth Amendment rationally to determine what are the badges and incidents of slavery, and the authority to translate that determination into effective legislation." The Court did not describe what limits Congress must observe in enforcing the amendment by "appropriate" legislation as required in Section 2. Again in *Runyon v. McCrary* (1976), the Court avoided the public/private distinction requirement of the Fourteenth Amendment legislation and held that exclusion of a black student from a private school was a denial of the right to make and enforce contracts guaranteed by the Civil Rights Act of 1866 and prohibited by the Thirteenth Amendment.

On the other hand, in cases outside of Congress's Section 2 enforcement power, the Court was more careful to limit the "badges and incident of slavery" doctrine to its historical context. For example, the Supreme Court found that a city's closing of its swimming pools, rather than operating them on a desegregated basis, was not a badge of slavery. *Palmer v. Thompson* (1971). In *City of Memphis v. Greene* (1981), the Court decided that the closing of a street in a white neighborhood, even if it had a disparate impact on blacks outside the neighborhood, was not a badge or incident of slavery in violation of the Thirteenth Amendment. These cases indicate that Section 1 of the Thirteenth Amendment, unaided by legislation, does not reach the badges and incidents of slavery not directly associated with involuntary servitude.

The most significant recent judicial exploration of the meaning of the Thirteenth Amendment reaffirms a narrow definition of involuntary servitude under federal statutes. In *United States v. Kozminski* (1988), the Supreme Court unanimously decided that private employers of two mentally retarded men, forced to labor in squalid conditions, violated statutes based on the Thirteenth Amendment. Controversy in the Court focused on the criteria used to determine the existence of involuntary servitude. The opinion of the Court stated that involuntary servitude is compulsory servitude by the use of physical restraint or injury, or by the use or threat of coercion through legal process. Disputing a concurring opinion, the majority declared that compulsion by psychological coercion is not involuntary servitude under the Thirteenth Amendment.

Slavery and involuntary servitude in constitutional law retain the essential meaning intended by the framers of the Thirteenth Amendment, and congressional legislation under its enforcement clause remains limited. Since the reappearance of the Thirteenth Amendment in civil rights litigation in 1968, Congress has chosen not to enact any further legislation identifying and proscribing "badges and incidents of slavery."

Herman Belz

See Also

Suggestions for Further Research

HERMAN BELZ, A NEW BIRTH OF FREEDOM: THE REPUBLICAN PARTY AND FREEDMEN'S RIGHTS, 1861–1866 (2000)

Sidney Buchanan, *The Quest for Freedom: A Legal History of the Thirteenth Amendment*, 12 HOUS. L. REV. 12 (1976)

1 CHARLES FAIRMAN, RECONSTRUCTION AND REUNION, 1864–1888 (1971)

Robert L. Kohl, *The Civil Rights Act of 1866, Its Hour Come Round at Last*, Jones v. Alfred J. Mayer Co., 55 VA. L. REV. 272 (1969)

EARL M. MALTZ, CIVIL RIGHTS, THE CONSTITUTION, AND CONGRESS, 1863–1869 (1990)

Ronald D. Rotunda, *Congressional Power to Restrict the Jurisdiction of the Lower Federal Courts and the Problem of School Busing*, 64 GEO. L.J. 839 (1976)

Michael Vorenberg, Final Freedom: The Civil
    War, the Abolition of Slavery, and the Thir-
    teenth Amendment (2001)
Michael P. Zuckert, *Completing the Constitution: The
    Thirteenth Amendment*, 4 Const. Comment. 7
    (1987)

Significant Cases

Civil Rights Cases, 109 U.S. 3 (1883)
Bailey v. State of Alabama, 219 U.S. 219 (1911)
United States v. Reynolds, 235 U.S. 133 (1914)
Taylor v. State of Georgia, 315 U.S. 25 (1942)
Pollock v. Williams, 322 U.S. 4 (1944)
Jones v. Alfred H. Mayer, Co., 392 U.S. 409 (1968)
Palmer v. Thompson, 403 U.S. 217 (1971)
Runyon v. McCrary, 427 U.S. 160 (1976)
City of Memphis v. Greene, 451 U.S. 100 (1981)
United States v. Kozminski, 487 U.S. 931 (1988)

Citizenship

**All persons born or naturalized in
the United States, and subject to
the jurisdiction thereof, are citizens of the United States and of the
State wherein they reside.**

(Amendment XIV, Section 1)

~

*B*efore the adoption of the Fourteenth Amendment, citizens of the states were automatically
considered citizens of the United States. In 1857,
the *Dred Scott v. Sanford* decision had held that
no black of African descent (even a freed black)
could be a citizen of the United States. The Fourteenth Amendment was thus necessary to overturn *Dred Scott* and to settle the question of the
citizenship of the newly freed slaves. The Fourteenth Amendment made United States citizenship primary and state citizenship derivative. The
primacy of federal citizenship made it impossible for states to prevent former slaves from
becoming United States citizens by withholding
state citizenship. States could no longer prevent
any black from United States citizenship or from
state citizenship either.

The Civil Rights Act of 1866 had previously
asserted that "All persons born in the United
States and not subject to any foreign power,
excluding Indians not taxed, are hereby declared
to be citizens of the United States." The immediate impetus for the Fourteenth Amendment
was to constitutionalize and validate the Civil
Rights Act because some had questioned
whether the Thirteenth Amendment was a sufficient basis for its constitutionality. A constitutional amendment would also have the advantage of preventing a later unfriendly Congress
from repealing it.

One conspicuous departure from the lan-
guage of the Civil Rights Act was the elimination
of the phrase "Indians not taxed." Senator Jacob
Howard of Ohio, the author of the Citizenship
Clause, defended the new language against the
charge that it would make Indians citizens of the
United States. Howard assured skeptics that
"Indians born within the limits of the United
States, and who maintain their tribal relations,
are not, in the sense of this amendment, born
subject to the jurisdiction of the United States."
Senator Lyman Trumbull, Chairman of the Senate Judiciary Committee, supported Howard,
contending that "subject to the jurisdiction
thereof" meant "not owing allegiance to any-
body else . . . subject to the complete jurisdiction
of the United States." Indians, he concluded,
were not "subject to the jurisdiction" of the United States because they owed allegiance—even if
only partial allegiance—to their tribes. Thus,
two requirements were set for United States citizenship: born or naturalized in the United States
and subject to its jurisdiction.

By itself, birth within the territorial limits of
the United States, as the case of the Indians indicated, did not make one automatically "subject
to the jurisdiction" of the United States. And
"jurisdiction" did not mean simply subject to
the laws of the United States or subject to the
jurisdiction of its courts. Rather, "jurisdiction"
meant exclusive "allegiance" to the United
States. Not all who were subject to the laws owed
allegiance to the United States. As Senator
Howard remarked, the requirement of "jurisdiction," understood in the sense of "allegiance,"
"will not, of course, include persons born in the

United States who are foreigners, aliens, who belong to the families of ambassadors or foreign ministers accredited to the Government of the United States."

Most revealing, however, was Senator Howard's contention that "every person born within the limits of the United States, and subject to their jurisdiction, is by virtue of natural law and national law a citizen of the United States." Almost everyone certainly would have understood "natural law" to refer to the social compact basis of citizenship, the basis for citizenship adumbrated in the Declaration of Independence.

The argument of the Declaration grounded citizenship in consent. The natural law argument of the Declaration was a repudiation of the notion of birthright citizenship that had been the basis of British citizenship (i.e., being a British "subject") ever since it was first articulated in *Calvin's Case* in 1608. Sir William Blackstone, in his *Commentaries on the Laws of England*, had argued that the idea of birthright citizenship was an inheritance from the "foedal system"—it derives from the "mutual trust or confidence subsisting between the lord and vassal." "Natural allegiance," says Blackstone, is "due from all men born within the king's dominion immediately upon their birth. [It] is a debt of gratitude which cannot be forfeited, cancelled, or altered, by any change of time, place or circumstance....[T]he natural-born subject of one prince cannot by any act of his own, no, not by swearing allegiance to another put off or discharge his natural allegiance."

In the *Summary View of the Rights of British America* (1774), Thomas Jefferson argued that it was a natural right possessed by all men to leave the country where "chance and not choice" had placed them. The notion of a natural right to expatriation has no place in the scheme of an indefeasible birthright citizenship. Furthermore, the natural right to revolution is the perfect antithesis of "perpetual allegiance." In 1868, the Reconstruction Congress passed an Expatriation Act. The act provided, in pertinent part, that "the right of expatriation is a natural and inherent right of all people, indispensable to the enjoyment of the rights of life, liberty, and

the pursuit of happiness." Senator Howard was an enthusiastic supporter of the bill, describing the right of expatriation as the necessary counterpart of citizenship based on consent. During debate, commentators frequently described Blackstone's view of birthright citizenship as an "indefensible feudal doctrine of indefeasible allegiance" that was incompatible with republican government.

In *Elk v. Wilkins* (1884), the Supreme Court decided that a native Indian who had renounced allegiance to his tribe did not become "subject to the jurisdiction" of the United States by virtue of the renunciation. "The alien and dependent condition of the members of the Indian Tribes could not be put off at their own will, without the action or assent of the United States" signified either by treaty or legislation. Neither the "Indian Tribes" nor "individual members of those Tribes," no more than "other foreigners" can "become citizens of their own will."

Beginning in 1870 Congress began extending offers of citizenship to various Indian tribes. Any member of a specified tribe could become an American citizen if he so desired. Congress thus demonstrated that, using its Section 5 powers to enforce the provisions of the Fourteenth Amendment, it could define who was properly within the jurisdiction of the United States.

In 1898, the Supreme Court in *United States v. Wong Kim Ark* declared that the Fourteenth Amendment adopted the common-law definition of birthright citizenship. Chief Justice Melville W. Fuller's dissenting opinion, however, argued that birthright citizenship had been repealed by the principles of the American Revolution and rejected by the framers of the Fourteenth Amendment. Nonetheless, the decision conferred birthright citizenship on a child of legal residents of the United States. Although the language of the majority opinion in *Wong Kim Ark* is certainly broad enough to include the children born in the United States of illegal as well as legal immigrants, there is no case in which the Supreme Court has explicitly held that this is the unambiguous command of the Fourteenth Amendment.

Based on the intent of the framers of the Fourteenth Amendment, some believe that Congress could exercise its Section 5 powers to prevent the children of illegal aliens from automatically becoming citizens of the United States. An effort in 1997 failed in the face of intense political opposition from immigrant rights groups. Apparently, the question remains open to the determination of the political and legal processes.

Edward Erler

Suggestions for Further Research

Edward J. Erler, *From Subjects to Citizens: The Social Contract Origins of American Citizenship, in* Thomas G. West & Ronald J. Pestritto, eds., The American Founding and the Social Compact (2003)

Edward J. Erler, *Immigration and Citizenship, in* Gerald Frost ed., Loyalty Misplaced: Misdirected Virtue and Social Disintegration (1997)

Robert J. Kaczorowski, The Nationalization of Civil Rights (1987)

James H. Kettner, The Development of American Citizenship, 1608–1870 (1978)

Significant Cases

Calvin's Case, 77 Eng. Rep. 377 (1608)

Dred Scott v. Sandford, 60 U.S. (19 How.) 393 (1857)

Elk v. Wilkins, 112 U.S. 94 (1884)

United States v. Wong Kim Ark, 169 U.S. 649 (1898)

State Action

No State shall make or enforce any law which shall abridge the privileges or immunities of citizens of the United States; nor shall any State deprive any person of life, liberty, or property, without due process of law....

(Amendment XIV, Section 1)

∼

*I*n the course of interpreting and applying the Fourteenth Amendment, lawyers, legislators, and judges have identified two broad state-action questions. First, are the directives in Section 1 aimed only at states and those acting under state authority? Second, is Congress's power under Section 5 to enforce the prohibitions in Section 1 limited to enacting laws aimed at states and those acting under state authority? The original understanding of the Fourteenth Amendment supports an affirmative answer to both these questions.

The prohibitions in Section 1 can be understood by placing the language in its relevant textual and historical context. Of first importance in determining the original meaning are the exact words of the provision. Those words identify three kinds of prohibited conduct: (1) a state making or enforcing any law "which shall abridge the privileges or immunities of citizens of the United States"; (2) a state depriving "any person of life, liberty, or property, without due process of law"; and (3) a state denying "to any person within its jurisdiction the equal protection of the laws." Although each prohibition seems to forbid a different kind of conduct, all three seem aimed at state action, or conduct fairly attributable to a state. The close proximity of these prohibitions in the text tends to reinforce the conclusion that the language of each individual prohibition points to state action.

The historical context of the adoption of the Fourteenth Amendment would have been known to the contemporary members of the amendment's intended audience and would no doubt have influenced greatly their understanding of its meaning. Congress drafted the Fourteenth Amendment and sent it to the states for approval in 1866, after the required supermajority of Congress had voted to overturn President Andrew Johnson's veto of the Civil Rights Act of 1866. In his veto message, President Johnson had questioned the constitutionality of that act. Sections 1 and 5 of the Fourteenth Amendment together were obviously intended to provide a solid constitutional base for the act, and Section 1 was intended to embed the essential proscriptions of the act in the Constitution itself, safe from subsequent repeal by mere legislative action. Congress had drafted the act to overturn the effects of the infamous "Black Codes" enacted by the reconstituted Southern state governments in 1865 and 1866 under President Johnson's Reconstruction policies. Those codes limited in important ways the basic civil rights of the freed slaves to contract, to own property, and to sue. To stop these evils, the Civil Rights Act of 1866 provided:

> That all citizens, of every race and color, without regard to any previous condition of slavery or involuntary servitude, shall have the same right, in every State and Territory in the United States, to make and enforce contracts, to sue, be parties, and give evidence, to inherit, purchase, lease, sell, hold, and convey real and personal property, and to full and equal benefit of all laws and proceedings for the security of person and property, as is enjoyed by white citizens, and shall be subject to like punishment, pains and penalties, and to none other....

Reading the words of Section 1 against this history, the contemporary reader would probably have concluded that they were aimed at the state actions that the Civil Rights Act of 1866 intended to outlaw, namely, actions by state officials that treated the freed slaves differently from whites with respect to basic litigation, contract, and property rights, or that imposed on the freed slaves different punishment, pains, or penalties than would be imposed on whites for the same conduct.

Some modern commentators argue for a broader interpretation of the state-action language than the likely originally understood meaning. One common modern argument is that Section 1 of the Fourteenth Amendment recognized a broad, general, constitutional principle of equality. Thus, any pattern of behavior by private individuals that undermines equality becomes state action if it is not prohibited by the state. This reading would wipe out the distinction between state action and private behavior that the prohibitions in Section 1 seem on their face to recognize and embody. The Supreme Court has rejected this argument.

One can identify the original understanding of Section 5, too, by focusing on its specific language and placing that language in its relevant textual and historical context. Section 5 gives Congress the *power to enforce* the other provisions of the Fourteenth Amendment. Section 1 contains prohibitions against certain state actions, directed at states and those acting on behalf of states. The ordinary understanding of the power to enforce those prohibitions, then, would be to enforce those prohibitions against those to whom they were exclusively directed. An earlier proposed amendment, proposed in 1865, would have empowered Congress to enact "all necessary and proper laws to secure to all persons in every State of the Union equal protection in their rights of life, liberty, and property." Congressman John A. Bingham, who later drafted the Fourteenth Amendment, was the author of this sweeping proposal. The Joint Committee on Reconstruction reported his proposal to Congress, but it was ultimately defeated precisely because many in Congress believed that the wording would give the federal government plenary power to protect life, liberty, and property by passing laws directed to the conduct of private individuals. Such a power could supplant state civil and criminal law. Comparing the language of this earlier, defeated proposal with the ultimate wording of Sections 1 and 5 supports the conclusion that the different language was used to make clear that Congress would have only the limited power to legislate against the states to enforce the prohibitions in Section 1.

Nonetheless, an argument for a broader interpretation of Congress's power under Section 5 arose not long after the ratification of the amendment. According to this line of argument, Section 1 forbids a state to deny a person the "equal protection of the laws." "The laws" in that directive would include the long-established common law that protected the right of any member of the public to be served by those who hold themselves out to provide a service to the public. For the courts of a state to refuse to enforce this common-law right when asserted by a newly freed slave would be to deny him the equal protection of the laws. Similarly, for a state legislature to overturn that common-law rule by simple, nondiscriminatory legislation would, for exactly the same reason, deny the equal protection of the laws. One way for Congress to rectify or to foreclose these violations of Section 1 would be to enact a general law under Section 5 protecting everyone's common-law right to public accommodations. This could plausibly be understood as Congress "enforcing" the right to equal protection of the laws recognized in Section 1.

Congress did exactly that in the Civil Rights Act of 1875, which mandated equal access to public accommodations, common carriers, and places of amusement. Because many of the Members of Congress who voted for the Civil Rights Act of 1875 were Members of Congress in 1866, when Congress approved the Fourteenth Amendment, some argue that their votes are evidence that the intended meaning of Section 5 was broad enough to support the 1875 act. Later conduct expressing the subjective understanding of legislators as to the meaning of a constitutional amendment is not controlling on the question of its proper interpretation, however, as the legislators can only act authoritatively by following the prescribed forms for proposing a constitutional amendment. The Fourteenth Amendment was ratified by the action of three-quarters of the state legislatures, following the procedures in Article V. There is no indication that those state legislatures would have understood Section 5 as a broad delegation of power to Congress to regulate private behavior.

The Supreme Court in the *Civil Rights Cases* (1883) held that the Federal Civil Rights Act of 1875, which had prohibited private racial discrimination in public accommodations, was unconstitutional. In holding that Congress had no power under Section 1 and Section 5 of the Fourteenth Amendment to enact that legislation, the Court reasoned:

> The prohibitions of the amendment are against State laws and acts done under State authority. [But the Civil Rights Act of 1875] makes no reference to any supposed or apprehended violation of the Fourteenth Amendment on the part of the State.... [It] lays down rules for the conduct of individuals in society towards

each other, and imposes sanctions for the enforcement of those rules, without referring in any manner to any supposed actions of the states or its authorities.

In *United States v. Guest* (1966), the Supreme Court held that Congress, under Section 5, could regulate the conduct of private individuals who conspired with state officials to deprive persons of their rights under Section 1. The conspiracy with state officials was enough to bring the conduct within the state-action requirement. In two concurring opinions, some Justices said that Congress could use its Section 5 powers to reach purely *private* conduct. However, no case since then has embraced the *Guest* concurrences, and the Court later avoided the issue in cases like *Katzenbach v. Morgan* (1966). Finally, in *United States v. Morrison* (2000), the Supreme Court reaffirmed the holding of the *Civil Rights Cases*, explicitly rejected the *Guest* dictum, and struck down the part of the federal Violence Against Women Act that had provided a federal civil remedy for victims of sex-motivated violence. The Court held that the act exceeded Congress's power under Section 5 of the Fourteenth Amendment because it was "directed not at any state or state action, but at individuals who have committed criminal acts motivated by gender bias."

The Supreme Court has consistently held that some sort of state action is a prerequisite to judicial enforcement of the prohibitions in Section 1 of the Fourteenth Amendment. The remaining question is what counts as state action. In cases raising that question, the Supreme Court has recognized that in certain unusual circumstances, conduct by a nominally private entity may qualify as state action. Many cases seem to fall into one of two categories: (1) when private entities perform public functions or exercise powers traditionally exclusively reserved to the state; and (2) when a government becomes so inextricably entangled with a private entity that the entity in effect acts as the government.

The leading public-function cases are the "white primary" cases, in which the Supreme Court repeatedly held that ostensibly private political parties could not constitutionally exclude blacks from their primary elections held to nominate candidates for office at the state's general elections. *Nixon v. Condon* (1932), *Smith v. Allwright* (1944), *Terry v. Adams* (1953). Additionally, the Court has held that actions by those in control of a company town or a public park operated by private trustees also constitute state action. *Marsh v. Alabama* (1946), *Evans v. Newton* (1966).

The leading cases finding an inextricable entanglement are *Burton v. Wilmington Parking Authority* (1961), in which racial discrimination by a restaurant leasing space in a publicly owned parking garage was held to be state action, and *Lugar v. Edmondson Oil Co.* (1982), in which a private entity's filing an *ex parte* petition for prejudgment attachment of an adversary's property, carried out by the court clerk and the sheriff, was held to be state action.

Examples in which racial discrimination by private action was authorized or enforced by seemingly neutral state actions are *Shelley v. Kraemer* (1948) and *Reitman v. Mulkey* (1967). In *Shelley*, the Supreme Court held that judicial enforcement of a private restrictive covenant barring occupancy of the restricted property by "any person not of the Caucasian race" was state action denying equal protection of the laws to the black buyer of the property. This was so, even though the law the court enforced was the racially neutral common-law rule that certain private restrictions on property use in restrictive covenants were valid and judicially enforceable. The fact that the state court was asked to use the state's judicial power to enjoin the private contract between a willing buyer and willing seller may have led the Court to find state action.

In *Reitman*, the Supreme Court held unconstitutional a California constitutional amendment that barred the enactment of any law limiting the right of any property owner to refuse to sell his or her property to any buyer for any reason. This was so, even though the Fourteenth Amendment did not require the state to enact fair-housing legislation, and the California amendment was on its face racially neutral. The Court appeared to argue that the state constitutional amendment itself was the state act that

violated equal protection because it singled out this type of legislation for special protection.

The Supreme Court has continued to limit state-action claims against private individuals or entities. It has held that the prohibitions in Section 1 of the Fourteenth Amendment do not reach electric utilities when they terminate service to its customers, *Jackson v. Metropolitan Edison Co.* (1974). Nor did it hold liable under Section 1 a warehouseman's sale of stored property to make good back payments, *Flagg Brothers, Inc. v. Brooks* (1978), or prominent sports accrediting organizations, *San Francisco Arts & Athletics v. United States Olympic Comm.* (1987), *National Collegiate Athletic Ass'n. v. Tarkanian* (1988).

Patrick Kelley

See Also

Suggestions for Further Research

Charles L. Black, Foreword: *"State Action," Equal Protection, and California's Proposition 14*, 81 HARV. L. REV. 69 (1967)

Erwin Chemerinsky, *Rethinking State Action*, 80 NW. U. L. REV. 503 (1985)

1 CHARLES FAIRMAN, RECONSTRUCTION AND REUNION 1864–1888 (1971)

ERIC FONER, RECONSTRUCTION: AMERICA'S UNFINISHED REVOLUTION, 1863–1877 (1988)

ROBERT J. KACZOROWSKI, THE POLITICS OF JUDICIAL INTERPRETATION: THE FEDERAL COURTS, DEPARTMENT OF JUSTICE AND CIVIL RIGHTS, 1866–1876 (1985)

EARL M. MALTZ, CIVIL RIGHTS, THE CONSTITUTION, AND CONGRESS, 1863–1869 (1990)

WILLIAM E. NELSON, THE FOURTEENTH AMENDMENT: FROM POLITICAL PRINCIPLE TO JUDICIAL DOCTRINE (1988)

Significant Cases

Civil Rights Cases, 109 U.S. 3 (1883)
Nixon v. Condon, 286 U.S. 73 (1932)
Smith v. Allwright, 321 U.S. 649 (1944)

Marsh v. Alabama, 326 U.S. 501 (1946)

Shelley v. Kraemer, 334 U.S. 1 (1948)

Terry v. Adams, 345 U.S. 461 (1953)

Burton v. Wilmington Parking Authority, 365 U.S. 715 (1961)

Evans v. Newton, 382 U.S. 296 (1966)

Katzenbach v. Morgan, 384 U.S. 641 (1966)

United States v. Guest, 383 U.S. 745 (1966)

Reitman v. Mulkey, 387 U.S. 369 (1967)

Jackson v. Metropolitan Edison Co., 419 U.S. 345 (1974)

Flagg Brothers, Inc. v. Brooks, 436 U.S. 149 (1978)

Lugar v. Edmondson Oil Co., 457 U.S. 922 (1982)

San Francisco Arts & Athletics v. United States Olympic Commission, 483 U.S. 522 (1987)

National Collegiate Athletic Ass'n v. Tarkanian, 488 U.S. 179 (1988)

United States v. Morrison, 529 U.S. 598 (2000)

Privileges or Immunities

No State shall make or enforce any law which shall abridge the privileges or immunities of citizens of the United States....

(AMENDMENT XIV, SECTION 1)

~

*A*lthough there is no agreement concerning a single original meaning of the clause, it is possible to identify three distinctly different yet plausible and credible original understandings of the clause. This essay first describes in general terms the nature of the disagreement, and then discusses in more detail the contending interpretations.

The initial division of opinion is over whether the clause was intended simply to require the states to make their laws apply *equally* to all their citizens or to mandate a certain *substantive content* to state law. The equality argument reads the clause to say nothing about the content of a state's law; rather, it simply says that whatever the content of a state's law, it must be the same for all citizens. The substantive argument reads the clause to mandate certain

content to state law—to prescribe or proscribe state law in order to deliver a substantive package of entitlements known as the privileges or immunities attaching to federal citizenship.

The substantive view is subdivided into two differing versions of the substance of the privileges and immunities of federal citizenship. The first view holds that these privileges or immunities consist of all of the rights and liberties contained in the Constitution, a category that includes such rights as habeas corpus and the protection against ex post facto legislation or bills of attainder, but, more importantly, the Bill of Rights, that is to say, the first eight amendments. Under this view, the principal function of the Privileges or Immunities Clause was to make the *entire* Bill of Rights binding on the states. A variant of this view is the contention that the clause was intended to do nothing more than to make the Bill of Rights applicable to the states. The second view is influenced by John Locke's view of natural rights and holds that the privileges and immunities of national citizenship are the natural rights of property and liberty possessed by free persons upon creation of government but never ceded to government.

The reason that it is so difficult to determine with confidence the original meaning of the Privileges or Immunities Clause is that the proponents of the clause in the Thirty-ninth Congress, particularly Representative John A. Bingham of Ohio, were vague and sometimes inconsistent in their statements of the intended effect of the clause. Historical evidence outside the congressional debates is inconclusive. Although each of the three plausible original understandings will be discussed, it is useful to begin with some common historical background.

A central focus of the Thirty-ninth Congress, the body that drafted and proposed the Fourteenth Amendment, was to protect newly emancipated slaves from discriminatory state laws, especially the "Black Codes," which severely limited the civil and political rights of African-Americans. The first effort in that direction was the Civil Rights Act of 1866, Section 1, which declared "all persons born in the United States and not subject to any foreign power, excluding Indians not taxed" to be United States citizens, and provided that all "citizens, of every race and color, without regard to previous condition of slavery... shall have the same right, in every State or Territory in the United States, to make and enforce contracts, to sue, be parties, and give evidence, to inherit, purchase, lease, sell, hold, and convey real and personal property, and to full and equal benefit of all laws... for the security of persons and property, as is enjoyed by white citizens...."

Because some supporters of the Civil Rights Act were concerned that Congress lacked constitutional authority to enact the law, Representative Bingham proposed a constitutional amendment that was a precursor to the Fourteenth Amendment. Bingham's proposed amendment gave Congress "power to make all laws which shall be necessary and proper to secure to the citizens of each State all privileges and immunities of citizens in the several States." Bingham's proposal was tabled because it did not go far enough. All it purported to do was to give Congress the power to provide by federal law "that no State shall discriminate between its citizens and give one class of citizens greater rights than it confers upon another," but it failed to bar the states directly (without such federal legislation) from excluding "any class of citizens in any State from the privileges which other classes enjoy." In its stead, the Fourteenth Amendment was proposed, but the Fourteenth Amendment addressed a number of important practical problems associated with Reconstruction, only one of which was the absence of authority for the 1866 Civil Rights Act.

Even though the text of the clause suggests substantive content to the privileges or immunities of national citizenship, the historical context credibly suggests that the clause may have been intended to require the states to make their laws, whatever their content, apply equally to all their citizens, rather than to proscribe or prescribe state law in any particular substantive manner.

The argument for the equality view is partly historical and partly textual and makes the following contentions. First, the Citizenship Clause of Section 1, which immediately precedes the Privileges or Immunities Clause, defines both national and state citizenship. Because a citizen of the nation is a citizen of a state (unless he resides abroad), the privileges or immunities of national citizenship necessarily include the privileges or immunities of state citizenship. Second, because both the Equal Protection and Due Process Clauses extend protection to all persons within a state's jurisdiction (rather than just *citizens*), the reference to "citizens" in the Privileges or Immunities Clause is best understood as a reference to a particular group of *individuals* rather than a reference to a particular set of *rights*. Third, although the debate in the Thirty-ninth Congress is not a model of clarity, it contains ample suggestions that many Members of Congress thought abridgment of a citizen's privileges or immunities consisted of state "legislation discriminating against classes of citizens" or that gave "one man... more rights upon the face of the laws than another man." Fourth, as a result of prior interpretation of the Privileges and Immunities Clause of Article IV, the drafters of the Fourteenth Amendment understood that the privileges and immunities of state citizenship were rights derived from state law, and understood that the function of the Privileges and Immunities Clause of Article IV was to ensure that states treated citizens of other states equally with their own citizens with respect to the privileges and immunities of state citizenship. Finally, when Congress debated adoption of what ultimately became the Civil Rights Act of 1875, which forbade private racial discrimination by persons *already subject to a legal duty to serve the public indiscriminately*, Members of Congress grounded that proposed legislation in the Privileges or Immunities Clause of the Fourteenth Amendment.

The idea that the privileges or immunities of national citizenship included substantive rights secured by the Constitution, especially those contained in the Bill of Rights, was partly grounded in the text of the clause, and partly in the comments of certain proponents of the Privileges or Immunities Clause, particularly Representative John A. Bingham, who repeatedly declared that "the privileges and immunities of citizens of the United States... are chiefly defined in the first eight amendments to the

Constitution." To be sure, Bingham was, in the words of one modern commentator, a "gasbag" who frequently failed to articulate the constitutional analysis underlying his pronouncements, and that failing has led many subsequent commentators to deride Bingham as "befuddled," "confused," and "distinguished for elocution but not for hard thinking."

This point of view was most notably expressed by historian Charles Fairman and by Justice Felix Frankfurter in his concurring opinion in *Adamson v. California* (1947). Fairman and Frankfurter argued that incorporation of the Bill of Rights would have immediately invalidated numerous practices of the states and that there was neither any indication that the framers of the clause expected this to happen nor any movement, after ratification of the Fourteenth Amendment, to alter such local practices to comply with the Bill of Rights.

Yet despite this dissonance and Bingham's failings as an articulate analyst, later interpreters of the record have argued that it was, indeed, the intention of the framers of the clause to make the Bill of Rights, along with all other rights associated with national citizenship, binding on the states. These commentators argue that such an intention was entirely consistent with the antebellum antislavery view of the Constitution, comports with the clause's textual suggestion of substantive content, and reflects the framers' lack of concern with or ignorance of incipient conflict between local practices and the demands of the Bill of Rights. On the other hand, subsequent to ratification, Congress approved new state constitutions from the reconstructed states that contained provisions that conflicted with the federal Bill of Rights.

The other substantive conception of the Privileges or Immunities Clause is that it secures a bundle of natural rights of property and liberty, rights possessed by people in the abstract state of nature prior to their voluntary cession of some of these rights to secure the order and stability afforded by government. This reading is based primarily on the fact that, at the time the Privileges or Immunities Clause was proposed and ratified, the Privileges and Immunities Clause of Article IV, which requires states to afford the citizens of other states the same privileges and immunities they extend to their own citizens, had been read in a dictum by Justice Bushrod Washington as securing "those privileges and immunities which are, in their nature, fundamental; which belong, of right, to the citizens of all free governments; and which have, at all times, been enjoyed by the citizens of the several states . . . from the time of their becoming free, independent, and sovereign." *Corfield v. Coryell* (1823). Justice Washington had summarized those rights as "[p]rotection by the government; the enjoyment of life and liberty, with the right to acquire and possess property of every kind, and to pursue and obtain happiness and safety; subject nevertheless to such restraints as the government may justly prescribe for the general good of the whole." This reading of the Privileges or Immunities Clause is consistent with the framers' concern, manifested in the 1866 Civil Rights Act, to secure important fundamental rights for all citizens on a racially nondiscriminatory basis, but this reading goes well beyond that immediate objective by suggesting that states lack the power to enact laws that offend the fundamental rights identified by Justice Washington. This view was echoed most forcefully by Justice Stephen J. Field in his dissent to the *Slaughter-House Cases* (1873), and, to a lesser extent, by Justice Joseph P. Bradley in his dissent to the same decision. For these two Justices, the Privileges and Immunities Clause of Article IV contained substantive protections that were carried over into the Privileges or Immunities Clause of the Fourteenth Amendment. (*See* Article IV, Section 2, Clause 1.)

The clause was effectively stripped of any meaningful substance by the Supreme Court's decision in the *Slaughter-House Cases* (1873). The majority concluded that the privileges or immunities of national citizenship were, indeed, substantive, but that they consisted of rights "which owe their existence to the Federal government, its National character, its Constitution, or its laws." The Court offered examples of these rights: the right "to come to the seat of government,... the right of free access to its seaports,... to the subtreasuries, land offices, and courts of justice in the several States ... to demand the care and protection of the Federal government ... when on the high seas or within the jurisdiction of a foreign government,... to peaceably assemble and petition for redress of grievances, the privilege of the writ of habeas corpus,... [t]he right to use the navigable waters, [and the right to] become a Citizen of any State of the Union by a bona fide residence therein, with the same rights as other citizens of that State."

Notably absent from these distinctively national rights were the fundamental natural rights identified by Justice Washington in *Corfield v. Coryell*, despite the Court's reference to the case, and also absent, despite the Court's reference to the Constitution, the rights secured by the Bill of Rights. The Court found it unthinkable that the Privileges or Immunities Clause could have been intended "to transfer the security and protection of ... civil rights ... from the States to the Federal government," or "to bring within the power of Congress the entire domain of civil rights heretofore belonging exclusively to the States." Such a change, said the Court, "would constitute this court a perpetual censor upon all legislation of the States," and "[w]e are convinced that no such results were intended."

After *Slaughter-House*, the Privileges or Immunities Clause became a virtual dead letter. The equality function of the clause, much altered in character, was assumed by the Equal Protection Clause, and the substantive functions, again altered, were assumed by the Due Process Clause. Both of these clauses of the Fourteenth Amendment applied to "persons," whereas the Privileges or Immunities Clause is limited to "citizens." Indeed, except for *Colgate v. Harvey* (1935), overruled five years later in *Madden v. Commonwealth of Kentucky* (1940), the Supreme Court did not rely on that clause as the basis for any decision until 1999, when it decided *Saenz v. Roe* (1999). In *Saenz*, the Court struck down a California law that set welfare benefits for new residents and citizens of California at the level provided by their former state

for the first year of their California residency. The Court concluded that one aspect of the right of travel, the right of new state citizens "to be treated like other citizens of that State," is one of the privileges or immunities of national citizenship.

Calvin Massey

See Also

Article IV, Section 2, Clause 1 (Privileges and Immunities Clause)

Amendment XIV, Section 1 (Due Process Clause)

Amendment XIV, Section 1 (Equal Protection Clause)

Suggestions for Further Research

Akhil Amar, The Bill of Rights: Creation and Reconstruction (1998)

Raoul Berger, Government by Judiciary: The Transformation of the Bill of Rights (1978)

James E. Bond, No Easy Walk to Freedom: Reconstruction and the Ratification of the Fourteenth Amendment (1997)

2 William Crosskey, Politics and the Constitution in the History of the United States (1953)

David Currie, The Constitution in the Supreme Court: The First Hundred Years, 1789–1888 (1985)

Michael Kent Curtis, No State Shall Abridge: The Fourteenth Amendment and the Bill of Rights (1986)

Charles Fairman, *Does the Fourteenth Amendment Incorporate the Bill of Rights?*, 2 Stan. L. Rev. 5 (1949)

John Harrison, *Reconstructing the Privileges or Immunities Clause*, 101 Yale L.J. 1385 (1992)

Earl Maltz, Civil Rights, the Constitution, and Congress, 1863–1869 (1990)

Bernard H. Siegan, The Supreme Court's Constitution: An Inquiry into Judicial Review and Its Impact on Society (1987)

Significant Cases

Corfield v. Coryell, 6 F. Cas. 546 (C.C.E.D. Pa. 1823) (No. 3,230)

Slaughter-House Cases, 83 U.S. (16 Wall.) 36 (1873)

Colgate v. Harvey, 296 U.S. 404 (1935)

Madden v. Commonwealth of Kentucky, 309 U.S. 83 (1940)

Adamson v. California, 332 U.S. 46 (1947)

Saenz v. Roe, 526 U.S. 489 (1999)

Due Process Clause

.... nor shall any State deprive any person of life, liberty, or property, without due process of law....
(AMENDMENT XIV, SECTION 1)

∼

*B*oth the Fifth Amendment and the Fourteenth Amendment to the United States Constitution prohibit governmental deprivations of "life, liberty, or property, without due process of law." The Due Process Clause of the Fourteenth Amendment serves three distinct functions in modern constitutional doctrine: "First, it incorporates [against the States] specific protections defined in the Bill of Rights .... Second, it contains a substantive component, sometimes referred to as 'substantive due process.'... Third, it is a guarantee of fair procedure, sometimes referred to as 'procedural due process.'..." *Daniels v. Williams* (1986) (Stevens, J., concurring).

Modern law interprets the Fifth and Fourteenth Amendments to impose the same substantive due process and procedural due process requirements on the federal and state governments. The doctrine of procedural due process under both amendments, as well as the definition of "life, liberty, or property" as the range of interests protected by the respective Due Process Clauses, is addressed in more detail in the entry on Due Process in the Fifth Amendment. (*See* the Fifth Amendment's Due Process Clause.) This entry addresses substantive due process and the use of the Fourteenth Amendment's Due Process Clause as a vehicle for incorporating selected provisions of the Bill of Rights against the states.

To understand the Fourteenth Amendment's Due Process Clause, one must start with the Fifth Amendment's Due Process Clause, from which the language of the Fourteenth Amendment's provision was drawn nearly verbatim. Although the phrase "due process of law" first appeared in the fourteenth century with a very narrow and technical meaning involving the service of appropriate writs, the American Founding generation likely identified the Fifth Amendment's Due Process Clause with the clauses, prevalent in state constitutions in 1791, that required governmental deprivations of life, liberty, or property to conform to "the law of the land."

There are certain respects in which "due process of law," understood as equivalent to "the law of the land," uncontroversially regulates the substance of governmental action. Most obviously, the core meaning of "law of the land" provisions, dating back to the Magna Carta, is to secure the *principle of legality* by ensuring that executive and judicial deprivations are grounded in valid legal authority. In this respect, the Fifth Amendment's Due Process Clause limits the substance of executive or judicial action by requiring it to be grounded in law.

The term "substantive due process" as used in modern discourse conventionally does not refer to the principle of legality or limitations on Congress's power to prescribe novel adjudicatory procedures for the deprivation of life, liberty, or property. Instead, it generally refers to limitations on the substance of legislation other than legislation that seeks to alter the core procedural meaning of "due process of law." Few constitutional doctrines generate more heat. Many doubt whether there is any legitimate doctrine of substantive due process, and there is a dispute among those who advocate some form of substantive due process about the scope and content of that doctrine.

Many advocates of substantive due process openly eschew any reliance on original meaning as support for their position, but some do not. Originalist defenders of substantive due process emphasize the Due Process Clause's links to "law of the land" provisions and the likely eighteenth-century American understanding of those provisions. Americans were familiar with, and influenced by, the writings of

English judges and legal scholars such as Sir Edward Coke and Sir William Blackstone. In the seventeenth century, Coke sought to check the arbitrary rule of the Stuart monarchs by emphasizing that the "law of the land" clause in the Magna Carta encompassed both procedural safeguards and substantive limitations on the power of government; monopoly grants, according to Coke, were invalid because contrary to "the law of the land." Scholars have debated whether Coke's understanding of the Magna Carta was correct, but there is no doubt that his views markedly influenced constitutional development in the American colonies. Sir William Blackstone, in his widely read and influential *Commentaries on the Laws of England*, also discussed the Magna Carta's "law of the land" provision in terms of both procedure and substance. Thus, some have argued, Founding-era persons conversant with Blackstone and Coke would be disposed to a broad reading of "law of the land" provisions so as to place certain fundamental rights beyond the reach of government, and the Fifth Amendment's Due Process Clause is best understood as part of this "law of the land" tradition.

Skeptics of substantive due process counter on several levels. First, they respond that British traditions of restraints on *royal* power do not readily translate into American constitutional restraints on *congressional* power. Second, they say that most of the substantive concerns voiced by pre-1791 writers are addressed by provisions of the Constitution other than the Due Process Clause, such as the Fifth Amendment's Takings Clause and the original Constitution's Ex Post Facto, Bill of Attainder, and Necessary and Proper Clauses. The skeptics maintain that there is no reason to force those concerns into the unpromising language of "due process of law." Third, they argue that attempts to draw too close a linkage between the Due Process Clause and broadly construed "law of the land" provisions run headlong into the Supremacy Clause, which says that all valid congressional statutes are, in fact, the "supreme Law of the Land." On balance, say the critics of substantive due process, the phrase "due process of law" is best read as compelling the government to act

according to traditional modes of procedure ("due process") and pursuant to valid legal authorization ("of law").

The scope of the Due Process Clause was not a serious topic of discussion in the decades immediately after the Founding. The Supreme Court did not decide a case squarely involving the Fifth Amendment due process guarantee until 1856. It did not invalidate a congressional statute under the Due Process Clause until the infamous *Dred Scott v. Sandford* decision in 1857, and the use of the Due Process Clause in that case was brief and cryptic: the Court said only that a statute that effectively frees any slave brought by his or her master into federal territory "could hardly be dignified with the name of due process of law."

State courts in the pre–Civil War era dealt more actively with issues of due process. Some courts equated due process with procedural requirements only, whereas others in the antebellum era wrestled with substantive interpretations of due process. State courts early established the principle that transfer of property from one person to another by legislative fiat violated due process. Further, in the landmark case of *Wynehamer v. People* (1856), the New York Court of Appeals struck down a prohibition statute as applied to the sale of liquor owned when the law became effective. Holding that the act constituted a deprivation of property without due process, the *Wynehamer* court anticipated later doctrinal development by invalidating a generally applicable regulation on due process grounds. Thomas M. Cooley, in his influential work *A Treatise on the Constitutional Limitations Which Rest Upon the Legislative Power of the States of the United States* (1868), insisted that due process was not satisfied by any duly enacted legislation. Rather, he argued that due process was not merely procedural but limited legislative authority to violate fundamental constitutional values.

In 1868, the Fourteenth Amendment was added to the Constitution. Historians have long debated the intentions of the framers and ratifiers of the Fourteenth Amendment. Clearly the amendment was designed to extend protection to the newly freed slaves against mistreatment by the states. Some thought that the Bill of Rights' guarantees would now limit the states through the Privileges or Immunities Clause. A few, like Justice Joseph P. Bradley, thought that, whatever "due process of law" meant in 1791, by 1868 it clearly signaled substantive restraints on legislation. Yet others no doubt believed that the Fourteenth Amendment's Due Process Clause had precisely the same meaning as the Fifth Amendment's Due Process Clause, so that if there was no legitimate doctrine of substantive due process under the latter, there could not be any such doctrine under the former either.

The Supreme Court at first construed narrowly the due process requirement of the Fourteenth Amendment. It adhered to the view that the Bill of Rights was not extended to the states by virtue of that amendment. It further held that the Due Process Clauses in the Fifth and Fourteenth Amendments had the same meaning, so that substantive due process under the two provisions had to stand or fall together. Disagreeing with the majority, Justice John M. Harlan argued that the Due Process Clause of the Fourteenth Amendment created a national standard of rights. And Justice Stephen J. Field forcefully maintained that the Due Process Clause protected the right to pursue lawful trades and contractual freedom from abridgement by the states. Field's understanding of the Fourteenth Amendment gained ground on the Supreme Court in the late nineteenth century.

Under Chief Justice Melville W. Fuller, the Court relied on substantive due process to uphold a variety of economic rights. In a line of cases, the Court held that under due process, regulated industries were entitled to charge reasonable rates. The Justices ruled in *Allgeyer v. Louisiana* (1897) that the right to make contracts was a liberty interest protected by the Due Process Clause, thereby establishing the liberty-of-contract doctrine. In the seminal case of *Lochner v. New York* (1905), the Court invoked due process to strike down a state law regulating the hours of work in bakeries as an interference with contractual freedom. Building on the liberty-of-contract principle, the Court later determined in *Adkins v. Children's Hospital of D.C.* (1923) that a minimum-wage law for women

violated due process. The Court also relied on substantive due process to safeguard other types of fundamental rights not enumerated in the Constitution. For example, *Pierce v. Society of Sisters* (1925) affirmed the right of parents to control the education of their children.

The political triumph of the New Deal and the resulting constitutional revolution of 1937 transformed the interpretation of the Due Process Clause. The Supreme Court signaled its rejection of substantive due process as a basis on which to review economic legislation in *West Coast Hotel Co. v. Parrish* (1937). Until this point state and federal courts had not carefully differentiated between the procedural and substantive components of due process. As the unitary understanding of due process shattered, judges began in the 1940s to employ the term "substantive due process" for the first time.

The Court further downplayed the rights of property owners in *United States v. Carolene Products Co.* (1938) by holding that economic regulations would not be found to violate the Due Process Clause so long as they satisfied a minimal "rational basis" test. Conversely, the Court indicated that other rights deemed fundamental would receive heightened scrutiny. It is difficult to reconcile *Carolene Products* with the language of the Due Process Clause, which draws no distinction between the right to property and other personal rights, especially because the Framers of the Constitution and Bill of Rights closely identified security of private property with political freedom. The opinion also ranked rights into categories not expressed in the Constitution. Nonetheless, *Carolene Products* virtually eliminated due process review of economic regulations. After the mid-1930s, the Supreme Court did not invalidate a regulatory statute on grounds of substantive due process until *BMW of North America, Inc. v. Gore* (1996), which concluded that there was a due process right not to be charged excessive punitive damages.

More controversial was the Supreme Court's revival of substantive due process to safeguard noneconomic rights not set out in the Constitution. Some modern critics, such as Robert H. Bork, have insisted that due process pertains entirely to matters of procedure, but the Court has decided that due process protects certain substantive liberties. Justice Antonin Scalia, in particular, has criticized the inconsistent picking among rights to receive substantive due process protection. In the discovery of new liberties protected by due process, the Court has more recently left behind both the text of the Constitution and historical tradition. These substantive personal rights include the right to marry and a right of privacy that encompasses the right of married couples to use birth-control devices. In *Roe v. Wade* (1973) the Court extended the concept of privacy to cover the right to obtain an abortion. In *Planned Parenthood of Southeastern Pennsylvania v. Casey* (1992), the Court grounded the abortion right in a highly subjective theory of the individual, extending the principle to protect private homosexual acts in *Lawrence v. Texas* (2003). On the other hand, in *Washington v. Glucksberg* (1997), the Justices held that the Due Process Clause does not encompass the asserted liberty to commit an assisted suicide.

Until the ratification of the Fourteenth Amendment, the accepted opinion was that the Bill of Rights restricted only the federal government, a principle affirmed in *Barron v. City of Baltimore* (1833). Some abolitionists thought otherwise, and some think that the Privileges or Immunities Clause of the Fourteenth Amendment was meant to undo *Barron* and apply the Bill of Rights protections (and perhaps others in the Constitution) to the states. In the *Slaughter-House Cases* (1873), the Supreme Court sheared the Privileges or Immunities Clause of any real strength. If there were to be any application to the states of the guarantees found within the Bill of Rights, it would have to come through some other route.

At first, the Court did not "incorporate" rights within the Bill of Rights into the Fourteenth Amendment. Rather, the Court determined that the same right that was protected by the Bill of Rights against federal infringement was also protected against state infringement by the Due Process Clause of the Fourteenth Amendment. Later, Justice Felix Frankfurter would state that the clause had an "independent potency," separate from that of the Bill of Rights.

In *Chicago, Burlington & Quincey Railroad Co.* (1897), the Justices unanimously determined that the Due Process Clause required the states to provide just compensation when they acquired private property for public use. Thus, the just-compensation principle of the Fifth Amendment became in effect the first provision of the Bill of Rights to be federalized. In *Gitlow v. New York* (1925), the Court similarly suggested that principles of free speech basically identical to those contained in the First Amendment applied to the states by virtue of the Fourteenth Amendment. From the 1940s onward, however, the view that the Fourteenth Amendment's Due Process Clause literally "incorporates" the text of various provisions of the Bill of Rights rapidly gained steam; by the 1960s, what we know today as the "incorporation doctrine" was complete. Under current law, most provisions of the Bill of Rights are deemed applicable to the states in precisely the same manner that they are applicable to the federal government. Notable exceptions to the rule of incorporation are the Fifth Amendment's requirement of indictment by grand jury, the Seventh Amendment's guarantee of jury trial in civil cases, and the Second and Third Amendments. (Similarly, ever since *Bolling v. Sharpe* in 1954, the Fifth Amendment's Due Process Clause has been held to "reverse-incorporate" the Fourteenth Amendment's Equal Protection Clause against the federal government.)

The doctrine, although settled as law, remains controversial in a number of respects. During the doctrine's formative years in the mid-twentieth century, Justice Hugo L. Black consistently maintained that *all* of the substantive provisions in the first eight amendments should be deemed incorporated against the states, not simply those that the Court considers to be sufficiently fundamental. *Adamson v. California* (1947). Justice Frankfurter, as noted, believed that the fundamental rights protected by the Due Process Clause were independent of those in the Bill of Rights, though they may coincide in some instances. The route the Court chose was "selective incorporation," often attributed to Justice Benjamin N. Cardozo's opinion in *Palko v. State of Connecticut* (1937). Through selective incorporation, the Warren Court brought most of the Bill of Rights into the Fourteenth Amendment, though the selective incorporation doctrine did not restrain some Justices from finding additional rights to add that were not in the Bill of Rights.

James W. Ely, Jr.

See Also

Amendment V (Due Process Clause)
Amendment XIV, Section 1 (Privileges or Immunities)
Amendment XIV, Section 1 (Equal Protection)

Suggestions for Further Research

Akhil Amar, The Bill of Rights: Creation and Reconstruction (1998)

Edward S. Corwin, *The Doctrine of Due Process of Law Before the Civil War*, 24 Harv. L. Rev. 366 (1911)

James W. Ely, Jr., *The Oxymoron Reconsidered: Myth and Reality in the Origins of Substantive Due Process*, 16 Const. Comm. 315 (1999)

Howard Gillman, The Constitution Besieged: The Rise and Demise of Lochner Era Police Powers Jurisprudence (1993)

Herbert Hovenkamp, *The Political Economy of Substantive Due Process*, 40 Stan. L. Rev. 379 (1988)

Earl M. Maltz, *Fourteenth Amendment Concepts in the Antebellum Era*, 32 Am. J. Legal Hist. 305 (1988)

Rodney L. Mott, Due Process of Law (1926)

Michael J. Phillips, *The Slow Return of Economic Substantive Due Process*, 49 Syracuse L. Rev. 917 (1999)

Robert E. Riggs, *Substantive Due Process in 1791*, 1990 Wis. L. Rev. 941 (1990)

Significant Cases

Calder v. Bull, 3 U.S. (3 Dall.) 386 (1798)
Barron v. City of Baltimore, 32 U.S. (7 Pet.) 243 (1833)
Murray's Lessee v. Hoboken Land & Improvement Co., 59 U.S. (18 How.) 272 (1856)
Wynehamer v. People, 13 N.Y. 378 (1856)
Dred Scott v. Sandford, 60 U.S. (19 How.) 393 (1857)
Slaughter-House Cases, 83 U.S. (16 Wall.) 36 (1873)
Munn v. Illinois, 94 U.S. 113 (1877)
Hurtado v. California, 110 U.S. 516 (1884)
Mugler v. Kansas, 123 U.S. 623 (1887)
Allgeyer v. Louisiana, 165 U.S. 578 (1897)
Chicago, Burlington & Quincey Railroad Co., 166 U.S. 226 (1897)

Lochner v. New York, 198 U.S. 45 (1905)
Muller v. Oregon, 208 U.S. 412 (1908)
Bunting v. Oregon, 243 U.S. 426 (1917)
Adkins v. Children's Hospital of D.C., 261 U.S. 525 (1923)
Meyer v. State of Nebraska, 262 U.S. 390 (1923)
Gitlow v. New York, 268 U.S. 652 (1925)
Pierce v. Society of Sisters, 268 U.S. 510 (1925)
Nebbia v. New York, 291 U.S. 502 (1934)
Palko v. State of Connecticut, 302 U.S. 319 (1937)
West Coast Hotel Co. v. Parrish, 300 U.S. 379 (1937)
United States v. Carolene Products Co., 304 U.S. 144 (1938)
Adamson v. California, 332 U.S. 46 (1947)
In re Oliver, 333 U.S. 257 (1948)
Rochin v. California, 342 U.S. 165 (1952)
Bolling v. Sharpe, 347 U.S. 497 (1954)
Williamson v. Lee Optical Co., 348 U.S. 483 (1955)
Mapp v. Ohio, 367 U.S. 643 (1961)
Gideon v. Wainwright, 372 U.S. 335 (1963)
Malloy v. Hogan, 378 U.S. 1 (1964)
Griswold v. Connecticut, 381 U.S. 479 (1965)
Pointer v. Texas, 380 U.S. 400 (1965)
Klopfer v. North Carolina, 386 U.S. 213 (1967)
Duncan v. Louisiana, 391 U.S. 145 (1968)
Benton v. Maryland, 395 U.S. 784 (1969)
Roe v. Wade, 410 U.S. 113 (1973)
Daniels v. Williams, 474 U.S. 327 (1986)
Planned Parenthood of Southeastern Pennsylvania v. Casey, 505 U.S. 833 (1992)
BMW of North America, Inc. v. Gore, 517 U.S. 559 (1996)
Washington v. Glucksberg, 521 U.S. 702 (1997)
Lawrence v. Texas, 539 U.S. 558 (2003)
Johnson v. California, 125 S. Ct. 1141 (2005)

Equal Protection

No State shall . . . deny to any person within its jurisdiction the equal protection of the laws.
(Amendment XIV, Section 1)

∽

*T*he Equal Protection Clause is one of the most litigated and significant provisions in contemporary constitutional law. The meaning of the clause is bound up with the entire drama of the Civil War and Reconstruction and, in particular, with slavery and emancipation. Thus the Equal Protection Clause can be understood only as an organic part of the Fourteenth Amendment and in the broader context of all the Reconstruction amendments.

Considered textually, the Privileges or Immunities Clause, the Equal Protection Clause, and the Due Process Clause of the Fourteenth Amendment can be read to form a coherent triad. A state's legislature could not deny to any citizen within its jurisdiction any privilege or immunity (however defined). Once a law was validly passed, the state or its agents could not arbitrarily enforce it against any person within the state's jurisdiction without violating the Equal Protection Clause. Finally, every person accused of violating a law would enjoy the full panoply of procedural rights before the courts of the state. However, early Court involvement, such as in the *Slaughter-House Cases* (1873), as well as the ambiguity of much of the congressional debates, has led to debate and disagreement as to the original understanding of the three clauses.

Debate on the original understanding of the Equal Protection Clause became intense in modern times after the Supreme Court ordered briefing and reargument on the question in *Brown v. Board of Education* (1954), the school desegregation case. Scholarly debate on the original intention of the Equal Protection Clause and, more broadly, on Section 1 of the Fourteenth Amendment, continues to the present day. Controversy centers on two primary questions. The first is how far, or in relationship to what rights, did the framers intend the command of equality to apply? In other words, equal as to what? The second is what does it mean to treat persons equally? In other words, what is equal treatment? Although these two questions have been answered by the Court since *Brown*, the original intention of the framers remains subject to ongoing dispute.

The scope of equal protection today is as broad as governmental action under the State Action doctrine. Thus in modern constitution-

al law, the command to treat persons equally extends to all actions by the government.

Most commentators agree, however, that the intended scope of the Equal Protection Clause was narrower. The framers were focused primarily on the status of the freed slaves, and thus the command of equal protection was debated primarily in racial terms. Congress had enacted the Civil Rights Act of 1866 largely in response to perceived southern oppression of the freed slaves, particularly in the form of "Black Codes" enacted in the former Confederate states. John A. Bingham, the primary author of Section 1 of the Fourteenth Amendment, did not believe that Congress had the authority to enact the Civil Rights Act of 1866, and he therefore intended to provide congressional authority for that enactment by constitutional amendment. When Bingham's version of Section 1 emerged from committee for consideration by the full Congress, it was received primarily as a means of legitimizing the 1866 Civil Rights Act. Thus, at a minimum, the framers intended that the command of equal protection apply to the rights protected by the Civil Rights Act of 1866, which provided for the "same right":

> To make and enforce contracts, to sue, be parties, and give evidence, to inherit, purchase, lease, sell, hold, and convey real and personal property, and to full and equal benefit of all laws and proceedings for the security of persons and property... and shall be subject to like punishment, pains and penalties, and to none other....

The methodology of the first section of the Civil Rights Act was to define national citizenship and to declare that all citizens, "of every race and color" should have the same benefit of the listed rights "as is enjoyed by white citizens." The language of Section 1 of the Fourteenth Amendment, by contrast, can be read to distinguish between citizenship rights protected by the Privileges or Immunities Clause and personhood rights protected by the Due Process and Equal Protection Clauses. Once the Supreme Court gutted the Privileges or Immunities Clause of the Fourteenth Amendment in the *Slaughter-House*

Cases, however, the Equal Protection Clause became the primary bulwark supporting the constitutionality of the Civil Rights Act and providing for the enforcement of its listed rights.

The framers' jurisprudence tended to lump together rights flowing from citizenship and personhood under the rubric of "civil rights," and to speak of them in religious or natural law and natural rights terms. In Section 1 of the Fourteenth Amendment, the framers attempted to create a legal bridge between their understanding of the Declaration of Independence, with its grand declarations of equality and rights endowed by a Creator God, and constitutional jurisprudence. However, the framers also prized federalism—although not in the absolutist sense of the Southern secessionists. Antislavery activists themselves had at times relied on state authority to resist federal policies protective of slavery and so shared that era's common mistrust of centralized authority. The Fourteenth Amendment's compromise between federal enforcement of civil rights and the maintenance of significant state authority was to amend the Constitution to provide clear warrant for the Civil Rights Act, but at the same time to provide additional federal protection for those fundamental rights flowing from citizenship and personhood.

The rhetoric of the time distinguished civil equality from two other kinds of possible equality: political and social. The framers of the Fourteenth Amendment chose not to include political rights (such as the right to vote, which the Fifteenth Amendment would later address) and social rights within the protections of the Fourteenth Amendment. The Fourteenth Amendment, including its then more prominent sections regarding representation and the political exclusion of certain former Confederates, was part of the Republican Party's Reconstruction program during the critical 1866 election. The program was popular because of its perceived moderation by Northern opinion of the time, which was generally negative or ambivalent in regard to political and social equality for African-Americans. After achieving political success in the 1866 election, Republicans became bolder, enacting the Fifteenth Amendment, explicitly protecting the right to vote.

However, the very passage of the Fifteenth Amendment indicates that voting rights were not protected by the Fourteenth Amendment.

The question of whether *Brown v. Board of Education*, invalidating segregated public education, was consonant with the framers' original intent has been much debated. Some scholars view the provision and integration of education as local, social, or political in nature, and hence as beyond the original scope of the Fourteenth Amendment. Others would point to post-1866 Republican efforts to desegregate schools as evidence that *Brown* is a plausible interpretation of the framers' intent. Antislavery rhetoric had been critical of Southern laws that outlawed basic education for slaves, and thus provision of education for the freed slaves would have been important to the framers. Arguably, then, education was neither a political nor social right, but rather was related to a person's right to the pursuit of happiness, or was a right equipping citizens for their civic responsibilities. In any event, by the time segregation swept the South, it was part of the Jim Crow program to reduce blacks to a status not unlike that imposed by the "Black Codes," which the Fourteenth Amendment was clearly intended to efface.

Brown posed the question of whether a doctrine of "separate but equal" was compatible with the Equal Protection Clause, as had been established by *Plessy v. Ferguson* (1896). The records of the Thirty-ninth Congress, which proposed the Fourteenth Amendment, provide little guidance on this question. The other parts of the Fourteenth Amendment received far more discussion within the Congress than did Section 1. Once John A. Bingham's version of the Fourteenth Amendment emerged from committee, it was treated primarily as providing constitutional authority for the Civil Rights Act of 1866, and it received relatively little comment. Nonetheless, in light of the concerns for the freed slaves that animated the framers of the Fourteenth Amendment, it is reasonable to believe that the framers would generally have presumed "equal *treatment*" to mean the same, rather than segregated, treatment. The framers would likely have accorded the system of racial oppression found in the Jim Crow laws the same hostility they had demonstrated toward the "Black Codes" of their own time, despite any legal differences between these methodologies of oppression.

The primary intent of the Equal Protection Clause was to require states to provide the same treatment for whites and freed slaves in regard to the class of personhood and citizenship rights enumerated in the Civil Rights Act of 1866. The clause is not limited to racial classifications, in large part because the framers were also concerned about white Union loyalists, who also suffered discriminatory treatment in the South. In addition, this general language reflected anti-slavery Republican jurisprudence, which drew links between the Declaration of Independence, natural law and natural rights, and constitutional jurisprudence. From an originalist constitutional perspective, application of the Equal Protection Clause to rights or issues beyond the scope of the 1866 Civil Rights Act can rest upon the broader principle enacted by the framers—their jurisprudence of equality linking the Declaration of Independence to the Constitution.

The Supreme Court's acceptance of white supremacist segregation in the period from 1896 to 1954 would not have pleased the framers. Even if the framers had viewed public accommodations and education as local or social rights not directly protected by the Equal Protection Clause, their sense of racial justice would have opposed the systematic, legally enforced racial caste system that emerged in the 1890s. In fact in the so-called Ku Klux Klan Acts (1871), Congress did attempt to thwart the violent racism that was the harbinger of Jim Crow.

Although the Equal Protection Clause may not have been intended to command integration, it also was not intended to countenance legally enforced segregation. In addition, the ultimate failure of the legal system to protect African-Americans against terrorist acts that enforced white supremacy was precisely the kind of failure that the Equal Protection Clause was designed to prevent. The framers undoubtedly would have recognized that government and private institutions had coalesced to enforce a racial caste system that oppressed African-Americans in a manner inconsistent with the fundamental principle of civil equali-

ty. As Justice John M. Harlan famously declared in his dissent in *Plessy v. Ferguson*, "In view of the Constitution, in the eye of the law, there is in this country no superior, dominant, ruling class of citizens. There is no caste here."

Generations of experience with segregation demonstrated that a partial permission of governmental racial classifications was an ineffective means of protecting the core principles and rights enacted in Section 1 of the Fourteenth Amendment. From this perspective, the Supreme Court's expansion of the Equal Protection Clause to all governmental action, without regard to distinctions among civil, political, and social rights, as well as the Supreme Court's overturning of "separate but equal" jurisprudence, was a realistic application of the core principles of the Equal Protection Clause. Governments that systematically demeaned and excluded African-Americans proved unable and unwilling to protect even the limited equality directly protected by the Equal Protection Clause.

Although its history demonstrates a primary concern with the protection of the freed slaves and African-Americans, the language of the Equal Protection Clause is general. The framers were also concerned with the protection of white Union loyalists in the South, and they thus clearly understood that the clause would not be limited to the protections of the freed slaves. The general language of the Fourteenth Amendment reflects the framers' commitment to constitutionalizing their natural-law understanding that all human beings are created equal as to their fundamental rights of life, liberty, and property. Thus it was inevitable that the question should arise as to how the clause would be applied to nonracial classifications.

All laws classify, and thus there are countless classifications in American law. All laws make distinctions, but not all laws violate equal protection. A law that limited driving to those sixteen years of age and older would not violate equal protection even though it treated fifteen-year-olds differently from sixteen-year-olds. Close judicial review of all classifications to ensure "equal protection of the laws" is a practical impossibility. Therefore the Supreme Court has had to find doctrinal means of managing the task of judicial review under the Equal Protection Clause. Although the clause protects all persons, the Court, as a practical matter, cannot give close scrutiny to all classifications that governmental action may create among persons.

During the era of "separate but equal" jurisprudence, the primary application of the clause to race was severely, although not entirely, eliminated. At the same time the Court had found the clause applicable to little else beyond race. The clause was not sufficient to stop the internment of Japanese-Americans during World War II, despite the Court precedents making the clause applicable to the protection of all races, and not to African-Americans only. With the clause generally ineffective as to racial matters and applicable to little else, the Equal Protection Clause became, in Justice Oliver Wendall Holmes's words, the "usual last resort of constitutional arguments ...." *Buck v. Bell* (1927).

After the Court resurrected the Equal Protection Clause in regard to racial classifications, it subsequently developed a two-tiered system of review. All classifications based on race were subjected to "strict judicial review," and they were thus subjected to a means-end test: the classification must be narrowly tailored to effectuate a compelling governmental interest. The Court determined which governmental interests (ends) were significant enough to be "compelling." As a practical matter, in many cases the government could at least claim to be implementing an end or purpose deemed compelling under the Court's precedents. Therefore the heart of strict scrutiny often rests in the means test.

Means-end testing involves essentially two questions: (1) Does the governmental action work, meaning does the governmental action actually serve the claimed interest? (2) If it does work, is there an alternative and less "suspect" (i.e., nonracial) classification that would work approximately as well, making use of the racial classification unnecessary to achievement of this goal? Under strict scrutiny, means-end testing involves a kind of public policy "second-guessing" by the legislative branch. By contrast, nonsuspect classifications are presumptively constitutional, and they are therefore reviewed under the very lenient rational basis test, which asks whether the classification is rationally related to a legitimate government interest. Under rational basis review there is generally little second-guessing as to whether the law works, and the analysis of alternatives is irrelevant. The burden is on the complaining party to show that the only purpose of the legislation was invidiously discriminatory. Rational basis review has understandably developed into a virtual rubber stamp.

The group of classifications subject to strict scrutiny is very limited: race and its corollaries, such as national origin or ethnic group; and legal alienage, except where the classification is either (1) created by the federal government (which has plenary control over immigration) or (2) excludes aliens from political functions "intimately related to the process of democratic self-government," such as serving as police and probation officers or public school teachers. Alienage classifications operating within the two exceptions are generally reviewed under the lenient rational basis test.

Beginning in the 1970s the Court developed a third, intermediary standard of review for two classifications: sex and legitimacy (the distinction between marital and nonmarital children). The test for intermediary scrutiny asks whether the law is substantially related to an important government interest. As to gender, a number of decisions have emphasized that there must be "an exceedingly persuasive justification" for any sex classification. *United States v. Virginia* (1996). Although some interpret this language as implying a creep toward strict scrutiny for sex classifications, officially gender remains subject to intermediary scrutiny.

The Supreme Court has thus far refused to extend heightened scrutiny (strict or intermediary scrutiny) to any other classifications, even though some, such as age, disability, and sexual orientation, are frequently included in antidiscrimination legislation. The Supreme Court's tendency to occasionally invalidate laws employing sensitive classifications, purportedly under the rational basis test, as in *City of Cleburne v. Cleburne Living Center, Inc.* (1985) (mental retardation) and *Romer v. Evans* (1996) (sexual orientation), only underscores the Court's reluctance to officially expand the classifications subject to heightened scrutiny. In fact a majority of the Court thus far prefers to rest their protection of same-sex relationships on a substantive view of due process rather than equal protection. *Lawrence v. Texas* (2003).

The methodology by which the Court determines which classifications receive heightened scrutiny, beyond that of race, is unclear. Commentators have invoked the classification of "discrete and insular minorities" from the famous footnote four of *United States v. Carolene Products Co.* (1938), but the relevance of that footnote in modern times is hardly clear. Women, for example, are neither minorities nor insular. Justices and commentators have sometimes compared the historical discrimination experienced by African-Americans to that experienced by women, the mentally retarded, and those with a same-gender sexual orientation, but it is unclear whether there is a clear scale for measuring tragic histories. In addition, once a classification is made suspect, under current precedents the Court will protect members of the historically favored, as well as historically disfavored, group. For example, the equal protection cases protect "sex," not the female sex. Thus, the Court has invalidated a law that limited a nursing school to women, *Mississippi University for Women v. Hogan* (1982), and a law that allowed women, but not men, to buy alcohol at age 18. *Craig v. Boren* (1976). Given these difficulties, the Court thus far has not developed a single methodology for determining the critical question of which classifications receive heightened scrutiny, nor for choosing between strict and intermediary scrutiny.

The question of affirmative action has spawned much litigation. Under current precedents, all legislative racial classifications are evaluated under strict scrutiny, even if they purport to be positive affirmative action programs favoring racial minorities. Although the primary impetus behind the Fourteenth Amendment (and its Equal Protection Clause) was to protect African-Americans, the framers of the amendment phrased the protection in general terms, and the courts have applied it in that fashion. Thus today, even classifications favoring African-Americans are presumptively unconstitutional absent of sufficiently weighty reason. The courts

have held that the protection of all races against discrimination effectuates the broader original purpose of the Equal Protection Clause, which constitutionalized the core concept of personal equality as described in the Declaration of Independence. Thus, the apparent tension between active efforts to promote the progress of racial minority *groups* and the promise of personal equality for each *individual*, regardless of race, have been resolved in favor of the latter.

The Supreme Court has recently upheld some forms of race-based affirmative action despite the application of strict scrutiny. Thus the Supreme Court has said that racially conscious acts by legislatures, courts, or other state actors will meet strict scrutiny if the racially conscious act rectifies, in a narrowly tailored fashion, a previous governmental violation of equal protection, or—more controversially—if it furthers the compelling interest of student body racial diversity in higher education by including race as a positive element in an applicant's profile. *Grutter v. Bollinger* (2003), *Gratz v. Bollinger* (2003). Given the close divisions on the Court it is possible that, as new Justices are appointed, the Court will revisit the issue of whether to apply a more lenient standard of review to affirmative action programs assisting racial minorities.

The Equal Protection Clause textually limits only state government, hence it is literally inapplicable to the federal government. However, since *Bolling v. Sharpe* (1954), the Court has developed the doctrine that the Due Process Clause of the Fifth Amendment has an equal protection component with equivalent requirements to the Equal Protection Clause of the Fourteenth Amendment. Equal Protection doctrine (if not literally the Equal Protection Clause) has thus become applicable to all governmental action, whether state, local, or federal.

David Smolin

See Also

Suggestions for Further Research

RAOUL BERGER, GOVERNMENT BY JUDICIARY: THE TRANSFORMATION OF THE FOURTEENTH AMENDMENT (2d ed. 1997)

Alexander M. Bickel, *The Original Understanding and the Segregation Decision*, 69 HARV. L. REV. 1 (1955)

JAMES E. BOND, NO EASY WALK TO FREEDOM: RECONSTRUCTION AND THE RATIFICATION OF THE FOURTEENTH AMENDMENT (1997)

John Harrison, *Reconstructing the Privileges or Immunities Clause*, 101 YALE L.J. 1385 (1992)

HAROLD M. HYMAN & WILLIAM M. WIECEK, EQUAL JUSTICE UNDER LAW: CONSTITUTIONAL DEVELOPMENT 1835–1875 (1982)

Patrick J. Kelley, *An Alternative Originalist Opinion for* Brown v. Board of Education, 20 S. ILL. U. L.J. 75 (1995)

Michael J. Klarman, *An Interpretive History of Modern Equal Protection*, 90 MICH. L. REV. 213 (1991)

EARL M. MALTZ, CIVIL RIGHTS, THE CONSTITUTION, AND CONGRESS, 1863–1869 (1990)

Michael W. McConnell, *Originalism and the Desegregation Decisions*, 81 VA. L. REV. 947 (1995)

WILLIAM E. NELSON, THE FOURTEENTH AMENDMENT: FROM POLITICAL PRINCIPLE TO JUDICIAL DOCTRINE(1988)

Significant Cases

Dred Scott v. Sandford, 60 U.S. (19 How.) 393 (1856)

Slaughter-House Cases, 83 U.S. (16 Wall.) 36 (1873)

Yick Wo v. Hopkins, 118 U.S. 356 (1886)

Plessy v. Ferguson, 163 U.S. 537 (1896)

Buck v. Bell, 274 U.S. 200 (1927)

United States v. Carolene Products Co., 304 U.S. 144 (1938)

Korematsu v. United States, 323 U.S. 214 (1944)

Sweatt v. Painter, 339 U.S. 629 (1950)

Bolling v. Sharpe, 347 U.S. 497 (1954)

Brown v. Board of Education, 347 U.S. 483 (1954)

Williamson v. Lee Optical, 348 U.S. 483 (1955)

Craig v. Boren, 429 U.S. 190 (1976)

Mathews v. Diaz, 426 U.S. 67 (1976)

Washington v. Davis, 426 U.S. 229 (1976)

Foley v. Connelie, 435 U.S. 291 (1978)

Regents of the University of California v. Bakke, 438 U.S. 265 (1978)

Mississippi University for Women v. Hogan, 458 U.S. 718 (1982)

Plyler v. Doe, 457 U.S. 202 (1982)

City of Cleburne v. Cleburne Living Center, Inc., 473 U.S. 432 (1985)

Adarand Constructors, Inc. v. Pena, 515 U.S. 200 (1995)

Romer v. Evans, 517 U.S. 620 (1996)

United States v. Virginia, 518 U.S. 515 (1996)

Vacco v. Quill, 521 U.S. 793 (1997)

Gratz v. Bollinger, 539 U.S. 244 (2003)

Grutter v. Bollinger, 539 U.S. 982 (2003)

Lawrence v. Texas, 539 U.S. 558 (2003)

Apportionment of Representatives

Representatives shall be apportioned among the several States according to their respective numbers, counting the whole number of persons in each state, excluding Indians not taxed. But when the right to vote at any election for the choice of electors for President and Vice-President of the United States, Representatives in Congress, the Executive and Judicial officers of a State, or the members of the Legislature thereof, is denied to any of the male inhabitants of such State, being twenty-one years of age, and citizens of the United States, or in any way abridged, except for participation in rebellion, or other crime, the basis of representation therein shall be reduced in the proportion which the number of such male citizens shall bear to the whole number of male citizens twenty-one years of age in such State.

(AMENDMENT XIV, SECTION 2)

～

*I*n his speech of April 11, 1865, President Abraham Lincoln described the Southern states that had rebelled in the Civil War as being "out of their proper practical relation with the Union." In setting the terms for the readmission of those states to the Union, the Reconstruction Congress had to deal with several issues in addition to that of the status of the freedmen: representation in Congress, the political status of high-ranking rebels, and the debts of the United States and Confederate States.

The abolition of slavery increased the political power of the former slave states in the House of Representatives. Under the Three-fifths Clause of the original Constitution (Article I, Section 2, Clause 3), five slaves had counted as three persons; now they would be counted as five persons, though none of the Southern states would have permitted them to vote. Section 2 was a major concern in the South. Paper after paper carried charts showing its impact on Southern representation in Congress. The framers of the Fourteenth Amendment intended Section 2 to encourage the Southern states to enfranchise blacks, without directly compelling them to do so—for very few Northern states allowed blacks to vote. Democrats condemned any congressional interference in the traditionally state-controlled matter of voting, and radical Republicans objected to the implicit approval of racial qualifications for voting. Section 2 was, therefore, a compromise position acceptable to the moderate Republicans who held the balance of power in Congress. Although Section 2 allowed the disenfranchisement of persons who had engaged in the rebellion, none were denied the vote on those grounds. Neither did Congress reduce the representation of any Southern state that restricted the franchise on the basis of race.

The Fifteenth Amendment made Section 2 superfluous concerning "race, color or previous condition of servitude," and Congress never seriously attempted to apply it when Southern states began to disfranchise blacks—largely because such disfranchisement was cast in racially neutral terms. As it turned out, the inability or unwillingness to enforce either Section 2 of the Fourteenth Amendment or the provisions of the Fifteenth Amendment was the Achilles' heel of Reconstruction and the years that followed because without federal enforcement, blacks were unable to protect themselves through the political process. In one federal case, a putative candidate for Congress from Virginia sued under Section 2 of the Fourteenth Amendment in order to compel the state to adopt an at-large electoral system, because the state, by the poll tax, was not entitled to the nine seats that Congress had apportioned after the 1940 census. The Court dismissed the suit as a "political question." *Saunders v. Wilkins* (1945).

Despite being written in a particular historical context, Section 2 is still in operation and would apply in future cases of rebellion. By referring to "rebellion, *or other crime*," it recognizes and makes an exception for purposes of apportionment for states' traditional disfranchisement based on non-race based criminal conduct. The Supreme Court has inferred from Section 2 that states may disenfranchise convicted felons subsequent to their prison sentences. *Richardson v. Ramirez* (1974).

In *Reynolds v. Sims* (1964), Justice John M. Harlan decried the Court's continuing disregard of Section 2. In dissenting from the Court's adoption of the one person, one vote rule, he stated,

I am unable to understand the Court's utter disregard of the second section which expressly recognizes the States' power to deny "or in any way" abridge the right of their inhabitants to vote for "the members of the [state] legislature," and its express provision of a remedy for such denial or abridgement.

Paul Moreno

See Also

Article I, Section 2, Clause 3 (Three-Fifths Clause)
Amendment XV (Suffrage—Race)

Suggestions for Further Research

Alfred Avins, The Reconstruction Amendments' Debates: The Legislative History and Contemporary Debates in Congress on the Thirteenth, Fourteenth, and Fifteenth Amendments (1967)

James E. Bond, No Easy Walk to Freedom: Reconstruction and the Ratification of the Fourteenth Amendment (1997)

HORACE E. FLACK, THE ADOPTION OF THE FOUR-
TEENTH AMENDMENT (1908)

JOSEPH B. JAMES, THE FRAMING OF THE FOURTEENTH
AMENDMENT (1956)

Significant Cases

Saunders v. Wilkins, 152 F.2d 235 (4th Cir. 1945)

Reynolds v. Sims, 377 U.S. 533 (1964)

Richardson v. Ramirez, 418 U.S. 24 (1974)

Disqualification for Rebellion

No person shall be a Senator or Representative in Congress, or elector of President and Vice-President, or hold any office, civil or military, under the United States, or under any state, who, having previously taken an oath, as a member of Congress, or as an officer of the United States, or as a member of any State legislature, or as an executive or judicial officer of any state, to support the Constitution of the United States, shall have engaged in insurrection or rebellion against the same, or given aid or comfort to the enemies thereof. But Congress may by a vote of two-thirds of each House, remove such disability.

(AMENDMENT XIV, SECTION 3)

∼

*T*he disqualification of former rebels for federal and state office was the most controversial of the sections of the Fourteenth Amendment. It appeared to be vindictive and to intrude on the President's pardon power. It certainly made the ratification of new state constitutions in the South less likely—and some Congressmen believed that this was a deliberate stratagem to keep the Southern states out of the Union until after the 1868 election. An original draft of the section would have disqualified all who had voluntarily aided the Confederacy until 1870, but

the Senate adopted Senator Jacob Howard's less severe but potentially more permanent version. Congress lifted the disqualification of many individuals, and in 1872 it did so for all but Members of the Thirty-seventh (1861–1863) and Thirty-eighth Congresses (1863–1865), federal judicial and military officers, heads of departments, and foreign ministers. In 1898, Congress removed all disqualifications for previous disloyal conduct. Despite being written in a particular historical context, the clause is still in operation and would apply in the case of future insurrections or rebellion.

Paul Moreno

Suggestions for Further Research

ALFRED AVINS, THE RECONSTRUCTION AMEND-
MENTS' DEBATES: THE LEGISLATIVE HISTORY AND
CONTEMPORARY DEBATES IN CONGRESS ON THE
THIRTEENTH, FOURTEENTH, AND FIFTEENTH
AMENDMENTS (1967)

JAMES E. BOND, NO EASY WALK TO FREEDOM: RECON-
STRUCTION AND THE RATIFICATION OF THE FOUR-
TEENTH AMENDMENT (1997)

HORACE E. FLACK, THE ADOPTION OF THE FOUR-
TEENTH AMENDMENT (1908)

JOSEPH B. JAMES, THE FRAMING OF THE FOURTEENTH
AMENDMENT (1956)

Debts Incurred During Rebellion

The validity of the public debt of the United States, authorized by law, including debts incurred for payment of pensions and bounties for services in suppressing insurrection or rebellion, shall not be questioned. But neither the United States nor any State shall assume or pay any debt or obligation incurred in aid of insurrection or rebellion against the United States, or any claim for the loss or emancipation of any slave; but all such debts, obligations and claims shall be held illegal and void.

(AMENDMENT XIV, SECTION 4)

~

The effort to make the national debt sacrosanct and to repudiate the Confederate debt was the least controversial of the sections of the Fourteenth Amendment, at least in the North. As Representative Thaddeus Stevens of Pennsylvania put it, "I need say nothing of the fourth section, for none dare object to it who is not himself a rebel." The only objection to it was from owners of slaves in the loyal slave states who thought they should be compensated.

In applying the section, federal courts held that no contracts involving Confederate bonds could be enforced and that "a court of the United States must hesitate to give them any recognition whatever." Contracts involving Confederate currency, on the other hand, were enforceable "to prevent injustice to people who, when war was flagrant, had no other currency in which to make the exchanges required in the ordinary business of life." *Branch v. Haas* (1883).

The issue of the repudiation of the United States debt again emerged when Congress took the United States off the gold standard, and some of the *Gold Clause Cases* (1935) involved United States bonds. The Supreme Court did hold that Congress had exceeded its power under the Constitution in refusing to repay the bonds in gold, but it concluded that the bondholders had suffered only nominal damages and could not recover. Although Section 4 "was undoubtedly inspired by the desire to put beyond question the obligations of the Government issued during the Civil War, its language indicates a broader connotation [that embraces] whatever concerns the integrity of the public obligations." *Gold Clause Cases.*

Paul Moreno

Suggestions for Further Research

ALFRED AVINS, THE RECONSTRUCTION AMENDMENTS' DEBATES: THE LEGISLATIVE HISTORY AND CONTEMPORARY DEBATES IN CONGRESS ON THE THIRTEENTH, FOURTEENTH, AND FIFTEENTH AMENDMENTS (1967)

JAMES BOND, NO EASY WALK TO FREEDOM: RECONSTRUCTION AND THE RATIFICATION OF THE FOURTEENTH AMENDMENT (1997)

HORACE E. FLACK, THE ADOPTION OF THE FOURTEENTH AMENDMENT (1908)

JOSEPH B. JAMES, THE FRAMING OF THE FOURTEENTH AMENDMENT (1956)

Significant Cases

Branch v. Haas, 16 F. 53 (1883)
Gold Clause Cases, 294 U.S. 330 (1935)

Enforcement Clause

The Congress shall have the power to enforce, by appropriate legislation, the provisions of this article.
(AMENDMENT XIV, SECTION 5)

~

Following the pattern of the Necessary and Proper Clause of Article I, Section 8, the enforcement clause of the Fourteenth Amendment grants to Congress the power to pass legislation directed at effectuating the provisions of Sections 1 through 4 of the Amendment. Like the enforcement clauses of the two other reconstruction amendments (the Thirteenth and the Fifteenth), as well as those found in the Nineteenth, Twenty-third, Twenty-fourth, and Twenty-sixth Amendments, Section 5 constitutes a delegated power granted to Congress in addition to those listed in Article I, Section 8, of the Constitution.

One specific purpose of the Fourteenth Amendment when it was passed in 1866 was to ensure that Congress had adequate power to adopt the Civil Rights Act of that year, of which current 42 U.S.C. § 1981 is a descendant. That act prohibited state legislation—specifically, the notorious "Black Codes"—that denied blacks certain rights afforded to whites, including the power to make and enforce contracts.

A significant limitation in the text of Section 5 is that Congress is authorized only to "enforce, by appropriate legislation" the provisions of the Fourteenth Amendment. Justice William J. Brennan, Jr.'s opinion in *Katzenbach v. Morgan* (1966) suggested that Section 5 might also give Congress authority to define the substantive scope of the rest of the Fourteenth Amendment, but this interpretation seems at odds with the text and history of Section 5, and more recent opinions of the Supreme Court have rejected it. As early as 1883 in the *Civil Rights Cases*, the Court declared that since the prohibitions of Section 1 of the amendment reached only actions committed by the state or its agents, Congress was not empowered to legislate against the discriminatory actions of private individuals. More recently, in *City of Boerne v. Flores* (1997), the Court struck down as unconstitutional the Religious Freedom Restoration Act, in which Congress tried to use Section 5 to overturn an earlier Supreme Court decision defining the scope of the Free Exercise Clause with respect to the states. In doing so, the Court explicitly rejected Justice Brennan's suggestion in *Morgan* that Section 5 allows Congress to expand the meaning of the rest of the amendment. Thus, for Congress to invoke its power under Section 5, the proposed legislation must be aimed at remedying or preventing actions that would violate some prohibition within the Fourteenth Amendment. The legislation cannot be aimed at changing the scope of the Amendment.

On the other hand, the Supreme Court has declared that Congress may, as a prophylactic matter, ban state actions that it has found to be generally violative of the Fourteenth Amendment, even if in some instances they might not be. A classic example is the literacy test for voting. *See Oregon v. Mitchell* (1970). In theory, a state could use such a test in a constitutional way, but Congress determined that these tests were so commonly abused that they should be banned across the board, and the Court upheld this ban. The law was aimed at preventing actual and potential violations of the Constitution; it did not change the Constitution's substantive meaning and guarantees.

In *City of Boerne*, the Supreme Court declared that there must be a "proportionality"

and "congruence" between the statute "and the legitimate end to be achieved." It follows that, before Congress invokes its Section 5 authority, it must ascertain that the actions it is concerned about are in fact violative of the protections within the Fourteenth Amendment and that legislation remedying such violations has a "proportionality" and a "congruence" in accomplishing the remedy. This, in turn, requires a careful analysis of the rest of the Fourteenth Amendment and the scope of its guarantees.

For instance, there must be "state action." Section 5 gives Congress no authority to legislate with respect to the private sector because, the Court has held, there can be no Section 1 violation without state action. *Civil Rights Cases*. Likewise, with respect to religious discrimination, the state action must amount to intentional discrimination. The Court found in *City of Boerne* that laws that are neutral in text and intention and that have only a disproportionate effect on a religious group are beyond Congress's authority to prohibit. The same kinds of distinctions and limitations apply with respect to other antidiscrimination legislation, For example, because the disabled are not "a suspect classification," state discrimination against the disabled violates the Fourteenth Amendment only if it is "irrational." Thus, the Court has recently held in *Board of Trustees of the University of Alabama v. Garrett* (2001) that Section 5 gives Congress authority only to ban irrational state discrimination against the disabled.

Roger Clegg

See also

Suggestions for Further Research

Alexander Bickel, *The Voting Rights Cases*, 1966 Sup. Ct. Rev. 79

Robert A. Burt, *Miranda and Title II: A Morganatic Marriage*, 1969 Sup. Ct. Rev. 81

Ronald D. Rotunda, *The Power of Congress Under Section 5 of the Fourteenth Amendment after* City of Boerne v. Flores, 32 Ind. L. Rev. 163 (1998)

J. TenBroek, Equal Under Law (pb. ed. 1965)

The Human Life Bill: Hearings on S. 158 before the Subcommittee on Separation of Powers of the Committee on the Judiciary, United States Senate, 97th Cong., 1st Sess. 310 (1982) (statement of Robert H. Bork)

Significant Cases

Civil Rights Cases, 109 U.S. 3 (1883)

Katzenbach v. Morgan, 384 U.S. 641 (1966)

Oregon v. Mitchell, 400 U.S. 112 (1970)

City of Boerne v. Flores, 521 U.S. 507 (1997)

United States v. Morrison, 529 U.S. 598 (2000)

Board of Trustees of the University of Alabama v. Garrett, 531 U.S. 356 (2001)

Suffrage—Race

Section 1. The right of citizens of the United States to vote shall not be denied or abridged by the United States or by any State on account of race, color, or previous condition of servitude—

Section 2. The Congress shall have power to enforce this article by appropriate legislation.

(Amendment XV)

≈

$\mathcal{P}$assed by Congress on March 3, 1869, and ratified in 1870, the Fifteenth Amendment was the last of the three Reconstruction Amendments. Though the language of the Fifteenth Amendment prohibits all race-based discrimination in qualifications for voting, the Framers were primarily concerned with the enfranchisement of African-Americans. As early as 1866, many of the Republicans were convinced of the need for a constitutional amendment that would require the states to allow African-Americans to vote. Indeed, at one point the Joint Committee on Reconstruction voted to report a version of the Fourteenth Amendment that explicitly embraced the principle of race-blind suffrage. However, many Northerners continued to oppose black suffrage in principle, and fears of a political backlash led the committee to abandon the issue before the proposed amendment came to the floor. By 1869, the situation had changed. Although the outcome of referenda on black suffrage in the North continued to reflect the opposition of critical swing voters, other factors persuaded mainstream Republicans in Congress of the need for a federal constitutional amendment to deal with the issue.

Republicans had a variety of different reasons for supporting such an amendment. In the Reconstruction Act of 1867, Congress had forced black suffrage on the ex-Confederate states by statute, and Republicans faced the charge that they were hypocritical in not imposing the same requirement on Northern states. Some also believed that if blacks were enfranchised in the states that had remained in the Union, they would provide critical support for Republican candidates in those states. Still others argued that, even in the South, black suffrage would be insecure without a constitutional amendment and that the governments of the ex-Confederate states could not be returned to local control until the political power of the freed slaves was guaranteed.

By 1869, these considerations, combined with the conviction that allowing blacks to vote was right in itself, convinced virtually all mainstream congressional Republicans that a constitutional amendment was desirable. Republicans were, nevertheless, deeply divided over the question of what precise language should be adopted. Initially, the House of Representatives adopted a proposal quite similar to the current Fifteenth Amendment. However, a number of prominent Republicans complained that this narrow language would allow states intentionally to disfranchise most African-Americans by adopting qualifications that, although neutral on their face, would in practice be impossible for most freed slaves to satisfy. Responding to these and other concerns, the Senate proposed to eliminate not only discrimination on the basis of race, color, and previous condition of servitude but also discrimination on the basis of nativity, property, education, or creed in both the right to vote and the right to hold elective office. In ordinary circumstances, one might have expected a conference committee to have been convened at this point. However, in the complex parliamentary maneuvering that followed, the Senate did not vote to enter into conference; instead, the entire drafting process began again in both houses. The House then produced a draft that tracked the original Senate version, except that it deleted the reference to discrimination on the basis of education. The Senate, by contrast, now passed a simple prohibition on racial discrimination with respect to the rights to vote and hold office. A conference committee was convened, and it produced the current language of the Fifteenth Amendment, which embraced only the prohibition on racial discrimination in voting, omitting any reference to the right to hold office.

In short, because of the difficulty of agreeing to the precise language, the framers adopted a simple prohibition on discrimination on the basis of race, color, and previous condition of servitude even though there was a risk that a court could interpret the language narrowly and thereby allow deliberate evasion by facially neutral statutes. At first, the Supreme Court did exactly that and refused to inquire into the motives of those who adopted facially neutral statutes, such as literacy tests. *Williams v. Mississippi* (1898). Subsequently, the Court took a slightly broader view and voided a grandfather clause, the effect of which was to allow illiterate whites to vote, on the ground that it could have no conceivable purpose other than racial discrimination. *Guinn v. United States* (1915). More recently, the Court has invoked both the Fourteenth and Fifteenth Amendments to invalidate facially neutral restrictions on voting rights where the legislative history reveals an intention to exclude or hinder African-Americans. *Rogers v. Lodge* (1982), *Hunter v. Underwood* (1985). The Court also invoked the

amendments in cases where there was evident racial gerrymandering designed to disenfranchise blacks. *Gomillion v. Lightfoot* (1960). On the other hand, the Court has held that race may be considered in the redistricting process only so long as racial considerations do not predominate, and there is no effort to dilute the voting strength of minorities. *Bush v. Vera* (1996).

Similarly, the Court adopted variable views on the sweep of allowable congressional authority under the enforcement clause. One critical issue was whether the amendment armed Congress with the power to regulate purely private action. Many of the congressional Republicans, who were responsible for passing the Fifteenth Amendment, apparently believed they had such authority: a section in a statute passed in 1870 made private, racially motivated interference with voting a federal crime. Nonetheless, although *Ex parte Yarbrough* (1884) suggested that this statute was constitutional, in 1903 the Supreme Court reversed course and held that the Fifteenth Amendment did not allow Congress to regulate purely private activity. *James v. Bowman* (1903). This basic principle was maintained until at least 1941, *United States v. Classic*, although the Court preferred to take the route of expansively defining nongovernmental activity as state action for purposes of the Fifteenth Amendment, applied particularly to the institution of the white primary. *Smith v. Allwright* (1944), *Terry v. Adams* (1953).

Although the legislative history of the Fifteenth Amendment provides little direct guidance on the precise scope of the enforcement authority under Section 2, recent decisions have upheld the constitutionality of sweeping remedial measures adopted to combat government-imposed racial discrimination. For example, when Congress had evidence of widespread racial discrimination in state elections, the Court allowed Congress to place the entire state and local electoral apparatus under federal supervision and to forbid the adoption of measures that had even the *effect* of diluting the voting power of racial minorities. *Thornburg v. Gingles* (1986). The Court, asserting that enforcement power had the same breadth as a necessary and proper clause, has also upheld the power of Congress to forbid literacy tests. *South Carolina v. Katzenbach* (1966).

Earl Maltz

See Also

Amendment XIII (Abolition of Slavery)

Amendment XIV, Section 1

Amendment XIX (Suffrage—Sex)

Amendment XXIV (Poll Taxes)

Amendment XXVI (Suffrage—Age)

Suggestions for Further Research

Michael Les Benedict, A Compromise of Principle: Congressional Republicans and Reconstruction 1863–1869 (1974)

James G. Blaine, Twenty Years of Congress: From Lincoln to Garfield with a Review of the Events Which Led to the Political Revolution of 1860 (1884–1886)

LaWanda Cox & John H. Cox, *Negro Suffrage and Republican Politics: The Problem of Motivation in Reconstruction Historiography*, 33 J. S. Hist. 303 (1967)

William Gillette, The Right to Vote: Politics and the Passage of the Fifteenth Amendment (1965)

Earl M. Maltz, Civil Rights, the Constitution and Congress, 1863–1869 (1990)

Xi Wang, The Trial of Democracy: Black Suffrage and Northern Republicans (1997)

Significant Cases

Ex parte Yarbrough, 110 U.S. 651 (1884)

Williams v. Mississippi, 170 U.S. 213 (1898)

James v. Bowman, 190 U.S. 127 (1903)

Guinn v. United States, 238 U.S. 347 (1915)

United States v. Classic, 313 U.S. 299 (1941)

Smith v. Allwright, 321 U.S. 649 (1944)

Terry v. Adams, 345 U.S. 461 (1953)

Gomillion v. Lightfoot, 364 U.S. 339 (1960)

South Carolina v. Katzenbach, 383 U.S. 301 (1966)

City of Rome v. United States, 446 U.S. 156 (1980)

Rogers v. Lodge, 458 U.S. 613 (1982)

Hunter v. Underwood, 471 U.S. 222 (1985)

Thornburg v. Gingles, 478 U.S. 30 (1986)

Bush v. Vera, 517 U.S. 952 (1996)

Johnson v. California, 125 S. Ct. 1141 (2005)

Income Tax

The Congress shall have power to lay and collect taxes on incomes, from whatever source derived, without apportionment among the several States, and without regard to any census or enumeration.

(Amendment XVI)

෨

*T*he Sixteenth Amendment, approved by Congress in 1909 and ratified in 1913, made it possible for Congress to enact an income tax without having to worry about whether, under the rules applicable to direct taxes, the tax had to be apportioned among the states on the basis of population.

Congress has the "power to lay and collect taxes," including an income tax, but, under two constitutional provisions (*see* Article I, Section 2, Clause 3; Article I, Section 9, Clause 4), direct taxes must be apportioned—a difficult requirement to satisfy. If an income tax is subject to apportionment, a state with one-tenth the national population, for example, has to bear one-tenth the aggregate tax liability, regardless of the state's financial condition. Suppose the populations of Iowa and Maine were equal, but Iowa's per capita income were twice Maine's. The rates for an apportioned income tax would have to be twice as high in Maine, the poorer state, as in Iowa. Such geographic variability makes it difficult, if not impossible, for anyone in Congress to support that kind of tax.

National real-estate taxes were enacted in antebellum America, with complex rules for apportionment—the Founders intended direct taxes to be difficult, not impossible—but, at the Founding, no one was thinking about an income tax. When this idea emerged and became politically possible, an income tax was assumed to be indirect, largely because Justices in *Hylton v. United States* (1796) had intimated, in dicta, that the term "direct taxes" was limited to capitation and real-estate taxes. Congress accordingly enacted an unapportioned income tax during the Civil War, and the Court, citing *Hylton*, upheld the tax in 1881. *Springer v. United States* (1881).

In 1894, with little attention to constitutional issues, Congress again enacted an unapportioned income tax with the clear goal of shifting the tax burden from regressive tariffs and excises to a levy based on ability of the individual to pay. Congressional debates were full of statements about how the well-to-do had not been paying their fair share. The authors of the income tax intended to accomplish what consumption taxes had not, and, to that end, the 1894 tax reached only the wealthiest one percent of the population.

This time the Supreme Court refused to approve the idea. In *Pollock v. Farmers' Loan & Trust Co.* (1895), a closely divided Court reinvigorated the direct-tax clauses, holding that the 1894 tax was direct and, because not apportioned, unconstitutional. With *Pollock* on the books, something had to be done if there was to be an unapportioned income tax.

Not every income-tax proponent thought a constitutional amendment was necessary after *Pollock*. Many believed the decision was so clearly wrong that the Court would decide differently if given another chance. In addition, supporters feared that if a campaign to amend the Constitution failed, the income tax would be doomed for years. In fact, some Congressmen "backed" the amendment precisely because they expected it to die in state legislatures.

Whether *Pollock* was wrongly decided was, however, almost beside the point. Enacting a new tax to challenge a recent Supreme Court decision was politically risky. Even if wrong, the Court might not change its mind, particularly if Congress seemed to be questioning judicial authority. By 1909, it had become apparent there would be no income tax until the apportionment issue had been resolved.

The Sixteenth Amendment did that for "taxes on incomes." By its terms, it exempted only such taxes from apportionment, leaving apportionment to apply to other direct taxes (including capitation and real-estate taxes, and, given *Pollock*'s expanded conception of direct taxation, maybe more, like a direct-consumption tax). The sponsor, Senator Norris Brown of Nebraska, said he intended to limit the amendment's application in this way, to make an unapportioned *income* tax possible, and he rejected changes that would have eliminated the direct-tax clauses.

Despite heated opposition, the amendment passed Congress with huge majorities. During ratification, Governor Charles Evans Hughes of New York raised a concern that the phrase "from whatever source derived" could be interpreted to permit national taxation of state and local bond interest, something the *Pollock* Court had said was inconsistent with intergovernmental immunity. Assured the amendment was not intended to overturn that doctrine, New York signed on and ratification proceeded swiftly.

Facilitating an unapportioned income tax was hardly trivial, but some say the amendment did even more. Bruce Ackerman, for example, argues it was intended to repudiate all of *Pollock*, to contract the notion of "direct taxes," and to revive the plenary taxing power. That interpretation gives more weight to the amendment than the "taxes on incomes" language comfortably bears, however, and it relies on the questionable assumption, derived from *Hylton* dicta, that modern forms of taxation are immune from limitation simply because the Court did not mention them in 1796.

Except in tax protester cases, where ineffectual arguments about the amendment's legitimacy are made, the amendment is not involved in litigation today. The Supreme Court has had no recent occasion to articulate the meaning of the amendment or to consider whether the amendment, which broadened congressional power, also contains restrictions on that power.

The general understanding among contemporary scholars is that the taxing power is so broad that Congress alone determines what can be reached by an income tax. This view of unbounded congressional power conflicts with the original, limited role of the amendment, however, and it requires rejecting several old Supreme Court decisions that took the language of the amendment seriously: for an unapportioned tax to be authorized by the Sixteenth Amendment, it must be on "incomes."

In *Eisner v. Macomber* (1920), for example, the Court struck down an income tax as it applied to a stock dividend (a distribution not of money, but of additional shares), the receipt of which, said the Court, was not income. Even if the Court misunderstood stock dividends, as some have argued, the case remains significant for what it says about how the amendment should be interpreted. Throughout the 1920s, the Court assumed the term "incomes" had content, stressing that Congress could not circumvent apportionment by simply labeling a levy an income tax. These cases have not been overruled, and the Court has cited *Macomber* favorably, on nonconstitutional matters, as recently as 1991.

In one respect, the Court has revised the understanding of 1913. Interest on state and local bonds is no longer constitutionally exempt from income taxation; the doctrine of intergovernmental immunity advanced by Governor Hughes has been discarded in this context (although not as a result of the Sixteenth Amendment). *See South Carolina v. Baker* (1988).

Erik M. Jensen

See Also

Article I, Section 2, Clause 3 (Three-fifths Clause)
Article I, Section 8, Clause 1 (Spending Clause)
Article I, Section 8, Clause 1 (Uniformity Clause)
Article I, Section 9, Clause 4 (Direct Taxes)

Suggestions for Further Research

Bruce Ackerman, *Taxation and the Constitution*, 99 COLUM. L. REV. 1 (1999)

Erik M. Jensen, *The Apportionment of "Direct Taxes": Are Consumption Taxes Constitutional?*, 97 COLUM. L. REV. 2334 (1997)

Erik M. Jensen, *The Taxing Power, the Sixteenth Amendment, and the Meaning of "Incomes,"* 33 ARIZ. ST. L.J. 1057 (2001)

Marjorie E. Kornhauser, *The Morality of Money: American Attitudes Toward Wealth and the Income Tax*, 70 IND. L.J. 119 (1994)

EDWIN R. A. SELIGMAN, THE INCOME TAX (1911)

Significant Cases

Hylton v. United States, 3 U.S. (3 Dall.) 171 (1796)
Springer v. United States, 102 U.S. 586 (1881)

Pollock v. Farmers' Loan & Trust Co., 157 U.S. 429 (1895)
Eisner v. Macomber, 252 U.S. 189 (1920)
South Carolina v. Baker, 485 U.S. 505 (1988)

Popular Election of Senators

The Senate of the United States shall be composed of two Senators from each State, elected by the people thereof, for six years; and each Senator shall have one vote. The electors in each State shall have the qualifications requisite for electors of the most numerous branch of the State legislatures.

(AMENDMENT XVII, CLAUSE 1)

~

*O*n May 12, 1912, the Seventeenth Amendment, providing for direct popular election of the Senate, was approved by the Congress; the requisite three-fourths of the state legislatures ratified it in less than eleven months. Not only was it ratified quickly, but it was also ratified by overwhelming numbers. In fifty-two of the seventy-two state legislative chambers that voted to ratify the Seventeenth Amendment, the vote was unanimous, and in all thirty-six of the ratifying states the total number of votes cast in opposition to ratification was only 191, with 152 of these votes coming from the lower chambers of Vermont and Connecticut.

Although state ratification of the Seventeenth Amendment came quickly and easily, congressional approval of the idea of popular election of the Senate did not. The first resolution calling for direct election of the Senate was introduced in the House of Representatives on February 14, 1826. From that date, until the adoption of the Seventeenth Amendment eighty-six years later, 187 subsequent resolutions of a similar nature were also introduced before Congress, 167 of them after 1880. The House approved six of these proposals before the Senate gave its consent. By 1912,

Senators were already picked by direct election in twenty-nine of the forty-eight states. As Senator William E. Borah said in 1911, "I should not have been here [in the U.S. Senate] if it [direct election] has not been practiced, and I have great affection [for this system]." What happened is that the people in most of the states gradually turned to nonbinding primary elections to select their Senator; state legislators promised to vote for the Senator that the people had selected in this "advisory" election. This "advisory" election had real teeth because many state laws provided that candidates for state legislator had to sign pledges (which were placed on the ballot) that they would promise (or refuse to promise) to vote for the U.S. Senate candidate that the people had selected in their nonbinding election. If the state legislative candidate refused to sign the pledge, the people would vote against him, and so the Senate gradually became populated with people who were, in effect, selected by popular, direct election.

The Seventeenth Amendment was approved and ratified to make the Constitution more democratic. Progressives argued forcefully, persistently, and ultimately successfully that the democratic principle required the Senate to be elected directly by the people rather than indirectly through their state legislatures. By altering the manner of election, however, they also altered the principal mechanism employed by the framers to protect federalism. The framers understood that the mode of electing (and especially reelecting) Senators by state legislatures made it in the self-interest of Senators to preserve the original federal design and to protect the interests of states as states (*see* Article I, Section 3, Clause 1). This understanding was perfectly encapsulated in a July 1789 letter to John Adams, in which Roger Sherman emphasized that "[t]he senators, being eligible by the legislatures of the several states, and dependent on them for re-election, will be vigilant in supporting their rights against infringement by the legislative or executive of the United States."

In practice, the state legislatures' election of Senators became more complicated. The members of the state legislators were often divided over whom to elect as Senator. Many state legislators simply voted for themselves, and their deadlock would result in no Senator being chosen, which then deprived the state of any representation in the Senate for a period of time that lasted a year or more.

In addition to its impact on federalism, the ratification of the Seventeenth Amendment has also had demographic, behavioral, and institutional consequences on the Senate itself. Demographically, popularly elected Senators are more likely to be born in the states they represent, are more likely to have an Ivy League education, and are likely to have had a higher level of prior governmental service. Institutionally, the states are now more likely to have a split Senate delegation, and the Senate now more closely matches the partisan composition of the House.

Ralph Rossum

See Also
Article I, Section 3, Clause 1 (Senate)

Article V (Prohibition on Amendment: Equal Suffrage in the Senate)

Suggestions for Further Research
Sara Brandes Crook & John R. Hibbing, *A Not-So-Distant Mirror: The Seventeenth Amendment and Congressional Change*, 91 Am. Pol. Sci. Rev. 845 (1997)

Jay S. Bybee, *Ulysses at the Mast: Democracy, Federalism, and the Sirens' Song of the Seventeenth Amendment*, 91 Nw. U. L. Rev. 500 (1997)

Christopher H. Hoebeke, The Road to Mass Democracy: Original Intent and the Seventeenth Amendment (1995)

Ralph A. Rossum, Federalism, the Supreme Court, and the Seventeenth Amendment: The Irony of Constitutional Democracy (2001)

Herbert Wechsler, *The Political Safeguards of Federalism: The Role of the States in the Composition and Selection of the National Government*, 54 Colum. L. Rev. 543 (1954)

Todd J. Zywicki, *Beyond the Shell and Husk of History: The History of the Seventeenth Amendment and Its Implications for Current Reform Proposals*, 45 Clev. St. L. Rev. (1997)

Vacancies in the Senate

When vacancies happen in the representation of any State in the Senate, the executive authority of such State shall issue writs of election to fill such vacancies: Provided, That the legislature of any State may empower the executive thereof to make temporary appointments until the people fill the vacancies by election as the legislature may direct.

This amendment shall not be so construed as to effect the election or term of any Senator chosen before it becomes valid as part of the Constitution.

(AMENDMENT XVII,
CLAUSES 2 AND 3)

~

*T*he Seventeenth Amendment, ratified in 1913, provided for the direct election of United States Senators, replacing the original method that had left the choice to state legislatures. Previously, state legislatures could choose Senators and fill vacancies at any time during a regular or special legislative session. After the ratification of the Seventeenth Amendment, it was recognized that the expense and inconvenience of election by popular vote made it necessary to schedule elections for Senators at regular intervals. To avoid the hardship to a state suffering a lack of representation pending a regular election, the Seventeenth Amendment also provided for methods of election or appointment to fill any unexpired term.

The language and history of the clause indicate that the states have the power to balance conflicting goals of a speedy popular election versus the state's interests in conducting elections on a regularized basis so as to maximize voter participation and minimize administrative expense. Thus, when the death of Robert F. Kennedy created a vacancy in New York's Senate delegation in June 1968, New York was permitted to postpone the election of his replacement

until 1970, rather than being required to hold both a primary and general election by fall 1968. *Valenti v. Rockefeller* (1969). Following the death of Senator John Heinz in 1991, Pennsylvania was permitted to fill the vacancy by a special election, with the candidates to be chosen by party conventions of the state's two major parties. The Court held that the Seventeenth Amendment did not mandate that party nominees be chosen by popular vote, so long as the actual election was by popular vote. *Trinsey v. Pennsylvania* (1991).

The clause does not define when a vacancy exists. During the 2000 election, the people of Missouri knowingly voted for the deceased Mel Carnahan for Senator. The governor of the state declared this election to have created a vacancy, which he filled by appointing Carnahan's widow, Jean Carnahan, and then issued a writ of election for 2002. It remains an open question, however, whether the voters can create a Senate "vacancy" by knowingly voting for an ineligible candidate and allowing the governor to fill the position with an individual of his choice, as opposed to simply declaring the votes to be improper or "spoiled" ballots.

Todd Zywicki

See Also

Article I, Section 3
Article I, Section 4
Amendment XVII (Popular Election of Senators)

Suggestions for Further Research

ROBERT BYRD, THE SENATE, 1789–1989 (1988)

2 THE RECORDS OF THE FEDERAL CONVENTION OF 1787, 231 (Max Farrand ed., rev. ed. 1966) (Madison's notes) (rev. ed. 1966)

GEORGE H. HAYNES, THE SENATE OF THE UNITED STATES: ITS HISTORY AND PRACTICE (2 vols. 1938)

S. REP. No. 961 (1911)

Todd J. Zywicki, *Beyond the Shell and Husk of History: The History of the Seventeenth Amendment and Its Implications for Current Reform Proposals*, 45 CLEV. ST. L. REV. 165 (1997)

Todd J. Zywicki, *The Law of Presidential Transitions and the 2000 Election*, 2001 BYU L. REV. 1573 (2001)

Todd J. Zywicki, *Senators and Special Interests: A Public Choice Analysis of the Seventeenth Amendment*, 73 Or. L. Rev. 1007 (1994)

Significant Cases

Valenti v. Rockefeller, 292 F. Supp. 851 (S.D.N.Y. 1968), *aff'd* 393 U.S. 405 (1969)

Trinsey v. Pennsylvania, 941 F.2d 224 (1991)

Prohibition

Section 1. After one year from the ratification of this article the manufacture, sale, or transportation of intoxicating liquors within, the importation thereof into, or the exportation thereof from the United States and all territory subject to the jurisdiction thereof for beverage purposes is hereby prohibited.

Section 2. The Congress and the several States shall have concurrent power to enforce this article by appropriate legislation.

Section 3. This article shall be inoperative unless it shall have been ratified as an amendment to the Constitution by the legislatures of the several States, as provided in the Constitution, within seven years from the date of the submission hereof to the States by the Congress.
(AMENDMENT XVIII)

≈

*T*he Eighteenth Amendment, enacted in 1919, was one of four "Progressive" Amendments passed and ratified in quick succession. Although the American involvement with alcohol and with temperance movements had been present from the beginning of the country's history, Prohibition rode to easy victory in an alliance with other elements of the Progressive Movement in the early twentieth century. The Sixteenth Amend-

ment, permitting the income tax, freed the government from dependence on the tax on liquor. The direct election of Senators, through the Seventeenth Amendment, made the Senate more amenable to electoral pressure for temperance. Although the Nineteenth Amendment, guaranteeing women the right to vote, was ratified in 1920, it reflected a general acceptance of woman suffrage (and temperance support) already present in the states, many of which allowed women to vote even before the Nineteenth Amendment came into effect.

Businesses supported the amendment to ensure a more reliable workforce, while prejudice against German-Americans and their breweries during World War I helped make Prohibition a patriotic cause. The amendment passed through both Congress and the states with amazing speed. There were no committee hearings in Congress, and debate took less than six hours, most of it centering on the time limit for ratification. The states ratified the amendment within a month.

The only problematic element of the amendment was Section 2, granting Congress and the states concurrent enforcement powers. Under its Section 2 powers, Congress enacted the Volstead Act in 1919 over President Woodrow Wilson's veto. The act defined "intoxicating liquors" as any drink with an alcohol content higher than .05 percent, a strict definition that prohibited even the intake of beer. It permitted exemptions for industrial, medicinal, and sacramental uses, and the act also contained a possession exemption for personal use within one's own private dwelling.

In the 1920 *National Prohibition Cases*, the Supreme Court ruled that, under the Supremacy Clause, states could not enact legislation that conflicted with congressional enactments regarding Prohibition. Because the states had been the engines of much Progressive legislation, the Progressive Movement assumed that the states would actively enforce the amendment, federal law, and their own state laws. The unexpected and widespread reluctance among the states to enforce Prohibition, along with the concomitant development of organized crime and the loss of tax revenues after the start of the

Depression, led to a national scandal that undid Prohibition in little more than a decade. Prohibition was repealed in 1933 by the Twenty-first Amendment.

David Wagner

See Also
Amendment XXI (Repeal of Prohibition)

Suggestions for Further Research
EDWARD BEHR, PROHIBITION: THIRTEEN YEARS THAT CHANGED AMERICA (1997)

RICHARD F. HAMM, SHAPING THE EIGHTEENTH AMENDMENT: TEMPERANCE REFORM, LEGAL CULTURE, AND THE POLITY (1995)

JOHN KOBLER, ARDENT SPIRITS: THE RISE AND FALL OF PROHIBITION (reprint, 1993)

THOMAS PEGRAM, BATTLING DEMON RUM: THE STRUGGLE FOR A DRY AMERICA, 1800–1933 (1998)

Significant Case
National Prohibition Cases, 253 U.S. 350 (1920)

Suffrage—Sex

The right of citizens of the United States to vote shall not be denied or abridged by the United States or by any State on account of sex.

Congress shall have power to enforce this article by appropriate legislation.

(AMENDMENT XIX)

~

Contrary to popular belief, the United States Constitution of 1787 is a gender-neutral document. Throughout the original text, the Framers refer to "persons"—as opposed to "male persons"—and use the pronoun "he" only in the generic sense. The word "male" did not even appear in the Constitution until the Fourteenth Amendment was ratified in 1868.

Nothing in the original Constitution bars women from voting. Instead, the Framers left the matter of determining who was eligible to participate in the election of House Members and presidential electors almost entirely to the discretion of the states. Article I, Section 2, minimally requires that each state's congressional electors "shall have the qualifications requisite for electors of the most numerous branch of the state legislature," and Article II, Section 1, simply directs each state legislature to appoint its presidential electors in whatever manner it chooses. Although it is true that almost every state opted to restrict the vote to men, New Jersey did not. Accordingly, between the late 1780s and 1807, when that state's legislature restricted the vote to men, many women participated in federal elections. Under the Constitution, in short, no change was needed to enable women to vote. This fact was ultimately reflected in the different strategies used by the advocates of woman suffrage to remove sexual qualifications for voting.

Although scholars typically trace the origins of the organized woman's rights movement generally, and the drive for woman suffrage particularly, to a famous 1848 gathering in Seneca Falls, New York, the woman suffrage movement began to affect policy only during Reconstruction. In this period, the advocates of woman suffrage began pursuing three main strategies. The first was a judicial strategy involving the Fourteenth Amendment. From the standpoint of the woman suffrage movement, the Fourteenth Amendment represented both a setback and an opportunity. It was a setback insofar as its second section introduced the word "male" into the Constitution and did so in a clause penalizing any state that abridged the right of its "male inhabitants" to vote in state or federal elections for reasons other than crime or rebellion. In so doing, woman suffrage advocates worried, the second section lent credibility to the idea that the Constitution restricted the right to vote to men. Nevertheless, they also viewed the amendment as an opportunity, because they believed the first section of the amendment contradicted the implication of the second. When the Citizenship

Clause was read in combination with the Privileges or Immunities Clause, they argued, the Fourteenth Amendment barred states from denying a woman's right to vote in federal elections. In its 1874 decision of *Minor v. Happersett*, however, the Supreme Court unequivocally disagreed, holding that voting was not one of the privileges and immunities of citizens of the United States.

At the same time, various elements of the woman suffrage movement began pursuing other strategies. Consistent with the Framers' arrangements in Articles I and II, the first such strategy involved persuading individual states and territories to eliminate sexual qualifications for voting. In 1869, the Wyoming territory became the first territorial government to do so; upon obtaining statehood in 1890, Wyoming became the first state since New Jersey to allow women to participate in federal elections on an equal basis with men. Although success was often slow in coming, by the time the Nineteenth Amendment was ratified in 1920, thirty states and one territory already permitted women to vote in at least some aspect in the selection of Members of the House (and by then the Senate) or presidential electors.

The other strategy begun in this period involved amending the federal Constitution in a way that would render such state action unnecessary. More precisely, the advocates of woman suffrage sought to reduce the power conferred upon the states in Article I, Section 2; Article II, Section 1; and eventually in the Seventeenth Amendment (which was ratified in 1913)—as well as their own constitutions—by explicitly barring the states from making sex a qualification for voting in federal and state elections. The first such amendment was introduced in Congress in 1869. In 1878, California Senator Aaron A. Sargent introduced the proposal that would, without any change in wording, be approved by Congress in 1919 and ratified by three-fourths of the states in 1920. Sargent's proposal simply repeated the language of the Fifteenth Amendment save for one change: whereas the Fifteenth Amendment forbids both the U.S. and state governments from denying or abridging their citizens' right to vote "on account of race, color, or previous condition of servitude," the Nineteenth forbids the same "on account of sex."

Unlike so many other clauses of the Constitution—including the Fifteenth Amendment itself—the Nineteenth Amendment has generated a remarkably small body of case law. In the first decade or so following ratification, a relatively small number of state courts implemented its restriction on the power of the states by striking down constitutional or statutory provisions that restricted the vote to men, made it more difficult for women to qualify than men, or otherwise treated male and female ballots differently. The amendment has generated even fewer federal cases. Although the Court has obliquely commented on the meaning of the amendment in various cases, it has confronted this question squarely on only one occasion. In *Breedlove v. Suttles* (1937), a Georgia law exempted payment of a one-dollar poll tax for unregistered female voters, but required male voters to pay the tax before registering to vote. In its decision, the Court stated that the amendment's restriction on the power of the federal and state governments to deny or abridge their citizens' right to vote "on account of sex" applied to men and women equally, and superseded all federal or state measures to the contrary. The Court concluded, however, that the amendment was not designed to restrict the state's ability to tax.

Tiffany Jones

See Also

Article I, Section 2, Clause 1 (Elector Qualifications)
Article II, Section 1, Clause 2 (Presidential Electors)
Amendment XVII (Popular Election of Senators)

Suggestions for Further Research

Eleanor Flexner & Ellen Fitzpatrick, Century of Struggle: The Woman's Rights Movement in the United States (1996)

Thomas G. West, Vindicating the Founders: Race, Sex, Class and Justice in the Origins of America (1997)

Marjorie Spruill Wheeler ed., One Woman, One Vote: Rediscovering the Woman Suffrage Movement (1995)

Significant Cases

Minor v. Happersett, 88 U.S. 162 (1874)
Leser v. Garnett, 258 U.S. 130 (1922)
Breedlove v. Suttles, 302 U.S. 277 (1937)

Presidential Terms

Section 1. The terms of the President and Vice President shall end at noon on the 20th day of January, and the terms of Senators and Representatives at noon on the 3d day of January, of the years in which such terms would have ended if this article had not been ratified; and the terms of their successors shall then begin.

Section 2. The Congress shall assemble at least once in every year, and such meeting shall begin at noon on the 3d day of January, unless they shall by law appoint a different day.

Section 3. If, at the time fixed for the beginning of the term of the President, the President elect shall have died, the Vice President elect shall become President. If a President shall not have been chosen before the time fixed for the beginning of his term, or if the President elect shall have failed to qualify, then the Vice President elect shall act as President until a President shall have qualified; and the Congress may by law provide for the case wherein neither a President elect nor a Vice President shall have qualified, declaring who shall then act as President, or the manner in which one who is to act shall be selected, and such person shall act accordingly until a President or Vice President shall have qualified.

Section 4. The Congress may by law provide for the case of the death of any of the persons from whom the House of Representatives may choose a President whenever the right of choice shall have devolved upon them, and for the case of the death of any of the persons from whom the Senate may choose a Vice President whenever the right of choice shall have devolved upon them.

Section 5. Sections 1 and 2 shall take effect on the 15th day of October following the ratification of this article.

Section 6. This article shall be inoperative unless it shall have been ratified as an amendment to the Constitution by the legislatures of three-fourths of the several States within seven years from the date of its submission.

(Amendment XX)

~

*T*he Twentieth Amendment appears simply to embody minor structural changes to the Constitution. That the amendment was ratified by the states more quickly than any other constitutional amendment before or since supports this impression of an uncontroversial technical revision. So does the absence of litigation surrounding the meaning of the amendment. But the Twentieth Amendment became part of the Constitution only after decades of congressional debate, and its meaning was debated as recently as the impeachment of President William Jefferson Clinton by the United States House of Representatives in December 1998.

The six clauses of the Twentieth Amendment are readily divided into three pairs. The first two sections shorten the "lame-duck" period after an election and before the new officials take office. The next two sections govern various presidential succession questions. The final two provisions are standard provisions specifying the manner of approval and the date of its coming into effect. The amendment was, in large part, the creation of Nebraska Senator George W. Norris, who championed it for over a decade until Congress approved it in March 1932 and three-fourths of the states ratified it by January 1933. Throughout its consideration by Congress and the states, it was known as "the lame-duck amendment."

The first two sections respond to the initial purpose for the amendment, which was the concern about lame-duck sessions of Congress. The framers of the Twentieth Amendment, however, wanted to eliminate such lame-duck sessions of Congress altogether, not just shorten them. Legislation enacted by lame-duck Congresses had been roundly criticized as undemocratic because the people had already selected the successors of the representatives who were enacting bills in lame-duck sessions. The text of the amendment failed to prohibit future lame-duck sessions, though, and that purpose was forgotten soon after the states ratified the amendment in 1933. Congress has met in lame-duck sessions thirteen times since the Twentieth Amendment became law. In recent years, a lame-duck Senate confirmed Stephen G. Breyer to a federal appeals court judgeship in 1980, and the House of Representatives impeached President Clinton after the 1998 election, despite calls from a number of scholars that such an action contradicted the spirit of the Twentieth Amendment. The original understanding of the Twentieth Amendment has thus become a policy argument against lame-duck congressional sessions, but no one has asked the courts to enforce that understanding.

There is another question that the framers of the Twentieth Amendment anticipated but which the language of the amendment fails to resolve. According to the Twelfth Amendment, the House of Representatives chooses the President if no candidate receives a majority of the electoral votes. Thomas Jefferson, John Quincy Adams, and Rutherford B. Hayes were all elected by the House—more specifically, the lame-duck

House, not the newly elected House. The supporters of the Twentieth Amendment wanted to ensure that any future selections of the President would be made by the new Members of the House. The text of the amendment does not express that purpose, and the question of which House could act was one of many unanswered constitutional questions discussed while the presidential election of 2000 was still in dispute.

Sections 3 and 4 address an issue unrelated to the concern about lame-duck Congresses, namely, the circumstances in which the President or the President-elect dies. In the words of Senator Norris, Sections 3 and 4 ensure that "there can never arise a contingency where the country will be without a chief magistrate or without the method of selecting a chief magistrate." The nation has never had the occasion to put Senator Norris's confidence to the test. A number of scholars, however, have imagined circumstances in which the selection of a new President would remain unclear, notwithstanding Sections 3 and 4. For example, Professor Akhil Amar has asked, "What happens if, God forbid, the person who wins the general election in November and the electoral college tally in December dies before the electoral college votes are officially counted in Congress in January? If the decedent can be considered 'the President elect' within the meaning of the Twentieth Amendment, then the rules would be clear, but it is not self-evident that a person who dies before the official counting of electoral votes in Congress is formally the 'President elect.'" The solution, proposes Amar, is for Congress to enact a statute that would (1) postpone the election if a major candidate dies or becomes incapacitated shortly before election day and (2) authorize the counting of electoral votes for candidates who died on or after election day. Thus far, Congress has failed to heed such advice.

John Copeland Nagle

See Also

Suggestions for Further Research

Bruce Ackerman, The Case Against Lame Duck Impeachment (1999)

Akhil R. Amar, *Presidents, Vice Presidents, and Death: Closing the Constitution's Succession Gap*, 48 Ark. L. Rev. 215 (1995)

Richard S. Beth & Richard C. Sachs, Lame Duck Sessions, 74th–106th Congress (1935–2000) (2000) (Congressional Research Service report summarizing the history of lame-duck congressional sessions from 1935 to 2000)

John Copeland Nagle, *A Twentieth Amendment Parable*, 72 N.Y.U. L. Rev. 470 (1997)

George W. Norris, Fighting Liberal: The Autobiography of George W. Norris (1946)

Repeal of Prohibition

Section 1. The eighteenth article of amendment to the Constitution of the United States is hereby repealed.

Section 2. The transportation or importation into any State, Territory, or Possession of the United States for delivery or use therein of intoxicating liquors, in violation of the laws thereof, is hereby prohibited.

Section 3. This article shall be inoperative unless it shall have been ratified as an amendment to the Constitution by conventions in the several States, as provided in the Constitution, within seven years from the date of the submission hereof to the States by the Congress.

(Amendment XXI)

~

*W*hen the nation repealed Prohibition via the Twenty-first Amendment in 1933, it vested primary control over alcoholic beverages in the states. The common understanding of the framers of the Twenty-first Amendment was that it grants each state the power to regulate alcoholic beverages within its borders without intrusion by federal law or regulation. The question remains, however, as to how much and what kind of federal intrusion the amendment blocks. The Twenty-first Amendment has three parts. Section 1 explicitly repealed the Eighteenth Amendment and brought an end to Prohibition. Accordingly, because many saw the Twenty-first Amendment as nothing but a repeal of the Eighteenth Amendment, Congress passed the resolution without much substantive debate. Most of the legislative debate centered on the issue of saloons and the ratification process codified in Section 3 of the amendment, which mandated the use of state conventions. The amendment was passed by the Senate on February 16, 1933, and by the House four days later. It became law on December 5, 1933.

In the original resolution there was an additional section, which granted Congress and the states "concurrent power to regulate or prohibit the sale of intoxicating liquors to be drunk on the premises where sold." This provision was designed primarily to authorize the prohibition of saloons. But Members of Congress finally agreed that such regulation belonged with the states, and the section was removed.

Section 2 became the Twenty-first Amendment's primary source of judicial conflict. The question was whether the amendment gave the states absolute control over alcohol, notwithstanding the Commerce Clause and the Import-Export Clause, or whether the amendment permitted the states only enough autonomy to be dry without infringing on the scope of the rest of the Constitution. The amendment tracks very closely the language of a pre-Prohibition federal statute, the Webb-Kenyon Act (1913), *current version* at 27 U.S.C. § 122 (1994), that gave states power to tax alcoholic beverages not only when sold in state, but also when sold through the mail in interstate commerce.

In *State Board of Equalization v. Young's Market Co.* (1936) and in *Ziffrin, Inc. v. Reeves* (1939), the Supreme Court originally interpreted the Twenty-first Amendment as an absolute exception to the Commerce Clause. However, this changed in 1964 with a string of Twenty-first Amendment cases. In *Hostetter v. Idlewild Bon Voyage Liquor Corp.* (1964), Justice Potter Stewart, writing for the majority, argued forcefully that the Twenty-first Amendment was not an absolute exception to the Commerce Clause as far as liquor was concerned. Likewise, in *Department of Revenue v. James B. Beam Distilling Co.* (1964), the Court held that Kentucky's tax on imported whiskey violated the Import-Export Clause. Justice Stewart, again writing for the majority, stated:

> To sustain the tax which Kentucky has imposed in this case would require nothing short of squarely holding that the Twenty-first Amendment has completely repealed the Export-Import Clause so far as intoxicants are concerned. Nothing in the language of the Amendment nor in its history leads to such an extraordinary conclusion. This Court has never intimated such a view, and now that the claim for the first time is squarely presented, we expressly reject it.

Similarly, in *Wisconsin v. Constantineau* (1971), the Court held that a Wisconsin statute, which empowered a police chief to post in all local retail liquor outlets a notice forbidding the sale of alcohol to the plaintiff because of his excessive drinking, without giving the plaintiff any advance notice or opportunity to contest it, violated the due process requirements of the Fourteenth Amendment.

Throughout the 1970s and early 1980s, the Supreme Court continued to chip away at the Twenty-first Amendment. *See, e.g., United States v. Tax Commission of Mississippi* (1975) (holding that the states could not tax the sale of liquor on military bases within their borders because the United States has concurrent jurisdiction over military bases); *Craig v. Boren* (1976) (noting that the Twenty-first Amendment does not override the equal-protection requirements of the Fourteenth Amendment); *California Retail Liquor Dealers Ass'n v. Midcal Aluminum, Inc.* (1980) (finding that the Twenty-first Amendment does not protect a state

regulation that violates the Sherman Act because of the Supremacy Clause); *Larkin v. Grendel's Den, Inc.* (1982) (stating that the state may not exercise its powers under the Twenty-first Amendment in a way that impinges the rights protected under the Establishment Clause). *But see New York State Liquor Authority v. Bellanca* (1981) (allowing a state to prohibit the sale of liquor on premises where topless dancing occurs because "[w]hatever artistic or communicative value may attach to topless dancing is overcome by the State's exercise of its broad power under the Twenty-first Amendment").

In *Capital Cities Cable, Inc. v. Crisp* (1984), the Court finally articulated a balancing test to determine when the state's powers under the Twenty-first Amendment trump the Commerce Clause:

> In such a case, the central question is whether the interests implicated by a state regulation are so closely related to the powers reserved by the Amendment that the regulation may prevail, even though its requirements directly conflict with express federal policies.

Utilizing this balancing test in *Bacchus Imports, Ltd. v. Dias* (1984), the Court struck down a Hawaiian tax law that favored certain liquors that were only manufactured locally because "[s]tate laws that constitute mere economic protectionism are . . . not entitled to the same deference as laws enacted to combat the perceived evils of an unrestricted traffic in liquor."

In *324 Liquor Corp. v. Duffy* (1987), the Court balanced the state's virtually complete control over the liquor distribution system within its borders against the policy behind the Sherman Anti-Trust Act and found the latter of more weight. In a sharp dissent, Justice Sandra Day O'Connor, joined by Chief Justice William H. Rehnquist, rejected the majority's conclusion. The dissent described in detail the legislative history and the subsequent state practices to show that the amendment was designed to give the states absolute control over the manufacturing and distribution of liquor within their borders. The "Senate discussions," she wrote, "clearly demonstrate an intent to confer on States complete and exclusive control over the commerce of liquor." The states understood the meaning as well. Immediately after the ratification of the Twenty-first Amendment, states enacted strong price-control measures, "the very type of statute that this Court strikes down today." The majority opinion answered Justice O'Connor's argument with a one-paragraph footnote that focused on maintaining federal economic power through the Commerce Clause and the Antitrust Laws.

That same year in *South Dakota v. Dole* (1987), the Court held that Congress could use its spending power to regulate indirectly interstate commerce with regard to intoxicating liquors. In *Dole*, Congress made certain highway funding contingent upon a state's acceptance of a minimum drinking age of twenty-one years. Justice O'Connor and Justice William J. Brennan, Jr., each filed dissents, with Brennan arguing that the Twenty-first Amendment limited the spending power.

In *44 Liquormart, Inc. v. Rhode Island* (1996), the Court held that Rhode Island's prohibition against certain advertisements stating the prices of liquor was an abridgment of the First Amendment's protection of free speech. Although the lengthy decision contained several concurring opinions, all nine Justices agreed that the Rhode Island law was not saved by the Twenty-first Amendment.

After a number of years in which the Supreme Court pruned state powers under the Twenty-first Amendment, the amendment now leaves a state with the power to become dry if it chooses. Beyond that, however, the Court has held that state control of liquor is subject to federal power under the Commerce Clause (Article I, Section 8, Clause 3), *Granholm v. Heald* (2005), the Spending Clause (Article I, Section 8, Clause 1), the First Amendment, and, it follows, the Necessary and Proper Clause (Article I, Section 8, Clause 18) and the Supremacy Clause (Article VI, Clause 2).

David Wagner

See Also
Article I, Section 8, Clause 3 (Commerce with Foreign Nations)
Article I, Section 8, Clause 3 (Commerce Among the States)
Article I, Section 10, Clause 2 (Import-Export Clause)

Suggestions for Further Research
EDWARD BEHR, PROHIBITION: THIRTEEN YEARS THAT CHANGED AMERICA (1997)

Duncan Baird Douglass, *Constitutional Crossroads: Reconciling the Twenty-first Amendment and the Commerce Clause to Evaluate State Regulation of Interstate Commerce in Alcoholic Beverages*, 49 DUKE L.J. 1619 (2000)

John Foust, *State Power to Regulate Alcohol Under the Twenty-first Amendment: The Constitutional Implications of the Twenty-first Amendment Enforcement Act*, 41 B.C. L. REV. 659 (2000)

JOHN KOBLER, ARDENT SPIRITS: THE RISE AND FALL OF PROHIBITION (reprint 1993)

Susan Lorde Martin, *Wine Wars—Direct Shipment of Wine: The Twenty-first Amendment, the Commerce Clause, and Consumers' Rights*, 38 AM. BUSINESS L.J. 1 (2000)

Russ Miller, *The Wine Is in the Mail: the Twenty-first Amendment and State Laws Against the Direct Shipment of Alcoholic Beverages*, 54 VANDERBILT L. REV. 2495 (2001)

THOMAS PEGRAM, BATTLING DEMON RUM: THE STRUGGLE FOR A DRY AMERICA, 1800–1933 (1998)

Significant Cases
State Board of Equalization v. Young's Market Co., 299 U.S. 59 (1936)
Joseph S. Finch & Co. v. McKittrick, 305 U.S. 395 (1939)
Ziffrin, Inc. v. Reeves, 308 U.S. 132 (1939)
United States v. Frankfort Distilleries, 324 U.S. 293 (1945)
Department of Revenue v. James B. Beam Distilling Co., 377 U.S. 341 (1964)
Hostetter v. Idlewild Bon Voyage Liquor Corp., 377 U.S. 324 (1964)
Wisconsin v. Constantineau, 400 U.S. 433 (1971)
United States v. Tax Commission of Mississippi, 421 U.S. 599 (1975)
Craig v. Boren, 429 U.S. 190 (1976)
California Retail Liquor Dealers Ass'n v. Midcal Aluminum, Inc., 445 U.S. 97 (1980)

New York State Liquor Authority v. Bellanca, 452 U.S. 714 (1981)

Larkin v. Grendel's Den, Inc., 459 U.S. 116 (1982)

Bacchus Imports, Ltd. v. Dias, 468 U.S. 263 (1984)

Capital Cities Cable, Inc. v. Crisp, 467 U.S. 691 (1984)

324 Liquor Corp. v. Duffy, 479 U.S. 335 (1987)

South Dakota v. Dole, 483 U.S. 203 (1987)

44 Liquormart, Inc. v. Rhode Island, 517 U.S. 484 (1996)

Granholm v. Heald, 125 S. Ct. 1885 (2005)

Presidential Term Limit

Section 1. No person shall be elected to the office of the President more than twice, and no person who has held the office of President, or acted as President, for more than two years of a term to which some other person was elected President shall be elected to the office of President more than once. But this Article shall not apply to any person holding the office of President when this Article was proposed by Congress, and shall not prevent any person who may be holding the office of President, or acting as President, during the term within which this Article becomes operative from holding the office of President or acting as President during the remainder of such term.

Section 2. This article shall be inoperative unless it shall have been ratified as an amendment to the Constitution by the legislatures of three-fourths of the several States within seven years from the date of its submission to the States by the Congress.

(AMENDMENT XXII)

∽

*A*lthough the Twenty-second Amendment was clearly a reaction to Franklin D. Roosevelt's service as President for an unprecedented four terms, the notion of presidential term limits has long-standing roots in American politics. The Constitutional Convention of 1787 considered the issue extensively, although it ultimately declined to restrict the amount of time a person could serve as President. But following George Washington's decision to retire after his second elected term, numerous public figures subsequently argued he had established a "two-term tradition" that served as a vital check against any one person, or the presidency as a whole, accumulating too much power. Congress expressed its interest in presidential term limits by introducing 270 measures restricting the terms of office of the President prior to proposing the Twenty-second Amendment.

Nonetheless, sustained political attention to this matter only developed with Roosevelt. In 1946, lawmakers made the President's four terms an issue in congressional election campaigns, pledging to support a constitutional amendment that would prevent a similarly lengthy presidency in the future. In January of 1947, prominent House leaders acted on these campaign promises, introducing an initiative that ultimately became the Twenty-second Amendment.

The turning point in the debates on the measure occurred when Senator Warren Magnuson argued for an amendment that would simply bar someone from being "elected to the office of President more than twice." Magnuson claimed that other proposals being considered were too "complicated" and comprehensive and might unfairly restrict a person who assumed the office of President "through circumstances beyond his control, and with no deliberation on his part...but because of an emergency," such as the death of an elected President. When some legislators countered that Magnuson's proposal provided insufficient controls on those who assumed the presidency through these "unfortunate circumstance[s]," a compromise was struck. The final proposal provided a general prohibition against a person being elected to the office of the President more than twice while imposing additional restrictions on some individuals who attained the office of President through nonelectoral means, such as succession. The resulting language is what we now know as the Twenty-second Amendment.

We can safely conclude that those who drafted the amendment sought somehow to prevent the emergence of a President with a tenure as lengthy as Roosevelt's. Many proponents of the measure further argued that they sought to codify the two-term tradition associated with Washington. But although these observations surely point us to the general aspirations of the amendment's authors, they do not establish a specific picture of how the framers intended their proposal to apply.

To begin with, congressional deliberations about the amendment were curtailed. For example, the House restricted debate to two hours. Furthermore, the discussions leading up to the proposing of the Twenty-second Amendment did not obviously suggest a consistent, clear legislative purpose. Lawmakers expressed, at various times, their interest in limiting a President's "service," "terms," "tenure," and "[eligibility for] reelection," without elaborating exactly how they understood these terms. Moreover, when Congress dropped early proposals to foreclose a person's eligibility for office if he had *served* in two prior terms and instead adopted the current text that focuses on limiting individuals twice *elected* to the presidency, it provided little explanation for this important shift beyond needing "compromise" as part of the lawmaking process. One should also note that the framers of the amendment did not obviously intend to create a two-term tradition in any narrow sense, because they specifically discussed allowing someone who became President through an "emergency" within the first two years of one term to secure election for two additional terms. We are therefore left with some uncertainty about the precise goals of the Twenty-second Amendment's creators.

The ratification debates over the amendment do not provide much additional insight into the particular wishes of those who supported the proposal in the states. In general, the amendment does not appear to have prompted a great deal of public or legislative discussion once proposed by Congress.

Although numerous court opinions make passing reference to the Twenty-second Amendment, its parameters have not been systematically examined by the judiciary. No doubt the low profile of the amendment in the courts reflects limited interest in and opportunity for testing the provision. Since the amendment was ratified, only five Presidents have been technically limited by it (Dwight D. Eisenhower, Richard M. Nixon, Ronald Reagan, William Jefferson Clinton, and George W. Bush were all twice elected), and, to date, none of these individuals seriously considered challenging the amendment's legal restrictions or meaning.

These facts should not lead one to conclude that the Twenty-second Amendment is so straightforward that it requires no further interpretation. Among other unresolved questions, the amendment seems to leave open the possibility that a twice-elected President could still become President through nonelectoral means. For example, such a person might still be elevated to the presidency after serving as Vice President, or, if authorized, to act as President through a presidential-succession statute.

Bruce Peabody

See Also

Article II, Section 1, Clause 5 (Presidential Eligibility)

Article II, Section 1, Clause 6 (Presidential Succession)

Amendment XII (Electoral College)

Amendment XX (Presidential Terms)

Amendment XXV (Presidential Succession)

Suggestions for Further Research

David Kyvig, ed. Unintended Consequences of Constitutional Amendment (2000)

Bruce G. Peabody & Scott E. Gant, *The Twice and Future President: Constitutional Interstices and the Twenty-second Amendment*, 83 Minn. L. Rev. 565 (1999)

Stephen W. Stathis, *The Twenty-second Amendment: A Practical Remedy or Partisan Maneuver?*, 7 Const. Comm. 61 (1990)

Electors for the District of Columbia

Section 1. The District constituting the seat of Government of the United States shall appoint in such manner as the Congress may direct:

A number of electors of President and Vice President equal to the whole number of Senators and Representatives in Congress to which the District would be entitled if it were a State, but in no event more than the least populous State; they shall be in addition to those appointed by the States, but they shall be considered, for the purposes of the election of President and Vice President, to be electors appointed by a State; and they shall meet in the District and perform such duties as provided by the twelfth article of amendment.

Section 2. The Congress shall have power to enforce this article by appropriate legislation.

(AMENDMENT XXIII)

≈

*T*he inability of the citizens of the District of Columbia to participate in federal elections has been controversial since the federal seat of government of the United States came into existence in 1800. In 1960, Congress rectified the situation concerning the District's participation in presidential elections by passing the Twenty-third Amendment. It enables the District to participate in presidential and vice-presidential elections in the same manner in which the states participate in those elections. The states swiftly ratified the proposed amendment in time for the District to cast electoral votes in the presidential election of 1964. The amendment did not address the District's lack of representation in Congress.

The legislative history of the amendment makes clear that the drafters sought to provide the seat of government of the United States, the District of Columbia, with the same method of selecting presidential electors in the Electoral College as the states employed to select their presidential electors. The legislative history also reveals that some of the key drafters were ignorant of the relevant constitutional history concerning the manner in which the states had selected their presidential electors. Early in U.S. history, some states chose electors by district, others by the state legislature, and others by a "winner-take-all" system. Despite this confusion, the Twenty-third Amendment clearly provides Congress the same leeway as the state legislatures in enacting the electoral vote selection procedures for the District.

The amendment contains some *sui generis* provisions. The amendment expressly caps the District's electoral votes at the number equal to the least populous state. This, in effect, provides the District with three electoral votes regardless of the population of the District. In addition, because the parallel constitutional provisions grant the respective state legislatures with plenary power over the method of selection of the presidential electors, a like power was necessarily given to Congress. The legislative history notes that "the language follows closely, insofar as it is applicable, the language of article II of the constitution."

Although not constitutionally required, Congress, by statute, has adopted a winner-take-all system, in which the winner of the plurality of votes receives all of the District's presidential electors. Such winner-take-all systems have been enacted in all fifty states except for Maine and Nebraska. Recently, controversies over the Twenty-third Amendment have arisen as part of efforts for District statehood or to provide the District with representation in the federal legislature. For example, if Congress, by statute, accepted the District of Columbia as the State of New Columbia, and the present "seat of government of the United States" was not eliminated but reduced to a small federal enclave containing the White House and the federal Mall, what would become of the Twenty-third Amendment?

Many District-statehood and District–voting-rights proponents generally seek to avoid amending the Constitution because of the difficulties of obtaining congressional approval and state ratification. They contend that the Twenty-third Amendment would become a "dead letter" without the necessity of formal repeal by constitutional amendment, because there would be virtually no residents left in the federal enclave. On the other hand, "the Seat of Government of the United States," the entity designated in the amendment to receive electoral votes, would still exist in its geographically reduced form. That constitutional entity, absent constitutional repeal, would still be constitutionally entitled to the electoral votes under the Twenty-third Amendment. Any congressional effort to repeal the enabling legislation, but not to repeal the Twenty-third Amendment, would likely face constitutional difficulty. For example, the concept that any constitutional provision can be deemed a "dead letter" by legislation runs contrary to basic principles of the American constitutional structure. Additionally, such a scenario could imply that a state legislature could exercise like authority and act to disenfranchise its citizens from participation in the Electoral College.

For decades, these concerns seemed academic and hypothetical. However, the 2000 presidential election and the controversy over Florida's electoral votes renewed focus on a state's constitutional prerogatives concerning the manner and selection of presidential electors. Those constitutional developments necessarily inform Congress's parallel obligations under the Twenty-third Amendment.

Adam Kurland

See Also

Article I, Section 8, Clause 17 (Enclave Clause)
Article II, Section I, Clause 2 (Presidential Electors)
Amendment XII (Electoral College)

Suggestion for Further Research

WALTER BERNS, ED., AFTER THE PEOPLE VOTE: A GUIDE TO THE ELECTORAL COLLEGE (1992)

Adam Harris Kurland, *Partisan Rhetoric, Constitutional Reality, and Political Responsibility: The Troubling Constitutional Consequences of Achiev-*

ing D.C. Statehood by Simple Legislation, 60 GEO. WASH. L. REV. 475 (1992)

U.S. Department of Justice, Report of the Attorney General: The Question of Statehood for the District of Columbia (April 3, 1987)

Significant Cases

McPherson v. Blacker, 146 U.S. 1 (1892)
Williams v. Rhodes, 393 U.S. 23 (1968)
Adams v. Clinton, 90 F. Supp. 2d 35 (D.D.C. 2000), *aff'd*, 531 U.S. 941 (2000)
Bush v. Gore, 531 U.S. 98 (2000)
Bush v. Palm Beach County Canvassing Board, 531 U.S. 70 (2000)

Poll Taxes

Section 1. The right of citizens of the United States to vote in any primary or other election for President or Vice President, for electors for President or Vice President, or for Senator or Representative in Congress, shall not be denied or abridged by the United States or any State by reason of failure to pay poll tax or other tax.

Section 2. The Congress shall have power to enforce this article by appropriate legislation.

(AMENDMENT XXIV)

∽

*S*outhern states enacted poll taxes of one or two dollars per year between 1889 and 1966 as a prerequisite to voting. A citizen paid the tax when registering and then annually thereafter; some laws required payment up to nine months before an election. Furthermore, many states had a cumulative feature that required an individual to pay all previous years' poll taxes before he could vote in the instant year.

Prior to the enactment of poll taxes, property ownership was frequently a prerequisite to voting. States instituted the poll tax early in the nineteenth century as a device to grant voting rights to individuals who did not own real property. Although most states had dispensed with both property qualifications and the poll tax by the time of the Civil War, the tax resurfaced in the South to dilute the effect of race-neutral voting provisions required in Southern states' constitutions as a condition for readmission to the Union following the Civil War.

Beginning in 1889, Southern states reintroduced the poll tax as a method of disenfranchising black voters. As delegate Carter Glass declared during the Virginia constitutional convention of 1902, the tax was designed "with a view to the elimination of every negro voter who can be gotten rid of, legally, without materially impairing the numerical strength of the white electorate." Additionally, poll taxes had the effect of disenfranchising the poor in general, including whites; later, it fell upon many women after the passage of the Nineteenth Amendment.

Legislation to eliminate poll taxes in federal elections was introduced in every Congress beginning in 1939, but no bill made it into law. By the time of the Twenty-fourth Amendment's ratification in 1964, only five states retained a poll tax. Nevertheless, Congress deemed the amendment necessary inasmuch as poll taxes had previously survived constitutional challenges in the courts, *see Breedlove v. Suttles* (1937), and they had become a notorious symbol of black disenfranchisement.

During the debates, some Members of Congress argued that because poll taxes were racially discriminatory, Congress should outlaw them directly under the enforcement powers of the Fourteenth and Fifteenth Amendments. However, Congress eventually decided against using its Fifteenth Amendment enforcement power because it did not directly reach the disenfranchisement of the poor. Early drafts of the Fifteenth Amendment had, in fact, sought to proscribe devices like poll taxes. Ultimately, however, the Fifteenth Amendment's drafters had settled on language forbidding only racial discrimination in the enjoyment of the franchise. A specific poll tax amendment would be both more sweeping and have greater symbolic status. In addition, the amendment's supporters

attacked the poll tax as a vehicle for fraud because the tax facilitated political corruption through vote buying by political machines that had made block payments of the tax. Some states allowed third parties to pay an individual's poll tax, so some businesses interested in the repeal of the Eighteenth Amendment were able to pay the poll tax for their patrons. Similarly, unions, frustrated with the resistance to unionization in the South, encouraged registration of their members in some cases by paying their poll taxes. Defenders of states' rights, however, fended off any attempt to extend the amendment's application to local elections. Nonetheless, not long after the ratification of the amendment, Congress enacted the Voting Rights Act of 1965, which made problematic the continuing validity of the poll tax as a qualification in state elections.

In *Harman v. Forssenius* (1965), the Supreme Court for the first time construed the Twenty-fourth Amendment, giving broad effect to its prohibition. In anticipation of the amendment's adoption, Virginia had enacted a statute amending its election laws to provide that a qualified citizen might vote in federal elections only if, at least six months prior to each election, he had either paid a poll tax or filed a certificate of residence. In declaring the new Virginia voting law unconstitutional, the Court stressed the broad language of the Twenty-fourth Amendment, which prohibits not only the denial but also the abridgement of the right to vote. The Court noted that the Twenty-fourth Amendment, like the Fifteenth, "nullifies sophisticated as well as simple-minded modes of impairing the right guaranteed." Continuing, the Court also found that the Twenty-fourth Amendment applies to "onerous procedural requirements" which effectively handicap, impede, or impair the "exercise of the freedom by those claiming the constitutional immunity."

The drafters of the amendment carefully limited its scope to federal elections. Two years after its ratification, the Supreme Court announced that the use of poll taxes as a prerequisite to voting in state elections violated the Equal Protection Clause of the Fourteenth Amendment, even though it seemed evident that the conclusion was at odds with the original understanding of the framers of the Fourteenth Amendment, a position emphasized in the dissents of Justices Hugo L. Black and John M. Harlan. *Harper v. Virginia State Board of Elections* (1966). In *Harper*, the Court dealt with a Virginia statute requiring the payment of a poll tax not to exceed $1.50 as a precondition for voting, an amount that Virginia argued was minimal and thus not a significant burden on the right to vote. Admitting "the right to vote in state elections is nowhere expressly mentioned," the Court nevertheless invalidated the statute because "it is enough to say that once the franchise is granted to the electorate, lines may not be drawn which are inconsistent with the Equal Protection Clause of the Fourteenth Amendment." Justice William O. Douglas, writing for the Court, explained: "[A] state violates the Equal Protection Clause... whenever it makes the affluence of the voter or payments of any fee an electoral standard. Voter qualifications have no relation to wealth nor to paying or not paying this or any other tax." The logic of the Court's opinion has made the Twenty-fourth Amendment virtually superfluous, as Justice John M. Harlan observed in his dissent.

David F. Forte

See Also

Article I, Section 2, Clause 1 (Elector Qualifications)
Amendment XIV, Section 1 (Equal Protection)
Amendment XV (Suffrage—Race)
Amendment XIX (Suffrage—Sex)

Suggestions for Further Research

Steven F. Lawson, Black Ballots: Voting Rights in the South, 1944–1969 (1976)

Frederic D. Ogden, The Poll Tax in the South (1958)

Ronnie L. Podolefsky, *The Illusion of Suffrage: Female Voting Rights and the Women's Poll Tax Repeal Movement after the Nineteenth Amendment*, 7 Colum. J. Gender & L. 185 (1998)

Significant Cases

Breedlove v. Suttles, 302 U.S. 277 (1937)
Harman v. Forssenius, 380 U.S. 528 (1965)
Harper v. Virginia State Board of Elections, 383 U.S. 663 (1966)

Presidential Succession

Section 1. In case of the removal of the President from office or of his death or resignation, the Vice President shall become President.

Section 2. Whenever there is a vacancy in the office of the Vice President, the President shall nominate a Vice President who shall take office upon confirmation by a majority vote of both Houses of Congress.

Section 3. Whenever the President transmits to the President pro tempore of the Senate and the Speaker of the House of Representatives his written declaration that he is unable to discharge the powers and duties of his office, and until he transmits to them a written declaration to the contrary, such powers and duties shall be discharged by the Vice President as Acting President.

Section 4. Whenever the Vice President and a majority of either the principal officers of the executive departments or of such other body as Congress may by law provide, transmit to the President pro tempore of the Senate and the Speaker of the House of Representatives their written declaration that the President is unable to discharge the powers and duties of his office, the Vice President shall immediately assume the powers and duties of the office as Acting President.

Thereafter, when the President transmits to the President pro tempore of the Senate and the Speaker of the House of Representatives his written declaration that no inability exists, he shall resume the powers and duties of his office unless the Vice President and a majority of either the principal officers of the executive department or of such other body as Congress may by law provide, transmit within four days to the President pro tempore of the Senate and the Speaker of the House of Representatives their written declaration that the President is unable to discharge the powers and duties of his office. Thereupon Congress shall decide the issue, assembling within forty-eight hours for that purpose if not in session. If the Congress, within twenty-one days after receipt of the latter written declaration, or, if Congress is not in session, within twenty-one days after Congress is required to assemble, determines by two-thirds vote of both Houses that the President is unable to discharge the powers and duties of his office, the Vice President shall continue to discharge the same as Acting President; otherwise, the President shall resume the powers and duties of his office.

(AMENDMENT XXV)

≈

*T*he original Presidential Succession Clause of the Constitution (*see* Article II, Section 1, Clause 6) appeared to be relatively simple in providing for succession to the presidency. There were, however, troubling ambiguities. What was the meaning of "inability" of a President "to discharge the Powers and Duties of said Office"? Who determined the existence of an "inability"? Did a Vice President become President for the rest of the presidential term in the case of an inability or in the event of death, resignation, or removal; or was he merely "acting as President"? It was clear that there was no procedure for filling a vacancy in the office of Vice President, although it authorized Congress to legislate a line of succession to cover situations involving the death, resignation, removal, or inability of both the President and Vice President.

Until the Twenty-fifth Amendment was adopted, the nation confronted a number of deaths in office of Presidents and Vice Presidents as well as periods when Presidents have been disabled. When President William Henry Harrison died in 1841, Vice President John Tyler, asserting that he was fully the President, ascended to the presidency for the rest of the term, claiming that was the proper interpretation of the clause. The precedent he established by assumption of the presidency was followed by other Vice Presidents when Presidents died in office. These Presidents were Zachary Taylor, Abraham Lincoln, James A. Garfield, William McKinley, Warren G. Harding, Franklin D. Roosevelt, and John F. Kennedy. The Vice Presidents who succeeded to the office were Tyler, Millard Fillmore, Andrew Johnson, Chester A. Arthur, Theodore Roosevelt, Calvin Coolidge, Harry S. Truman, and Lyndon B. Johnson, respectively.

Although the Tyler precedent was helpful in providing for continuity and stability, it caused future Vice Presidents to hesitate in asserting any role in a case of presidential inability as opposed to the death of the President. There was the question of whether the Vice President succeeded to the presidency for the rest of the term, even in a case of temporary inability, as well as the problem of the Vice President's being seen as a usurper because of the constitutional silence about his role in determining whether there was an inability. This hesitancy occurred during the eighty days when President Garfield lay dying after being shot by an assassin in 1881; in the period after President Woodrow Wilson suffered a stroke in 1919; and when Dwight D. Eisenhower suffered a heart attack, an attack of ileitis, and then a stroke. To cope with any future inability, President Eisenhower and Vice President Richard M. Nixon developed an informal protocol. Although it did not have the force of law, it gave assurance that a case of inability would be handled with due regard for stability. It provided for the President to declare his own inability and, if unable to do so, enabled the Vice President, with appropriate consultation, to make the decision. In either event, the Vice President served as Acting President until the President recovered his powers and duties upon his own declaration of recovery. This protocol was followed in turn by President Kennedy and Vice President Johnson, and by President Johnson and Vice President Hubert H. Humphrey. It was a useful protocol, but many in Congress wanted a more formal long-term solution.

Compounding the problem of presidential inability was the problem of vice presidential vacancy. Such a vacancy occurred whenever a President died in office, on the seven occasions when Vice Presidents died in office, and when Vice President John C. Calhoun resigned in 1832. In the absence of a mechanism for filling a vacancy, a statutory line of succession provided the necessary backup. This line changed twice in the country's history. The original line, reflected in a law of 1792, placed the President Pro Tempore of the Senate next in line after the Vice President. In 1886 the Secretary of State was made first in line, followed by other Members of the Cabinet. Then, in 1947, the Speaker of the House of Representatives and President Pro Tempore of the Senate, respectively, were placed ahead of the Secretary of State and the other Cabinet officers.

When President John F. Kennedy was assassinated in 1963, a movement developed to change the Constitution to constitutionalize these practices and to provide more certainty. The Twenty-fifth Amendment captures the history of succession in its provisions providing for the Vice President to become President in the event of the death, resignation, or removal of the President and to serve as Acting President for the duration of any inability. It allows a President to declare his own inability and resume his powers and duties when it has ended. This provision has been used when Presidents underwent surgery—in 1985 by President Ronald Reagan and in 2002 by President George W. Bush. For situations where the President is unable to declare his own inability, the amendment authorizes the Vice President, acting with a majority of the Cabinet, to do so and then act as President. If the President disagrees, Congress resolves the issue. The amendment also gives Congress the power to replace the Cabinet and substitute another body to function with the Vice President. It was not an accident that the amendment did not define "inability." The term was left vague in order to provide maximum flexibility to the constitutional decision makers, at a time of crisis, to do what they thought was in the best interests of the country. It was intended to cover cases of both physical and mental inability, such as when a President undergoes surgery, is kidnapped, or becomes infirm.

The amendment, recognizing the importance of the vice presidency, added a procedure for filling a vacancy in that office, namely, nomination by the President and confirmation by both Houses of Congress. This procedure was used when Vice President Spiro T. Agnew resigned and was replaced by Gerald R. Ford, and when Richard M. Nixon resigned as President. Vice President Ford became President and Nelson A. Rockefeller became Vice President by the same process.

John Feerick

See Also

Article II, Section 1, Clause 6 (Presidential Succession)

Amendment XX (Presidential Terms)

Suggestions for Further Research

BIRCH EVANS BAYH, ONE HEARTBEAT AWAY: PRESIDENTIAL DISABILITY AND SUCCESSION (1968)

JOHN D. FEERICK, FROM FAILING HANDS: THE STORY OF PRESIDENTIAL SUCCESSION (1965)

JOHN D. FEERICK, THE TWENTY-FIFTH AMENDMENT: ITS COMPLETE HISTORY AND APPLICATIONS (1976 and 1994)

ROBERT E. GILBERT ED., MANAGING CRISIS: PRESIDENTIAL DISABILITY AND THE TWENTY-FIFTH AMENDMENT (2000)

RUTH C. SILVA, PRESIDENTIAL SUCCESSION (1968)

Suffrage—Age

Section 1. The right of citizens of the United States, who are eighteen years of age or older, to vote shall not be denied or abridged by the

United States or by any State on account of age.

Section 2. The Congress shall have power to enforce this article by appropriate legislation.

(AMENDMENT XXVI)

~

The Vietnam War provoked many draft-age youngsters and like-minded adults to proclaim, "If eighteen-to-twenty-year-olds are old enough to die for their country, they're old enough to vote." That slogan is commonly cited as the impetus for the Twenty-sixth Amendment. The truth is somewhat less colorful. The amendment was crafted primarily to overturn the holding of a fractured Supreme Court in *Oregon v. Mitchell* (1970). That case had invalidated an attempt by Congress to regulate voting age in state and local elections. Essentially, the Twenty-sixth Amendment did what Congress could not do.

Earlier in 1970, Congress had amended the Voting Rights Act of 1965, lowering the minimum voting age to eighteen in all federal, state, and local elections. When the revised law was challenged, primarily on federalism grounds, Justice Hugo L. Black wrote an opinion reflecting the position of two separate five-Justice majorities. One contingent agreed with Black that Congress could establish a minimum voting age for federal elections, but found contrary to Black that Congress could also exercise that power over state and local elections. A different four Justices joined Black in restricting Congress's power over state and local elections, but would have restricted its power over federal elections as well. Thus, Black's opinion became the Court's holding: Congress had the authority to extend the vote to eighteen-year-olds in federal elections but not in state or local contests.

After *Oregon v. Mitchell*, states unwilling to set their minimum voting age at eighteen would have been required to maintain separate voting systems for federal and nonfederal elections. To avoid that complication and expense, the states opted for national uniformity and ratified the Twenty-sixth Amendment in record

time—a mere 107 days after it was proposed by Congress.

Almost immediately, the courts had to resolve issues peripheral to the new amendment. For example, did the right to vote for a candidate include eligibility to sign and vote for initiative petitions? In *Colorado Project-Common Cause v. Anderson* (1972), a state court found that enactment of the Twenty-sixth Amendment entailed participation by young voters in the entire political process—initiatives included.

Could states restrict voting by minors by denying them residency at schools or other places away from their parents? In *Jolicoeur v. Mihaly* (1971), the California Supreme Court found that denying minors voting residence where they actually lived—whether at school or elsewhere—constituted a violation of the Twenty-sixth Amendment; the amendment was held to have emancipated minors for all purposes related to voting. In the same vein, a New Jersey court added that the Twenty-sixth Amendment secured the rights of bona fide campus residents to register in the counties where their campuses were located. *Worden v. Mercer County Board of Elections* (1972).

On the other hand, a state constitution could, without offending the Twenty-sixth Amendment, institute twenty-one as the minimum age for holding elective public office. *Opatz v. City of St. Cloud* (1972). And the amendment does not mandate that persons under twenty-one years old be seated as jurors under state law. *Johnson v. State* (1972); *Commonwealth v. Cobbs* (1973); *State ex rel. McNary v. Stussie* (1974).

Robert Levy

See Also

Amendment XIX (Suffrage—Sex)

Amendment XXIV (Poll Taxes)

Suggestions for Further Research

William H. Danne, Jr., *Annotation: Residence of Students for Voting Purposes*, 44 A.L.R. 3D. 797 (1972)

Kenneth J. Guido, *Student Voting and Residency Qualifications: The Aftermath of the Twenty-sixth Amendment*, 47 N.Y.U. L. REV. 32 (1972)

Voting Rights Act Amendments of 1970, Pub. L. 91–285, 84 Stat. 314

Voting Rights Act of 1965, 42 U.S.C. 1971 et seq.

Significant Cases

Oregon v. Mitchell, 400 U.S. 112 (1970)

Jolicoeur v. Mihaly, 5 Cal. 3d 565 (1971)

Colorado Project-Common Cause v. Anderson, 178 Colo. 1, 495 P.2d 220 (1972)

Johnson v. State, 260 So.2d 436 (Miss. 1972)

Opatz v. City of St. Cloud, 293 Minn. 379, 196 N.W.2d 298 (1972)

Worden v. Mercer County Board of Elections, 61 N.J. 325, 294 A.2d 233 (1972)

Commonwealth v. Cobbs, 452 Pa. 397, 305 A.2d 25 (1973)

State *ex rel.* McNary v. Stussie, 518 S.W.2d 630 (Mo. 1974)

Congressional Compensation

No law, varying the compensation for the services of the Senators and Representatives, shall take effect, until an election of representatives shall have intervened.

(AMENDMENT XXVII)

∾

On June 8, 1789, James Madison proposed the Congressional Compensation Amendment as one of many that he presented to the House of Representatives that day. After debate, the House of Representatives and the Senate approved the proposed amendment and forwarded it and eleven others to the states. Only six states ratified it, however, and thus it did not become part of the Bill of Rights. The proposed amendment languished for almost two hundred years before becoming the object of a successful ratification campaign in the 1980s, ultimately resulting in its formal acceptance by Congress as the Twenty-seventh Amendment on May 20, 1992.

At the Constitutional Convention, the Framers heatedly debated the question of whether individual states or the new national government would compensate elected representatives. The Compensation Clause of Article I, Section 6, was the result, providing that the central government would pay the representatives from the federal treasury as established by federal law.

The Anti-Federalists and others at state ratifying conventions found this compensation arrangement deeply worrisome; because the Members of Congress enacted the very law that set their salary, there was no check on Congress's ability to enrich itself. It was a classic case of the danger of self-dealing corruption. Madison responded to that criticism with the proposed Compensation Amendment, which would prevent representatives from granting themselves a pay raise that would take effect during the term in which they sat. Instead, Congress would only be able to pass the pay raise prospectively and would thereby face the electorate before it could take effect. Madison believed the amendment was necessary because of the "seeming impropriety in leaving any set of men without controul to put their hand into the public coffers, to take out money to put in their pockets."

The issue of congressional compensation was the subject of periodic legislation and attendant political maneuvering in succeeding years. Particularly unpopular with the electorate was the notorious "Salary Grab" Act of 1873, which not only granted a pay raise to legislators but also made it retroactive. One of the Ohio General Assembly's responses to the act was ratification of the dormant Compensation Amendment, thus becoming the seventh state to do so, eighty-four years after Maryland, which was the first state to ratify.

Over a century later, the amendment became the object of a grassroots ratification campaign initiated by a college undergraduate who had authored a term paper on the subject in 1982.

Despite widespread doubt about the propriety of actually adopting the long-dormant amendment should it ever be fully ratified, the ratification campaign gathered momentum. On May 7, 1992, Michigan became the thirty-eighth state to ratify the Compensation Amendment, completing the process initiated over two hundred years earlier by the First Congress in 1789.

The unique history of the Compensation Amendment raised initial questions about the validity of its ratification. In *Coleman v. Miller* (1939), the Supreme Court declared that disputes about ratification procedures and the time within which an amendment could be ratified were political questions assigned to the province of the legislative branch under Article V of the Constitution and, therefore, not subject to adjudication by the federal courts. *Coleman* seemed to envision some sort of formal congressional review of the constitutional validity of a fully ratified amendment prior to its official addition to the Constitution. Despite initial comments about formal review by rather stunned federal legislators following Michigan's ratifying vote on May 7, 1992, Congress, sensing the public mood, scheduled no formal hearings on the Compensation Amendment. On May 18, 1992, the National Archivist certified the amendment. Two days later, overwhelming majorities in both chambers of Congress confirmed the Twenty-seventh Amendment.

The first, and thus far, only, case to explore the scope of the amendment's compensation limitation was *Schaffer v. Clinton* (2001) where four plaintiffs challenged the now-traditional annual cost-of-living pay increases to legislators. The district court interpreted *Flast v. Cohen* (1968) to limit general taxpayer standing to challenges under the Establishment Clause only (and thereby refusing to treat the Twenty-seventh Amendment as a comparable explicit restriction on spending). The court denied standing to three of the plaintiffs, who came to the court as taxpayers. However, the district court reached the merits for the remaining plaintiff, Congressman Bob Schaffer, whose salary was increased under the statute (to the detriment, he asserted, of his antitax reputation). The court held that periodic cost-of-living pay increases were not discretionary acts of Congress and were therefore not independent laws that varied compensation in violation of the amendment. It is true that cost-of-living increases, though "automatic" under congressional legislation, may, like any other governmental expenditure, only take effect upon enactment of an appropriation statute, but the court did not find that procedure to be dispositive.

On appeal, the Tenth Circuit declined to reach the merits, finding instead that Congressman Schaffer also lacked standing, noting that "the standing inquiry must be 'especially rigorous'" when the dispute involves two branches of government. The circuit court held that the Congressman "was not injured for standing purposes simply because he received a higher salary." If followed by later courts—the Supreme Court denied the petition for a writ of certiorari in the case—the Tenth Circuit's reasoning would appear to foreclose standing to any plaintiff challenging a statute under the Twenty-seventh Amendment. Ironically, after lying dormant for two hundred years, this amendment may now have been put back to sleep. Nevertheless, it is clear that Congress still has the option of voluntarily abiding by the amendment.

John C. Eastman

See Also

Article I, Section 6, Clause 1 (Compensation Clause)
Article I, Section 9, Clause 7 (Appropriations Clause)
Article III, Section 2

Suggestions for Further Research

Richard B. Bernstein, *The Sleeper Wakes: The History and Legacy of the Twenty-seventh Amendment*, 22 FORDHAM L. REV. 497 (1992)

Ronald Rotunda, *Running Out of Time: Can the E.R.A. Be Saved?*, 64 A.B.A. J. 1507 (1978)

Significant Cases

Coleman v. Miller, 307 U.S. 433 (1939)
Flast v. Cohen, 392 U.S. 83 (1968)
Boehner v. Anderson, 30 F.3d 156 (D.C. Cir. 1994)
Schaffer v. Clinton, 240 F.3d 878 (10th Cir. 2001), *cert. denied sub nom.* Schaffer v. O'Neill, 122 S.Ct. 458 (2001)

TABLE OF CASES

ADDITIONAL RECOMMENDED READING

Here is a brief list of books that provide general historical and intellectual background to the formation, implementation, and early application of the U.S. Constitution.

Primary Sources and Collected Documents

WILLIAM B. ALLEN AND GORDON LLOYD, EDS., THE ESSENTIAL ANTIFEDERALIST (1985).

This volume of essays offers an accessible selection of leading Anti-Federalist opinion. After a nice interpretative essay by the editors, the selections are grouped to focus on the origins of the Anti-Federalists' thought and their views on federalism, republicanism, capitalism, and democracy.

BERNARD BAILYN, ED., DEBATES ON THE CONSTITUTION (1993).

This is a very nice two-volume collection of Federalist and Anti-Federalist speeches, articles, and letters written during the struggle over ratification of the Constitution, focusing on debates in the press and correspondence between September 1787 and August 1788, as well as on the debates in the state ratifying conventions of Pennsylvania, Connecticut, Massachusetts, South Carolina, Virginia, New York, and North Carolina.

WILLIAM BLACKSTONE, COMMENTARIES ON THE LAWS OF ENGLAND (University of Chicago Press, 1991) (1833).

Originally lecture notes designed as a general introduction to the law, these volumes of British legal thinking and common-law analysis were significant in England and the American colonies in the century after their initial publication in 1765, and were thus especially influential during the formation of the American legal system.

MAX FARRAND, ED., THE RECORDS OF THE FEDERAL CONVENTION OF 1787 (1986).

This definitive work, originally published in 1937, gathers into three volumes (and one supplemental volume) all of the records written by participants of the Constitutional Convention of 1787, including the extensive notes taken by James Madison.

JACK P. GREENE, COLONIES TO NATION, 1763–1789: A DOCUMENTARY HISTORY OF THE AMERICAN REVOLUTION (1975).

This collection tells the story of the American Founding using documents ranging from government papers and popular pamphlets to diary accounts and personal letters. Each section has a full introduction, and each entry is prefaced by an introductory note, thus placing all the documents in a coherent framework.

ALEXANDER HAMILTON ET AL., THE FEDERALIST PAPERS (Clinton Rossiter ed., Mentor Books 1999).

First published between October 17, 1787, and April 12, 1788, as a series of newspaper articles intended to sway New Yorkers in the debate over ratification, this famous collection of essays written by Alexander Hamilton, John Jay, and James Madison in defense of the Constitution remains the greatest work of American political philosophy. The classic edition, edited by the late Clinton Rossiter, has now been published with a fine introduction by Charles Kesler.

CHARLES HYNEMAN AND DONALD LUTZ, AMERICAN POLITICAL WRITING DURING THE FOUNDING ERA (1983).

This two-volume set includes pamphlets, articles, sermons, and essays written by various political authors between 1762 and 1805. It is a gold mine of seventy-six less well-known, but equally colorful and highly reasoned, popular writings of the revolutionary era. Each entry is introduced by a brief note on the author.

PHILIP B. KURLAND AND RALPH LERNER, EDS., THE FOUNDERS' CONSTITUTION (2000).

Originally published by the University of Chicago Press to commemorate the bicentennial of the Constitution, this extensive work consists of extracts from the leading works on political theory and law, as well as letters, speeches, and notes from the Constitutional Convention, as they relate to each clause of the Constitution. Liberty Fund has prepared a paperback edition of the entire work in five volumes. It is also available online at *http://presspubs.uchicago. edu/founders*.

JOSEPH STORY, COMMENTARIES ON THE CONSTITUTION OF THE UNITED STATES (Carolina Academic Press, 1987).

The *Commentaries* are a classic and substantive work on the meaning of the U.S. Constitution by one of its early scholars, and also one of the greatest Justices of the Supreme Court. Originally a three-volume work, this one-volume reprint of the 1833 edition includes histories of various colonies and of the revolutionary and Confederation periods; it also includes straightforward commentaries on the clauses of the Constitution.

Secondary Sources and Collected Documents

WALTER BERNS, TAKING THE CONSTITUTION SERIOUSLY (1987).

This brief work makes a defense of the original meaning of the Framers by relating the Constitution back to the principles of the Declaration of Independence and considering how the Founding dealt with various challenges to the idea of constitutionalism.

STANLEY ELKINS AND ERIC MCKITRICK, THE AGE OF FEDERALISM: THE EARLY AMERICAN REPUBLIC, 1788–1800 (1993).

This lengthy work traces the development of the new nation from the time after the Constitutional Convention through its first three Presidents. It is a comprehensive analysis of the early national period, including all the achievements and fights of the chief figures.

DON E. FEHRENBACHER, THE SLAVEHOLDING REPUBLIC: AN ACCOUNT OF THE UNITED STATES GOVERNMENT'S RELATIONS TO SLAVERY (2001).

Fehrenbacher's detailed study, stretching from the First Continental Congress to the Civil War, argues persuasively that early trends in the colonies were against slavery and that the U.S. Constitution is not a proslavery document, despite later policies that supported the institution.

ROBERT GOLDWIN, FROM PARCHMENT TO POWER: HOW JAMES MADISON USED THE BILL OF RIGHTS TO SAVE THE CONSTITUTION (1997).

Goldwin's clear and convincing historical study of the constitutional issues surrounding the creation of the Bill of Rights looks at the philosophical arguments behind these guarantees and how Madison crafted the Constitution's first amendments and then shepherded them through the First Congress.

CHARLES KESLER, ED., SAVING THE REVOLUTION: THE FEDERALIST PAPERS AND THE AMERICAN FOUNDING (1987).

In a very approachable collection of fourteen essays, leading scholars explain and interpret the eighty-five essays of James Madison, Alexander Hamilton, and John Jay on topics such as republicanism, federalism, foreign policy, the separation of powers, executive power, and the original purposes of the Constitution.

LEONARD LEVY AND DENNIS MAHONEY, EDS., THE FRAMING AND RATIFICATION OF THE CONSTITUTION (1987).

Twenty-one essays on the Framing and ratification of the Constitution address various topics, ranging from the colonial background and the events leading up to the Constitutional Convention to questions of original meaning and organization of the new government.

JOHN E. NOVAK AND RONALD D. ROTUNDA, PRINCIPLES OF CONSTITUTIONAL LAW (2004).

This concise treatise on American constitutional law (condensed from a five-volume legal text) provides law students and nonstudents with a basic understanding of the most fundamental principles of constitutional law. The text is designed to explain and analyze those principles, and it provides a guide as to how judges and legal practitioners apply them in the world outside the classroom, thus forming the foundation used to develop new precedents.

JACK N. RAKOVE, THE BEGINNINGS OF NATIONAL POLITICS: AN INTERPRETIVE HISTORY OF THE CONTINENTAL CONGRESS (1979).

Rakove follows the flow of events to reconstruct the circumstances and decisions of the First Continental Congress of 1774 and the Second Continental Congress (which began in 1775 and became the Congress of the Confederation in 1781), including the administration of the Revolutionary War, the framing (and breakdown) of the Articles of Confederation, and the reform movement that culminated in the Constitutional Convention of 1787.

CLINTON ROSSITER, 1787: THE GRAND CONVENTION (MacMillan Company, 1966).

The editor of the most widely read edition of *The Federalist* examines the meeting that created the Constitution in this very readable (and trustworthy) work, focusing on the setting, men, events, and consequences of the Constitutional Convention through the early years of the new Republic. A number of related documents are also included.

HERBERT J. STORING, WHAT THE ANTI-FEDERALISTS WERE FOR: THE POLITICAL THOUGHT OF THE OPPONENTS OF THE CONSTITUTION (1981).

Storing offers a brief introduction to the thought of the Anti-Federalists, who opposed the ratification of the Constitution and wanted a small republic, more federalism, and a bill of rights, among other things. It also considers their effect on enduring themes of American political life, such as a concern about big government and the infringement of personal liberty.

ABOUT THE EDITORS

Edwin Meese III, Chairman of the Editorial Advisory Board, served as the 75th Attorney General of the United States. Meese is a graduate of Yale University and holds a law degree from the University of California at Berkeley. He is a Distinguished Visiting Fellow at the Hoover Institution, Stanford University, a Distinguished Senior Fellow at The University of London's Institute of United States Studies, and currently holds the Ronald Reagan Chair in Public Policy at The Heritage Foundation.

Matthew Spalding, Executive Editor, is the Director of the B. Kenneth Simon Center for American Studies at The Heritage Foundation. Spalding is a graduate of Claremont McKenna College, holds a Ph.D. from The Claremont Graduate School, and has taught at George Mason University, the Catholic University of America, Claremont McKenna College, and Hillsdale College. An Adjunct Fellow of the Claremont Institute, he is co-author of *A Sacred Union of Citizens: Washington's Farewell Address and the American Character*, and the editor of *The Founders' Almanac: A Practical Guide to the Notable Events, Greatest Leaders & Most Eloquent Words of the American Founding*.

David F. Forte, Senior Editor, is the Charles R. Emrick, Jr.-Calfee Halter & Griswold Professor of Law at Cleveland State University. Forte is a graduate of Harvard College, and holds a Ph.D. from the University of Toronto and a law degree from Columbia University. A former Chief Counsel to the United States Delegation to the United Nations, and a National Endowment for the Humanities Fellow, Forte writes and lectures on a wide range of topics, including international law, constitutional law, natural law, and jurisprudence.

The Heritage Foundation

The Heritage Foundation is a research and educational institute—a think tank—whose mission is to formulate and promote conservative public policies based on the principles of
free enterprise, limited government, individual freedom, traditional American values, and a strong national defense. Governed by an independent Board of Trustees, The Heritage
Foundation is a nonpartisan, tax-exempt institution. Founded
in 1973, it is one of the world's largest public policy research
institutions.

heritage.org

INDEX

Americans with Disabilities Act (ADA), 376

Annals of Congress (1789-1824), 77

Annapolis, Md., 8

Anti-Federalists: Allocation of Representatives Clause and, 57, 58; Appellate Jurisdiction Clause and, 258; Army Clause and, 133; Bill of Rights and, 10, 367; Commerce with Foreign Nations Clause and, 100; congressional compensation and, 433; constitutional amendment and, 285; Debt Assumption Clause and, 290; Declaration of War Clause and, 197; election regulations and, 72; Eleventh Amendment and, 375; Enclave Clause and, 143; Executive Vesting Clause and, 180; House of Representatives and, 49; judiciary and, 251, 252, 253; Jury Trial Clause and, 350; Militia Clause and, 139, 141; Navy Clause and, 135; Ninth Amendment and, 368; Obligation of Contract Clause and, 172; Patent and Copyright Clause and, 121; Port Preference Clause and, 162; Preamble and, 44; Quartering of Troops Clause and, 323; Ratification Clause and, 299; Reexamination Clause and, 362; Right to Jury in Civil Cases Clause and, 359; Right to Keep and Bear Arms Clause and, 320; standing armies and, 45; State Coinage Clause and, 169; Third Amendment and, 323; Trial by Jury Clause and, 262

Antiterrorism and Effective Death Penalty Act of 1996, 154

APA. *See* Administrative Procedure Act

Appeal to the Inhabitants of Quebec, 311

Appellate Jurisdiction Clause, 123, 247, 256, 258–61

appointment power: Appointments Clause, 124, 207, 209–12, 213; Commissions Clause, 224–25; Inferior Courts Clause, 123–26; Recess Appointments Clause, 60, 66, 215–16; Supreme Court and, 5

Appointments Clause, 124, 207, 209–12, 213

apportionment: Enumeration Clause and, 56; House of Representatives and, 49–50; population and, 49; taxation and, 55. *See also* representation

Apportionment of Representatives Clause, 404–6

Appropriations Clause, 163–66

Archbald, Robert, 70

Aristotle, 16, 283

Army Clause, 132–35

Arraignment Clause, 352–53

Arrow, Dennis W., 244–46

Arthur, Chester A., 184, 192, 430

Articles of Confederation: amendment of, 7; Appropriations Clause and, 163, 164; Bankruptcy Clause and, 112; Bill of Rights and, 80; Captures Clause and, 131; Citizen-State Diversity Clause, 255; Coinage Clause and, 114; Commerce among the States Clause and, 104; Commerce with Foreign Nations Clause and, 100; Commerce with Indian Tribes Clause and, 108; compensation of Congress and, 79; constitutional amendment and, 285; Constitutional Convention and, 4, 8, 9; Constitution and, 43–44; Debt Assumption Clause and, 290; Define and Punish Clause and, 126; executive and, 7, 180; Full Faith and Credit Clause and, 267; Guarantee Clause and, 282; Incompatibility Clause and, 84; Land Grant Jurisdiction Clause and, 255; Military Regulations Clause and, 136; national government and, 4, 7; Naturalization Clause and, 109; Pardon Power Clause and, 203; Post Office Clause and, 119; Privileges and Immunities Clause and, 269, 271; Qualifications and Quorum and, 75; religion and, 43; representation and, 63; revenue power and, 55; sovereignty and, 43; Speaker of the House and, 59–60; states and, 7, 43–44; Supremacy Clause and, 291; taxation and, 7, 85, 97, 159; treaties and, 7; Treaty Clause and, 205–6; war powers and, 195; weaknesses of, 4, 7; Weights and Measures Clause and, 116

Ascertainment Clause. *See* Compensation Clause

Assimilative Crimes Act, 145

Attestation Clause, 301–2

auxiliary precautions. *See* checks and balances

Backus, Isaac, 309

Bail Reform Act of 1984, 363

Baker, John, 302–7

Bank of the United States, 98, 99, 292

Bankruptcy Clause, 112–14

Chase, Samuel: Ex Post Facto Clause and, 156–57; impeachment of, 61, 226–27; State Bill of Attainder and State Ex Post Facto Clause and, 170–71

checks and balances: Allocation of Representatives and, 58; Appointments Clause and, 211; Constitution and, 3, 10–11; faction and, 3; *The Federalist Papers* and, 10; impeachment and, 62, 71; President and, 195; republican government and, 3; tyranny and, 3

Chiappinelli, Eric, 116–17

Chief Justice of the Supreme Court, 67, 68

CIA. *See* Central Intelligence Agency

citizenship: Citizenship Clause, 384–86; Declaration of Independence and, 385; discrimination and, 110; dual, 111, 265; Fourteenth Amendment and, 384–86; Naturalization Clause and, 109–12; Privileges and Immunities Clause and, 390–93; treason and, 265

Citizenship Clause, 386–90

Citizen-State Diversity Clause, 252–53, 255

civic virtue, 4, 10

Civil Rights Act of 1866, 381–82, 384, 390–91, 399–401

Civil Rights Act of 1875, 390–91

Civil Rights Act (1964), 149

Civil War, 58, 65, 72, 76, 95, 99, 115, 116, 134, 194, 200

Claims Clause, 281–82

Clay, Henry, 91

Clegg, Roger, 51–53, 407–9

Clinton, Robert, 260

Clinton, William Jefferson, 83, 425; impeachment of, 61, 68, 69, 70, 226, 227–28, 237, 419, 429; Pocket Veto Clause and, 91; President as Commander and Chief and, 198; Recess Appointments Clause and, 215

Coinage Clause, 114–16; Counterfeiting Clause and, 118; Obligation of Contract Clause and, 115; original understanding of, 114–15; Supreme Court and, 115–16

Coke, Sir Edward, 170, 264, 338, 345, 347, 349, 395

COLAs. *See* cost-of-living adjustments

Cold War, 133, 142

Commentaries on the Constitution of the United States (Story), viii; Admiralty Clause and, 247; Allocation of Representatives and, 58; Appellate Jurisdiction Clause and, 258; Appointments Clause and, 210; Appropriations Clause and, 164; Claims Clause and, 282; Compensation Clause and, 79; constitutional amendment and, 285; Convening of Congress Clause and, 220; Counterfeiting Clause and, 117; Enclave Clause and, 144; House Journal and, 77; judiciary and, 251; Meetings of Congress Clause and, 74; Military Installations Clause and, 145; Military Regulations Clause and, 136; Oaths Clause and, 295; Post Office Clause and, 119; Preamble and, 43; Presentment of Resolutions Clause and, 92; President term of office and, 183; Public Trial Clause and, 347; Qualifications and Quorum and, 75; Sinecure Clause and, 83; Speech and Debate Clause and, 81; State of the Union and, 216; State Treaties Clause and, 168; Vice President in Senate and, 66

Commentaries on the Laws of England (Blackstone), 44, 110, 152, 333, 347, 350, 385, 395. *See also* Blackstone, Sir William

Commerce among the States Clause, 101–7; Import-Export Clause and, 106; Necessary and Proper Clause and, 105; Privileges and Immunities Clause and, 106; Supremacy Clause and, 105; Supreme Court and, 101–6

Commerce Clause: Commerce with Indian Tribes Clause and, 108; Counterfeiting Clause and, 118; economy and, 47; Export Taxation Clause and, 161; Import-Export Clause and, 177; Obligation of Contract Clause and, 174; Original Jurisdiction Clause and, 257; Prohibition and, 421–22; Slave Trade Clause and, 151

Commerce Department, 117

Commerce with Foreign Nations Clause, 100–101

Commerce with Indian Tribes Clause, 107–9

Commissions Clause, 224–25

Commodity Futures Exchange Commission, 240–41

Compact Clause, 178–79

Compensation Clause (Congress), 78–79

Compensation Clause (executive), 192–93

Compulsory Process Clause, 355–57

Confrontation Clause, 354–55

liberty (cont.)

people of the United States, 1; Preamble and, 43, 45; preservation of, 3; separation of powers and, 3, 4; states and, 44

Libya, 198

Lilburne, John, 352–53

Lincoln, Abraham, 151, 153, 194, 202, 204, 235, 380, 404, 430

Lindh, John Walker, 266

Line Item Veto Act (1995), 88–89

Livermore, Samuel, 303

Livingston, William, 150

Locke, John, 46, 309

Louis XVI, 167

Lund, Nelson, 97–98, 162–63, 322

McAffee, Thomas, 366–71

McClurg, James, 8

McConnell, Michael, 308, 309

McDonald, Forrest, 43–46, 298–99

McGinnis, John, 209–12

McKinley, William, 430

Maclaine, William, 222

McPherson, Isaac, 156, 170

Madison, James: Allocation of Representatives and, 57–58; Ambassadors Clause and, 221; apportionment and, 49; Appropriations Clause and, 164; Army Clause and, 132; Bankruptcy Clause and, 112; Bill of Attainder Clause and, 154; Bill of Rights and, 367; checks and balances and, 3, 10–11; Claims Clause and, 282; Coinage Clause and, 114; Commerce with Foreign Nations Clause and, 100; Compact Clause and, 178; congressional compensation and, 433; constitutional amendment and, 285; Constitutional Convention and, vii, 8, 9, 12; Counterfeiting Clause and, 118; Cruel and Unusual Punishment Clause and, 363; Debt Assumption Clause and, 290; Declaration of War Clause and, 128, 196, 197; Define and Punish Clause and, 126; Direct Taxes Clause and, 159; Diversity Clause and, 253–54; Double Jeopardy Clause and, 333; Electoral College and, 187; Elector Qualifications Clause and, 51–52; Eleventh Amendment and, 375; Emoluments Clause and, 166; Enclave Clause and, 143; Estab-

lishment of Religion Clause and, 304; Export Taxation Clause and, 161; faction and, 8, 76; *The Federalist Papers* and, viii, 10; First Amendment and, 302, 303, 308, 309; Free Exercise of Religion Clause and, 308, 309; Fugitive Slave Clause and, 275; Full Faith and Credit Clause and, 267; Guarantee Clause and, 283; House Journal and, 77; House of Representatives and, 49, 50; impeachment and, 61, 226; Import-Export Clause and, 177; Inferior Courts Clause and, 123; internal improvements and, 45; Judicial Compensation Clause and, 238; judiciary and, 242, 251, 252–53; Meetings of Congress Clause and, 74; militia and, 199; Militia Clause and, 140; national government and, 4, 44; Naturalization Clause and, 109; Ninth Amendment and, 368–69; Oath of Office Clause and, 194; Obligation of Contract Clause and, 172; Opinions Clause and, 201; Origination Clause and, 86; Patent and Copyright Clause and, 121; Pocket Veto Clause and, 90; Presentment Clause and, 87; Presentment of Resolutions Clause and, 92; Presidential Succession Clause and, 191; President qualifications and, 189; President term of office and, 182; Privileges and Immunities Clause and, 271; Qualifications and Quorum and, 75; qualifications for Representatives and, 53, 54; Qualifications for Senators and, 65; Ratification Clause and, 299–301; Recommendations Clause and, 218; religion and, 302, 303; representation in Senate and, 288; republican principle and, 49; reserved powers of states and, 11; Right to Keep and Bear Arms Clause and, 320; Second Amendment and, 320; Senate and, 63; Senate term of office and, 64; separation of powers and, 3, 9, 11; Sinecure Clause and, 82–83; Slave Trade Clause and, 151; sovereignty and, 4; Spending Clause and, 93, 94, 95; State Bill of Attainder and State Ex Post Facto Clause and, 170; State of the Union and, 216–17; State Title of Nobility Clause and, 176; State Treaties Clause and, 168; Supremacy Clause and, 291; Supreme Court and, 234; Takings Clause and, 341; Tenth Amendment and,